D1104260

SOCIAL SCIENCE AND
THE CHALLENGE OF RELATIVISM

SOCIAL SCIENCE AND
THE CHALLENGE OF RELATIVISM

VOLUME 1

A WILDERNESS OF MIRRORS

—On Practices of Theory in a Gray Age

LAWRENCE HAZELRIGG

THE FLORIDA STATE UNIVERSITY PRESS
TALLAHASSEE

University Presses of Florida
The Florida State University Press
© 1989 by the Board of Regents of the State of Florida
⊛ Printed in the U.S.A. on acid-free paper.

Library of Congress Cataloging-in-Publication Data

Hazelrigg, Lawrence E.
  Social science and the challenge of relativism.

  Includes bibliographies and indexes.
  Contents: v. 1. A wilderness of mirrors—
v. 2. Claims of knowledge.
  1. Social sciences. 2. Relativity. I. Title.
H91.H42 1988   300   88-19132
ISBN 0-8130-0917-0 (set : alk. paper)
ISBN 0-8130-0873-5 (vol. 1)

UNIVERSITY PRESSES OF FLORIDA is the central agency for scholarly publishing of the State of Florida's university system, producing books selected for publication by the faculty editorial committees of Florida's nine public universities: Florida A & M University (Tallahassee), Florida Atlantic University (Boca Raton), Florida International University (Miami), Florida State University (Tallahassee), University of Central Florida (Orlando), University of Florida (Gainesville), University of North Florida (Jacksonville), University of South Florida (Tampa), University of West Florida (Pensacola).

ORDERS FOR BOOKS published by all member presses of University Presses of Florida should be addressed to University Presses of Florida, 15 NW 15th Street, Gainesville, Florida 32603.

EDITORIAL INQUIRIES should be addressed to the Florida State University Press, Dodd Hall, Florida State University, Tallahassee, Florida 32306.

Contents

A*cknowledgments*

THESE THREE VOLUMES TOOK SHAPE, initially as one, during years of discretion (1975–80) given to me through the National Institutes of Health as an award of money from their Research Scientist Development Program. But for some reworking of the early pages of chapter 1, this volume was set to paper while I enjoyed facilities of the Institute for Social Research, Indiana University. The second volume was written partly in Bloomington, partly in Tallahassee. A third volume, both older and newer than the first, is underway.

"Acknowledgments," a *reconnaissance* in the economy of the book, is a sort of action of distributive justice in which the beneficiary gets to write the size and provenance of benefactions already received. How then shall I confess my indebtedness and name my benefactors? How indeed, when the productivity of memory always exceeds its past, and the ownness of "what is mine" is always open to rescission. How does a wood carver? —or a sand sculptor? It is not a question of simple forgetfulness or of a failure of double-entry bookkeeping.

I am much indebted to Jeanne Ruppert, director of the Florida State University Press, for sharing the guidance of her improbable combination of scholarly acumen and administrative skill. I can recite the names of those—especially Melissa Hardy and Russ Carpenter—whose enduring support and encouragement nurtured, enlivened, continually rejuvenated an arduous yet pleasurable journey. I do recite, throughout succeeding pages, the names of a great many people in whose names arguments are used and re-used. The long conversations held with those names—sometimes frustrating and sometimes saddening but always beneficial and very often exhilarating—have been immensely rewarding to me. But what of all the others, those who, wittingly or not, directly or indirectly, join in this production without leaving their names explicitly in its registers? Those who subsidized my "years of discretion"; those who have read the manuscripts along the way and left behind anonymous words of commentary, sometimes kind and sometimes fierce; those who have participated in the responsibilities of a *Bildung*: not nameless but unnamed, their differences are reassembled in "my own."

And, to repeat in conclusion what I said at the beginning: man would rather will nothingness *than* not *will.*
—Nietzsche, 1887

*B*eginnings

BEGINNINGS ARE DIFFICULT—in part because they resist the singularity of "*That* is the beginning" or "*Now* I shall begin." Is the three-word phrase "Beginnings are difficult" the beginning of this book? Or is it rather the heading of "Chapter 1"? Or perhaps not the "Chapter 1" that you will read, but as it first was? Or is it all of this, and yet none of this alone? Surely we can intelligibly say that the paragraph you are now reading began *before* these words were set to paper just so. But where is the site and what is the date of that fissure between a "before" and an "after"? From Hegel's famous preface to his *Phenomenology* (1807) to Derrida's outwork (1972) and Erving Goffman's provocations of authorial framing of *Frame Analysis* (1974), we recognize differently the signals of prefacing. And so now a question we may put before us is: Just what work do we cradle in aspirations of that ritual of difference of an "order of presentation" versus an "order of production"? Have Derrida and Goffman asked only that now we should preface with embarrassment?

I hope that answers to those questions, answers that I intend, will become known by you through the project of which this volume is *a* beginning. For now, suffice it to suppose three opinions, here very loosely uttered. First, it is impossible for me to spell it all out "in the beginning." Second, what I want to have spelled out eventually, for you as for me, has to do with the process and product wherein "anything," including my/your answers to those questions, has "become known." Third, the throat on which you stand while reading this book is no less mine than yours. The first of these suppositions should serve as forewarning that this volume is doubly open-ended. I attempt in the third section of chapter 1 to describe the character and circumstances of the incompleteness. The second supposition poses a question that will not, therefore, receive a full, explicit

1

answer in these pages. I return to the *question* of an answer in the second section of chapter 6. The third supposition is offered as reminder of the *activity* of what we call "reading"—a "writing" without pen, as it were. Presentation is production under another name; regardless of name, its idiom is neither that of the "fresh start" nor that of the "once and for all."

Having thus acknowledged the workings of an agon, I shall offer some brief remarks about the manner of my "writing" this volume: remarks about the place of advocacy, about the inescapable practice of rhetoric, about the labor of a "writer" as "someone for whom language is a problem, who experiences its profundity, not its instrumentality nor its beauty" (Barthes 1966, 46), yet for whom "the problem of language" is, after all, *still* a matter of instrumentalities and beauties as well as profundities.

When Charles Lyell had published his three volumes concerning various *Principles of Geology* (1830–33), he was criticized by Adam Sedgwick for having employed "the language of an advocate." As a matter of record, Lyell *had* been instructed and *had* practiced as a barrister; but that biographic detail was neither uncommon in those early days of the modern natural science of geology, especially in Britain, nor the main point of concern. The asperity of Sedgwick's criticism was directed against a "style of presentation," argumentative and openly persuasional, that was deemed to be at odds with the "Baconian ideal" of a dispassionately reasoned exposition. Already the admonition to "let the facts speak for themselves," to refrain from any embellishment of the discovered "is," was very much in force. Yet the lesson that Lyell could have gained from his critic's disapproval was not that the discourse of science had to be "style-free" but that the requirements of acceptable (i.e., "proper") style had changed. The flexibility that Hobbes or later Rousseau, or even Bacon himself, could enjoyably carry to such advantage in the "jurisprudential" uses of language—languages of conviction shaped and trimmed to fit the characteristics of different audiences—no longer seemed necessary to the tasks of these "new model scientists" of Baconian inspiration.[1] The language of this science was meant to be neutral, a placid medium through which the facts

---

1. Bacon himself did not disavow the relevance of rhetoric or its "proper uses," but insofar as natural science was concerned these uses were regarded as integral to the transmission, and not to the constitution, of knowledge (see the eighteenth chapter of book 2 of his *Advancement of Learning*).

Concerning the persuasive uses of language by Hobbes and by Rousseau, see, e.g., the studies by Gavre (1974) and Strauss (1947). In the same vein, see Strohm's (1977) study "Chaucer's Audience," Strauss's essay *Persecution and the Art of Writing* (1952), Hauser's ([1958] 1963, 253–76) general observations on the relation of artist and audience, and the many relevant passages of Skinner's splendid essay *The Foundations of Modern Political Thought* (1978). Many other examples from what is by now a massive literature could be cited in illus-

of reality could pass with no, or minimal, alteration ("distortion"). Conviction of the validity of scientific knowledge was to be obtained not by the persuasions of a barrister's tricks or of a parson's divine passion but by demonstration of the universal replicability and consistent fruits of a precisely enacted methodical process of discovery, all to be conveyed in a "plain style" of reportage. In this new science the force of advocacy was removed from an overt agon of protagonist and antagonist, the dialogue of the court and the pulpit, and placed behind the shield of an allegedly neutral language in the locus of "the facts themselves."

Today geology and its sister sciences are regarded as being quite different from their "ancestral forms" in the days of Charles Lyell and Adam Sedgwick. Among other circumstances, Kantian problematics entered the conscious relations of "doing science." Even as evidence of "accumulation" and "mastery" abounds experientially, confidence in claims of "progressive accumulation" and "progressive mastery" is weaker, less surefooted. But for all the differences between his time and ours, Sedgwick's strong sentiment against the scientist-as-barrister continues in current opinions and images of the "purity" of the ideal of scientific knowledge. Anyone who would startle the limpidity of "scientific report writing" with anything at all like a "moral earnestness" risks being described as Freud was: "Irrepressible moral earnestness [colored] his attitude of scrupulous scientific neutrality"—and rebuked for it (Rieff 1959, 3–4). We are reminded always that there are essayists and there are scientists.

Be that as it may, much of what I try to construct in these following chapters *is* a work of advocacy, not the hidden advocacy that slides through a supposedly neutral language of discovery but, as best I could make it, an open advocacy and an earnestness of desire to convince. Not that I claim any special revelation of self-knowledge: I cannot stand behind myself any more effectively than can the next person—which is to say, finally, not at all. Nevertheless, I have struggled against sedimentations of a socialization in what Martin Green (1972) has called the "Erasmian" position and temperament—the liberalist-humanitarian mentality of "intellectual life"—in order *not* to inscribe what I want to say in the pretense of an impassive, impersonal, ethically neutral, disinterested "proper style."

At the same time, I might acknowledge also that portions of this work are not conducted in what some would deem an "easy, straightforward style." This transgression, if it be that, was premeditated and willfully conducted: Because much of what I set out to construct was, by intention,

tration of the point that (paraphrasing Gavre 1974, 1,543) one mark of what comes to be consumed as a "great work" of theory is its diversity of appeal to a great many different consumers, including those who otherwise hold opposing points of view.

to be antagonistic to certain conventions of "thinking," I sometimes chose unconventional words, phrases, or artifices such as hyphenated compounds, alienations by scare quotes, "awkward" negations, etymological reminders, uncommon couplings and associations, redeployments of prepositional space. The desire was not—is not—to conjure mystery; it is rather the desire to be read by *my* choice of dictations and moldings, instead of those of the conventions against which I argue. Yet I appreciate well enough the labor of reading to be aware of the "hazards" that lie in wait for such intentionalities of production. Each effort to enforce "my choice" was an exercise in recall of the opening paragraphs of *The Eighteenth Brumaire of Louis Bonaparte*:

> Hegel remarks somewhere that all facts and personages of great importance in world history occur, as it were, twice. He forgot to add: the first time as tragedy, the second as farce. Caussidière for Danton, Louis Blanc for Robespierre, the *Montagne* of 1848 to 1851 for the *Montagne* of 1793 to 1795, the Nephew for the Uncle. And the same caricature occurs in the circumstances attending the second edition of the eighteenth Brumaire!
>
> Men make their own history, but they do not make it just as they please; they do not make it under circumstances chosen by themselves, but under circumstances directly encountered, given and transmitted from the past. The tradition of all the dead generations weighs like a nightmare on the brain of the living. And just when they seem engaged in revolutionising themselves and things, in creating something that has never yet existed, precisely in such periods of revolutionary crisis they anxiously conjure up the spirits of the past to their service and borrow from them names, battle-cries and costumes in order to present the new scene of world history in this time-honoured disguise and this borrowed language. . . . [A] beginner who has learnt a new language always translates it back into his mother tongue, but he has assimilated the spirit of the new language and can freely express himself in it only when he finds his way in it without recalling the old and forgets his native tongue in the use of the new. (Marx [1852] 1979, 103–4)

Anyone who has striven to learn a new language surely appreciates how difficult it is *not* to recall the old in the use of the new; appreciates, too, that speaking/writing is never a private affair, never effectively accomplished independently of auditing/reading.[2] I have struggled to inscribe

---

2. "Language is as old as consciousness, language *is* practical, real consciousness that exists for other men as well, and only therefore does it also exist for me" (Marx and Engels [1932] 1976, 44).

words conscientiously and unspontaneously in order to work a critique of that which, because it "fits" so "naturally," typically passes as the background by which the old colors of criticism show up *as* criticism. By virtue of such design to interrupt, this "writing" was not "easy." Perhaps, in the labor of a reading, it will not *be* "easy." But the difficulty of it did not begin in a swelter of perverse ingenuity.

1

$U_{nder\ the\ Thesaurus}$

According to a very old and often repeated adage, "One picture is worth a thousand words." A few years ago, when planning the composition of this first chapter, I thought to place among its initial pages some number of pictures, mostly photographs. The thought came as a quiet confession of the deficiency of my skills of verbal alliance. I wanted to encourage a certain understanding of this presentation of written words by reproducing on the flat white page something of the emotion that gave this work its intent. But anger and tears do not live well in the dwellings my pen can make; my writing has been molded too tightly by the puritan prescriptions of "cool reason" and "detachment." So I thought to use, in place of the halted images of my words, some images of a pictorial kind: pictures that would incite the reader's eye, disrupt its comfortable gaze, and redirect it toward the neglected relations of "material" support beneath our modern *thēsauros*.

I "knew," in a manner of speaking, the pictures I wanted to use. These are not pleasant images. They are thin memoirs of the slimy gore of atrocity that some human beings have inflicted on other human beings, both directly and indirectly, both recently and currently. They are special images, but they are not extraordinary images; they tell of the normal worries of most of the people of our world.

I "knew," in a manner of speaking, where to find the pictures, at least some of them. For the rest, I began to explore various archives. The decisions of selection and order of placement proved to be even more difficult than I had anticipated—partly because there were so many pictures from which to choose (photographs, I tried to remind myself, tend to be "cost-inhibi- tive" for publishers), and partly because it seemed absurd that there could

6

be any framework by which to prefer one picture over another or to decide the difference between "enough" and "one too many." But I decided.

I also "knew," in a manner of speaking, how I wanted to use these pictures. They would do most of the "talking." Simply by their presence these images would impassion the reader's sensibilities. They would tell as my words could not of the concrete conditions that comprise the support as well as the context and "subject matter" of this work of words. It would thus be sufficient for me simply to ask you, the reader, to keep your now-impassioned sensibilities to the fore while reading the stream of words that follow. I would encourage you to appreciate the pictures with great care, each in its turn, none too quickly: "Consider their possibilities. Say them to yourself. Feel them. Think of your parents, and of their parents. Think of yourself. Find your own possibilities within each image, thinking of yourself. And most of all, in these images of torture-swollen bodies, see your children, and their children—the children of earth. Small faces looking back at you."

Such was the initial plan. It was troubled from the start. The pictures I wanted to place among these pages are special; my desire was that you would read and speak them in a very particular way. Yet, I was aware that, contrary to the repeated wisdom, pictures not only do *not* speak more voluminously or more loudly than words; they, like words, do not speak at all. It is *we* who read and speak pictorial images, just as we read and speak the images of words, and any picture can be read and spoken in a variety of ways. I "knew" that I could not compel you to grasp them, or to be grasped by them, just as I wanted. I remembered all the warnings issued by Walter Benjamin and Roland Barthes, for example, and now again most recently by Susan Sontag: pictorial images can either strengthen or corrupt sensibilities of conscience, and the difference of effect is finally told not by any presence or absence within "the picture itself" but by the presence or absence, within us, of an attunement of political consciousness.[1] Surely I did not intend to corrupt. Yet it was evident that I could not enforce an exclusive reading of the pictures I had thought to include among these pages. Their meaning would not be constituted independently of what you, the reader, were prepared to see and able to feel. Even so, I said to myself, I can *plead* for a particular reading.

As I reviewed the manuscript of this volume one last time, I considered once again my decision. Despite my best efforts of special pleading, the

---

1. See, for example, Sontag's essay *On Photography* (1977, esp. 19–20) and Barthes' series of essays on the rhetoric of images, "Shock-Photos," and related matter (e.g., 1957, 1961, 1964a).

decision remained a troubled one. I tried to improve those efforts; but the trouble persisted. Then I remembered Stanley Simmons. That is, I remembered "a man"—or a trace of a man—whose name, Stanley Simmons, I had forgotten. Stanley Simmons, an unemployed cement mason and father of two young children, died October 7, 1980. He was crushed between the boarding platform, from which he had fallen, and the third car of a four-car train in an underground State Street station in downtown Chicago. There were dozens of bystanders: not only did they refuse to come to his aid, they laughed and jeered as this man with one arm in a sling tried frantically to climb out of the path of the roaring subway train.

The trouble with my decision to place some pictures among these pages was now inescapably clear: it was a decision already antiquated by the progress of our world. Wanting to strengthen sensibilities, I had worried (such was my naïveté) that my "special pictures" might corrupt instead. But we have progressed far beyond that range of effect of mere *pictures* of the hideous. What Lawrence Langer has said about images formed in narration applies as well to the imagination of pictures: "The sheer quantity of lives wasted by atrocity has corrupted the redeeming power of tragic insight" (1978, xii).

So my poor words will have to do the best they can, alone, amid whatever sensibilities or political consciousness they encounter. I have nothing that is competitive for a next level of our escalation of the threshold to horror.

2. TELLURIAN NOTES

Do we now know better "the meaning of a text" (or the conditions of its failure) told to us by so "esoteric" a "thinker" as Martin Heidegger?— "not just any kind of humanity is suited to bring about unconditional nihilism in a historical manner. . . . a struggle is even necessary about the decision as to which kind of humanity is capable of the unconditional completion of nihilism" (Heidegger [1954a] 1973, 103).

Item: "A Fortnight in the Wilds," Tocqueville's notebook from his journey of July 1831 across New York State to Buffalo, thence up the Great Lakes to Detroit, contains this entry:

> How many times during our travels have we not met honest citizens who said to us of an evening, sitting peacefully by their fires: the number of Indians is decreasing daily. However it is not that we often make war on them but the brandy that we sell them cheap every year carries off more than our arms could kill. This world here belongs to us, they add. God, in refusing the first inhabitants the capacity to become civilized, has destined them in advance to inevitable destruction. The true owners of this continent are those who know how to take advantage of its riches.
>
> Satisfied with this reasoning, the American goes to church, where he hears a minister of the Gospel repeat to him that men are brothers and that the Eternal Being who has made them all in the same mould has imposed on them a duty to help one another. (Tocqueville [1860] 1971, 354)

Less than a quarter-century later, in 1855—long before the word "genocide" was coined and long before phrases such as "the destruction of lives devoid of value" were added to the vocabulary of scientific diagnosis—President Franklin Pierce of the United States of America received from Chief Sealth of the Duwanich people this letter:

> The Great Chief in Washington sends word that he wishes to buy our land.
>
> How can you buy or sell the sky—the warmth of the land? The idea is strange to us. Yet we do not own the freshness of the air or the sparkle of the water. How can you buy them from us? Every part of the Earth is sacred to my people. Every shiny pine needle, every sandy shore, every mist in the dark woods, every clearing and humming insect is holy in the memory and experience of my people.
>
> We know that the white man does not understand our ways,

one portion of the land is the same to him as the next, for he is a stranger who comes in the night and takes away from the land whatever he needs. The earth is not his brother but his enemy, and when he has conquered it he moves on. He leaves his father's graves, and his children's birthplace is forgotten.

There is no quiet place in the white man's cities. No place to hear the leaves of spring or the rustle of insect wings. But perhaps I am savage and do not understand—the clatter only seems to insult the ears. And what is there to life if a man cannot hear the lovely cry of the whippoorwill or the arguments of the frog around the pond at night.

The whites too shall pass—perhaps sooner than other tribes. Continue to contaminate your bed and you will one night suffocate in your own waste. When the buffalo are all slaughtered, the wild horses are all tamed, the secret corners of the forest heavy with the scent of many men, and the view of the ripe hills is blotted by the talking wires. Where is the thicket? Gone. And what is to say goodbye to the swift and the hunt, the end of the living and the beginning of survival.

Item: A soldier of the army of Henry V, one John Page, returned to London with this account of his master's laying siege to Rouen in 1418:

One might see wandering here and there children of two or three years old begging for bread as their parents were dead. These wretched people had only sodden soil under them and lay there crying for food—some starving to death, some unable to open their eyes and no longer breathing, others cowering on their knees as thin as twigs. A woman was there clutching her dead child to her breast to warm it, and a child was sucking the breast of its dead mother. There one could easily count ten or twelve dead to one alive, who had died so quietly without call or cry as though they had died in their sleep.[2]

John Toland described another scene of laying siege, this to what had been only minutes earlier a city of 245,000 people (Hiroshima, August 6, 1945, 8:15 A.M.):

350 young girls from the Girls Commercial School had been working in an empty lot, clearing an evacuated area. They wore blue *mompei*

---

2. John Page's account of the Siege of Rouen is quoted in part by Seward (1978, 176). See also Scattergood (1971, 60–69).

[pajamas] and jackets but no hats or fire hoods, and those who turned, curious, toward the *pika* [flash]—almost 300 of them—were instantly doomed. Twelve-year-old Miyoko Matsubara's instinct was to bury her face in her arms. She regained consciousness in unimaginable desolation—no people, no buildings—only limitless rubble. Where were her *mompei*? All she had around her waist was a white cloth belt and it was on fire. . . . She started to beat out the flames with her right hand, but to her horror she saw strips of skin, her skin, dangling from it. (Toland [1970] 1971, 882)

Do we now know better the reason of such destruction? Who tells the truth of it?—Martin Heidegger, when he says, "This long war in its length slowly eventuated not in a peace of the traditional kind, but rather in a condition in which warlike characteristics are no longer experienced as such at all and peaceful characteristics have become meaningless and without content" (Heidegger [1954a] 1973, 104–5)?—or the anonymous young scientist who says to his interviewer-confessor, "What I'm designing may one day be used to kill millions of people. I don't care. That's not my responsibility. I'm given an interesting technological problem and I get enjoyment out of solving it" (quoted in Kevles 1977, 408 n. 4)? It is not simply "too easy"; it is the height of perversity to segregate such destruction as "senseless." It *has* "a sense"; it *is* reason. Willing the void is, after all, willing; and contrary to our convenient compartmentalizations, "the will" does not will without reason. So if we regard Kevles's young scientist as a latter-day example of that new breed of scientists described by Brecht as "a generation of inventive dwarfs who can be hired for any purpose," must we not consider also those who do the hiring, and those who support the marketplace? Such is the gangrene in *our* lovely places.

Still, there are pressures for us to persist in our struggle to decide the edge of that true empirical difference that segregates "the kind of humanity" who reaps "senseless" enjoyments from puzzling out the means of instant genocide, "the kind of humanity" that *is* suited to bring about unconditional nihilism. Surely there are some among us who are *both* full-sized human beings *and* inventive. We may recall with Joravsky (1979) that Brecht also told, in his *Galileo* (Brecht [1943] 1966, 38), how an ancient thinker, Keunos, was confronted one day by an official who demanded, "Will you serve me?" Keunos served many years, silently, until the official died; whereupon he dragged the corpse out of his house, straightened up, and said, "No." But what matters the difference between "*real*" inventive dwarfs and a stooped Keunos? What is the point of deciding such difference? Perhaps only this: once our psychoneurological and sociobiological sciences have completed their unriddling of Nature's final mysteries of "human nature," so that "the congenitally evil" can be discriminated unmistakably from those of us who are "basically good (even if occasionally weak)," we will then be able to practice a *selective* genocide, without fear of harming innocent people. Thus we will know what the savage Chief Sealth could not know—what we did not then know, because (we take comfort in saying) our science was still too weak.

The argument I hope to sustain in this volume is at its surface about the conditions of knowledge, including most importantly the knowledge that we qualify as "scientific." But if its most visible focus is the claim of knowledge, the terrain that constitutes both the substance and the support for that which is focalized must also have presence in the argument. An argument about conditions of knowledge cannot escape being simultaneously an argument about conditions of human society, and vice versa. Yet many of our specialist "purveyors" of knowledge, especially those of scientific knowledge, would have us believe otherwise. They insist on a certain segregation of conditions, by which they seek to achieve certain immunities. They argue that knowledge is the ultimate good, of which there can never be "too much."[3] Knowledge is the ultimate benefactor of humanity, they say, and if destructive effects can sometimes be traced back to one or another of its benefactions, that is not because the knowledge was destructive but because it was misused by some of its recipient political actors. In other words, the favored segregation presumes a logic of temporality in which knowledge—or, more to the point, scientific knowledge—precedes the realm of uses. By this presumption, the scientist can disclaim responsibility for destructive uses, even while receiving accolades as the progenitor of scientific benefactions. But this segregation, though real insofar as it is practiced, is false. The conditions of human society described in preceding paragraphs—indeed, the entire array of conditions onto which

3. Note, for instance, the responses to Robert Sinsheimer's (e.g., 1976, 1978) suggestion, heretical to many, that perhaps it is time to consider the desirability of placing limits on scientific research:

If . . . one believes that there may be other values to be held even higher than the acquisition of knowledge—for instance, general human welfare—and that science and possible other modes of knowledge acquisition should subserve these higher values, then one is willing to (indeed, one must) consider such issues as: the possible restriction of the rate of acquisition of scientific knowledge to an "optimal" level relative to the social context into which it is brought; the selection of certain areas of scientific research as more or less appropriate for that social context; the relative priorities at a given time of the acquisition of scientific knowledge or of other knowledge such as the effectiveness of modes of social integration, or of systems of justice, or of educational patterns. (1978, 23)

For examples of the reaction to Sinsheimer's suggestion, see the issue of *Daedalus* in which the above-quoted passage appeared.

those brief paragraphs open as the smallest of windows—were and are conditions of knowledge, including scientific knowledge.

No doubt some will see in this contention the seeds of a rabid "anti-intellectualism"—or, perhaps more to the point, an "antiscience" bias. Such contention as this, the response will be, surely betrays a distrust of reason, in particular the reason of modern science. It could only have been written by one of those who somehow "feel that even in the midst of great wealth they must live by an ethic of social despair"; or perhaps even by one of those who, having lived in despair so long, are now encased in a windowless fatalism, one of those who have taken the clockface on the *Bulletin of Atomic Scientists* a bit "too literally." Never mind that for every person who works to erase that timepiece, or at least to turn back its hand, there are thousands who oil its movement and still other thousands who tune its balance wheel. We must "hope that in the long run the constructive uses of knowledge will prevail." And we must remember that *science* "does not flourish amidst preoccupation with its own potential evil."

But what is "knowledge" apart from its uses, actual and potential? No different from fantasy? Not even that can be said, for fantasy too exists only in its uses.

Remembering that C. P. Snow did warn about a spreading gulf between "the two cultures," some will see in this evidence of a nascent (or fully blown?) bias "against science" the nevus of "poetic" despair: a despair for all the lost nonrationals and irrationals of an enchanted, magical world. A late example of the well-known "Romantic Reaction," in other words: "poetic language," no longer able to comprehend the precisions of "scientific language," is angry that the village idiot has been supplanted by abstract tables of electrochemical malfunctions, chromosomal fractures, and calculations of heritability. The great monuments of this "reactionary movement"—typically nominated as Stéphane Mallarmé, Gottfried Benn, T. S. Eliot, among others—still cast a long and dangerous shadow of retreat: their criticisms of the rationalism of their times, the modern science of their times, promoted nothing less than "a retreat from meaning and coherence." Indeed, abundant evidence has been collected and assayed and catalogued to show that "a retreat from meaning and coherence" has, since the late nineteenth century, increasingly characterized "modern art" generally.

But are we to suppose that Mallarmé or Benn or Eliot imagined his work was *meaningless* and *incoherent*? Has Kristeva's (1974) investigation of a "revolution of poetic language," for example, been the study of transformations of coherence into incoherence, of meaning into unmeaning? If there *was* a "retreat," was it not rather from a *historically specific* "meaning and coherence," and toward at least the glimmering potentiality of another?

We must not also suppose, however, that the claim of "a retreat from meaning and coherence" is itself meaningless or incoherent. There is not only a substance but also a support to that claim. Although I will not here attempt a full excavation, it is easy enough to see first of all that such a claim rests (at one level of lamination) on the presumption of a numerical identity of "meaning and coherence" with an eternalized science ("science in the abstract," we might say, or "the *idea* of science"), in which the former is assimilated entirely by the latter. Of course, this crucial presumption *of* the claim is occulted *by* the claim: the identity is not announced; it resides in the not-said that gives force to the said and strives to make the claim functionally sufficient. And just here, in the facticity of this presumed identity, is also located (is it not?) the hierarchical principle that declares with each gift of modern science, "Here. Do with it what you will. You are free, so do what you will." As Glucksmann has recounted through the fable of Thélème, such presentation spans (occultatively) an empowering "predicament," that is, a predicated relation that deeply perplexes those who experience its occulted force. For the pronouncement "Do what you will" is prefaced implicitly by a specific instance of what linguists have termed "illocutionary force"—namely, "Obey me when I say, . . .";[4] but "Do what you will" is formally open, in the transitivity of its force ("what you will"), to "Disobey me, if that is what you will."

> Modern logic has carefully examined paradoxes such as this. All the solutions which have been put forward consist either in ruling out such propositions as nonsenses, absurdities, or in accepting them while making a hierarchical distinction between the proposition and its terms, the whole and its parts, the statement and what is stated. In all cases, an irreversible subordination.
>
> Do what you will, but do not rebel against the one who tells you to, lest you become bogged down in insuperable contradictions. A device that produces only one difference—the hierarchical difference. A device for governing. (Glucksmann [1977] 1980, 13)

So, that which presses upon us as "a retreat from meaning and coherence," as a "distrust of reason" (read: "science"), is the surface of a crisis of authority, the authority of a particular regime of meaning and coherence, regarded from the opacity of claims about differences between "the poetic" and "the scientific" and between "living by an ethic of social despair even in the midst of great wealth" and "hoping that in the long run the constructive uses of knowledge will prevail." Those who so regard the crisis—that

---

4. Admittedly I have collapsed a distinction that linguists prefer to observe (see, e.g., Searle 1976). I might rather have said "an instance of what linguists have named 'illocutionary act,' which is characterized by variable 'illocutionary force.' " The point, however, is unaffected.

is, as an undermining assault directed peculiarly, or at least primarily, against the foundation of modern science—thereby demonstrate indirectly the enormous exaggeration of place in which they hold the twin "institutions" of an "autonomous" science and scientific technology. This attitude describes both those who applaud such "assault against science" ("reason") and those who oppose it.

It has been said (as axiologic assertion) that to assume there is one basis for life and a different basis for science is as a matter of course a lie.[5] If with that I concur, and I do, then I can no more stand against "science in general" than against "life in general." One stand would be as vacant as the other. But if there are concrete conditions of life that I must try to oppose, then I must try to oppose those same conditions of science. Claims of autonomy notwithstanding (including "relative autonomy," whatever *that* difference), conditions of the one are conditions of the other. Thus, the question, What to say of a science that "gives us" (as if science were some Otherness that bears gifts from its theo-ontological domain) enormous powers but does not simultaneously provide the means to prevent the enormous destruction that is inherent in enormous powers? is a fatality of its own conception. Rather: What to say of a *mode, a regime, of producing life* that favors the manufacture of enormous powers (along with "hope for their constructive use") over the manufacture of means to prevent the enormous destruction that inheres in enormous powers? Certainly we cannot abolish risk; a risk-free world would be a world totally predetermined and predestined, held in the ironclad guarantee of a singular "worldline" by just the sort of universal law that some still regard as the hallmark of a "*true* science."[6] But surely the prudent gambler is one who assesses and limits risks—and indeed refuses the gamble when risk is of such proportion as to jeopardize all gain, no matter how large the anticipated gain

5. The reference is to Marx's argument in his *Economic and Philosophic Manuscripts* of 1844 (Marx [1932] 1975, 303). Here and elsewhere I would insist on a discrimination between "Marx" and "Marxism" (or "Marxisms") were it not for the futility of it. Never mind that Marxism generally has long been a travesty of the best in Marx; it is the multiplicity of "Marxisms" that today rules Marx. What answer to Lévy ([1977] 1979, 171, 182) would now make a difference?— "Fact-worshipping, pragmatic, realistic, and at the service of *Realpolitik*, Marxism is in the process of becoming the modern form of the consensus through which the republic of the wise and learned have always established their communion"; and, "When will we have an elementary anti-Marxism that will say that the left, which extends to the reformist right, is materialist, materialist from top to bottom, even if it understands nothing—in fact, because it understands nothing—about the uniqueness of the Marxian epistemological break?"

6. We must remember, too, not to succumb to any pure formalism of "risk," as if it were an intrinsically vacant term of statistical formulae. It is "risk," for example, that is given as the moral justification of profits. We are treated to the

might be. What do we say of a mode of producing life that has practiced a domestication of madness?—and that has theorized the domestication in a language of "the autonomy of science" and "knowledge for its own sake" and "distrust of reason," a language of separated realms named "the technical," "the political," and "the ethical"? What do we say of a regime of producing life that has abandoned its children to a "hope that in the long run the constructive uses of knowledge will prevail"?—and that has simultaneously manufactured such an enormous growth of scale of *destruction* that "in the long run" can easily end in a few minutes? Not more than a generation ago the common practice was for parents to warn their children of the dangers of young life, dangers both small and large, with a comforting measure of confidence: "Be careful with that stick." "Don't play with matches." "Don't swim alone."—and so forth. But do we today warn our children against the dangers of playing too close to chemical plants?—or "hazardous-waste" dumps?—or microwave transmitters? How *can* we, when the dangers are so widespread, so often invisible, so complicated in the proportions of their danger? And just where *do* we find "safe territory" today? How are we to delineate its boundaries—as once we did by the yard fence, the playground, or the look of a horse's eye—when acid falls from the common sky, lethal liquids bubble up from the common soil, and radiations do not respect the yard gate? What words can suffice to warn our children against heavy halogenated hydrocarbons such as the polychlorinated biphenyls or hexachlorobenzene or Agent Orange?—against an airdrop of botulism?—against MIRVs and neutron bombs? How do you explain to children a mode of producing life in which the assessment of danger occurs primarily by mass-marketing each new commodity and waiting to see if a statistically significant number of people die because of it?— and in which such effects of the danger are segregated and depreciated by naming them "*side* effects"?[7] How do we explain it to ourselves? Or do we

picture of an atomized individual living by his or her (typically his) wits in a hostile environment, who risks his capital in an investment venture. Risk! But deprive that formula of its abstractions, and see what is sacrificed by actions morally justified by "risk."

7. How often do official enunciations of "public policy" concerning "risk" remind us of Raskolnikov's words about the bleak fate of a drunken girl (or about the "harmony" of "statistical rule")?

But what does it matter? That's as it should be, they tell us. A certain percentage, they tell us, must every year go . . . that way . . . to the devil, I suppose, so that the rest may remain chaste, and not be interfered with. A percentage! What splendid words they have; they are so scientific, so consolatory. Once you've said 'percentage,' there's nothing more to worry about. If we had any other word—maybe we might feel more uneasy. (Dostoyevsky [1866] 1956, 47)

merely call it "senseless," an "absence of reason"? Perhaps we settle on the explanation/expiation that points to an underlying "animal beastliness" of our "human nature"—the same primordial ghost that has periodically threatened to overwhelm our "cultivated reason" and destroy "civilization," the same primordial ghost that our psychoneurological and sociobiological sciences will, they promise, eventually conquer by learning to observe the laws of its nature.[8]

Some readers may wish to object that the sorts of questions I have been mobilizing to the service of an argument have been asked in "every period of human history"—the implication, *qua* moral lesson, being that we will survive our questions, just as our predecessors survived theirs. We may. But is there no difference between then and now? When our predecessors confronted *their* questions of survival, did the boundaries of failure encompass annihilation of *all* potentiality? When they calculated risk, did they conclude that *their* dangers had a half-life of twenty-four thousand years? Several recent commentaries (see, e.g., Ophuls 1977) have tried to argue the case for such difference, a difference formulated primarily in terms of "the problem of scale." While these arguments typically suffer serious deficiencies, especially those that result from efforts to ground the argument in naturalistic presuppositions, they do serve as a beginning for a redirection of consciousness regarding matters of scale.

Considerations of "the problem of scale" are not unprecedented, of course. Galileo wrote of "the impossibility of increasing the size of structures to vast dimensions either in art or in nature," for example (Galileo [1638] 1914, 130), and Hegel concluded that change in quantity eventually results in change in quality (Hegel [1830a] 1974, 203). Both of these enunciations share in the notion that scale is of special significance insofar as it pertains to a phenomenon as a nonlinear property. Or, as Georgescu-Roegen has put it, "the problem of scale" is a problem uniquely of "quality-related processes":

> If the variables immediately connected by a phenomenon are cardinally measurable, then they can all be increased in the same proportion and still represent the same phenomenon. The formula describing the phenomenon then must be homogeneous and linear or, more generally, a homogeneous function of the first degree. On the other hand, if some variable is a quantified quality [or indeed a "nonquantifiable

---

8. "Human nature"—what would our "Reason" be without it? As Cioran put it, "Since we all believe that our merits are misunderstood or flouted, how admit that so general an iniquity could be the doing of mere man? It must go back further and belong to some ancient dirty work, to the very act of the Creation" ([1969] 1974, 6).

quality"], nothing seems to cast doubt over our expectation that the formula will be nonlinear. (1971, 105)

Phenomena that are indifferent to scale (i.e., formulated as a homogeneous function of the first degree) seem to be comparatively rare in our earthly world. But those who would put forward the sort of objection noted in the preceding paragraph apparently are convinced that they have hit upon a whole collection of them: the dangers I have been mentioning in my argument by interrogation are just such phenomena, it would seem. That is, "dangers to survival" may have been increasing in size (as the "inevitable" "*by*-products" of growing benefactions), but despite those increases the dangers are phenomenally unchanged in their "whatness"; they are still the *same* phenomena, only bigger, about which, therefore, the same kind of questions and the same kind of answers remain appropriate. By this assertion of indifference to scale and "phenomenal sameness," we are encouraged to believe that a war fought with strategic nuclear weapons would be the same kind of phenomenon as World War II or the Great War before that—bigger, to be sure, and no doubt quicker to its conclusion, but survivable just as previous world wars were survivable. That the nearly twenty-nine million "battle deaths" inflicted in all "interstate" wars during the century and a half following 1815 would equal merely a small fraction of the "battle deaths" from a nuclear war (however, and by whomever, such deaths might then be discriminated) is irrelevant to the rationality of phenomena that are indifferent to scale.[9]

Karl Mannheim began his *Diagnosis of Our Time* by emphasizing historic differences of scale in "the new social techniques," that is, in "those methods which aim at influencing human behavior and which, when in the hands of Government, act as an especially powerful means of social control." Prominent among such methods, he noted, was "a new military technique [that] allows a much greater concentration of power in the hands of the few than did the technique of any previous period" (including the generation of Durkheim and Sorel, for example, who also had stressed for their time the significance of scale). "Whereas the armies of the eighteenth and nineteenth centuries were equipped with rifles and guns," Mannheim observed, "our armies work with bombs, aeroplanes, gas, and mechanized units. A man with a rifle threatens only a few people, but a man with a bomb can threaten a thousand" (1943, 3, 4). This renovation of Aristotle's famous rule must surely impress us as already antiquated. Had Mannheim

---

9. The estimate of nearly 29 million "battle deaths," that is, "combat-connected deaths of military personnel only" in wars fought between or among two or more "nation-states," is from Singer and Small (1972, table 4.2).

lived to revise his *Diagnosis* but a decade later, he would have written of yet another increase of scale, this one still much greater than the last: not a thousand or even ten thousand but several million people could be threatened by "a man with a bomb."

And today? Are the numbers sufficiently impressive? As of 1980, the world population of nuclear "bombs" had reached about 40,000. That translates into a ratio of approximately one "bomb" for every 100,000 of the world population of men, women, and children—which is less than the "prompt kill factor" of one of the small "bombs" in a metropolitan area. More than 15,000 of the "bombs" are designated "long-range strategic warheads"; three-fifths of these were manufactured during the past dozen years, when there was also much talk about "strategic arms limitation." Ten very small warheads (one megaton each, or nearly seven times the explosive force of the Hiroshima bomb) exploded over "strategic sites" in the greater Boston metropolitan area would promptly kill at .ast 1.3 million people. No more than a few hundred of the "strategic warheads" in the arsenal of the United States would be sufficient to annihilate the largest Soviet cities, two-thirds of the Soviet industrial base, and one hundred million people just from the immediate effects of the nuclear detonations.[10]

Still, everyone—or everyone who seems to count in such decisions—wants more. And the people who want more continue to undertake the most marvelous calculations of "survivability," in their rationality of phenomena indifferent to scale. Sidney Drell, deputy director of the Stanford Linear Accelerator Center and onetime consultant to the President's Science Advisory Committee, recently observed, "Nuclear war would be so great an extrapolation of the scale of disaster in human experience, and so great a physical disturbance of our environment and ecosphere, that the unknowns of a nuclear conflict clearly far outweigh the knowns or predictables. Yet there appear more and more detailed calculations that describe how hundreds of millions of people will behave in all-out conflict, when deadly radioactive rain will fall for many months. These calculations also predict casualty levels and recovery times with incredible precision" (1980, 183). The expansion of scale and, simultaneously, of concentration that Mannheim found so disturbing forty years ago has continued to accelerate throughout the world hierarchy of human societies, with consequences that have yet to be seen or felt in the full register of social formations. Drell's sad query—"Do we even still remember what nuclear explosions do?"

---

10. None of this takes into consideration the morbidity and death that would result as delayed effects; see, for example, Glasstone and Dolan (1977) and the study of long-term effects by the National Academy of Sciences (1975).

(1980, 177)—may be massively answered tomorrow; and we, or any "survivors" among us, may then diagnose from the visible surface of such consequences a final rush to exhaustion of the "inner logic" (Weber's *Eigengesetzlichkeit*) of a world order that has held sway during the past two hundred years. Like the famous owl of Minerva, we may conclude our diagnosis both of and in a world that is indeed already there, cut and dried.

Assuming that the planet earth is *not* a wasteland of radioactive debris, not even in its northern hemisphere, by the year 2000, what sort of world shall we expect? That has been a principal question of most of those scholars—e.g., Ophuls, Eckholm, Dumont, Peccei—who recently have been trying to argue the case of "problems of scale."[11] It is important to note that, in posing such a question, we must not say "the future," as if an ordainment by some divine, natural, or historical law had already measured the boundaries and densities of the definite article, robbed it of all potentiality except that of an abstract schedule of random occurrence, and ensconced it in a universal time as a series of sites and dates awaiting human actualization. Nevertheless, the productions and habituations of human activity do figure in the moment of any here and now, constraints that channel potentialities into the more and the less visible, the more and the less desirable, the more and the less difficult of realization. Even as "the future" always remains historically indefinite within a range of potentialities, human constraints of and in the production of life continually alter the limits and composition of those potentialities, making some futures, at any moment, "more likely" than others. At their best, these recent commentaries on the question "What world in the year 2000?" have tried to extrapolate from trends established in the existing complex of governing conditions. This is, of course, both their strength and their weakness. It is their strength when the extrapolations are constituted from the standpoint of projected valuations of a future-to-be-made. It is their weakness when the extrapolations are constituted from the standpoint of a value neutrality of technical competence, in which the "pure facticities" of a serialized presentation-of-the-past reduce potentialities to the regularities of current habituations.

What world in the year 2000?—assuming our world does not become, between now and then, a radiant legacy of the struggle to decide "which kind of humanity is capable of the unconditional completion of nihilism" (Heidegger [1954a] 1973, 103). One of the most striking features of the literature addressing that question is the recent shift in its balance of an-

---

11. Ophuls's book is one of the best instances of this "literature of global predicament," as it has been called, a literature already very large and highly variable in its sensitivities to the enormous complexities of "the problem of societal reconstruction" (as it has been known in the tradition of Karl Mannheim, Bertrand Russell, and others).

swers. Who now takes seriously the amazing scenario prognosticated in Kahn and Wiener's *The Year 2000?* Instead of luxuriating in imageries of endless abundance, the typical scenario now offers images of a plundered earth, a suffocating contamination of our bed, an ecology of scarcity. This scenario tells "about shortages of the vast array of energy and mineral resources necessary to keep the engines of industrial production running, about pollution and other limits of tolerance in natural systems, about such physical constraints as the laws of thermodynamics, about complex problems of planning and administration, and about a host of other factors Malthus never dreamed of" (Ophuls 1977, 9). It is a naturalistic scenario that speaks of the necessity of adopting a "spaceman economy" (Kenneth Boulding's notion) and, without noticing the promise of irony, encourages us to replace the traditional imagery of Mother Nature with a new, supposedly more fitting imagery of Spaceship Earth.[12] National governments as well as individual scholars and organizations such as the Club of Rome have been embracing one or another version of this scenario of scarcity, providing thereby a stamp of legitimacy to arguments that not long ago were widely regarded as the fanciful mutterings of sour cranks and "nattering nabobs of negativism." A case in point is the U.S. government's study *The Global 2000 Report to the President,* published in three volumes and conducted under the direction of the Council on Environmental Quality and the Department of State in 1977–80. Like most other studies of the kind, this report emphasizes problems of scale primarily in terms of logistic curves of profligate consumption and finite reserves of natural resources.[13]

12. The promise of irony is foretold by the contrasting "aesthetics" of the two imageries: the one, a warm, enveloping home of homes, colorful in a soft palate of blues, greens, browns, reds, and yellows; the other, a cold vehicle silently rushing through a near-void, its almost colorless sheen of icy metallics contrasting against an infinite blackness of absent background—the ultimate in homeless transience, the sense of alienation taken to its limit.

13. An illustration of the central thrust of this emphasis can be drawn from Ophuls (1977, 63–65). Assume we have a beginning stock of 50,000 units of resource X, an initial rate of consumption of 100 units per year, and a constant rate of growth of consumption at 3.5 percent per year. Our stock would be exhausted in 83 years. But let's assume that our beginning stock was actually 10,000 percent larger than we initially thought—i.e., 5 million units. The effect of this huge "discovery" is relatively small: our stock will now last 217 years, which is a gain of only 261 percent or slightly more than one-fortieth the increase of beginning stock. Moreover, let's assume in this latter case that one day we suddenly notice we have consumed nearly a third of our huge stock; so we somehow abruptly reduce to zero the 3.5 percent annual rate at which consumption had been growing. Again the effect is relatively small: we would gain only an additional 31 years—i.e., the beginning stock of 5 million units would now have a total longevity of 248 rather than 217 years.

It is flawed in a variety of ways, some of them fundamental. Even so, it gives an instructive look at what has become the governing scenario of a world not yet actualized but drawing near in the habituations of this one.

According to the *Global 2000 Report*:

● The human population of the world will be at least 50 percent larger, at 6.35 billion. The annual rate of growth will still be a rapid 1.7 percent, as compared with 1.8 percent in 1975. The number of people per unit of arable land will increase from approximately six persons per acre in 1975 to nearly ten persons per acre in 2000.

● More than 90 percent of this enormous growth of human population will occur in the poorer countries of the world (the so-called LDCs, or "less developed countries"). Four of every five people will be inhabitants of countries that now collectively account for less than one-fifth of the world total of GNP. Moreover, if current trends of rural-to-urban migration as well as natural increase should continue during these remaining decades of the century, cities such as Lagos, Bogotá, Karachi, Tehran, Manila, Delhi, Seoul, Jakarta, Greater Cairo, Greater Bombay, Calcutta—urban concentrations that already are huge, unmanageable ecological sinks—will each have a human population of ten to twenty million, Mexico City, thirty million.

● The gap between the few rich and the many poor countries of the world will continue to widen. In terms of the crude comparisons of GNP per capita (calculated on an exchange-rate basis), for example, the highly industrialized countries will average an increase of $20 for every $1 gained on average by the poorer countries. Indeed, the total GNP for *all* of the poorer countries of the world (four-fifths of the world population) will still be less than the total GNP of the United States alone (about 4 percent of the world population).

● The real price of food will double. In the richer countries, per capita food consumption will increase by about 21 percent; these populations are already well fed, on average, and often overfed. In the poorer countries, where malnourishment and starvation already affect hundreds of thousands of people, food consumption per capita will increase by an average of only 9 percent. Among some populations of sub-Saharan Africa, per capita food consumption will probably *decrease*, and in areas of South Asia, the Middle East, and North Africa it will increase very little, if at all. Relative to the standard of minimum caloric intake set by the Food and Agriculture Organization of the United Nations, food consumption among the poorest groups of people living in regions of the Asian rimland, in the Middle East, in Central Africa, and in parts of North Africa will simply be insufficient to meet the nutritional requirements of children for normal body weight and mental functioning.

● Sources of usable energy will continue to diminish in quantity. Real prices will continue to escalate rapidly. Here, too, of course, the effects will be manifested differently in rich and poor countries. In the words of the *Global 2000 Report* (1:2), "The richer industrialized nations will be able to command enough oil and other commercial energy supplies to meet rising demands through 1990,"[14] at which point "world oil production will approach geological estimates of maximum production capacity, even with rapidly increasing petroleum prices." But with the expected increase in the price of commercial energy supplies, "many less developed countries will have increasing difficulties meeting energy needs. For the one-quarter of humankind [who depend] primarily on wood for fuel, the outlook is bleak. Needs for fuelwood will exceed available supplies by about 25 percent before the turn of the century." Indeed, already in some parts of Sahelian Africa as many as 360 person-days of work per household are devoted each year to the collection of firewood. In some cities of West Africa, where surrounding territory has been stripped of collectible wood, families often spend 20 to 30 percent of household income for the purchase of firewood.

• At the current rate of deforestation—43 to 48 million acres, or an area about half the size of California, each year—Latin America, Africa, Asia, and Oceania will lose nearly half of their forest covers and growing stocks of commercial-size wood. Among the consequences of this loss are soil erosion and depletion; siltation of rivers, lakes, and estuaries; extinction of huge numbers of plant and animal species; depletion of groundwater; and possible climatic changes. In the poorer countries, where as much as 90 percent of current wood consumption is for cooking and heating, per capita growing stocks will decrease by more than 60 percent.

• Regional water shortages and general deterioration of water quality, already serious problems in many areas of the world, will continue to worsen because of a variety of factors, including increased demand for water for domestic, agricultural, and industrial uses and increased pollution from denuded, eroding soil, commercial fertilizers, persistent pesticides and herbicides, inadequate sanitation and wastewater practices (in industrial plants and in massive urban population centers of ten to twenty million) that include continued dumping of domestic and industrial wastes in rivers, lakes, and coastal waters. In nearly half of the countries of the world, demand for water will double, relative to demand in 1971, simply from population growth alone.

14. Energy consumption per capita in the United States will be about 422 million British thermal units per year by 1990; in the poorer countries it will be only 14 million Btu (as compared with 11 million in 1975), or about one-thirtieth of the U.S. figure. Moreover, this estimate for the poorer countries includes component estimates of per capita consumption in the several member-states of the OPEC petroleum cartel.

• Consumption of commercial nonfuel minerals will continue to accelerate,[15] for example: the consumption of phosphate rock, a crucial ingredient of commercial fertilizers, will increase at an annual rate of 5.2 percent; aluminum, at least 4.3 percent, perhaps 6.4 percent; silver, 2.5 percent; zinc, 3 percent. Most of the increased consumption will be in rich countries, which will continue to absorb more than three-fourths of the world production of nonfuel minerals. Although none of these minerals will have been exhausted by the year 2000, virgin supplies of some of them may be approaching exhaustion. In terms of the geologist's category "identified reserves" (mineral sources that are known to exist), and assuming that the annual rates of growth of demand that are projected for the next two decades continue indefinitely, the estimated "life expectancies" of selected minerals are: silver, 17 years; copper, 36 years; aluminum, 33 years; phosphate rock, 51 years; lead, 28 years; and mercury, 21 years. Although most of the ore-deposit regions of the planet have been identified and geologically mapped already, additional deposits of nonfuel minerals will probably be identified during years ahead. In general they will be of lower grade and less accessible; therefore, the minerals will be more costly to extract and refine. Even if very large deposits should be newly identified, however, the life-expectancy estimates would probably not be greatly modified. Thus, for example, if we add to the identified reserves the geologist's categories of "hypothetical" and "speculative" mineral resources—resources not now "identified" but geologically predictable from current information, plus the speculative estimates of resources that *may* exist in unexplored areas or forms—and then recalculate the longevity estimates using the same annual rates of growth of demand, the revised figures are generally not much larger: silver, 23 versus 17 years; copper, 46 versus 36 years; aluminum, 49 versus 33 years; lead, 119 versus 28 years; and mercury, 44 versus 21 years.

• Approximately thirty million square kilometers of land (nearly one-quarter of the ice-free land area of the planet) are currently classified as undergoing "severe desertification." At the current rate of conversion, an area the size of Maine is lost to desert conditions each year. About half of this loss consists of rangelands; most of the remainder consists of croplands, including irrigated farmlands. Should the current rate of desertification continue, desert areas will have expanded by about one-fifth at century's end. But because of probable accelerations of land-use pressure—deforestation, overgrazing, intensified food production through increased appli-

15. In this paragraph I have supplemented the information supplied in the *Global 2000 Report* with data and analyses from Meadows et al. (1974, fig. 5-1) and Ophuls (1977, 66–68).

cations of commercial fertilizers—the rate of loss to desert conditions will probably increase during the next twenty years, with the result that the total desert area will be about 60 percent larger in the year 2000. Even in areas that escape desertification, the deterioration of soils will increase rapidly. In some semiarid regions, pressures due to urban settlement will continue to accelerate watersheds, lower the underlying aquifers, and, as in areas of California, intensify the conditions that result in firestorms. Deforestation will increase erosion and leaching. Depletion of the organic content of soils will continue at a quickened pace, not only because of deforestation and greater usages of commercial fertilizers but also because of the growing shortage of firewood, "the poor people's oil." As firewood becomes scarce in the poorer countries, dung and crop wastes are substituted as domestic fuels, thereby additionally depriving the soil of nutrients and degrading its moisture-retention characteristics.

• If food production per capita is to increase during the last two decades of this century despite reductions of the amount of arable land per capita, much of the increase will come from the higher-yield capabilities of irrigated farmland. In 1975 approximately 15 percent of the arable land of the planet was under irrigation; by 1990 another 120 million acres will have been added, an increase of more than 20 percent. But maintenance of irrigated soil is both difficult and costly, because of the continuous threats of waterlogging, salinization, and alkalinization. Serious damage from these sources already characterizes about half of the current area of irrigated land, and much of the land that is expected to be brought under irrigation during the years ahead will be even more vulnerable to degradation. Even if the current rate of loss does not increase, however, enough irrigated farmland to supply the food requirements of nine to fifteen million people will be out of production by the year 2000.

• Increased combustion of fossil fuels, especially coal, during the next twenty years will result in further deterioration of atmospheric quality, both in increased particulate pollution and in growth of the conditions that yield highly acidic rainfall. In recent years the acidity of precipitation over large areas of the eastern United States, southeastern Canada, Norway, and Sweden has increased by more than a factor of ten. No doubt the acidity will continue to increase, and acid rain will continue to affect larger and larger areas of the planet's surface. Particulate emissions from fuel combustion will double by 1990 (to a total of about seventy-three million short tons per year), resulting in especially heavy concentrations in the local atmospheres of large urban areas. Atmospheric concentrations of carbon dioxide will continue to increase at an accelerating rate, because of fuel combustion, deforestation, and depletion of soil humus. During the last one hundred years, atmospheric carbon dioxide has increased about 15 percent, but one-third of that increase occurred during the last twenty years;

if recent trends continue, the concentration could double by the middle of the next century and stimulate catastrophic changes of global climate.

• As a result of increased pollution and destruction of habitats, as many as one-fifth of all species of life now on the planet may be extinct by the end of the century. In absolute numbers, this means the extinction of at least five hundred thousand species, perhaps as many as two million species. Consequences of this enormous reduction of diversity are for the most part simply incalculable. The loss will constitute an irrevocable enforcement of our current ignorance of the potentialities that dwell within that diversity. It will surely be one of the gigantic legacies of a regime of human economy that, in its characteristic fetishism of commodities, occults its severe discounting of potentiality. Or, as Garrett Hardin has typified the modern economist's explanation, "the higher the interest rate [on money, the exchange standard of present value], the more heavily the purely rational man must discount the future" (1979, 315).

The collective picture of "the world in 2000" that is implied by these several of the many individual projections from the *Global 2000 Report* is of a world that will be much more unstable, to say the least. Yet even this picture is inadequate in a number of respects. For one, as the authors of the study acknowledged, because the model from which those projections came did not include most feedback and interactive effects or linkages, the projections undoubtedly *underestimate* the magnitude of plundering and devastation of habitat that may occur by the end of this century. However, there is another and vastly more important reason for concluding that this scenario, even if corrected for underestimations, gives an inadequate glimpse of probable future conditions of human habitat: the collective scenario focalizes the substance and support of "structural crisis" within an imaginary space that is created by a certain abstraction, the "naturalization of the social," and in consequence the governing vector of this crisis is seen to be a scarcity of *the supply of natural resources*.[16] But what is regarded as crisis due to current and impending scarcities of the supply of "natural resources" is concretely a crisis of human price or cost.

Consider the example of the well-advertised "scarcity of petroleum supplies." When the sources of deep-basin petroleum are finally exhausted, as they almost surely will be in another few decades, the crisis will not

---

16. True, the scenarists could not but notice the logical complement of "supply," in their equations of scarcity, namely, accelerations of "social demand." But this too was naturalized, though less completely, through the imagery of "development": the rich countries of the world are seen not as rich but as "developed," and being a "developed country" is "naturally" preferable; the poor countries are seen not as poor or impoverished but as "less developed," and the site of any "problem of development" is to be found there, in the "less developed countries."

consist in an absence of usable sources of energy; other sources—coal, oil shale, nuclear reactors, solar cells, and so on—will be substituted for the exhausted petroleum supplies. Rather, the crisis will be, as it has been already, one of price or cost: not simply the question "Who can afford the more costly substitution?" but the question "When the substitution is made, where will it be made, and at what cost to whom?" It will be made by the rich; the price will be increased exploitation of the poor.[17]

To be sure, the scenario constructed by the *Global 2000 Report* acknowledges the existence and the expected intensification of our enormous segregation of the conditions of human life between the rich and the poor. But this segregation and the expected intensification of its effects are regarded altogether too passively within the scenario's naturalistic focus on "scarcity of supply of natural resources"; consequently, important structural contradictions in this segregation are neglected. For example, the scenario virtually ignores the dynamic relations of the so-called multinational (better termed *trans*national, since they are mostly U.S.-based) corporations, which establish factories and offices in poorer countries in order to reduce the costs of labor, reduce taxes by avoiding accumulation of capital in rich countries, increase possible sources of financial subsidies through access to a larger number of national treasuries, avoid unwanted regulatory pressures, and, of course, thereby generate high rates of profit. These organizations constitute a huge increase of scale of centralization and concentration of markets, and in attendant efforts of normalization of populations (labor power, financial services, consumers) toward a "fitting" model of behavior. On the one hand, this process has meant an acceleration of the rate of plunder and transfer (of "raw materials" and labor power)

17. Other costs of the increased scale of danger will almost certainly include intensifications of state efforts of social control. Consider the case of plutonium recycling. Plutonium is a "by-product" of uranium-fueled power plants. It is extremely toxic, and it has a half-life of hundreds of centuries. As uranium supplies diminish, there will be increasing pressures to build plutonium-recycling plants for the purpose of making additional fuel for nuclear-power plants. What legal structures will be put in place as "security precautions"? Compare the dangers resulting from a theft of coal from a coal-fired power plant with those resulting from a theft of plutonium: what "extraordinary measures" will seem "reasonable" when that question of "security precautions" is asked in state councils? As one legal scholar has noted, should it be decided that some quantity of plutonium has been stolen, "the case for literally turning the country upside down to get it back would be overwhelming" (Ayres 1975). Winner (1980, 134, 135), from whom I learned of Ayres's study, summarized one aspect of the basic point: "In our times people are often willing to make drastic changes in the way they live [in order] to accord with technological innovation [yet] at the same time they would resist similar kinds of changes justified [explicitly] on political grounds."

from the poor to the rich. But on the other hand, it has also meant a reduction of variability across countries (most crucially, of course, across the rich countries) in the cycling of market dynamics and an acceleration of structural inflation on a world scale (see Levinson 1971).

Moreover, the very circumstances that in the short run encourage these corporations to undertake this partial or dependent form of industrialization in the poor countries will, in the longer run, increase their vulnerability to popular movements of the peoples of those countries—people who will be subject to increasing, and increasingly visible, exploitation and impoverishment. Resistance from such peoples will probably accelerate. Whether the events of that resistance are labeled "internal insurrection" or "struggles of national liberation," because of the increasingly precarious situation of the rich in a world of growing "scarcities," internal upheavals in poor countries may lead to imperialistic wars conducted by rich countries "in defense of the national interest." When the *Global 2000 Report* says that "the richer industrialized nations will be able to command enough oil and other commercial energy supplies to meet rising demand," it leaves in silence the concrete semantic space of "to command."

A number of "diagnosticians of our time" have been pondering once again the questions that Mannheim raised several decades ago about "a very marked and painful disproportion between the vastness of scientific machinery and the value of ultimate results" (Mannheim [1932] 1953, 189). Their concern is formulated not from the nostalgic dreams of a Luddism but from an understanding that, in the words of one of them, "much more effort and skill will be needed to cope with the increasing vulnerability to disorder (entropy) and failure" (Ophuls 1977, 124). While this "need" seems straightforward enough, they argue, the means of satisfaction do not: "To count on perfect design, skill, efficiency, or reliability in any human enterprise is folly, [since] all man's works, no matter how perfect as self-contained engineering creations, are vulnerable not only to . . . natural disasters . . . , but also to deliberate disruption by madmen, criminals, terrorists, and military enemies. Nevertheless, despite the patent impossibility of achieving any such thing, modern society seems to be approaching a condition in which nothing less than perfect planning and management will do." And it would seem that "nothing less than perfect planning" must now be of a temporal scale rather longer than the customary biennial or decennial calendar. As any of the textbook illustrations of a logistic growth function demonstrate (e.g., Ophuls 1977, 63–65), once a certain level in those dynamics has been attained, significant alterations of subsequent outcomes require an extraordinary range of foresight and planning.

Planning and foresight are effects of theory—indeed, of *social* theory. No matter how "arcane" or "mundane" a design of "physical" or "natural" engineering, it is inescapably a social production in its imagination, in its materials, in its motive or purpose, in its execution and realization. It is a social design, both embedded in and a statement of social theory—however foggy or occulted that theory may be. Thus, any expectation of "nothing less than perfect planning and management" is necessarily an expectation of effective social theory, in particular from those sciences that have been named "the social sciences" or "the human sciences" or "the sciences of man"—disciplines of inquiry and design that were constituted during the late eighteenth and early nineteenth centuries as formulative responses to "the problem of order" (of "the economy," of "the polity," of a newly fashioned realm of "the social"; cf. Foucault [1966] 1970; Donzelot [1977] 1979) and that have displayed remarkable growth characteristics during the past century and a half. From Smith, Tocqueville, and Comte to Durkheim, Marshall, and Mosca, to Freud, Mannheim, and Keynes, the substance and support of these sciences have consisted in configurations of order/disorder within an unfolding regime of industrialism. To be sure, some of these disciplines have been more forthright than others in acknowledging their utility in (a "public function" of) planning and policy: thus, for instance, an economist can say without apparent discomfort, even while addressing the embarrassments of failed theory, that "the only meaningful evaluation of [economic theory] turns on its being 'not false' [i.e., by reason of "its nature, economic theory cannot be taken as complete or 'true' "] and its being useful in supporting and directing research and policy endeavors" (Chase 1978, 71), a statement that few sociologists, on the other hand, have so comfortably uttered. Perhaps the modern science of economics, as also that of politics, can offer such self-accounting with comparative equanimity because of a heritage in disciplines that spoke "Advice to the Prince," whereas a discipline such as sociology had its beginnings in a liberalist regimen whose dominant language was already one of "disinterested knowledge" and "knowledge for its own sake." In any case, the expectation for *all* these modern "sciences of man" has been, above all else, the provision of effective theory and designs from and through which plans, policies, and policings can be made. All have provided such designs, even if the designs provided have usually been regarded more for their anemic resemblances to whatever conventions prevail as the "common sense" of the moment and less for any similarity to the latest "esoteric" designs contributed by "the exact sciences" ("the *real* sciences"). But now the expectation of theory has escalated: it has been underwritten by the charge that "artful" designs for "muddling through" by exercises of trial and error, "common sense," or whatever, are acceptable no longer—not when the scale of error and its consequences is so enormous. Perhaps it is not surprising that in this same moment social scientists are both warning themselves that "the elites can do without us" (Gibbs 1979) and pleading that the scale of expectation for their wares should be reduced (see, e.g., Lindblom and Cohen 1979).

3. FAILURES OF THEORY AND THE DILEMMA OF STANDPOINT

Several years ago, in a late-night session at the kitchen table, a friend remarked that "Gouldner's 'coming crisis' came—even before he had announced its coming. But then obituaries typically do follow the event of a death, don't they?" My friend is one of a growing number of scholar-critics who argue with conviction that we have witnessed the death of the disciplines of social science in all aspects but the occupational. It is clearly not an argument calculated to win them high praise among their social-scientist colleagues, of course, many of whom are quick to counter the judgment of fatality by pointing to evidences of professional expansion during the last quarter-century: in number of personnel, students, journals, and textbooks; in quantities of research, research grants, data, and "scientific machinery," as Mannheim called it; in expanded occupational assignments with government agencies and industrial enterprises, as well as in the academy; and in various other dimensions of occupational or professional import—all of which are conventionally treated as emblems of success. But surely it is apposite to ask whether the object of a social science is merely the production of social science. If we think to interrogate the disciplines of social science beyond the aspects of their occupational reproduction, should we not ask what they have offered in the way of effective theory from and through which foresight and planning of the social productions of, say, a physics or a biology—indeed, the productions of human life—can now be made? What designs of consequence have these disciplines to offer to human societies that are now hurtling into social productions called "cloning" and "recombinant-DNA engineering" and "private patent rights to life-forms" and "scarcity of natural resources" and "first-strike capability" and "survivable nuclear exchanges"? Just such questions have been animating not only the "human futures" commentaries by Ophuls, Hardin, and others; they have also stimulated many of the recent declarations of the failure of social science. Perhaps "declaration" is more often than not too strong a designator, since many of the statements of failure are only implicit—as in the appeals for a lowering of expectation. Thus, when Lindblom and Cohen (1979, vii) addressed the acknowledged situation of widespread "dissatisfaction with social science and social research as instruments of social problem solving," they did so less in terms of the quality of nutrients brought to table and more in terms of "excessive" demand by those who expect some sustenance. But some of the statements of failure have been quite explicit and forceful, sometimes in conjunction with an appeal for the quick preemption of social science. Consider, for instance, the recent statement by Rosenberg, who has constructed in terms of a strict naturalistic standard of empiricism a rigorous argument in "explanation of the failures of the social sciences," that is, in "explanation of why these subjects [the disciplines of social science] have yet to produce scientifically respectable results" (1980, 3, 4).[18] His statement is noteworthy in a number of respects, one of the most salient being his assumption that, even while directing his argument to an audience of social scientists as well as philosophers of science, he did not need first of all to demonstrate any evidence of the failure of social science "to produce scientifically respectable results." Here—as with Lindblom and Cohen's notice of "dissatisfaction with social science"—the condition of failure could be regarded as an already demonstrated condition, about which there is wide (if hardly unanimous) consensus.

Critics such as Rosenberg locate the failure of social science not in terms of an insufficiency of personnel, funding, "scientific machinery," numerical-analytic techniques, or maturity of discipline (i.e., the still-invoked defense that the disciplines of social science are "too young" or "immature"). The failure is, they argue, rather more fundamental: it is a failure of theory. But what does it mean to say of the disciplines of social science that they have suffered a "failure of theory"? Certainly it does not mean an *absence* of theory: social science may not be rich in theories, yet theorization is abundantly present. No pursuit, not even the much reviled "dustbin empiricism" that is so often used to describe one or another activity of social science, is atheoretical. No matter how feeble or indirect or unacknowledged it may be, theory is inescapable; it is integral "even" to such ordinary and "simple" acts as those of observing and counting.

Nor does "failure of theory" mean an absence of *effective* theory: surely theorization in social science does have effects, although these effects may be more or less weak, occulted, indeliberate, unpredicted, and unwanted (or the reverse). Moreover, insofar as other social scientists are prepared to concur with the economist Chase (1978, 71) in his view that part of the "meaningful evaluation of [theory] turns on . . . its being useful in supporting and directing research," then we must admit that at least this effect of theory has been quite robust during recent decades. After all, the quantity of social-science research *has* grown larger and larger, as has the number of organs of its reportage.

Rather, the "failure of theory" must be regarded as a statement constituted in reference to *desired* effects in a project of making. Approached in more conventional terms, it is a judgment about the claim to knowledge—more particularly, about the claim of scientific social theory to represent truthfully or validly the "*is*" of the-world-that-is-there. Scien-

18. I do not mean to suggest that I am in agreement with Rosenberg's critique as it stands or, more importantly, with his prescriptive proposal (which is implicated in the critique as part of its condition). To accept his proposal is to accept that all is lost—where "all" includes a great deal more than traditional social science.

tific social theory has traditionally held out the promise of being superior—more efficient, more powerful, and, most important of all, more accurately reflective and penetrative of the world as it is—in comparison to ordinary opinion or common sense, magical operations of simple trial and error, ambiguous myths and folk wisdoms, all sorts of speculative philosophizing, dogmatisms of sacred or secular authority, and similar other sources of representational claims. By the methodical exercise of techniques of scientific discovery and systematization, scientific social theory would accumulate the pieces of a truthful representation of the dynamic being of human life in all its peculiarly human essentials ("the cultural," "the economic," "the political," and so on), and on the basis of this cumulative representation any of the "problems," the undesired conditions, of human society would become increasingly susceptible of rectification or at least amelioration. The proper object of social science surely would *not* be merely the production of social science. That is, its aims would extend far beyond the occupational or professional concerns of its own reproduction, and just the sort of expectation voiced by Ophuls and his colleagues would comprise the proper expectation of disciplines of social science. Scientific social theory would be a germinal act: by re-presenting clearly and truthfully the distinctively human world as it really is—not as we wish it to be or as we guess it to be, but as it *is*—validated theory would serve as an empowering base from which other actions ("citizen actions") could be launched toward goals of improving the human condition. Such has been the promissory tradition of a scientific social theory. I am aware, of course, that social scientists have been uncomfortable with the qualification of *true* representation and have substituted the qualification "valid"; that they have generally preferred a probabilistic mode of the representational claim; that some of them prefer to speak not in terms of "validation" or "verification" but in terms of "conjecture and refutation" (for example, Chase's locution, "not false," quoted above); that they often prefer to speak not of "causal explanation," or not exclusively of that, but also of "understanding" and "interpretive explanation"; that they have often eschewed the natural-science goals of "universal laws," and have argued accordingly for expansions of the authorized boundaries and techniques of "the scientific method." Even so, however, social scientists typically do not imagine that their representations are never anything more than fairy tales. Despite the various shadings and nuances of their claim to knowledge, it has remained a claim to the factual, not the fictive or the fanciful, and it has remained centrally fixed to the criterion of a correspondence between the-world-that-is-there and the re-presentation of that world by scientific theory. Social scientists expect that a "good theory" will be coherent; they expect that a consensus can develop around it; they expect that it will be useful—but most of all, they expect that it will correspond to its object, that which it claims to re-present from the-world-that-is-there.

But scientific social theory has been unable to make good its claim to knowledge. I do not mean that the disciplines of social science have failed utterly to hold an allegiant following (though some of them—e.g., economics—have been more successful at it than others): that is not the point; no doubt the claims to knowledge struck by astrology or oneiromancy or the plumbing of goat carcasses still retain adherents. Rather, I mean that the claim to knowledge argued traditionally by scientific social theory has not been demonstrated sufficiently and self-consistently; its substance and its support are not what it proclaims them to be. This representational claim, in terms of which the self-understanding and valorization of scientific social theory are constituted, rests on a convention that can be held in place only insofar as, and only so long as, the convention is segregated from the domain of representational objects. Once that segregation is breached, as it has been by the persistent gaze of social theory itself, the representational claim is radically destabilized. Definitive limits between "the factual" and "the fictive" dissolve, and any effort to restabilize the representational claim by reinvigorating the convention cannot escape the unseemly appearance of imperialistic fiction-mongering.

Such is now the setting in which social scientists have been slowly awakening to the unsettling sound and sight of what one has called "blurred genres":

> This genre blurring is more than just a matter of Harry Houdini or Richard Nixon turning up as characters in novels or of midwestern murder sprees described as though a gothic romancer had imagined them. It is philosophical inquiries looking like literary criticism (think of Stanley Cavell on Beckett or Thoreau, Sartre on Flaubert), scientific discussions looking like belles lettres *morceaux* (Lewis Thomas, Loren Eiseley), baroque fantasies presented as deadpan empirical observations (Borges, Barthelme), histories that consist of equations and tables or law court testimony (Fogel and Engerman, Le Roy Ladurie), documentaries that read like true confessions (Mailer), parables posing as ethnographies (Castaneda), theoretical treatises set out as travelogues (Lévi-Strauss), ideological arguments cast as historiographical inquiries (Edward Said), epistemological studies conducted like political tracts (Paul Feyerabend), methodological polemics got up as personal memoirs (James Watson). Nabokov's *Pale Fire*, that impossible object made of poetry and fiction, footnotes and images from the clinic, seems very much of the time; one waits only for quantum theory in verse or biography in algebra. (Geertz 1980, 165–66)

Given the network of conjunctions that were thought to exemplify the "blurring of genres," it is perhaps tempting to conclude that the social scientist's self-understanding has finally caught up with that of the litterateur, who has more or less wittingly struggled with the bankruptcy of theories of literature and literary criticism for half a century and more (see the recent accounts and diagnoses by Graff 1979; Goodheart 1978; and Ellis 1974). Yet such a conclusion is apparently belied by at least two circumstances: on the one hand, there is little indication that more than a handful of social scientists are aware that the failures of theory in social science and in literary production are in any important way related, much less that they have the same structure; on the other hand, social theorists at least as early as Karl Mannheim and Max Weber—that is, as early as the presence of Gottfried Benn and Rémy de Gourmont, and well before the New Criticism movement—displayed more than a glimmer of familiarity with the predicament of social science's claim to knowledge, even if they chose mostly to ignore the depth and breadth of that predicament. Moreover, we would be remiss were we not to appreciate the well of resistance from which that peculiar amalgam of familiarity and ignorance continues to be refreshed.[19] Concern for a "blurring of genres," as for the general predicament of which it is part, manifests an anxiety about the privileged voice of social science. The valorization of social-scientific knowledge as superior to "mere opinion" or "ideology" or "literary storytelling"—that is, a valorization that is integral to social science's traditional claim to knowledge—constitutes the visible surface of social scientists' central privilege, namely, the privileged status of their speaking/writing, the authorization of their words. A "blurring of genres" signifies destabilization of that visible surface of privilege: the field of speaking/writing, previously traversed by multiple lines of demarcation that both separated and ordered the various regions called "social-scientific knowledge," "ideology," "literary storytelling," etc., has been undergoing a relentless homogenization. It should be hardly surprising, therefore, if these symptomatic "irregularities" and "disappearances" that comprise such phenomena as "blurred genres" should strike the registers of social scientists as serious threats to the authority of their occupational credentials—and as threats to be resisted, even if only by denial and amnesia.

In view of the preceding remarks, it is appropriate that I should interject a thread of commentary on "epistemological activity" and, more particularly, on the relative situation of the activity of this book, which might be characterized as a critical "exposition" of the epistemological arguments of social theory. Because the activity of this book, in both conclusion and beginning, is implicated in a structure of ironization, I must address the question posed by the author of *Sherston's Progress* when he asked whether "my neatly contrived little narrative would come sprawling out of its frame" (Sassoon 1936, 7).

| 19. See, e.g., Overington's (1979) expository essay and the appended responses.

Excepting the opinions of a small number of academic philosophers, the self-conscious pursuit of epistemology has not been a well-regarded activity in recent times. Indeed, even among people who ostensibly have to do with the birth and nurturance of new knowledge, there are a great many who either exhibit little or no regard for inquiries into the grounds and warrant of knowledge claims or view such inquiries with a mixture of impatience and disdain. Perhaps the most common expressions of this latter attitude can be summarized by analogy to the "warning" of a celebrated comment about the concept of "face," so much discussed in connection with cultures of the East: "It is very well if you don't stop to think, but the more you think the more confused you grow" (Lu Hsün [1934] 1960, 4:129). There have been more forceful enunciations of the warning, of course. The strongest version I have encountered, more than once, is pronounced injunctively, sometimes with a paternalistic air of concern, but almost always with a finality that would brook no argument: "Don't bother with those questions, or you will destroy whatever chance you have of becoming a good scientist!" Such challenge can be quite enough to make many a young student of science pull up short and research his or her professional conscience.

No less disdainful, if less crudely uttered, was the position argued by Max Weber at the turn of the century, and subsequently ritualized by much of twentieth-century social science. After conducting a brief but highly critical review of essays written by one of his contemporaries, Weber shared the thought that "all this makes one wish that the current fashion according to which every first work must be embellished with epistemological investigations would die out as quickly as possible" (Weber [1905–6] 1975, 187n). Yet even while greatly perturbed that "something like a methodological pestilence prevails within our discipline" (Weber [1913] 1964, 139), Weber would still accept the worth of inquiry into the grounds and conditions of knowledge, under specified and exceptional circumstances. In this, he took a stance that was later to be made fashionable by certain philosophers of science (e.g., Kuhn 1970a; Toulmin 1961): when "considerable shifts of the 'viewpoint' from which a datum becomes the object of analysis" have taken place, in consequence of which "the idea emerges that the new 'viewpoint' also requires a revision of the logical forms in which the 'enterprise' [of science] has heretofore operated," then at such time, Weber conceded, one may worthily undertake an epistemological inquiry (Weber [1906] 1949, 116).[20] Whether Weber would have diagnosed the current scene as such a time I do not pretend to know. Perhaps not. Clearly

---

20. Thus it was that Weber's own time qualified, particularly in view of his and others' efforts to formulate properly "the logic of the cultural sciences" and thereby expand the accredited limits of scientific method.

there are many Weberian scholars today who do not believe that this is such a time. Be that as it may, in the following chapters I shall undertake examinations of some issues of epistemology—though not of that alone, and not as an end in itself.

In conducting the critical "exposition" of epistemological arguments both explicit and implicit in twentieth-century social theory, I shall make certain constrictions, omissions, and promissory "managements" of irony. Those of which I am aware may be acknowledged in advance.

First, and most notable of all, there is the matter of standpoint. The argument of this book is governed by a shorter and a longer aim. The shorter aim—to evaluate the epistemological foundations of twentieth-century social theory—is necessarily and severely limited by virtue of the fundamental "premise" (at this point I shall not name it otherwise) that an adequate theory of knowledge must simultaneously be a theory of society, of history. Because scientific social theory has traditionally presupposed the existence of a stable and self-consistent epistemic structure (that which accredits its claim to true or valid knowledge of the-world-that-is-there), this beginning of my project must focalize those alleged beginnings, that is, the various epistemic structures that have been presupposed by a variety of twentieth-century social theorists. This critical exegesis comprises, first, limited expositions of what was said and attempted epistemologically in the written word and, second, critiques thereof, insofar as limited descriptions of the said and the attempted in relation to the destination of a self-consistently demonstrated warranting of the claim to true or valid knowledge can be said to be critique. Insofar as that destination was not reached in a given venture, the "why" of such failure has not been addressed except in a preparatory way. The inquiry offered in chapters 2 through 5 is situated in the midst of a dilemma: exegesis must take place on the basis of some sort of "knowledge of history"—this, in order to judge what was said in the context of the unsaid, the desired, and the done—yet it is the claim to true or valid knowledge, the claim of epistemic judgment, that is here put to question as to its possible foundedness. Thus, these chapters answer nothing concretely. I surely do not imagine them to be a "sociology of knowledge" or even an "intellectual history," insofar as those activities are accredited differently from "myth" or "literary storytelling" or "ideology." I do not pretend that these chapters provide an adequate account of why various theorists adopted, explicitly or implicitly, one or another epistemic stance. Yet these chapters do, I believe, clarify some of the questions regarding those stances and the conditions of a claim to knowledge; and in that, they prepare a way to some answers—which is the longer aim not only of this volume as a whole but also of the project of which it is a first installment.

I do not attempt in these chapters a wholesale inventory of all those scholars who have striven to formulate analyses or doctrinal positions regarding epistemological relations, or who have otherwise manifested such analyses or positions. Numerous figures whose works might well qualify for inclusion in a general library of "epistemological studies" appear not at all or only fleetingly.[21] Such an undertaking would require much more space and patience, the point of diminishing returns would be reached very quickly, and I do not intend in these pages to write a general history of epistemology. My purpose is rather more modest: to feature a broad range of current views, as these have been given explicitly or implicitly in the works of selected major theorists. While I freely concede that other scholars, neglected below, may be equally deserving of the appellation "major theorist," I do not believe that the principal conclusions of my critical study would be different were they included. Nevertheless, I acknowledge that such question of difference cannot be answered by recourse to any sort of sampling theory, for example; and it is partly with that circumstance in mind, in a proleptic context of audience, that I include as many theorists as I do. To be sure, readers as well as publishers expect to see a justification of choices, some giving of "reasons" within a prefabricated rationality of difference and preference: why *these* cases, just this one and that one, but not some other. I can respond with opinion, with "reasons ad hoc": for instance, the theorists treated below "represent the wide variety of epistemological positions and theoretical perspectives that have been central to twentieth-century social theory"; these theorists have been, and in one degree or another continue to be, "influential on the conduct and self-understanding of social science"; and so forth. But in the absence of a demonstrably warranted theory of knowledge—which is to say also, theory of society, of history—I cannot here invoke in a responsible way fully grounded and warranted "reasons" for the choices made. Indeed, insofar

21. There are other "exclusions"—those that figure in the deferral of an argument, marking both its incompletion and its spilling over the apparent frame of its pages. A wilderness of mirrors multiplies variety endlessly until the vanishing point, which is where we can catch different sight of the functioning of wilderness (much as Duerr [1978] has recently urged). This strategic theme—in which the question of an epistemics, an ethics, a politics, a technics, an aesthetics, is always already one unitary question of poiesis—circulates throughout this volume and into its successors. But of course it circulates much more widely, too: in Derrida's growing provocations, in one of the trajectories being built in "radical feminist theory," and elsewhere. Because these materials (what I now make them) are implicated in the completion of argument "in" this volume, they are exclusions only in the most exiguous sense. I hope to redeem that promise (to the extent it *can* be redeemed by the institution of the book) in succeeding volumes, more especially the third.

as that theory is not yet wholly constructed, I cannot guarantee that these choices *are* "correct" choices. I only believe them to be so.

I also acknowledge that my expository critique of the epistemological structures of particular scholars makes no pretense of being an account of the entire scholarly product of any of the considered theorists. I am quite aware that by concentrating my attention on theorists' epistemological arguments, to the neglect of what some would call their "substantive" studies, readers may charge me with having engaged in unfair criticism, oversimplification, and distortion, because of oversight of possible complications in a theorist's "œuvre" between prescriptions of "methodological principle" and the actuality of a "logic in use" as this latter spreads throughout the theorist's conduct of his project. It does seem to be the case that theorists have laid down "rules of method" only to violate them in the conduct of their own subsequent endeavors. But to that potential charge I must oppose the following answer.

In the first place, my concern is not with "rules of method" in the small sense; rather it is with theorists' studies of and/or positions with regard to fundamental epistemological questions—that is, those pertinent to the possibility of and the conditions of a veridical knowledge. Whether one of the theorists, in the practice of this or that particular study, diverged wholly or partly from methodological prescriptions previously set down by his own hand is itself relatively unimportant to my purpose of argument. That Durkheim, for example, sometimes only weakly obeyed his own admonitions regarding proper rules of sociological method does not imply that the basic epistemological statement attempted in the introduction to his study *The Elementary Forms of the Religious Life* is contradictory to that behind his methodological primer.

In the second place, where a theorist does not undertake systematic study of epistemological matters (or even where the theorist does) but addresses them selectively and perhaps rather casually, one may expect to find that the conclusions drawn and the positions adopted are marked by raw edges, inconsistencies, and a touch of the enigmatic. But I am much less concerned to trace all the ambages and reticulations than to emphasize the predominant stance. (When a product is invented and distributed to markets, the nuances separating the ensuing versions or "brand names" of that product are undoubtedly important both to the firms competing for shares of the markets and to the chroniclers of inventions and promotional techniques; but if in its basic constitution that product is the materiality of a madness, nuances offer no salvation.)

Third, and most importantly, we must be very clear about what is assumed in the posture of the claimant who would argue the trace of a line between that which is "substantive" and that which is "procedural" in order to show that a given theorist's disquisition on "principles of knowing" was merely preliminary exercise to the *really* important task of investigating one or another topical object in the discipline's domain—in other words, that epistemological disquisition occupies a peripheral location in the space of the theorist's total work. Whether explicitly or not, the epistemological position adopted by a theorist (even if unwittingly or half-wittedly adopted) addresses the actuality of that "logic in use" which is manifested in his or her own subsequent studies and passes judgment upon it. To be sure, in a given case the judgment may be wholly wrong, because the position adopted and the disquisition behind it were crucially flawed. Indeed, it must also be said that the judgmental relation is reciprocal; the actuality of a "logic in use" (to continue to use these inadequate terms) passes judgment upon the principles of the adopted position—which, of course, implies an epistemological space greater than that defined by those principles. Indeed, further: the actuality of the scholar's conduct of knowledge may be *fundamentally different* from the prescriptions offered in those epistemological principles; such is, in fact, precisely the burden of argument toward which I work in my critical review. But to say that the space of the disquisition, whatever its conclusions, and the impulse of the position, whatever its stripe, are marginal or peripheral within the theorist's "œuvre" by virtue of the category to which they belong, is to say that the *warrant* for a knowledge claim, that is, the possibility and conditions of its existence, must be marginal or peripheral to the existence of the claim as such.

I am well aware of the abundance of those who preach just that marginality—the very same marginality as that of the marketplace seller who, behind the doublespeak of a "caveat emptor" sign, promotes the commodity itself and therewith its commodious masking of the conditions of its production. Indisputably, there are many who counsel their successors to avoid the "self-debilitation" of epistemological inquiry; and they do so even while proceeding merrily with their own profound works of science, any one of which may be enough to evoke memory of a justly famous exemplification of such "profound" thinking:[22]

observation:	"The cat eats the mouse."
reflection:	"Cat = nature, mouse = nature; consumption of mouse by cat = consumption of nature by nature = self-consumption of nature."
discovered generalization:	"Devouring of the mouse by the cat is based upon the self-consumption of nature."

22. I have slightly modified the phrasing of this example (see Marx and Engels [1932] 1976, 5:481).

Finally, I should note that the critique presented in these chapters is partial in the sense that emphasis is given largely to the negational side of critique. Sooner or later, in their reading of these chapters, some may feel a strong urge to voice Samuel Johnson's complaint, "To object, is always easy, and, it has been well-observed by a late writer, that 'the hand which cannot build a hovel, may demolish a temple' " (1757, 306). I would be pleased to have the reader's forbearance at those times, as at others. While a solely negative critique is indeed partial, and is surely inadequate because of that partiality, the negational side of critique is indispensable. My activity is not negation for the sake of negation; rather, it is to prepare a construction by demonstrating first what that construction cannot be, thereby making a space *for* that construction. I agree that the task of a critic is, in part, "to awaken congealed life in petrified objects," as Adorno once said of Walter Benjamin's activity (Adorno [1955] 1967, 233). Whether I shall accomplish as much during the course of my project I do not know. I cannot know. But in any case, it is too great a task to hope to accomplish within the compass of this volume. My desire in these chapters is to show certain ossifications and petrifactions for what they are. In subsequent volumes I hope to work toward redemption of the promise of that necessary complement to the negational side of critique.

As to the import of this volume, I would recommend a pair of cautions above all others. On the one hand, there must be no confusion of a critique of science or more generally of epistemologies for a critique of society. A critique of society is necessarily implicit in this volume, but it is necessarily also partial, and that partiality makes the critique inadequate as an account, even of the various conditions whereby the objects of the critique of epistemologies (which objects comprise the explicit material of the following chapters) are as they are. On the other hand, in the construction of critique (whether of epistemologies or of society generally) we must avoid the ineffectuality of placing ourselves vicariously in an imagined space of some *Wunschwelt*. The world one wishes to make in consequence of a full critique is not the world wherein one stands when formulating and promoting that critique. (Such an obvious caution; yet so much of the putatively critical activity I have observed argues otherwise.) Short of consigning oneself to a destiny of iconoclastic sniping, there is no escape from the tension of that nexus of relations constituted simultaneously as the object *and* the condition of one's critical activity. The temptation to transport oneself to the projected space of that which one desires to make concrete, through critical activity, and then to assume that localization as provisional of the concrete circumstances of one's activity, is a notoriously strong temptation. But it is finally disastrous. Insofar as one desires to be effective in the world—not simply to "understand" it but to change it in desired ways—one must engage it as it is. To do otherwise concretely is quite impossible. To do otherwise in abstraction is to purchase a ticket of passage to those distant bleachers of the world where sit the romantics and the rebels, wishing and sighing, hissing and spitting—and dying with the rest of us.

4. MADNESS IN REASON, REASON IN MADNESS

Have we lost our capacity for revulsion? Have we witnessed, been party to, so much plunder and devastation and brutality that we are now thoroughly corrupt? How otherwise would you describe our apparent success in, to use that ludic expression of the past quarter-century, "learning to live with the bomb"?—in adjusting to the prospect that, one day soon, our devices may create the final devastation? Are we already beyond sensibilities of revulsion—the revulsion that can father a great refusal, "No more!"? I wonder. Others have wondered. Some have decided, either for the claims of pessimism or for a haze of optimism. Some still wonder. Some sleep. Stanley Cavell must have wondered, when, in his public letter to Alceste, he wrote the following lines:

> Montaigne is appalled by the human capacity for horror at the human. I think I know what he means and I think you do too. But the world during my lifetime rather shows that it is yet more horrible to lose this capacity for horror. . . . [A]ren't Nazis those who have lost the capacity for being horrified by what they do? They are our special monsters for *that* reason, monsters of adaptability. (Who knows whether what they did, apart from scale, was really that different from what others have done? Who knows whether the only real Nazis were created by a particular time and place and by a particular set of leaders and led? Who does not know that Nazism cannot succeed apart from the human capacity for *going along*? And what political thinker does not recognize that most of us will mostly go along with the tide of events, and even argue that we (mostly) ought to? But who does not see that there must be *some* limit to this? I am saying that Nazism specifically turns this human capacity for adapting into a mockery of itself, a mockery of being human.) And was hypocrisy really the charge that the students brought against America the other day? Their claim was to be in revolt because revolted, because horrified, by what they were asked to consent to. I do not raise the question whether their response was pure. *My question here is whether one is prepared to credit revulsion and horror as conceivably political responses, as perhaps the only epistemological*

access to the state of the world; as possible forms of conscience.
(1979a, 31; last emphasis added)[23]

Cavell's is one of the most crucial questions we face today. You do not agree? But open your eyes! Look at what we *have* consented to, already, in our global dwelling, in our lands of patriotism, in our daily existences. Consider how "well" we have adjusted to the injuries of class, race, and gender—injurer and injured alike; to the pollution of our biosphere; to scenes of mass starvation; to the manipulations of commodity fetishism; to the ghettos of our discourse. Consider that the average male in this country, still somewhat younger than thirty years of age, has witnessed the annual ritual of introducing the new-model automobiles from Detroit fifteen or twenty times, for a total of perhaps a thousand different "models"; the chances are very good that he can correctly name four of every five automobiles he sees on the street. During the past two decades he has also seen hundreds and probably thousands of pictorial images—photographic and electronic—of a variety of atrocities. Can he correctly name them? Can he, for instance, discriminate Tuareg starvation from Biafran or Bengali?—the survivors of Nagasaki from those of Minamata? If such critics as Barthes and Sontag are correct that atrocities have become "too familiar" to us through the congealed presence of their photographic images—so that the price of our horrification has soared—then what must be said of our "political consciousness"?

At some point in our modern times, it seems, our notion, our sensibility, of "crisis" grew tired. There is a level of irony in that, a level of irony beneath the naturalistic explanations that tell of satiations and overstimulations of sensory receptivity: in the midst of so much material for a sensibility of crisis, in the midst of that "pile of debris" that "grows skyward" before Klee's aghast *Angelus Novus*,[24] our sensibility of crisis was

---

23. The essay from which this passage is quoted has been incorporated in Cavell's *The Claim of Reason*, one of the rare, exquisite gems of thinking/writing during this century. I regret that my "dialogue" with Cavell's book did not begin until after the core of this volume had been fashioned.

24. I am here referring to Paul Klee's painting, as narrated by Walter Benjamin circa 1940 in his "Theses on the Philosophy of History":

> A Klee painting named "Angelus Novus" shows an angel looking as though he is about to move away from something he is fixedly contemplating. His eyes are staring, his mouth is open, his wings are spread. This is how one pictures the angel of history. His face is turned toward the past. Where we perceive a chain of events, he sees one single catastrophe which keeps piling wreckage upon wreckage and hurls it in front of his feet. The angel would like to stay, awaken the dead, and make whole what has been smashed. But a storm is blowing from Paradise; it has got caught in his wings with

starving; for "crisis" is a construction, a condition, always rooted in criticism, and criticism is an activity that since the eighteenth century we have minimized in our conduct of "objective knowledge" and assigned principally to a "peripheral" domain of "subjectivity" called "art." In the absence of the activity of criticism, an activity that figures a rupture of the conventional, the possibility of "crisis" gives way to the blasé, to ennui, or to a certain brand of cynicism. On the one side, there is the sort of elicitation exemplified in a remark by Robert Merton—all the more significant because of its light-handed, even amused touch, and because Merton is surely very far from being among the least erudite of scholars—that social science (or sociology in particular) "has been in a condition of crisis throughout its history," indeed a condition of "chronic crisis, intermittently broken by short surprising periods of relative calm" (1975, 21–23). Cautioning against undue worry about this state of affairs, Merton recalled the comment of a historian (Eisenstein 1966, 38) that "every era once regarded as 'transitional' is now presented as an age of 'crisis' " and advised that sociologists as well as historians "may be indulged" in their self-referential thoughts of "crisis," although it be a "faded metaphor." On the other hand, there is our apparent willingness to endure any loss, any evil, no matter how terrible, so long as we can imagine to have *explained* it within a frame of "objectivity." Explanation puts the event in place, measures it for the shroud of amnesia. And when enough explanation of enough loss has passed into the fibers of biography, knowing that amnesia will hold it amidst a company of equals, the accumulation transforms into that which Burke (1953, 2) once named "the cynicism of analysis"—and exemplified by quoting Flaubert: "I dissect unceasingly; that gives me amusement; and when finally I have uncovered the corruption in something that was thought pure, the gangrene of lovely places, I raise my head and laugh."

In his dazzling study of "insanity in the age of reason," Foucault observed that during "the Middle Ages and until the Renaissance, man's dispute with madness was a dramatic debate in which he confronted the secret powers of the world; the experience of madness was clouded by images of the Fall and the Will of God, of the Beast and the Metamorphosis, and of all the marvelous secrets of Knowledge. In our era, the experience of madness remains silent in the composure of a knowledge which, knowing too much about madness, forgets it" (Foucault [1961] 1965, xii).

such violence that the angel can no longer close them. This storm irresistibly propels him into the future to which his back is turned, while the pile of debris before him grows skyward. This storm is what we call progress. (Benjamin [1950] 1968, 259–60)

The silence of madness, madness locked away, segregated from reason by the asymmetry of a one-way window through which reason claims the privilege of peering as if an unobserved observer of madness: but *is* there a Maxwellian Demon, keying the locks of tiny trapdoors in that window so as to direct a magical stealth of segregation, keeping each side homogenous relative to the other? Is it his breath (perhaps he is a demonic trickster) that gives the chill to our confidence, now and then, regarding the space of that segregation? Who does not shiver, Foucault implicitly asked, when confronted with the awareness that, in our era, in our segregation of the mad and the not-mad, we confine madness, fix it to the plane of a medical table and to the tininess of individual as patient-inmate, and we address our cures to the space of an individualized "personality"?

So it is by that feat that we can count among ourselves, in our world, legions of the certifiably not-ill who daily warn their children and their children's children against the dangers of playing with matches and then march off to toy with nuclear firesticks; legions of the certifiably not-ill who daily seek to neutralize "snot" by folding it into a clean pressed handkerchief and carefully concealing "the whole soggy parcel" in a pocket, as if it were to the contrary a most valuable possession,[25] and then march off to insert in our food chain thousands of chemical agents the teratogenic effects of which have seldom been considered. Such is indeed madness, the madness of reason outside the medical corridors of our world, madnesses not of the clinically isolated individuals of "unreason" or "dementia" but of the rationality of the structure of us all, explicit and complicit. It is the madness of our uses of our world. It is the madness Husserl tried to appreciate when he charged that the crisis *of* modern science consists in an abandonment of "radicalness of scientific self-responsibility" (Husserl [1929] 1969, 4). It is the reason Graff tried not to appreciate as a "finally aimless and irrational mode of calculation that serves the goals both of arbitrary terror and dull commercialism" (1979, 41).

What stance can we take against madness that flourishes not from an absence of reason, as we have long been taught to believe, but from the very presence of reason, *as* reason? What claims of future being already ferment in the yellow juices that have condensed from the alembics of our philosophies and sciences?

During those fleeting periods when amnesia fails us, we experience

25. Significations of "the riddle of snot"—"what is it that the rich man puts in his pocket that the poor man throws away?"—have been considered by Thompson (1979), from whom the suggestion of my contrast derives.

again the novelty of being the posthumous citizens of our own era, the era of Progress. Whereas dying once secured the release of an end, living now offers the captivity of an interminable dying: we have "learned to live" with the constant threat, the likelihood, of planetary immolation. How do we respond to a world marked by this transfiguration of Life and Death?

Amnesia is a cold-stone certainty: therein its great appeal—if not as a response, strictly speaking, then as an effect.

Or, as some still do, we can lend our voices in appeal for the case of social science, the "sciences of man" and "humanistic study" of the social condition. "Take us seriously," these vaunted servants say, "give us enough money, a large-enough computer, and we will build a complete causal model of the world social system." But the "sciences of man" are idler wheels in the industrial machine, and social scientists have come lately to realize that the engineers of our world have devised other, more efficient means for the transfer of motion from one set of gears to another.

Again, we might respond to the normality of lunacy by deliberately crafting a philosophy of pessimism. I mean by this not the pessimism of a great fatigue—though that is probably the more common variety, since fatigue comes easily in our world of accelerated synaptic expectations—but the pessimism that is spawned in the dashing of hot excitements. Recent announcements by the French orphans of May 1968 have resuscitated this more energetic sort of pessimism, perhaps for the final time. I mean such declarants as Bernard-Henri Lévy, born in 1948, whose *Barbarism with a Human Face* has been by all accounts a very popular book in France (winner of the 1977 *Prix d'Honneur de l'essai*) and in translated editions—a work of diagnosis that tells of "this stricken world," full of "black mornings" and "twilights without dawn," wherein "nature is even more livid than the culture it apes" (Lévy [1977] 1979, 43). Lévy and his companions are archaeologists of the present, necromancers of future possessions. They have picked through the rubble of their springtime, weighed etiologies of the patently inutile, interrogated the lineages and unions of personal genealogy, and come upon a reconfirmation of Marx's famous verdict, rendered in the wake of 1848–49: "All revolutions perfected this machine [the state] instead of breaking it" (Marx [1852] 1979, 11:186). Those red morning rays of 1968 were black after all, as black as boot-dried blood. The enemy is tenacious, unrelenting, pervasive, these newly orphaned witnesses say to us; the enemy populated our own imaginations from the beginning, possessed our champions' bodies long before the heat of puberty, grew in strength at the bosom of our hopes. Our "stricken world" is novel for having shown us the paradigm of Greek tragedy in its true meaning: previously we knew only to beware the fatal flaw that always lurked within the unique excellence; now we can taste "unique excellence" for what it really is. "Peoples are there, they resist as much as they can, they fight and they die—and nothing prevents the Pinochets from ruling the world" (Lévy [1977] 1979, 133).

Lévy and his kin are casualties of the socialist/communist fraud. Do we chide them for having been duped so easily, and for so long?—for having promoted the fabulous remedies of a socialist homeopathy?—for having refused sight and smell of the suppurating proof of Stalin's cure, until, as Lévy has acknowledged, Solzhenitsyn's Gulag chronicles forced them "*to believe* what [they] were satisfied with *knowing*" (Lévy [1977] 1979, 154), namely, that carbuncular pus signifies necrosis of deep and vital tissues? Perhaps. But surely not at the cost of neglecting their lesson, as if it were solely theirs in source and fit. Turgot, Condorcet, Guizot, and the rest got it wrong, they tell us, but so have the skeptics: Progress is *not* an illusion, *not* a fantasy nurtured in unhappy consciousness, *not* a fraud perpetrated as some "stage theory" by the "haves" of this world against the "have-nots." Progress is real; it thrives; it does promote a unity of the world. Not only the *philosophes* and their inheritors but also their skeptical critics got it wrong because of their underlying optimism. Though "the world may have wandered, marked time, and got bogged down," its movement has nonetheless traced the thin line of an upward trend, a genuinely progressive movement up the slopes of barbarity—"a uniform and linear progression toward evil." In the opening era of uniformity and "generalized servitude," there will indeed be but a single class, "the class which fails to give birth to the good society, but succeeds, on the contrary, by consecrating the barbarian state" (Lévy [1977] 1979, 130, 163).

Is it true? Is Lévy *totally* without hope for a different future? It would seem so: "As far as I'm concerned, the game is over. For us in the West, the barbarism to come will have the most tragic of all faces: the human face of a 'socialism' that will take on itself all the flaws and excesses of industrial society" (151–52). His talk of what is to come, of what face it will have, is doubtlessly accurate extrapolation. Yet his talk is not only to himself. He did bother to write an announcement of his pessimism. Why? If the extrapolation is already locked in the grip of inevitable destiny, a chunk of unwitherable necessity, why bother to shake the amnesiacs among us? What is the point of it? Perhaps self-therapy for a betrayed revolutionary? More francs for his pocket? A wicked delight in robbing victims of their anesthesia, as he was robbed? Perhaps there is another answer—though I doubt it is to be found in his *Barbarism* or its sequel, *Le Testament de Dieu*.

2

Science and
the Pursuit of Knowledge

I. INTRODUCTION

> *All the social sciences are in a state of crisis. Some manifestations of this crisis are the intellectual sterility and practical futility of much policy-orientated research, the prevalence of "behavioural" survey-based investigations, the proliferations of descriptive studies, particularly of minutiae, the neglect of fundamental theoretical and philosophical work, and the reduction of the social sciences to problems of research technology.*

SO BEGAN THE INAUGURAL EDITORIAL of one of the many new journals to have been founded in recent years. This one, according to its name, traffics in articles of "Economy and Society" (presumably to be distinguished from articles that somehow pertain to one but not the other). The passage just quoted is not, as a statement of introduction and justification, peculiar to this journal alone, however. We have witnessed a spate of new journals, book-length essays, and anthologies that speak in much the same vein: of "reinventing anthropology" (Hymes 1972), of "an end to political science" (Surkin and Wolfe 1970), of "the coming crisis of Western sociology" (Gouldner 1970), of the bankruptcy of Western Marxism (Anderson 1976; Gouldner 1976), of a "restructuring of social and political theory" (Bernstein 1976; also Dunn 1979), of "economists at bay" (Lekachman 1976; Georgescu-Roegen 1971; Hutchison 1977), of history as "a discipline in crisis" (Handlin 1971; 1979), of *Contemporary Crises* (a journal), of exaggerated understandings of the possible contributions of social science to policy making and problem solving (see, e.g., Lindblom and Cohen 1979), and to other appeals for self-scrutiny. The tables of symptoms cited, the diagnoses tendered, the cure prescribed—all may vary from physician to physician, engineer to engineer, but there is general agreement that the collective patient is gravely ill and that serious address of the malady and its conditions of existence takes us quite unavoidably into mysteries of "the philosophy of science"—or, though on this there is less agreement, into the still darker recesses of epistemology, ethics, and aesthetics. Discussions of doctrines wholly or partially comprising theories of knowledge are clearly more in evidence among scientists today than was the case twenty or thirty years ago. Various doctrinal positions, the wooly labels of which are by now common words to most eyes, have been staked out in networks of strophic alliance and intermittent disputation: there are, or there purport to be, "positivist," "fallibilist," "phenomenological," "pragmatist," "structuralist," "Marxist," etc., theories of knowledge and corresponding versions of philosophy of science, none of which has actually accomplished very much beyond its own reproduction (which is, of course, occupationally fruitful); and, in evident exasperation with that sorry record of accomplishment, most recently we had put before us the proposal of an "anarchist" or "dadaist" theory of knowledge, the sole tenet of which (allegedly) is "*Anything goes.*"[1]

A sense of crisis, even of epistemological crisis, has grown appreciably larger and more insistent among the various disciplines of science, yet in most quarters of the scientific academy epistemological inquiry is not well regarded. Part of the legacy of the high doctrine of positivism consists of a frayed raiment of that proclaimed identity of all valid and useful knowledge with science itself and, on its obverse reflection, the banishment of metaphysics, taken in its broadest sense, to a residence in history's garbage heap alongside all other remainders of the "prescientific age." This part of the positivist legacy (in which I would include the notion of the basic unity of science, the natural sciences being exemplary) is deeply imprinted in the sentience of many members of the academy, and for them the whole matter of *epistemic* questioning is pointless: all issues of epistemology, or at least all of those that truly mattered, have been settled, and there is simply no point in rehashing dead issues. Other members strive to share conviction in that belief, but the failure of their effort is told by their prevailing attitude toward proposals to raise once again those "dead" issues—not so much

---

1. Feyerabend (1975, 21 n. 12), the recent proponent of this "doctrine of no doctrine," took pains to distinguish his "anarchistic" thesis from the political anarchism of, say, Kropotkin, preferring to that, or any other "Puritanical dedication and seriousness," the dadaist attitude of being "utterly unimpressed by any serious enterprise."

dismissive as suspicious, distrustful, scornful. For these working scientists the very suggestion of inquiry into the grounds and warrant of claims of knowledge can be profoundly threatening. Faced with the prospect of such an investigation, they sometimes join with Tevye, who, unable to rationalize his daughter's marriage to a Gentile, because that would necessitate thinking the unthinkable, declared, "My daughter is dead."

There are many in the practice of science who believe if not that they are a special people then that science is a special, privileged activity, the fruits of which are quite unlike any other. While some of these people are oblivious to the possibility that the constitution of science might actually be something less, others manifest their concern that "unthinkable thoughts" might win credence if epistemological self-scrutiny is taken seriously. They typically discount such examinations as the work of cranks and malcontents (or perhaps of those who, having shuffled off to intellectual retirement, at whatever age, are no longer capable of adding to the cumulative product of *real* science). To be sure, there *is* much chicanery and there *is* much simple foolishness in the whole array of that which has been passing before us as serious epistemological critique of the foundation of science. No doubt a diversity of silent motivations—including all sorts of fuzzy-headed romanticism, anxieties induced by confrontations with the numerical or the mathematical, apprehended opportunities to acquire stature within less populated niches, and so on—stands behind those proffered critiques. No doubt, too, much of that speaking and writing is marked by a hebetude fully equivalent to the standard defined in the corpus of utterances emitted by business-as-usual scientists. But the great folly is to dismiss the *very possibility* of clarifying critique, to prejudge the destination and thus to discount the worth of the journey, by calling up such bogus arguments as that which points to the independence of our ability to walk whether or not we know anything about anatomy and the kinesiology of human locomotion.

Epistemological self-consciousness is not, of course, an unprecedented happening in the academy of science. One need not be an accredited historian of modern science in order to appreciate the controversies of the pragmatists in the United States or the *Methodenstreit* in turn-of-the-century Germany—or indeed the quarrels during that most auspicious seventeenth century when Baconian optimism gradually took hold. While the late sixteenth-century Botero could join formulations that strike us as distinctly medieval in their emphasis on "divine plan" with other formulations having a more modern look—for example his Malthusian-like proposition of the limits of population growth (Botero [1588] 1956, bk. 3, chap. 2), or his argument that a ruler ought to undertake all manner of environmental improvements, since "the products of the manual skill of man are more in number and of greater worth than the produce of nature, for nature provides the material and the object but the infinite variations of form are the result of the ingenuity and skill of man" (Botero [1589], 1956, bk. 8, chap. 3)—many others were not so confident of the professed powers of traditional science and its applications. For them it appeared increasingly that the *liber naturae* was not so easy to read as once had been thought, that it was proving to be a bewildering and indecipherable *mysteria naturae*. There, as elsewhere, we can count on Montaigne for colorful observations of the skepticism with which the traditional science had come to be held by many. In his "Apology for Raimond de Sebonde" (*Essays*, II.2), written during the same decade as Botero's treatises, Montaigne asked whether "we have a little more light in the knowledge of human and natural things" and then answered with another, mocking question: "Why will not Nature please, once for all, to lay open her bosom to us, and plainly discover to us the means and conduct of her movements, and prepare our eyes to see them? Good God, what blunders, what mistakes should we discover in our poor science! I am mistaken if it apprehend any one thing as it really is." There was no bashfulness in Montaigne's pronouncement of verdict: the practice of science had been a display of fake lights, dazzling the multitudes away from the proper path of *prudentia* and *sapientia*.

> Just as women for themselves make use of teeth of ivory where the natural are wanting, and instead of their true complexion make one of some foreign matter; legs of cloth or felt, and plumpness of cotton, and in the sight of everyone paint, patch, and trick up themselves with false and borrowed beauty: so does science (and even our law itself has, they say, legal fictions whereon it builds the truth of its justice); she gives us, in presupposition and for current pay, things which she herself informs us were invented. (Montaigne [1580–88] 1952, 258–59)

Not that Montaigne was skeptical about the lawfulness of nature: he found it "credible that there are natural laws" (282). The problem was rather one of proper method—and in particular, for Montaigne, the instrument of human reason, which was "everywhere so insinuating itself to govern and command, as to shuffle and confound the face of things, according to its own vanity and inconstancy; . . . reason finds appearance for divers effects: 'tis a pot with two ears that a man may take by the right or left" (282).

Bacon, who was composing his famous treatises only a few years after Montaigne's *Essays*, settled accounts in favor of a theory of knowledge that emphasized methodical accumulation of experientially tested scientific knowledge, on the basis of which ever greater control of nature would be attained. His play to the manifold audiences of his time was carefully wrought, as the following passage testifies:

> If therefore there be any humility towards the Creator, any reverence for a disposition to magnify His works, any charity for man and anxiety to relieve his sorrows and necessities, any love of truth in nature, any hatred of darkness, any desire for the purification of the understanding, we must entreat men again and again to discard, or at least set apart for a while, these volatile and preposterous philosophies [of a mind-constituted reality], which have preferred theses to hypotheses, led experience captive, and triumphed over the works of God; and to approach with humility and veneration to unroll the volume of the Creation, to linger and meditate therein, and with minds washed clean from opinions to study it in purity and integrity. (Bacon [1622] 1870–82, 9:371)

Bacon's attendance to religious duty would not suffer neglect because of this unrolling of the book of nature, for nature and the creation were one. Nor would he propose to deny the ancients' "possession of their honors" (Bacon [1620] 1952, I, Aphorisms 18–22). But the instauration of science required a different and superior method—a carefully disciplined method that does not permit the mind to "avoid labor" by hurrying "rapidly from the senses and particulars to the most general axioms" but that follows the true path of "investigating and discovering truth" through the meticulous design and conduct of experiments of the senses and particulars and "by ascending continually and gradually, til it finally arrives at the most general axioms." By obeying nature, it would be possible to gain genuinely the light of her secrets. Such obedience necessitated extirpation of various "false notions" or *idola mentis:* those of the tribe, being a failure to appreciate the innate limits of human intelligence; those of the den, a failure to appreciate that one's perception is always from the point of view of one's "individual den or cavern, which intercepts and corrupts the light of nature"; those of the market, a failure to appreciate the obstructions that language can create; those of the theater, or the dogmas of received tradition that "have crept into men's minds." Because these "idols," or their effects, are errors of human understanding rather than of the nature of things, they are open to correction. Although those who seek "to unroll the volume of Creation" must approach it "with minds washed clean" of all dogmatic opinion, they cannot approach as "blank slates," strictly speaking, for with the exceptions of the idols of the theater and certain of those of the market, the conditions of the *idola mentis* are "native" rather than acquired. However, their effects on human understanding can be avoided: "The formation of notions and axioms on the foundation of true induction is the only fitting remedy by which we can ward off and expel these idols" (Bacon [1620] 1952, I, Aphorisms 32–68).[2]

I do not here intend to write a history of modern science or of theories of scientific knowledge. Several well-known, conventional histories are currently available, and I would not attempt at this juncture to improve upon any of them. A properly constructed history requires first that one has elucidated a self-consistent theory of knowledge, and, at a minimum, that means (as I shall argue later) the construction of the basic framework of a theory of society. Rather, my concern in this chapter is to set out some general considerations of features of the current relationship between epistemology and the enterprise of science—or, to be more specific, circumstances of what has become an equation of "epistemology" with "philosophy of science." If we are to appreciate the better part of that recent literature, which, like the inaugural editorial quoted at the beginning of this chapter, speaks of "crisis"—not so much a crisis in science as the crisis *of* science—then we must approach it at its rooted references to the conditions and consequences of this dissipation of epistemic issues.

The demarcation of epistemology as philosophy of science with no remainder, a movement that school philosophy itself has often promoted, means that the presuppositions of modern science are shielded from the eye of critical inquiry, not perfectly, to be sure, but nonetheless effectively in most circles of science. Especially since the late nineteenth century, science has increasingly subjugated its own philosophical scrutiny through the promotion of a philosophy of science (its variations matter little in this regard) that is itself "scientized."[3] To the extent that this

2. Although certain of the "aphoristic" passages of *Novum Organum* could be read as propositions of, say, the social constitution of language and thought, or the partiality and relativity of observational perspective, or the reproduction of "received opinion" and interpretation, Bacon's thesis of the idols was deployed primarily as a wedge with which to open space for his formulation of a new scientific method. It was rather the *philosophes*—Condillac and Diderot, for instance—who generalized the thesis and extended the Baconian optimism regarding the potency of a restored science to the knowledge of "the social" as well as "the natural." Diderot's *Encyclopédie*, crown jewel of the French movement, expressed "two leading features of the fundamental ideas of the Enlightenment," as Goldmann saw it: "the great importance attached to making knowledge as comprehensive as possible," and "the idea that this knowledge is a *sum* of items of information to be conveyed in alphabetical order" (Goldmann [1968] 1973, 1).

3. To select but one of the host of examples at hand, in 1910 the philosopher/social scientist John Dewey was lamenting the misguidedness of traditional epis-

subjugation has won credibility as a matter-of-fact regularity and propriety, external challenges to the foundation of science can be exploded harmlessly in the wasteland of "anti-intellectualism," "religious quackery," and "metaphysical nonsense."[4] The critique of theories of knowledge is dissolved into a "house philosophy" that refuses to take seriously a wider examination of its own bases (indeed, it pretends to be without presuppositions), that purports to distinguish itself from the discourse of ordinary language by the conceit of possessing its own special discourse ("anti-poetical"), that empties itself of all questions of ethics and aesthetics except insofar as they may be treated as objects of the scientific method (and excepting the narrow ethic of the method itself), that suspends "values" in a realm separate from that of "facts" (perhaps acceding to the possibility that "values" can be based on, or derived from, or directed by, verified "facts"—that is, "scientifically guided policy"—but never to the possibility that the constitution of "facts" is based in "values"). Such a philosophy of science dissembles as having greatly simplified the classical problem of how true and necessary knowledge is possible. Indeed, the matter would seem to have been settled: the methodical conduct of modern science begets an ever more extensive progeny of proven knowledge. By virtue of the peculiar involution, there is even a parthenogenesis of

temology, arguing that it was far removed from its proper concern for the creation of "a theory that takes knowledge as it finds it and attempts to give the same kind of account of it that would be given of any other natural function or occurrence" (Dewey [1910] 1965, 97).

4. Despite its disclaimers, of course, this philosophy and the scientism that inspires it practice their own peculiar metaphysics; thus, for instance, consider the concerns of a science that has become so attentive to exactitude of measurement of the degree to which its formulae diverge from the "real-world" facticities those formulae purportedly organize and interrelate. (As Eddington remarked, just "because a man works in a laboratory it does not follow that he is not an incorrigible metaphysician." Eddington [1939] 1958, 33.) Ironically, it was Bergson ([1903] 1912) who, already by the turn of this century, in his romanticist attack on positivism, argued that the definitiveness of a proper definition of metaphysics could be referenced only after the practice of the scientist had been considered; his claim was that one must examine science not simply in regard to its successes, that is, to its finished formulae, but also in regard to those margins of error, "stochastic disturbances," and indeterminacies that spread between the formulae and their *explacanda*, for there, in that presupposed intimacy of science to a world that is both referenced by science and prior to the objects of science, one finds the space for a metaphysics. Bergson's proffered salvation of "the metaphysical approach" (a metaphysics subject to science, nevertheless) was not fundamentally unique, nor has it been entirely ignored (even though most philosophers of science have dismissed it). Merleau-Ponty ([1961] 1964), for example, has expressed his sympathy for the Bergsonian claims regarding the site of metaphysics.

proven scientific knowledge of the practice of science itself, for once this "scientized" philosophy of science acquired supremacy, the way was clear for the emergence of those species of "science of science" that, via their quickly flowing spew of specialty journals, books, and symposia, have taught us many strange and profound things about "science as a social enterprise" (for example, that scientists are susceptible to intangible as well as material rewards; that they squabble among themselves about such crucial matters as "priority of discovery" and eponymy but have developed ways of regulating their disputes; that many scientists, like many generals and many theologians, give their first loyalty not to the place of their legal employment but to their "profession"; that budding scientists are trained to be objective, impartial, and totally disinterested in any goal other than the pursuit of knowledge but sometimes stray from the correct path and seek eponymous glory or some other emblem of personal recognition and monetary reward; that the organization of work differs in specifiable fashion as between physics or chemistry, say, and anthropology or political science; and numerous other findings that would equally tax the nonscientist's intellect and credulity).

But matters are not so simple as a "scientized" philosophy of science would have us believe. Thus, we may ask, with Husserl (1936), with Gadamer (1965), and others, how it is possible to construct an adequate theory of knowledge based on the products of experimental science, when to do so would be tantamount to a presupposition of the veracity of those very criteria of scientific knowledge that are in question, that is, that are the problematics to be addressed by such theory! If the grounds of scientific knowledge are susceptible of even the possibility of error or falsity (and of course there are those who will not allow even that much), can we possibly rely on the results of science to test those grounds? One need not champion the resuscitation of any of the traditional epistemological theories in order to see that most of them addressed issues that are either ignored or answered noncritically by the subjugated philosophy of science. Indeed, I do not propose the revival of any of those traditional theories; their frailties are so great that abandonment, not revitalization, is required. But it must also be said that this subjugated philosophy of science is no better endowed (though perhaps no worse, either, even though it does neglect many of the questions of classical epistemology). The evidentiary product of modern science, no matter how great its lionization by the philosophers of science, cannot sustain this philosophy of science that seeks to demonstrate the warrantability of scientific knowledge. This philosophy of science suffers a constitutional defect of fundamental self-reflective critique, in consequence of which it is left ignorant of its own false existence. Whatever its variant—whether the old positivism of Mach (1883), the reductionist formalism of Duhem (1914), the logical positivism of the Vienna Circle (see Kraft 1950), the physicalism of Neurath (1931), the operationalism of Bridgman (1948), the logical empiricism of Carnap (1936–37, 1956), the falsificationism of Popper (1935), the *commodisme* of Poincaré (1905), etc., nearly all of which still have adherents—philosophy of science has not demonstrated the claimed veracity of scientific knowledge. Given its actual presuppositions and constitution, I shall argue, it cannot demonstrate as much.

2. QUESTS FOR CERTAINTY AND THE PROBLEM OF RELATIVISM

Some authorities have contended that epistemology, as the general study of the possibility, the conditions, and the nature of knowledge, originated within the matrix of sophistical skepticism. By that account we can attribute this species of dialogue to the wandering Sophists of fifth-century Athens, who allegedly first cast into systematic doubt a theretofore untrammeled "naive realism" regarding the configuration of "knowing that," "knowing about," "knowing how," and so forth. Once the gauntlet had been thrown, so the story goes, it became the obligation of those who profess "to love wisdom" to demonstrate by refinements of reason and experience, with or without the aid of final appeal to a revelatory monologue, the universal possibility, conditions, and nature of human knowledge, including foremost those categories of knowledge the truth of which is necessary, absolute, incorrigible, apodictic.

Whatever the concrete genesis of that doubt, the recorded efforts of epistemological inquiry can be read as a serially authored journal of a collective quest made in "devotion to an ideal of certainty" (Dewey [1922] 1930, 236; Dewey 1929). Now, the philosophical notion of "certainty" is complexly variegated, as we might expect such an important term of the philosophical tongue to be, and I have no desire to document all the nuances and divagations of meaning that have been crafted. Suffice it to say in general outline that the quest for certainty has manifested the concern that there must be demonstrably indubitable grounds for claims of knowledge, that absolutely true and necessary knowledge-statements are possible and can be made in specifiably methodical, replicable ways. Traditionally the possibility of certitude has been entertained principally with regard to three sorts of claims: claims of faith, claims of reason, and claims of sense experience. With the movement to dissociate philosophy from theology, claims of faith diminished in stature as a concern of epistemological inquiry—although as late as Kant the epistemological significance of articles of faith remained great (faith in the Summum Bonum, for example, was held to be a necessary consequence of the undoubtable reality of freedom even though such entailment could never be demonstrated theoretically). Claims of reason have often been assigned the distinction of certitude. The prime case consists of claims that are tautological—that is, strictly entailed within the rules of an abstract logic—but nontautological structures as well have been accorded the status of incorrigibility. In Kolakowski's words, "Philosophy has never given up its attempt to constitute an autonomous 'Reason' " (Kolakowski [1966] 1969, 210). Likewise with claims of sense experience: not only in the supposedly bedrock case of the *sensa* of oneself, but generally with sense experiences of other objects, there have been those who argue the applicability of a universal, absolute certitude.

In the course of arguing the respective merits of the methodical ways of rationalism and empiricism, some authors of that figurative journal have displayed a lassitude of purpose in regard to the quest for certainty. Understandably so: long before the advent of this century, the arguments had become tediously involved, often obscure, and none seemed to carry final solution. The suspicion was increasingly voiced that perhaps the standard insisted upon by radical skepticism—namely, that knowledge must be characterized by certainty, otherwise it can have no more authority than mere opinion—was simply too stringent. One measure of this suspicion can be found in the course of work produced by Bertrand Russell. It is well known to students of academic philosophy that the convictions of this most prolific writer changed enormously during the first three decades of his major work. Unlike many philosophers, he was usually candid about his changing views and failures of proof. While it would not be accurate to say that he threw over entirely the search for the grounds of certain knowledge, his later epistemology was devised in terms of an effort of increasing approximation to the certifiably true, a *connaissance approachée*. The earlier Russell (as in *Our Knowledge of the External World*, 1914) held to a strong criterion: a claim of knowledge must be characterized as that which cannot possibly be false. Hewing to a kind of phenomenalism wherein the "material object" itself was put aside in favor of sense data or "percepts" as the object of knowledge, he stressed the possibility of certitude with respect to further statements of knowledge constructed inferentially (e.g., about events not directly experienced: "Is my desk in my study when I am not?"). But by the time of *The Analysis of Matter* (1927), he had reconsidered that earlier position. Moving from the phenomenalist stance to his position of "logical constructionism," he had loosened the standards of what could qualify as acceptable knowledge. For the later Russell (e.g., 1948), sense data continued to serve as the foundation for claims of knowledge but without the assertion that their external causes can be known indubitably; and the possibility of inferential knowledge rested in the argument that if we are to give credence to *any* of our inferences about unobserved happenings in our everyday world, as of course we do, there is a minimal set of basic assumptions that we necessarily accept, and, while we cannot be assured of the truth of those assumed conditions of the world, we can, under specifiable circumstances, be "safe" in treating specific claims of knowledge as justified.

Whereas Russell persisted, if with reduced confidence, in allowing the possibility of certitude of true knowledge of the world, others have altered the focus of "truth" and therewith the applicability of the notion of "certainty." According to Tarski's (1931; 1944) "semantic theory of truth," the word "true" is a metalinguistic adjective that may be applied in description of a statement in a given language, that is, a descriptive "metastatement" about a statement.[5] In its original formulation Tarski's theory is tantamount to a version of the so-called correspondence theory of truth; but if to say that a knowledge statement "is true" requires use of a metastatement S^1 from a metalanguage L^1 about a statement S in a language L, then to say that we "are certain" that the knowledge statement "is true" requires a *meta-metastatement* from a *meta-metalanguage* about the metastatement S^1 from the metalanguage L^1 about the statement S in language L. Faced with this spiraling complexity, some philosophers of science not surprisingly have sought to dispense with the relevance of "truth-falsity" altogether, arguing that science creates theories that simply are useful—neither true nor false but simply more or less useful devices, fictions, or rules of inference and conduct that enable us to explain and predict observations of events in our world—and that therefore the notion of *certainty* of true knowledge is a useless relic of metaphysical thinking.[6]

Among the circumstances that led eventually to this sort of conclu-

5. Kolakowski has aptly referred to Tarski's theory as a "legalization of the semantic notion of truth" ([1966] 1969, 206): "truth," in other words, "refers to the relation obtaining between linguistic signs and elements of experience and does not prejudge or even raise the question concerning the metaphysical meaning of experience itself."

There is, of course, an affinity between this position and that of the "ordinary-language" theorists' preference for a coherence theory of truth (initiated from the emphasis of the linguistic model on criteria of coherence—phonological, semantical, syntactical—within language structure, rather than on criteria of correspondence), wherein the truth criterion of facticity refers not to referenced objects but to a discursive justifiability of the claim of a proposition. Among others, Habermas (e.g., 1973a, 169; 1973b, 245–47), following to some extent the truth doctrine of Strawson (1949), has recently attempted to develop this thesis and the connections between the classical alternatives of "correspondence" versus "coherence."

6. "Thought today is only too often compelled to justify itself by its usefulness to some established group rather than its truth" (Horkheimer [1947] 1974, 86).

sion, one of the most profound in its ramifications was the so-called discovery of language, for the infinite recession of the privilege of an original language sucked away all claims of privileged authority that had inhered in the office of "original author." By the early years of the nineteenth century, a stunning self-consciousness had intruded into the intimate relationship of "knowing subject" to "known object," as the problematics posed by a no-longer-neutral medium were realized more and more in the reflections of theory: "Language was burying itself within its own density as an object and allowing itself to be traversed, through and through, by knowledge" (Foucault [1966] 1970, 300).[7] As the century grew old, the sense of this discovery was being articulated still for the most part as a negativity (a feature very much with us today): "the societal" and "the historical," on the one hand, and "the linguistic," on the other, do not stand mutually exclusive as object-to-be-described and description-of-object.[8] As Cassirer later related this realization (in his characteristically neo-Kantian fashion):

> Man lives in a symbolic universe. . . . No longer can man confront reality immediately; he cannot see it, as it were, face to face. Physical reality seems to recede in proportion as man's symbolic activity advances. Instead of dealing with the things themselves man is in a sense constantly conversing with himself. He has so enveloped him-

---

7. Foucault argued further, however, that at the same moment language was being suspended in this doubled convolution, it was also being reconstituted elsewhere in a formation "difficult to access, folded back upon the enigma of its own origin and existing wholly in reference to the pure act of writing" ([1966] 1970, 300). This Faustian "irrationalism"—for example, the formations of the Marquis de Sade, Hölderlin, or Nietzsche—constituted a counterdiscourse to the standard scientific discourse: "Literature becomes progressively more differentiated from the discourse of ideas, and encloses itself with a radical intransitivity; it becomes detached from all the values which were able to keep it in general circulation during the Classical age (taste, pleasure, naturalness, truth), and creates within its own space everything that will ensure a ludic denial of them (the scandalous, the ugly, the impossible)." Compare Sontag: "The subject of literature has pre-empted much of the energy that formerly went into philosophy, until that subject was purged by the empiricists and logicians" ([1963] 1965, 132).

8. Inevitably, it would seem, this realization of "linguistic mediation" and "the duality of language" became itself the launching pad of new subject matters and new disciplines *within* science, even while it posed the most serious questions about the basis of science. Among the several treatments of "language and culture" that stimulated development of these disciplines, some of the better known works include von Humboldt (1880), Sapir (1921), Whorf (1956), Öhman (1951), and Segerstedt (1947). See also the collection of essays in Pinxton (1976).

self in linguistic forms . . . that he cannot see or know anything except by the interposition of this artificial medium. His situation is the same in the theoretical as in the practical sphere. (Cassirer 1944, 25)

Denied the possibility even of peering at physical reality without the complications of a medium that could no longer be assumed to have the neutrality of a vacuum, the human knower faced the curious predicament of being less able to demonstrate the surety of claims of knowledge at the very moment that science was yielding ever greater fruits, the palpability and effects of which were being readily confirmed in the practice of daily life. As one philosopher of science would impatiently remark (in the early 1970s), "The greatest scandal of philosophy is that, while all around us the world of nature perishes—and not the world of nature alone—philosophers continue to talk, sometimes cleverly and sometimes not, about the question of whether this world exists" (Popper 1972, 32).

One of the many casualties of this "discovery of language" was the notion of an unsullied, theory-free or theory-neutral "observation language," that is, the belief that direct observation of the real external world, with no "intervention" of any theoretical discourse and with no dependence on covert processes or nonobservables, was not only possible but had in fact been accomplished. The attempt to define, as a basic element of scientific method and norms, a theory-free observation language had been conducted beneath the auspices of that innocent doctrine characterized by Foucault as "the great myth of a pure Gaze that would be pure language: a speaking eye [which] would scan the entire . . . field, taking in and gathering together each of the singular events that occurred within it; and as it saw, as it saw ever more and more clearly, it would be turned into speech that states and teaches. . . . This speaking eye would be the servant of things and the master of truth" (Foucault [1963a] 1973, 114–15). Of course, that doctrine had not escaped completely from the realm of the disputable; among the several cases called upon as illustration of that point, the most commonly cited is Galileo's "astonished" though approving notice of the "ability" of Aristarchus and Copernicus to reject their "unmediated" (as some would put it) observations, and "to make reason so conquer sense that, in defiance of the latter, the former became mistress of their belief" (Galileo [1632] 1967, 328).[9] And it had been generally recognized that algorithms of measurement necessarily rely

9. The Salusbury–de Santillana translation gives a bit more flair to the passage: "to commit such a rape upon their senses as, in despite thereof, to make herself mistress of their belief."

on number theory, although such theory was taken to be perfectly neutral. But the understanding that, in Cassirer's words, we "cannot see or know anything except by the interposition of this artificial medium" of language posed the greater question of whether there can be *any* distinction between theory and experience, between method and result.[10] If theory is to be tested against experience as a gauge of its truth (or "validity"), and if experiences—our methods of observation and the methodical observations themselves—are theory-endowed, then how can we interrupt the circularity so as to proclaim a demonstrably true or valid knowledge of anything? If claims of knowledge are conditioned historically-culturally, new claims of knowledge at any moment are conditioned by (*inter alia*) the truths and falsities decided at previous moments; "old" knowledge, that is, acceptances of at least some truth claims, must be cou⌐.ted among the material causes of "new" knowledge (as illustrated in the approach of Gombrich [1959], for instance). But where, then, can one find a present place from which to judge the "old" knowledge, to assess it independently and without unknown (and unknowable) bias?[11]

According to one of our contemporary philosophers of science (Harré 1972, 25), it "seems to be generally agreed . . . , now, that the ideal of a descriptive vocabulary which is applicable to observations, but which is entirely innocent of theoretical influences, is unrealizable."[12] Yet in the epistemologies of many philosophers of science—not only the empiricist variety of Carnap (1956, 41), for example, but also in the views of sworn antagonists (e.g., Smirnov [1964] 1970, 29–30, 41–43)—there is continued reliance on a dichotomy of "observation language," the terms of which purportedly have direct empirical referents, and a deductively articulated "theoretical language," the terms of which "refer to unob-

10. As we will later see, Foucault (e.g., 1963a; 1966) has attempted to define, as one of the fundamental relations of discourse, a level at which there is *no* distinction, a level of that which binds intelligibilities of theory with intelligibilities of experience (and vice versa) so that they are mutually, each to the other, sensible as field and gaze, gaze and field.

11. Compare Goldmann's notice of the hard question that faced the *philosophes*: "How was prejudice to be overcome if the corrupted thought of the time, itself determined by prejudice, was the inevitable product of a corrupt social situation which could be made healthy or abolished only by sane thought untainted by prejudice?" ([1968] 1973, 35).

12. As for himself, Harré agreed that "there is no term used in describing observations upon the nature and behavior of things and materials, whose meaning is able to be grasped without some knowledge of the relevant theory or theories" (1972, 26). One of the strongest critics of the thesis of "theory-laden observation" has been Scheffler (1967), but his criticisms do not withstand careful scrutiny, as Suppe ([1974] 1977, 192–216) has partly demonstrated.

servable events, unobservable aspects or features of events." And there is continued adherence to the ahistoricist view of a single, uniform, capitalized Logic which is applicable uniformly to each and every allowable object of scientific knowledge (e.g., Popper 1972, 6). The current situation is better approximated, I believe, by Feyerabend's (1975, 165–68, 169 n. 4; 1978) characterization: referring to his own studies of Galileo's "actual conduct," and citing Popper ([1935] 1959, 97) as a major proponent of the dominant view of science, he averred that "all these discoveries cry out for a new terminology that no longer separates what is so intimately connected in the development both of the individual and of science at large. Yet the distinction between observation and theory is still upheld and is defended by almost all philosophers of science."[13] It is not simply that the "analytic-synthetic, observational-theoretical distinctions" are delineated with vagueness, as some have charged (e.g., Giedymin 1970, 261). Whether formulated in these terms or in terms of a "context of discovery" versus a "context of justification," or some related variant, such distinctions may be "pleasing to simple minds," but they are "*irrelevant* for the running of science."[14]

It is clear that the underlying issues are both broader and deeper than disputation about the comparative merits of apparently different terminologies. The awakening to language, together with a parallel discernment of the spatiotemporal instability or heterogeneity of perspective, entailed a general relativization of thought that threatens the very

13. Nevertheless, one must acknowledge the impact of papers by Putnam (1962) and Achinstein (1965; see also 1968), which have been acknowledged by several philosophers of science (e.g., Suppe [1974] 1977, 80–86; Stegmüller [1973] 1976, 26–29) as containing very persuasive arguments against the "observational-theoretical" distinction. Stegmüller's "Sneedian" answer to Putnam consists of a relativization of "theoretical terms" to the given theory of which they are terms: "The concept *theoretical* is relativized to a particular theory T, so that the new predicate reads '*x* is a T-theoretical term,' and not '*x* is a theoretical term'" (Stegmüller [1973] 1976, 29; see also Sneed 1971).

14. Feyerabend made a great deal of the Galilean case: witness his several chapters of recitation of Galileo's "demonstration" of relative motion—the point being that a basic change in the experience of naive realism was involved. As a result of Galileo's "attempt to support Copernicus," experience ceased to be "the unchangeable fundament which it is both in common sense and in the Aristotelian philosophy" and became "'fluid' in the very same manner in which [the Galilean argument] makes the heavens fluid, 'so that each star roves around in it by itself' [Galileo 1632, 120]. An empiricist who starts from experience, and builds on it without ever looking back, now loses the very ground on which he stands. Neither the earth, 'the solid, well-established earth,' nor the facts on which he usually relies can be trusted any longer" (Feyerabend 1975, 89).

intelligibility of that classic ideal of a certitude of true and necessary knowledge. Not that relativism is entirely of recent vintage: while it has been a matter of some contention, for instance, whether the Protestant Reformation sprang from a looseness of Ockhamite skepticism left in the wake of a declining Catholic tradition, as argued by Lortz (1939–40) and Iserloh (1956), or emerged as a "continuist" development of theology from a still-vital late-medieval matrix, as argued by Moody (1935) and Preus (1969), the sighting of a medieval relativism runs throughout much of those arguments (see Ozment 1971).[15] And, by the same token, much has been written about the connections of the Reformation, the "quarrels of the Ancients and Moderns," and modern science (e.g., Jones [1936] 1965, esp. chapters 5–7; Merton [1938a] 1970; Feyerabend 1970a). But for a science that had disabused itself of matters theological and, more generally, "metaphysical" or "prescientific," the redoubled challenges came from within its own domain. Among these, the most stimulating proved to be the constructions of quantum physics and Einsteinian relativity. Already before those "discoveries," debates of physical realism versus phenomenalism had been joined in the lecture halls and in the laboratories of physical science (e.g., Boltzmann on the one side, Mach on the other). But the debate quickened with the advent of such curious images of the physical world, for they entailed strong challenges to the hitherto fundamental notion of natural properties independent of the observer. Quantum theory, with its view that there are processes not interpretable in terms of definite spatiotemporal localizations, introduced a kind of "subjectivism": not that microphysical entities are purely mind-constituted, as it were, but that their properties are dependent upon our observation of them—e.g., the "superposition principle" (see Dirac 1947, chap. 1), according to which the state of an entity is not singular but consists in the superposition of all possible constituent substates.[16] In short, there entered not only a fundamental indeterminacy and uncertainty but also a fundamental dependence of property specification on the act of the observer. Some years after the Planckian upheaval, a noted physicist would ponder the argument that a solipsism is

15. Ozment (1975, 5) has reminded us that such matters of contention can be taken quite seriously, for it is on the resolution of such issues that the fate of Martin Luther turns: whether he was "an ignorant and immoral heretic" or "an intelligent and sincere heretic"—or, in the tolerance of ecumenicism, "not only intelligent and sincere, but also no longer properly heretical." Who now argues in such manner about the scientist Galileo? Or about Velikovsky (see de Grazia 1966)?

16. Thus, prior to observation of a specific state (velocity or position) of an electron, say, it is considered to have been in the "superposition" of all possible substates of velocity or position.

more in tune with quantum theory than is the traditional doctrine of physical realism; while he could not endorse a solipsistic view, he as much as concluded that physical realism is no longer "useful" (Wigner 1967, sec. 3).[17]

Some philosophically inclined observers of the amazing issue of physical science during the first third of the twentieth century expressed displeasure that academic philosophy was being mostly silent toward these progeny. Bachelard (1928; 1934), for one, charged that philosophy had abdicated any serious claim to analyze the implications of these new theories, inasmuch as its epistemic traditions were tenaciously those of Newton: "There is no transition between Newton's system and Einstein's system. One cannot get from the former to the latter by collecting knowledges, taking double pains with measurements, slightly modifying principles. On the contrary, an effort of total novelty is required" (Bachelard 1934, 42).[18] For another—and with notable similarities to Bachelard—George Herbert Mead (1917; 1938) displayed both a fascination for the new physical theories and a rejection of the obsolescent "metaphysical speculations" of academic philosophy, as he urged consideration of the ramifications of those theories (and experimental results) for a philosophy of science and for the sciences of "the social." Of course, in the case of the social sciences many if not all of the issues that were being finely drawn from apparent implications of the new physical science had figured already in the storm of controversy that centered in Germany during the closing years of the preceding century. But from Mead's point of view, as from that of many others, the social sciences had little to show for it, in the way of either a realistic philosophy of science or, more importantly, effective scientific knowledge. The "sciences of man" simply did not compare at all well with the "sciences of nature."

In the face of seemingly overwhelming evidence of the paucity of effective social-science knowledge, the defender often pleads the equiva-

17. Planck himself would have none of it, however, despite the reading one might make of his oft-cited argument that "a new scientific truth does not triumph by convincing its opponents and making them see the light but rather because its opponents eventually die, and a new generation grows up that is familiar with it" (Planck [1928] 1949, 33–34). As Scheffler has cautioned, it is a mistake to read that as an endorsement of relativism (Scheffler 1972, 370–71). This old Prussian, brave antagonist of Nazism, never acceded to the positivists' interpretation of quantum theory.

18. "To sum up, a general view of the epistemological relations between contemporary physical science and Newtonian science reveals that there is not a *development* from the old doctrines toward the new, but far rather an *envelopment* of the old thoughts by the new ones" (Bachelard 1934, 58).

lent of *nolo contendere,* a plea typically supported by evocations of "an immature science" tackling a uniquely complex subject matter.[19] To wit: "the science of man is concerned with too complicated an object, it embraces a multitude of too varied facts, it operates on too subtle and too numerous elements always to give to the immense combinations of which it is capable the uniformity, evidence, and certainty that characterize the physical sciences and mathematics." Considerations of such complexities, and of the gap between the object of the physical sciences and that of the social sciences (the "hard" and the "soft"), were central to the battles of that *Methodenstreit* at the close of the 1800s. Yet the plea and the evocation are hardly of recent vintage. The passage just quoted, though its string of words could just as well have been fashioned last year or in 1885, was published in the Year XII of the French Republic (Dumas 1804, 27–28). And what Foucault (from whom the quotation was taken) said about its attitude in regard to the art of medicine applies just as well to the breadth of the social sciences:

> Out of this defect the eighteenth century, in its last years, made a positive element of knowledge. In the period of LaPlace, either under his influence or within a similar movement of thought, medicine discovered that uncertainty may be tested, analytically, as the sum of a certain number of isolatable degrees of certainty that were capable of rigorous calculation. Thus, this confused, negative concept, whose meaning derived from a traditional opposition to mathematical knowledge, was to be capable of transforming itself into a positive concept and offered to the penetration of a technique proper to calculation.
>
> This conceptual transformation was decisive: it opened up to investigation a domain in which each fact, observed, isolated, then compared with a set of facts, could take its place in a whole series of events whose convergence or divergence were in principle measurable. It saw each perceived element as a *recorded event* and the uncertain evolution in which it found itself an *aleatory series.* It gave to the clinical field a new structure in which the individual in question was not so much a sick person as the endlessly reproducible pathological fact to be found in all patients suffering in a similar way. (Foucault [1963a] 1973, 97)

19. It goes without saying that there have been those who have judged the matter somewhat differently (e.g., Machlup 1961; Lindblom and Cohen 1979). No doubt, too, there have been some who not only have judged accumulation as being tiny but also have deemed that to be a good circumstance.

It gave to the social sciences a structure of probabilistic or statistical empirics—the same statistical empirics scored by Raskolnikov (Dostoyevsky [1866] 1956, 47)—and it gave to the scientists, as to the clinical physicians in Foucault's example, a gaze within "an unlimited space, made up of isolatable events," the solidarity of which was that of an open-ended "order of the series." The task was not now "to see the essential truth beneath the sensible individuality" but was instead "the task of perceiving, and to infinity, the events of an open domain" (Foucault [1963a] 1973, 97–98).

Not long after Dumas's inditement about the several difficulties of "the science of man," Auguste Comte composed his proposition of a "positive philosophy" within which all the historical modes of knowledge were precisely staged and the order of modern science was carefully devised in ascending tiers, with a discipline of social science ensconced at the top. The grandeur of Comte's original scheme has been matched perhaps only by its train of controversy, much like the tail of some comet in pursuit of a star. "Positivism" and its adjectival uses have assumed such a sturdy presence in the armament of dismissive epithets that hardly anyone will now admit to being a "positivist."[20] Indeed, as a label for a distinctive and coherent school of philosophy, "positivism" no longer serves so well as it once did (e.g., for Ernst Mach or Richard Avenarius, to say nothing of Comte himself); it was no less immune to "the hazards of historical development," to borrow Horkheimer's ([1947] 1974, 73) phrase, than any other systematic construction—though to say that, of course, does not deprive it of its legacy.

According to classical positivism, the "knowing subject" is an essentially passive presence, in the sense of being marginal (when following proper method) or contaminating (when not) to objective inquiry. The Comtean tenets have been well summarized for us by Habermas:

> Comte's philosophy of science can be reduced to methodological rules, all of which are supposed to be covered by the term "positive": the "positive spirit" is linked to procedures that guarantee scientific objectivity (*Wissenschaftlichkeit*). . . . He uses "positive" to refer to the actual in contrast to the merely imaginary (*reél-chimérique*), what can claim certainty in contrast to the undecided (*certitude-l'indécision*), the exact in contrast to the indefinite (*le précis–le vague*), the useful in contrast to the vain (*l'utile-l'oiseux*), and, finally, what claims

---

20. Witness the so-called Adorno-Popper debate of a few years ago, which one commentator (Giddens 1974, 18) likened to "Hamlet without the prince."

relative validity in contrast to the absolute (*le relative–l'absolu*). (Habermas [1968a] 1971, 74)

Thus, Habermas continued, Comte followed first of all the basic empiricist rule regarding *le reél*, that all knowledge must "prove itself through the *sense certainty* of systematic observation that secures intersubjectivity" (Habermas [1968a] 1971, 74–77). But that alone does not guarantee *la certitude* of knowledge: "*Methodical certainty* is just as important as sense certainty"; because science addresses a multiplicity of facts, in principle infinitely numerous and thus outside the limits of total comprehension, scientific knowledge can achieve surety only through "unity of method." Third, Comte's tenet of *le précis* asserted that the "exactitude of our knowledge is guaranteed only by the formally cogent construction of theories that allow the deduction of lawlike hypotheses."[21] Fourth, the demand for *l'utile* continued the juxtaposition of empiricist and rationalist views by asserting, on the one hand, that "scientific cognitions must be technically utilizable," so that through the harmony of science and technology there can be "technical control over processes of both nature and society," and by asserting, on the other hand, that "the power of control over nature and society can be multiplied only by following rationalist principles—not through the blind expansion of empirical research, but through the development and unification of theories."[22] Finally, as a necessary implication of the foregoing, Comte formulated his tenet of *le relative*—not in the sense of a generalized relativization and partiality of possible world-constitutions or objectifications of reality but simply as a denial of any "metaphysical" or "prescientific" closure in a realm of essences. All scientific knowledge is "in principle *unfinished and relative,* in accordance with the 'relative nature of the positive spirit.' " This, of course, as Habermas pointed out, constituted part of the central paradox of early positivism: it was "repeatedly compelled to move within the metaphysical antithesis of essence and appearance—of the totality of the world and absolute knowledge on the one hand and contingent manifoldness and

---

21. Of this conjunction of empiricist and rationalist traditions—often commented upon as the uneasy marriage that it was—Habermas ([1968a] 1971, 76) remarked: "The reason that he can freely combine rationalist and empiricist principles is that they are functioning not as components of a theory of knowledge, but as normative rules of scientific procedure, through which science itself receives its definition." That is a bit of an oversimplification, of course; the "reason" had more to do with existent criteria of acceptability at the hands of an audience than the abstract qualifications of "a theory of knowledge."

22. Compare the discussion by Botero ([1589] 1956, bk. 8, chap. 3), previously mentioned.

relative knowledge on the other—while simultaneously declaring the positions advanced by metaphysics to be meaningless" (Habermas [1968a] 1971, 79).

Insofar as major tenets of classical positivism have been reproduced in works of subsequent authorities—nearly all of whom would reject the appellation of "positivist"—one of the most important has continued to be the postulation of a basic unity of science and the universality of "the scientific method" (e.g., see Popper 1972; Rudner 1966; Nagel 1961). By this argument the methodical procedures of the natural sciences are founded in a universally applicable "logic of inquiry" and therefore are those of "science in general."[23] Included in that tenet are a particular view of the proper goals of scientific inquiry—ethically neutral explanation and prediction, leading to capacities of control—and a particular view of the proper relationship of theory to practice—a "technical" relationship anchored in the premise that scientific theory is "value-free" or at least "value-neutral," that is, that while the construction of an axiological principle or ethical rule may draw upon the results of scientific inquiry, science itself remains neutral on all axiological questions—except that of the value of scientific knowledge—and does not dictate ethical rules. In the recent chronicles of modern science, strenuous challenges to the unity movement can be dated from the time of the Schmoller-Menger controversy during the last quarter of the previous century and followed through to the present day in such works as Husserl's struggle for a pure transcendentalism, Winch's (1958) deployment of the later Wittgenstein's "language-game" argument, Gadamer's (1965) version of hermeneutics, and a host of others (see the reviews by Radnitsky 1968, vol. 2; Habermas [1968a] 1971; Habermas 1970c; Palmer 1969; Apel 1955; Apel [1965] 1967).

Although the original Schmoller-Menger *Methodenstreit* was woven complexly of issues regarding proper method in economics ("historical," "theoretical," and "applied" economics),[24] it soon broadened into general reconsiderations of the relationship between natural and historical or sociocultural sciences. New doctrines of Kantian provenience imparted energy to the greater range of disputes, out of which the highly consequential brands of *verstehende* sociocultural science were developed (e.g., Dilthey,

---

23. It may seem curious that so little attention has been paid to the reverse claim, that the "human sciences" include the "natural sciences." But of course that would be an absurdity inasmuch as nature is (taken to be) larger than and prior to the human world.

24. Of the original antagonists, it would seem that Menger's work (e.g., 1883) has held the greater attention, especially in Anglo-American social science.

Rickert, the Webers, Mannheim).[25] The key figures on the one side of this "methods controversy"—which included arguments concerning the proper status of value judgments (i.e., the *Werturteilsstreit*)—were Dilthey and Rickert. Dilthey's sally against positivism, resulting in the formation of the *Geisteswissenschaften* (e.g., [1883] 1959), rested in a discrimination of "the natural" and "the historical" on the basis of a doctrine of *Verstehungspsychologie,* a psychologistic individualism characterized by emphasis on individual psychic experience. Rickert's (e.g., [1899] 1921) antipositivist alternative to Dilthey, on the other hand, gave emphasis not to the facticities of individual psychic experience but to the cultural significance of normativities. Believing that the Kantian method of "critical philosophy" was the only way to universally true and necessary knowledge of the social world (Rickert [1892] 1928), he rejected any notion of a "natural science of history" and proposed instead his *Kulturwissenschaft,* the objectivity of which rested on his claim of an epistemological demonstration of the universality of historical-cultural values, not on any *naturwissenschaftliche* capability of nomothetic generalization from unique particulars. All historical thinking, according to Rickert, is inherently individualizing thinking; that is, it constitutes an individuation of universal values into unique experiences. A science of history can be objective insofar as its values are universal *and* insofar as its subject matter is studied in terms of significance vis-à-vis those values. Universal value principles constitute the only proper foundation of an objective world history (Rickert [1896–1902] 1921, 200–205; Rickert [1899] 1921, 63, 118–32; see also Makkreel 1969; 1975).

As Habermas has shown rather cryptically, Rickert became irretrievably caught up in the gap of his fact-value separation (Habermas [1968a] 1971, 159 n. 40; Habermas 1970c, 74–77). Nonetheless, the impact of this so-called Marburg school of neo-Kantianism has been enormous, not the least of the reasons being that its putatively epistemological solutions were precisely those of an analytical philosophy of science, extended and applied in such endeavors as Weber's interpretive-causal sociology, Cassirer's philosophy of symbolic forms, Wittgenstein's transcendental logic of language,

---

25. In his survey of the literature on "The Dualism of the Natural and Cultural Sciences," written in 1967, Habermas (1970c, 71) contended that "the lively discussion" initiated by the neo-Kantians "is forgotten today," and the problematic no longer seems real or important. That conclusion is slightly exaggerated; one recent example of an explicitly neo-Kantian epistemological position can be found in Kreckel (1972), wherein the "discovery argument" (i.e., the discovery of "invariant laws"), the individualist-reductionist method, and the nominalist conception of the social are all allegedly rejected in favor of a counterposition that maintains an epistemic split between the *Naturwissenschaften* and the *"Human-Wissenschaften."*

and in the revisions of positivism itself. Although generally preserving the unity-of-science claim, the revisionist brands of positivism increasingly conceded the "influence" of theoretical formation on observation and, under the heading of logical consistency, directed attention to conceptual and semantic rigor as well as to methodical procedures of empirical testing. Popper, for example, came to treat the knowing subject's theoretical framework (including the "experiential") as a heuristic element of inquiry (Popper [1935] 1959). Hanson (1958), Kuhn (1970a), Bohm (1965), and others moved still further from some of the tenets of classical positivism and have directed attention to the social collectivity of knowing subjects as a "context of discovery" that molds successive frames of reference or paradigmatic constructions.

3. FROM THE BOOK OF SAND

The current condition of philosophy of science is notoriously confused and occluded. On the one hand, the dominant views are suffused with relativistic premises and implications; on the other, there are tenacious resistances to acknowledgment of those features and their annihilative consequences for the central claims of science itself. It can still be said, as Feyerabend recently did, that "interests, forces, propaganda and brainwashing techniques ["professional socialization," etc.] play a much greater role than is commonly believed in the growth of our knowledge and in the growth of science" (Feyerabend 1975, 25). Of the great number and variety of illustrations of the confused circumstances of philosophy of science that could be presented, I shall here give only two.[26] One pertains to Kuhn's well-known study; the other, rather longer than the first, concerns the work of Popper.

Clearly the most interesting aspect of Kuhn's study, first published in 1962 as a contribution to the *International Encyclopedia of Unified Science* (vol. 2, no. 2), is the reception that it has received. Kuhn acknowledged in his preface the significant inspiration that he found in an obscure study by Fleck (1935), which "anticipates many of [Kuhn's] own ideas," but one could point as well to similarities to less obscure works by Bachelard or George Herbert Mead, among others.[27] However that may be, Kuhn's

26. See the useful review by Suppe (1974) for discussions of these and other philosophers of science. Stegmüller (1973) has provided an often sensitive analysis of several of the recent major proposals, especially the Kuhnian.

27. On the matter of overturning established conventions, for example, Znaniecki (1940, 164) observed: "All new developments in the history of knowledge have been due to those scientists who did more in their social roles than their circles wanted and expected them to do." A young Russian scientist, V. F. Turchin (1977,

original presentation and subsequent emendations have become a major chapter in the philosophy of science by virtue of his thesis regarding "normal" and "revolutionary" science.[28] As is by now well known, that thesis is oriented in terms of what he called a *paradigm* (an idealist construction not unlike the late Wittgenstein's "language-games"), which was posited as having two central dimensions: a constellation of values, beliefs, apodictic cognitions, rules of order, techniques of procedure, and applications, all of which are shared by a given community; and a set of exemplars, or "concrete" puzzle-solutions that serve as sculptured recipes for subsequent problem-solving activity.

Whereas the first of these dimensions was posited as common to all science always—indeed, one could find it equally well in Ngorongoro or Caduveo mythology and magic, or in Catholic rituals of exorcism—it is the second dimension, according to Kuhn, which serves to distinguish paradigmatic from preparadigmatic science (Kuhn 1970a, 175, 179; see also Kuhn 1970b). It is not clear whether he meant his account of paradigmatic shifts in a sequence of "normal-revolutionary-normal" science to be merely descriptive or also prescriptive, but it is clear that he saw the matter of formation and reformation of paradigms as an unequivocally social process and the selection of competing theories as unequivocally context-dependent.[29]

56–57, 290–91), has recently spoken of the crucial process of "metasystem transition," a vertical cumulative process in science. Of the several resemblances to earlier works that one might construct, however, the most notable are to Mead (e.g., 1917, 1938)—the sections of his writing least often read by social scientists—and to Bachelard (1928, 1934).

28. There have been several challenges to the descriptive accuracy of Kuhn's thesis—e.g., Zahar's (1973, 237–39) charge that his account of "paradigm change" is not applicable to the "Einsteinian revolution." Such challenges are not my principal concern here, however, and I shall ignore them.

29. The response to Kuhn's thesis has been very large in size, if not always of good quality. With respect to the social sciences, Urry (1973, 462–64) proposed recently a characterization of a part of this response. (Actually, Urry spoke of sociologists, but his characterization extends as well to other of the social-science divisions.) The response, he said, consisted of three main views. First, there are some who have concluded (or re-concluded) that social science is still immature, still in the preparadigmatic stage with respect to the second of Kuhn's definitive criteria, and that it must be quick to build a paradigm. Then there are the apocalyptic "radicals" who have called for revolt against the allegedly existent ruling paradigm of a "normal-phase" science and replacement by another paradigm that is everything the ruling paradigm is not, and vice versa. Finally, there are some who have perceived the existence of a plurality of paradigms—but incommensural paradigms that, precisely because of their incommensurability,

Nevertheless, Kuhn's thesis is badly marred by failures of consistency and capability. In his conception of "normal" science, for example, if it is the given paradigm that constitutes the "norm" of normal science, then what is the constitution of the normativity of a paradigm? Kuhn proposed two different answers to that question, between which he did not make a clear choice. On the one hand, he contended that what is "normal" is simply a matter of pragmatic consensus on the part of the group or community undertaking the decisions about competing paradigms (Kuhn 1970a, 94). This position has been attacked by various scholars (e.g., Feyerabend 1970b, 199–201; Watkins 1970, 33; Toulmin 1970, 41) as inadequate because it cannot discriminate among the activities of science, those of theologians, and those of a band of thieves. These critics are correct in a very limited sense; but in the end their counterarguments prove to be powerless, for they implicitly accede to the basic suppositions that made the question posable to begin with. As I shall propose later in this volume, it is not so much the answer as the question that is fallacious. Kuhn's second but no more satisfactory answer was formulated with reference to the Stratton and Bruner-Postman psychological experiments: Kuhn argued here, by analogy, that paradigmatic change consists in a mutation of the structure of scientists' world view. However, Kuhn could not specify the meaning of his analogy, that is, whether it refers to an apriorism in which the discontinuity of science through paradigmatic shifts is accountable in terms of "the nature of the mind" (1970a, 62–64), or whether the analogy is very loose and refers to a similitude, which, after all, explains "nothing about the role of paradigms" (1970a, 112).[30] In addition to these lapses in the constitution of the normativity of a paradigm, there are difficulties of commensurability across paradigms and of the associated ramifications for whatever version of a theory of truth Kuhn may have had in mind. Not

can be simply ignored while new and preferred paradigms are fabricated. While this classification offers a useful sense of much of the reaction to Kuhn, no doubt, it should be noted that all of its categories assume acceptance of Kuhn's basic thesis. But there have been reactions against the basic thesis itself. Urry himself (1973, 471–72) expressed one of the most central complaints, that Kuhn fell victim to a relativist stance by adapting a communitarian criterion of validity: "the fact that [we] may begin to explain why people *believe* that they know the truth does not mean that there is any account of whether in fact they do" (see Overington 1977). Urry's criticism is reminiscent in both manner and conclusion of Grünwald's (1934) older critique of the sociology of knowledge.

30. In neither case is his answer at all satisfactory, of course. The point is, Kuhn got terribly caught up in the idealist concern of certifying the certitude and objectivity of scientific knowledge, even at the very moment he was forced to relinquish some vital clauses of the traditional guarantee (e.g., a theory-neutral observation language).

only the distinction between *preparadigmatic* and *paradigmatic* but also differences within the latter are purportedly sensible within some vocabulary of "progress" (that is, different paradigms are related "vertically" rather than "horizontally"), yet there is supposedly a fundamental shift between paradigms which is of such a nature as to involve a substitution of alternative "universes of meaning" and as a consequence of which even the constitution of facts changes (compare the Bachelardian "rupture").[31] This "incommensurability of paradigms," the argument of which was considerably weakened in the second edition of Kuhn's book, involves at its very core, of course, all of the difficulties of the well-known "problem of synonymity," a problem yet to be solved by the philosophers of language (see the review in Alston 1964, chaps. 1, 2); indeed, Austin (1961, chap. 2) was of the opinion that an analysis of the meaning of terms is impossible: "What is the meaning of a word?" is an incoherent question.

Quite simply, Kuhn has been caught between the proverbial horns of dilemma. His own anxiety about the matter was revealed clearly enough in a brief lamenting paragraph, when he asked:

> Is sensory experience fixed and neutral? Are theories simply man-made interpretations of given data? The epistemological viewpoint that has most often guided Western philosophy for three centuries dictates an immediate and unequivocal, Yes! In the absence of a developed alternative, I find it impossible to relinquish entirely that viewpoint. Yet it no longer functions effectively, and the attempts to make it do so through the introduction of a neutral language of observations now seem to me hopeless. (Kuhn 1970a, 126)

His unease can be seen also in the ironic awkwardness of certain of his expressions—as in, for example, his attempts to preserve the "objective" use of "to contemplate" and "to look at" (that is, to contemplate or to look at "things as they really are"), while using "to see" when referring

---

31. Some efforts to explain the "shift-learning" between "universes of meaning" have drawn on the function of metaphor. One example is the Quinean position argued by Hesse (1974), according to which different uses of a common language (the notion of different languages for theory and observation is rejected) are distinguishable only pragmatically and relative to a given network of statements. Scientific language is linked by the operation of metaphor to "ordinary language" (though with the special "poetics" of the former preserved). However, the operation of metaphor is no substitute for a self-consistent theory of knowledge. Nor can Stegmüller self-consistently relegate the whole matter "to the philosophy of language, not the philosophy of science" or, alternatively, bury it within the recesses of a "theoretical-nontheoretical dichotomy" ([1973] 1976, 152, 231–40).

to the observer's "subjective" experience (e.g., 1970a, 120). Despite such statements as the one just quoted, Kuhn has insisted continually that he is not a relativist, citing as supporting evidence his "progressivism," among other features (e.g., 1974, 507–8). These disclaimers notwithstanding, and regardless of how he may prefer to describe himself, the relativistic implications of his constructions are plain to be seen.[32] Indeed, it is by virtue of those implications that he has been totally unable to demonstrate an anchorage even for his own thesis of "the structure of scientific revolutions" and totally unable to devise a self-consistent alternative to the various theories of truth (including Popper's version of a correspondence theory) that he has rejected.

Popper's work, the central part of which (Popper 1935) antedates Kuhn's celebrated study by a quarter of a century, began chiefly as a response to the logical incapacity of the classical model of induction to escape the uncertainty of "the next observation."[33] Although often labeled a "positivist," Popper has consistently rejected that description, preferring instead to be known as a "scientific realist" (e.g., [1935] 1959, 252; 1972, 35, 38n.6, 40n.9).[34] His main argument, repeated many times, is that scientific knowledge does not and cannot proceed by the verification of theories through empirical testing but proceeds, and progresses, on the basis of a "critical method" of "bold conjectures" fol-

---

32. It may be that Kuhn was not entirely cognizant of the relativism of his own constructions. Note, for example, the relativist theme of his discussion of the "exceedingly artificial" distinction "between fact and theory" (1970a, 52–56, and *passim*). Of course, "exceedingly *artificial*" makes sense only against the possibility of a distinction that is "of nature."

33. Bacon ([1620] 1952, I, Aphorism 105) argued that the greatest change in scientific practice introduced by his efforts was "in the form itself of induction and the judgment made thereby." His method of induction was not one "which proceeds by simple enumeration," for that "is puerile, leads to uncertain conclusions, and is exposed to danger from one contradictory instance, deciding generally from too small a number of facts, and those only the most obvious."

34. Nevertheless, Popper (e.g., 1972, 183–85) has not rejected the unity-of-science thesis, although he has altered it a bit (in comparison with Mach's view, for example). Thus, he has admitted to being "quite prepared to accept the thesis that understanding is the aim of the humanities. But I doubt whether we should deny that it is the aim of the natural sciences also. Of course, it will be 'understanding' in a slightly different sense." And: "Science, after all, is a branch of literature; and working on science is a human activity like building a cathedral [why "cathedral," rather than "monastery" or "dungeon" or "battleship"?]. . . . Labouring the difference between science and the humanities has long been a fashion, and has become a bore. The method of problem solving, the method of conjecture and refutation, is practised by both. It is practised in reconstructing a damaged text as well as in constructing a theory of radioactivity."

lowed by rigorous efforts of refutation, that is, by falsifying rather than confirming propositions of knowledge. "The quest for certainty, for a secure basis of knowledge, has to be abandoned"; indeed, "all that can possibly be '*positive*' in our scientific knowledge is positive *only* in so far as certain theories are, at a certain moment of time, preferred to others in the light of our *critical* discussion which consists of attempted refutations, including empirical tests," in other words, "only with respect to *negative methods*" (1972, 37, 63, 20).[35]

What we should do, I suspect, is to give up the idea of ultimate sources of knowledge, and admit that all knowledge is human; that it is mixed with our errors, our prejudices, our dreams, and our hopes; that all we can do is grope for truth even though it be be-

---

35. The view here attributed to Popper is not entirely unique to him, of course. One of the strongest expressions of the argument that verification can never be conclusive was given by Lewis in 1929 and thereafter (see Lewis 1929, 279–81; 1946, 180). Regarding a statement such as "A piece of white paper is now before me," Lewis argued that such

> judgment will be false if the presentation is illusory; it will be false if what I see is not really paper; false if it is not really white but only looks white. This objective judgment also is capable of corroboration. . . . any test of the judgment would pretty surely involve some way of acting—*making* the test, as by continuing to look, or turning my eyes, or grasping to tear, etc.— and would be determined by finding or failing to find some expected result in experience. But in this example, if the result of any single test is as expected, it constitutes a partial verification of the judgment only; never one which is absolutely decisive and theoretically complete. This is so because, while the judgment, so far as it is significant, contains nothing which could not be tested, still it has a significance which outruns what any single test, or any limited set of tests, could exhaust. No matter how fully I may have investigated this objective fact, there will remain some theoretical possibility of mistake; there will be further consequences which must be thus and so if the judgment is true, and not all of these will have been determined. The possibility that such further tests, if made, might have a negative result, cannot be altogether precluded; and this possibility marks the judgment as, at the time in question, not fully verified and less than absolutely certain. To quibble about such possible doubts will not, in most cases, be common-sense. But we are not trying to weigh the degree of theoretical dubiety which common-sense practicality should take account of, but to arrive at an accurate analysis of knowledge. This character of being further testable and less than theoretically certain characterizes every judgment of objective fact at all times; every judgment that such and such a real thing exists or has a certain objectively factual property, or that a certain objective event actually occurs, or that any objective state of affairs actually is the case. (Lewis 1946, 180).

yond our reach. . . . If we thus admit that there is no authority beyond the reach of criticism to be found within the whole province of our knowledge, however far it may have penetrated into the unknown, then we can retain, without danger, the idea that truth is beyond human authority. And we must retain it. For without this idea there can be no objective standards of inquiry; no criticism of our conjectures; no groping for the unknown; no quest for knowledge. (Popper 1965, 29–30)[36]

At most, scientists can determine only the falsity of their theories, which is to say that any given theory may actually be true but that scientists cannot "establish its truth, even if it is true"; they can only try to refute the theory and, having failed to do so at any particular date, can regard it as possibly true and as the "best-tested" of the competing theories. As the Popperian philosopher of science Lakatos (1970) has argued—though not in contradiction of Popper himself (see Popper 1972, 53, 81)—this "falsificationist thesis" must be formulated in other than a "dogmatic" or "naive" fashion, meaning that one theory can be refuted only relative to another that both duplicates and extends the explanatory range of the first.[37] In Popper's own words, "the logical basis of the method of science—the method of bold conjectures and . . . attempted refutations"—consists in the assertion that "the theory with the greater content," that is, the bolder and hence the riskier theory, "will also be the one with the greater verisimilitude unless its falsity content is also greater" (1972, 53; emphasis deleted).

For Popper epistemology is nothing more than "the theory of *scientific knowledge*." Moreover, the only defensible interest of such theory is in regard to the actual procedures and products of science. As with members of the so-called school of logical empiricism, he has proclaimed his complete disregard for questions of the genetic conditions of knowledge.

---

36. One suspects that Popper was not fully aware of the implications of some of the sentences in this passage. Nevertheless, it is curious that Popper has held that the view that "human knowledge is a product of men" and that "all our theories are of our own invention"—a view to which he subscribed—is "a kind of idealism" (1972, 99n.59, 158–61; see also 1965, 117). Precisely what "kind of idealism" is unclear, but in one discussion (1972, 38–44) he identified idealism with a solipsistic idealism, to which he preferred "realism."

37. Nevertheless, as we shall see, this stipulation in no way solves the "contamination" of theory-testing that accrues from the "theory-impregnation" of observations (which Popper continued to acknowledge [e.g., 1972, 30, 71–74]) on the basis of which the testing, whether principally justificatory *or* refutational, proceeds. Nor does it give necessary anchorage to Popper's "verisimilitude" thesis.

I see the problem of knowledge in a way different from that of my predecessors. Security and justification of claims to knowledge are not my problem. Instead, my problem is the growth of knowledge. In which sense can we speak of the growth or the progress of knowledge, and how can we achieve it? (1972, 37)

The clarification and investigation of the process of growth or progress is "the fundamental problem of the theory of knowledge." As we have seen, the Popperian scheme organizes this supposed process of progressive achievement in terms of a "negative method" of continual criticism or attempted refutations (thus, Popper's 1962 defense of a liberalist doctrine of "the open society," wherein supposedly all diverse views can compete freely and without "extrinsic" hindrance).[38] That which in science grows through the method of "bold conjecture and attempted refutation" has the character of *objective* knowledge, that is, knowledge consisting of "linguistically formulated expectations submitted to critical discussion" in an "open society" (as opposed to "subjective knowledge," which "consists of dispositions and expectations, . . . is not subject to criticism, . . . [and] grows or achieves better adjustments by the Darwinian method of mutation and elimination of the organism"). Objective knowledge—composed of "the logical content of our theories, conjectures, guesses (and, if we like, of the logical content of our genetic code)" and exemplified by "theories published in journals and books and stored in libraries"—changes and grows not by elimination of the organism, as with the inseparable subjective knowledge, but through "the elimination (killing) of the linguistically formulated conjecture" (Popper 1972, 35, 66, 73, 108, 142).[39]

Popper's epistemology-as-theory-of-scientific-knowledge is, he has claimed, an "epistemology without a knowing subject" (1972, 106–52). Its focus is exclusively an "objective knowledge," which occupies a separate, distinct, and at least partly autonomous world of its own.[40] This

38. One of the points of disagreement between Popper's and Kuhn's views concerns this principle of continual criticism; according to Kuhn's account, this principle is one of the hallmarks of preparadigmatic discourse (for example, the social sciences).

39. Popper's "subjective knowledge" is a rather curious species: apparently it is something unique to but not "linguistically formulated" by the given "organism" or individual person, but it excludes "the logical content of our genetic code."

40. Compare this assertion by a well-known "scientist of science" (Ben-David 1971, 1; emphases added): "Sociologists study structures and processes of social behavior. Science, however, *is not behavior* but knowledge that can be written down, forgotten, and learned again, *with its form or content remaining unchanged.*"

"world 3," as he has called it (in contrast to "world 1," the physical world, and "world 2," which is "the world of our conscious experiences"), is the special province of science. It is "a natural product of the human animal, comparable to a spider's web," and, even though it is of our own making and "has a strong feed-back effect upon us ... qua inmates" of worlds 1 and 2, this third world is "largely autonomous" in the sense that once we produce a theory—or, in general, some "unit" of objective knowledge—that theory or "unit" usually proves to have unanticipated characteristics of internal logic. For example, Popper has referred approvingly to Brouwer's view, formulated early in this century, that "the sequence of natural numbers is a human construction," but claimed further that "although we create this sequence, it creates its own autonomous problems in its turn"—an instance of this being the "distinction between odd and even numbers," which distinction "*is not created by us:* it is an unintended and unavoidable consequence of our creation." In other words, it is not only possible but also fruitfully evident that we "can discover new problems in world 3 *which were there before they were discovered*" (Popper 1972, 74, 112, 118; emphasis added).

Now, while we must "give up ... the quest for justification," in the sense of justifying a claim that our "objective knowledge" is true, this in no way means, according to Popper, that "truth itself is just an illusion" (1972, 29–30, 40, 46–47, 59). The notion of truth "is absolutist, but no claim can be made for absolute certainty: *we are seekers of truth but we are not its possessors.*" To be sure, "science aims at truth in the sense of correspondence to the facts or to reality."[41] Yet we can never demonstrate a claim that our conjectures *are* true. (An "*advocatus diaboli*" is sensible and proper; an "*advocatus dei*" is neither.) Rather, we "test for truth, by eliminating falsehood"; and so long as the procedures of our "critical method" do not break down ("for example, because of antirationalist attitudes"), it is the case that "our conjectural theories tend progressively to come nearer to the truth." Popper has consistently rejected the "relativist" label (e.g., 1972, 126; 1965, 4–5, 66), arguing that whereas relativism denies the existence of objective truth, his method "makes possible the approximation to (absolute) truth." That is, his method supposedly maximizes "nearness to truth"—or "verisimilitude," as he has preferred to term it (e.g., 1972, 17–26, 143)—and while there is "no criterion of truth at our disposal," a "fact" that "supports pessimism," nevertheless "we do possess criteria which, *if we are lucky,* may allow us to recognize error and falsity" (1965, 28).

41. Popper has stated on several occasions his preference for a correspondence theory as refined by Tarski, which he has called "the commonsense theory" (see, e.g., 1972, 44).

But Popper's "epistemology without a knowing subject" does indeed amount to a relativism, his claim to the contrary notwithstanding.[42] Consider these components of his argument: observations, and thus facts, are inescapably theory-impregnated; the truth of conjectured theories can never be demonstrated; conjectures can be subjected only to efforts of falsification, the first step of which involves the test of facts; through successive falsifications, objective knowledge progresses in increasing approximation to truth, that is, in verisimilitude or that which has the appearance of truth, which is an effect of falsification. Popper's dilemma is obvious. First of all, if observations and facts are theory-impregnated, why should any given observation or fact, or any set thereof, be accorded the significant virtue of being able to falsify a theory? What possible criterion will limit the rescue of theory from threatened refutation? Clearly the stipulation of "greater explanatory range" cannot salvage the refutation thesis, for the "greater explanation" can only be conjectured in relation to facts that are, again, theory-laden. Such stipulation merely widens the circle—or makes explicit the already infinite radius. Second, Popper's formula of "approximation to truth" or "verisimilitude" lacks cogency. It requires demonstration that there exist only a *finite* number of alternative conjectures to be discriminated and selectively discarded through refutations: What could the basis of that discrimination possibly be? Moreover, the notion of approximation requires an existent referent to which one can achieve proximity, yet how can we know that existence? According to Popper, we cannot; but if we cannot, then how are we possibly to judge the question of proximity? How can we possibly know which is the better and which the poorer approximation—whether to truth or to the truthlike—when we cannot know the definitive measure of our arbitral act?

And so we must ask of Popper, "What of the truth of *your* conjectures? Why should we not reject them? Are you, when all is said and done, finally about the *absence* of standards? Do you, as Horkheimer ([1947] 1974, 73) said of some earlier positivists, hand science over 'to the hazards of historical development' and in promoting 'its investiture as *arbiter veritatis . . .* make truth itself subject to changing social standards'?"[43] Indeed, when all *is* said

---

42. As Barnes has commented, the "truly remarkable thing is how rarely this is noted" (1977, 21 n. 25).

43. Horkheimer's protest was directed not only against *positivism* (which served him as an easy catchword) but also against the general doctrine of relativism in whatever version. The standard that he imagined in implicit contrast was one of sanitary quality, elevated beyond the "vagaries" and the "impurities" of "social process." I shall return to Horkheimer's work in a later chapter.

and done, the Popperian theory of knowledge *is* a relativism of the very sort that Horkheimer so round'y assaulted.

Obviously Popper is no the only philosopher of science to have strenuously resisted the relativist character and implications of his or her own construction. Nagel (1961, 459–66, 498–502), for example, managed somehow to avoid the reflexivity of his own acknowledgment that "social phenomena are 'historically conditioned' or 'culturally determined,' " in order that he could reject "self-defeating skeptical relativism" and defend, undaunted, the scientist's claim to "objective (that is, value-free and unbiased)" knowledge. And there are those who, like Turchin (1977, xv), pretend that phantasmagoric alienation of perspective known as "stepping outside" or "stepping behind." Thus, in answer to his own query, "What is scientific knowledge of reality?" Turchin stated quite matter-of-factly that "from a scientific point of view" it means that we "look at the human race from outside, from outer space so to speak."[44] A great many scientists, as well as many philosophers of science, still speak of and through their adherence to what Feyerabend quite appropriately called the "fairy tale" of that "special method" of science according to which science is immune to the "relativization of all forms of thought" and is "a *neutral structure* containing *positive knowledge* that is independent of culture, ideology, prejudice" (1975, 302).

It is the case, of course, that in the social sciences philosophers and scientists of the *Geisteswissenschaft* persuasion have recognized the fairy tale as such; but they have been at pains to salvage the authority of a fulcrum from which they can lift *their* claims to knowledge above the level of alternative fairy tales. Following Husserl's failing effort to construct (or to explicate) the conditions of a presuppositionless knowledge, several scholars came to adopt a notion of an incontrovertible "circle of knowledge"—for instance, in their various ways, Schutz's phenomenological social science, Gadamer's hermeneutics, Winch's late-Wittgensteinian social science, Garfinkel's ethnomethodology.[45] According to the more or

44. Schrödinger ([1958] 1967, 127) once remarked that scientists typically "exclude the Subject of Cognizance from the domain of nature that we endeavor to understand. We step with our own person back into the part of an onlooker who does not belong to the world, which by this very procedure becomes an objective world." While this "stepping back" enables scientists to reach "a moderately satisfying picture of the world," he continued, it does so "at the high price of taking ourselves out of the picture, stepping back into the role of a non-concerned observer ([1958] 1967, 128). This fantasy of teleportation is a popular self-understanding among scientists; it is seldom recognized as the terrible madness that it is.

45. I shall return to some of these efforts in the chapters that follow.

less shared premise of these formations regarding methodical knowledge of "the social world," hermeneutic understanding or interpretive analysis characterizes the object of knowledge (the actor-in-the-world) as well as the approach of the scientifically disciplined knowing subject, insofar as both proceed in the respective activities of accomplishing actions/ meanings or intersubjectivities necessarily within "frames of meaning" or "traditions" or "language-games" (or "paradigms," etc.). In adopting a fundamental premise of "the hermeneutic circle" of inescapably presuppositioned knowledge, these scholars have attempted to construct methodical procedures based on an ontologic parallel between the "skilled accomplishments" of the so-called ordinary actor and those of the hermeneutical scientist-observer, a parallel the orthogonal dimension of which is asymmetrically loaded if the observer's claims of superior "accomplishments of meaning" are to be granted. Thus, it is an attempt to make a virtue of relativism while at the same time providing insulation from the epistemological specters of infinite regress and self-annihilation.[46] But these efforts have been marked (albeit in varying degree) by a naturalistic tendency to neglect the scientist-observer's reflexivity in its concrete circumstances, to neglect the force of historical structures of domination, including implications of false consciousness and false "accomplishments" at the level of their methodical hermeneutics no less than at the "lower" or less methodical level of "the ordinary actor." The crucial, and fundamentally incriminating, presumption is that the hermeneutic circle of knowledge is *benign*. The untenability of that presumption results in a partiality that deprives argument of a grounding or a justification that would be more compelling (save for the powerful aura of "science" itself; that is, a structure of domination) than that which is enacted at any moment by "the ordinary actor." Although having different (yet closely interdependent) ancestries, the philosophy-of-science legatees of *Geisteswissenschaft* suffer entrapment in the

---

46. Another effort to neutralize the epistemological threat of relativism consists in an analytic separation of distribution from production. According to this view, relativism is a problem of distribution, so to speak; that is, the relativity and partiality of facts and theories are considered to be a matter of selection of questions that are asked, facts that are seen, and so on. Max Scheler's social science, which I examine in chapter 4, rested on such an approach. An extreme (and less honest) version of this effort at neutralization can be illustrated by a passage from a book that was given much attention a few years ago: "To include epistemological questions concerning the validity of sociological knowledge in the sociology of knowledge is somewhat like trying to push a bus in which one is riding" (Berger and Luckmann 1966, 12). Even though these writers modestly cautioned that epistemological questions cannot be brushed aside, they did just that through a trick called "bracketing." (And one must ask: How, then, does *your* bus move?)

spiral of relativism as much as do the legatees of positivistic and naive empiricist doctrines.

Cannot the endless spiral of relativism be conquered? Some scholars have argued that, because the logical conclusion of the relativist doctrine is a radical skepticism and therefore an absolute inaction, we must replace it with reliance on "articles of faith." Cioran ([1964] 1970, 81, 83), for example, argued that, whereas the practice of negation in criticism is aggressive denial, which is to say a product of conviction, the radical doubt entailed in relativism has only itself for sustenance yet nonetheless must call even itself into question; "rather than see its perplexities degenerate into articles of faith," it chooses "to abolish itself" and to leave us in the stupor of total inaction. But can we afford the cost of such "solutions" as Cioran proposed (even if it were possible now to enact them)? For all the bite of his call for conviction—and it is not to be denied—that which he would celebrate is also a stupor, the absence of critical reflection in thought and action: "Anyone who is carried away by his reasoning *forgets* that he is using reason, and this forgetting is the condition of all creative thought, indeed of thought itself."[47] To "think that we are thinking," he continued, conversely produces the sterility of ideas opposing each other, neutralizing each other, "within an empty consciousness" (Cioran [1964] 1970, 79). It is clear that Cioran, not unlike James Agee in his autobiographical journey from *Let Us Now Praise Famous Men* to *A Death in the Family,* spoke from a sense of loss—the loss of identity in secure knowledge. But that sense of loss has been as constipating for the purveyors of "articles of faith" as doubt has been for the radical skeptic.

---

47. The equation of "creative thought" with a sort of "possessed thinking" (being "taken out of oneself"; or a "blessed madness," as Dodds [1951, 64] termed it, following Socrates) expresses a profound disaffection from the conditions of existence inasmuch as it indicts those conditions as being so alienated, and so alienating, that one can respond to them accurately and with dignity only by dipping silently into the unconscious well of one's life-urge. As Hamburger put it, with particular reference to Hölderlin, it is "to identify evil with consciousness itself, to deify Energy and discredit Intellect" (1957, 15). In Hölderlin's case, "when he could no longer accept any of the philosophical explanations of evil current in his time," his vision turned into a tragic vision: the human urge to seek self-betterment ends in a hubris, as a result of which we suffer estrangement from nature and entanglement in the raw words of our intercourse. Caught between the desire to be in easy union with the cosmos—that enhanting, archaic image of a cosmos that is a hologram to its own eyes, overdetermined in such a way that there can be no localization of causal agents—and the reason that told only of unique isolations within the analytics of distinct vectors, moments, and perspectives, Hölderlin said his choice through Hyperion: "Man is a god when he dreams, a begger when he reflects."

The conclusion of relativism has meant both a rejection of belief in intelligible essences and an acceptance of the power of language: there can be no neutral "language of observation," and all facts are what they are by virtue of categories and classifications that are socially constructed, related, and dependent. But we find that conclusion to be a source of great discomfort, inasmuch as it seems to carry the implication that our pursuit of scientific knowledge (*especially* scientific knowledge, but then also other, "lesser" kinds of knowledge) is really just a gigantic, meaningless play of games in which we are ever learning the rules of the smaller, historically conditioned games *seriatum*, while the game of games is ruled mysteriously and inaccessibly by some higher, unimaginable, ineffable being of rulership itself—or perhaps it is simply unruled. If that is what the pursuit of knowledge is all about, finally and inevitably, then one is apt to ask, as many nascent scientists have asked: Why bother? Why not instead admire the daisies, bake bread, and live life unquestioningly? This understandable attitude—often referred to, ironically, as anti-intellectual and contributing to the "embattlement of reason"—has just as understandably been cause for alarm among those who have interests (and who does not?) in the establishment of science and the pursuit of knowledge. As did Einstein, we recoil from this image of our universe as some godly play of the dice—even as we feel ourselves immersed in the froth of relativistic standards of judgment and the uncertainty whether our claim of knowledge may be a false consciousness. "Such a man," in Nietzsche's words, "no longer believes in himself or his own existence" ([1874a] 1957, 6).

Yet we also point to the patently obvious benefits of a patently obvious accumulation of scientific knowledge and its applications, all of which seems to prove beyond doubt that our efforts in search of certain knowledge have not been for naught; that there *is* a world of real things and real events, which are as they are, whether or not we know them to be or like them to be as they are; that we do have, after all, *real* grounds for selecting among alternative theories and discarding or modifying the invalid. In short, we succeed in creating an antinomial space between "the theoretical" and "the factual." On the one hand, the doctrine of relativity tells us, seemingly incontrovertibly, that facts are always theory-impregnated, partial, historically socially relative; on the other hand, our continued belief in the quest for certainty shows itself in the everyday practice of science, wherein we proceed matter-of-factly to gauge the validity of theories by reference to an independent realm of facts.

Why is the absurdity so seldom seen, or admitted? If relativism and the abolition of intelligible essences cannot be controverted, how can we consistently believe that the results of scientific experiments, social surveys, mathematical peregrinations, and the like—our scientific facts—are not intelligible solely and inescapably through the interpretive lens of our theories, the very objects that we propose to assess and discriminate on the basis of those facts? One very common response to that incoherence has been to manage our consciousness of it by stretching the incoherence so far as to discredit the one side in the name of the other. The discredited side we have associated with pursuits of philosophy, that foremost mental discipline of the prebourgeois, preliberal, preindustrial world. With the development of science first as an oppositional discourse and then as a master discipline, philosophy was recast more and more into the image of the merely speculative—harmless, perhaps, as long as there is no interference with the business of making and doing, but futile if one wants to learn about the concrete reality of this world in which we actually live. And, indeed, in due course academic philosophy became bankrupt. Science has largely ignored not only metaphysics but also aesthetics, ethics, and epistemology (aside from the "scientized" philosophy of science). Although science does consist fundamentally in epistemological assumptions, it sharply discounts the worth of inquiries into the possibility and the constitution of knowledge. Although science does consist fundamentally in desires of liking, of the pleasurable, the tasteful, and the elegant (and their opposites), it dismisses any relevance of aesthetics in regard to itself. Although science does consist fundamentally in moral judgments of oughtness, of the good, the right, and the responsible (and their opposites), it proclaims an inherent ethical neutrality in which its only obligation is an evenhanded, nonpolitical discovery of the facts and their explanation.

4. OBJECTIVE TRUTH, SUBJECTIVE TASTE

One of the most remarkable features of the consciousness of modern science has been the persistent idiocy of regard for questions of relationship between theories of scientific knowledge, on the one hand, and concerns of axiology, aesthetics, and ethics, on the other. That idiocy has reached what must be its pinnacle in the consciousness displayed by those "scientized" philosophies of science discussed in the previous sections of this chapter. When reading the literature accumulated by those philosophers and their followers, one cannot fail to notice the almost total disregard in which such questions are held. It is as if the construction of scientific knowledge were a uniquely "privileged" enterprise, an activity that is quite independent of considerations of sensual desire, the good and the evil, the beautiful and the ugly. True, at the very moment that some philosophers of science and some research scientists have allowed the relativization of observation and thought as seemingly incontrovertible properties of scientific knowledge, a few have also begun to reconsider the relation between science and "traditional" issues of axiology and ethics.

In part, these reconsiderations have been directed by concerns for what is taken to be a disproportion between the apparent limits of scientific knowledge as uncertain approximation to truth and the destructive antagonism of science toward "traditional" axiological and ethical pursuits, including those of the world religions. Clearly that was one of the themes of Monod's very popular essay (1970), as it has been also of the popular writings of other eminent scholars such as Dubos, Dumont, Bronowski, and Eddington. And while there has been less readiness by scholars of the social sciences to voice such concerns—no doubt because of the perception that the social scientist's object of knowledge is less securely ensconced vis-à-vis "value contaminations" and the like—even here one can recall the outstanding example of Campbell's (1975) controversial presidential address to the American Psychological Association, a central argument of which was that "behavioral and social scientists" too often arrogantly ignore the epistemic relativism that makes their own assertions of knowledge "well-edited approximations" at best, while they persist in being unnecessarily and even dangerously antagonistic toward other sources of truth and morality.[48] Nevertheless, the predominant self-understanding of science continues to be one in which the foundation of scientific knowledge is thought to rest in some equation or linkage of dispassionate observation of facts and dispassionate reasoning, with no intrusion of the inventory of concerns proper to aesthetics, ethics, or axiology in general. One may speak of an experiment or a theory as being "more beautiful" or "better" or "more valuable" than another, but only after the fact of its scientific epistemology, so to speak, which is to say only in terms derived from its theory of knowledge. While proponents of this general position may or may not side with Cohen's (1931, 348) exemplary appraisal of the social vis-à-vis the natural sciences—namely, that the former, unlike the latter, are faced with "the subjective difficulty of maintaining scientific detachment in the study of human affairs," because of the "interference" of values—they do agree among themselves about the allegedly "inescapable fact that we cannot at the same time be moralists (or policy makers) and scientists" (Barnett 1948, 353).

Certainly the analytic dispersion of human judgment into separate terrains of epistemology, ethics, aesthetics, and so on, has not been peculiar to the philosophers of science. At least from the time of Plato's writings, these have been regarded in the larger traditions of academic philosophy

---

48. Part of the ensuing controversy was recorded in the May 1976 issue of the APA's journal, *American Psychologist* (more than 40 pages of commentary in response to Campbell's address) and in the September 1976 special issue of *Zygon*. No doubt Campbell has now been redefined by some of his colleagues as "someone who lets his religious beliefs interfere with his science."

as separate disciplines of inquiry about more or less distinct sorts of problems—even though in all cases these activities of inquiry are also activities of "knowing about" or "knowing how," that is, knowing the good from the evil, the beautiful from the ugly, the just from the unjust, as well as the factual from the fictitious and truth from falsity. Thus, whereas the principal conscious interest of ethicians—to elucidate universal standards for appraisal of the morally good or rightful action—supposedly parallels the classical interest of epistemology—to elucidate universal principles of knowledge (whether "true and necessary," "reasonable," "approximate," or whatever)—most practitioners of each discipline, including the so-called metaethicians and metaepistemologists, have agreed at least in rejecting any claim that the chief interests of one can be reduced to those of the other.[49] Similarly, nonreducibility has usually been regarded as a property of the relationship between epistemology and aesthetics, the latter conceived at its most general as the consideration not of claims of knowledge but of qualities of art (*Ars*), including skills of craft (*technē*)—although allowance must be made for notions of "the aesthetic experience of nature," as in the naturalistic doctrines that emphasize the arts as a "culmination of nature" (see Dewey 1925, chap. 9; Dewey 1934, *passim*).[50] From the standpoint of epistemology, a theory of knowledge or a positive claim of knowledge can be devised without any consideration of aesthetic or ethical judgment whatsoever, nor need there be any reference to or consideration of values other than those proper to epistemology itself (e.g., criteria of the worthiness of knowledge). After the event of its constitution, the theory or the positive claim may be subjected to moral judgments regarding its character and possible uses, it may be experienced aesthetically as pleasing or displeasing ("elegant simplicity" or "confusing complexity"), its worthiness may be assessed from the point of view of some "extraepistemological" value (e.g., soteriological values revealed in religious scripture); but the conditions and process of the constitution itself are free of all such considerations. Much the same can be said with respect to sensual desire or passion.

According to a story circulating in the south of France during the 1540s, a certain king once swore vengeance against God for having been struck by the Divine Hand. With great confidence in the power of *his* word, the king proclaimed that no one within the realm should speak the

---

49. There have been exceptions. Chisholm, for instance, has argued that the terms of epistemology are reducible to those of ethics (1957; 1961).

50. Again there are exceptions of one sort or another. For example, Cassirer's (1923–29) "philosophy of symbolic forms" amounts to a philosophical anthropology *qua* general aesthetics of the "great symbolic forms of culture" (language, myth, art, science); insofar as these incorporate all questions of axiology, epistemology, and ethics, his aesthetic claims a superordination.

name of God, utter prayers to God, or even believe in God, for the duration of ten years to come. Montaigne, who related this story allegedly from boyhood memory, observed that, whereas the original storytellers had meant it to show "not so much the folly as the vainglory of the nation" in question, the real point of the tale was that "such actions as these have in them still more of presumption than want of wit" (Montaigne [1580–88] 1952, 10–11). That is, Montaigne's recitation was intended to illustrate for us the title of his essay: "that the soul discharges her passions upon false objects, where the true are wanting." Everywhere we look, he said, "we see that the soul, in its passions, inclines rather to deceive itself, by creating a false and fantastical subject, even contrary to its own beliefs, than not to have something to work upon." Why? Because otherwise "the soul, being transported and discomposed, turns its violence upon itself, if not supplied with something to oppose it." Aroused passion will not be stilled even by the inaccessibleness of its true object, and lest "discomposition of the soul" become too fierce, passion's stablemate, "wit," sets out to find a surrogate object.[51] Now, presumably we have come to understand these matters of "psychic energy," "defense mechanisms," and the like, much better since the years of Montaigne (who, it may be noted, made no pretense of being the first to discover some subtle truth about passion; Plutarch, for instance, had recorded much the same observation when discussing the human propensity "for small dogs and monkeys"). But how remarkable it is that our characterization of the matched horses, Reason and Passion, has changed so very little: two separate principles of action, one the finely bred guide horse, keen of eye and sensitive to the reins of instruction; the other a ruggedly original, vibrant stallion, powerful and given to amazing feats of vitality. The relationship between these competing, mutually dependent principles has been formulated most often in a core image of symbiosis-in-duality. For Hobbes, the reciprocity of a principle of motive energy and a principle of directive control was made sensible in the following way:

> The passions that most of all cause the difference of wit are principally the more or less desire of power, of riches, of knowledge, and of honour. All of which may be reduced to the first, . . . [for] riches, knowledge and honour are but several sorts of power.
> And therefore, a man who has no great passion for any of these things, but is as men term it *indifferent*; though he may be so

---

51. Compare Nietzsche's discussion of the "slave morality," wherein those "who are denied the real reaction, that of the deed," seek compensation in "an imaginary revenge" and so are buried in *ressentiment* (e.g., 1887).

far a good man as to be free from giving offence, yet he cannot possibly have either a great fancy or much judgment. For the thoughts are to the desires as scouts and spies to range abroad and find the way to the things desired, all steadiness of the mind's motion, and all quickness of the same proceeding from thence. For as to have no desire is to be dead; so to have weak passions is dullness; and to have passions indifferently for everything, giddiness and distraction; and to have stronger and more vehement passions for anything than is ordinarily seen in others is that which men call *madness*. (Hobbes [1651] 1952, 68)

Thought offers "celerity of imagining" and a "steady direction to some approved end," but it is nothing without passion, the want of which means the absence of motion. Desire gives to mind and soul their puissance.

Nevertheless, the assumed relationship between the motive force of sensual desire or passion and the regulative presence of rational desire or reason (or reasoned "will"; e.g., Locke 1690, II.21.30) has been characterized almost always by a definite asymmetry. According to nearly all doctrines of academic philosophy, and certainly according to our common philosophies of science, one may properly display a "passion for knowledge," signifying both the privation of ignorance and the promise of satisfying that privation through learning, but passions or sensual desires are not allowable as properties of the content of knowledge (except in certain cases of religious and mystical knowledge, e.g., a "passionate knowledge of God," or a "passionate knowledge of life"). Already before Hobbes wrote his words about the indifference of that which is without great passion, Bacon had cautioned that while "the greatest impediment and aberration of the human understanding proceeds from the dullness, incompetency, and errors of the senses," the passions "imbue and corrupt" human understanding "in innumerable and sometimes imperceptible ways" (Bacon 1620, I, Aphorisms 49–50). In aesthetics, when sensual desire rules the imagination, the result is "fantasy," which is very often a more or less positively valued aesthetic object. In ethics, when passion rules action, the result is "incontinence," which is sometimes negatively valued, as in an incontinence of "sexual appetite," and sometimes positively valued, as in the passion of wartime heroics. In epistemology, however—that is, in the secular epistemology of the modern world—when passion rules thought, the result is "wishful thinking" or "rationalization," outcomes that are nearly always negatively valued. But more than that, whereas the duality of sensual and rational desire has been reproduced in the discipline of aesthetics by Dionysian and Apollonian doctrines and in ethics by doctrines stressing reason (e.g., Kant) and doctrines stressing sensual desire (e.g., Benthamite utilitarianism), in the epistemology of science it is the *absence* of passion from the epistemological object and constitutive process that is consistently valorized. There is presumption of a *singular* true knowledge, since things and events are as they are regardless of our thoughts about them, and there is presumption of a multiplicity of desire, for desires are considered to be subjective and arbitrary. It is partly this latter component of human nature that supposedly accounts for the diversity of perception and understanding: different sensual desires, life-urges, interests, and so on, influence the course of the faculty of reason in this way or that, resulting in different statements of how the world is. Thus, if true knowledge is to be discovered, all untoward desires must be neutralized. There may be acceptance of a "passion to know" or a "passion for knowledge," the existence of which in the particular case is understood as manifesting some species-general premise of human nature ("the human by nature desires to know"), but such passion must be carefully harnessed by the reason-as-form of the scientific method, lest the outcome be a product that is corrupt and even venal because of an impassioned content. By the standards of scientific method, knowledge must indeed have the quality of *indifference,* in the very sense meant by Hobbes. Not only is passion itself not knowledge, it properly plays only the most elemental and initial part in the production of knowledge: while the scientist may be passionate about an abstract "principle of knowledge," as in "knowledge is better than ignorance" (though even that is not necessary), this same scientist must be strictly *dispassionate* in regard to the contents of a concrete knowledge product and the range of its possible consequences. Internal dialogue should be conducted in the manner of irenics, the discourse of conciliation and achievement of unity. Even eristic dialogues, involving as they do disagreements of the interpretation of specific facts or the merits of competing hypotheses, are to be acted out in an irenical way. Polemics, the discourse of disputation and passionate persuasion (and in theology, the refutation of errors), has no place in the theoretical scripts of science: to utter polemically is to mark oneself as a lout and a boor, incapable of the measured, dispassionate enunciations of intellect. In the culture of modern science, the polemical is properly submerged and "pacified" by the "civilizing" constraints of a Freudian superego and the *Staatsmonopol* of physical force and violence.[52]

With the ascendance of science as a virtually exclusive way of knowl-

---

52. See Elias's characterization of these "internal" and "external" structures as mutually linked components of the "process of civilization" (Elias [1939] 1976, 2:320–26).

edge, this asymmetry of the relation between sensual and rational desire, passion and reason, has spilled over from epistemology to the disciplines of aesthetics and ethics, with profound ramifications for their constitution. On the one hand, that classic triad of dichotomies—"the good and the evil," "the beautiful and the ugly," and "the true and the false"—has undergone another level of partitioning: the first two couplings are considered to be matters of "subjective judgment" or "taste," while judgments of truth versus falsity are "objective" because they are factually demonstrable and, therefore, alone of the three, belong to science. This partitioning has come to be accepted in many quarters as so obvious a *fact*, hardly anyone sees that it is *anything but* "obvious." On the other hand, aestheticians and ethicians have grown increasingly troubled about the foundations of their respective endeavors, although not all aestheticians and ethicians, to be sure. Notable developments in each of the two disciplines consist in concerted efforts to fashion groundings in the evidences of science. Of the numerous examples that could be cited, consider Fechner's (1876) opening of a "scientific experimental aesthetics" and the subsequent approaches through experimental psychology (see, e.g., Valentine 1913); Arnheim's (1954) attempt to ground aesthetics in the empiricities of Gestalt psychology, the "ordinary-language" aestheticians' grounding in analyses of talk about art, including the talk of art critics (see, e.g., Stolnitz 1960); the approaches through the science of semiotics (see Rudner 1951; Ballard 1953),[53] and so on. No doubt one could even find an aesthetics founded in the facticities of a social survey or a public-opinion poll. As for ethics, its central problematic has become by nearly all accounts the question whether "ought" can be derived from "is"—which is also to say, whether ethical rules can be derived from scientific facts. Those who deny the possibility of such derivation typically invoke the authority of David Hume, who, in what has come to be a famous if still rather ambiguous passage of *A Treatise of Human Nature* (1739–40, 3.1.1), supposedly made clear, according to the most common reading of it, that factual and moral judgments pertain to entirely separate realms and that there is no possible relation of entailment from the former to the latter (or vice versa). Recent adherents to this view include Popper (1972)

---

53. In the general category of "semiotic approaches," one of the most important statements was by Ogden and Richards (1923), who distinguished "the referential" from "the emotive" as language functions and contended that this functional separation constituted the difference between (respectively) "scientific" and "poetical" modes of discourse. It may be recalled that Bacon—for example, in his *Advancement of Learning* (1605)—treated imagination or "fancy" as a human faculty separate from the faculty of reason and to the former assigned poetics.

and Hare (1952; 1964).[54] On the other side of the argument, numerous scholars have striven in recent years to show that moral views and principles are founded on and derivable from demonstrable facts—for example, the facts of "human good." These include Anscombe (1958), von Wright (1963), Black (1964), and, of course, Searle (1964; 1969, 175–98), with his well-known "performative solution." At least one student of the question (Zimmerman 1962) has argued even that "ought" is totally reducible to "is," that is, that all "ought statements" are superfluous and might just as well be banished from language.

In much of the literature devoted to the relation between "the factual" and "the moral," arguments have frequently been cast in a somewhat confused way because of indiscriminate uses of the category "value." Insofar as the category of "value" pertains to that which is "desired" or "wanted" or "needed," one can speak appropriately of "value" in respect to epistemology (and science) as well as in respect to aesthetics or ethics. It is clear, however, that when a contributor to this literature writes, "values must be based on our factual knowledge of reality," more than the value of "disinterested factual knowledge" is intended. For instance, when the quantum physicist Schlegel wrote, "Our primary values must rest on our conception of the universe; for if values are not consonant with what we find the universe to be, there can be no hope of realizing them" (1973, 201), the reference of this stupendous insanity must have been to ethical and perhaps aesthetic values. When Durkheim argued that social values must be based on scientifically factual knowledge, he was referring especially to moral as well as to aesthetic values (Durkheim [1895] 1964, 47–49).[55] Likewise, when Rickert wrote of the doc-

---

54. Popper, for instance, has emphasized the critical need for "purely rational arguments, including empirical arguments," and has distinguished "the point of view of the theoretician—the seeker for truth, and especially for true explanatory theories—from that of the practical man of action" (Popper 1972, 13, 17, 21–22). In at least one respect, however, he has weakened his stand against "is-ought" derivation, by arguing that from the viewpoint of this "practical man of action" it is clear that "we should *prefer* as basis for action the best-tested theory"— meaning scientific theory, of course.

55. There is some evidence that Durkheim may have retreated a bit, in the direction of the "separate realms" view; see, for example, his response to Deploige's criticism (Durkheim 1912a, 327). Durkheim's argument had been formulated in terms of an alleged necessity of certain facticities; as he expressed it in *The Elementary Forms*, "it is an essential postulate of sociology that a human institution cannot rest upon an error and a lie, without which it could not exist. If it were not founded in the nature of things, it would have encountered in the facts a resistance over which it could never have triumphed" (Durkheim [1912b] 1965, 14). Of course, it has not been in question that "human institutions" have

trine of *Wertbeziehung,* or "value relevance"—that values are relevant to
the formulation and choice of scientific problems but not to the problem-
solving activity or the validity of its results—the relation of ethics and
aesthetics was at issue (Rickert [1896–1902] 1921). Weber's agnostic image of struggling gods who rule the different spheres of the world—and
over whom "Fate, and certainly not 'science,' holds sway"—was informed by the same calculation of "value relevance" (Weber [1919b]
1946, 148). It has been cogently said that this "irreconcilable struggle
between the heterogeneous values of modern life has the practical result
. . . of dividing the realm of *Realpolitik* as irrevocably from the preoccu-
pations of ethics as at the end of the Baghavad-Gita, where Arjuna is
admonished, in spite of his horror of killing, to return to the battle and
'do what must be done' " (Jameson 1974, 62). The economist von Mises,
a critic of Weber in some respects, similarly adopted a premise of "ethical
neutrality": "Praxeology and economics, its up to now best developed
branch, are neutral with regard to any moral precepts" (von Mises 1961,
133; see also von Mises [1933] 1960, 35–37). And when critics of
Searle's (1964; 1969) halting effort to demonstrate the derivability of
"ought" from "is," through analysis of the performative act of promising, argue that the performative already contains a value premise, they
are speaking of moral values, of course. Throughout this large volume of
literature concerning the mutual address of "value" (moral and aesthetic)
and "fact"—and I shall stop with that smattering of specific examples—
the basic issue of the division or separation itself has been left in a rather
confused state. Whether the thesis is one of strict separation and incommensurability or one of deriving "ought" from "is" (and who today argues that "is" has its foundation in "ought"?),[56] the sense of the difference between "fact" and "value," by nearly all accounts a radical
difference, is terribly mistaken. Typically, the presumption is that one

socially real foundations. The question is not the presence of an existent "is" but
the relation of the existent "is" to some projected value. From this latter standpoint, institutions *can and do* often "rest upon an error and a lie." To presume
otherwise as a matter of the possible is to assert that "what is" exhausts the "could
be"; potentiality is relegated to an ever-receding "nature of things" and our human
world is apprehended as some gigantic maze of successive goal-boxes, the gates
of which are controlled by Nature, God, a Spirit of History, or the ghost of some
rat.

56. It *has* been argued that moral views determine what will and what will not
qualify as a fact relevant to a moral question (e.g., Phillips and Mounce 1965),
but that is not the same argument. Of course, to assert that "is" has foundations
in "ought" would be to fly in the face of the "primordial" asymmetry of *Natura*
and *Ars.*

side of the duality is an "objective reality" and is, therefore, empirically demonstrable, while the other is "merely" a matter of "subjective judgment" and "subjective desire" (see, e.g., Pap 1949, 124). But, as we have seen, it is not at all clear that the "empirically factual" is less relative to some theoretical standard and its historical-sociocultural embeddedness than is the "subjective judgment" of an aesthetic or ethical pronouncement. Nor is it clear how the concrete formation of any of these theoretical standards (though not necessarily consciousness of them, obviously) could be devoid of desires and valuations at once epistemological, ethical, and aesthetic.

In his discussion of the "self-relativization of thought" and commensurate "unmaskings of ideologies," Mannheim (1925) observed that the replacement of an immanentist by an extrinsic and manifestational interpretation has been paralleled in the replacement of an ecstatic or religious anchorage by that of the findings of empirical science, in consequence of which the ethical and aesthetic (as well as epistemological) value discrimination of ideas and ideational saliencies of action are subject to definitive understanding by the factual (see also Grünwald 1934, 79–88). "We arrive at this level when we no longer make individuals personally responsible for the deceptions which we detect in their utterances, and when we no longer attribute the evil that they do to their malicious cunning" (Mannheim [1929] 1936, 54). Although this passage understates the force of dominations that exist as (what we might call) "nonconscious structure," it does point up the twin loss of "the evil" and "the ugly," and the consequent evisceration of "the good" and "the beautiful," in our science-dominated discourse. The Homeric play of tragedy, wherein truth, beauty, and goodness are in the epic, not in the individual players, has been reconvened in the laboratory of science as an epic of statistical laws of reality—a "statistical play of chance, with the individual as its victim" (Kuznetsov 1972, 83).[57]

I would be remiss, of course, were I not to acknowledge the existence within science of a literature of critical commentary on the condition and philosophy of science. However, these commentaries have been ineffectual, by and large, fraught as they are with the very dilemma they seek to address. Of the several commentaries that are available, two recent examples illustrate that charge. The first, *The Social Function of Social Science,* conducted by a social scientist, concerns a "coexistence"

---

57. Or, as Kuznetsov asked the question à la Dostoyevsky: "Can thought, freed from faith and tradition and pursuing its ideas to their conclusion, escape the danger of disregarding a microscopic fate, and of transforming this fate into an insignificant detail in the macroscopic harmony?" (Kuznetsov 1972, 87–88; cf. Turchin 1977, 323–44).

of "reliable scientific knowledge of man and nature" with a "rational ethical discourse" (MacRae 1976). As an instance of current probing for a viable, acceptable relationship between the ethical and the epistemological in science and for some solution to the difficulties of policy choice entailed by the academic fragmentation of consciousness and practice ("specialization," as it is more generally called), this study presents some useful descriptions of a visible surface of serious troubles. But in the end there is total failure, due to the author's insistence that "scientific propositions and ethical assertions, while clearly distinguishable, may be fruitfully combined in academic disciplines concerned with the study of man and society." Rather than an integral discourse that is at once ethical-aesthetic-epistemological, we are given the proposal of a new academic compartment of "policy analysts," who, together with that platitudinous abstraction called "informed citizens," would deliberate over the ethical questions of policy choices as these appear in the light of factual knowledge presented by the scientists (MacRae 1976, 5, 98, 277–307). This is an ethic of a "social-welfare function," aggregated somehow from the congeries of individual choices, demands, and utilities, with no effective recognition of their character as social productions.

The second example comes from Feyerabend's "outline of an 'anarchistic' theory of knowledge," wherein Feyerabend claims that his "frequent use of such words as 'progress,' 'advance,' 'improvement,' etc., does not mean that [he] claim[s] to possess special knowledge about what is good and what is bad in the sciences and that [he] want[s] to impose this knowledge upon [his] readers. *Everyone can read the terms in his own way* and in accordance with the tradition to which he belongs" (Feyerabend 1975, 27). Appropriately, it might seem, Feyerabend meant to remain faithful to his central tenet—"anything goes"—and therefore would resist any temptation to enunciate his views with the conviction of moral force. But what a terrible conceit that is! On the one hand, he has insinuated the morality of amorality, the ethic of total tolerance, by disclaiming any but the most abstract responsibility for his own constructions; and, on the other, insofar as there are evils in science as elsewhere (surely Feyerabend would not admit, say, the Nazi genetic experiments into his central tenet),[58] he has abdicated any responsibility for the extirpation of those evils. It is the liberalist proclamation of "knowledge for its own sake" all over again, his critique notwithstanding. We may expect

58. Indeed, Feyerabend recognized the possibility "that science as we know it today, or a 'search for the truth' in the style of traditional philosophy, will create a monster," that it may "harm man, turn him into a miserable, unfriendly, self-righteous mechanism without charm and humour" (Feyerabend 1975, 175, also 189, 216–17).

the physicians to be responsible for their product, and the carpenters and mechanics theirs; but apparently we need not, by this accounting, expect the scientists to be responsible for their productions of scientific knowledge, except for the responsibility to obey the scientific method of accomplishing those productions. The notion that science can be unfettered and maximally open to "progressive development" by giving up antiquated, never-very-accurate philosophies of its method, and replacing them with Feyerabend's anarchism-*cum*-dadaism, is quaint, to say the least. What of the larger society? It is within those historical structures of domination that modern science is supported; whatever its ideology, it cannot avoid those concrete forces and constraints. But then, what Feyerabend's anarchism is mainly about is *not* the alteration or "correction" of the actual practice of science: *that,* he averred, has been generally good, healthy, and proper. Rather, his anarchism is about the need to align the *ideology* of science—its own philosophical enunciations of what it is and does— with the actual practice of science. Feyerabend's joining epistemology and ethics is not so far removed from the natural scientist Monod's "solution" to the dilemma of modern science:

> In the course of three centuries science, founded upon the postulate of objectivity, has conquered its place in society—in men's practice, but not in their hearts. Modern societies are built upon science. They owe it their wealth, their power, and the certitude that tomorrow far greater wealth and power still will be ours if we so wish. But there is this too: ... the choice of scientific *practice,* an unconscious choice in the beginning, has launched the evolution of culture on a one-way path; onto a track which nineteenth-century scientism saw leading infallibly upward to an empyrean noon hour for mankind, whereas what we see opening before us today is an abyss of darkness. (Monod [1970] 1972, 170)

The ailment, we were told, has consisted in the contradiction between "objective knowledge" accumulated by modern science and anachronistic "traditional systems" of belief and thought, which "have placed ethics and values beyond man's reach." And Monod's solution? Inasmuch as "the very definition of 'true' knowledge reposes in the final analysis upon an ethical postulate,"[59] the general values and ethical principles of life in today's world must be brought into correspondence with the basic values and the "ethic of knowledge" on which modern science is founded. "The

---

59. A rare statement by a scientist—or so it would appear, until we reach into its conclusion.

ethic of knowledge that created the world is the only ethic compatible with it, the only one capable, once understood and accepted, of guiding its evolution" (Monod [1970] 1972, 170–80).

5. THE ATROPHY OF UTOPIA

At this juncture I want to introduce explicitly some further considerations of the critique of modern science and its subjugated philosophy that were partially captured in a statement made by Roberto Mangabeira Unger a few years ago. Unger reminded us that in order to "construct we must criticize, but criticism cannot be clear and effective unless it anticipates what is to be built" (Unger 1975, 12). That is so. In order to be effective, a critique must build beyond the one-sidedness of negation—though negation is surely indispensable—otherwise it will dissolve in its own acidic juices. This production depends upon the presence of a clear, consciously formulated project, not merely of "epistemological" or "ethical" or "aesthetic" countenance but simultaneously of all these, without division, and more: a project of the production of life. Unger's remark invites us to reconstitute the potentiality of utopia—not, however, the utopia of a *Wunschwelt*, through which we only reconfirm our pathos; rather, the utopia that joins *outopos* with *eutopos*,[60] through which we can reconvene our productions of the world, first imaginatively and then concretely.

In its best classical uses the force of utopia consisted in the projection of values to be realized in the production of life. This force resided equally and indistinguishably in the reflexivity of the project as critique and as anticipation. True, the projection always failed to break through the limits of imagination or fancy and thus, without exception, remained an impotent vision which more often than not was turned back upon itself in recriminations of "the impossible." Imaginations without material determination—imaginations that are sustained simply in a consciousness of the positivities of existing material determinations—are destined

---

60. The connection was made, it may be recalled, in a prefatory poem composed by the poet laureate of More's *Utopia*:
> NOPLACIA was once my name,
> That is, a place where no one goes.
> Plato's *Republic* now I claim
> To match, or beat at its own game;
> for that was just a myth in prose,
> But what he wrote of, I became,
> Of men, wealth, laws a solid frame,
> A place where every wise man goes:
> GOPLACIA is now my name. (More [1516] 1972, 26)

to be a reproduction of those determinations, often with horribly malignant consequences. But we must not conclude from this fact of life that material determinations without imagination can be less malignant, that the imagination of a production is epiphenomenal. In the modern consciousness, however, the force of utopia has shriveled to inanition. One manifestation of this inanity consists in latter-day versions of Hegel's "unhappy consciousness," in which despair over radical skepticism gives way to more or less silent articulations of noncritical "articles of faith" regarding some ultimate Otherness, whether this Otherness be "godly" (in the remaining sense of that reference) or "naturalistic." But the supreme manifestation is to be found in the recalculation of potentiality into that continuous arithmetic of analytic prediction that extends the existent "is" indefinitely and with neither remainder nor insufficiency. It has had its counterpart in an "ideology of non-ideology" which is "the justification of the administered world," to borrow Jacoby's phrase, an ideology that "interprets the lack of a concept of what ought to be, and the decline of public opinion, as the positive result of the progress and prosperity which have now been achieved" (Jacoby [1969] 1973, 206). In place of the creative impulse of utopia, a perverted Nietzschean pessimism, nurtured on the substance of an eschatological deterministic history and its inevitably victimized individual, has been substituted, and the concrete being of man-woman-child has correspondingly suffered a quiet, almost imperceptible dissipation, its space having been claimed by the progressive spiritualization of a rationality that prefigures "*the* future" (singular in number and with definite article!), always as an analytic-predictive extension of a present. In the end, said Max Weber—who was impressed by his readings of Dostoyevsky and Nietzsche—the iron cage triumphs.

It has been argued that the atrophy of utopia has crucial links to the general hostility toward rationalism, reformism, and radicalism displayed in romanticist and existentialist critiques (see, e.g., Shklar 1957). No doubt links of that sort, even important ones, can be constructed; certainly the rationalist denigration of sensual desire and the material sensuality of life, the disenchantment of language, and the vapid proposals of movements for reform and reconstruction, including "utopian socialism," were important stimulants of the romanticist reaction in particular. And it would be well to remember that this reaction was sometimes more than mere escape, though it was often only that. However, in the dialectical course of such oppositions, the reactive critique assumed aspects of that to which it was reacting.[61]

61. Thus, taking Burke's satiric *Vindication of Natural Society* (1756) as an early instructive example, Pollard has observed that such response was "not so much a denial of the Enlightenment as an enlargement of it. If he denies ration-

The crucial site of the atrophy of utopia was not within the critiques as such—they were never as powerful in material effect as were their adversaries—but rather was within scientific rationalization itself. It was there, in that burgeoning dominance of instrumentalism, that the utopic impulse was overwhelmed—and already before the reactions of Goethe, Stendhal, or Schopenhauer had been felt. Apprehensions of the utopic changed fundamentally from the eighteenth to the nineteenth century. (Witness the almost instantaneously vulgarized apprehensions of Marx's utopic impulse: as a mechanistic determinism of blind forces of history, or as a hayfork uprising of messianic romanticism.) Certainly by the end of the last century, what once had been, in the sense of its etymological space, a *poetic* of the true-good-beautiful was now transmuted into a vocabulary of "poetics" in its degenerated vernacular sense. "Utopia" became a fanciful lexicon of impossibilities. In the words of one commentator, we are asked to keep in mind, when attending to works of utopic imagination, that we can

> understand these stories and legends as saying nothing other than that anything to be found in Eden, Arcadia, or the Golden Age is, by its very nature, unattainable outside those perfect places, never to be expected in the real world: to say that something existed in, for example, Arcadia, is *only* to say that it cannot exist in the world: Arcadia is *only* that which cannot be, that which we cannot legitimately hope for, not a land that people once inhabited and lost, much to their incredible misfortune. (Kateb 1963, 7n.7)

It must have been by such understanding that a social scientist of international standing could find so much significance (though in this, by no means atypically) in the observation that all "utopias from Plato's Republic to George Orwell's brave new world of 1984 have one element in common: they are all societies from which change is absent. . . . The social fabric of utopias does not, and perhaps cannot, recognize the unending flow of historical process" (Dahrendorf 1968, 107).[62]

---

alism, and declares that men are in reality moved by passion rather than exclusively by reason, he accepts Utilitarianism and he uses history to learn what has made men happy in the past. If he believes that history never makes jumps, he also holds that individuals or the multitude may be wrong, though not mankind as a whole" (Pollard [1968] 1971, 101).

62. One is here reminded of all those insipid arguments whether the projected object of Marx's utopic impulse—i.e., his "communist society," for which, it is clear, he *necessarily* refused to draw up a blueprint—would be "free of conflict and change."

In place of utopic vision, the modern consciousness has become suffused with an ideological "non-ideology" of something called "social planning," which dispassionately conceives its tomorrow (whether near or far) not as antithetical to a present but as an extensional prediction from that present—that is, as a process of routinization of "the future," wherein the object of imagination, the project-to-be-realized, is localized in the here of a hereafter. Aspects of this process have been addressed in a little-known book written by Polak during the early 1950s. It must be said in advance that Polak's argument is marred by the one-sidedness of a thoroughgoing idealist viewpoint;[63] nevertheless, if treated with appropriate caution, his discussion does lend some insight into the demise of utopic vision. In particular his argument shows (sometimes despite itself) that the crystallization of anti-utopic sentiment must be well within the matrix of technical rationalism inspired by the development of natural science and its imitators. One indication of this is, of course, the strongly antitechnological theme of such "dystopian" stories as Huxley's *Brave New World*, Orwell's *1984*, and Zamiatin's *We*. Another, yet related, indication is the wedge driven by the "non-ideological" ideology of social planning between the constitution of its engineering and whatever memory of an ethic-aesthetic may have survived in the ahistoricity of its projects. "The scientist's ideal of a differentiation between what is and what ought to be," Polak warned, "condemns the social utopia to a nonscientific status as a useless pastime when it is judged by the standards of empirical science" (Polak [1955] 1973, 190). That which "ought to be" is recast in the scientific calculations of the limits of that which "can be done." Reason deployed within the narrow channels of modern science and its technology, through which an incrementally achieved "mastery of nature" is promised even for those who would have none of it, replaces the impassioned reason of utopic projection; concordantly, the ethical innocence pretended by science rules out the claim to responsible self-consciousness that properly informs the utopic impulse. Faced with the overwhelming social power of the machinery of this perversional science, the utopic impulse succumbs more and more to aspirations to scientific

---

63. Thus, Polak was of the opinion that the "primary forces of history are not propelled by a system of production, nor by industrial or military might, but rather by the underlying ideas, values, and norms that manage to achieve mass appeal" (Polak [1955] 1973, 14, 13). (He also held that "images of the future are always aristocratic in origin.") Perhaps this view was partly inspired by—at the very least it was correlated with—his (not uniquely) poor understanding of Marx, a mechanistic and fundamentally pessimistic version that would make us total captives of naturalistic, universal laws.

standing, in consequence of which its shadow "assumes the character of an extrapolation of existing trends."

> Today all images of the future, utopian and eschatological alike, have been driven into a corner and out of time. They appear to be the victims of a common conspiracy, and yet they themselves set in motion the processes of their own dissolution. . . .
>
> The most remarkable aspect of this entire development is the blindness of our generation in regard to it. How is it possible that this abrupt breach in our times, occurring midway through the century and already challenging the future historian to find a new label for this period, goes unnoticed? . . . We do not understand and respond to the degeneration of our images of the future because we do not understand their function; our lack of understanding and response hastens the silent death of our visions. (Polak [1955] 1973, 183)[64]

This silent death of our vision reveals the empty space of our consciousness, destitute of passion and as hopeless as the pure fool.

The function of the utopic impulse is to give conscious design to the destiny of man-woman-child, by demanding a constantly self-reflective, self-critical consciousness of the incontrovertible value (desire-want-fact) of our responsibility for our destiny, our concrete dignity. It begins in imagination—in wanting, desiring, projecting. If it is to be the imagination of that which is not, the imagination of an "ought to be," it cannot begin otherwise. It does not rest in imagination alone, however; it does not find its constitution in the one-sidedness of a "mind-constituted" configuration. If it is to be other than its own degeneration into the ineffectualities of wishful thinking and mere hope (as with Bloch 1918; 1954–59, for example), or into the vulgar effects of a "social-planning" ideology, critical awareness of its own conditions of existence is indispensable at a practical level. The effective impulse is indissolubly, concretely critique-and-anticipation; for as the one without the other cannot surmount its own negativity, so the other without the one cannot realize its own imagination. The creative impulse will not survive the pretense of prolepsis, of

---

64. Perhaps that was partly what Cioran had in mind when, in his essay of "the skeptic and the barbarian," he said that "skepticism, as a historical phenomenon, is to be met with only at moments when a civilization no longer has a 'soul' in the sense Plato gives the word: 'what moves of itself.' In the absence of any principle of movement, how could it still have a present, how especially a future?" (Cioran [1964] 1970, 89–90).

fashioning a utopia within the confines of existing conditions, like some pupated microcosm within a polluted sea (cf. Frye 1970, 113). The point is not to "idealize" the existent conditions of our world, "leaving out the shadows," as Korsch put it (1938, 53); rather, the point is, still, to *change* those conditions, and *that* is to anticipate a difference.

6. MINERVA'S BIRD

It was Hegel who had to say, in the penultimate paragraph of his preface to *Philosophy of Right*,

> One more word about giving instruction as to what the world ought to be. Philosophy in any case always comes on the scene too late to give it. As the thought of the world, it appears only when actuality is already there cut and dried after its process of formation has been completed. ... When philosophy paints its grey in grey, then has a shape of life grown old. By philosophy's grey in grey it cannot be rejuvenated but only understood. The owl of Minerva spreads its wings only with the falling of dusk. (Hegel [1821] 1952, 7)[65]

That is the attitude of our modern science, our governing consciousness: to "discover" more and more the "secrets" of our world-as-it-is-made, even our world-in-the-making, but always after the fact, "when actuality is already there cut and dried," always too late to say what the world "ought to be" and to strive to make it so. All of our pseudoscientific doctrines of "social planning" notwithstanding, this consciousness signals our self-removal from responsibility, which we have given over to an alien authority (whether it be the godhead of a Pauline eschatology or the abstract laws of an equally abstract nature, or the soteriologic message of beings from some Saturnine world). It is a terrible and terrifying conceit. It is *our* conceit, for which we are condemned already by children born to starvation and barren souls, and by children yet to be born to a chemical wasteland, to bodies malformed and polluted, perhaps to incineration in the fire of charmed particles and mad solutions.

Perhaps there was once a time, when secular philosophy and the germ of modern science were struggling for a space free of the constraints of church dogma, when a thoughtful person could say, without foretell-

---

65. Hegel's "grey in grey" is a reference to Goethe's *Faust*, wherein Mephistopheles informs the Student, "Dear friend, all theory is grey, / and green the golden tree of life" (1832, pt. 1, lines 2038–39).

ing a terror, that one ought to seek knowledge *for its own sake,* as, for example, Bruno did say, though to the dread of many (Bruno [1584b] 1964, 141–43). It was a clever fiction, "knowledge for its own sake," and a fiction that rapidly became its own unquestionable dogma. Much can be done in the name of such an abstraction, much that could not be done in the unclothed reality of the concrete (a lesson that was abundantly available to the new science from the church itself). But even during that earlier time, the fiction *was* a fiction, a masking of material interests; if all variety of benefits to human health and longevity ensued from its enactment, it was no less reprehensible for that. "Enlightenment," in the very way that it was emancipation from the dominations of "prescientific" or mythical dogmas, has also constituted new dominations, many of which, through the mythology of "mastery of nature" and "freedom of the individual," have been destructive of other emancipations previously achieved. Speaking of the present age, Feyerabend has warned that science "has become too powerful, too pushy, and too dangerous to be left on its own" (1975, 217, 300–301). Unquestionably so, even though it has never been exactly "left on its own." The elitism of science—as illustrated, for example, by the only apparently benign belief that, in Turchin's words, "science is the highest level of the hierarchy in the organization of cosmic matter" (1977, 316)—*is* powerful and pushy and dangerous. The liberalist fiction of "knowledge for its own sake" must be abolished. The production of knowledge must be directed consciously and critically for and as its use-values. The evil and the ugliness that we do, no less than the good and the beautiful, must be self-consciously *ours*—not those of some abstraction.

But "science" and "theory of knowledge" are not sustained in a vacuum. Self-understandings of science and of epistemology, just as with the making and doing of science and of epistemology, are fed in the concrete act of producing life; and so it is in the latter that our destiny will be made.

3
E*pistemological Arguments*

I. FROM DESCARTES TO NIETZSCHE

THE COURSE OF ACADEMIC PHILOSOPHY in this century has been described by one philosopher of merit as "the true expression of an age which no longer succeeds in presenting to itself—by means of reflection—an unclouded mirror of its being. The dimming and eventual shattering of this mirror corresponds to the fractured state of philosophy itself which in its attempted self-understanding has become questionable to itself" (Landgrebe [1957] 1966, 2–3). It is worth emphasizing that Landgrebe chose to say "*expression of an age.*" Undoubtedly mindful of the professionalization of philosophers as one more group of intellectual smallholders, he took care not to exaggerate the endurance or the effects of philosophical activity. Thus, what is held up to us most in his remark is not a claimed singularity of the academic philosopher's perspicacity, not a testimony to the sure grasp of a mature philosophical discourse, but instead a very commonplace expression of an uncertainty that is felt at the base of percipience in all quarters of the consciousness of life. This is not a feeling revealed to us originally by the philosophers of the academy; even less have they provided a convincing interpretation. The course of philosophical understanding during this century has been traversed chiefly within the naturalistic consciousness of the sciences, including the "human sciences" and their affiliates in the industry of "mass culture and psychic relief." And what we have received most often by way of "interpretation of the world" is not only instantly gray; it also begs the question of its own insinuation in the predicament of a consciousness that, as Landgrebe said of academic philosophy, is "no longer capable of establishing some firm ground upon which it might gain certitude as to where it stands and whither it intends to go."

Somewhere among the fragments of that once "unclouded mirror" lies the shattered image of a self-certain and autonomous "knowing subject" whose innovation we conventionally credit to Descartes (1596–1650). There is more than a little eponymic deception in that assignment, of course, for the innovation was collective, and it came to be in conjunction with the gradual transformation of a medieval world order of divine providence— a process that predated Descartes and, what is more important, had its roots more in the practical activities of common people's self-governance within their guilds, unions, and village associations, than in the super-ordinate implementations of theoreticians' official doctrines of authority and rulership.[1] By the time of Descartes' century, much of the medieval-Christian ontological unity of the world was already in shambles, and the replacement of a unity imposed by "the perceiving subject" was well underway. It did remain, however, to express this subjective unity in a compelling theoretical systematization—of which the first major instance, the Cartesian system, has cast by far the longest shadow.

The Cartesian subject was constituted as a self-certified *res cogitans*, a secular subjectivity in control of itself and free to master the whole externality that stood as "objectness" to its autonomous presence. The systematization of this new principle of knowledge originated, so we are told, from the midst of a "hyperbolical" doubt that Descartes had under-taken as a necessary condition of his quest for truth. He proposed to doubt everything, "to reject as absolutely false everything as to which I could imagine the least ground of doubt, in order to see if afterwards there remained anything in my belief that was entirely certain." Despite his most strenuous efforts, however, Descartes said he noticed "immediately after-wards" that

> whilst I thus wished to think all things false, it was absolutely essential that the "I" who thought this should be something, and remarking that this truth "*I think, therefore I am*" was so certain and so assured

1. Ullmann, for example, in sketching the outlines of the complex dialectical relation between ruler and ruled, and between the theory and the practice of rulership in medieval Europe, remarked that "the customary practices and usages in the lower strata assumed great historic significance, although the layman, precisely because he was a layman, was held by doctrine to be incapable of taking part in government and in the making of law, the reason being that he lacked the appropriate knowledge, that he did not possess *scientia*" (Ullmann 1966, 62; see also Ullmann 1961). But indeed this layman was an increasingly active, though by no means autonomous, subject, who predicated much in the arrangements of day-to-day life. Even among the theoreticians, whose doctrines typically celebrated a facelessness of service to divine authority, there was by the twelfth century, according to the survey by Curtius, a marked tendency to assert their individuality of authorship (Curtius [1948] 1963, 515–18).

that all the most extravagant suppositions brought forward by the sceptics were incapable of shaking it, I came to the conclusion that I could receive it without scruple as the first principle of the Philosophy for which I was seeking. (Descartes [1637] 1952, 51; see also Descartes [1641] 1952, 77–81)

The truth that he did think, and therefore the truth of his being, consisted for him in the circumstance that he doubted as much; for the very doubting meant that he was thinking.[2] Such "proof" (or posit) of a certain self-consciousness became the point of departure for a revision of the skein of philosophy. It would be a philosophical order that increasingly took its cues from the procedures and subtantive lessons of modern science.

This *ego cogito*, an "immaterial substance" ("the ghost in the machine," in Gilbert Ryle's famous coinage), "the whole essence of nature of which is to think,"[3] was postulated as an indubitable, unanalyzed primordial. Of the separate poles in this duality, "subject" enjoyed distant priority over that which was then set against it, "object." Evidently Descartes had not researched the archives of skepticism very carefully when testing his thesis against their "most extravagant suppositions," but the fact that such failures of procataleptic argument did not impede the flowering of his system testifies to the conditions of receptivity of his audience. The justification or warrant for the claimed indubitability of Descartes' *ego cogito* was in the posited existence of a God who steadfastly refuses to play the trickster—that is, a God "whose idea is in me . . . , who is liable to no errors or defect" and who therefore "cannot be a deceiver, since the light of nature teaches us that fraud and deception necessarily proceed from some defect" (Descartes [1641] 1952, 88). Descartes had entertained the possibility that some powerful and deceitful "evil genius" had made a point of mustering all his energies to the task of deceiving Descartes: that, for example, the human body is not what we see by our eyes and feel by our hands but is really quite different (perhaps, as the physics of mechanistic atomism would later tell us, a concert of many tiny particles whirling through volumes of space). But, having established to his satisfaction the certitude of *cogito*, Descartes traversed to "the objective external world"

---

2. There is, of course, the hidden premise of Descartes' privileged position. It was Hume who later pointed out that in trying to obtain an "experience of oneself," one acquires only a *perception* (Hume 1739–40, I.4.6). As well, there is the hidden presupposition of an ideal model of science, based on the existing mathematical natural science (see Husserl 1936; Gilson 1930).

3. "To think," meaning to engage in *cogitatio* in any of its "modes," which for Descartes were several in number and more inclusive than the English "thought."

by invoking the surety of a God who will not play tricks—that is, who would not give us *real* self-consciousness and then have it falsify, always or occasionally, that which is outside *cogito*.

The seat of the autonomous law-giving and mastery was postulated to be not the concrete, undivided whole of "man," however, but instead a special faculty of the human being, an immaterial substance with which the human creature was uniquely endowed. This substance and seat of the knowing subject, from whence the unity of the world is predicated, was literally the *logos spermatikos*, the seminal reason, order, and providence, of the created world. Thus, from its very beginning in modern philosophy the autonomization and self-certification of a knowing subject who would freely exercise the force of reason for the formation of community, and for the mastery of nature to the service of that community, constituted its own contradiction in the category of its remainder, which included not only the *non*rational but, by virtue of the extreme positivity of this self-assured mastery, the *ir*rational as well.

This *abstraction* of an autonomous subject was proclaimed by historically real men, of course, but men whose consciousness had become the unleashed imagination of a universal lawgiver—a teller of *logos* whose self-mastery was defined without remainder. The abstraction was materially consequential through practical realizations of a doctrine of "free agency," which liberated the subject *from* its subjection in the communal identity of a preordained quality—an intrinsic "whatness" securely limited by its place in the divine order—*to* its situation of a supposedly autonomous *self-identification* enacted in its actions on the external world. And the fruits of "working on the world" confirmed the powers of this emancipated *ego cogito*, though its cost in a cosmic loneliness resisted the anodynic promises of the secular *procursus* only slightly less than those of the increasingly privatized theology. But the stoicist elements transported by this world-constituting subject included a good deal more than the principle of "seminal reason."

Inasmuch as the postulated autonomy of *ego cogito* was conceived in relation to its opposite—both at the level of parallelism in the Cartesian mind-body duality and in the contrast of the "clear and distinct" issue of *cogito* vis-à-vis deceptions and fake images that might be induced by demons—the "ego" of the *ego cogito* could not avoid having an "underside" that was by definition "the dark side" of human nature, opaque to the light of reason. In the very positivity of its powers of world-predication, the knowing subject reproduced stoicist notions of the exhaustibility of "the good" in nature, including human nature, which fed into both a secular version of that Protestant doctrine characterized by Kant (1798a) as "moral terrorism"—that is, that "mankind is in continual regression toward the worse"—and renewed cyclical themes of a basic human nature that, by virtue of mixtures of its diverse passions with *heimarmene* or "fate" (the world-regulative form of the stoicist "seminal reason"), persists as the unchanging center point of the historical drama.[4]

Descartes, together with Bruno, Galileo, Bacon, and a few other stellar figures of the seventeenth-century premiere, succeeded in fashioning systematic linkages between human knowledge and earthly power; but the preceding tradition of churchly admonitions against an unbridled search for knowledge (the "lust of the mind") was never far removed. Moral lessons of regression or "abderitism" would continue to find their occasions. And always there was that shudder of solitude whenever the autonomous "I think" contemplated the tininess of its "I am"—a shrinking proportion within an unfeeling, mechanistic universe, whose spheres and orbits had been constituted from the design of three-dimensional indifference curves.

The systematic imposition of subjectivist unity by the perceiving subject, this consciousness-in-itself, did not occur in a single stroke. Descartes' proposed system was as attractive, for some, as it was startlingly new—the first fundamentally new system after Aristotle, it has been called. But neither Descartes' demonstration nor his defense of his system was very persuasive. A proper history of these developments, even a conventional history of ideas, would attend to numerous correlative developments—for example, aspects of Hobbes's "solution," Vico's comments about "the history of man" versus that "of nature," Leibniz's monadology, and, of course, Hume's thesis of the unknowability of any "ultimate cause" of our "mental actions" (from which he concluded that we engage merely in a "leap of faith" when linking our sense experiences with rational principles). But this is not a proper history, so I shall beg indulgence to pass directly from Descartes' proposal to the close of the eighteenth century and Immanuel Kant (1724–1804), who, in the preface to the second edition of *Critique of Pure Reason*, described his goal thusly:

> It has hitherto been assumed that our cognition must conform to the objects; but all attempts to ascertain anything about these objects *a priori*, by means of conceptions, and thus to extend the range of our knowledge, have been rendered abortive by this assumption. Let us then make the experiment whether we may not be more successful in

---

4. Kant referred to three alternative views of the "moral dynamic" of human history: "moral terrorism," "eudaemonism," and "abderitism" (i.e., cyclical change about a constant point). Rejecting all three as oversimplifications—and, in any case, as impossible of proof—he argued his preference for a simple moral wager: belief in the *possibility* of human betterment as an article of faith, which, although not susceptible of proof, remained necessary to the continued purposefulness of the "crooked stick" (cf. Manuel 1965, 70–91).

metaphysics, if we assume that the objects must conform to our cognition. (Kant [1787] 1952, 7)

Kant was a critical scholar of Hume and Rousseau, as well as of Christian Wolff and Leibniz.[5] He began his deliberations on metaphysics within the "dogmatic slumbers" (as he later described it) of Leibniz's subjectivistic "windowless monads," both directly and via Wolff's "development" of Leibnizian subjectivism, but then turned to the Humean critique and to Rousseau's "practical philosophy." Agreeing with Hume that the first or fundamental causes of our intellection cannot be known, Kant nevertheless rejected the empiricist conclusion on which Hume's thought had come to rest, namely, that there can be no warrantable or explicable basis for connecting our sense-experiences to rational principles, only the belief of articles of faith. Against this conclusion he argued that, although the duality of "I" that obtains in the consciousness of self-as-self—once as subject and once as object—is indeed completely beyond the powers of human explanation, its undoubted facticity nonetheless demonstrates the existence of a founding faculty of intellect that is pretersensuous and that constitutes the unity of the perceiving subject. Discerning the weakness of the Cartesian thesis of a substantial, intuitively known *ego*, Kant counterposed the "I" as the final, ultimate subject to which all else (including the

---

5. Gottfried Wilhelm Leibniz (1646–1716), German polymath of the seventeenth century, had been a persistent promoter of unification in nearly every area of his involvements. Not least of these were his interrelated proposals for a universal language of inquiry (often depicted as the "forerunner" of symbolic logic), a universal calculus of reasoning, and a universal encyclopedia of knowledge. In these respects, no doubt, Kant was sympathetic with the Leibnizian efforts; but not with his rationalistic metaphysics. The centerpiece of Leibniz's philosophy was his doctrine of "monadism," according to which the universe consists of indivisible, nonextended, incorruptible, and entirely self-contained "monads" (*monos*, or "oneness," "unit"), each of which has its own body. Each monad is "windowless," that is, nothing passes into or out of it; but each is aware of externality, and of events or happenings outside, because of impacts or forces on its body. Furthermore, each monad is related to all others in a hierarchical network of substantial unity, such that each is a microcosmic localization of the universe. All events of a particular monad derive from its own force of beingness, and in perfect harmony with all events of every other monad. The universe was preestablished by God as a continuous and harmonious unity of monads—that is, in "the way of preestablished harmony," as Leibniz phrased it.

Kant came initially to Leibniz's work by way of his teacher, Martin Knutzen, who in turn was a student of Christian Wolff (1679–1754), a popular systematizer and teacher during the first half of the eighteenth century who proposed to construct an exhaustive, coherent system founded on Leibnizian principles of ontology (though without the doctrine of monadism).

objectness of self) is object. This "I," as "transcendental unity of apperception," as the *pure* I (which is to say, *not* the empirical selfhood), is neither "thingness" nor "concept" but is, in its purity, empty.[6]

It is the dynamic unity of consciousness, within which any range and sequence of empirical selfhoods phenomenally constituted are given articulation. Therewith, the "Kantian synthesis": an effort to construct a total system by joining a rationalism with a phenomenal empiricism. Such effort centered in Kant's proposal to demonstrate the possibility of "synthetic judgment *a priori*," that is, a proposition which is neither analytic nor, even though it may be elicited by experience, based necessarily in experience. Kant sought to demonstrate that in our synthetic experiences, in our syntheses of experience, we can connect experiences so as to form claims of knowledge that are neither analytically necessary nor empirically probable, yet are true and necessary claims.

The Kantian effort turned on his postulation of an ontically fundamental duality: *noumena* and *phenomena*. The noumena (from *noumenon*, "that which is perceived"; a passive form derived from *noein*, "to perceive") comprise the reality of "things-in-themselves." They trace from their side the thin edge of the limit of human cognition; "things-in-themselves" are independent of the epistemological subject and thus are epistemically inaccessible (though intelligible by faith). The phenomena (from *phainomenon*, "that which appears"; derived from *phainein*, "to show," which is the root also of "fantasy"), on the other hand, comprise the reality that we have in perception, that which we experience. This duality is required, according to Kant, by reason of the following: if the world of our experience were directly a world of things-in-themselves, we could not possibly have a priori knowledge; but, since we do have a priori knowledge, our knowledge must be not of things-in-themselves but of their effects.

Indeed, he argued, the noumenal reality causes the material part of our experiences, that is, the "sensations"; the phenomena consist of these "sensations" plus something else, "phenomenal form," which is a priori and has its origin in the structure of the mind, that is, in that fundamental faculty of intellect. We can have no knowledge of noumenal reality; it is the realm of belief and faith. Phenomenally, we have both empirical and a priori knowledge. We have a priori knowledge of an analytic kind, that is,

---

6. This "emptiness" of the "pure subject" has affinities with the Christian doctrinal version of the Greek notion of *kenosis* ("emptying"), wherein Jesus was "emptied" in order to serve as a "vessel." In Kant's ethic it is the pure, rational will, the so-called categorical imperative, as a function of this pure subject, that dictates proper action.

judgments wherein the predicate is rigorously implied by the propositional subject.

Also, however, we have a priori knowledge of a synthetic kind—that is, apodictically certain judgments the epistemological ground of which consists neither of experience (as in a correct judgment that my desk is in my study when I am not) nor of the necessity of rules of logical inference (as in a correct judgment the predicate of which is not contained already by the propositional subject). Objectively valid synthetic *a priori* knowledge is possible because of the transcendence of reason, which, as the universally active basic constructs of mind, constitutes the objects of such knowledge. These constructs of mind *are* the ordering of our noumenally caused "sensations" in space and time and according to certain categories.

This synthetic function of "transcendental apperception" proceeds in terms of fundamental "forms of *Anschauung*"—that is, "view" or, more conventionally, "intuition"; the "original forms of sensibility" (Kant [1787] 1952, 59)—which are "space," or the external ordering, and "time," or the internal ordering, and in terms of a priori "categories" or "pure conceptions of the understanding," which are those of "quantity" (unity, plurality, totality), those of "quality" (reality, negation, limitation), those of "relation" (substance-and-accident, cause-and-effect, reciprocity), and those of "modality" (possibility, existence, necessity). Together, these two forms of "intuition" and the twelve "categories" are constitutive of the rational faculty, the *ratio* and *informatio* of mind, and thus of the mind-constituted objects of synthetic a priori knowledge of phenomena.

> *Understanding* is, to speak generally, *the faculty of cognitions.* These consist in the determined relation of given representation of an object. But an object is that, in the conception of which the manifold in a given intuition is united. Now all union of representations requires unity of consciousness in the synthesis of them. Consequently, it is the unity of consciousness alone that constitutes the possibility of representations relating to an object, and therefore of their objective validity, and of their becoming cognitions, and consequently, the possibility of the existence of the understanding itself.
>
> The first pure cognition of understanding, then, upon which is founded all its other exercise, and which is at the same time perfectly independent of all cognitions of mere sensuous intuition, is the principle of the original synthetical unity of apperception. . . . The synthetical unity of consciousness is . . . an objective condition of all cognition, which I do not merely require in order to cognize an object, but to which every intuition must necessarily be subject, in order to become an object for me; because in any other way, and without this

synthesis, the manifold in intuition could not be united in one consciousness. (Kant [1787] 1952, 50–51)[7]

Thus, the Kantian principle of systematization consists in the postulation of a necessary Reason (*Vernunft*) that is, from the point of view of any human knower, completely circumscribed in the architecture of the Understanding (*Verstand*). This schemata of understanding, the means by which mind intersects in a knowable world of objects, is nonetheless of inexplicable origin, a hidden art deep in the human soul.[8]

The Kantian system must be appreciated in part as an effort to create a space of authority for modern science. Kant was very much an enthusiast of Newtonian mechanics. One of his earliest works (1755) was a treatise in natural history and cosmology, in which he conjectured, before Laplace, that solar systems originate in the shrinking of spiral nebulae (and in which he speculated on the existence of intelligent creatures in other solar systems). He sought to provide for the new physics a foundation of objective validity and certitude. At the same time, his *Critique of Pure Reason* may be appreciated as a sustained effort to fathom the founding meaning of the then-century-old "modern science"—that reason had become "legislative of experience"—and to work out generally the systematics of a "revolutionized" philosophy. Given his orientation to the new physical science, it is not surprising that the resulting epistemology concerns primarily a knowledge of "things" rather than "people."

On the one hand, Kant argued, science is necessarily empirical. But, on the other, a collection of empirical generalizations, learned from experience, can be a true science only when there is also a rational part that establishes its a priori foundation and the possibility, therefore, of apodictically certain claims of knowledge (Kant [1787] 1952, 17–19; see also Kant [1786] 1970). In addition to its empirical part, a true science must contain the transcendental principle of the a priori "intuitions" and "categories," which constitute the very possibility and the actual conditions of experience as such, and the rational principles of the metaphysics of body and mind, which constitute the qualification of what can be known a priori about body and mind. Physics, according to Kant—that is, Newtonian physics—met the test: its empirical generalizations were founded in both

---

7. See Kant's parallel discussion of "infant socialization" in terms of unity of consciousness and unity of object vis-à-vis the "I" (Kant [1798b] 1974, 9–12).

8. The passage reads: "This schematism of our understanding in regard to phenomena and their mere form, is an art, hidden in the depths of the human soul, whose true modes of action we shall only with difficulty discover and unveil" (Kant [1787] 1952, 62).

the necessary transcendental principle and in principles of the metaphysics of mind and body that, although necessarily dependent on sense-experience, can be demonstrated a priori. By contrast, the empirical study of "soul," or the psychology of mind, must always fall short of the status of genuine science, for such study cannot claim for itself a complete "rational part." It is rather an example of "pretended science" (e.g., Kant [1787] 1952, 121–29), although, as empirical "guidance of experience," it can be useful pragmatically, that is, in the course of conducting affairs of life, as Kant strove to show in various passages of his *Anthropology* (Kant [1798b] 1974, 3–4, 20, 183–85; see also Kant [1785] 1952, 253).

While the Kantian system was designed epistemologically to provide an indubitable basis for the claims of knowledge of modern science, it was at the same time, and as its other aspect, an attempt to establish such a basis without violating the integrity of an *autonomous* ethic, that is, an ethic independent of the empirical generalizations of science. Thus: his study of the practical use of reason, uses of reason as connected with morals (1788), and his effort to develop a metaphysic of morals that would be totally isolated, self-contained, and autonomous within itself, having its own purpose; in short, a "supreme principle of morality" (Kant [1785] 1952, 255). Arguing against Hume that "moral actions" comprise the one class of actions in which reason rather than sensual desire is fully governing, Kant located moral concepts as originally and finally embedded in the a priori of reason. The fulcrum of his moral system is the "categorical imperative." In contrast to all "hypothetical imperatives" (or "technical imperatives," as he called them in the general introduction to his *Metaphysic of Morals*), which are contingent, or means-end relative, and refer to skills and to prudence, the categorical imperative is singular, absolutely, objectively necessary, and a priori synthetic. It consists of one supreme principle: "Act only on that maxim whereby thou canst at the same time will that it should become a universal law." Again: "Act as if the maxim of thy action were to become by thy will a universal law of nature." True duty and true virtue consist not in any honesty of self-interest or in the fulfillment of any technical goal, nor even in obedience to law because of considerations of possible alternative consequences, but simply and purely in the necessity to act in accordance with the maxim, without any regard for consequences. The compulsion of this a priori moral consciousness gives rise to the three supreme affirmations, according to Kant: the affirmations of one's freedom, one's immortality, and one's conviction in the *Summum Bonum* (Kant [1785] 1952, 260, 265–68).

Aside from the purely formal criterion, Kant had nothing definitive to say about the constitution of the correct "maxim of thy action"; the supposition was that if one follows such a maxim (however one is to know it), the consequences *will* be good and the action virtuous. But his "ethic" clearly reveals, in a way that his "epistemology" does not, that for Kant the authentic ground of reality was truly the inaccessible noumena and that his construction came to rest in a position of agnosticism despite his "epistemological" struggles against skepticism and agnosticism. As Hegel was later to note, rather cryptically: "All that is left . . . for the making of a law is the mere form of universality" (Hegel [1807] 1977, 256). Kant's a priori concepts were authorized in his theory of the synthetic function of consciousness as a means by which to surmount the disjunction of "thought" and "thing"—that is, crucially to establish claims of a truth-in-correspondence. But his solution was conducted by the formal categories of logic, categories that could establish only criteria of coherence and consistency (see, e.g., Kant [1787] 1952, 49).[9]

At the end of the "Analytic" section of Critique of Pure Reason Kant argued, as if to anticipate objections, that his concept of noumena was meant to serve only as a "negativity," as a that-which-is-but-not-knowably (Kant [1787] 1952, 96, 98); yet the entirety of his "positive" construction is crucially dependent on that inaccessible "negativity," for it is the necessary material and efficient cause of that which can be known. His duality of noumena-phenomena reproduces his initial problematic outside of logic, so to speak, and in an anteriority of the "thought-existence" relation from which he began.

The status of the noumenon was tenuous indeed. For many of his neo-Kantian followers, the noumenal world came to be regarded not as an externally existent though unknowable realm but simply as a limiting concept, a construct of "minding." For some, the thing-in-itself was dropped altogether, leaving the phenomenal world without an otherness; that is, the phenomenal world was elevated to identity as the realm of true being, wherein the subject is the constitutive thought of an objective world of which it, the subject, is the supreme manifestation. In various expressions, this strongly subjectivist (and later the positivist) idealism comprised one avenue of consequence from abandonment of Kant's noumena (see e.g., Fichte 1808; Cohen 1914).[10]

---

9. One of the most finely documented criticisms of Kant's penchant for argument by formal symmetries and analogies was given by Schopenhauer, in an appendix to his principal work (1844).

10. See, for example, Heidegger [1962a] 1967, 58–61. Hermann Cohen (1842–1918), a principal figure in the Marburg or Southwestern German school of neo-Kantianism during the quarter-century ending with World War I, identified the phenomenal and the real, making the real world totally a creative act of thought. Among later scholars of the Marburg School, Heinrich Rickert (1863–1936) and Ernst Cassirer (1874–1945), though differing sharply from Cohen's proclivity for a mathematical-physical model of the real, nonetheless continued this subjectivist side of neo-Kantianism.

Another and different avenue was the absolutist-objectivist idealism of G. W. F. Hegel (1770–1831). It was Hegel who most systematically addressed the Kantian system from the point of view of its fundamental predicament, in an all but devastating critique. The cogency of Kant's argument depended on acceptance of the supposition that we can have the experiences that we do have *only if* such and such conditions genuinely obtain. Already, then, his argument was contingent on *presuppositions*: presuppositions of the *experiences* we do have, and of the experiences *we* do have. Hegel brought these presuppositions out of the shadow of Kant's transcendental apperception.

To begin with, there is the presupposition of a specific normative concept of science.[11] As already noted, Kant relied on a particular category of knowledge, chiefly Newtonian science, as the prejudged model of that which qualifies as the veridical knowledge that we do have (and for which he set about to demonstrate full warrant). But this science, countered Hegel, "just because it comes on the scene, is itself an appearance: in coming on the scene it is not yet Science in its developed and unfolded truth" (Hegel [1807] 1977, 48–49). This presupposed science, by presuming to assure us of its stature, that is, that it is "a quite different sort of cognition for which . . . ordinary knowledge is of no account whatever," declares "its power to lie simply in its *being*"; yet that "ordinary" and putatively "untrue knowledge likewise appeals to the fact that *it is*, and *assures* us that for it" this science is irrelevant. Why, then, should one choose this science over another "sort" of knowledge? "*One* bare assurance is worth just as much as another."

Moreover, Kant relied on the presupposition of a specific normative concept of the knowing subject. The "I" of the "I think" came on the scene as an already constituted mind, the rational apparatus of which passes judgment on all else. But in fact it passes judgment on all else *except* its own formative embeddedness. In other words, in the Kantian formulation the "*education* of consciousness itself to the standpoint of Science" is represented "simplistically as something directly over and done with" in the making of the resolution to know genuinely (Hegel [1807] 1977, 50). An already completed and undoubted constitution of consciousness cannot, however, distinguish the "I think" as illusion or hallucination from the "I think" as truth. Rather, the genuine power of consciousness rests in its *self-reflection*, that is, in consciousness of its self-formative process through its constitution of its objects *for itself*. In its process of constitution in the reflection of consciousness, what first appeared naively as the object-in-itself "sinks for consciousness to the level of its way of knowing it, and . . .

11. This characterization is borrowed from Habermas, whose treatment of the Hegelian critique my own follows in part (see Habermas [1968a] 1971, 7–20).

the in-itself becomes a *being-for-consciousness* of the in-itself," which is now a *new* object. This "*origination* of the new object . . . presents itself to consciousness without [the latter's] understanding how this happens"; that is, it

> proceeds for us, as it were, behind the back of consciousness. Thus in the movement of consciousness there occurs a moment of *being-in-itself* or *being-for-us* which is not present to the consciousness comprehended in the experience itself. The *content*, however, of what presents itself to us does not exist *for it*; we comprehend only the formal aspect of that content, or its pure origination. *For it*, what has thus arisen exists only as an object; *for us*, it appears at the same time as movement and a process of becoming. (Hegel [1807] 1977, 56)

The Hegelian phenomenological observer, who, as Goethe spoke of Hegel himself, "places himself between object and subject by means of his philosophy of identity" (quoted by Löwith [1941] 1967, 5), can detect this consciousness at work, as it were, wherein the object-in-itself is transformed to an object-for-consciousness and whereby consciousness itself is transformed in a series of successive stages.

In a third presupposition the Kantian system proceeded from a separation of theoretical and practical reason. Yet, Hegel argued, in the mode of reflection wherein consciousness becomes conscious in and for itself, the theoretical and the practical are undivided, inasmuch as the successive negations of objects and formations of new objects, through which the self-formative process of consciousness unfolds, is at once a theoretical and a practical linking. The "*dialectical* movement which consciousness exercises on itself and which affects both its knowledge and its object, is precisely what is called *experience* [*Erfahrung*]." Our knowledge of an object, or the "being-*for*-consciousness" of this in-itself, "itself becomes the second object." Although it may *seem* to us that "our experience of the untruth of our first notion comes by way of a second object which we come upon by chance and externally, so that our part in all this is simply the pure *apprehension* of what is in and for itself," such is a purely negative skepticism which "ends up with the bare abstraction of nothingness or emptiness" and which, accordingly, "must wait to see whether something new comes along," so that it too can be thrown into "the same empty abyss." Actually, however, the true object "shows itself to have come about through a *reversal of consciousness* itself." As our knowledge changes from knowledge of "true object" to that of "untrue object," so, too, does the object-in-itself-for-consciousness, and this transpires not simply as some "pure apprehension" but through that which is necessarily cognitive-and-normative action. Lest we forsake ourselves amidst random movements of completely disconnected surprises, Hegel urged, the "result of an untrue mode of knowledge must not be allowed to run away into an empty nothing, but must necessarily be grasped as the nothing *of that from which it results*—a result which contains what was true in the preceding knowledge" (Hegel [1807] 1977, 51, 55–56).

In his proposal to demonstrate the conditions of the possibility of apodictically certain knowledge as a necessary condition of the credence of our sense-experience, Kant was captured *from the beginning* in an oscillation of assertions that were unfailingly self-denying. For, if the critical demonstration *is* apodictically certain knowledge—and surely Kant proposed to speak therein the truth—then Kant failed to account for his own cognitive faculty in "knowing about knowing." In short, Hegel concluded, Kant presumed to construct as his epistemology what it could not possibly be, a strictly presuppositionless primal philosophy (*Ursprungsphilosophie*).

Any study of the existence and indeed the possibility of knowledge is always in a position of contingency with respect to conditions that are prior to it. This criticism extends to all theories of knowledge that postulate the existence of an "organon" of knowledge, whether it be in terms of a "medium" through which one discovers the that-which-is or an "instrument" which operates on a that-which-is-received (e.g., "sensations") and constitutes this as our object-world.[12] Whether "medium" or "instrument," Hegel argued, these are useless constructions. If, for example, "we remove from a formed thing what the instrument has done to it, then the thing . . . is once again just what it was before this exertion, which thus was superfluous." Here again, of course, Hegel's own basic standpoint is revealed: the "organon" theory of knowledge presupposes that cognition is real, yet that it stands independent of absolute reality; that cognition, "which, since it is excluded from the Absolute, is surely outside the truth as well, is nevertheless true." Such thinking signifies a "fear of the truth," namely, "the fact that the Absolute alone is true, or the truth alone is absolute" (Hegel [1807] 1977, 46–47). Thus, while Hegel's critique shattered the dark pane that had obscured the actual presuppositions of Kant's "solu-

---

12. The premise of an "organon" is embedded in the varieties of so-called faculty psychology, of which the most prominent instance during the century preceding Hegel had been Christian Wolff's *Rational Psychology*, published in 1734. A fundamental fault of this or any other "faculty psychology" is the circularity of its argumentative structure. In postulating "mind" as the unity of specific "faculties" (e.g., "will," "intellect," "emotion") each of which serves in the explanation of different observable processes, or different "components" of behavior (e.g., "willing," "intellecting," "emoting"; or "volitional processes," "cognitive processes," etc.), that which is purportedly the *explicans* is simply the reified abstractedness of that which is the *explicandum*.

tion," it was not to the advantage of an alternative demonstration of that which Kant had questioned. As Habermas has remarked with admirable clarity, the very idea that

> Hegel imputes to transcendental philosophy, namely, "that the Absolute is located on one side and knowing, located on the other, is still something real by itself and in separation from the Absolute" [Hegel (1807) 1977, 47]—this idea belongs rather to Hegel's own frame of reference. For Hegel is referring to the absolute relation of subject and object. In this relation a mediating organon of knowledge can in fact be thought of only as the cause of subjective interference and not as the condition of the possible objectivity of knowledge. For critical philosophy [i.e., for Kant] it is otherwise. The organon produces the world within which reality can appear at all; thus under these conditions of its functioning it can always only disclose reality and not obscure it. Only presupposing that reality as such simply appears can this or that individual real element be obscured—unless we presume an absolute relation between reality and the cognitive process that is independent of that instrument. But from the presuppositions of transcendental philosophy we cannot even meaningfully talk of knowledge without identifying the conditions of possible knowledge. Accordingly Hegel's critique does not proceed immanently. For his objection to the organon theory of knowledge presupposes just what this theory calls into question: the possibility of absolute knowledge. (Habermas [1968a] 1971, 12)

The Hegelian rejection of a noumena-phenomena dualism and the positive formation of his own system did indeed proceed from an absolutization of the subject-object relation. As early as 1802, with publication of his essay "On the Scientific Modes of Treatment of Natural Law" in the *Kritisches Journal der Philosophie*, Hegel began his assessment of *Geist* ("Spirit") in superordination to *Natur*. Accepting Kant's distinction between reason and understanding (*Vernunft* and *Verstand*) initially, Hegel argued that the understanding is a necessary but limited prephilosophical stage of knowing, that its fixed categories are in fact uncritical. The course of reason, on the other hand, is a dialectical movement toward its own completion in terms of categories that are self-amending as they surpass themselves at each stage of the process. The reason of Spirit, the essence of Spirit, is not an eternally fixed "givenness" but consists instead in its eschatological design of becoming-for-itself, an unfolding through which the in-itself is transformed to the for-itself of consciousness. In this process of self-knowledge the one concrete principle of the world, of truth, is articulated: the reflection of difference, opposition, contradiction, a reflection into identity, eventually the identity of the Whole. The unfolding of Spirit as thought-thinking-itself (with no remainder, as it were) results in its own consummation of its beginnings, the consummation of the Absolute Totality.

The Hegelian system differs vitally from the Kantian not only by virtue of Hegel's interdiction of the noumenal mystery and his realignment of nature as objectification of spirit (i.e., the presenting of nature always as predicate, though ultimately not of "man") but also by his systematic effort to be fully incorporative of an "actual human history."[13] In Hegel's hands the veil of arbitrariness and nonessential quality, the "accident of events," that had shrouded the history of the world was to be cast off, as philosophy would become self-consciously its own time apprehended in thought, "the self-thinking Idea, the truth aware of itself" (1830c, §574).

Not that Hegel's history was a simple apotheosis of his own time and place, as it is sometimes crassly imagined to be.[14] Nor was his historical sensibility itself ahistorical (within his own framework): before Waterloo, in the preface to his *Phenomenology*, he spoke of his own epoch as a time of birth, "a period of transition to a new era," although "the initial appearance of the new world is, to begin with, only the whole veiled in its *simplicity*" (Hegel [1807] 1977, 6–7); after Waterloo, in the preface to his *Philosophy of Right*, he spoke of philosophy as "the thought of the world" always coming on the scene "only when actuality is already there cut and dried" (Hegel [1821] 1952, 12, 13)—only at the dusk and not, as in 1807, at the dawn. But while Hegel's periodization of world history changed in response to Napoleonic events and the revision of the Prussian state,[15] the fundamental construction of his identity theory remained intact.

> Self-manifestation is a determination belonging to Spirit as such; but it has three·distinct forms. The first mode in which Spirit, as [only] in itself or as the logical Idea, manifests itself, consists in the direct release (*Umschlagen*) of the Idea into the immediacy of external and particularized existence. This release is the coming-to-be of Nature.

13. It is hardly incidental that Hegel was the first philosopher of stature, after the European "Age of Discovery," to consider seriously the idea of, and to compose, a "*world* history."

14. Even though Hegel became more accepting "of German society as it was" after the "modernization" of the Prussian state, "the 'owl of Minerva' never became the carrion-crow of reaction under the Restoration" (Lukács [1954] 1976, 461; cf. Avineri 1972, 34–130).

15. Lukács dated the re-periodization as having taken place sometime between 1817, the year of the first edition of Hegel's *Encyclopedia*, and 1820 (Lukács [1954] 1976, 460).

Nature, too, is a posited existence; but its positedness has the form of immediacy, of being outside of the Idea. This form contradicts the inwardness of the self-positing Idea which brings forth itself from its presuppositions. The Idea, or Spirit implicit, slumbering in Nature, overcomes, therefore, the externality, separateness, and immediacy, creates for itself an existence comformable to its inwardness and universality and thereby becomes Spirit which is reflected into itself and is for itself, self-conscious and awakened Spirit or Spirit as such.

This gives the second form of Spirit's manifestation. On this level, Spirit which is no longer poured out into the asunderness of Nature but exists for itself and is manifest to itself, opposes itself to unconscious Nature which just as much conceals Spirit as manifests it. Spirit converts Nature into an object confronting it, reflects on it, takes back the externality of Nature into its own inwardness, idealizes Nature and thus in its object becomes for itself. But this first being-for-self of Spirit is itself still immediate, abstract, not absolute; the self-externality of Spirit is not absolutely overcome by it. The awakening Spirit does not yet discern here its unity with the Spirit concealed and implicit in Nature, to which it stands, therefore, in an external relation, does not appear as all in all, but only as one side of the relation; it is true that in its relation to the Other it is also reflected into itself and so is self-consciousness, but yet it lets this unity of consciousness and self-consciousness still exist as a unity that remains so external, empty and superficial that in it self-consciousness and consciousness still fall asunder; and Spirit, despite its self-communion is at the same time in communion not with itself but with an Other, and its unity with the Spirit implicitly present and active in the Other does not as yet become *for* Spirit. Here, Spirit posits Nature as a reflectedness—into-itself, as *its* world, strips Nature of its form of otherness and converts the Other confronting it into something it has itself posited; but, at the same time, this Other still remains independent of Spirit, something immediately given, not posited but only presupposed by Spirit, as something, therefore, the positing of which is antecedent to reflective thought. Hence from this standpoint the positedness of Nature by Spirit is not yet absolute but is effected only in the reflective consciousness; Nature is, therefore, not yet comprehended as existing only through infinite Spirit, as its creation. Here, consequently, Spirit still has in Nature a limitation and just by this limitation is finite Spirit.

Now this limitation is removed by absolute knowledge, which is the third and supreme manifestation of Spirit. On this level there vanishes, on the one hand, the dualism of a self-subsistent Nature or of Spirit poured out into asunderness, and, on the other hand, the merely incipient self-awareness of Spirit which, however, does not yet comprehend its unity with the former. Absolute Spirit knows that it posits being itself, that it is itself the creator of its Other, of Nature and finite Spirit, so that this Other loses all semblance of independence in face of Spirit, ceases altogether to be a limitation for Spirit and appears only as a means whereby Spirit attains to absolute being-for-self, to the absolute unity of what it is in itself and what it is for itself, of its Notion and its actuality.

The highest definition of the Absolute is that it is not merely Spirit in general but that it is Spirit which is absolutely manifest to itself, self-conscious, infinitely creative Spirit, which we have just characterized as the third form of its manifestation. Just as in philosophy we progress from the imperfect forms of Spirit's manifestation delineated above to the highest form of its manifestation, so, too, world-history exhibits a series of conceptions of the Eternal, the last of which first shows forth the Notion of Absolute Spirit. (Hegel [1830c] 1971, §384 *Zusatz*)

For the old as for the young Hegel, Spirit works its will through its otherness in the world; it actualizes itself dialectically in its manifestations in world activity. And the dialecticity is not merely "of the method" but is rather of the very essence of reality, that is, of Spirit in its becoming for-itself.

At each stage of the unfolding of Spirit, its self-reflection in the object of its otherness reveals to itself its limitations, its difference and contradiction, which must then be negated in the next stage or form of its manifestation. This negation is not, however, merely a shuffling of that which was true but now is untrue into an abyss of nothingness—as if it had become a that-which-never-was, a quaint but nugatory presence. Rather, it is negation as the contradiction of opposing moments of the act of Spirit "laying-itself-down"—that is, of "thesis-antithesis," if you will—in the reflectedness of which a new "synthesis" emerges as a higher and incorporative stage, the limitations of which as a new thesis-of-itself are revealed to Spirit in its new otherness and are then sublated in yet another stage of the becoming of Spirit.

Thus, in the act of Spirit unfolding to itself the "identity of identity and nonidentity" proceeds as an "eschatological movement" of annulment-preservation-elevation, of sublation (*Aufhebung*). It is a "movement" in which each stage preserves and elevates the abrogated content, the essence, of all previous stages as moments of the becoming of the whole. Spirit "inheres" in the world, yet the process is a not-quite-immanent process; for while its consummation is a consummation as pure self-knowledge of the Whole, the pure being of Absolute Spirit, it is consummation of its beginnings.

The true history of the world is the biography of Spirit, inasmuch as the actualization of Spirit necessarily takes place through the activity of generations and nations of people. Spirit constitutes true consciousness as it constitutes itself, but it does so behind our backs, so to speak, for we are only falsely conscious (except insofar as we "see" as Hegel's phenomenological observer). Spirit operates with "cunning" (the famous "*List der Vernunft*"), so that we, as world-historical actors, may act even from the most selfish and crassest of motives and yet remain, as it were, the material expression of Spirit's motive in the moment of its unfolding. Our activity is the necessary agency of change through which Spirit works its will; but our subjective views and understandings are as such of no fundamental importance. The force of "cunning of reason" wills through us. In the Reason of Spirit, "the cognitive" and "the normative" are one; they are identified in a *Theoria*, which, as pure thought or "vision" ("seeing"), is itself the highest form of activity—simultaneously the spectator and that which produces the spectacle by acting it.

The course of human knowledge was described by Hegel in multifaceted relation to species history and the biography of Spirit, first in the *Phenomenology* (its very structure is a mapping of the process) and again in the *Encyclopedia*, though this time from the completed philosophical viewpoint of objectively true history. According to Hegel, the course of human knowledge is a triplicated recapitulation of history, each traversing being the sublative culmination of the preceding one, until the only true history, that of the Whole, is reached. In the biography of Spirit, it is the course of Spirit working toward the culmination of its beginnings through the dialectic of Idea-Nature-Spirit, each of which can be complete only in the relation formed with each of the others in the Whole.

The first trajectory, that of subjective spirit, proceeds as ordinary consciousness of the world as a given externality, a consciousness marked by "sense-certainty" of the world as a real and independent externality of ruled relations and forces. In the course of this trajectory, the simple but necessary consciousness of sense-certainty becomes "perception" and that, in turn, becomes "understanding"; consciousness becomes a self-consciousness of agency, from which derives a consciousness of "observing reason" that shows the necessity of a second traversing of history. As Hegel formulated it in part 1 of the *Encyclopedia*, the very least that we can say of something is that it *is*, and then that it has such and such qualities, and so forth; beyond these simple descriptive levels of a sense-certain knowledge, we can say of something that it is explicable in terms of causes or essences inhering in the ruled relations and forces that exist behind the sense-certain immediacy of our observations; but, finally, with cognition of that anteriority of phenomena, we become conscious of the origin of those ruled relations and forces in our own activities, and thus that the most that can be said of "something" can be said only in terms of its embeddedness in human life, that is, in terms of purpose and will. Our knowledge of "externalities" becoming a knowledge *that* and *of* that which we have devised, therefore, it becomes a self-knowledge, though not yet of the whole (that is, a self-certainty, though not yet truth; see Hegel [1830c] 1971, §416). It becomes increasingly a self-consciousness of the tragic relations of a consciousness that, having glimpsed the origination of externalities in itself, tries to put the world to its service. This is the dialectic of the not-yet-absolute Spirit attempting to master Nature and vouchsafe freedom.[16]

In Nature the Idea, as a unity of subjectivity and objectivity, encounters its Otherness—though not yet at the level of Absolute Spirit (wherein, by Hegel's identity principle, Nature attains equivalent status; see e.g., Hegel [1830c] 1971, §§575–77). This otherness is constituted in the circumstance that the notion of Nature offers that within which a knowledge of experienced nature is first of all possible, yet Nature is impotent in that "it preserves the determinations of the Notion only *abstractly*, and leaves their detailed specification to external determination" (Hegel [1830b] 1971, §§250–51).[17]

---

16. Here, then, the dialectical relations of domination (lord and slave) and freedom in thought (the stages of stoicism, skepticism, and the unhappy consciousness of Christianity).

17. Hegel thus remarked by way of clarification that in this "impotence of Nature to adhere strictly to the Notion in its realization, lies the difficulty and, in many cases, the impossibility of finding fixed distinctions for classes and orders from an empirical consideration of Nature." That is:

> Nature everywhere blurs the essential limits of species and genera by intermediate and defective forms, which continually furnish counterexamples to every fixed distinction; this even occurs within a specific genus, that of man, for example, where monstrous births, on the one hand, must be considered as belonging to the genus, while on the other hand, they lack certain essential determinations characteristic of the genus. In order to be able to consider such forms as defective, imperfect and thus deformed, one must presuppose a fixed, invariable type. This type, however, cannot be furnished by experience, for it is experience which also presents these so-called monstrosities, deformities, intermediate products, etc. The fixed type rather presupposes the self-subsistence and dignity of the determination stemming from the Notion. (Hegel [1830b] 1970, §250)

The place and meaning of "monstrous forms" in the table of living nature was a matter of great concern in the transforming natural sciences of the early nineteenth century. Referring to classic natural history as well as folkloric constructions, the historian Jules Michelet recounted in his *La Mer* the conserving view: "Everything that did not conform to animality and everything that also came close to man, passed for a *monster*, and they did away with it. The mother who had the misfortune of giving birth to a malformed son could not defend it; they smothered

It is in labor that embodied Spirit confronts its manifestation in the otherness of objects and their rules and regularities—that is, the object manifested as an externalization of the laborer, and, in the double aspect of the dialectic of that origination, as an alienated otherness. This self-consciousness arises, moreover, in the concrete subjugation of the servant by the master: the master, who enjoys the fruits of the bondsman's labor, does not, however, confront the object of labor in its origination directly but only through the bondsman; it is, then, the servant whose consciousness is elevated by virtue of confrontation with the objective otherness of labor (the alienated externalizations manifested as such), an elevation that shows itself in the historical stages of servile consciousness, including latterly the Unhappy Consciousness or "consciousness of self as a dual-natured, merely contradictory being."[18]

The culmination of history in its first trajectory was, according to Hegel, expressed in the systems of Kant and Fichte and their "abstract morality" (*Moralität*): reason as a contentless universal and therefore a merely formal standard within which we would do what we would do. But this self-consciousness of subjective Spirit confronting its externality and trying to master it having been attained, the course of history must be traversed again—this time in the revised terms of objective Spirit, that is, consciousness of the rationality of reality as the real historical activity of human creation. This objective knowledge, which Hegel surveyed briefly in the *Phenomenology* (especially chapter 6), more extensively in the *Encyclopedia*, and again in his *Philosophy of Right* (and subsequent lectures),

---

it between mattresses" (Michelet 1836, 256; quoted in Orr 1976, 39). The new evolutionism would not be daunted by the "impotence of Nature to adhere strictly to the Notion in its realization," however; within a few years of Hegel's exposition of "the difficulty" and even "the impossibility of finding fixed distinctions," Étienne and Isidore Geoffroy Saint-Hilare, father and son zoologists and comparative anatomists, published their landmark catalogue of "monstrous forms" or "teratoids," *Traité de tératologie* (1836). Fabulous genealogies gave way to serial orderliness and statistical regularities. (For additional description, see Jacob [1970] 1973, 26–27, 123–24; Foucault [1966] 1970).

18. Quoting from Hegel's *Phenomenology of Spirit*:
   The *truth* of the independent consciousness is . . . the servile consciousness of the bondsman. This, it is true, appears at first *outside* itself and not as the truth of self-consciousness. But just as lordship showed that its essential nature is the reverse of what it wants to be, so too servitude in its consummation will really turn into the opposite of what it immediately is; as a consciousness forced back into itself, it will withdraw into itself and be transformed into a truly independent consciousness. . . . Through his service [the bondsman] rids himself of his attachment to natural existence in every single detail; and gets rid of it by working on it. (Hegel [1807] 1977, 117)

is knowledge of the actuality of history, the dialectical moments of which are Family (Antiquity), Civil Society (post-Reformation), and State (the modern epoch).[19] Having reconstituted its consciousness at this level, Spirit traverses to its absolutization, its consummation of the in-and-for-itself, and as such beholds history reflexively as self-knowledge of its moments in Absolute Truth.

From this vantage point, history is comprehended as moments of the Whole by a philosophy that, having completed the threefold recapitulation, is itself the retrospective description of the that-which-is, the actuality (*Wirklichkeit*, as opposed to *Dasein* or "existence") which is real-rational-good.[20] It is a movement, a philosophy, which "finds itself already accomplished, when at the close it seizes its own notion—i.e., only *looks back* on its knowledge"—in its self-characterization as a cognition of the necessity of rationality. "This notion of philosophy is the self-thinking Idea, the truth aware of itself—the logical system, but with the signification that it is universality approved and certified in concrete content as in its actuality" (Hegel [1830c] 1971, §§573, 574).[21]

In the coming-to-close of the age, as Hegel's philosophy prepared to paint "its grey in grey," the institutional embodiment and penultimate dialectical moment of the objectification of Spirit was seen to be the modern state. Dialectically, "the state" occupies a place at the pinnacle, so to speak, of the objective embodiment of Spirit—that is, objective Spirit, the three moments of which are law, *Moralität*, and *Sittlichkeit* ("ethical life"). The state is the third moment of *Sittlichkeit*. As such, it is inferior to Absolute Spirit—the embodied moments of which are art, religion, and philosophy—but consists as the mediation to Absolute Spirit. In other words, as the

19. In the *Phenomenology* the mediative and transitional period was defined in terms of the Enlightenment and the ensuing world-crisis of the French Revolution (Hegel [1807] 1977, 328–55). Later, however, in his *Philosophy of Right* and in revised editions of the *Encyclopedia*, he redefined the beginning of the period (and the chief condition of the modern state) in terms of the Reformation (for a brief discussion, see Lukács [1954] 1976, 460).

20. The reference is to Hegel's statement that "what is rational is actual and what is actual is rational"—which sentence aroused considerable controversy when it appeared in the preface to his *Philosophy of Right* (Hegel [1821] 1952, 6). Hegel tried to clarify the matter in the second edition (1827) by pointing out that by "the real" (*Wirklichkeit*) he meant not the merely empirical existence but actuality as identified with the notion of reason (see his Addition to §270).

21. It must be emphasized that the "description" referred to above is not the positivistic sense of "description" as separate from "prescription." For Hegel, "the cognitive" and "the normative" are fused in the consummated embodiments of Spirit; the philosophic retrospect of an age coming to its close was not meant to yield precepts for an open future.

sublation of the historical moments of "family" and "civil society" as modes of "ethical life," the state, with its corresponding "universal class," bureaucracy, dialectically preserves and elevates the unity-in-duality of subjective individuality and objective universality. At the level of subjective Spirit, the state exists as an instrument of (collected) individual motives and goals; at a higher level, the state is also embodiment of the immanent necessity of Spirit, through which we attain realization of the Absolute Whole (albeit not initially *as* a whole). It is, then, the mediation of the identity of individuality and universality, a mediation dialectically constituted by the actuality of the state as simultaneously instrument and immanent necessity and by corresponding actuality of the person as simultaneously "civilian" (*bourgeois*) and "citizen" (*citoyen*). For Hegel, this identified duality of the third moment of "ethical life," doubly of "modern society" and "modern man," is the locus of integration of the one and the many, the individual and the universal, "man" and "society." The state, with its universalist bureaucracy at the apex of "class" (*Stand*) structure, serves as the annealing force by which the ills, the errors, and the limitations of modern society—in early nineteenth-century industrial Europe—would be overcome. (See e.g., Hegel [1830c] 1971, §§535–46; Hegel [1821] 1952.)

It is here, of course, that the quietistic compulsion of Hegel's purportedly closed system stands out most transparently, as Marx demonstrated first in his critical notebook on Hegel's *Philosophy of Right*, composed in 1843, and then in the so-called Paris manuscripts of 1844, dealing principally with the *Phenomenology*. On the one hand, Hegel had formulated a remarkably sharp indictment of the ills of "modern society" (see, e.g., Hegel [1805–6] 1967, 231–57; Hegel [1821] 1952, §244, et passim; Hegel [1830c] 1971, §§524–36): the impoverishment of "whole masses" as a result of rapid "change in fashion," marketplace inflation, and obsolescence of the old by ever-newer inventions; the attraction of wealth to wealth, and the centralization of production to the exclusion of smaller firms; the erection of factories on "the misery of a class"; the condemnation of large masses of people to a "dullness in labor" that makes of them a "rabble" suffering "raggedness of the will, an inner indignation [*Empörung*] and hatred"; and so forth.[22] On the other hand, the Spirit of his philosophy would merely interpret the world, in its backward look at itself as already accomplished knowledge, which is *all* philosophy *can* do: only

---

22. *Empörung*, translated by Knox as "(inner) indignation," also means "uprising" or "rebellion," in this context an internal rebellion in anger at the meanness of conditions, but an inward-turning anger that, as Nietzsche later characterized the *ressentiment* of slave morality, is wanting of the deed.

the spiritual is real; to think is to act. But its interpretation was such as to make of the being who *does* have the potentiality to accomplish more than mere interpretation, more than mere thinking, a helpless cipher of an absolutized abstraction, the hypostatized "metaphysical necessity" of rationality. The future is determined, but nowhere does the consciousness of man-woman-child enter into that determination (cf., e.g., Hegel [1821] 1952, §§274, 297 plus Addition; and Marx [1843] 1975, 19, 44–54). The concrete sensuous being of man was reduced once again, in this reinforcement of false consciousness, to the predication of a lifeless abstraction, which itself derived from the existence of "man." Such was, and is, the inevitable conclusion of any idealism—which, in whatever version, can, by its own premises, unite "man and nature," "mind and body," "subject and object," *only in words*, never in deeds. Marx's critique of the Hegelian mystification, precisely because it owed so much to "kernels" of insight from Hegel, was devastating. Ironically, and this is truly the irony of tragedy, the devastation took root much more widely than did the cleansing and reconstitution for which it had been merely the preparation. And in that, the sheer negativity of Marx's critique has been turned back upon it, and has sucked it dry of any reconstituting life. But it never claimed for itself any existence in the anteriority of a "metaphysical necessity."

Before Marx, and contemporary with Hegel's growing stature in the German academy, an altogether different line of attack on the Hegelian architecture was taking shape at the hands of Arthur Schopenhauer (1788–1860), whose chief work, *The World as Will and Idea*, was first published in 1818, the same year Hegel assumed Fichte's chair at the University of Berlin. A vociferous critic of Hegel's absolutization of reason (as well as his "barbarous and mysterious speech"), Schopenhauer returned to elements of the Kantian scheme for his starting point. In particular, he accepted both the noumenal-phenomenal distinction as a fundamental condition of reality and the correlative claim that our "cognitive experience" can be only of the phenomenal world—or, in his terms, of the world as "idea" or "representation" (*Vorstellung*: "a putting forward"). However, he also argued that the in-itself of noumenal being *is* accessible to a human experience, despite the cognitive limit marked by the edge of phenomenal reality: this is the inner experience of a *willing* being. It is not through a perceptual consciousness that one has access to the in-itself, rather it is in the inner experience of an active principle of willing that one *is* joined in the in-itself (see, e.g., Schopenhauer [1844] 1883–86, 1:39). Thus, according to Schopenhauer, an absolute reality of creative Will, and not some rational Absolute, constitutes the being-given of the phenomenal world. Will is the supreme real, the one undivided and timeless whole of the universe, of which our phenomenal distinctions (e.g., the perceptual consciousness of *my* being) are illusions.

Kant, too, had situated "will" in the noumenal reality (and therein the point of all inquiry of moral law, as the synthetic a priori). But Schopenhauer's Will was constituted differently. This Will is a raw, untamed nonrational—a naturalistic original force that articulates no grand purpose, no compulsive doctrine of progress-in-enlightenment, but only its own compulsion of immediate survival. This Will, and not some rational and rationalizing Intellect, is the master in human nature, as indeed in the universe at large.[23] The human creature always does just what he wills, but the doing is always the doing what is necessary by virtue of the identity of being and willing. Put otherwise, while we may "feel" that we do only what *we* will, our activity is actually nothing other than the pure expression of our very being-given in Will, and even the lowest natural creature, assuming it could *have* such "feeling," would indeed have the *same* "feeling" (see Schopenhauer [1841] 1960, 98–99).

Schopenhauer's confession was one of an enduring evil: the extension of Will is meaninglessness, which is to say the meaninglessness of opposing Will and the recurrent conflicts of its contending forces, which have only the purpose, or meaning, of survival. The knowledge gained from our sciences cannot turn Will from that course, even as it serves to satisfy the "wants" of Will. To be sure, that which the sciences claim to know, they do often know truly; but it is, after all, the knowledge merely of phenomena and can muster of itself, therefore, only the means by which to alleviate phenomenal manifestations, symptoms, of the inevitable evils of life. Although Schopenhauer sought to reserve a capacity whereby this world-pattern of evil could be rejected (through a self-denying "turning of the will") and whereby moral virtue could be approached, the enactment of that alleged possibility was imprisoned in mystery by his characterization of deterministic Will. No doubt Schopenhauer formed an important reaction to the one-sided rationalisms of philosophic discourse. But his recalling of attention to the force of "nonreason" transpired through a perverting "willing" that would enslave the sensuous creativity of human life to an indomitable will whose destiny is horror and doom. He "spoke of the 'will'; but nothing is more characteristic of his philosophy than the absence of all genuine willing" (Nietzsche [1901] 1967, §95). For all the great fury of his disillusionment with the post-Enlightenment world, there is nothing in his doctrine that constituted in any way an effective contradiction of the dominant structure of scientific-technological-philosophical self-understanding

---

23. Cf. Hegel's comment that the "distinction of Intelligence from Will is often incorrectly taken to mean that each has a fixed and separate existence of its own, as if volition could be without intelligence, or the activity of intelligence could be without will" (Hegel [1830c] 1971, §445).

of the world (see Lukács 1953, 156–98). It told rather the quietism of a great fatigue.

This prophetic fatigue displayed in Schopenhauer's radical "pessimism" has been retrospectively marked for us by Löwith (1941), among others, as part of "the revolutionary break in nineteenth-century thought." Certainly between the first and the last great philosopher of the nineteenth century, between the second edition of the *Encyclopedia of the Philosophical Sciences* and the first edition of *The Gay Science*, we encounter a disparity of profound significance.

Most often, the difference marked on the one side by the work of Friedrich Nietzsche (1844–1900) is memorialized for us in an image of "Nietzsche the mad prophet." It is the mockingly personal statuary of "the differently different"—the sort of memory that can tell us, for instance, that Van Gogh did in fact cut off part of his own ear, but cannot say whether he had a hand in the creation of a "Garden of the Asylum" or an "Old Man in Sorrow." It is of such images that paradoxes are made. If Nietzsche remains important to us today in any "positive" way, then he must be important somehow *despite* his refusal to fashion a "system," found a "school," or cultivate "disciples" (and who today is "a Nietzschean"?), that he wrote in a most unorthodox "style" (so fragmented, so fleeting, so "poetic"; full of etymological allusion and pun; language deflected back upon itself), that he seemed to engage even gleefully in ad hominem arguments, that he railed against morality, that he gave voice— and this is undoubtedly his most infamously different "difference"—that he gave voice to an underworld of unspeakable perversion and lunacy: God is dead! Christianity, rotten to the core! Yet the difference of Nietzsche, the difference that established such an enormous distance from Hegel in so short a time, has survived all the idiotic consumption of "paradox" and the "shockingly different."

And it *has* survived precisely because of that which gives to the severity of his critique its continuing relevance. The madness Nietzsche suffered was not, as *he* well knew, a unique presence beneath his skin, autochthonous from the seed only of his soul. When, in 1889, he stepped from lonesomeness to an emphatic solitude, we were granted occasion to individualize the madness once again—to translate it into this or that instance in the medical tables of insanity, where it would thereafter serve as a double-edged instrument with which we could not only expiate Nietzsche of responsibility for his many offending passages but also vilify him, and any who dare take his utterances seriously, under the heading "conditions of insanity." But that is our abuse, not Nietzsche's. And any who *would* dare to listen seriously to Nietzsche could not fail to conclude that he was not merely the last great philosopher of the nineteenth century but also virtually the first of this century. "A nature such as Nietzsche's," Hesse wrote, "had to suffer our present ills more than a generation in advance. What he had to go through alone and misunderstood, thousands suffer today" (Hesse [1927] 1963, 23–24). Thousands? But do not we all? Nietzsche's charity was a "presentiment of *universal* disaster."[24]

What is the meaning of Nietzsche? Although there are parts of his argument that lack sufficient clarity (some of which are discussed below), the central thrust of his critique is unmistakable. It begins with the specter of nihilism. From notes composed during the last five or six years before his silence, we have the following examples of Nietzsche's keen insight:

> Nihilism stands at the door. . . . what does nihilism mean? *That the highest values devaluate themselves.* The aim is lacking; "why?" finds no answer. (Nietzsche [1901] 1967, §§1–2)

> The most universal sign of the modern age: man has lost *dignity* in his own eyes to an incredible extent. For a long time the center and tragic hero of existence in general; then at least intent on proving himself closely related to the decisive and essentially valuable side of existence—like all metaphysicians who wish to cling to the *dignity of man*, with their faith that moral values are cardinal values. Those who have abandoned God cling that much more firmly to the faith in morality. (Nietzsche [1901] 1967, §18)

> The nihilistic question "for what?" is rooted in the old habit of supposing that the goal must be put up, given, demanded *from outside*—by some *superhuman authority*. Having unlearned faith in that, one still follows the old habit and seeks *another* authority that can *speak unconditionally* and *command* goals and tasks. . . . One wants to get around the will, the willing of a goal, the risk of positing a goal *for oneself*; one wants to rid oneself of the responsibility (one would accept fatalism). (Nietzsche [1901] 1967, §20)[25]

---

24. This phrase, minus the emphasis, is from Walter Kaufmann (1968, 98)—who, it must be said, has done more than any other writer in English to bring Nietzsche out of the sideshow of slavering freaks and into the "respectable world" (there is irony in that, to be sure, but it does not mean a conversion of Nietzsche to a figure of Christian morality). Perhaps it is only because of Kaufmann's sensitive hand that I find remarks such as Barth's—that Nietzsche is so difficult to understand because "he hid his true face behind many masks" (Barth [1961] 1976, 137)—to be an exaggeration.

25. *Per contra*, this "is the manner of noble souls: they do not want to have anything for nothing; least of all, life. Whoever is of the mob wants to live for nothing; we others, however, to whom life gave itself, we always think about what we might best give in return" (Nietzsche [1883–85] 1954, III.§12).

The distressful yearning for a self-certain authority, an authority situated in some ultimate externality beyond the tininess of "mankind," has produced all variety of "true worlds"—worlds behind the merely apparent and the relativistic, worlds which, even at the cost of a rigid determinism, would obviate the necessity of one's own responsibility.

But even those "true worlds" have failed us. They melt away with our recognition of their sustenance and provenience in us: conjurations undertaken as a desperate search for external validation. Nihilism rushes upon us in thick black waves. Our world has become fundamentally meaningless, valueless, void. Our science does not find its answer: since Copernicus, "man has been rolling from the center toward X," an inconceivably tiny speck floating in cosmic vastness. No voice of God speaks to us: God is dead—only the "great unholy lie" that is Christianity, the "most fatal seductive lie that has yet existed," continues to chirp in our ear. Today our "philosophical sensibility" assumes the form of fatalism, which is a consequence of our "long belief in divine dispensation, an unconscious consequence: as if what happens were no responsibility of ours." We can no longer convince ourselves of the validation offered by "categories of reason" or by any "leap of faith." The doubled relativization of thought and values—a historical consciousness of the epochal contingency of world views, facticities, normativities; a psychological consciousness of the reductive contingency of all valuation in an interiority of drives, dispositions, impulses—has resisted all effort to salvage an absolute, supratemporal authority (Nietzsche [1901] 1967, §§1, 12, 200, 243; Nietzsche [1883–85] 1954, prologue; Nietzsche [1887] 1968, III.§§24–26; Nietzsche [1889] 1954, chaps. 3–4).

In the Platonic-Christian-Kantian tradition of dualism, Nietzsche argued, we have been taught to repudiate our actual world as the merely apparent and to favor this or that "true world" as the authorization of our true significance and composition. But with successive recessions of those "true worlds," we find ourselves holding only the consequence of our own self-repudiation. We have been enslaved in "a poor ignorant weariness that does not want to want any more: this created all gods and afterworlds." All previous philosophies, Hegel's and Schopenhauer's included, proliferated the error, because of their moral origins, and therefore must be cast aside. We must expose traditional morality, show its nullity, bare its hidden suppositions, experimentally question each claim of a "will to truth." In short, "we need a *critique* of moral values, *the value of these values themselves must just be called in question*." The metaphysician's "true world" must be abolished, for it has been contrived in an attitude of "contradiction to the actual world," and the actual world has been remade thereby as apparition—even though the "reasons for which 'this' world has been characterized as 'apparent' are the very reasons which indicate its reality; any other kind of reality is absolutely indemonstrable" (Nietzsche [1883–

85] 1954, I.§3; Nietzsche [1887] 1968, preface §6, I.§26, III.§24; Nietzsche [1886] 1968, §6; Nietzsche [1889] 1954, III.§6).[26]

The deceit of metaphysical "true worlds" has a tenacious grip that must be appreciated for what it is in the actual world. Can it be simply an effusion of "unattached" or "disembodied" thought? Or is that explanation itself part of the deceit? Regardless of the "philosophical standpoint one may adopt today," Nietzsche warned,

> from every point of view the *erroneousness* of the world in which we think we live is the surest and firmest fact that we can lay eyes on: we find reasons upon reasons for it which would like to lure us to hypotheses concerning a deceptive principle in "the essence of things." But whoever holds our thinking itself, "the spirit," in other words, responsible for the falseness of the world—an honorable way out which is chosen by every conscious or unconscious *advocatus dei*— whoever takes this world, along with space, time, form, movement, to be falsely *inferred*—anyone like that would at least have ample reason to learn to be suspicious at long last of all thinking. Wouldn't thinking have put over on us the biggest hoax yet? And what warrant would there be that it would not continue to do what it has always done? (Nietzsche [1886] 1968, §34)

Our moralities of virtue have castrated us by the excision of passion and our "dark undersides," by nurturing mediocrity and polishing rubble, all the while concealing the sources of strength of those moralities. Error and illusion, "the lie," have been and continue to be compelling presences, which, though nonetheless still error and illusion, are supportive of life. Fantasy, dreams, "forgetting" as an active affirmative process, sublimations of unacceptable drives, creations of necessary fictions: all these illusions constitute a falseness of judgment; but the falseness of a judgment is not necessarily an objection to it. The critical question asks not about a judgment's "truth" or "falsity" as such, as in the traditional calculus of propositions, but rather "to what extent it is life-promoting, life-preserving, species-preserving, perhaps even species-cultivating." Indeed, Nietzsche argued, it is the falsest of judgments that are "the most indispensable for us":

> Without accepting the fictions of logic, without measuring reality against the purely invented world of the unconditional and self-iden-

---

26. In his account, "How the 'True World' Finally became a Fable," Nietzsche remarked that if these "true worlds" are unattainable, or at least unattained, they are *unknown* and cannot be redeeming or obligating (Nietzsche [1889] 1954, IV.§4).

tical, without a constant falsification of the world by means of numbers, man could not live— . . . renouncing false judgments would
mean renouncing life and a denial of life. To recognize untruth as a
condition of life—that certainly means resisting accustomed value
feelings in a dangerous way; and a philosophy that risks this would
by that token alone place itself beyond good and evil. (Nietzsche
[1886] 1968, §4)

In contrast to all previous philosophies, psychologies, and histories, which
had "remained stuck in moral prejudices and apprehensions" and "did not
dare go into any depths," Nietzsche's approach would risk the depths,
explore the drives and their transformations, experiment with morality's
evil and search therein for hidden sources of greatness of life. It would be
an unmasking psychology, an experimentive philosophy, conceived as "the
morphology and theory of the evolution of the will to power" (Nietzsche
[1886] 1968, §23; emphasis deleted).

What is the meaning of Nietzsche? Simmel captured part of it when
he remarked that we can "inquire into knowledge and morality, self and
reason, art and God, happiness and suffering," only after we have solved
the "puzzle" of "the meaning of life, . . . its value merely as life." The
solution to this puzzle "decides everything else. It is only the original fact
of life which provides meaning and measure, positive or negative value"
(Simmel [1918] 1968, 15; see also Simmel 1907). While we must not
confuse Nietzsche as a *Lebensphilosoph*, nor confuse his emphasis on
"drives" and "impulses" as simply a reversal of polarity in the traditional
dualism of "spirit" and "life-urge," it is indeed the case that the reality of
that which in life decides the positive and the negative, truth and falseness,
good and evil, the beautiful and the ugly, health and sickness, constituted
the sensibility of Nietzsche's experiments. A passage from one of his later
books, already quoted, bears repeating: "To recognize untruth as a condition of life—that certainly means resisting accustomed value feelings in
a dangerous way; *and* a philosophy that risks this would by that token
alone place itself *beyond good and evil*" (emphasis added). How one reads
the statement therein conveyed, how one constructs its textual limits and
density, reveals a very large portion of the hypocaust of one's own "philosophy." What is the "beyond" of this fearsome proclamation?[27] Surely,
one might say, if Nietzsche's argument was not a doctrine of total indifference, then he must have preserved the idea of morality in general. But
"morality in general" or any "general notion of morality" is only abstrac-

---

27. *Jenseits*, as in the title of his book, *Jenseits von Gut und Böse*, translates as
"beyond," or etymologically as "on the other side (of)"; in nominative form it
translates also as "the hereafter" or "the life to come."

tion, an empty phrase of grammarians and metaphysicians: if it does not refer to the collectivity of actually existing moralities, all of which Nietzsche castigated, then it refers to nothing concrete. Empty phrases no longer purchase salvation.

Yet this hardly makes Nietzsche into an axiological nihilist, a confirmed proponent of "deep and total Nihilism," as some have claimed (e.g., Danto 1965, 30–34).[28] Were his critique bereft of axiological contrast, his ruthless attacks on mediocrity, on the moral excisions of passion, on the presuppositions of metaphysicians' exercises in good and evil, would of course be total gibberish. The force of his *diagnosis* of nihilism—an unyielding contempt for the traditional system of values, not merely as utterances of hallowed principles (the famous "in principle") but as actuality of effect—had its footing in an otherness that sought realization through a "revaluation of all values."[29] Thus, Nietzsche declared: "Now that the shabby origin," that is, the genealogy, of that traditional system is being revealed for what it is, "the universe seems to have lost value, seems 'meaningless'—but that is only a *transitional stage*" (Nietzsche [1901] 1967, §7; Nietzsche [1883–85] 1954, II.§12). In what may be termed the "hypomorality" of his critique, Nietzsche saw himself at most as a "herald and precursor" of the creation of "philosophers of the future"—genuine philosophers, beyond the conceit of pretending "to solve all with one stroke, with one word," as if thunderstriking "unriddlers of the universe," and ever alert to the danger of opacities engendered by the stealth of presuppositions. Such philosophers would be willing to argue "boldly at any time ... *against* [their] previous opinion" (Nietzsche [1881] 1923–27, §547; Nietzsche [1882] 1974, §296).

> A new species of philosophers is coming up: I venture to baptize them with a name that is not free of danger. As I unriddle them, insofar as they allow themselves to be unriddled—for it belongs to their nature to *want* to remain riddles at some point—these philosophers of the future may have a right—it might also be a wrong—to be called *attempters*. This name itself is in the end a mere attempt and, if you will, a temptation.
>
> Are these coming philosophers new friends of "truth"? That is probable enough, for all philosophers so far have loved their truths.

28. Kaufmann (1968) has surely laid to rest this queerest of claims. (See also Schacht 1973.)

29. The title of Nietzsche's projected *opus magnum*, only the first book of which, *The Antichrist* (1895), he was able to finish, was *Revaluation of All Values*. Kaufmann (1968, 113–14) has reprinted Nietzsche's brief "plan," consisting of four book titles, for the projected work.

But they will certainly not be dogmatists. (Nietzsche [1886] 1968, §§42–43, also 211–12).

These "attempters" will be free spirits, "*very* free spirits," although not merely that "but something more, higher, greater, and thoroughly different." They must not be confused with any of the "goodly advocates of 'modern ideas'" or with any existing morality. Proponents neither of a "master morality" nor of a "slave morality," they will understand that the "strongest and most evil spirits have so far advanced humanity the most," or at least as much as their opposites, for just these evil spirits are responsible for having "always rekindled the drowsing passions" (Nietzsche [1882] 1974, §4; Nietzsche [1886] 1968, §44; Nietzsche [1883–85] 1954, III.§10).

The program of these free-spirited, risking, tempting philosophers of the future can be foreseen only in the most general of outlines, and only through the foreshadowing of the program in Nietzsche's own programmatic, the revaluation of all values—which also can be discerned only partially, not only because the *opus magnum* was never finished but also because of the existence of certain difficulties in the main threads of his argumentation. About the vital thrust of the Nietzschean programmatic there can be no doubt, however. In part, it was aimed at the idiocy of that long tradition of pretending to displace and neutralize passion in the name of virtue. "*Destroying* the passions and cravings, merely as a preventative measure against their stupidity and the unpleasant consequences of this stupidity—today this itself strikes us as merely another acute form of stupidity" (Nietzsche [1889] 1954, V.§1; see also Nietzsche [1883–85] 1954, I.§§3–4). One who is without passion, without impulse, cannot be moral, for being moral is *overcoming* impulse. The so-called morality of civilization, a morality of domestication, is "anti-natural" inasmuch as it stands "*against* the instincts of life: it is *condemnation* of these instincts, now secret, now outspoken and impudent." By contrast, every "naturalism in morality—that is, every healthy morality—is dominated by an instinct of life" (Nietzsche [1889] 1954, V.§4).[30] What is required, Nietzsche

---

30. Compare the essay, "Why I Am a Destiny" (1908), wherein, in section 7, Nietzsche reminded us that what truly horrified him was "*not* error as error" but, instead,

> the utterly gruesome fact that *antinature* itself received the highest honors as morality and was fixed over humanity as law and categorical imperative. . . . That one taught men to despise the very first instincts of life; that one mendaciously invented a "soul," a "spirit" to ruin the body; that one taught men to experience the presupposition of life, sexuality, as something unclean; that one looks for the evil principle in what is most profoundly necessary for growth, in *severe* self-love (this very word constitutes slander); that, conversely, one regards the typical signs of decline and contradiction

averred in one of his notes, is a "doctrine strong enough to have the effect of *breeding*: strengthening the strong, paralyzing and breaking the world-weary" (Nietzsche [1901] 1967, §862). This doctrine must be founded not in either side of the oppositions of traditional dualism but in that actuality of being from which derive passion and reason, drive and spirit, impulse and intellect, in their putative separateness.[31] All the deep forces of being, passion no less than reason, must be put to work in self-creation, a self-overcoming that carries "the effect of breeding." The locus of that dialectic unity of passion and reason, and the centerpiece of Nietzsche's proposed doctrine, is the "will"—described by Nietzsche (characteristically) as an experiment: "the experiment of positing the causality of the will hypothetically as the only" causality, and, further, experimentally positing "*one* basic form of the will," namely, "the will to power" (Nietzsche [1886] 1968, §36). This concept of *will* must be approached first in terms of what it is not; and it is not "drive" or "impulse" or "urge" or "want," or any of their cognates, in the sense of being one side or one pole of the traditional dualism of faculties. Rather, the will is distinguished from all these one-sided constructs "by the affect of command," which is to say that "something is commanded" and this commanding thought is inherent in the will (Nietzsche [1901] 1967, §668). As Heidegger remarked, there is no "characteristic phrase which occurs more often in Nietzsche than . . . to will is to command" (Heidegger 1961a, 1:70). The will is neither mere "drive" or "impulse" nor mere "spirit" or "intellect"; it is constituted as Nietzsche's attempt to fathom life-value at the level of that which must exist beneath all such dualisms of "spirit and drive," "mind and body," and which makes them possible *as* fictions. This is the Dionysian of Zarathustra, who does not merely believe but creates: the will to power *is* creative force, a creative force that creates its own normativities and its own facticities. In this Dionysian image it is foremost a self-creating, a self-mastery, and *not* the chaotic effluence of unregulated or helter-skelter impulse (see, e.g., Nietzsche [1883–85] 1954, III.§19; Nietzsche [1886] 1968, §36).

Given these formulations, it is clearly to be expected that we would find that Nietzsche's "epistemology," if it may be called such, rests in this creative will to power. Passages such as the following, among the most potent in all his writing, are decisively telling—even if they are confused by other of his statements (discussed below):

> of the instincts, the "selfless," the loss of a center of gravity, "depersonal-ization" and "neighbor love" (*addiction* to the neighbor) as the *higher* value—what am I saying?—the *absolute* value!

31. This, it may be noted, is the Dionysian image of the later Nietzsche, which had absorbed the Apollonian-Dionysian polarity displayed in his early works (e.g., 1870). In Kaufmann's phrase, it "represents passion controlled" (1968, 129, 202).

God is a conjecture; but I desire that your conjectures should not reach beyond your creative will. Could you *create* a god? Then do not speak to me of any gods. But you could well create the overman. Perhaps not you yourselves, my brothers. But into father and fore-fathers of the overman you could re-create yourselves: and let this be your best creation.

God is a conjecture; but I desire that your conjectures should be limited by what is thinkable. Could you *think* a god? But this is what the will to truth should mean to you: that everything be changed into what is thinkable for man, visible for man, feelable by man. You should think through your senses to their consequences.

And what you have called world, that shall be created only by you: your reason, your image, your will, your love shall thus be realized. And verily, for your own bliss, you lovers of knowledge. (Nietzsche [1883–85] 1954, II.§2)[32]

There are few statements in the *procès-verbal* of philosophy as profoundly important as the statement that defines the depth of that passage. The knower, the creator, the lover are constituted as a unity, and it is in this constitution that we find the very possibility of good and evil, truth and falsity, beauty and ugliness. One's conjectures "should be limited by what is thinkable"—which is to say, by what one can create, for the actual condition of "knowing something" consists in the attempt to create it. And for Nietzsche, that is the will to power, "the unexhausted procreative will of life." Thus the so-called will to truth:

A will to the thinkability of all things: this *I* call your will. You want to *make* all being thinkable, for you doubt with well-founded suspicion that it is already thinkable. But it shall yield and bend for you. Thus your will wants it. It shall become smooth and serve the spirit as its mirror and reflection. That is your whole will, you who are wisest: a will to power—when you speak of good and evil too, and of valuations. (Nietzsche [1883–85] 1954, II.§12)

Although we must not neglect Nietzsche's disdain for the epistemologists (e.g., Nietzsche [1901] 1967, §410), and while we must respect his resis-tance to systematization (e.g., Nietzsche [1887] 1968, I.§26), we can none-theless construct from those passages and their correlates the framework of *his* "epistemology" (the term no longer easily applies). The positing of knowledge as an always contingent and interested invention, an imper-

32. See also section 8 of his commentary on *Zarathustra* in *Ecce Homo* (1908), where he repeated much of this passage.

manent effect of the struggles of willing, is unmistakably the decisive formation in Nietzsche's argument, and it is one that lends itself to the charge of relativism. Formulations of "the true," as well as those of "the good" and "the beautiful," are inherently relative to the historical and psychological conditions of their making. But more than this, Nietzsche's argument would seem to lead unavoidably into the Epimenidean predicament. As Kaufmann has remarked, although Nietzsche did not engage this question, "it would seem that his own *conception* of the will to power must be admitted by him to be a creation of *his* will to power" (1968, 204; emphasis added), and that is tantamount to the Cretan's proclamation that all Cretans are liars.

Is this self-annihilative stance a necessary "conclusion" of Nietzsche's argument concerning the "origin" (that is, the antecedence of *Herkunft*, *not* a first-beginning or *Ursprung*) of knowledge, truth, good and evil, value? In the absence of Nietzsche's explicit answer, we can only speculate about his intentions—all of which too easily degenerates into the drum-beating of "what Nietzsche *really* meant." Still, consideration of this question may prove to be fruitful in an altogether different way. There is at least the glimmer of an answer, to which Kaufmann has already pointed, in the Nietzsche text: it rests in his conception of the will to power as, in Kaufmann's phrase, "a universal feature of the human constitution, whose fictions must be considered necessary (for man) because they are not subjective: they leave no leeway for individual differences between one man's thinking and another's" (Kaufmann 1968, 206). The implication of this is that Nietzsche's "theory of the will to power might be the one and only interpretation of human behavior"—of a (the) reality of human being— "of which we are capable when we consider the evidence and think about it as clearly as we can." Or, to state the matter more pointedly, it is not Nietzsche alone who is in the "dilemma" of positing that which defines one's positing as a fiction; *everyone*, the entire human world, is fixed precisely within the bounds of this "dilemma"—"however ridiculous it might seem to the angel Gabriel." Kaufmann treated this "answer" rather gingerly; understandably so. I shall argue below that there are severe difficulties with it, as an answer to the question about Nietzsche, because of the relation formed with another level of Nietzsche's argument.

Before turning to that set of issues, however, we would do well to consider the possibilities of Kaufmann's suggestion in terms of Nietzsche's trenchant critique of the metaphysician's "true world." According to that critique, it may be recalled, the enforcement in traditional morality of an "other world" as the "true world" has always been fashioned from "contradiction to the actual world," therein lowering the actual world to mere appearance. As each in the string of "true world" candidates has fallen from the grace of faith, the merely apparent world, consistently disqualified because of its remaindering, speaks to us ever louder its claim of being the *only* story of existence—which is, then, the story of nothingness. But, Nietzsche argued, the "reasons for which [the actual world] has been characterized as 'apparent' are the very reasons which indicate its reality; any other kind of reality is absolutely indemonstrable." Moreover:

> The true world—we have abolished. What world has remained? The apparent one perhaps? But no! *With the true world we have also abolished the apparent one.* (Nietzsche [1889] 1954, IV.§6; also III.§6)

Analogously, one might say for Nietzsche: "An absolute, noncontingent knowledge (Truth), a knowledge the ground and warrant for which lay in the 'true world' that is to be discovered from its hiddenness—that we have abolished. So, what knowledge has remained? The merely contingent and relative knowledge perhaps? But no! Along with absolute, noncontingent knowledge, *we have abolished also all contingent and relative knowledge.*" That is, just as the abrogation of all "true worlds" cannot be stayed by a limit that no longer "exists" but necessarily annuls all "apparent worlds" as well, thereby granting us the presence of our *actual* world, so the abrogation of an "absolute, noncontingent knowledge" or "Truth" means also that all "relative, contingent knowledge" is abrogated by the same stroke, and what "remains" is neither more nor less than actual knowledge.

This is not to deny the Nietzschean thesis of "perspectivism"—that is, that our claims of knowledge are historically and psychologically conditioned—any more than his rejection of an "apparent world" along with all "true worlds" denies that our being-in-the-actual-world is so conditioned. What is abolished is the invidiousness that speaks of "perspective" and "relative, contingent knowledge" while secretly dreaming of "the absolutely real and true."[33] As Nietzsche said of the Aristotelian "law of contradiction":

> Are the axioms of logic adequate to reality or are they a means and measure for us to *create* reality, the concept "reality," for ourselves?— To affirm the former one would . . . have to have a previous knowledge of being—which is certainly not the case. The proposition [i.e.,

---

33. This brings to mind Ryle's simile—that "there can be false coins only where there are coins made of the proper materials by the proper authorities" (1954, 95)—which points up the circumstance that Nietzsche, in order to reject traditional morality, did indeed assert a standard against which that morality existed as a "false coin." The failure of Nietzsche, from my point of view, has to do with his constitution of that standard.

the Aristotelian "law" as a certainty] therefore contains no *criterion of truth*, but an *imperative* concerning that which *should* count as true. (Nietzsche [1901] 1967, §516)

The will to know, to know truly, is of the will to power; and the "standards" by which knowledge claims are judged, by which to select *this* "knowledge" from *that* "ignorance," are the values of life-preserving or life-enhancing "fictions."[34]

By this surrogation "for Nietzsche," then, one might conclude that the Nietzschean "revaluation of all values" posited experimentally and nondogmatically the cosmic perspective of an *axios* of "self-overcoming" by which claims of knowledge can be judged. This speculation, it must be noted, is not strictly consonant with Jaspers' claim that Nietzsche's argument "involves two distinct concepts of truth"—one, that which "appears as the kind of error that supports life"; the other, a "completely indeterminate and indeterminable truth" which, though "unattainable as it may be from the level of life," perseveres in the transcendence of *Existenz* (Jaspers [1935] 1965, 186, 219–28). (Here, as elsewhere, Jaspers arranged Nietzsche to fit the orchestral requirements of his own *Existenz* doctrine.) Whatever else Nietzsche's "revaluation," "self-overcoming," and "overman" may or may not be, they clearly were *not* proposed as unattainable or unrecognizable or as the mere perseverance of some transcendental *Existenz*.[35]

---

34. Heidegger, who characterized Nietzsche's work as a "subjectivism" that signified the beginning of the end of a philosophic tradition extending from the early 1600s (Descartes), found Nietzsche guilty of making "the world thought of after the image of man" and asked rhetorically, "Is not such thought pure anthropomorphism?" (Heidegger 1961a, 1:653–54). According to Heidegger's account (see, e.g., Heidegger [1961b] 1973, 30; Heidegger [1954a] 1973, 95), Descartes' *Meditations on First Philosophy* was "a decisive beginning" of "the true start of the metaphysics upon which the modern period rests." On the other hand, "with Nietzsche's metaphysics, philosophy is completed. That means: It has gone through the sphere of prefigured possibilities."

35. Jaspers ended his section "A Transcending Breakthrough to Truth" with this combination of sheer rubbish and appropriate caution:
>As we deliberately go through the dialectical movements in which the truth never attains its goal (since it can never be possessed but in the end even denies itself), we are forced back to find fulfillment in our own historically present *Existenz*. Through our knowledge of the movement we become aware of not possessing the truth. Only perseverance in this movement can overcome the danger of deception which will result if we thoughtlessly use Nietzsche's isolated and isolating formulae as deadsure dicta and, with the aid of these dialectical thoughts, arbitrarily justify or condemn everything. (Jaspers [1935] 1965, 228)

Nevertheless, for all the suggestiveness of the foregoing response to Nietzsche's encounter with the "Epimenidean predicament," it is stymied by the naturalistic understructure of Nietzsche's programmatic formation. A sense of his naturalistic bent can be obtained from an early fragment "On Truth and Lie in an Extra-Moral Sense," written in 1873, which begins with a fable: "In some remote corner of the universe, poured out and glittering in innumerable solar systems, there once was a star on which clever animals invented knowledge. That was the haughtiest and most mendacious minute of 'world history'—yet only a minute. After nature had drawn a few breaths the star grew cold, and the clever animals had to die" (*The Portable Nietzsche*, 42–47). Although the chief lesson of this fragment had to do with the illusory character of truths and the "functionality" of lies,[36] on route to his destination Nietzsche averred that one "might invent such a fable and still not have illustrated sufficiently how wretched, how shadowy and flighty, how aimless and arbitrary, the human intellect appears in nature." The ontic statement is here perhaps only ambiguously at hand, but in later works its train of crisp sentences and nuances is more surely grasped. Early in *Beyond Good and Evil*, for example, there is the argument that "without measuring reality against the purely invented world of the unconditional and self-identical, without a constant falsification of the world by means of numbers, man could not live" (Nietzsche [1886] 1968, §4)—an argument that offers the contrast between a world (or worlds) of our invention and the real world which we do not invent but only falsify in order to live.

And consider his concept of "power" (as in "will to power"), which was conceived as "self-overcoming" and as such was taken to be the *key* process of all nature. Nietzsche rejected notions of any disjunction of "nature" and "spirit," "body" and "mind"; rather, for him human life is *of* nature, and the fundamental striving of human life is power—that is, this "self-overcoming"—just as it is for the entirety of nature:

> In order to understand what "life" is, what kind of striving and tension life is, the formula must apply as well to trees and plants as to animals [not to human creatures alone]; all expansion, incorporation, growth

---

36. Thus, later in the fragment Nietzsche wrote:
   What, then, is truth? A mobile army of metaphors, metonyms, and anthropomorphisms—in short, a sum of human relations, which have been enhanced, transposed, and embellished poetically and rhetorically, and which after long use seem firm, canonical, and obligatory to a people: truths are illusions about which one has forgotten that this is what they are.
At this juncture in his thinking, 1873, Nietzsche could also say: "We still do not know where the urge for truth comes from."

means striving against something that resists. . . . For what do trees in a jungle fight each other? For "happiness"?—*For power!* (Nietzsche [1901] 1967, §704)

Thus the fundamental relation, "will to *power*," was posited as existing at a level of life anterior to human consciousness or conscious self-reflection; that is, it is *in and of nature* at that anterior level. Such is the basis from which "the subject"—which is our "fictitious insertion"—was declared *to be* a fiction (see, for example, Nietzsche [1901] 1967, §§632, 483–85, 547–52).

Likewise, the notion of successive states of cause and effect: "the psychological necessity for a belief in causality lies in the inconceivability of an event divorced from intent; by which naturally nothing is said concerning truth or untruth (the justification of such a belief)! The belief in *causae* [that is, efficient cause] falls with the belief in *télē* [that is, final cause]" (Nietzsche [1901] 1967, §§627, 477, 550–54). Behind the fiction of "cause-and-effect" succession there is simply "a struggle between two elements of unequal power: a new arrangement of forces is achieved according to the measure of power of each of them. . . . [The] essential thing is that the factions in struggle emerge with different quanta of power" (Nietzsche [1901] 1967, §663).[37] Moreover, on the same basis Nietzsche argued "there are no things," that is, no "things-in-themselves," except as "fictions invented by us." The Kantian dichotomy of "thing-in-itself" versus "thing-as-appearance" is itself fictitious, as are separately existent "facts" (Nietzsche [1901] 1967, §§481, 553–58, 562, 568–69, 634).

These would be enormously powerful statements were they not finally undercut by Nietzsche's naturalistic value theory, his Archimedean posturing on some pivot in a cosmic nature. Consider this claim, for example:

> "The *real* and the *apparent* world"—I have traced this antithesis back to value relations. We have projected the conditions of *our* preservation as predicates of being in general. Because we have to be stable in our beliefs if we are to prosper, we have made the "real" world a world not of change and becoming, but one of being. (Nietzsche [1901] 1967, §507)

---

37. Accordingly, our sense of "regularity in succession" actually exists as "only a metaphorical expression, *as if* a rule were being followed" (Nietzsche [1901] 1967, §632). See also Nietzsche's corresponding comments on the concept of "motion," which "always supposes . . . a thing that produces effects—i.e., we have not got away from the habit into which our senses and language seduce us" (Nietzsche [1901] 1967, §§634–35).

Such claim was robbed by his naturalistic location of the will to power in the recesses of "a kind of instinctive life in which all organic functions are still synthetically intertwined along with self-regulation, assimilation, nourishment, excretion, and metabolism—as a *pre-form* of life" (Nietzsche [1886] 1968, §36; see also §4). The promise of his proclamation (for example) that "there are no things" except as we invent them, no "syntheses and unities" except as we invent them, was robbed by the naturalistic premise that

> that which becomes conscious is involved in causal relations which are entirely withheld from us—the sequence of thoughts, feelings, ideas in consciousness does not signify that this sequence is a causal sequence; but apparently it is so, to the highest degree. Upon this *appearance* we have founded our whole idea of spirit, reason, logic, etc. (—none of these exist: they are fictitious syntheses and unities), and projected these *into* things and *behind* things! (Nietzsche [1901] 1967, §524)

In other words, that which is in consciousness is only the appearance of causality, being, thinking, and so on (it may or may not *be*) that we *project into* and *behind* things; and the coming-into-consciousness was itself involved "in causal relations which are *entirely withheld from us*"!

The greatness of Nietzsche's affirming thesis—that genuine knowing and genuine being consist in the activity of creation, beginning most profoundly with self-creation, self-overcoming—was finally spoiled in the posit of *Natur* as the "pre-form" within which is constituted the *very possibility* of this upwardly propelling self-overcoming. Such preformation "stands behind," as it were, as an inaccessible, directive realm of enablement, of which we (and, if we act cooperatively with and in aid of the forces of that realm, our successors) are predications.[38]

This conception of a primal wellspring is not incongruous with a "leitmotif of Nietzsche's life and thought," as Kaufmann characterized it: "the theme of the antipolitical individual who seeks self-perfection far from the modern world" (1968, 418). Indeed, Nietzsche spoke of being "away from the tyranny of stimuli and influences that condemns us to spend our

---

38. Cf. Kaufmann, especially his "Epilogue," wherein he concluded that Nietzsche's "projection of the will to power from the human sphere to the cosmos is an afterthought—an extreme conjecture that is not substantiated by the evidence and is at variance with Nietzsche's own critical principles" (Kaufmann 1968, 174–77, 420). That there is such "variance" is indisputable. That its provenience was that of an "afterthought" cannot be more than speculation; in any case, it is there.

strength in reactions, and does not permit us any more to let it *accumulate* to the point of *spontaneous* activity" (Nietzsche [1901] 1967, §916).[39] Who today does not suffer that anguish of being exhausted of one's strength by all the tininess, the pettiness, the fatuousness that press upon us? And of failing to muster the wherewithal by which to return one's own lethal arrow? Who today does not "need *solitude*—which is to say, recovery, return to myself, the breath of a free, light, playful air" (Nietzsche [1908] 1968, I.§8)? But for all the appeal of an unspoiled monastery or a distant mountaintop, the "self-education" and "self-creation" so necessary to such effective-creation-of-the-world as Nietzsche desired cannot be achieved by an *"antipolitical* individual," nor by the fiction of "an *individual.*"

*

Hegel's absolutization of subject as Absolute Spirit offered to the nineteenth century its first and last great system of the metaphysics of supreme being and essential genesis. Closely on Hegel's heels the grand edifice of German idealism began to dissolve, partly because of the reconsiderations undertaken by the so-called left-Hegelians and especially through the solvent peering of Marx. Later, in conjunction with the almost immediate trivializations both of Marx's radically constructed critique and of Nietzsche's "mad prophecy" of the specter of nihilism, the space of a general system of metaphysics was increasingly appropriated by alternative versions of late-nineteenth-century positivism (a crude materialism, often labeled "Marxism," or a sense-certain, idealist operationalism) and by the naive instrumentalism of adaptive-behavioralist formulations of pragmatism. It was only after the demise of the nineteenth-century order, marked in popular consciousness by World War I, that diagnoses of nihilism began to gain credibility and, at the same time, that a self-consciously devised "resurrection" of metaphysical system took place.[40]

39. Nietzsche then added parenthetically: "One should observe our scholars closely: they have reached the point where they think only 'reactively,' i.e., they must read before they can think."

40. The awakening to nihilism was less profound in the Anglo-American than in the continental-European academy and was more nearly confined by an "anti-metaphysical" tradition of science and science-subjugated philosophy. Within the Anglo-American social sciences, for example, the renewed efforts to discover "cultural universals," which became a central concern as the debate over cultural relativism was gradually joined (see, for example, Herskovits 1942; Aberle et al. 1950; Kluckhohn 1951), were formulated from presuppositions that nomothetic rules governed the essential givens of "human institutions" at an analytic level beneath the idiographic-ethnographic manifold of human life. The principal "successful" instance of renewed "theorizing on a grand scale" took the form of nearly vacuous abstractions in the work of Talcott Parsons (1937; 1951).

Whereas Marx had demonstrated, justifiably in theory and as the possibility of concrete life, the *Aufhebung* of metaphysics, neither positivism nor pragmatism (to say nothing of the Marxist epigone, of whom Nietzsche had offered an appropriate description) could fathom the claim of that demonstration and justification—not even before the name of Marx had become identified with the most grotesque forms of human management. Consequently, when advocates of this positivism or that pragmatism stood to proclaim the uselessness of all metaphysics, and their own superiority as methodical successors of all prescientific thought, they failed to see, yet could only reveal, the metaphysical sand beneath their feet. Their "anti-metaphysical" or "postmetaphysical" doctrines were based in metaphysical presuppositions, though not self-consciously so.

Thus it was that the so-called resurrection of metaphysics, overseen most assiduously by Husserl and his followers, stood forth both as critique and as recovery in respect to the quest for a confrontation with "the things themselves," that is, an unabridged reality known with certitude. But this search for "the absolute zero-point," as it were, which was to be conducted through clarification and annulment of all the hidden presuppositions that had hitherto thwarted rigorous metaphysical thinking, was predominantly an event of continental Europe. Philosophical thought in the Anglo-American academy persisted, by and large, with self-delusions of a "postmetaphysical" science.

2. HUSSERL: "TO THE THINGS THEMSELVES"

One of the most persistent attempts during this century to overcome the crisis of relativism and skepticism by establishing the absolute zero-point of an apodictically certain knowledge can be read in the philosophical writings of Edmund Husserl (1859–1938). Keenly aware of the profound threat to "Western culture" posed by this crucial absence, Husserl sought to demonstrate an unshakably founded Archimedean point outside the sheer facticity and contingency of human existence by going "back to the things themselves"—meaning a "return," a clarified return, to direct "objects" of human insight—and, correspondingly, by creating a truly rigorous or strict science, one that would not rest on hidden or unclarified presuppositions, not even those that are insinuated in a supposedly pure formalism of logic.

In following his quest for certitude, Husserl produced a complicated and occasionally obscure literature. Much of it reads as an emended replication of itself, for Husserl was, or so he reportedly said of himself, "a perpetual beginner," trying first this and then that construction as possible solutions to the task of his quest. In detail, Husserl's project underwent a course of development that involved reconsiderations as well as extensions, especially with regard to the self-founding of his transcendental phenomenological method. Some commentators have seen in his later writings a slackening of conviction in the realizability of absolute certitude.[41] Important though the various divagations and nuances of reformation may be, especially to Husserl scholars, I shall not attend to them here. Rather, the central thrust of his attempted solution, which, whatever the strength of his late conviction may have been, remained basically intact, is my main interest.

Husserl began with training as a mathematician. His dissertation concerned "the theory of the calculus of variations," and his first major publication, only the first volume of which was brought to completion, was a study in the philosophy of arithmetic (1891). Already in this examination of the foundations of his chosen field of scholarship, Husserl had turned to issues of general philosophy, largely under the stimulus of Franz Brentano's late-nineteenth-century "psychology of intentionality" and the midcentury studies of logic by Bernard Bolzano; but as a result of sharp criticisms by Gottlob Frege of the psychologism of his inquiry, Husserl was led to undertake fundamental reconsiderations.

This undertaking became the long quest for rigorous demonstration of an epistemological absolutism (which required an ontological absolutism), that is, the possibility of an *epistēmē* totally anterior to mere *doxa* and founded in an absolutely original insight, an insight that is independent of any concrete knowing-subject-as-contingent-being. From his preliminary investigations, Husserl quickly concluded that "since the middle of the nineteenth century" all of Western philosophy had suffered unmistakable

---

41. Much of Husserl's work appeared in print only after long delay. Following publication of the first edition of his *Logical Investigations* in 1900–1901), Husserl delivered in 1904–5 (and after) his lectures on internal time-consciousness (1928), then in 1907 a series of lectures later published as *Ideas* (1913). His *Formal and Transcendental Logic* (1929) was published soon after completion, as were the *Cartesian Meditations* (1931) and *The Crisis of European Sciences* (1936). But *Experience and Judgment* (1948), composed during the period 1910–20 and then revised in 1929–30, was not published until 1938, and then only in a very small quantity. In the discussion that follows, I have relied mainly on the later works—especially the *Meditations*, *The Crisis*, and *Experience and Judgment*. As noted above, there is in Husserl scholarship a major issue regarding the continuity of his work: in particular, whether he abandoned transcendentalism by the time he wrote *The Crisis*. Several of his students (for example, Landgrebe 1962) have argued that he did. My own view is closer to that of Gadamer's claim of basic continuity and retention of transcendentalism (see, for example, Gadamer [1963] 1976, esp. 157–62), although this does not deny that Husserl was aware of difficulties attending the matter of "intersubjectivity" and historicity (see, for example, Ricoeur [1949] 1967, 174).

decline, due to the self-involution of the various constructions of "the epistemological subject" and, correlatively, an abdication of responsibility to original questions. The positive sciences were one-sided, "lost in the world," but because of their "prosperity" in action they had nonetheless become the exclusive determinant of "the total world-view of modern man." Even those sciences that seemed most "theoretical" were only technique [*techne*], devoid of "sight into the *ratio* of [their] accomplished production."[42] Without important exception, modern science had abandoned "the ideal of genuine science that was vitally operative in the sciences from the time of Plato; and, in its practice, it has abandoned radicalness of scientific self-responsibility." More than the form of an "ideal" was at stake, however: "Merely fact-minded sciences make merely fact-minded people" (Husserl [1931] 1960, §§2, 64, Husserl [1929] 1969, 2–4; Husserl [1936] 1970, 5–6).

In seeking to locate the conditions of philosophy as truly rigorous science, Husserl abjured all claims offered by psychologism, historicism, indeed any version of empiricist contingency, and especially the general revaluation of logic in empirical categories. All psychologism rests in a naturalistic posit of consciousness as object-in-the-world, which posit turns back on itself and denies the independence of place from which to know the world and therefore what it does and does not contain. The contingencies proposed in historicism suffer the same fate.[43] And the exclusive empiricity of view that had pervaded science in general was most objectionable, for such an attitude "excludes in principle precisely the questions which

42. Nonetheless, Husserl remarked, he was "quite in earnest in admiring the great discoveries of classic and post-classic physics and their thinking" (Husserl [1936] 1970, 53). Such thinking was "not at all depreciated" by Husserl's "clarification of it as *techne*."

43. Regarding the increasingly popular "existentialism," Husserl (e.g., [1936] 1970) argued that exactly because it so successfully gave expression to the feeling of crisis of values and the drift of human life, it was itself only a symptom and not even the barest beginning of a solution. (See also Bachelard [1957] 1968, 142–43; Ricoeur [1951–52] 1967, 52, 75.) Indeed, the differences between existentialism—say, the existentialism of Sartre—and the analytic philosophy of Carnap or Wittgenstein are hardly so great, and the fields not nearly so clearly demarcated from each other, as a good many commentators have seemed to believe in recent years. We have witnessed even the tendency of some members of the social-science academy to view the prospect of an "existential sociology" (anthropology, psychology, historiology, etc.) as their long-sought "humanistic" bulwark against the "sterilities" of positivist analytics especially. That makes for an ironic championing: for, whatever it is that these proponents think they are defending, both positivist analytics and existentialism profess to feel secure in the conviction that essential being is radically mysterious.

man, given over in our unhappy times to the most portentous upheavals, finds the most burning: questions of the meaning of meaninglessness of the whole of this human existence."

The very sciences one would otherwise assume are trying to answer those questions, Husserl observed, are instead dozing through the upheavals in a perverted pursuit of "rigor." Practitioners of these sciences, which claim to be "the sciences of man," foist on us the high celebration of their "rigorous scientific character," which, they say, requires

> that the scholar carefully exclude all evaluative positions, all questions of the reason or unreason of their human subject-matter and its cultural configurations. Scientific, objective truth is exclusively a matter of establishing what the world . . . is in fact. But can the world, and human existence in it, truthfully have a meaning if the sciences recognize as true only what is objectively established in this fashion, and if history has nothing more to teach us than that all the shapes of the spiritual world, all the conditions of life, ideals, norms upon which man relies, form and dissolve themselves like fleeting waves, that it always was and ever will be so, that again and again reason must turn into nonsense, and well-being into misery? Can we console ourselves with that? Can we live in this world, where historical occurrence is nothing but an unending concatenation of illusory progress and bitter disappointment? (Husserl [1936] 1970, 6–7)[44]

The "logic" in which these sciences find the scope and the scale of their discourse is the exclusively empiricist logic of a contingent ego—the biologically, culturally, historically contingent ego who says, "I think, therefore I am, and I am in the world of which I think." But this "logic," supposedly a neutral, pure instrument, has no clarified foundation, no self-

44. The diagnosis offered here and elsewhere by Husserl may be fairly compared with another, which it recalls—a well-known commentary on the despair of contingency in sheer facticity, written nearly a century earlier.

> My life has been brought to an *impasse*, I loathe existence, it is without savor, lacking salt and sense. . . . One sticks one's finger into the soil to tell by the smell in what land one is: I stick my finger into existence— it smells of nothing. Where am I? Who am I? How came I here? What is this thing called the world? What does this word mean? Who is it that has lured me into the thing, and now leaves me there? Who am I? How did I come into the world? Why was I not consulted . . . ? How did I obtain an interest in this big enterprise they call reality? Why should I have an interest in it? . . . And if I am to be compelled to take part in it, where is the director? I should like to make a remark to him. (Kierkegaard [1843] 1946, 114; cf. Pascal [1670] 1960, 116)

consistent authorization, no adequacy of self-evidence, only a welter of hidden presuppositions that already "establish" in the quiet of their pre-givenness to us "what the world is in fact." The other face of this exclusivity is an attitude of total denial toward the possibility of a metaphysics, a disregard that has become nothing less than "a collapse of the belief in 'reason,' understood as the ancients opposed *epistēmē* to *doxa*." This collapse has been devastating to modern life, for it is *reason* that "ultimately gives meaning to everything that is thought to be, all things, values, and ends—their meaning understood as their normative relatedness to what, since the beginnings of philosophy, is meant by the word 'truth'—truth in itself—and correlatively the term 'what is' " (Husserl [1936] 1970, 12–13).

With this general diagnosis (here vastly adumbrated) as background,[45] Husserl set about the construction of his program of clarification and correction: the demonstration of a complete and absolute grounding of philosophy as strict science by returning to the object in its immediacy of originality (see Husserl [1910–11] 1965; Husserl [1913] 1967; Husserl [1931] 1960). As a point of departure for this program, Husserl held up to view the lesson of Descartes' failing effort of "doubting to the true": the Cartesian answer was inadequate because of its failure to radicalize beyond the empirically substantial "I think." The empirical ego of the *cogito* is necessarily bound within the circumstances of its presence and therefore is contingent, partial, and ultimately ambiguous. It may be certain of itself, but its evidence of its certain self is not adequate.[46]

The Cartesian epistemology and its successors pretended to have

---

45. I am, of course, here compressing the sequence of Husserl's writings. The "diagnostic" passages just quoted are from *The Crisis*, a later work composed against the backdrop of teratogenic scum known as Nazism. This work manifests what could be called Husserl's "awakening to history" during the early 1930s, after three decades of a decided attitude of avoidance of notions of the historical character of human endeavor (see, e.g., Ricoeur [1949] 1967; [1967] 1971). But it would be wildly mistaken to suggest that Husserl's diagnosis of the crisis of European civilization came to him only with the appearance of, and only in the terms of, the Nazi evil. No doubt events in Germany after 1930 heightened Husserl's sensitivity to his own "life world" context, and to what Ricoeur designated "the historical character of culture" (Ricoeur [1949] 1967); but the crisis to which Husserl responded (or which he constituted) was much more pervasive and of longer antecedence.

46. Gadamer appropriately characterized Husserl's relation to this problem of adequacy of evidence, when he referred to his program as a search for a method that would distinguish "within what was given in self-evident intuition something whose nonbeing was absolutely absurd and impossible" (Gadamer [1963] 1976, 153).

answered the question how the ego, conceived as a self-conscious priority consisting of a determinate structure of representations, can know the external world with apodictic certitude, when that consciousness is *in* the world. There was, in other words, only the pretense, the presupposition, of a clean separation between the representations in consciousness ("theoretical language") and the consciousness of external things ("empirical language") to which those representations may or may not correspond ("verification"). Such an epistemological subject is rootless.

In contrast, Husserl argued, the necessary anchorage cannot be *in* the world, that is, the absolutely certain ground from which the *cogito* has meaning cannot itself be a part of the empirical world. But how to discover such grounding? The empiricist program, especially in its more positivist variety, proposes a method of "abstraction," according to which only the immediately given and verifiable, the sense-certain "things themselves," can be assigned meaning—all else being discarded as useless "metaphysics." Yet this method assumes implicitly that "immediacy of experience" ("sense experience") can obtain only with respect to the atomistic particular, that we cannot directly experience anything but already differentiated singularities, and, correlatively, that the generalities and universals that we then "derive" from such abstractedness must already have been contained in the singular experiences themselves, without remainder. This implicit assumption entails the conclusion that "universals" could not, therefore, offer us anything new or additional in experience. Because of their anchorage and essential identity in the singular, such "abstraction" and its product of "universals" would necessarily be bound in the contingency of time and space. The positivist method of abstraction cannot avoid the relativist dilemma. True universals, Husserl reaffirmed, are timeless and spaceless, and they are immediately given as such.

In attempting to radicalize the Cartesian terminus, and to complete the program of a strict science, Husserl found himself confronting—"unintentionally," according to his student and longtime assistant, Landgrebe ([1957] 1966, 28)—what appeared to be a new approach to the epistemological problematic. A central issue remaining from the *cogito ergo sum* had been the status of its consequent term, the "I am" or "objectness." The positive sciences insisted on directly given, sense-certain "things themselves" but could not avoid the annihilative involution of their claims because the objectness of their "I am," and thus of their thinking subject, was posited as simply another empirical objectness in the manifold of objects-in-the-world.

The question remained, how can the criterion of an undistorted, noncontingent, adequately evidenced experience of the "givenness" of "things themselves" be constituted? How to judge what will and what will not qualify? How to get truly "back to the things themselves"? Husserl concluded that the answer could depend neither on the empirical ego (a localized object-in-the-world) nor on any seemingly independent empirical object of perception (which, after all, could be illusory).[47] Rather, the determination of that which is truly an "originary experience" ("originary" [*originär*] in the sense of "firsthand," unmediated experience) must come from consciousness itself—not, however, a consciousness-as-object-in-the-world, but a pure *consciousness-itself*.

The world of our everyday experience, the world in and of which our everyday consciousness exists and acknowledges, is already given to us as an interpreted world, just as the empirical ego who thinks, wills, judges, and so forth, within that everyday world is always spatiotemporally contingent. Such experience, which is that of the positive sciences as well as that of the "ordinary" *cogito*, is always given as already linguistically interpreted and therefore always as a mediated, contingent experience. Relative to the truth of the absolutely real, it is adventitious, partial, "contaminated" by the specific givenness of the world. It cannot claim for itself the efficacy of a presuppositionless, immediately grounded judgment. Thus, the import of what Husserl referred to as his "first methodological principle":

> It is plain that I, as someone . . . striving toward the presumptive end, genuine science ["presumptive," because I do not yet know whether the end *can* be realized], must neither make nor go on accepting any judgment as scientific *that I have not derived from evidence*, from "experiences" in which the affairs and affair-complexes in question are present to me as "*they themselves*." Indeed, even then I must at all times reflect on the pertinent evidence; I must examine its "range"

47. There is the pseudo-issue, considered from its affirmative side by some who designate themselves Husserlian students or Husserlian social theorists (for example, Alfred Schutz, who will be treated in chapter 4, below), that Husserl "slipped into" a psychologism and authorized a psychologistic framework of the empirical ego and the life-world. This is in large part a consequence of the more general issue of whether, as of the composition of *The Crisis*, he abandoned his transcendentalist effort. No doubt, too, the pseudo-issue gained sustenance from the circumstance that already in volume 2 of *Ideas* Husserl formulated a notion of "the personal self": a "personal 'I' " who in the matrix of intersubjectivity constitutes culture. Ricoeur ([1951–52] 1967, 80–81) was correct, I believe, in locating this "personal self" between the pure transcendental Ego and the empirical ego. In any case, it is clear that Husserl consistently strove to demonstrate (and to overcome) the limitations of any science that takes as its starting point an "empirical ego"—whether in a positivistic version or in any of the purportedly nonpositivistic projects of "understanding-psychology" or "understanding-sociology" (see, e.g., Ricoeur [1951–52] 1967; Gadamer [1963] 1976).

and make evident to myself *how far* that evidence, how far its "perfection," *the actual giving of the affairs themselves*, extends. Where this is still wanting, I must not claim any final validity, but must account my judgment as, at best, a possible intermediate stage on the way to final validity. (Husserl [1931] 1960, §5; see also Husserl [1913] 1967, §24)

By this principle, all evidences of experience and all suppositions must be subjected to radical doubt. For example, consider the notion of externally caused "sensations" that are constituted as our sense-data of the empirical world (a notion common to the positive sciences as to much of our "everyday thought"): according to one doctrine, those sensations are directly caused by the particular objects that are externally "there," and, although in a given case "distortions" may occur because of defects of sensory apparatus or because of untoward prejudices or failures to remain "ideologically neutral," the direct relation of causation/constitution is already present, as something *of* reality that *can be* "distorted."

Yet, Husserl admonished, the notion of externally caused sensations is itself a presupposition—one that refers to an already physically interpreted world of externally causative agents, objects that are themselves presupposed and that are presupposed to have certain effective properties (but see Husserl [1948] 1973, 54–58). What is required as general solution can be nothing less than a fully warranted basis of a *self-evident act of judging*, and that in turn calls attention to the requirement of a general method by which the "originary *cogitationes*," the immediate content of consciousness itself, can be revealed as such, that is, without the interference of any received opinion, prejudice, interpretation, or any already-given linguistic or predicative judgment whatever. In contrast to the neo-Kantian idealist concern for the grounds of *scientific* knowledge, as this was presumed to be the singular ideal of *all* knowledge, Husserl's search was for the grounds of self-evidence that establish the ontic validity of anything thinkable (judicable, willable, sayable, etc.) whatever, including that in the "natural attitude" of "everyday life" no less than that in the logico-deductive attitude of mathematical science (see, e.g., Husserl [1931] 1960, §§4–8; Husserl [1948] 1973, 11–27).[48]

Put otherwise, the Husserlian program was conceived as an effort to clarify the necessary basis of logic and, indeed, most generally, of anything that *can* be thought, willed, said. Landgrebe has nominated Husserl's effort

---

48. By "*cogitatio*" Husserl intended the all-embracing Cartesian category, which encompasses more than the English "thought" and "cogitation" in their usual limits—i.e., willing, judging, desiring, etc., as well as thinking and pondering.

to clarify the foundation of mathematics (and in particular the number concept) as the beginning of his project (Landgrebe [1957] 1966, 29)—in support of which nomination he quoted Husserl's own retrospect on *Philosophy of Arithmetic*, that it was an attempt to clarify "the authentic originary and true meaning of the basic concepts of the doctrine of quantities and numbers by retrogression to the spontaneous activities of colligating and counting in which collections (such as totalities [*Inbegriffe*: "includedness"] or multiplicities [*Mengen*]) and quantities are given in an original-creative manner." While we must suspect the presence of reauthorization in such retrospects, the early endeavor did nonetheless lead to considerations of the meaning of the categories of logic in general, and therewith to an effort to retrieve logic from the contingency into which it had been transported. Husserl sought to restore a universal, a priori, timeless logic that is completely independent of the empirical being of any sentience or intellect, immune to (because wholly prior to) any empirical test of confirmation, and true apodictically. Just this logic and its pure meanings can comprise the *possibility* and the *foundation* of *cogitatio*. Thus, Husserl's program may be understood generally as an attempted "clarification of the essence of the predicative judgment by means of an exploration of its origin," that is, its originary seat (Husserl [1948] 1973, 11).

By the traditional understanding of predicative judgment (or *apophansis*), it "has been established from the beginning" (from Aristotle) that

> the most general characteristic of the predicative judgment is that *it has two members*: a "substrate" (*hypokeimenon*), about which something is affirmed, and that which is affirmed of it (*katēgoroumenon*). . . . Every judging presupposes that an object is on hand, that it is already given to us, and is that about which the statement is made. Thus tradition provides us, so to speak, with an original model of the judgment which, *qua* judgment, we must interrogate as to its origin. (Husserl [1948] 1973, 14)

What, then, are the *prepredicative* conditions of predicative judgment? What are the conditions whereby not only the actual but also *all possible* "logical thematizings"—including those that are presupposed in the already interpreted object—*can* be offered as predications of "the real"? Here we must remember, Husserl cautioned, that logical thematizing is always "two-sided." On the one side there are rules of formal logic, which dictate the truth-conditions of "judgments considered purely according to their form, quite apart from the material content of that which, as the object or substrate of the judgment, is inserted in the empty form." So separated in that analytic disjunction, such rules may be characterized as necessary conditions, conditions but for which a predicative judgment could not possibly be true. Nevertheless, these are "the *merely negative conditions of the possibility of truth.*" In addition, there must be conditions that produce a "self-evident act of judgment," that is, "the subjective conditions of the attainment of self-evidence"; for a judgment could be such as to satisfy fully the formal requirements and yet fail to qualify as a *true* judgment. We must therefore consider an act of judgment not merely from the side of rules and principles of empty form (which, as such, refer to presuppositions) but in its "two-sidedness," that is, as "an achievement of consciousness in which the formations, with all their claim to be the expression of cognitions, originate — an area which traditional logic has never placed at the center of its concerns" but has preferred instead to leave as a matter for genetic psychology (Husserl [1948] 1973, 16–17).[49]

Interrogation as to the conditions of a possible self-evident act of judgment must begin with the completion of Descartes' project: a complete radicalization of doubt even of the Cartesian *cogito*, which had been left standing on its presupposition of an "ideal of science"—"the ideal approximated by geometry and mathematical natural science"—and which had retained for itself, again through presupposition, a space *in* the world ("a little *tag-end of the world*") as a substantial empirical presence. We must place in doubt *everything* of the manner and expression of predicative judgment—including all the idealizations and interpretations of science, plus the very notion of "a genuine science" itself. This means, it bears repeating, that even the possibility of the Husserlian goal must be treated, to begin with, as a mere presumption wanting of its rigorously demonstrated grounding. "Consequently," Husserl acknowledged,

> if our presumptive aim is to be capable of becoming a practically possible one, we meditators, while completely destitute of all scientific knowledge, must have access to evidences that already bear the stamp of fitness for such a function, in that they are recognizable as preceding all other imaginable evidences. Moreover, in respect of this evidence of preceding, they must have a certain perfection, they must carry

---

49. With regard to the traditional treatment, Husserl affirmed the view that men believed that they knew in advance what self-evidence is. They believed that they could measure every other item of cognition against ideal, absolute, apodictically certain knowledge. They did not suspect that this ideal of knowledge (and with it the cognitions of the logician, which imply a claim of apodicticity for themselves) could for its part also require a justification and originary foundation. Thus these laborious psychological analyses [i.e., the genetic psychology of judgment] never applied to the *self-evidence itself.* (Husserl [1948] 1973, 18)

with them an absolute certainty, if advancing from them and constructing on their basis a science governed by the idea of a definite system of knowledge— considering the infinity presumed to be part of this idea—is to be capable of having any sense. (Husserl [1931] 1960, §5)[50]

In short, according to Husserl's diagnosis and program, we require evidences that are *immediate*, "evidences that are first in themselves" (Husserl [1931] 1960, §§3, 5; Husserl [1948] 1973, 16–21).

Such evidences must be founded phenomenologically through application of a method of reduction whereby that which is originary in consciousness can be revealed, that is, without the mediation of any meanings that accrue from reception of the world as already interpreted and that thereby obscure the pure givenness-in-consciousness-itself. This is the "transcendental reduction": revelation of the constitutive act of consciousness, which is the constitution of the givenness of objects by modes of the directedness or intentionality of *cogitatio*.[51] This phenomenological method seeks to create for itself its own ground, which is to say that the accomplished reduction is only a means to constitution —that is, the constitutional investigation of all possible (including actual) interpretations, life-worlds, and so on, which gain the space and temporality of possible as well as actual being only from the ground of the transcendental Ego. Husserl's phenomenological meditator must assume the "attitude" of pure *theoria* and suspend all belief in reality of the objective world and all that is in (of) it—including the empirical ego, the contingent "I think," which, because

---

50. ". . . to be capable of having any *sense*": this "sense" is *noema* (the noematic unities of objects-intended, the noematics of *cogitata*), not the noetic act or process of "meaning." Thus, it is a question of whether "a science governed by the idea of a definite system of knowledge" can have demonstrably founded *cogitata*.

51. It *might* be said of Husserl's proposed method that it is simply an obscurely described version of the classic method of idealist philosophy, witnessed from Plato onward, namely the method of abstracting from "the common essence" of one's objects so as to be able to speak of the essential remainder as one's *true* object *in the singular*, and hence indicative of the universal; in other words, to delaminate "observed things" of the manifold of particularities until "a common essential core" is reached, which is then taken as the space of "the unity of science" and as the basis for elaboration of a complete and universal theory of knowledge. But that was *not* Husserl's proposed method of "reduction," for the "that-which-is-abstracted" (or delaminated) to "essential core" is still held in a presupposition of already-given existence. Husserl's "reduction" was proposed as an "eidetic" reduction, which, in contrast to "the factual" or empirical, incorporates the purely possible as possible singularizations of the universe of possibility (see, e.g., Husserl [1948] 1973, 348–54; Husserl [1931] 1960, §46).

of spatiotemporal contingency, varies in the actuality of its manifold possibilities from one locality to another—and then investigate the *cogitatio*, the "contents" of this purified consciousness itself. Such suspension is accomplished by application of the "phenomenological *epoché*," which puts in "brackets" [*Einklammerungen*] the already-given world, "inhibits acceptance of [that] Objective world as existent, and thereby excludes this world completely from the field of judgment." The *epoché* (from *epechein*: "to hold back") does not abolish that which is bracketed but holds it in suspension in order to achieve a cessation of its effects. In the acme of doubting that which is given as the relation of "conscious act" and "object of consciousness," we withhold judgment whether "objectness" is illusion or reality, in order to regard that it *is* present to consciousness. The suspension is coextensive not merely with the set of interpretations already given of the particular experiences confronted by the phenomenological meditator but also with the *entire range* of correlative and co-implied interpretations that always "go along with" the givenness of any particular experience, since, Husserl argued, the "horizons" of particular experiences all share within a common, universal "world-horizon" of the entirety of our existence as intending beings (i.e., the universal horizon of the *eidos* of "life-world"). With that exclusion accomplished, "the realm of my *psychological self-experience*" is reduced completely "to my transcendental-phenomenological Ego," which thereby "posits exclusively himself as the *acceptance-basis* of all Objective acceptances and bases." As a result of the *epoché*, we obtain access to "*an infinite realm of being of a new kind*, as the sphere of a new kind of experience," the experience of the transcendental Ego: it is the place of prepredicative, ultimate substrates, the "core of determinate quiddity, of the truly given as 'itself there' " (Husserl [1931] 1960, §§11–12; Husserl [1948] 1973, 31–41).

Accomplishment of this "universal depriving of acceptance"—this leaving "all expression out of play," by which we then "obtain *pure universal nature*" as the passively pregiven ground of experience (Husserl [1948] 1973, 56)—does not, therefore, "leave us confronting nothing."

> On the contrary we gain possession of something by it; and what we (or, to speak more precisely, what I, the one who is meditating) acquire by it is my pure living, with all the pure subjective processes making this up, and everything meant in them, *purely as* meant in them: the universe of "phenomena" in the (particular and also the wider) phenomenological sense. The *epoché* can also be said to be the radical and universal method by which I apprehend myself purely: as Ego, and with my own pure conscious life, in and by which the entire Objective world exists for me and is precisely as it is for me. (Husserl [1931] 1960, §8)

What we confront, in other words, is direct experience of "phenomena" as intentional objects of the pure act of consciousness. Whether "I" as empirical ego truly exist is still unknown, for the evidence of its self-certainty cannot be adequate until interrogation of that direct experience has shown it to be so. Likewise, whether the phenomena confronted are indicative of some "thing" or presence "behind" them is still unknown. Whereas for Kant the phenomenon, or its "sensational" component, was caused by an agency from the noumenal background, for Husserl that assertion itself must be included within the brackets, since it is an already interpreted givenness.[52] The "being of the transcendental Ego" and its *cogitatio*, "as a being that is prior in itself, is antecedent to the natural being of the world"— that is, the world of "the natural attitude," the empirical world "of which I always speak, the one of which I *can* speak." This latter realm is one "whose existential status [*Seinsgeltung*] is secondary; it continually presupposes the realm of transcendental being" (Husserl [1931] 1960, §§8, 45; Husserl [1948] 1973, 19, 72).

The quest for an absolutist epistemology presumes an absolutist ontology. Accordingly, the Husserlian project was not a "solely epistemological" quest but was fundamentally an attempted ontological construction that would provide the structure of the possibility and conditions of apodictically certain knowledge. The substrate of phenomenologically reduced consciousness is allegedly made available to the Husserlian meditator for "phenomenological description," simultaneously as *noēsis*, *noema*, and *hylē* (to use Husserl's earlier choice of descriptions)—that is, as noetic "act," noematic "content" or "intended object," and hyletic "body," all of which are distinguishable but are given only together.

This substrate is the place of the constitution of the *cogito* and the *cogitatum*. "Objects exist for me, and are for me what they are," Husserl contended, "only as objects of actual and possible consciousness" (Husserl [1931] 1960, §30). The conditions of a self-evident act of judgment must be sought in the conditions of self-evidence of *cogitatio*, as this is revealed in the transcendentally reduced place of constitution. Through interrogation of this pure *cogitatio* the phenomenological meditator may describe both the self-evident *cogitatum* (the intended object) and the self-evident *cogito*—not, however, by reason of an assimilation of "object" and "sub-

---

52. Whereas for Kant the transcendental conditions of knowledge included only "form" (the a priori forms of intuition and the categories), for Husserl they included both "form" and "content" entirely. For Kant, "mind" is already structured as the a priori forms and categories; for Husserl, consciousness has "in itself" no structure except insofar as it is determined in objects-of-its-intentionality.

ject" to the *cogitatio* but by virtue of their constitution in the place given by experience with the substrate, that is, by "sensuous experience."

> The world, as it is always already pregiven entire in passive *doxa*, furnishing the ground of belief for all particular acts of judgment, is at bottom given in simple experience as a world of substrates apprehensible simply by sense. Every sensuous experience, in other words, every experience with the being-sense [*Sinnssein*] of a simple substrate, is *sensuous* experience—the existing substrate is a body, i.e., a body which confirms itself in the harmony of experience and as such has the validity of a body truly existing. (Husserl [1948] 1973, 54)

As phenomenological meditators, we behold this experience of substrate as a "field of passive data"—that is, as the passive genesis of a field that exists before *any* "activity of the ego has as yet carried out any sense-giving operations whatever with regard to it," and which is not *accessible* to doubt. Even so, however, the field is not chaotic: although not yet a terrain defined by products of any "objectivating operation of the ego," the field is not "a mere 'swarm' of data," as Husserl put it, but possesses "a determinate structure, one of prominences and articulated particularities."

This structure can be most easily understood in terms of its simplest model, namely that of a "field of sensuous data" such as the optical data of "color." Although the articulated unity of "color" is not an *immediately* given object in experience—that is, "colors are always already 'taken' in experience as colors of concrete things"—nevertheless, because the "apperceptive substratum" beneath the color of a colored thing *can* be made into an object, the sensuous data so brought into prominence must themselves already be "unities of identity which appear in a multiform manner and which, as unities, can then themselves become thematic objects." In other words, already there is a unity of identity such that "whiteness," for example, exists among a manifold of white-colored different things. Thus, the sensuous data

> are themselves also already the product of a constitutive synthesis, which, as the lowest level, presupposes the operations of the synthesis in internal time-consciousness. These operations, as belonging to the lowest level, necessarily link all others. Time-consciousness is the original seat of the constitution of the unity of identity in general. But it is a consciousness producing only a general form. The result of temporal constitution is only a universal form of order of succession and a form of coexistence of all immanent data. But form is nothing without content. Thus the syntheses which produce the unity of a

field of sense [i.e., always as a "formed content"] are already, so to speak, a higher level of constitutive activity. (Husserl [1948] 1973, 73)

There is, then, still the question of the structure of "a unitary field of sense as it is given in an immanent present"—that is, the constitution of field as having a formed content such that there can be consciousness of "prominence" within it (Husserl [1948] 1973, 72–74, 162–67).

At this point Husserl postulated "the phenomenon of associative genesis," which is "established on the basis of syntheses of internal time-consciousness" and according to which "*the most general syntheses of sensuous data,*" in regard to their formed content, are "*raised to prominence within a field*" in terms of "*affinity (homogeneity)* and *strangeness (heterogeneity).*" This term, "association," Husserl cautioned, must not be confused with the psychological or psychophysical notion; in the phenomenological context it denotes "a form belonging essentially to consciousness in general, a *form of the regularity of immanent genesis,*" that is, as exclusively "the *purely immanent connection of 'this recalls that.'* " All phenomenological data are governed by "an absolutely fixed law" of internal time-consciousness, a lawfulness of "intentional *modification in the realm of pure passivity,*" which takes place "without any participation of the activity radiating from the ego-center." This modification, which "belongs to the regularity of the original constitution of immanent temporality," occurs both as *retention,* in the process of which "every impressional having-consciousness of an original momentary now is constantly changed into the still-having-in-consciousness of the same in the mode of the just-past (the just-having-been-now)," and as *protention,* in which "every new experience in the flow of lived experience" takes place within "a horizon of original, even if entirely empty, expectation, an expectation at first purely passive." These fundamental syntheses in *cogitatio,* by which a field of sensuous data is constituted as a field of prominences-from-homogeneous-background, are not, however, "passive occurrences in consciousness." On the contrary,

these syntheses of coincidence have their own affective power. We say, for example, of that which, in its nonsimilarity, stands out from a homogeneous background and comes to prominence that it "strikes" us, and this means that it displays an *affective tendency* toward the Ego. The syntheses of coincidence, whether it is a matter of coincidence in undifferentiated blending or of coincidence together with the opposition of the unlike, have their own affective power; they exert a stimulus on the Ego which makes it turn toward, whether it obeys the stimulus or not. If there is an apprehension of a sensuous datum in the field, this always takes place on the basis of such a prominence. Through its intensity, the datum stands out from a multiplicity of coaffecting data. This occurs, for example, when, in the sensuous sphere, there is a sound, a noise, or a color which is more or less obtrusive. These lie in the field of perception and stand out from it and, although not yet apprehended, exercise on the ego a stimulus more or less powerful or weak, as the case may be. (Husserl [1948] 1973, 76)

The intensity or insistence of this "standing out" (stimulus) is determined by "the mode, more or less abrupt, of coming-to-prominence," that is, by the modalizations of givenness, such as "problematic possibility," "open possibility," "probability," and so on (Husserl [1948] 1973, 74–76, 87–101, 110–11; Husserl [1931] 1960, §§37–39; see also Husserl [1928] 1964).

Here we must take care to maintain a dual distinction and therewith avoid the temptation of resolution by means of assimilation. On the one hand, we must distinguish "between *that which obtrudes* and *the Ego on which it obtrudes*." If the that-which-obtrudes (and its "corresponding stimuli for the Ego") obtrudes with adequate intensity, *and if "the Ego yields to the stimulus*," then in such conjoint conditions of *cogitatio* "a new element enters"—namely, the Ego's "turning-toward" [*Zuwendung*] the that-which-obtrudes and, correlatively, its "apprehending it by contact." In this "accomplishment of the turning-toward"—referred to by Husserl also as "the being-awake of the Ego"—we are in the midst of the lowest level of the activity of the Ego, namely "the receptivity of the Ego." This new element is constituted as "a tendency coming from the Ego and directed toward" that which is obtrusive. However, we must also distinguish between this "tendency as stimulus"—which has as its two sides (as just mentioned) the obtrusion on the Ego, and, from the side of the Ego, "the being-attracted, the being affected of the Ego itself"—and the "turning-toward *as compliance with* the tendency." In the tendency of the Ego "to give way" to the obtrusion on the Ego, the *cogito* is not yet present; rather, this "tendency as stimulus" (with its internal distinction) constitutes a condition, but not yet the realization, of the *cogito*. It is with the compliant turning-toward of the Ego that the *cogito* as such arises. "The Ego is now turned toward the object; it has *of itself* a tendency directed toward the object": a "tending toward" or "intentionality." Although the object may not yet be fully thematized (i.e., perceived and then thoroughly examined), this general act of compliant turning-toward, whether in a transitory or a continuous way, is the basic "act of the Ego's being-with [*inter-esse*: "interest"]."⁵³ The Ego, now as *cogito*, has its intended object (Husserl [1948] 1973, 77–78, 86).⁵⁴

Thus arise both the active *cogito*, as intentional ego, and the *cogitatum*, as intended-object-of-consciousness, as meaning-constituted-object intended by and for ego in the intentional act of *cogito*. "Consciousness" is always "consciousness-*of* . . . "; that is, it is always constituted as self-transcendence.

Because the already given objectness was bracketed—not abolished, not negated, but "put out of play"—all mediation between *cogito* and *cogitatum* was removed, according to Husserl, and the certitude of *cogito* as constituted with adequate self-evidence in the act of *cogitatio* extends to the *cogitatum*. But this shrinking of distance between "I think" and "object thought" to an absolute immediacy has been achieved (if indeed it has) only as a meaning-constitutive act of consciousness performed by the transcendental-phenomenological Ego, that is, as an intentional meaning-constitution always after the brackets are in place. Truth-falsity, good-evil, and so on, are located entirely within the constitutiveness of transcendentally reduced consciousness.⁵⁵ It is here that we encounter the fundamental weaknesses, and ultimately the failure, of Husserl's projected formation: for example, the obscurity of his "method," the problem of his treatment of language, and most importantly the question of "constitution" with regard to the transcendental Ego and temporality.⁵⁶

---

53. Husserl offered as an empirically approximate exemplification of the difference between general "turning-toward" and "thematizing" the situation in which "I can be engaged thematically with something, e.g., some scientific labor, and be disturbed by a noise from the street. The noise breaks in on me, and I turn toward it for a moment. Nevertheless, my previous theme has not been abandoned because of this but only sinks into the background for this moment. It still remains my theme, to which I return immediately, as soon as the disturbance is over" (Husserl [1948] 1973, 86).

54. It is appropriate to consider here the Latin etymology of *object*: namely, *ob* + *jacere*, "to throw" + "against," "before"; or, in nominative case, "that which is thrown against" or "that which stands against" (as in "*Gegenstand*").

55. "The predicates *truth* (*correctness*) *and falsity*, albeit in a most extremely broad sense, relate to [the transcendental-phenomenological] reduction to our pure meaning" (Husserl [1931] 1960, §23).

56. On the issue of "obscurity of method," it has been observed—fairly, I think—that

> what one tried to learn was almost like a craft-secret of philosophy. A man could say, for instance, that he had "worked with Husserl" or "with Pfänder" [Alexander Pfänder, an early student and colleague of Husserl], just as a practitioner has special credentials because he served his appren-

The Husserlian project held at its center the task of cutting through the "vicious circle" of relativism by founding a noncontingent standpoint, an Archimedean site outside the contingency of being-in-the-world, from which to think all. The transcendentally reduced consciousness was thought to form that site in the manner of pure *theoria*: a "beholding" of the "spectacle" in the act of its constitution. Clearly the method of phenomenology, by which the phenomenological meditator could traverse all the layers or stratifications of received predication and behold the site of the *cogitatio*, had to be self-referential. That is to say, it faced the requirement of founding itself, by its own method and free of any unexamined and unclarified suppositions. This self-referential circle of phenomenological method was a crucial requirement of Husserl's own interrogations, and it is with regard to such requirement that we must be prepared to notice his difficulty in speaking/writing the structure of "reduced consciousness" without importing the not-yet-demonstrated. The instances of such notice are numerous. For example, in his attempt to stipulate a "preknowledge"— that is, a prepredicative, prelinguistic "knowing" in immediate experience—he stated that such "preknowledge is indeterminate as to content, or not completely determined, but it is never completely empty" (Husserl [1948] 1973, 32). But by what point of reference could Husserl think the "emptiness/fullness" (and its gradations) of a "preknowledge"? By what coordinates for thinking the limits and interior possibilities of "volume" could he fix a scale so as to distinguish the "nearly empty" from the "completely empty," the "completely determinate" from the "partly determinate"?[57]

Presumably such knowledge of prelinguistic, prepredicative knowing is somehow grasped by the phenomenological meditator in the "pure consciousness" of the transcendental Ego. But, while it is evident that Husserl meant this "transcendental Ego" as "something" fundamentally different

ticeship under a great experimental scientist or a great doctor. Yet the question, "What is phenomenology?" was posed by almost every scholar whom we can assign to this movement, and the question was answered differently by each one. (Gadamer [1963] 1976, 142–43)

This observation relates to the problem of language, and in particular to the problem of didactic communication, to which I will return shortly.

57. A different level of difficulty is exemplified by Husserl's reminders (e.g., [1948] 1973, 77–78, esp. 77 n. 1), to himself as to others, that he had to be careful in his use of the word *object*. In a related vein, it is noteworthy that Landgrebe apparently found it necessary, when presenting an account of Husserl's critique of the inadequacies of the efforts of empirical science, to mobilize in behalf of that critique and its larger project various empirical "findings" of such existing particular sciences as Gestalt psychology and psychopathology (Landgrebe [1957] 1966, 70–71).

from, and prior to, the empirical ego of the particular thinking subject who speaks and writes, it is not at all clear what that Ego *is* or, indeed, what it *can be*. Nor is it at all clear what the "whatness" of his "originary substrate," to which the Ego relates in immediacy, can be. Husserl appears to have identified "the world of simple, sensible experience," by which he meant the immediately experienced substrate, with "pure nature"—not, of course, the "nature" of the empirical natural object but the *original nature* that exists entirely before all predication or interpretation and is of passive genesis (Husserl [1948] 1973, 33; Husserl [1931] 1960, §61).[58] In "the world of experience," he argued,

> nature is the lowest level, that which founds all others. The existent in its simple, experienceable properties as nature is the substrate which lies at the basis of all other modes of experience, of all evaluation and conduct. Nature is the invariable foundation for all the changing relativity of evaluative judgments which bear on it and for all the changes in its usefulness with regard to the various ends which are set in order to produce something different from naturally given "material." The existent is always given, at bottom, *qua* natural body, provided with natural properties accessible to simple experience— although often interest need not be directed toward them. (Husserl [1948] 1973, 54; see also 56)[59]

The substrate is always given as "natural body," which is "*provided* with natural properties" that are "*accessible* to simple experience."[60] But what,

---

58. Ricoeur, a generally insightful critic of Husserl, has often noted the solipsistic difficulties that surround Husserl's endeavor (e.g., Ricoeur [1949] 1967; 1967; see also [1955] 1965) but left unremarked Husserl's problematic presumption of "original nature" (e.g., Ricoeur [1951–52] 1967, 39–41; Ricoeur [1949] 1967, 147).

59. In order to avoid confusion in terminology, it must be noted that the "simple experience" discussed here and in related passages is "simple" [*schlicht*] in the sense of "straightforward," "plain," and "direct" or "unmediated" experience, experience before "the understanding of an expression." Thus: "Wherever we meet with animals and men and cultural objects (implements, works of art, or whatever), we no longer have mere nature but the expression of mental being-sense. Then we are carried beyond the domain of what is given in simple sensuous perception. Perception, as pure sensuous perception, is *directed toward pure corporeality*, simply and straightforwardly" (Husserl [1948] 1973, 33 n. 2, 55).

60. Similarly, regarding "the problem of time" Husserl had this to say:
> Just as a real thing or the real world is not a phenomenological datum, so also world-time, real time, the time of nature in the sense of natural science including psychology as the natural science of the psychical, is not such a datum.

we may ask, is the origin of that "provision"? And how does it come to be a "provision" that is unequivocally "accessible"? The genesis cannot be from the self-evident Ego, for this Ego is not identified with, but is only immediate to, "that which obtrudes" on the Ego and toward which the Ego turns. Yet if this original substrate that "obtrudes" is not, properly speaking, constituted in the constitutive act of the Ego, then its genesis must be preserved in some anterior privileged space of being, and such preservation introduces at least the risk of unclarified presuppositions.

Moreover, while it may be said that the Husserlian formation does serve to reinforce the Kantian argument regarding one necessary condition of the *cogito* as a reflectedly conscious ego that endures in its own consciousness—namely, that it must be a self-consciously object-constituting ego—it is also the case that in Husserl's formation that which is constituted is object-*sense*, in the manner of ideal object. Gadamer has drawn this point very well:

> Who will contest the fact that the concept of production with respect to the thing perceived can mean nothing else than the production of its valid sense? But when we take Husserl's transcendental intention seriously, the same holds too for the constitution of the life-world and of the other ego. Constitution is nothing but the movement of reconstruction that follows the accomplished reduction. Just as the latter is transcendental, that is, intends no real negation but only the suspension of ontic validity, so too the process of building up out of the accomplishments of subjectivity is not the real engendering of anything, but rather the way of understanding everything that is to have meaning. (Gadamer [1963] 1976, 165)

It is in the problematic from which that critical statement is drawn that we can appreciate the circumstance, noted by Gadamer and others, that Hus-

> When we speak of the analysis of time-consciousness, of the temporal character of objects of perception, memory, and expectation, it may seem, to be sure, as if we assume the Objective flow of time, and then really study only the subjective conditions of the possibility of an intuition of time and a true knowledge of time. What we accept, however, is not the existence of a world-time, the existence of a concrete duration, and the like, but time and duration appearing as such. These, however, are absolute data which it would be senseless to call into question. (Husserl [1928] 1964, 23)

In other words, Husserl stipulated that as a phenomenologist he was "concerned with reality only insofar as it is intended, represented, intuited, or conceptually thought" (Husserl [1928] 1964, 28). Thus, with regard to "the problem of time, this implies that we are interested in *lived experiences* of time," not the absolute time of the human-independent celestial spheres.

serl's project never came into contact with the classical opposition of "ideal" and "material" but remained on this side of it. Husserl's concern was "with reality only insofar as it is intended, represented, intuited, or conceptually thought," by which he meant only as "phenomenological data." To be sure, there is the claim that in the phenomenological method one rejects all distinction of "being" and "meaning" (or "intended sense"); yet such rejection occurs only against the background posit of "original substrate" and "transcendental Ego," for that which is constituted phenomenologically is a texture of understanding, object-as-intended-sense, which is constituted in the transcendentally reduced place of "original substrate obtruding on Ego" and "Ego compliantly turning toward substrate."

This constitution of object-as-intended-sense transpires as a phenomenologically described process only after the 'brackets' have been introduced. What happens once these brackets have been removed? Indeed, we must ask first "when and under what conditions the 'brackets' . . . *can* be removed" (Lukács 1953, 383; emphasis added). In pursuing the implications of that question, we again confront "the problem of language" and Husserl's exiguous attention to it.[61] Not that he was unaware of "problems of language," especially as conceived from the point of view of impedimenta. Consider, for instance, the following passage from his *Cartesian Meditations*:

> Owing to the instability and ambiguity of common language and its much too great complacency about completeness of expression, we require, even where we use its means of expression, a new legitimation of significations by orienting them according to accrued insights, and a fixing of words as expressing the significations thus legitimated. That too we account as part of our normative principle of evidence, which we shall apply consistently from now on. (Husserl [1931] 1960, §5)

Ordinary or "common language" is inadequate to the task and must be set aside in favor of "significations" that are newly legitimated from within phenomenological description "by orienting them according to accrued insights," that is, phenomenological insights accrued by "explication" (*Auslegung*), which does not "create" but "discovers" (Husserl [1931] 1960, §59). It is the building of a new language of expression, the assumption being that the merely "expressive" can be effectively split away from the "constitutive." This language must be neutral a priori; it will be originally

---

61. For a detailed treatment of Husserl's attention to "language," with special reference to *Experience and Judgment*, see Eley's (1973) critical essay.

enacted, in the place created by reduction, as an accurate, stable, unambiguous "fixing of words as expressing [those] significations" legitimated by proper orientation to phenomenological insights.

What, we may ask, is the genesis of those words so to be fixed? Do they come from the prepredicative, prelinguistic realm that is revealed after the brackets are firmly in place, or do they come from within the brackets? There is an answer in Husserl's account, but, as Eley has pointed out, that answer involves a contradiction: "what is prelinguistic and objective," that is, the prepredicative substrate, "is encountered in the horizon of language; on the other hand, language is secondary to what is objective" (Eley 1973, 408), that is, language is "mere communication," mere expression. Whatever the special genesis of Husserl's newly fixed words, the phenomenological meditator surely faces an enormous feat, either of total mental cleansing or of strict compartmentalization, in order to "hear" those newly created words precisely and without contamination by all the historical-cultural "baggage" that words ordinarily carry. Kolakowski well described this puzzle when he remarked in his Cassirer lectures that it "seems hardly possible, as Husserl appears to believe, that we could go back to the intellectual innocence of a newborn baby and still remain phenomenologists" (1975, 56). How does one excise the residuals of language and yet remain in the human world? But if our phenomenologically meditating minds retain even the faintest hint of language, we can have "no guarantee at all against illusions" and therefore "no source of certitude." Given the embeddedness of language in the entire production of concrete, sensuous life—not simply this or that "theoretical discourse" or world view but the entirety of life production—the phenomenological meditator is faced with the interminable task of purging all linguistic formations, all residuals of language, including those that are integral to each succeeding act of purging.[62]

The puzzle does not end there, however. Even if the Husserlian meditator *could* somehow accomplish this infinitely progressive feat, by what means could the attained "insights" (whatever their coinage could possibly be) be conveyed from the total and pure privacy of the meditation of prepredicative experience? As we saw in the above-quoted passage from *Cartesian Meditations*, Husserl was aware of the requirement of "a new legitimation of significations" and, correspondingly, "a fixing of words" that would "express" just those significations. The crucial question re-

---

62. Relatedly, Ricoeur commented on the tension between a notion of historicity and Husserl's transcendental project: "At least Husserl did mark out the shape of the true problem: How can one escape from the solipsism of a Descartes seen through Hume, in order to take seriously the historical character of culture and its evident power to form man?" (Ricoeur [1949] 1967, 174; cf. Husserl [1931] 1960, §62).

mained unanswered, however: what can be the provenience of the language that judges all other languages without being subject to the "contaminations" of linguistic or predicative experience and that thereby serves as a pure instrument for the conveyance of phenomenological insights to others? Perhaps, then, it is not without reason that Husserlian phenomenology has succeeded in talking only of itself, and of itself only as the "perpetual beginning" of a projected method.

3. DEWEY, RUSSELL, AYER

Twentieth-century Anglo-American philosophy has been especially subservient to the claims of modern science. That which science, particularly the "sciences of nature," may offer at any given moment as reigning facticities of its universe are characteristically taken as clear evidence of the epistemic propriety of "*the* scientific method" and as constituting a model of true knowledge. With few exceptions, the task of philosophy has been defined in terms of clarifying investigations and formalizations of this method of science—its "strategies of logical inquiry," its "logical syntax," and so forth. Until midcentury the Husserlian charge went generally unheard in the Anglo-American academy, and much of the subsequent hearing of it, today as yesterday, has been filtered through a pseudepigraphical screen of peculiarly empiricist phenomenologies. Wittgenstein's later critique, as limited as it was (see section 5, below), proved to have little impact until several years after the posthumous publication of his *Philosophical Investigations*.

In this section I shall direct attention to the epistemological positions of three of the central and most widely known figures of the first half-century of Anglo-American philosophy—John Dewey, Bertrand Russell, and A. J. Ayer—whose arguments are often associated respectively with the labels "pragmatism," "logical empiricism" (or "logical constructionism"), and "logical positivism." While it would be foolish to contend that these three scholars fully represent the variety of epistemological views presented during this period of Anglo-American philosophy (one thinks of the disagreements between Russell and A. N. Whitehead, for example, or of those between Dewey and William James), they were hardly marginal to the existing philosophical enterprise, and considerations of their views will serve well enough to characterize the ambient issues of the period.

John Dewey (1859–1952) is usually categorized as a proponent of pragmatism, although he himself generally preferred to describe his view as an "experimentalism" or "instrumentalism." Various sources have been cited in regard to the "origins" of pragmatism, including the seemingly ubiquitous Socrates and Aristotle. Those who are fond of ferreting out "anticipations" and "precursors" have sometimes latched onto a sentence by Francis Bacon, in *Novum Organum*, as just such an "anticipation" of pragmatism: "What is most useful in practice is most correct in theory"

(Bacon [1620] 1952, book 2, aphorism 4).[63] By the same token, a major root of pragmatism has been located in Kant, not only because of his discussion of "the pragmatic point of view" in regard to the conduct of "affairs of life" (e.g., Kant [1798b] 1974), but also by the argument that since his thesis of the unreachable *noumena* precluded any criterion of truth based on some ultimate correspondence, the only suitable criteria must refer simply to phenomenal understandings that pass tests of problem-solving and adaptive performance.[64] But the full deployment of a systematic pragmatism was given by the nineteenth-century engineer and philosopher, Charles Sanders Peirce (1839–1914),[65] and it was from this man's corpus of essays that Dewey, among others, gained his pragmatic inspiration. By the early years of the current century, the general view of pragmatism flourished in the philosophical academy—most especially in the United States, although it did not go unnoticed in Europe (among some advocates of *Lebensphilosophie*, for example).[66]

63. A word of caution: Bacon did not thereby propose a doctrine of "bargained truth," so to speak. His presupposition was that the structure of reality is so nomothetically determinant and regular that any effect that has been proved in experimental practice necessarily corresponds to the real and therefore verifies the theory. Much the same presupposition later informed the views of pragmatists, Dewey included.

64. An instance in the neo-Kantian tradition would be the argument of Hans Vaihinger, who someplace referred to pragmatism as "the most expedient form of error" (e.g., [1911] 1935). To be sure, the argument described above was not Kant's but that of some of his self-designated successors.

65. For a critical assessment of Peirce's work, see Habermas [1968a] 1971, 91–139. As will be seen in chapter 5, Habermas's own effort to separate the process of the constitution of objects of possible experience and the "higher" process of a discursive formulation of rationally grounded truthful statements about those objects brings to mind Peirce's distinction between a "pragmatist theory of meaning" (i.e., concerning the construction of objects of experience) and a "consensus theory of truth" (see, e.g., Habermas [1971a] 1973, 19–21).

66. Simmel, for example, said favorably of pragmatism that it "deprives truth (*Erkennen*) of its old claim to be a free-floating domain ruled by independent and ideal laws. Truth has now become interwoven with life, nourished by this source, guided by the totality of its directions and purposes, legitimized through its basic values. Life has thus reclaimed its sovereignty over a previously autonomous province" (Simmel [1918] 1968, 20–21). In other words, Simmel appreciated pragmatism as a manifestation of the revolt of "life-urge" (or a hypostatized "Life") against "spirit." But it may be noted, if "life-urge" is self-conscious, it is so, for pragmatism, through "spirit" or "thought" or something "like" that. Because pragmatism maintained the duality-as-opposition behind a screen of "the natural condition" (expressed variously in the different versions of pragmatism), it was left with a "life-urge" that could produce only an alienated self-consciousness—or, as Simmel put it, "the tragic conflict of life as spirit."

To Dewey's mind, the central fault of all traditional theories of knowledge lay in their commonly intended though differently executed efforts to account for "the relation of thought at large to reality at large." He rejected such efforts as futile, and worse: they are "not so much true or false as . . . radically meaningless," for they purport to abstract from the actual knowing process its specific actual contexts, and such abstraction breaks what he considered to be "the natural connection" of knower and known, subject and object. What is needed, he said, is "a theory that takes knowledge as it finds it" and then strives to provide "the same kind of account of it that would be given to any other natural function or occurrence" (Dewey 1903, 6–10; Dewey 1929, 117–18; Dewey 1938, 515–34; Dewey [1910] 1965, 97).

Thus, in his own work Dewey claimed to be less concerned to demonstrate the relation of knower to known—for him, a "natural connection"—than to elucidate processes of inquiry and validation. Eschewing all versions of the so-called spectator theory of knowledge, he regarded knowledge as a product of inquiry undertaken in specific circumstances in order to solve some "problem" with which the inquirer and others ("we") have been confronted. Knowledge (or "warranted assertion," as he sometimes preferred) is simply "a name for the product of competent inquiries," and it is acquired "whenever our inquiry leads to conclusions which settle the problem out of which it grew." The process of "knowing" is primarily instrumental rather than apprehensional: "an existential overt act." It is the experimental process of "inquiry," defined by Dewey as "the controlled or directed transformation of an indeterminate situation into one that is so determinate in its constituent distinctions and relations as to convert the elements of the original situation into a unified whole." This latter description of the consequence of inquiry perhaps mildly suggests a coherence criterion of "true knowledge," but such was not Dewey's choice. It has been argued that Dewey subscribed to neither the coherence nor the correspondence theories as countenanced in academic philosophy but tried to fashion a different sort of truth-criterion, after Peirce. In any case, Dewey himself expressed great admiration for Peirce's definition of truth, calling it "the best definition . . . from the logical standpoint" that he had encountered. According to Peirce, "The opinion which is fated to be ultimately agreed to by all who investigate, is what we mean by the truth, and the object represented in this opinion is the real" (Peirce [1878] 1960, para. 407).[67] Dewey's version of this definition held that truth is that which

67. Dewey (1938, 345 n. 6) also quoted another of Peirce's attempts at definition: "Truth is that concordance of an abstract statement with the ideal limit towards which endless investigation would tend to bring scientific belief, which concordance the abstract statement may possess by virtue of the confession of its inaccuracy and one-sidedness, and this confession is an essential ingredient of truth"

satisfies the conditions of inquiry (Dewey 1929, 189, 233; Dewey 1938, 8–9, 35, 104–5, 118, 345).

More specifically, truth is an effective characteristic of ideational or conceptual imaginations applied experimentally toward the removal of a perplexity or obstacle that has created a problematic situation. Successful removal of the obstacle or perplexity signifies the truthfulness of the experimentally applied hypothetical. As such, "truth" cannot be a single, monolithic, and unchanging state or condition, either of our theoretical statements or of our practical operations; rather there are multiple truths, in correspondence with the manifold of problems solved or perplexities removed. "Truth is a collection of truths," Dewey contended, "and these constituent truths are in the keeping of the best available methods of inquiry and testing as to matters-of-fact." Although a collection of truths may have attained at any moment some level of internal integration and coherence, any one or all of the constituents are subject to change as the situations on which they depend change and as the methods of inquiry—"which are, when collected under a single name, science"—are enhanced in technical apparatus. Because the "subject-matter of science, for better or worse, is . . . 'there,' " that is, because it consists in "a definite body of facts and principles" and has "a kind of independent external existence" of continuous process, so the multiplicity of truth is constantly pulsating with alteration and improvement, and therefore always retains "a hypothetical quality." Truth stands in relation to that external reality as the appropriateness of an invention stands in relation to "the conditions which the invention was intended to meet." It is an "answering," just as "a key answers the conditions imposed by a lock" (Dewey 1925, 3, 155–56, 172, 410; Dewey 1916, 24–25, 304; Dewey 1946, 343).

In view of such circumstances, Dewey argued, the ancient philosophical quest for a monolithic, immutable certainty of truth is pointless. Although a firm believer in the progress of science, he rejected all pursuits of an apodictic certitude, including the "contemporary hankering after ultimate 'sense-data' [and the] conviction that mathematical logistic is at last to open to philosophy the arcana of ultimate truth." Not only is there no single all-encompassing truth, no ultimate truth; such truths as do exist at any moment of the process of experience are the truths of science, which are never final. Philosophy "has no pre-eminent status" in regard to true knowledge of the world; "it is a recipient, not a donor" (Dewey 1925, 13, 410; Dewey 1929).

Dewey's account of the process and procedures of knowing—of

(Peirce [1901] 1960, para. 565). Peirce continued, with regard to the object: "Reality is that mode of being by virtue of which the real thing is as it is, irrespectively of what any mind or any definite collection of minds may represent it to be."

knowing "the true" by his criterion of "adaptational workability," as it has been called—rests primarily on his image of the experimental method of modern natural science and, equally important, on his notion of "experience." As to the latter, it served as the opaque lens through which we were meant to see the matter-of-fact continuity of subject and object. The opacity is unbreakable. In Dewey's words, "experience"

> denotes both the field, the sun and the clouds and the rain, seeds, and harvest, and the man who labors, who plans, invents, uses, suffers, and enjoys. Experience denotes what is experienced, the world of events and persons; and it denotes that world caught up into experiencing, the career and destiny of mankind. Nature's place in man is no less significant than man's place in nature. (Dewey 1925, 28)

This notion of experience signified for Dewey an unsullied "method of denotation" that simply points to the world that is "there," which world "has the last word in all human inquiries and surmises." One might suppose, Dewey allowed, that this special "cautionary and directive" concept of experience would be unnecessary, given the actual practices of empirical science. But we would suppose wrongly, for that view neglects the vast confusion that abounds because of the muddleheadedness of so much metaphysical speculation. Thus, the notion of experience has particular value for philosophy, inasmuch as

> it asserts the finality and comprehensiveness of the method of pointing, finding, showing, and the necessity of seeing what is pointed to and accepting what is found in good faith and without discount. Were the denotative method universally followed by philosophers, then the word and the notion of experience might be discarded; it would be superfluous, for we should be in possession of everything it stands for. But as long as men prefer in philosophy (as they so long preferred in science) to define and envisage "reality" according to esthetic, moral or logical canons, we need the notion of experience to remind us that "reality" includes whatever is denotatively found. (Dewey 1925, 11)

For any inquiry of the real, the proper procedure involves denotation "first and last"; with any question, or any problematic situation, "we must go to some thing pointed to, denoted, and find our answer in that thing" (Dewey 1925, 10–12, 28, 101–19, 463–69).[68]

---

68. Dewey was here referring to the value of "the real thing," of course. As to moral and aesthetic values, he took the view that "the constituents of the object of cognitional experience" in the natural world "are *the* means and the *only* means of regulative appraisals of values, of their revision, rectification, of their regulated generation and fortification" (1925, 424; emphases added).

As understood by Dewey, the process of inquiry always begins with the experience of a "felt difficulty"—that is, "jars, hitches, breaks, blocks," or "incidents occasioning an interruption of the smooth, straightforward course of behavior." In terms of the definition of "inquiry" previously quoted, this is the experience of a situation characterized by an "indeterminateness." If the "felt difficulty" or indeterminateness of situation is such that we desire to eliminate or rectify it, we formulate it as a problematic to be solved, then imagine hypothetical situations of transition from indeterminate to determinate distinctions and relations, and finally we test the various hypotheses experimentally. If one of the experiments proves to remove the "felt difficulty," as indicated by a successful return to "the smooth, straightforward course of behavior," we have verified the claim of "truth" or "warranted assertability" proposed in the tested hypothesis. This process is both open-ended and self-corrective; that is, while any particular inquiry necessarily begins from a background of *some* rules and claims of knowledge that are taken for granted, none of these is absolutely or eternally established, and any one or all of them (though not all of them simultaneously) may become the focus of later inquiry and may be altered therefrom. This capacity of self-correction in the process of inquiry allows for the progressive movement of science, according to Dewey, even though none of its constituent truths can be accorded a finality of moment (Dewey [1910] 1965, 72–77; Dewey 1938, 104–19, 278–83; Dewey 1946, 347–50; Dewey and Bentley 1949, 315).

This valorization of science and its "self-evident" accomplishments solved at once, for Dewey, a number of epistemological puzzles. But the "solution" consisted of an almost happenstance mixture of fiat and neglect. Asserting that "the subject-matter of science" is simply "there," an independently and externally existent "definite body of facts and principles," he covered the complexities of relation of subject and object with a supposedly self-evident, and equivalently "there," reality of "natural connection." Similarly, the opacity of his concept "experience," through which somehow we have a denotative sentience of discriminated "empirical occurrences," is matched by the occultation of the process through which "imagined hypotheses" and "existential observations" are supposedly brought into mutual alignment, thereby creating decisive tests and the possibility of successful solutions to problems. There are "operations of two kinds," we are told, one dealing "with ideational or conceptual subject-matter" and the other consisting of "activities involving the techniques and organs of observation" (Dewey 1938, 117–18); somehow these operations "are in functional correspondence with each other," when we conduct an inquiry by proper procedures. But the foundations of such key notions (and the burden they carry) as "functionally correspondent operations" and "proper procedures"—just as with the foundation of his truth criterion—

are matters not of consistent demonstration but of immense presuppositions. As numerous commentators have remarked, once the existence of
those presuppositions is revealed, the circularity of Dewey's argument becomes readily evident.

One of those who quickly rejected the pragmatist proposal associated
with Dewey, among others, was Bertrand Russell (1872–1970). Russell
disputed any proposal "to abandon the concept of 'knowledge' altogether
and substitute 'beliefs that promote success'—and here 'success' may perhaps be interpreted biologically"—for, he pointed out, determination of
that which qualifies *as* "success" already presupposes the existence of a
certified knowledge (Russell 1948, 156–57; Russell 1908a).[69] Put another
way, he found in pragmatism the same specious acceptance of received
scientific "conclusions" that had bothered him in the efforts of his god-
father, John Stuart Mill.

Russell must surely be counted the preeminent heir of Humean empiricism in twentieth-century Anglo-American philosophy. Although the
inwardness of Hume's psychological account of knowing gave way to a
rigorous formal-logical construction, Russell carried through the emphasis
on empirics in a realist-correspondence view of the relation between subject
and object of knowledge. As noted previously (chapter 2), the course of his
own epistemological thinking changed markedly during the first quarter of
this century, as he found it necessary to shift from a strong to a weaker
version of the correspondence criterion. In the early period, ending just
after World War I, his attention was given primarily to developments of a
mathematical logic in a series of works reckoned by many evaluators to be
his greatest: the *Principia Mathematica*, of course, coauthored with A. N.
Whitehead, but also such preceding works as the essays in which he proposed his theory of descriptions and his theory of types (Russell [1905]
1956; Russell [1908b] 1956).[70] These tools of formal logic would enable
him to accomplish what Hume could not, or so he believed, for he was
decidedly of the opinion that most of the problems of philosophy were
tractable by rigorous analysis of the logical elements from which propositions are formed, that is, by an analysis of the structure of language in terms
of a "logical atomist" theory of meaning. While he later modified certain
of his views regarding epistemic structure, he persisted in the belief that an
analytic understanding of the logical construction of propositions from

69. It is telling, nonetheless, that Russell was of the opinion that pragmatism
"was first promulgated by Marx," the alleged site being no less than the second
and eleventh theses on Feuerbach (see Russell 1948, 421–22).

70. See Pears (1972) for a critical study of Russell's early period, especially 1904–
19. Here I shall concentrate on the modified epistemological position later argued
by Russell.

atomistic elements is central to our understanding of the structure of reality. For the later as for the early Russell, the meaning of words was thought to consist in their referential function, such that words "have 'meaning' when there is an association or conditioned reflex connecting them with something other than themselves." The meaning of a word depends ultimately on some ostensive referral (i.e., either directly or by way of one or more other words already ostensively founded); the basic function of words consists in their referring to external objects; and the basic category of meaning is "naming" (Russell 1948, 63–73, 113, 262–65).[71]

Whereas the early Russell insisted on a very strong epistemic criterion and regarded sense-data as physical entities existing just beyond "mind" in the nervous system (see, e.g., Russell 1914; Russell [1918] 1956; also Russell 1959, 134–36), he subsequently retreated to the weaker position that sense-data, or "percepts," are constituents of objects and events but are neither identified with them nor exhaustive of them. The object of knowledge, independent of the subject but mediated by sense-data, is "a collection of qualities existing at the place in question," that is, a spatio-temporally structured complex of qualities and not a substance. The atomistic object, according to Russell, consists in "a complete complex of compresence," by which he meant a collection or group of qualities all of which are compresent, or "overlapping in space-time," and "nothing outside the group is compresent with every member of the group."[72] Sense-data, on the other hand, are not in, or identified with, the object of knowledge but are of our minds and ultimately of the neural circuitry of our brains. Insofar as the sense-data constitute the terminus of "causal lines" extending without interruption from an object to a human brain, they are structurally isomorphic with that object, and it is this correspondence that allows us to infer from sense-data knowledge of the object.[73] However, Russell conceded, there may exist intrinsically to the object itself certain

71. Russell categorized words into "naming words" and "relationals" (i.e., spatio-temporal relations), which together comprise a minimum vocabulary necessary for expressions of knowledge, plus two additional categories, "logical terms" (e.g., "and," "all") and "egocentric particulars" (e.g., "I," "this") (1948, 83–86, 119–20).

72. An "event" is distinguished as an "incomplete complex," by Russell's account. Whereas an "object," or "complete complex of compresence," qualifies as "a space-time point-instant," an "event" does not so qualify but instead "occupies a continuous region in space-time." Thus, the vernacular "things" referred to by such naming-words "as 'Socrates,' 'France,' and 'the sun' apply to continuous portions of space-time which happen to interest us" (Russell 1948, 303–5).

73. Russell's brief attempt at a neutral monistic solution, with its premise that both "mind" and "matter" are commonly founded in the same neutral "elements," led him to argue in The Analysis of Mind that

qualities beneath those that are sensible, and these, given the absence of a necessary "medium," are not accessible (Russell 1948, 226–31, 303–5; Russell 1940, 122).

Given such relations between sense-data and object as were posited by Russell, and holding aside for now the question how he could ground this initial posit, we are led to consider the structure of inference whereby valid and reliable knowledge of the external world can be inferred from the causal-line terminus of our sense-data. Russell rejected all coherence versions of rationalism, arguing that a coherence criterion must simply assume its own foundation; that is, it rests on some initially credible proposition, the credence of which it can, by its own terms, only assume (Russell 1940, 174–77; Russell 1948, 157–58). He continued to insist that a correspondence rule, a criterion of correspondence of the structures of sense-data and object, is indispensable (Russell 1912, 188–90; Russell 1940, 175–77; Russell 1948, 148). Yet he was compelled to reject a pure empiricism because of its inability to account for its own basis in nonempirical principles of induction even while it professed to credit only sense-experience as the foundation of valid evidence (1948, 496–98).[74]

The course taken by Russell began with his notion of a "basic belief," which supposedly we acquire from direct experience:[75] it is "a proposition

> physics and psychology are not distinguished by their material. Mind and matter alike are logical constructions; the particulars out of which they are constructed, or from which they are inferred, have various relations, some of which are studied by physics, others by psychology. Broadly speaking, physics groups particulars by their active places, psychology by their passive places. (Russell 1921, 307)

That last sentence reveals that it was a fragile neutrality, haunted by a barely suppressed asymmetry, and soon after the publication of this work he reverted to a Lockean causal theory of perception, in which the external object was treated as that to which a claim must conform (or correspond) in order to be true (see, e.g., Russell 1927).

74. Thus, Russell also differed from logical positivism to the extent that he disputed the verificationist doctrine (which must either be defined so broadly as to be meaningless or face paradoxes such as the proposition—which, he said, "we all believe"—"that there was a time before there was life on earth") and to the extent that he felt compelled to admit the "awkward conclusion for an empiricist," namely, that nondeductive scientific inference can reach only probable conclusions and only "by assuming postulates, or a postulate, for which there is, and can be, no empirical evidence" (Russell [1950] 1956, 372–74).

75. A "belief," according to Russell (1948, 94–95, 145) is a "collection of states of an organism bound together by all having in whole or part the same external reference." It is available in prelinguistic experience: language "immensely increases the number and complexity of possible beliefs and ideas, but is not, I am convinced, necessary for the simplest beliefs and ideas" ("ideas" here meant as "a state of an organism appropriate . . . to something not sensibly present").

which arises on occasion of a perception, which is the evidence for its truth, and has a form such that no two propositions having this form can be mutually inconsistent if derived from different percepts" (1940, 174). But evidences occasioned by "direct experience," whatever the veracity of that, cannot accredit claims of knowledge of objects and events beyond immediate experience, and for this larger requirement Russell had to face the hoary problem of demonstrating a self-consistent general principle of induction. Such was the task: to demonstrate a general principle of induction in a manner wherein the demonstration itself would remain strictly independent of actual inductions, which would depend upon that very principle.

Finding no solution to that puzzle, Russell offered instead a set of five assumptions, or postulates, summarized here, that he deemed to be necessary to the existence of claims of knowledge that we do make:

1. The postulate of "quasi-permanence"—"Given any event A, it happens very frequently that, at any neighboring time, there is at some neighboring place an event very similar to A." Such postulate is necessary to our knowledge of material objects.
2. The postulate of "separable causal lines"—"It is frequently possible to form a series of events such that from one or two members" of the series something can be inferred as to all the other members. This allows the differentiation of "things" and the connection of percept to object.
3. The postulate of "spatio-temporal continuity"—There "must be intermediate links in the causal chain" between two noncontiguous but causally related events; i.e., there can be no "action at a distance." This is necessary to our "inferences to unobserved occurrences, both in science and in common sense."
4. The postulate of "structure"—"When a number of structurally similar complex events are ranged about a center in regions not widely separated, it is usually the case that all belong to causal lines having their origin in an event of the same structure at the center."
5. The postulate of "analogy"—"Given two classes of events A and B, and given that, whenever both A and B can be observed, there is reason to believe that A causes B, then if, in a given case, A is observed, but there is no way of observing whether B occurs or not, it is probable that B occurs; and similarly if B is observed, but the presence or absence of A cannot be observed." Our inferences regarding unobservables, especially "other minds," are governed by this postulate. (Russell 1948, 487–93; emphases deleted)

These postulates or assumptions of "what is probable" pertain to our "knowledge of connections between facts" and not to the knowledge of particular facts themselves. They are, Russell contended, entirely "indispensable in reaching conclusions that we all accept" (1948, 156, 487–95).

The postulates are not definitively demonstrated, however, and so in the end they prove nothing. Russell sought to "ground" the worth of his set of assumptions in an argument of physical-physiological-psychological suppositions of "the natural world," but the argument fails to convince.

> Knowledge of connections between facts has its biological origin in animal expectations. An animal which experiences an A expects a B; when it evolves into a primitive man of science it sums up a number of particular expectations in the statement "A causes B." It is biologically advantageous to have such expectations as will usually be verified; it is therefore not surprising if the psychological laws governing expectations are, in the main, in conformity with the objective laws governing expected occurrences. (Russell 1948, 495)

This view of the ordered and ordering force of "animal expectations" had its background, in turn, in suppositions more generally of a physical universe:

> The physical world has what may be called "habits," i.e., causal laws; the behavior of animals has habits, partly innate, partly acquired. The acquired habits are generated by what I call "animal inference," which occurs when there are the data for an induction, but not in all cases where there are such data. Owing to the world being such as it is, certain kinds of inductions are justified and others are not. If our inductive propensities were perfectly adapted to our environment, we should only be prone to an induction if the case were of the sort which would make the induction legitimate. In fact, all except men of science are too prone to induction when one of the characters concerned is interesting, and too little prone to it when both characters are not easy to notice. When both characters are interesting, the popular mind finds the impulse to induction irresistible: comets foretell the death of princes, because both are felt to be noteworthy. (Russell 1948, 495)[76]

For all that, one cannot avoid the verdict that this complex posit, upon which Russell's claims regarding "knowledge of connections between facts" rests, fares no better than his initial posit of the definitive relation between object and sense-data, whereby the latter are to be taken as necessary, true

---

76. As this passage illustrates, at times Russell came perilously close to the very sort of criterion of acceptable knowledge claims that he had criticized in pragmatism. That is, "certain kinds of induction" are justified because they "work" in "the world as it is."

evidence of the former (i.e., knowledge of "the facts" themselves). His sense-data, or percepts, conceived as separate entities caused by the external world, stand as impenetrable mediators between a pre-given reality of object and the mind of subject. But by his own terms we cannot demonstrate whether and how such causation exists, nor, if it should happen to exist generally, which of our sensory experiences are genuinely "linked" to the "real objects" and which are mere hallucinations, some other dreamlike state, or the products of a socially enforced false consciousness. For we cannot penetrate these mediators so as to reach the object immediately.

In the end, Russell was forced to admit not only that our "knowledge of connections between facts" can be at best only a probable knowledge but that even our sense-data are characterized by "degrees of credibility" and always present to us the possibility of being either more or less credible than we suppose. "All knowledge is in some degree doubtful, and we cannot say what degree of doubtfulness makes it cease to be knowledge." Reluctantly, Russell came to the conclusion that "all human knowledge is uncertain, inexact, and partial. To this doctrine we have not found any limitation whatever" (1948, 391, 396, 497, 527).[77]

Quite aware at least of the formal limitations of his own construction, Russell settled finally for the ungrounded supposition that "we may be said to 'know' what is necessary for scientific inference, given that it fulfills the following conditions: (1) it is true, (2) we believe it, (3) it leads to no conclusions which experience confutes, (4) it is logically necessary if any occurrence or set of occurrences is ever to afford evidence in favor of any other occurrence" (1948, 496). Of course, whether it *is* true, whether a "confuting experience" *is* confuting, and so on—these remain open questions. Russell admitted that a radical skepticism or a "solipsism of the moment" (regarding the privacy of sense-data) "cannot be refuted," but he countered with the promise that he would be "profoundly skeptical" of the sincerity of anyone who should utter such a challenge. Throughout the length of his effort to ground the claims of science through a demonstrable

---

77. Russell's displeasure with the failure to demonstrate solid grounding in "the world as it is" can be appreciated in part from remarks he made in reference to the rational system of mathematics. In a letter to C. W. K. Mundle, dated 20 December 1968, Russell Archives, McMaster University, Hamilton, Ontario; quoted in Ronald W. Clark's biography, *The Life of Bertrand Russell* (New York: A. A. Knopf, 1976), p. 370, Russell wrote of his reaction to Wittgenstein's *Tractatus* that initially he "did not appreciate that his work implied a linguistic philosophy. When I did we parted company," for, he continued, he "felt a violent repulsion to the suggestion that 'all mathematics is tautology.' I came to believe this but I did not like it. I thought that mathematics was a splendid edifice, but this shows that it was built on sand."

structure of correspondence, his basic conviction regarding the constitution of reality is clear and consistent. Shortly after the turn of the century, he wrote the following:

> That Man is the product of causes which had no prevision of the end they were achieving; that his origin, his growth, his hopes and fears, his loves and his beliefs, are but the outcome of accidental collocations of atoms; . . . that all the labours of the ages, all the devotion, all the inspiration, all the noonday brightness of human genius, are destined to extinction in the vast death of the solar system, and that the whole temple of Man's achievement must inevitably be buried beneath the debris of a universe in ruins—all these things, if not quite beyond dispute, are yet so nearly certain, that no philosophy which rejects them can hope to stand. (Russell [1903] 1910, 60–61)

Many years later he reaffirmed this view of "man's place in the cosmos" (Russell 1957, 104)—not only the ontologic conviction in a naturalistic captivity of cosmic nihilism but, as well, the ethical implication he had drawn from it: while in our actions and desires "we must submit perpetually to the tyranny of outside forces," in our thoughts and aspirations "we are free, free from our fellow men, free from the petty planet on which our bodies impotently crawl." And so we must learn, he asserted, "that energy of faith which enables us to live constantly in the vision of the good," and (somehow) we must "descend, in action, into the world of fact, with that vision always before us"—even though we cannot be sure which of the world is "fact" and which is "fiction."

In view of the fate of Russell's epistemological proposals, it may seem redundant to consider another, closely related, train of argumentation. But the general approach defined by the varieties of logical empiricism has been a stalwart presence in the self-understanding of modern science, especially in the Anglo-American academy, and it is therefore appropriate to examine the offerings of a philosopher frequently associated with logical-positivist constructions, Alfred J. Ayer (b. 1910). Certainly the strain of ambivalence that has characterized much of the twentieth-century Anglo-American discourse of and about epistemology can be appreciated quite readily from the work of Ayer, the core of which began in the mid-1930s after Russell had made clear his conversion to a rather weaker criterion of truth. Even in its pattern of modification and reconsideration over four decades, Ayer's argument fits well enough within the broadly defined movement of logical positivism; and within that, it has displayed certain characteristic ambivalences and ambiguities. On the one hand, his argument has exhibited aspects of a phenomenalism, insofar as he has consistently rejected any notion of elusive "essences" and has emphasized a manifest experience as the touchstone of knowing. On the other hand, he has also rejected any subjectivist doctrine of mind-constituted reality; and in that, he has leaned toward a physicalism, even though his proposal of an ultimate or final criterion of valid or true knowledge has to do with the subject's "right to be sure" about his or her own experiences.

Ayer's initial view, strongly argued in *Language, Truth and Logic* (1946; first published in 1936), amounted to an eclecticism of Vienna-Circle positivism, a reductive empiricism after Hume and Russell, Moore's analytical approach, and some aspects of pragmatism.[78] His central thesis was that the object of knowledge can be defined ultimately in terms only of "sensible manifestations" (i.e., sense experiences), that any claim to true knowledge not based on sensory experience is a meaningless claim (all metaphysical propositions are, without exception, meaningless), and that the justificatory basis of propositions about reality consists in empirical verifiability. While conceding that total verification is apparently impossible, he argued that the factual meaningfulness of any proposition nevertheless rests in its verifiability at least to the extent that *some* sensory experiences are "relevant to the determination of its truth or falsity." The task of philosophy is not to discover empirical knowledge as such—that is for science to do—but to clarify the propositional language of science, and thus to clarify meaning, through an analysis of its fundamental concepts (Ayer 1946, 31–39, 41–43, 48–49, 60, 65–66, 75–78; see also Ayer 1940 and Ayer [1964a] 1970).

Subsequently, in his introduction to the second edition of *Language, Truth and Logic* (1946, 15–16), he conceded that his earlier formulation of the central "principle of verification" had not been entirely adequate, and that the principle itself escapes factual verification. Despite the recognized shortcomings of that early presentation, however, Ayer has remained "in sympathy with the spirit of the book."[79] As for its central principle, he most recently confessed: "I still broadly adhere to what may be called the verificatory approach" (1977, 155–56)—though not without awareness of some of the "difficulties" that haunt it. Indeed, in his modified statement "sense-experience" and "verifiability" continue to occupy center stage, but they fail to project enough of a sturdy presence to convince us that what

78. See Ayer's acknowledgment of these sources of his thinking, the sum of which he described as "a blend" rather than an eclecticism (1977, 154).

79. With regard to the proper task of philosophy, he persisted in the opinion that it is only to clarify "by refashioning the structure of language" so as to "help to determine what facts there can be"—and not to change the world materially, which latter task "must be left to science" (Ayer [1962] 1970, 93). There is in this an ambiguity of which Ayer was probably never aware.

we are watching are not simply the chimera of a nonexistent play. Thus, sense-experiences continue to serve as the central criteria by which the truth claims of a proposition are to be judged. The sense-experiences themselves "are neither certain nor uncertain"; they "simply occur," and it is by their mere occurrence that verification, which consists "in our having the appropriate experiences," proceeds. Truth and falsity are categories of judgment that pertain only to linguistically expressible statements or propositions of facticity (and to analytic or tautological propositions); and adjudication of the claims of such statements or propositions can take place only through the measure of concordance between the given statement or proposition and the "appropriate" sensory experiences of that to which the statement refers.[80] The proper goal of verification consists in ascertaining whether the necessary and sufficient conditions of a true statement are satisfied, that is, whether a knowing subject has "the right to be sure" about a claim. A necessary first condition of true knowledge is of course that that which is claimed to be known must itself be true. This condition alone is not sufficient, however: while "it is necessary that if something is known it is true," this hardly means "that for a fact to be known it must be such that no one could be mistaken about it or such that it could not have been otherwise." And a claimant could be "completely sure of something which is in fact true, but yet not know it." Rather, the claimant must have the *right* to be

80. Regarding moral propositions, Ayer originally argued that "in saying that a certain action is right or wrong, I am not making any factual statement, nor even a statement about my own state of mind. I am merely expressing certain moral sentiments," which is not the same as "asserting a genuine proposition" (Ayer 1946, 105, 108–9). In this sharp separation of the factual from the ethical, Ayer contended that "it is impossible to find a criterion for determining the validity of ethical judgments, ... not because they have an 'absolute' validity which is mysteriously independent of ordinary sense-experience, but because they have no objective validity whatsoever." Moreover, he continued (here in explicit opposition to G. E. Moore), we do not actually argue about questions of ethical value as such but instead about "the facts of the case": it is impossible "to construct even an imaginary argument on a question of value which does not reduce itself to an argument about a question of logic or about an empirical matter of fact." Subsequently, Ayer said of this "moral theory" that it was, "though to some extent along the right lines, ... much too crude" (Ayer 1977, 155). An interesting footnote to his discussion of ethics concerns his view that "our ordinary ideas of freedom and responsibility are very muddle-headed" (Ayer [1964b] 1970, 238–39), about which he allowed that such ideas "are also very firmly held" and surmised that if a social survey were conducted, he would "expect it to indicate that if it were shown to them that a man's action could be explained in causal terms, most people would take the view that he was not responsible for it. Since it is not at all clear why one's responsibility for an action should depend on its being causally inexplicable, this may only prove that most people are irrational."

sure: "the necessary and sufficient conditions for knowing that something is the case are first that what one is said to know be true, secondly that one be sure of it, and thirdly that one should have the right to be sure." Such right to be sure "may be earned in various ways," according to Ayer—although he has never given a precise and consistent exposition of how those "various ways" of earned entitlement are constituted, but he has admitted that he has found it "not at all easy to determine exactly" what such standards are. Yet "even if one could give a complete description" of those ways in which the right to be sure must be earned, "it would be a mistake to try to build it into the definition of knowledge," since, in Ayer's estimation, "the questions which philosophers raise about the possibility of knowledge are not at all to be settled by discovering what knowledge is. For many of them reappear as questions about the legitimacy of the title to be sure,"[81] and just those questions comprise "the main concern of . . . the theory of knowledge." Where one draws the line demarcating true knowledge from mere opinion or belief is simply a matter of agreement; the key question is rather that of the constitution of the standard by which *any* line is to be drawn (Ayer 1956, 20, 25, 31–35, 52; see also Ayer [1962] 1970 and Ayer [1967] 1970).

Ayer's account of the necessary and sufficient conditions of knowing truly reveals his own ambivalence most strikingly in his refusal to elucidate what otherwise amounts to a sort of referential opacity (see Ayer [1968] 1970, 54). There is no provision of any means or connection by which the knowing subject can know whether that which "one is said to know be true" *is* true. It has been Ayer's contention that

> we do just have to see that certain proofs are valid, and it is through having some experience that we discover the truth or falsehood of any statement of empirical fact. . . . To take a simple example, what verifies the statement that I have a headache is my feeling a headache, not my having a feeling of confidence that the statement that I have a headache is true. . . . [My] knowing that I am having the experience is just my having it and being able to identify it. . . . [My] justification for accepting the statement is not that I have a cognitive, or any other attitude toward it: it is simply that I am having the experience. (Ayer 1956, 21)

Yet there is the question of "being able to identify" it correctly. That is, identification of the putatively verifying experience itself, as *this* or *that* empirical fact—for instance, as a headache, or the feeling of a headache,

81. Since only "many of them reappear" in this guise, it is not clear how the remaining questions are to be settled, nor how they differ from those of the first category.

rather than, say, a bee-sting, an infected hair follicle, possession by the devil, or a hallucination—is also susceptible of doubt, a circumstance that Ayer recognized when, for example, he invoked the truism that "the proof must start somewhere." His choice of starting-point consisted in the givenness of experience, as in "having an experience." At that point Ayer's general argument is up against the skeptic's challenge. To be sure, in recognizing this confrontation Ayer retorted that radical skepticism, which proposes the dubitability not just of some but of *all* claims of true judgment, places itself in the position of being experientially unjustifiable. Experience cannot justify radical skepticism, but neither can it refute it. However, as Ayer rightly acknowledged, the nonskeptic is not therein relieved of the obligation to demonstrate the justification and warrant of positive claims put forward by his or her own hand. "Even granting that it makes no sense to say that all our perceptions are delusive, any of them still may be. We have to make good our claim to know that some particular ones are not. ... From the fact that our rejection of some of them is grounded on our acceptance of others it does not follow that those that we accept are true" (Ayer 1956, 20–21, 38).

So, how indeed are we to decide *which* claims to accept? How, even, are we to judge the existence of physical objects? Ayer's answer still turns on a sense-experience standard, but with an element of conventionalism about it: "the reason why our sense-experiences afford us grounds for believing in the existence of physical objects is simply that sentences which are taken as referring to physical objects are used in such a way that our having the appropriate experiences counts in favour of their truth" (1956, 132). Presumably, the "agreement" that governs linguistic usages in any given community of subjects extends also to the determination of experiential qualification, that is, to the determination of what will count as "*appropriate* experience" and what will not.[82] In any case, none of these determinations, and therefore no verified claim of knowledge, can be taken as infallible. All claims of knowledge are contingent, partial, and uncertain. To be sure, *if* something *is* known, it is true; nothing that is in fact known can be false. But any claim to know truly cannot itself be infallible: "the philosopher's ideal of certainty has no application"—which is just as well, since "security is sterile."[83] Yet, Ayer could not let the matter of truth claims

---

82. It may be remembered, however, that Ayer also suggested that decisions as to where the line between verified knowledge and mere opinion ought to be drawn are a matter of consensus but that the question of the standard by which any division at all *can* be made requires a different sort of answer (Ayer 1956, 34).

83. In carrying his point, Ayer referred to the aphoristic case of the Heraclitean philosopher, Cratylus of Athens, of whom it was recorded "that, having resolved never to make a statement of whose truth he could not be certain, he was in the end reduced simply to wagging his finger" (Ayer 1956, 52).

rest just there, in an insecure if fertile terrain of plausibilities, for the subject would still lack some definitive standard by which qualifications of "appropriate sense-experience" can be effected and, commensurately, by which verifications of claims can proceed. Accordingly, he argued further that, while there can be no infallible states of consciousness, and any claim of knowledge, no matter how well verified, must be treated as yet fallible, it would nonetheless be a mistake to conclude that "nothing is really certain." Rather we are given to understand that there are "a great many statements the truth of which we rightly do not doubt; and it is perfectly correct to say that they are certain." Thus, we "should not be bullied by the sceptic into renouncing an expression for which we have a legitimate use" (Ayer 1956, 52, 68, 22–23; also Ayer [1967] 1970, 127–28, 135–36; Ayer [1964a] 1970).

What is the sense of this conjunction of declarations? What is the sense of this proffered entitlement of the "legitimate use" of a linguistic expression, when the referential backing of that expression rests on an impossible typification of our statements of factual knowledge—namely, infallibility? For Ayer, the sense of it consisted in an effort to limit contingency and to escape what would otherwise be an infinite regress of doubt. If, he argued, "one holds that to know a proposition p to be true normally involves accepting it on the basis of some other true proposition q which strongly supports p, then it seems to be required that one should also know q to be true." With that, one accepts the radical skeptic's invitation to enter the unending spiral of a receding series of supportive propositions. But, as his phrasing "*seems* to be required" signals, Ayer declined the invitation on the proposed ground that, while there can be no claim of knowledge that is itself immune to error, there *are* propositions that are *incorrigible*; and just such propositions stop the regress. Such incorrigible propositions are most likely those that refer to the enunciating subject's "present thoughts and feelings or to the way things currently appear to him." In answer to the obvious objection that even these propositions may be false (see, e.g., Austin 1962a, 104–31),[84] Ayer conceded as much, saying only that in his view it ought to be the enunciating subject who is "the final authority with regard to their truth" (Ayer [1967] 1970, 145–46; Ayer [1964a] 1970, 119–23; Ayer 1956, 54–56, 67–68).

It is clear that Ayer arrived at this concluding position as a kind of resignation in "the best that we can do," as it were, because he could not devise a better alternative to the radical skeptic's "impeccable logic" and

---

84. Indeed, Austin held that "there is no kind of sentence which *as such* is surprising, or doubtful, or certain, or incorrigible, or true." Any sentence is always dependent "on the circumstances of particular cases" (1962a, 111).

"empty victory" (1956, 68). That he was quite aware of the ambiguity and finally the dilemma inherent in his argument is abundantly evidenced by the forthright manner in which he tried to navigate a course through the maze of obstacles. The ambivalence shows, for example, in his addressing the relation between one's sense-experiences, which "simply occur," and the quiddity of which they are sensory experiences. On the one hand, he rejected as being far too simple the "realistic" view of a world that is simply there, waiting "to be discovered and explained"; the putative distinction between "fact" and "theory" is not at all clearly drawn or drawable: "What counts for us as the world depends upon our conceptual system," and it is "at least conceivable that our conceptual system should be radically different," in which case "the facts would be different too." On the other hand, he did not opt for "the idealist mistake of concluding that nothing is true or false but thinking makes it so." The natural world is as it is: for example, the "stars pursued their courses before human beings ever began to think about them, and would have pursued the same courses even if no creatures with conceptual systems had ever come into existence" (Ayer [1962] 1970, 89–92; see also Ayer 1956, 27). Yet for all this, Ayer never succeeded in saying precisely what does constitute the relation of sense-experience to that which is experienced: if facticity "depends upon our conceptual system," but if that system is both fallible and mutable and perhaps "should be radically different," what can possibly constitute a standard by which to judge the "correctness" of that "conceptual system" and its contingent facticities? Notwithstanding that dilemma, Ayer could only propose that experiences enunciated by the experiencing subject, in incorrigible though possibly false propositions of what is, somehow comprise a criterion by which we may verify claims of knowledge. The possibility, indeed the likelihood, that any one or more of these individual, self-authorizing enunciators of their "simply existent" sense-experiences actually suffered a false consciousness was readily acknowledged. But as to a definitive ground from which such false consciousness (or false experience) could be recognized as such, a ground from which the experienced world could be taken as potentiality (and shown its absences) rather than as this or that selective congeries of uncorrectable propositions of what is, there was only silence.

The analytic approach championed somewhat differently by Russell and Ayer (among others) encountered severe criticism in the Anglo-American academy increasingly often after World War II.[85] The central thrust

85. For example, several objections to Russell's theory of descriptions were summarized by Strawson in an oft-cited paper published in 1950. Strawson ended his account with this programmatic sentence: "Neither Aristotelian nor Russellian rules give the exact logic of any expression of ordinary language; for ordinary language has no exact logic" (Strawson [1950] 1971, 27).

against an analytics conceived as the search for real or contextual definitions (as in Russell's denotational theory of meaning) and as the investigation of the syntactical properties of scientific language through applications of a formal-logical calculus of facts (as with Ayer) emerged from Wittgenstein's (1953) rejection of the "picture theory" of language—that is, from his attack on the notion of a basic isomorphism of structure between language and the world, wherein meanings are alleged to be the objects denoted. This new chapter in the "discovery of language"—which, in relation to Nietzsche's statement on language, cannot but seem anachronistic to us— will be examined below in section 5 of this chapter. But first let us return to the European "return to the object."

4. HEIDEGGER AND THE END OF PHILOSOPHY

It has been said that, today, we are all "existentialists," whether we choose to be or not. This is so, according to Löwith, not because of some "failure of nerve" on our part, or on the part of our predecessors, but because of a failure of belief: the death of God meant the death of "our belief in a divinely ordered universe in which man could feel himself at home" (Löwith [1950] 1966, 105). When the gods, or God, died, all basic ontology died with them, and no mere humanly contrived "social order" or "contract," whatever its hue or timber or texture, "can possibly make up for that lack of fundamental order in the universe." We have been left in the midst of an enormous absence: grounds recede into nothingness; boundaries that once divided and connected, arranging different from different and like with like, now vanish into a blur of equivocality; field and figure blink in and out of mutuality; centers decay into infinite dispersion; hard edges fade into shapeless vacuum. And each of us, caught up in that absence, must call into imagination the fluid scenery of a day when the "I am" predicates nothing. Before the failure of belief, we were secure in a two-fold conviction that "all that is" *is* and that this "*is*" is originally and finally the responsibility of an omniscient Summum Bonum, an omnipotent Unmoved Mover. What now, we ask, is responsible for "all that is?" Nothing? We find that we do "exist," do we not? In this absence of fundamental order, Löwith continued, "we have indeed 'to be,' or exist, in all those descriptive terms of sheer factuality, contingency, and absurdity that existentialism has brought to light. For how can one feel at home in an 'exploding' universe, the chance result of statistical probabilities?"[86] In such a place as that, and

---

86. Compare Jonas's discussion of existentialism as seen through the lens of his studies of gnosticism (1963, 320–40). Jonas there remarked that, when turning to those studies, he "found that the viewpoints, the optics as it were, which I had acquired in the school of Heidegger, enabled me to see aspects of gnostic thought that had been missed before. And I was increasingly struck by the familiarity of

among creatures whose highest certainty is that each is destined, in a destining about which it prefers not to think, to slip from being into nothingness—what there can "truth" be? And for what matter?

The fashion of "existentialism," once the profession of many good intellectuals, is itself now dead. In this age, all "-isms" are expressed through our common profligacy of consumption as rapidly as any other commodity. But the question of "existence"—it has often been referred to as Leibniz's question, though it is hardly his alone[87]—still rattles around in the cellar of our reflection: *Why is there anything at all, and not nothing?* Such is the dirge of our long funeral for divine providence. We ask: "What is the 'beingness' that remains?" "How came it 'to be,' and what is its sense?" Our interrogation is about more than the particular of this or that being— although the question of "*I am*" is never far from its spoken sound. Our interrogation is about the "beingness" of any and all beings: the *Being* of beings, the "*is*" of "it is this" or "it is that." And when we attempt to approach *that* question, the question of "the Being of beings," and weigh the significance of its aim, we notice the lack of discriminability between the interrogation of the interrogated and the interrogation of the interrogator. For, when we ask the question, "What is Being?" we already assert the very whatness we suppose to interrogate: we assert "*is*" in our very asking, "What is being?" And we cannot speak otherwise. As just this interrogator, we interrogate interrogation about the interrogated, which we ourselves are even as we interrogate.

In this century—close on the heels of Nietzsche's proclamation and

the seemingly utterly strange." Among the similarities between Heidegger's think-ing and categories of gnostic thought suggested by Jonas, one of the most striking pairs the Heideggerian *Geworfenheit* ("thrownness-into-the world") with "a standing phrase" from Mandaean literature—namely, that "life has been thrown into the world, light into darkness, the soul into the body" (Jonas 1963, 320, 334).

87. Löwith's nomination of Pascal as the true "forerunner" of modern existen-tialism—"It is my thesis here that we 'exist' (in the sense of existentialism) because we are lost in the universe of modern natural science," a condition that "was clearly realized by Pascal, but not by Kierkegaard and his followers"—is highly relevant as background to the "Leibnizian question" (see Löwith [1950] 1966, 102–3). In one of his memorable fragments, Pascal expressed the frightful awe-someness of being "cast into the infinite immensity of spaces of which I am ignorant and which know me not"; contemplating that "thrownness" (to insert Heidegger's term), Pascal continued: "I am frightened, and shocked at being here rather than there; for there is no reason why here rather than there, why now rather than then. Who has put me here? By whose order and direction have this place and time been allotted to me?" (Pascal [1670] 1960, 116). And in another fragment: "The everlasting silence of these infinite spaces frightens me" (Pascal [1670] 1960, 392).

already after Husserl's failed effort to go "back to the things themselves"—
the most famous "thinker" of the question of Being and the question of
Truth has been Martin Heidegger (1889–1976). A student of Carl Braig (a
theologian and professor of dogmatics at Freiburg University) and Heinrich
Rickert, and later of Husserl's phenomenology,[88] Heidegger was soon expected to become the continuator of the Husserlian project (he served as
Husserl's assistant during the early 1920s). Instead, with publication of the
first half of *Being and Time* in 1927,[89] Heidegger announced both his
fundamental disagreements with Husserl's transcendental phenomenology
and the beginning of his own different way—though not without granting
an indebtedness to his mentor's guidance (see, e.g., Heidegger [1927] 1962,
38 n. 5). Among the disputations, Husserl's failure to take his inquiry to the
fundamental tension of the beingness of beings meant, by Heidegger's
thinking, that the Husserlian notion of "constitution" was ambiguous at
best. Indeed, Husserl's attempt to formulate a phenomenology of constitution was destined to remain incomplete, and incompletable, inasmuch as
his approach did not appreciate that thematizing is necessarily and inevitably caught in the tension between disclosing and concealing. A thematizing
purports to be a constitutive revealing of "what is"; but insofar as a
revealing *does* reveal, it also cannot avoid concealing. As Gadamer later
put it, with respect to the meaning of a word (any word): "The 'essence'
of the word does not lie in being totally expressed, but rather in what is
left unsaid, as we see especially in speechlessness and remaining silent"
(Gadamer [1967] 1976, 234). Husserl neglected the basic and inescapable
mutuality of hiddenness and disclosure. In any revealing or disclosing of a
being from its hiddenness, that which makes this or any other revealing
possible in the first place is in concealment:

> What is it that by its very essence is *necessarily* the theme whenever
> we exhibit something *explicitly*? Manifestly, it is something that prox-

88. See Heidegger's (1963) brief account of his "way to phenomenology."

89. *Being and Time* was never completed as such. According to the original plan,
the treatise was to have two parts, each consisting of three divisions (see Heidegger
[1927] 1962, 63–64). Only the first two divisions of part 1 were published in
1927: "the preparatory fundamental analysis of *Dasein*" and "*Dasein* and temporality." Later essays, such as "Time and Being" (1968), dealt with many of the
questions that had been scheduled for treatment in the unfinished divisions of
Being and Time, but these essays cannot be regarded as late-arriving chapters of
that book. In his preface to the seventh edition, Heidegger noted that the designation "First Half," borne in the title of all previous editions, "has now been
deleted. After a quarter of a century, the second half could no longer be added
unless the first were to be presented anew." (That sentence does not mean,
however, that Heidegger had turned away from the investigation of *Being and
Time*, only that he had found much of his analysis to be inadequate to his task.)

imally and for the most part does *not* show itself at all: it is something that lies *hidden*, in contrast to that which proximally and for the most part does show itself; but at the same time it is something that belongs to what thus shows itself, and it belongs to it so essentially as to constitute its meaning and its ground. (Heidegger [1927] 1962, 59)

Knowing a disclosed being never escapes its condition in the concealed.

Heidegger's writings are laden with intricacies of meaning that often seem to be familiar and foreign simultaneously. More than once, his works have been held up to ridicule as prime instances of philosophical jabberwocky, especially by some proponents of logical empiricism and ordinary-language analysis. Of course, a reader may be expected to exert some effort in order to read a complex work intelligently—even (or especially) if then only to criticize the work as "mistaken" or "misbegotten"; and the whole of Heidegger's work demands considerable effort, including a willingness to travel his "way" with him, tentatively and experimentally.[90] Without such effort, it is always easy to dismiss Heidegger as an obscurant, etymologizing "existentialist" who hid behind a prattle of idiosyncratic words

90. A remark by Kolakowski is fitting: "Carnap made a detailed analysis of Heidegger's statement, 'Nothing nihilates,' in order to show that it is purely verbal, devoid of empirical meaning. (Incidentally, this is the only sentence from existentialist philosophy the majority of contemporary positivists appear familiar with)" (Kolakowski [1966] 1969, 181–82). Kolakowski's reference is to Carnap's essay "The Elimination of Metaphysics through Logical Analysis of Language" (1932), in which Carnap fixed on a particular passage from Heidegger's *What Is Metaphysics?* (1929). Heidegger's reply, to the extent that he made a specific reply, can be found in part in lectures given in 1935 on "the question concerning the thing":

> With the help of mathematical methods people attempt to calculate the system of connectives between assertions. For this reason, we also call [symbolic] logic "mathematical logic." It proposes to itself a possible and justified task. However, what symbolic logic achieves is anything but logic, i.e., a reflection upon λόγος. Mathematical logic is not even logic of mathematics in the sense of defining mathematical thought and mathematical truth, nor could it do so at all. Symbolic logic is itself only a mathematics applied to propositions and propositional forms. All mathematical logic and symbolic logic necessarily place themselves outside of every sphere of logic, because, for their very own purpose, they must apply λόγος, the assertion, as a mere combination of representations, i.e., basically inadequately. The presumptuousness of logistic in posing as the scientific logic of all sciences collapses as soon as one realizes how limited and thoughtless its premises are. (Heidegger [1962a] 1967, 156)

Somewhat later, in speaking of the dominance of a calculative-representational knowledge, Heidegger observed that "the elevation of logistics to the rank of true logic" is the "sign of the degradation of thinking" (Heidegger [1961d] 1973, 80).

and phrases.[91] No doubt a part of the difficulty of Heidegger's work does have to do with what seems to have been a penchant for devising strange terms and locutions.[92] Throughout the later as well as the early writings, we confront numerous demonstrations of the great expansiveness of German vocabulary by means of word-compoundings, many of which are best rendered in English by means of long hyphenations. But, although we may be reminded of Mark Twain's (1880) caustically humorous commentary "The Awful German Language," we must not be too quick to disparage Heidegger's devisings and etymologizings as emblems of a will to obscure. His cultivations of new, or "newly reawakened," meanings in commonly uttered words, his etymological bridges between Greek and German, his compoundings and hyphenated separations—all were part of a calculated response to the historicity of words.[93] It was an effort not to "surmount" the historical embeddedness of words but rather to bring to view the subtle and not-so-subtle changes of meanings that have occurred, and, by the same stroke, to try to clear a space within that historicity in order that he could maximally speak *his* meanings without interference from unwanted semantic inheritances.[94] Heidegger's project was meant to challenge the received

91. Even to say that Heidegger was an "existentialist" is a serious misassignment, if by "existentialist" one also means without much additional qualification Jaspers or Sartre; the differences outweigh the similarities. See Heidegger's own comments in his "Letter on Humanism" (1947; also see Heidegger [1954d] 1975, 81–82).

92. Heidegger's work is complex also because of the relations that establish the differences of his later from his earlier writings—differences that are collectively marked, in many accounts of his work, by his so-called turning during the 1930s. (The reference is not to Heidegger's terrible "error," as it has been called, of defending National Socialism but to alterations in his "thinking of Being.") I cannot see that this "turning" was in any way a radical change in his project; although he concluded that his earlier thinking had been fundamentally inadequate and attempted corrections of his course, the basic "path" or "way" of his project remained the same. In any case, I shall not follow the chronological ordering of his writings (either in terms of dates of composition or in terms of dates of publication, which were often separated by decades) but shall instead attempt to read his early works, in particular *Being and Time*, in light of the later essays and lectures.

93. Schöfer (1962) has made an extended study of several of Heidegger's word constructions (especially his "substantivization of verbs" and predilection for gerunds) and syntactical characteristics.

94. With regard to such effort, Heidegger reckoned that the greatest difficulty through which his task of thinking had to pass "lies in language. Our Western languages are languages of metaphysical thinking, each in its own way. It must remain an open question whether the nature of Western languages is in itself marked with the exclusive brand of metaphysics, . . . or whether these languages

tradition, to "overcome" metaphysics (see, e.g., Heidegger [1954a] 1973), to question doctrines and meanings of terms or concepts—especially each one that seems as if it "had fallen from heaven as a truth as clear as daylight" (Heidegger [1954b] 1977, 6).

Heidegger judged that Descartes' *Meditations* constituted "a decisive beginning" of modern metaphysics, "the metaphysics upon which the modern period rests" (Heidegger [1961b] 1973, 30). Among other distinctive features of this departure, the priority assigned to the "subject"—the "knowing subject" of an epistemological quest for apodicticity—has figured prominently in the heritage of the *cogito ergo sum*. But, Heidegger also reminded, the *Meditations* had as their chief matter and goal a *First Philosophy*, that is, an ontology of the *sum*. The proclamation of the *cogito* was not merely "I think clear and distinct ideas" or "I think truthfully." It was instead "I think, therefore (it must be that) I *am*." Epistemology presupposes ontology. True, Kant had convincingly refuted, by his own report, "the ontological argument," that is, the apriorist argument of reasoning from "definition" to "thing defined." But this argument was not the whole of ontology (it did not encompass, for example, Spinoza's or Leibniz's ontological arguments); and, while Heidegger was appreciative of Kant's effort to treat "the ontological question" within the context of the temporality of the beingness of human beings (see especially Heidegger [1951a] 1962 and Heidegger [1962a] 1967), he could not accept Kant's foreshortened answer to the question of the groundedness of that being.[95] From Heidegger's point of view, the "modern form of ontology is transcendental philosophy which becomes epistemology"—that is, a doctrine of "truth as the certainty of guaranteed representation," which is, as well, "the title for the increasing, essential powerlessness of modern metaphysics to know its own essence and the ground of that essence" (Heidegger [1954a] 1973,

---

offer other possibilities of utterance" (Heidegger [1957] 1969, 73). But throughout his work, and nowhere more pointedly than in his 1955 lecture entitled "What Is That, That Which is Called Philosophy?" ([1956] 1958), Heidegger reserved an exceptional place for the Greek language of old, the language of Anaximander, Heraclitus, Parmenides: this language, *if* we hear it "with a Greek ear," is no "mere language" like those to which we are accustomed today; for it alone is *logos*, and what it says is also "that which it is called." Next to this Greek language, only his German was held in high regard for its possibilities (indeed, a characteristic *Kultur*-centrism—though never anything like a crass irredentism or jingoism—undulates through much of Heidegger's published writing).

95. For an extended account of Heidegger's relation to Kant and the matter of temporality, see Sherover 1971. This seems to be one of the few instances of a Heidegger study that approaches his critical construction of Kant as other than a "bad reading" of Kant.

88–89; Heidegger [1927] 1962, 30–31, 252–54; Heidegger [1962a] 1967, 98–106).

The matter of the *sum*, the question of Being, has been locked in oblivion, and it has been locked there by the course of metaphysics itself.

> Do we in our time have an answer to the question of what we really mean by the word "being"? Not at all. So it is fitting that we should raise anew *the question of the meaning of Being*. But are we nowadays even perplexed at our inability to understand the expression "Being"? Not at all. So first of all we must reawaken an understanding for the meaning of this question. (Heidegger [1927] 1962, 19)

We must, Heidegger concluded, "work out the question of the meaning of *Being*." And we must "do so concretely." This task requires first of all a "reopening" of questions that have long been quiescent (Heidegger [1962a] 1967, 49–50); and it requires a "de-struction," or an "unbuilding," of the history of metaphysics, that is, "metaphysics as history of Being." Already before Descartes, metaphysics had confused "the ontological difference" (Heidegger's name for the difference between beings and the *Being* of beings) with Plato's distinction between the *existentia* ("thatness") and the *essentia* ("whatness"). In the tradition of this latter distinction, we are told that "*Essentia* answers the question *ti estin*: what is (a being)? *Existentia* says of a being *hoti estin*: that it is"; and between the "that it is" and the "what is" there stands the posit of an asymmetry such that "essential being" is purportedly the "first cause" or "first principle" of "existential beings" and therein is conceived as the *summum ens*, "the highest of beings" (Heidegger [1961b] 1973, 4). Yet, inasmuch as neither the *ti estin* nor the *hoti estin* asks the question of the *Being* of beings, Being is maintained as the *oblivion* of Being. Consider, for example, the suggestion that we try to grasp this long-assumed distinction between "whatness" and "thatness" by investigating "the common element that determines what is divided."

> What is it that still remains as "—is" if we disregard the what and the that? But if this search for what is most general leads to emptiness, must whatness be grasped as a kind of thatness or, on the contrary, must the latter be grasped as a degeneration of the former? Even if this were successful, the question about the origin of the distinction would still remain. Does it come from Being itself? What "is" Being? How does the coming of the distinction, its origin, result from Being? Or is this distinction merely attributed to Being? If so, by what kind of thinking and by what right? How is Being given to such *attribution* for such attribution? (Heidegger [1961b] 1973, 3)

Heidegger concluded that if we think through those questions "even roughly," we find that the distinction between *essentia* and *existentia*, which purportedly *"stands for all metaphysics,"* is indeed groundless insofar as "metaphysics simply tries again and again to define the limits of what is divided, and comes up with numbering the manners of possibility and the kinds of actuality which float away into vagueness, together with the difference in which they are already placed." Insofar as metaphysics itself tries to account for its own essence by means of the distinction between the what and the that, and seeks the ground of its essence therein,

> it can never of itself come to a knowledge of this distinction. It would have to be previously and as such approached by Being which has entered this distinction. But Being refuses this approach, and thus alone makes possible the essential beginning of metaphysics—in the manner of the preparation and development of this distinction. The origin of the distinction of *essentia* and *existentia*, far more so the origin of Being thus divided, remains concealed, expressed in the Greek manner: forgotten. (Heidegger [1961b] 1973, 3)[96]

96. Apropos of the foregoing, Heidegger remarked on the relationship of Aristotle to Plato that it is
> established even today by explanations, variously nuanced, as follows: In contradistinction to Plato, who held that the "Ideas" were "what is truly existent," allowed for individual beings only as seeming beings (*eidelon* ["imaginary beings"; see below]), and demoted them to that which really ought not to be called beings (*me on*), Aristotle took the free-floating "Ideas" back from their "supraheavenly place" and planted them in actual things. In doing this, Aristotle thought the "Ideas" as "forms" and conceived these "forms" as "energies" and "forces" housed in beings.
> This curious explanation, inevitable in the progression of metaphysics, of the relationship between Plato and Aristotle with regard to the thinking of the Being of beings calls forth two questions: How should Aristotle be able at all to bring the Ideas down to actual beings if he has not in advance conceived the individual actual being *as* that which truly presences? But how should he reach the concept of the individual real being's presence, if he doesn't previously think tne Being of beings in the sense of the primordially decided essence of Being in terms of presencing in unconcealment? (Heidegger [1961b] 1973, 9).

I shall return to Heidegger's notion of "presencing in unconcealment" and its relation to a truth concept later. (Regarding those "seeming beings": the *eidola* were "images" of the mind or "phantoms." Democritus had postulated *eidola* as groupings of very tiny particles given off by substantial bodies and impressive on the human senses—a notion not so far removed from later formulations of "sensations" and "sensibilia.")

Along with this concealment, "man" is concealed in his own metaphysically constructed world. In his self-representation metaphysically, "man" is thought as a creature endowed with distinct faculties and a compound nature that sets off his essential difference: "man" is *animal rationale*, the unique combination of nonsensuous sensuousness. Thus restricted within metaphysical representation, "man is caught in the difference of beings and Being which he never experiences." As a consequence of this captivity in "the emptiness of the abandonment of Being," modern "man" everywhere increasingly partakes of the uniformity of beings. Finding only the metaphysically constructed world in his representations of the real, which are characterized by "the uniformity of calculable reckoning," modern man has been destined to "enter monotonous uniformity in order to keep up with what is real." The attitude of awe and ecstasy (*ekstasis*, from *ex* + *histanai*: "to stand out") has been swept under the leveling force of an unchallenged calculative-representational thinking. As Heidegger put it in one of his best-known sentences: "A man without a uni-form today already gives the impression of being something unreal which no longer belongs" (Heidegger [1954a] 1973, 87, 108).[97]

As these preceding passages suggest, Heidegger developed a particular critique of the technologizing modern age and its supporting metaphysics around the notion of the oblivion of Being. Before pursuing that critique further, it is advisable to consider the meaning of his argument concerning "the end of philosophy" and the attendant need to "overcome" metaphysics. To begin with, clarification of the phrase, "end of philosophy," is called for. The simple word, "philosophy," signifies not an infinitely open region of discourse among all who ever have had, and all who ever will have, a "love of wisdom"; it does not signify an eternal necessity of human thinking that rained down from the heavens one day and thereby created in us a great thirst: it signifies simply a historically determinant "tradition" of thinking, a path of thinking, which, in the conditions of its origin and its development of regions of speaking, was differentiated in just so many ways—and was differentiable in finite ways. Hence, to say "the end of philosophy" signifies only the *completion*, the final working out and

---

97. The essay in which that sentence appears, though not published until 1954, was composed as a series of notes during the period 1936 to 1946, a time when military and militaristic uniforms were ubiquitous in Germany. It is clear, however, that Heidegger meant "uni-form" in much more than this vernacular sense of "uniform": not only the uniformity of military attire, the "businessman's suit," and the "lady's dress" but also the uniformity of thinking, acting, being. It was, moreover, a diagnosis of uniformity that treated the cleavages of domination as secondary.

through, of the "prefigured possibilities" of philosophy.[98] Such was the meaning of Heidegger's "talk about the end of philosophy": not a "mere stopping" or cessation, still less the "perfection" of metaphysics (since neither the criterion that "would permit us to evaluate the perfection of an epoch of metaphysics," relative to another epoch, nor the "right to this kind of evaluation" is available), but completion in the sense of "the gathering into the most extreme possibilities." According to the Heideggerian reading, the site and date of this completion can be found in the Nietzschean metaphysics—that is, in the reversal of Platonic metaphysics that nonetheless preserved the fundamental absence in that metaphysics.[99]

But what, then, in this "age of completed metaphysics," has become of philosophy? What does it speak? It has become a "philosophical anthropology," and it speaks as an "empirical science of man": "anthropology" as the science of *anthropos* and as "human studies."[100] The process whereby the sciences separate from philosophy and seek to establish their independence may appear to be the "dissolution of philosophy," yet on closer inspection we can see that "in truth" it is nothing other than "the legitimate completion of philosophy"—a process in which philosophy "turns into the empirical science of man, of all of what can become the experiential object of his technology for man, the technology by which he establishes himself in the world by working on it in the manifold modes of making and shaping." In the self-consciousness of this empirical science, interest is

98. This was one instance in which Heidegger cautioned us not to be *misled* by the etymology of a word: that "philosophy" literally means "love of wisdom" does not imply that philosophy as a historically conditioned tradition of thinking has a monopoly on wisdom, or even that it speaks wisely at all.

99. In at least one passage, however, Heidegger ([1964] 1972, 57) averred that with "the reversal of metaphysics . . . accomplished by Karl Marx, the most extreme possibility of philosophy" had already been obtained.

100. Habermas has faulted Heidegger's critical account of the history of metaphysics for having allegedly failed to recognize "that since Descartes there has run alongside the line of calculative-manipulative [*verfügbar machenden*] thinking a line of meaning, understanding, receptive thought [*Vernehmenden*]" (Habermas [1971f] 1977, 162). However, it seems to be clear enough that Heidegger neither failed to recognize this "other" line of thinking nor—what is more important— exempted it from his criticism. That he did not single out this "other" line for exceptional treatment was due rather to a conviction that such distinctions as might be observed were only superficial and that the "humanistic" or "meaning-understanding-interpretive" thinking was fundamentally as calculative-representational and manipulative as the most blatantly naturalistic versions of positivism. In my opinion, Heidegger was correct in this conviction: Freud's "interpretive" theoretic is only the most obvious example.

directed to a notion of "theory" that has come to mean "supposition of the categories which are allowed only a cybernetical function, but denied any ontological meaning." What now passes as "theoretical" thinking is exclusively a "representational-calculative thinking." In short, the end of philosophy, its legitimate completion in its own independence-seeking progeny, "proves to be the triumph of the manipulable arrangement of a scientific-technological world and of the social order proper to this world." Even so, Heidegger argued, "the sciences still speak about the Being of beings in the unavoidable suppositions of their regional categories. They just don't say so" (Heidegger [1964] 1972, 56–59; Heidegger [1953] 1959, 60; Heidegger [1954a] 1973, 95–96, 99; Heidegger [1961c] 1973, 70; see also Heidegger [1952b] 1977, 132–33; Heidegger [1947] 1962).

Although the end of philosophy means the completion of philosophy, it does not signify also "the complete realization of all the possibilities in which the thinking of philosophy was posited." Philosophy was *one* historical tradition of thinking, and it was itself posited by thinking. There does remain for our attention, then, a task of thinking: this remaining task of thinking calls forth the difference between *calculative* thinking, in which "we always reckon with the conditions that are given" and "take them into account with the calculated intention of their serving specific purposes," and *meditative* thinking, which "contemplates the meaning which reigns in everything that is." Each kind of thinking is "justified and needed in its own way"; yet, despite that justification and especially that need, "man today is in *flight from thinking*," that is, from meditative thinking. Thus, according to Heidegger, the task for thinking that remains after the completion of philosophy—a "preparatory" rather than a "founding" task— "is that of freeing itself and keeping itself free for what is to be thought in order to receive its determination from that." But this task of and for thinking cannot rely on the now-dominant representational-calculative thinking, with its "operational and model character," for this remaining task is "accessible neither to philosophy as metaphysics," including epistemology, "nor, and even less so, to the sciences stemming from philosophy." If we are to undertake this task of and for thinking, we must *overcome* metaphysics. We must undo our received tradition of thinking, free ourselves of the grip that moves us away from meditative thinking, and reopen our questioning to the priority of a thinking that can manifest the relation between "man" and Being.

> When tradition . . . becomes master, it does so in such a way that what it "transmits" is made so inaccessible, proximally and for the most part, that it rather becomes concealed. Tradition takes what has come down to us and delivers it over to self-evidence; it blocks our access to those primordial "sources" from which the categories

and concepts handed down to us have been in part quite genuinely drawn. Indeed it makes us forget that they have had such an origin, and makes us suppose that the necessity of going back to these sources is something which we need not even understand. (Heidegger [1927] 1962, 43)

In the modern epoch the historicality of the "being-there," the presencing and opening of human being, has been "thoroughly uprooted by tradition," and in consequence a veil has been drawn around "the fact" that the "being-there" of human beingness "has no ground of its own to stand on," though it does not appreciate that fact. If we are to think with Descartes in his metaphor of the tree—namely, that "the whole of philosophy is like a tree: the roots are metaphysics, the trunk is physics, and the branches that issue from the trunk are all the other sciences"[101]—then should we not ask what is the "whatness" in which those "roots of the tree of philosophy have their hold" and find their vital fluid? Accordingly, Heidegger proposed again and again that we must strive in preparatory effort to overcome the tradition of metaphysics and its deliveredness as self-evidence. This repeated urging to accomplish an overcoming was meant by Heidegger not in the sense of a mere banishment or a turning away from metaphysics, however. Rather the overcoming must be a "restoring surmounting," an overcoming that over-comes and restores; it would be, he said, "similar to what happens when, in the human realm, one gets over grief or pain," that is, when one "gets the better of" pain or grief.[102] Thus, Heidegger's exercise in the destruction (unbuilding) of "metaphysics as history of Being" was conceived in terms of an overcoming by which thinking would be redeemed from the end of philosophy and put "in transition to another beginning" (Heidegger [1964] 1972, 59–60; Heidegger [1959a] 1966, 45–46; Heidegger [1969] 1972, 35; Heidegger [1927] 1962, 41–49; Heidegger [1962b] 1977, 39; Heidegger [1954a] 1973, 95–96).

In the Heideggerian view, the need for overcoming was and is urgent.

101. This common metaphor was enlisted by Descartes in a letter to Picot, the translator of his *Principia Philosophiae* (see Heidegger [1949] 1956, 207).

102. Heidegger's notion of "overcoming" is suggestive of "sublation," although the "elevative" process is to be understood only as a matter of possibility, not of necessity (see, e.g., Heidegger [1957] 1969, 49). By way of partial contrast, "overcoming" calls to mind Hegel's discussion of the error of supposing that that which was but is no longer "true" was in fact a naughtness all along: the "result of an untrue mode of knowledge must not be allowed to run away into an empty nothing, but must necessarily be grasped as the nothing *of that from which it results*—a result which contains what was true in the preceding knowledge" (Hegel [1807] 1977, 55–56).

Modern technology has taken to the point of great danger the tradition that, from the time of Plato, has represented beings as already given, distinctly constituted entities. We are immersed in an idolatrization of things—things made by us to work for us. Not that we could ever be uninvolved in the making of things. But the *Being* of beings is not what is made; the Being of beings is not a made thing, although it *has* been silenced to us by our making, and we no longer hear the claim of Being in our makings. Being is the ultimate Whatness within which any and all things that we do make, including the idolatry of technical things, are brought forth. It is not Being we make; we make "things" within the possibilities of making, that is, within the whole of all possibilities that is Being. Husserl had asked whether we can experience how Being comes to presence today by equating Being with technology. "Obviously not," Heidegger reaffirmed, because "every analysis of the situation" falls short of the mark inasmuch as the "totality of the world of technology is interpreted in advance in terms of man, as being of man's making" (Heidegger [1957] 1969, 34). Even when we approach technology in its "broadest sense and in its manifold manifestations," technology is still only "the plan which man projects, the plan which finally compels man to decide whether he will become the servant of his plan or will remain its master." From that way of thinking the totality of the world of technology, everything is reduced to "man, the maker"—"and at best we come to the point of calling for an ethics of the technological world." In that thinking we merely "confirm our own opinion that technology is of man's making alone"—an opinion that has deafened us to "the claim of Being that speaks in the essence of technology." Rather than persisting in the tenacious conception that calculates the meaning of "technology as something purely technical, that is, in terms of man and his machines," Heidegger pleaded, we ought to "listen to the claim placed in our age not only upon man, but also upon all beings, nature and history, with regard to their Being." If we listen to the claim of Being, we will hear that the essence of technology is itself nothing technical (see also Heidegger [1953] 1959, 62–63; Heidegger [1952a] 1977; Heidegger [1954b] 1977).

In order to grasp better the placing of Heidegger's critique of technology, consider the following passage:

> The unnoticeable law of the earth preserves the earth in the sufficiency of the emerging and perishing of all things in the allotted sphere of the possible which everything follows, and yet nothing knows. The birch tree never oversteps its possibility. The colony of bees dwells in its possibility. It is first the will which arranges itself everywhere in technology that devours the earth in the exhaustion and consumption and change of what is artificial. Technology drives the earth beyond the developed sphere of its possibility into such

things which are no longer a possibility and are thus the impossible. The fact that technological plans and measures succeed a great deal in inventions and novelties, piling upon each other, by no means yields the proof that the conquests of technology ever make the impossible possible. (Heidegger [1954a] 1973, 109)[103]

The statement that comes to us adumbratively in this passage turns on a contrast between a "letting be," or a "letting presence" of earth in the bounds of its own possibilities, and a human willing that "devours the earth," puts forth "what is artificial," and provokes the possible to yield the impossible. It is a contrast between a "letting-be" that is open to reception of "the blessing of the earth"—a nonwillful willingness "to become at home in the law of this reception in order to shepherd the mystery of Being and watch over the inviolability of the possible"—and the willfulness of a will "just to use the earth." It is a contrast between "a thinking that is not a willing" but a preparing for hearing the claim of Being—a "mood" of *Gelassenheit* (conventionally, "calmness" or "self-possession," but more especially for Heidegger, "releasement")—and a thinking that is a willing, a will to will, a will to sub-ject every thing (ob-ject) to its own innermost domination.

The tradition of metaphysics, with its central posit of the priority of "subject" conceived as the active, willing, all-energizing principle of "is" (i.e., "*I* think; *therefore, I* must be"), has been consummated in the modern epoch as *Technik*—that is, as the technicity of a willfulness to subdue the earth and all its beings. In this "darkening of the world," a sense of technical achievement, as well as a technological pride of proof in those achievements, cannot be denied (over and over, Heidegger insisted that he was not merely espousing an "antitechnology" manifesto, which would be absurd). Nonetheless, such achievements as can be paraded ostensively before us have besotted this willing "subject" into a forgetfulness of Being: the "made thing" is indeed "made by man"; and yet the *Being* of beings, within which *all possibilities* of being are "presenced," is neither a "thing" nor "made." Even the Nietzschean "revaluation of values"—proposed in critique of and in answer to the nothingness of all previous (i.e., devalued) values—does not escape this dangerous forgetfulness, according to Heidegger, for the notion of "value" itself is a characteristic positing by the very "subject" who wills to will in the oblivion of Being (Heidegger [1954a] 1973, 109; Heidegger [1959a] 1966, 60, et passim; Heidegger [1952a] 1977).

Once again, then, we must return to the question—no longer "Leib-

103. See also Heidegger's contrasting of "earth" and "world" in his essay "The Origin of the Work of Art" (Heidegger [1950a] 1971, esp. 39–78).

niz's question" in any way whatsoever (see Heidegger [1949] 1956, 219–21; Heidegger [1929] 1949)—"Why is there any being at all, and not rather Nothing?"

But what means this "Nothing?" It is a strangeness to us, we who "stand in the very twilight of the most monstrous transformation our planet has ever undergone, the twilight of that epoch in which earth itself hangs suspended" (Heidegger [1950b] 1975, 17). Our being-there-in-the-world is determined by science, and science does not take nothingness seriously (see Heidegger [1929] 1949, passim). Science seeks to probe "the thing itself," the entity "as it is"; and science claims its "objectivity" of attitude and pronouncement on the basis of its self-submission to "the things themselves." Yet in carrying out this activity of science, and especially when most stringently defending the claim of this view, the scientist reveals an orientation to what can in no sense be a "thing" or an "entity"—that is, an orientation to nothingness. For the scientist is wont to say: "I as scientist explore entities and only entities; beyond that, nothing." But, what *is* this nothing? A meaningless question. To say "nothing" is to say "*not is*" or "to nothing," to make nothing, no entity; but if "no entity," no kind of thing, then science must be mute in its presence and in the silence of its possibility. Even so, we must remember, the silence of the not-said always is figured in the presence of the said, including the said of science. There is, however, a "mood" or an "attunement" of being-there-in-the-world that does bring forth the nothing, even though we cannot think the nothing as an object—namely, the anxiety of the what-is slipping into the nothing. And it is just such attunement that reveals things as things and not as nothing.[104] What *is* so revealed is that nothingness is at the basis from which there *is* anything at all (i.e., the Being of beings). But of this, modern science says nothing. Nothingness—and therefore the awe and the amazement of *there being* anything at all—cannot be found on the tongue of science. They are repelled by calculation and uniformalization and leveling. They are rather the matter of poetry, of the rigorous thinking of "poetics" (see, e.g., Heidegger [1929] 1949; Heidegger [1936] 1949; Heidegger [1950c] 1971).

In the modern epoch, "man" experiences profound homelessness because, in the determination of this world by modern science and tech-

104. "Attunement" translates *Stimmung* and *Bestimmung*, the root of which (*Stimme*) is "voice"; no doubt Heidegger intended his usage to elicit associations with *Einstimmigkeit* ("unanimity" or "consonance") and *einstimmig* ("unanimous"; literally, "of one voice"), as well as the more common meanings of *Bestimmung* ("determination," "ascertainment," "destination"). This case exemplifies the many cases in which Heidegger called upon etymological connections and allusions in his German, which for the most part are lost in English translation.

nology, "man" strives "to be at home" solely among entities, among things manifested by technology. Whereas *technē*, as understood by the early Greeks, belonged to *poiēsis*—that is, to a bringing-forth or revealing of "whatever does not bring itself forth and does not yet lie here before us"— in modern technology the revealing that holds sway is different. Certainly it too is a bringing-forth. But it is not *poiēsis*. "The revealing that rules in modern technology is a challenging [*Herausfordern*], which puts to nature the unreasonable demand that it supply energy that can be extracted and stored as such." It "*sets* upon nature," challenges nature to yield to its categorical demand, extracts nature's energies and puts them "on call" in a stockpile of readiness, as transformable, interchangeable means to be called upon for distribution. Thus, the bringing-forth of modern technology is a bringing forth of "that which comes to stand forth" as being on call, as being ready in the ordering of readiness, and as being uniform in the uniformity of "resources." In modern technology, entities come to presence as a "standing-reserve" (*Bestand*), the chief characteristic of which is "disposableness"; the entity is manifested precisely in the manner of, and only insofar as it is, a "being-ready" or a "being-disposable-for . . . "; such is its manifest being-present-in-the-world. This Heideggerian notion of being-a-standing-reserve was meant not simply as another name for "objectification." With the subject-object dichotomy, wherein "object" stands over against the priority of "subject," objectified entities are still extant entities with a quasi-independence of their own. By contrast, when the objectified entity is further transformed into the standing-reserve, its existence is transformed into that which is mastered as a disposable instrument for doing— for doing "something." In the sway of modern technology, Heidegger insisted, "everywhere everything is ordered to stand by, to be immediately at hand, indeed to stand there just so that it may be on call for a further ordering." It is "man," of course, who operates technologically, and who drives technology forward. And in so doing, "man" is captured in the sway of technology to the extent of being ordered in the ordering, too—though *not* to the extent of being converted wholly to the standing-reserve. For it is only

> to the extent that man for his part is already challenged to exploit the energies of nature [that] this ordering revealing [can] happen. If man is challenged, ordered, to do this, then does not man himself belong even more originally than nature within the standing-reserve? The current talk about human resources, about the supply of patients for a clinic [for example], gives evidence of this. The forester who, in the wood, measures the felled timber and to all appearances walks the same forest path in the same way as did his grandfather is today commanded by profit-making in the lumber industry, whether he

knows it or not. He is made subordinate to the orderability of cellulose, which for its part is challenged forth by the need for paper, which is then delivered to newspapers and illustrated magazines. The latter, in their turn, set public opinion to swallowing what is printed, so that a set configuration of opinion becomes available on demand. Yet precisely because man is challenged more originally than are the energies of nature, i.e., into the process of ordering, he never is transformed into mere standing-reserve. Since man drives technology forward, he takes part in ordering as a way of revealing. But the unconcealment itself, within which ordering unfolds, is never a human handiwork, any more than is the realm through which man is already passing every time he as a subject relates to an object. (Heidegger [1954b] 1977, 18)

Thus, according to Heidegger, even while "man" participates in and furthers the standing-reserve, and is profoundly affected by it, "man" is not converted to standing-reserve.[105] Nor is this state of affairs, this condition of modern technology whereby all things are rendered as disposables-standing-ready, merely the result of human whim or fancy or careless making. It is "never a human handiwork"—so Heidegger argued (Heidegger [1954b] 1977, 13–14, 17–18).

Never a human handiwork: a rather startling statement, to be sure; and in the face of it we may be excused for asking, Of what provenience, then, is this condition of modern technology in which we stand? Whence comes this "challenging" in which "man is challenged more originally than are the energies of nature," and in which entities are brought forth merely as standing-reserve, but which is not a human making? According to the Heideggerian answer, it originates as a mode of Being—a particular mode of Being which Heidegger named as "Enframing" (Gestell, or Ge-stell). "Enframing" is neither a thing nor an entity nor a world view or a conception of reality.[106] Nor is it a process resulting from human making within the sphere of technological activity; it is prior to all things and indeed to the activity of making, which it challenges forth. Enframing is one of the possible modes of Being's "coming to presence"—the mode in which Being manifests in the modern world of technology. Its "essence," that is to say,

---

105. In a later passage in the same essay, however, Heidegger spoke of the possibility of "a precipitous fall," a point at which "[man] himself will have to be taken as standing-reserve" (Heidegger [1954b] 1977, 26).

106. "That the world becomes picture is one and the same event with the event of man's becoming subiectum in the midst of that which is" (Heidegger [1952b] 1977, 132).

its "enduring as presence," consists in "the gathering together of that setting-upon which sets upon man," and which "challenges him forth," to manifest "the real, in the mode of ordering, as standing-reserve." In other words, "Enframing" means the prior that comprises the possibility and the way of the real coming into presence just so—namely, as entities that are merely disposable readiness in standing-reserve. As a particular way of revealing, Enframing belongs to the "destining of revealing," which always holds "complete sway over man." But to say that each and every way of revealing, each and every mode of the coming to presence of Being, is a "destining" (*Geschick*) does not mean that Enframing, as one of these ways, carries with itself the inevitability of an eternal necessity or of a natural law of determination. It *is* fateful; but it is not "fate" in the sense of "the inevitableness of an unalterable course." On the contrary, Enframing as a destining of revealing "in no way confines us to a stultified compulsion to push on blindly with technology or, what comes to the same thing, to rebel helplessly against it and curse it as the work of the devil"— though, of course, we may find ourselves doing either, or both. Insofar as we do not hear the other claim of Being, however, we approach ever more closely "the brink of the possibility of pursuing and pushing forward nothing but what is revealed in ordering, and of deriving all [our] standards on this basis."[107] That approach, or its continuation, Heidegger appealed, constitutes "the supreme danger"—namely, that enframing will reign henceforth as the sole mode of destining, as the sole way of the coming to presence of Being (Heidegger [1954b] 1977, 19–23, 25–26; Heidegger [1962b] 1977, 36–37, 40–41; Heidegger [1951b] 1975, 76).

The scope of the danger that is brought forward with (as) enframing— characterized by Heidegger in numerous passages, especially in his later essays on technology, "the turning" ("*Die Kehre*"), and "the danger" ("*Die Gefahr*")—is perhaps best conveyed in the following paragraphs from his essay "The Question concerning Technology":

This danger attests itself to us in two ways. As soon as what is unconcealed no longer concerns man even as object, but does so,

---

107. With regard to the death of God, for example, Heidegger drew the following illustration: "where everything that presences exhibits itself in the light of a cause-effect coherence, even God can, for representational thinking, lose all that is exalted and holy, the mysteriousness of his distance. In the light of causality, God can sink to the level of a cause, of *causa efficiens*. He then becomes, even in theology, the god of the philosophers, namely, of those who define the unconcealed and the concealed in terms of the causality of making, without ever considering the essential origin of this causality" (Heidegger [1954b] 1977, 26).

rather, exclusively as standing-reserve, and man in the midst of objectlessness is nothing but the orderer of the standing-reserve, then he comes to the very brink of a precipitous fall; that is, he comes to the point where he himself will have to be taken as standing-reserve. Meanwhile man, precisely as the one so threatened, exalts himself to the posture of lord of the earth. In this way the impression comes to prevail that everything man encounters exists only insofar as it is his construct. This illusion gives rise in turn to one final delusion: It seems as though man everywhere and always encounters only himself. Heisenberg has with complete correctness pointed out that the real must present itself to contemporary man in this way [Heisenberg 1954]. *In truth, however, precisely nowhere does man today any longer encounter himself, i.e., his essence.* Man stands so decisively in attendance on the challenging-forth of Enframing that he does not apprehend Enframing as a claim, that he fails to see himself as the one spoken to, and hence also fails in every way to hear in what respect he ek-sists [i.e., "stands-out-from"], from out of his essence, in the realm of an exhortation or address, and thus *can never* encounter only himself.

But Enframing does not simply endanger man in his relationship to himself and to everything that is. As a destining, it banishes man into that kind of revealing which is an ordering. Where this ordering holds sway, it drives out every other possibility of revealing. Above all, Enframing conceals that revealing which, in the sense of *poiēsis,* lets what presences come forth into appearance. As compared with that other revealing, the setting-upon that challenges forth thrusts man into a relation to that which is, that is at once antithetical and rigorously ordered. Where Enframing holds sway, regulating and securing of the standing-reserve mark all revealing. They no longer even let their own fundamental characteristic appear, namely, this revealing as such. (Heidegger [1954b] 1973, 26–27)

Enframing hides the possibility of the "otherwise," the possibility of a different mode of revealing, because it conceals the fact of its own presence *as a* revealing and thereby conceals all revealing as such. Caught in this condition, "man" deludes himself in the predatory view that everything that is, and that can be, is of his making; and, at the brink of the "precipitous fall," the delusion itself becomes so hidden that all possibility of an "otherwise" is forgotten, and the delusory condition becomes simply that-which-is. In its enduring presence, Enframing conceals that it is a revealing (and therefore but one possible mode of coming to presence), in the manner that a lie, in order to attain its height of effectivity, seeks to conceal its presence as an alternative—namely, as the self-disguised entrapping of the truth of its own coming to presence.[108]

Since Enframing, as the essence of the coming to presence of technology, is a mode of the coming to presence of Being itself, and indeed a self-disguising mode, how can we ever succeed in overcoming this Enframing? To begin with, Heidegger argued, an answer to that question must acknowledge that, inasmuch as the essence of technology is Being itself, "technology will never allow itself to be mastered, either positively or negatively, by a human doing founded merely on itself." Just as the essence of technology is nothing technological, so technology cannot be overcome technologically. But if technology "will never allow itself to be overcome by men"—which would, after all, mean "that man was the master of Being"—Being has nevertheless revealed itself in the modern condition as Enframing (*why* it has done so, we do not know). And because the coming to presence of "man"—in whatever condition, whether that of modern technology or some other—always "belongs to the coming to presence of Being," it follows that "the coming to presence of technology cannot be led into the change of its destining," that is, cannot be coaxed into a changing of way, so to speak, "without the cooperation of the coming to presence of man." Such change cannot happen as an activity of *Technik*, nor can it come to pass as a Nietzschean "revaluation of values"; both approaches, because they fail to reach the source of the danger, can only reproduce the danger. However, since any destining of revealing, including that which is the coming to presence of Enframing, "comes to pass from out of a granting" of Being, "and as such a granting," we are thrust not only into the danger but therewith also into "what we least expect"— namely, "the possible arising of the saving power." This is, by Heidegger's account, the mystery of all revealing: the "granting that sends in one way or another into revealing is as such the saving power." Consequently, we still have before us, precisely *in* the danger, the possibility of "the arising of the saving power"—if only we will look into the danger, "ponder this

---

108. The dynamic can be described also in terms of "forgetfulness": "Enframing disguises even . . . its disguising, just as the forgetting of something forgets itself and is drawn away in wake of forgetful oblivion. The coming-to-pass of oblivion not only lets fall from remembrance into concealment; but that falling itself falls simultaneously from remembrance into concealment, which itself also falls away in that falling" (Heidegger [1962b] 1977, 46). Likewise, one could speak of the false consciousness that is beyond all tenor of witting conspiracy, among those whose interests are served by it no less than among those whose interests suffer from it: the false consciousness that knows not its own falsity, nor the ground of its possibility as falseness.

arising," and "watch over it." How to do so? "Above all," Heidegger answered, "through our catching sight of what comes to presence in technology, instead of merely staring at the technological," that is, to see that the coming-to-presence of technology is itself nothing technological; for, as long as we continue to "represent technology as an instrument, we remain held fast in the will to master it," and thus we continue to "press on past the essence of technology" (Heidegger [1954b] 1977, 32–33; Heidegger [1962b] 1977, 38–39).

Heidegger's diagnosis of "the danger" carries the warning that time is short—that the darkening of the world, and our teetering at the precipice, may soon reach the point of irreversibility. Not that the "belongingness of man within granting" is itself susceptible of disjunction and a falling away; indeed, that belonging-together is "indestructable." Nevertheless, it will not "come to light" until we "begin to pay heed" to it (for we are needed and used in *any* coming to presence); and, while there is in Heidegger's writings some suggestion that his calling our attention to the danger and its source has contributed to a "growing light of the saving power" (see, e.g., Heidegger [1954b] 1977, 33; but also Heidegger [1976] 1977, 18–21), still "we are not yet saved," and the danger continues to increase.

The coming to presence of technology threatens revealing, threatens it with the possibility that all revealing will be consumed in ordering and that everything will present itself only in the unconcealedness of standing-reserve. Human activity can never directly counter this danger. Human achievement alone can never banish it. But human reflection can ponder the fact that all saving power must be of a higher essence than what is endangered, though at the same time kindred to it. (Heidegger [1954b] 1977, 33–34)

The great peril is that it may yet be denied to us, and soon, to undertake that pondering and to enter into the more primordial mode of disclosing that is given as the possibility of Being. With such denial, all revealing other than that granted in Enframing as one particular mode of Being will be closed off, and thenceforth everything, "man himself" included, will be present solely as standing-reserve.

Insofar as we have caught a glimpse of the essence of technology,[109]

109. This "glimpse," as I have called it, is meant to suggest something less than the "sudden flash of the truth of Being" which Heidegger named "insight into that which is." When such insight does come "disclosingly to pass," Heidegger argued, "then men are the ones who are struck in their essence by the flashing of Being" (Heidegger [1962b] 1977, 47). But, as any reader of Heidegger can testify, before full "insight" there are first glimpses, and it is on the basis of those glimpses

however, we may still respond in a way that allows the coming to presence of an alternative mode of Being. This possibility might be called the Heideggerian version of "the problem of reconstruction"—or, as Heidegger himself preferred to name it, the "restorative surmounting" of Enframing as the manifest mode of Being's presencing: how to restore Being, when the manifest presence of Being is its oblivion as Enframing. A more conventional phrasing of the issue would ask, how can we surmount manifest historical conditions from the inescapable basis of being *in* and *of* those very conditions? But such phrasing merely leads us in a circle within the tradition of Enframing itself, according to Heidegger, inasmuch as it dictates its own dilemma by proposing that the source of overcoming manifest historical conditions consists in the willful, conquering subject. On the contrary, the source of the restorative surmounting is prior to history, in the Being of beings.

This does not mean that we have nothing to do, that we are passive slaves to a Being that reserved solely for itself a willful and even arbitrary dictatorship: "Unless man first establishes himself beforehand in the space proper to his essence and there takes up his dwelling, he will not be capable of anything essential." But neither are we active sources, creators who hold sway over Being. The saving power, which can come to presence only through our cooperation, is not a historically conditioned power of ours. Rather it is the still-preserved possibility of Being, the mystery of Being. "As the danger, Being turns about into the oblivion of its coming to presence, turns away from this coming to presence, and in that way simultaneously turns counter to the truth of its coming to presence." However, there is also at the same time the possibility of another turning, which Heidegger called "the turn homeward," that is, the "turning of the oblivion of Being into the safekeeping belonging to the coming to presence of Being." Thus the saving power. No one knows when or how, or even *if, this* turning will come to pass; "probably," Heidegger conjectured, it "will finally come to pass only when the danger, which is in its concealed essence ever susceptible of turning, first comes expressingly to light as the danger that it is." But when that will be, no one knows. Nor is it necessary that we know. On the contrary, such knowledge "would even be ruinous for man": whereas "his essence is to be the one who waits, the one who attends upon the coming to presence of Being in that in thinking he guards it," a foreknowledge of the date and manner of this "turn homeward" would stimulate "man" to move further away from attendance. Yet, having said that, Heidegger did proceed to tell of certain necessary characteristics of this

---

that one decides to travel, or not to travel, further with Heidegger on his path of thinking.

turning of the danger expressly to light. For example, this "turning of the danger comes to pass suddenly," even instantaneously, and without any mediation whatever (since "Being has no equal whatever" and neither is "brought about by anything else" nor brings about anything else). "In this turning, the clearing belonging to the essence of Being suddenly clears itself and lights up"; therewith, "the truth of Being flashes" (Heidegger [1962b] 1977, 39–42; Heidegger [1968] 1972, 9; Heidegger [1957] 1969, 72; see also Heidegger [1952c] 1971).

If we can be neither passive bystanders nor the active makers in this turning homeward, just what is it we are to be, when we cooperate as the needed and the used in the restorative surmounting of Enframing? The answer has to do with that "attitude" or "mood" described by Heidegger as *Gelassenheit* and translated as "releasement" or "letting-be." We are to *do,* in the traditional sense of that word, nothing. It is only "when man, in the disclosing coming-to-pass [*Ereignis*] of the insight by which he himself is beheld, renounces human self-will and projects himself toward that insight, away from himself," that he can possibly "correspond in his essence to the claim of that insight." This means to give up "all mere willing and doing," to turn away from willfulness and toward the insight into that which is—which turning puts us within the "task of thinking" that Heidegger found remaining after the completion of philosophy. This task is a "thinking of the possibility that the world civilization which is just now beginning might one day overcome the technological-scientific-industrial character as the sole criterion of man's world sojourn." Such "thinking," in its Heideggerian mittance, is "thinking" in the full original sense, which predates the fateful separation of "theory" and "practice." It is a total engagement in "taking-heed-of," a bringing to fulfillment through which "the relation of Being to the enduring presence of man" is brought into its fullness. Neither a "willing" nor a "means" or "usefulness"—nor indeed in any respect characterizable as the "efficaciousness" associated with the representational-calculative approach of *Technik*—this thinking is a "letting-be," a "releasement," a "waiting" that releases itself into openness (Heidegger [1962b] 1977, 39–40, 47–48; Heidegger [1964] 1972, 59–60; Heidegger [1947] 1962, 271–272; Heidegger [1959a] 1966, 58–90).

In a lecture composed in 1964, Heidegger described the entire course of his work as an "attempt undertaken again and again ever since 1930 to shape the question of Being and Time in a more primal way" (Heidegger [1964] 1972, 55). The comparative of that description—"a more primal way"—was measured with reference to his own earlier efforts, no doubt, as well as to those of his predecessors, but it was not meant to suggest that Heidegger had in the meantime turned away from *Being and Time*. Some commentators have put forward the opinion that Heidegger's claim of basic continuity through all his work was exaggerated, perhaps a bit too self-serving. That there *were* "rethinkings" is quite clear; Heidegger himself acknowledged as much—in a way, even celebrated their sequence and significance. As Mehta has poi.ited out—to note one major dimension of Heidegger's rethinking—the differences between those lectures and essays that were published as the first volume of *Nietzsche* and those that were published as the second volume, all of which were composed during the years after 1935, are striking in regard to Heidegger's relation to Nietzsche (Mehta 1971, 112). Even so, the aim and the way of Heidegger's quest remained basically constant throughout the course of his work.

In the preceding sketch I have emphasized the basic continuity of Heidegger's argument, mostly to the exclusion of marking of any changes in vocabulary, details of recasting, and corrections of earlier by later statements. Heidegger's position with regard to the priority of ontology over epistemology, the character of metaphysics as history of Being and technology as Enframing (the oblivion of Being, the darkening of the world), the need to overcome metaphysics and Enframing, the importance of the preparatory step of going back and rethinking the meaning of the question of Being—in all these interrelated aspects of the Heideggerian argument I have sought to construct an exposition by reading his early works through the eyepiece of his later works. However, in his own description of the course of his work, quoted above, Heidegger spoke of the "attempt undertaken again and again"—a phrasing that draws our attention to the *re*thinking that was itself integral to the basic continuity of his aim and way. Heidegger as thinker of "the task of thinking," which was to rethink the question of Being, would himself engage in *re*thinking as he followed the path of that task.

In order to bring into focus the foundational character of this rethinking, let us consider the following questions: Where stands this rethinker who would rethink the question of Being? Of what, and how, is this rethinker constituted? What is the primordial connectedness whereby the rethinker who rethinks the question of Being, who interrogates the question of Being anew, can accomplish that rethinking and interrogation even as a being within Being? What is the way, or the "linkage," by which the rethinker, as a historical being in and of *this* historical world, could "overcome" the metaphysics that is the foundation of this world today (the metaphysics that is full in the very language that we speak), and thereby be open and free to rethink the question *anew*?[110] In Heidegger's thinking, such queries were raised and considered in the following manner:

110. There are still other questions, consideration of which will be postponed: for example, how did it come to pass, on what basis and by what authority, that *Heidegger* "knew" or "discovered" such connectedness (whatever it may be) wherefrom he could speak as he did about "the oblivion of Being"?

To lead our thinking on the way on which it may find the involvement of the truth of Being in human nature, to open up a path for our thinking on which it may recall Being itself in its truth—to do that the thinking attempted in *Being and Time* is "on its way." On this way—that is, in the service of the question concerning the unconcealedness of Being—it becomes necessary to stop and think about human nature; for the experience of the oblivion of Being, which is not specifically mentioned because it still had to be demonstrated, involves the crucial conjecture that in view of the unconcealedness of Being the involvement of Being in human nature is an essential feature of Being. But how could this conjecture, which is experienced here, become an explicit question before every attempt had been made to liberate the determination of human nature from the concept of subjectivity and from the concept of the *animal rationale?* To characterize with a single term both the involvement of Being in human nature and the essential relation of man to the openness ("there") of Being as such, the name of *Dasein* was chosen for that sphere of being in which man stands as man. (Heidegger [1949] 1956, 212–13)

In *Being and Time,* Heidegger approached those questions of "primordial connectedness" in the terms of *Dasein,* that is, in terms of the "entity which each of us is himself and which includes inquiring as one of the possibilities of its Being." When interrogating the question what it means "to be," we notice that there are all sorts of beings and different senses in which "things" are designated as beings. But we also notice that only the human being, "man," is the being who asks the question of the meaning of the Being of beings; moreover, "man" is the only being of whom the question can be asked. This double presence of "man" as both interrogator and interrogated is the unique imperative of human "existence"— that is, of "man's" unique *ek-sistence* or "standing-out-of" the surrounding. "Man" is not mere entity, a that-which-is in the manner of other entities; "man" is a special way of being, which is *Dasein:* a "being-there," a "being-in-the-world," a "standing-out" from entities. *Dasein* is not the "doing-knowing subject" of the metaphysical tradition. *Dasein* is not the Cartesian subject, who is separate from the world of the "object" and who must devise means of certifying the results of subjective efforts to represent that external world. *Dasein* is the way of being in which, without differentiation, "both the involvement of Being in human nature and the essential relation of man to the openness of Being as such" are a residing presence. Thus: "We are ourselves the entities to be analyzed. The being of any such entity is *in each case mine*"—that is, the Being of *Dasein* is the Being-ness that each of us claims as own-most. "These entities, in their Being, comport themselves towards their Being. As entities with such Being, they are delivered over to their own Being. *Being* is that which is an issue for every such entity." Mere entities, entities as things that are merely "present-at-hand," merely "are" in such a way that they neither care about nor are indifferent to "their" Being. *Dasein,* on the other hand, is for each of us a "mineness," a *my* Being, and "in each case *Dasein* is mine to be in one way or another" (Heidegger [1927] 1962, 24–28, 67–68; Heidegger [1953] 1959, 68–69).

The undertaking of a description of the ontological structures of experience which reveal the unique being of "man" as *Dasein*—the only being for whom own-being is at stake—was central to the inquiry of *Being and Time.* It was as such description that Heidegger examined the experience of "thrownness-into-the-world," "facticity," the authentic and inauthentic modes of being-in-the-world as alternative modes of Being, "care," the presence of the "they" in "average everydayness,"[111] the revealingness of "being-toward-death," and so on. Throughout such description Heidegger was attempting to look behind the subject-object distinction and find the way to a fundamental ontology that would be simultaneously its own "epistemology." *Dasein* was thought by Heidegger as a *"being-*

---

111. Heidegger referred to this attitude as the "dictatorship" of the neuter, indefinite "they," a dictatorship that is unfolded in "inconspicuousness and unascertainability":

We take pleasure and enjoy ourselves as *they* take pleasure; we read, see, and judge about literature and art as *they* see and judge; likewise we shrink back from the "great mass" as *they* shrink back; we find "shocking" what *they* find shocking. The "they," which is nothing definite, and which all are, though not as the sum, prescribes the kind of Being of everydayness. (Heidegger [1927] 1962, 164)

Moreover, Heidegger argued, the ways of Being of the "they"—"distantiality," "averageness," "levelling down"—are constitutive of what we call "publicness" [*die Öffentlichkeit*], by which "everything gets obscured, and what has thus been covered up gets passed off as something familiar and accessible to everyone" (Heidegger [1927] 1962, 165).

There are, it may be noted, some resemblances between Heidegger's treatment of "average everydayness," authenticity-inauthenticity, and death, and certain discussions of authenticity of life by the early Lukács, especially in his essay on the metaphysics of tragedy (Lukács [1910] 1974). Goldmann briefly examined these and other aspects of the relation of Heidegger and Lukács, in some of his last lectures; he sometimes overdrew the resemblances. For example, he reproduced from Lukács's essay on tragedy a passage that reads almost as if it had been written by Heidegger himself, many years later, about the "sudden flash" and "lighting up" of "the truth of Being" (Goldmann [1973] 1977, 47). However, Goldmann's version of the passage (see also Goldmann [1973] 1977, 48 n.3) does not correspond very well with either the wording or the tone of the original (see Lukács [1910] 1974, 153).

there," a being-in-the-world that is concerned with being-in-the-world, including *own*-being—hence, with Being.

Consequently, the issue of the possibility (and variability) of "correspondence" or "agreement" between an external thing-that-stands-against (object) and the "subject's" perception or apprehension of that outsideness that stands-against the "subject" does not arise. In the tradition of philosophy, this notion that "truth" must be defined in the terms of "correspondence" or "agreement" or ὁμοίωσις—the correspondence between a proposition or a subject-judgment and the "that which is" or object to which the proposition or judgment refers—had been accepted as a fundamental possibility since the time of Descartes.

No less a critical philosopher than Kant had taken the possibility for granted:

> The old question with which people sought to push logicians into a corner, so that they must either have recourse to pitiful sophisms or confess their ignorance, and consequently the vanity of their whole art, is this: "What is truth?" The definition of the word *truth*, to wit, "the accordance of the cognition with its object," is presupposed in the question; but we desire to be told, in the answer to it, what is the universal and secure criterion of truth of every cognition. (Kant [1787] 1952, 36)

Whether there could be a universal *criterion* with which to test correspondence between the "matter" or "content" of our cognitions and their objects was open to question, according to Kant; but the possibility of correspondence itself as the definition of truth was not. As he expressed his view in his introduction to the "Transcendental Dialectic" section of the *Critique of Pure Reason*, "Truth or illusory appearance does not reside in the object, insofar as it is intuited, but in the judgment upon the object, insofar as it is thought. . . . Hence truth and error . . . are only to be found in a judgment, that is, in the relation of an object to our understanding" (Kant [1787] 1952, 108).

But of the traditional posit of truth—*veritas est adaequatio rei et intellectus*—Heidegger asked us to think not simply the question of necessary and sufficient *criteria* of correspondence, of what qualifies as *adaequatio* and what does not, but instead the question of the posit itself: "*What ontological character does that which is thus posited have itself?*" (Heidegger [1927] 1962, 258–59). From what condition and in "what way is the relation possible as a relation between *intellectus* and *res*?" What is it, in short, that *is* the possibility of such a relation? The epistemological tradition had failed to answer that fundamental query, Heidegger concluded; indeed, it had hardly even posed the question. If we but think for a moment on that traditional formulation of the relation of truth, that *veritas est adae-quatio rei et intellectus,* we notice a fateful ambiguity: the *adaequatio* may be taken to mean the correspondence of *intellectus* to *res,* or it may be taken to mean the reverse, the correspondence of *res* to *intellectus.* If, for the sake of argument, therefore, we accept the traditional formulation of *veritas,* we find that the notion of "being correct" in an epistemic judgment can be rendered equally well in two ways: "firstly, the correspondence of a thing with the idea of it as conceived in advance, and secondly, the correspondence of that which is intended by the statement with the thing itself" (Heidegger [1943] 1949, 295). So, what is the condition that provides the possibility, and the measure, of both? (see also Heidegger [1950d] 1970, 38–41, 55–71; Heidegger [1964] 1972, 71; Heidegger [1962a] 1967, 117–18).

In the medieval view, such condition of possibility and measure was presupposed in the form of a divine wisdom. Insofar as both "thing and proposition are to an equal extent in conformity" to God's Idea, they must therefore "find themselves conforming to one another in the unity of the divine creative plan." With that presupposition ensconced in the seat of thinking, in the age of belief, the warrant of truth-as-correspondence was self-evident, assured, and in no ultimate sense susceptible of any ambiguity. In its "essence," *veritas* always meant "*convenientia,* the accord of 'what-is' itself, as created, with the Creator, an accordance with the destining of the creative order."

When the medieval order unraveled, the hold of a divinely creative plan dissipated; but the notion of truth as "correct agreement" survived with a new principle of authorization. In place of a Divine Creator as presuppositional condition, that of a World Reason was substituted, and the "creative order as conceived by theology" was replaced by "the possi-bility of planning everything with the aid of worldly reason"—that is, a rational-natural order that stands as "a law unto itself" and that claims that its operations "are immediately intelligible" (at least to "reasonable men" insofar as they abide by the rules of "proper method"). What happens, however, if we interrogate the self-evidence of this presuppositional con-dition? Or may we not attempt that interrogation?—that is, "Is the onto-logical meaning of the relation between Real and ideal (μέθεξις) something about which we must not inquire?" If not, why not? "Is it accidental," Heidegger asked, "that no headway has been made with this problem in over two thousand years?" (Heidegger [1943] 1949, 295–97; Heidegger [1927] 1962, 259).

If we do interrogate the notion of correspondence—what it can be, its condition of possibility—we notice first that it proposes a relation of representation, a re-presenting as a "letting something take up a position opposite to us, as an object." In this opposing, the "thing so opposed must, such being its position, come across the open towards us and at the same time stand fast in itself as the thing and manifest itself as something constant." The thing moves into "the realm of the open" and shows itself as presencing in the open just as the being to whom the thing is opposed must also stand in the open. Hence, the "relating" that hides behind the notion of "correspondence" or "agreement" is itself a "standing-in-the-open" *and* a "being-open-to-what-presences-in-the-open" (Heidegger [1943] 1949, 300–301; Heidegger [1927] 1962, 260–61).

It bears stating more emphatically that Heidegger's "realm of the open" was thought as "the opening," or "clearing," within which *both* "the thing" *and* the being who is open-to-the-thing-showing-itself necessarily stand. This is to say, "the opening" was not in any sense to be thought as the product of consciousness of an "epistemological subject" who stands thereby in opposition to it as "object." Manfred Frings has offered a helpful imagery in the introductory comments of his collection of essays on Heidegger (see Frings 1968, 14–15) which I shall reproduce here, with some modifications. Imagine that you have been thrown or hurled into a total darkness, a totally dark realm which I as storyteller know to be a forest but of which you, as character in the story, know nothing more than darkness. Imagine, then, that by way of a gradual clearing, things begin to emerge from the darkness—trees and stones arrayed here and there, paths traversing the forest-floor, a brook running beside you. They are "becoming 'lit up,' so to speak, by the way of the clearing so that they stand in bold relief." Immediately your attention falls on "such different things in this emerging forest as have never been seen before." The "clearing," then, is a bringing-forth of all those beings: "a 'letting' such things 'be' whatever they are." Yet the clearing itself "is neither any one of these things nor the forest," even though it brings them forth "to be." So, we ask, what *is* this "clearing" or "opening"? It cannot be assigned to our conventional scheme of categories under the heading "object," for that category includes only that which stands outside you and against you or in opposition to you, yet you are *in* the clearing as it clears. Rather, it must be your *being-in-the-clearing* that "makes" the clearing clear, that is, through which the things are "lit up." The clearing itself is not a being but Being, the Being of beings.

Standing in the realm of the open, *Dasein* is a "letting be"; it is a "participating in the open and its openness, within which every entity enters and stands." By committing itself to stand fast in the open, and therein "to consent or yield to what is," *Dasein* can inquire into what-manifests-itself-in-the-open, not as an interrogator of a thatness-which-stands-against-it (i.e., not as "subject" interrogating "objects"), but as an inquirer who lets beings manifest their own beingness in the open. In this "letting be," there is disclosure of truth: "the revelation of what-is, a revelation through which an openness occurs" (Heidegger [1943] 1949, 306–9). *This,* in the Heideggerian view of *Being and Time,* describes the most fundamental way of "knowing," a way to knowledge that long preceded the origin of the subject-object dichotomy: *phainesthai,* "to show itself," "to be in the light"; "being just there, in the light."

> "Being-true" ("truth") means Being-uncovering [*entdeckend-sein*]. But is not this a highly arbitrary way to define "truth"? By such drastic ways of defining this concept we may succeed in eliminating the idea of agreement from the conception of truth. Must we not pay for this dubious gain by plunging the "good" old tradition into nullity? But while our definition is seemingly *arbitrary,* it contains only the *necessary* Interpretation of what was primordially surmised in the *oldest* tradition of ancient philosophy and even understood in a pre-phenomenological manner. If a λογος [*logos:* here, "assertion"] as ἀπόφανσις [*apophansis:* "illuminating statement"] is to be true, its Being-true is ἀληθεύειν [*alētheuein:* "disclosing"] in the manner of αποφαίνεσθαι [*apophainesthai:* "appearing in the light"]—of taking entities out of their hiddenness and letting them be seen in their unhiddenness (their uncoveredness). The ἀλήθεια which Aristotle equates with πρᾶγμα [*pragma:* "things," "deeds"] and φαινομενα ["phenomena"] in the passages cited above [*Metaphysics,* A.984a.18ff.; A.986b.31], signifies the "things themselves"; it signifies what shows itself—*entities in the "how" of their uncoveredness.* (Heidegger [1927] 1962, 262)

"Knowing," in this original, primordial sense, has nothing to do with a correspondence of a "subject's" cognition to an "object's" qualities and actions, or vice versa. Indeed, it refers instead to the "something" from which arises "the belonging-together of subject and object" and which "first imparts their nature to both the object and its objectivity, and the subject and its subjectivity, and hence is prior to the realm of their reciprocity" (Heidegger [1954c] 1975, 103). This fundamental knowing as *aletheia* ("uncoveredness," "unconcealment") is not a matter of a "subject's" moving out of some inner sphere of encapsulation, examining one or another entity in externality, and then "returning with one's booty to the 'cabinet' of consciousness." *Dasein*'s dwelling among "entities which it encounters and which belong to a world already discovered" is always still a dwelling "inside," in the sense of a "Being-in-the-world which knows." Because entities *become* entities by being uncovered, they are true in their uncoveredness in a derivative sense; that is, their true presence derives from *being-uncovered.* Truth itself, on the other hand, that is, "Being-true," is *uncovering,* which is a fundamental "way of Being for Being-in-the-world," a mode of Being for *Dasein.* "*The most primordial phenomenon of truth is first shown by the existential-ontological foundations of uncovering.*" And it is "only with *Dasein*'s disclosedness," the disclosure of *Dasein* as such, that "the *most primordial* phenomenon of truth" is attained. In short, "*Dasein is 'in the truth'* " (Heidegger [1927] 1962, 89–90, 262–63).

To return to our question, what is the primordial connectedness whereby the thinker who rethinks the question of Being can accomplish that rethinking even as a historical being? Heidegger's answer in *Being and Time* was, as he increasingly appreciated during its composition, insufficiently radical to comprise a fundamental ontology. The linchpin of that answer was his postulation that the very process which emerges as the disclosure of *Dasein* is also the process that gives truth. Because *Dasein* discloses its relation to its ground (Being), truth likewise emerges as a grounded process. To say that *Dasein* is "in the truth," he argued, is to say something about *ontological* structure. However, *Dasein* was conceived as a Being-emerging—that is, as the result of a process to which it is therefore relative, and relative as a derivative being the truth of which can be only secondary. Since *Dasein* depends on "something else," from which it is given, thinking has not yet arrived at the fundamental groundedness. Hence, the famed "turning" in Heidegger's thinking: not a turning against his efforts in *Being and Time,* but an attempt to think ever more radically, in terms that are not merely ontic (and therefore dependent on and relative to the priority of a primordial "something") but in terms fully and solely ontological, the primordial ground.

In Heidegger's rethinking the question of Being (see especially 1943), the question itself changed from one of the mutuality of Being and truth—as it had been described in the statement that " 'Being-true' ('truth') means Being-uncovering" (Heidegger [1927] 1962, 262)—to one of the foundation of both Being and truth. This renewed interrogation meant that Heidegger's earlier identification of "truth" with *aletheia* had to be rejected. To begin with, the so-called principle of identity was in need of clarification: what does *it* say? and what is *its* foundation? In his essay on *Identity and Difference* (which Heidegger is said to have considered his single most important publication since *Being and Time*), he argued that the principle presupposes its own meaning and therein conceals its foundation.

The claim of identity speaks from the Being of beings. However, where the Being of beings appears, most early and most authentically in Western thought—with Parmenides—there speaks τὸ αὐτὸ, that which is identical, in a way that is almost too powerful. One of Parmenides' fragments reads:

τὸ γὰρ αὐτὸ νοεῖν ἐστίν τε καὶ εἶναι

"For the same perceiving (thinking) as well as being."

Different things, thinking and Being, are here thought of as the Same. What does this say? It says something wholly different from what we know otherwise as the doctrine of metaphysics, which states that identity belongs to Being. Parmenides says: Being belongs to an identity. What does identity mean here? What does the word τὸ αὐτό, the Same, say in Parmenides' fragment? Parmenides gives us no answer. He places us before an enigma which we may not sidestep. We must acknowledge the fact that in the earliest period of thinking, long before thinking had arrived at a principle of identity, identity itself speaks out in a pronouncement which rules as follows: thinking and Being belong together in the Same and by virtue of this Same. (Heidegger [1957] 1969, 27; see also Heidegger [1954d] 1975; Heidegger [1953] 1959, 136–96)[112]

The principle of identity, usually considered to be "the highest principle of thought," is conventionally formulated as "A = A." But this says nothing directly about "the nature of *identity*." Rather, that conventional formulation "already presupposes what identity means and where it belongs," for when we say "A is A" what we really say is "A *is* A," and the "*is*" calls us to view a *relation* of "belonging-together-in-the-Same." In other words, this "*is*" is not a neutral copula that denotes some juxtaposition or causality of one "A" to another "A"; the "*is*" of "A *is* A" (i.e., the *relation* called belonging-together-in-the-Same) is prior to ("more original than") the "thatnesses" which are related (Heidegger [1957] 1969, 23, 26–28).

According to the Heideggerian argument, this relation which he names "belonging-together" has to be thought in just a certain way, with a very deliberate distribution of emphasis. In the "customary way" of thinking the phrase, emphasis is placed on the "together," in which case the "belonging" then takes its reference from some scheme of categories or classes, and can be rendered as meaning this and nothing more: "to be assigned and placed into the order of a 'together,' established in the unity of a manifold, combined into the unity of a system, mediated by the unifying center of an authoritative synthesis." It is thus that we have charts and tables of this or that. Priority is lent to the "thatnesses," which are *only then* "assigned and placed *into* the order" of a togetherness—that is, a "*nexus* and *connexio*" thought as "the necessary connection" of one thatness with another thatness. But the phrase in question can also be thought in another way: as "*belonging* together." Thought in this way, the "together" is now a togetherness-in-the-Same, and it finds its determination from the belonging. That such a seemingly small and subtle difference of thinking could be of any import to our interrogations of the question of Being might strike us as a bit far-fetched; and yet, Heidegger recommended, consider that difference in terms of the problem of representation:

112. Heidegger's rendering of Parmenides' Fragment III has been a point of controversy—a matter to which I shall return below.

> When we understand thinking to be the distinctive characteristic of man, we remind ourselves of a *belonging* together that concerns man and Being. Immediately we find ourselves grappling with the questions: What does Being mean? Who, or what, is man? Everybody can see easily that without a sufficient answer to these questions we lack the foundation for determining anything reliable about the *belonging* together of man and Being. But as long as we ask our questions in this way, we are confined within the attempt to represent the "together" of man and Being as a coordination, and to establish and explain this coordination either in terms of man or in terms of Being. In this procedure, the traditional concepts of man and Being constitute the toe-hold for the coordination of the two. (Heidegger [1957] 1969, 30)

In other words, "to coordinate" means to bring into an arrangement some thatnesses which (in some sense) "need" to be brought into arrangement. But, Heidegger asked, how "would it be if, instead of tenaciously representing merely a coordination of the two in order to produce their unity, we were for once to note whether and how a belonging to one another first of all is at stake in this 'together'?" Could we not think the element in which the belongingness dwells? But to do so means that we must break away from our habit of representational-calculative thinking—the thinking by which "we represent everything only in categories and mediations" and therewith consign ourselves to the circularity of finding only those connections that we ourselves have already established presuppositionally as an *inter*-twining of man *and* Being, either from the standpoint of "man" rather than Being or from the standpoint of Being rather than "man." We must break away from the tenacious "attitude of representational thinking" and "spring" (as in the abrupt entry of a leap) into "the realm from which man and Being have already reached each other in their active nature [*Wesen* as *physis*]." By springing into this new way of thinking the *belonging*-togetherness, we may hear the claim of the ground of Being and truth (Heidegger [1957] 1969, 29–34; Heidegger [1954d] 1975, 92–95).[113]

This belonging-together exists in the element of unconcealment—that is, in that *aletheia* which Heidegger found to have been "named at the

---

113. It is apposite to note that in this conjunction of "*belonging*-togetherness" and "hearing the claim of Being," Heidegger was calling upon certain etymological connections in German. The verb *zusammengehören*, given lexically as "to belong together," "to be in solidarity or intimate congruity," has as its verbal root *hören*, which means "to listen," "to hear." Hence, *Zusammengehörigkeit* ("belonging-togetherness") could be rendered also as "hearing-togetherness" or, more properly, "the state of having-heard-together."

beginning of philosophy" (Parmenides' Fragment III) but of which philosophy knows nothing. Of course, philosophical thinking is always "already admitted to the free space of the opening" of *aletheia,* whenever it attempts to move to "things themselves." Indeed, language itself—not merely the communicative act of language-using, but its priorness as a being-together of human beings—dwells in the opening as "the custodian of the disclosed, the unconcealed."[114] Even as philosophy exists in the opening of *aletheia,* however, it does not find itself there.

> Philosophy does speak about the light of reason, but does not heed the opening of Being. The *lumen naturale,* the light of reason, throws light only on openness. It does concern the opening, but so little does it form the opening that it needs the opening in order to be able to illuminate what is present in the opening. This is true not only of philosophy's *method,* but also and primarily of its *matter,* that is, of the presence of what is present. (Heidegger [1964] 1972, 66)

The possibility of the presencing of what is present, even "the possibility of the path to presence," is granted by the opening—by *aletheia,* unconcealment, "the element in which Being and thinking and their belonging together exist." It is in the opening that there can be a "letting-presence" and the turning by which the danger that is Enframing comes expressly to light *as* the danger (Heidegger [1964] 1972, 66–68; Heidegger [1953] 1959, 155; Heidegger [1936] 1949, 276; Heidegger [1962b] 1977, 41–48; Heidegger [1951b} 1975, 77–78).

In Heidegger's later effort to think the question of Being, that is, to think the question still more radically, the relation between "truth" and

114. We are always confronted by this priority, Heidegger declared, whenever we try "to get our inquiry into language and the investigation of its nature started" (Heidegger [1959d] 1971, 71). All of our attempts will be in vain until we see that, when "we put questions to language, questions about its nature, its being, . . . clearly language itself must already have been granted to us." Heidegger then generalized his point: "Inquiry and investigation here and everywhere require the prior grant of whatever it is they approach and pursue with their queries. Every posing of every question takes place within the very grant of what is put in question." This, of course, may be referred to his demonstration in *Being and Time* that all knowing takes place within a *Vorgriff* (pre-concept) or a "pre-knowing" that is historically-culturally determined (see, e.g., Heidegger [1927] 1962, 190–95). Elsewhere, Heidegger rephrased the point in a slightly different way, and with an important addendum: no one can "jump over one's own shadow. No one can do this. However, the greatest effort in attempting this impossibility— that is the ground-movement of the action of thought" (Heidegger [1962a] 1967, 150).

aletheia was rethought. No longer could he propose a direct equation of "truth" and *aletheia,* for such proposal simply reproduced the metaphysical tradition. Metaphysics searches for the ground of "what is," a ground that it designates as "being" and that it interprets as the creative or productive force, cause, or prime reason for the reality of "what is." The central characteristic of this "metaphysical thinking which grounds the ground for beings," and thereby gives "reasons" for what is present, is "the fact that metaphysical thinking departs from what is present in its presence, and thus represents it in terms of its ground as something grounded." In so grasping after the "what is" as present, *and,* moreover, in so grasping after its "reason" or "ground" as also a "ground" that is present (i.e., as an *ontically* real "what is" that grounds the grounded), we struggle to capture the *results* of an activity and fail to see the activity itself. In metaphysical thinking, according to Heidegger, we seek to interpret the "what is present" by inquiring into its "ground," which is thought in the manner of a prior (and persisting) "is present," and therein neglect the very *presencing* of the present. Our metaphysical thinking, as shown by its grammar, focuses on the static predication of "is present"—that is, our representation of "the grounds" of that which is grounded—to the exclusion of the gerunds of activity: "presencing," "letting-presence," "unconcealing," "giving," and so on. With Heidegger's later course of thinking, then, the "opening" becomes the element in which Being-presencing, thinking, and truth all have their very *possibility* of "being present" (*parousia*). The opening is the *presencing* of presence and is always prior to it (Heidegger [1964] 1972, 54, 69; Heidegger [1950d] 1970, 150–54).

And so we must ask, with Heidegger, "Where does the opening come from and how is it given?" (Heidegger [1964] 1972, 73). But first of all, what does it mean to say, "It is given"? That is, in the giving, what means the "*It*"?—"What speaks in the 'It gives'?" Whence comes the "It gives?" Does it drop from heaven—even after the gods have died? Does it come from nothingness?[115] When we speak the idiom "It gives" (as in "It gives

<hr/>

115. There is indication of just that answer in Heidegger's (1950b) essay on the celebrated Anaximander fragment—although some Heidegger students have doubted that he pursued this line of thinking in his other works (see, e.g., the commentary by Arendt 1978, 188–94). In any case, it must be remembered that, if nothingness *is,* then Being is no less the Being of nothingness than the Being of beings. Moreover, several relevant passages from the Anaximander essay exhibit full concordance with other presentations of the *aletheia/lēthē* axis (i.e., uncon-cealment/concealment, the said/the not-said, etc.). For instance: "Certainly we can translate γένεσις [*genesis*] as origination; but we must think this originating as a movement which lets every emerging being abandon concealment and go forward into unconcealment. Certainly we can translate φθορά [*phthora*] as pass-

such and such" or "There is such and such"), we are saying something different from "It is"; but what means the "It" of which we speak? This "enigmatic It" to which we refer in our idioms ("*Es gibt*" in German; "*il y a*" in French; "*c'è*" in Italian; "there is" in English) "presumably indicates something distinctive." Can we bring this distinctiveness out of the idiom and into view? Heidegger attempted to do so, "by thinking the 'It' in the light of the kind of giving that belongs to it: giving as destining, giving as an opening up which reaches out." This is "the task of thinking" after the end of philosophy. But here Heidegger's forward motion began to flag. He introduced a new term, "the event of Appropriation" (*Ereignis*),[116] by which to try to overcome and leave behind all of the metaphysical impregnation of the term "Being"—impregnation which had so tenaciously haunted his previous attempts to rethink the question of Being. "Appropriation," or the "event of Appropriation," is the name of what determines both "time and Being, in their own, that is, in their belonging together."

ing away; but we must think this passing away as a going which in its turn abandons unconcealment, departing and withdrawing into concealment" (Heidegger [1950b] 1975, 30). "The coming forward into . . . and the departure to . . . *become present* within unconcealment between what is concealed and what is unconcealed. They initiate the arrival and departure of whatever has arrived" (Heidegger [1950b] 1975, 30; ellipses in original). "The *gegen* in *gegenwartig* [presently] does not mean something over against a subject, but rather an open expanse [*Gegend*] of unconcealment, into which and within which whatever comes along lingers"—that is, comes to pass, lingers "awhile in the expanse of unconcealment," and then passes away into concealment (Heidegger [1950b] 1975, 34). "What is present *is* arriving or lingering insofar as it is already departing from unconcealment toward concealment" (Heidegger [1950b] 1975, 37). Presencing is presencing of the absent as well as the present. Being, as enduring presencing, gives the transiency of beings as they come forward into *aletheia* (unconcealment), linger awhile, and pass away into *lēthē* (concealment).

116. *Ereignis* translates convenfionally as "event" or "occurrence"; in the Heideggerian context "coming to pass" is preferable (see Pöggeler 1959). *Ereignis* means the "event of Appropriation" in total, a lexical equation that draws upon the circumstance of a common etymological root. *Appropriation* can be rendered in German as *die Aneignung*; the verb *aneignen* ("to appropriate") shares with the verb *ereignen*, ("to come to pass," "to occur") the intransitive verbal root *eignen*, which (with *zu*) can be translated as "to belong to" (also as "to be qualified for" or "to be adapted to"), and the adjectival form *eigen*, meaning "own" or "individual" or "proper" (among others). Moreover, *eignen* developed from a verbal form (*äugnen*) of *Auge* ("eye"). The prefix *er-* in *ereignen* signifies accomplishment or completion of the aim of the action (i.e., the "belonging to" has "come to pass"); the *an-* in *aneignen* signifies direction relative to the speaker (as in movement of that which "belongs to" toward the being to whom it belongs, in a "*belonging*-together").

Appropriation is not a "realm" or a "ground"; it is a *relation* and an "*activity*"—the relation of "man" and Being, the "activity" of coming-to-presence, letting-presence—and as such it is primordial to that which is related and that which transpires in the "activity." It is "not simply an occurrence, but that which makes any occurrence possible." Appropriation appropriates. Appropriation is "the It that gives in 'It gives Being,' 'It gives time' "; the event of Appropriation neither *is* nor is *given*. Appropriation is not "the encompassing general concept under which Being and time could be subsumed."

In the face of these and other stipulations of what Appropriation is *not*, we may be quick to ask: "But just what *is* Appropriation?" Heidegger would remind us, however, that Appropriation is *not* an "*is*." In other words, our "seemingly innocent question," as he called it, is one that "demands information about the Being of Appropriation," and such demand only takes us "back to what first of all demands its own determination: Being in terms of time." Appropriation appropriates the *belonging-together* of Being and "man." Since "Being and time are there only in Appropriating, Appropriating has the peculiar property of bringing man into his own as the being who perceives being by standing within true time." Because of that, "we can never place Appropriation in front of us, neither as something opposite us nor as something all-encompassing." Although Heidegger described this formulation as only preliminary and as an inadequate saying of Appropriation—that is, "this thinking can only be concerned with preparing entry into Appropriation"—we are at the limit of thinking. "What remains to be said? Only this: Appropriation appropriates" (Heidegger [1968] 1972, 5, 16–24, 42; see also Heidegger [1969] 1972).

In what "place" do we stand, when rethinking the history of metaphysics and rethinking the question of Being, so as not to be *in* and *of* that history? For Heidegger, such "place" was integral to the very matter of the task of thinking that remains after the completion of metaphysics—a matter of thinking that not only remains, still unfulfilled, but also predated metaphysics as the realm of thinking within which the discourse of metaphysics emerged and staked out its claim. This thinking, the definitive character of which predates the distinction of "theory" and "practice," transpires as the "presencing of presence," as a "letting-be" in the "opening," and as a "waiting" to attend the "enduring presencing of Being." Exactly who we are in such thinking, and what will come out of the waiting, cannot yet be said. In Heidegger's "conversation on a country path" among a scientist, a scholar, and a teacher, we read this exchange:

> *Scientist:* With the best of will, I cannot re-present to myself this nature of thinking.

Teacher: Precisely because this will of yours and your mode of thinking as re-presenting prevent it.

Scientist: But then, what in the world am I to do?

Scholar: I am asking myself that too.

Teacher: We are to do nothing but wait.

Scholar: That is poor consolation.

Teacher: Poor or not, we should not await consolation—something we would still be doing if we became disconsolate.

Scientist: Then what are we to wait for? And where are we to wait? I hardly know any more who and where I am.

Teacher: None of us knows that, as soon as we stop fooling ourselves. (Heidegger [1959a] 1966, 62)

Homeless in our world, deaf in the oblivion of Being, and caught up in a plundering of the earth, none of us knows who we are, why we are here rather than there, now rather than then, or for what we wait. But in asking the question, "Who are we?" we must "remain cautious in our answer," Heidegger advised, for "it might be that that which distinguishes man as man is determined precisely by what we must think about" in the renewed task of thinking: "man, who is concerned with and approached by presence, who, through being thus approached, is himself present in his own way for all present and absent beings" (Heidegger [1968] 1972, 12). If, then, there is in the Heideggerian scheme a "place" in which Heidegger stood as preparatory rethinker, it was in this "presence"; indeed, "all the definitions of being . . . are grounded in, and are held together by, that wherein the Greeks unquestionably experienced the meaning of Being, and which they called *ousia,* or more fully *parousia*" (Heidegger [1953] 1959, 61). Παρουσια: lexically translated as "presence" (from *para + ousia,* the latter deriving from *eimi,* "to be"); in Christian theology, it may be noted, *Parousia* is the Second Coming, at which transpires the Last Judgment.[117]

Already in *Being and Time* Heidegger spoke of "the necessity of going back" to "primordial 'sources' " and to "an origin" (Heidegger [1927] 1962, 43). *Necessity? Primordial* sources? On what basis did he make such judgments? Heidegger could not claim, as Nietzsche had for the philoso-

---

117. I shall not attempt to pursue here the complicated relation between Heidegger's thinking and Christian eschatology; it is far from the seemingly simple matter of parallels and transplantations. As noted earlier, Heidegger began his course of studies in theology and for some time thought of himself as a theologian (Gadamer [1977, 44] quoted from a letter Heidegger wrote in 1921 to Karl Löwith, "Ich bin ein christlicher Theologe"); but by his own account it was the *tension* between "ontology and speculative theology" that served as stimulus to his thinking (see Heidegger [1963] 1972).

phers for whom he was "herald," that he had a "right" to assert his statement by his own authorization, inasmuch as he had rejected the Nietzschean argument regarding the "will to create." What is more, Heidegger eschewed any notion of his authorization of his speaking as *his* authority— a position that has been a focus of scathing criticism (e.g., by Adorno [1964] 1973).[118] But how can we tell if Heidegger got it right? When discussing the point of his "conversation with early Greek thinking," Heidegger said that "our sole aim is to reach what wants to come to language in such a conversation, provided it comes of its own accord" (Heidegger [1950b] 1975, 25). (That which "comes to presence of its own accord" is another way of naming *physis,* in Heidegger's "pre-Socratic" sense of that word—i.e., that which "arises from out of itself"; see, e.g., Heidegger [1962a] 1967, 70 and Heidegger [1954b] 1977, 10–11.) Now, as rethinkers, this is "*our aim*"; that is, we have something to *do,* even if it is merely to be "attendant" to "the claim of Being." How are we to know when we have realized our aim? How are we to ascertain that "what wants to come to language" *has* come to language, and whether it has come of its own accord? (How to judge whether that which *has* come to language is fitting to our aim?) The "flashing of Being": is it *the* "flashing of Being" of which Heidegger spoke, or is it the spangled field of my private hallucination? The "vision of Christ": is it the foretold Second Coming, the *Parousia* of Christianity, or is it the dying hope of some world-weary soul?

Language, that "most dangerous of possessions," was "given to man," according to Heidegger, "so that he may say what he is" (Heidegger [1936] 1949, 275–76; Heidegger [1953] 1959, 155; Heidegger [1951b] 1975, 77–78; Heidegger [1959b] 1971). Language is, of course, a "communicative function"; but more than that and before that, it is a being-together of human beings, a dwelling-in within which we can *be:* "language is the custodian of the disclosed, the unconcealed."[119] It was in this way, as "*the custodian*" of *aletheia,* that language was of such crucial importance to Heidegger (though Greek, and German, peculiarly more so than all others; see, e.g., Heidegger [1953] 1959, 56–57). His "task of thinking" included

118. Adorno was mistaken in some of his particulars, but in the kernel of this criticism he was on target.

119. In *Identity and Difference* Heidegger put it this way: "In the event of Appropriation vibrates the active nature of what speaks as language, which at one time was called the house of Being" (Heidegger [1957] 1969, 39). (Note: "active nature" was Stambaugh's translation of *Wesen*—which could also be translated as "essence" in the Heideggerian sense, i.e., as "enduring presence." The phrase "active nature" was meant to capture the sense of *physis* as that which comes to presence of its own accord.)

thinking "what the Greeks have thought," but "in an even more Greek manner"—meaning not to try to exceed their self-understanding but "to pursue more originally what the Greeks have thought, to see it in the *source* of its reality" (Heidegger [1959c] 1971, 29; emphasis added). In thinking to such "source," even more "originally" and with the aim of *letting* come to language what wants to come of its own accord, Heidegger engaged in etymologizings that have been seriously criticized. While we must preserve the meaning of Heidegger's effort to "overcome" the metaphysical tradition and to clear a space for *his* conceptual semantics, the criticisms do raise some troubling queries about the constitution of his effort. Various critics have argued that in asserting particular definitions, etymologies, and translations of terms that were allegedly central to the matter of pre-Socratic philosophy, and asserting them *as* pre-Socratic thinking, Heidegger produced "arbitrary" re-creations. Among the several instances of challenged definitions, etymologies, and translations, one of the most controversial pertains to Parmenides' Fragment III, which in the Greek has come to us as: τὸ γὰρ αὐτὸ νοεῖν ἐστίν τε καὶ εἶναι. Diels and Kranz (1960, 1:231) rendered it in German as: "*Dasselbe aber ist das Denken und das Sein*"— which I would translate, without regard to Heidegger, as "Thinking and being are but the same." Heidegger's translation to the German differs from that of Diels and Kranz: "*Das Selbe nämlich ist Vernehmen (Denken) sowohl als auch Sein*" (Heidegger [1957] 1969, 90)—which has been rendered in English, apparently without objection from Heidegger himself, as "For the same perceiving (thinking) as well as Being" and as "For thinking and Being are the same."[120] By contrast, Zeller's ([1876] 1881, 584n.1) translation of the Greek fragment has been rendered in English as: "For the same thing can be thought and can be"; a slightly different rendering is "only that which can be, can be thought." Burnet ([1892] 1957, 173), who apparently followed Zeller's example, as did Kirk and Raven ([1957] 1963, 269n) and Freeman (1946, 147n.1), translated the Greek into English as "It is the same thing that can be thought and that can be." Clearly these latter readings construct a meaning different from that proposed by Heidegger. This is not to say that there is a unanimity among conventional classicists themselves, however; Heidel, for instance, translated Parmenides'

---

120. The respective translations are by Stambaugh (from *Identity and Difference*) and Capuzzi (from "Moira"). Perhaps a somewhat "closer" translation would be (by treating "*nämlich*" in its sense of the evidentiary "for," and respecting Heidegger's distinction between *Sein* and *Seiende*): "For the Same is not only perceiving (thinking) but also Being." This translation is in keeping, I believe, with Heidegger's argument concerning "the principle of identity" (see above; and Heidegger [1957] 1969, 38–41).

fragment still another way: "For it is one and the same thing to think and to think that it is" (Heidel 1912–13, 720).[121]

I do not presume to settle the question of "proper translation" of Parmenides' Fragment III on classicists' terms, or anything like them. *Who knows* what Parmenides himself had in mind by those few words in just that sequence, or what their immediate context was—or, indeed, whether those who preserved the fragment got it right? Who *can* know? The far more interesting question, here with regard to Heidegger, is: What is the point of this great concern with "the proper translation" of what Parmenides and other pre-Socratic philosophers "really said"?

In a passage from his essay "The Anaximander Fragment," Heidegger acknowledged the abundance of evidence, from every standard lexicon, that ὄν and εἶναι are "correctly translated" as "being" and "to be"; but then he asked "whether in this correct translation we also *think* correctly" (my emphasis), that is, "whether in this most common of all translations anything at all is thought." By way of an answer he continued thusly: "It becomes manifest," once we examine the case,

that in this correct translation everything is embroiled in equivocal and imprecise significations. It becomes clear that the always hasty approximations of usual translations are never seen as insufficient; nor are scholarly research and writing ever disturbed by them. Perhaps great effort is expended in order to bring out what the Greeks truly represented to themselves in words like θέος, ψυχή, ξωή, τύχη, χάρις, λόγος, φύσις, or words like ιδέα, τέχνη, and ἐνέργεια. But we do not realize that these and similar labors get nowhere and come to nothing . . . so long as they do not cast sufficient light on ὄν and εἶναι in their Greek essence. (Heidegger [1950b] 1975, 23–24)

Surely we can join Heidegger part way in the course of his argument here: the Greek words were integral to a larger fabric of thinking, and too often "we thoughtlessly catalogue" them within the categories of "what we mean by the corresponding . . . words of our own mother tongue." In so doing, "we never ascribe a significance to the Greek words at all: we immediately adopt them from our stock of common knowledge, which has

---

121. Heidegger was not alone in having a propaedeutic interest in "the proper translation" of the pre-Socratics. Popper, for example—a philosopher of science not otherwise known to have shared cause with Heidegger—fastened upon particular fragments of Anaximander, Heraclitus, and Parmenides as support of his thesis that all good (true) philosophy and science proceed through the method of "conjectures and refutations" (Popper [1958–59] 1965).

already endowed them with the common intelligibility of its own language" (see also Heidegger [1951b] 1975, 59–60). After all, the Greek words *could* have meant, to the Greeks, something quite different. However, Heidegger did not rest with acknowledgment of the "*could*." By what standard did he speak so matter-of-factly of "equivocal and imprecise significations"? And of "the always hasty *approximations*" that typify "usual translations" but that are "never seen as insufficient"? One possibility is, of course, relativism—that is, the argument that, because each and every production (of words, meanings, etc.) is historically culturally contingent, one can never know the measure of a "precise, unequivocal, exact translation" across epochs and cultures. But such was hardly the touchstone of Heidegger's conviction (see, e.g., Heidegger [1954c] 1975, 105), for his speaking of equivocation and imprecision and approximation implied the foundation of a noncontingent scale on which "usual translations," though they may well be lexicographically correct, fail the test (his test) of unequivocacy, precision, exactness, sufficiency.

So, what *was* the Heideggerian zero-point from which deviations could be marked? When Heidegger argued in his "dialogue on language between a Japanese and an Inquirer" (Heidegger [1959c] 1971, 29) that the task of thinking "what the Greeks have thought in an even more Greek manner" means that we must think within the limits that they set for themselves and pursue what they thought, though "more originally," he was not proposing again the Diltheian feat of understanding the Greek authors better than they understood themselves (Dilthey [1900] 1976, 259–60). Rather, Heidegger was urging us to pursue, more originally then we now do, "what the Greeks have thought"—to think what they thought within their limits. Still, the question: Why the continuing "conversation" with the early Greeks? Why "the necessity of going back" to "primordial 'sources' "? And by what standard for gauging "their limits" and *our* arrival?

In his essay on Heraclitus's Fragment B 16, among other places, Heidegger demurred at the notion of offering "the one absolutely correct way" of reading Heraclitus, claiming instead that his "task limits itself to getting closer to the words of the Heraclitean saying." To assert an "absolutely correct way" presumably would display the burden of willfulness and would endanger the entry into *Gelassenheit*. Yet, "getting closer" implies the possibility of knowing the destination, of knowing when one has arrived at this "thinking more originally what the Greeks have thought." We are all aware, Heidegger said, "that Heraclitus speaks in one way to Plato, in another to Aristotle, in another to a Church Father, and in others to Hegel and Nietzsche." But it is not historiological thinking that is needed.

If one remains embroiled in a historical grasp of these various interpretations, then one has to view each of them as only relatively correct.
Such a multiplicity necessarily threatens us with the specter of relativism. Why? Because the historical ledger of interpretations has already expunged any questioning dialogue with the thinker—it probably never entered such dialogue in the first place. (Heidegger [1954c]
1975, 105)

Heidegger sought in his thinking a letting-come-to-pass that would be the
presencing of the primordial foundedness of Being. Yet his own historical,
contingent, "ontic" being could not be passed over or nullified in a generality; and it was in *his* thinking—*his* "conversations" with pre-Socratic
thinkers, for example—that we were to catch sight of the turn of Being
"back out of oblivion."[122] In his fundamental, lifelong effort to think the
primordial foundedness of Being, Heidegger did not succeed.[123] By his own
terms, even, he was agnostic in regard to the destination of his effort: "No
one can know *whether* and when and where and how this step of thinking"—i.e., this "step back . . . out of the oblivion" and "into the destiny
of the withdrawing concealment of perdurance"—"will develop into a
proper (needed in appropriation) path and way and road-building" (Heidegger [1957] 1969, 72; emphasis added). That statement, albeit not the
admission of failure that some commentators have designated it to be,
nonetheless denies to Heidegger's efforts, including his readings of the pre-
Socratics, the claim of being anything more than an "On-the-Way-to . . ."
—no one knows where or what. It was undoubtedly with this image in

122. A remark by Gadamer, concerning Heidegger's assimilation of history to
his own uses, is apropos:

> For Heidegger, it was fate, not history (remembered and penetrable by
> understanding), that originated in the conception of being in Greek meta-
> physics and that in modern science and technology carries the forgetfulness
> of being to the extreme. Nevertheless, no matter how much it may belong
> to the temporal constitution of man to be exposed to the unpredictability
> of fate, this does not rule out the claim continually raised and legitimated
> in the course of Western history to think what is. And so Heidegger too
> appears to claim a genuinely historical self-consciousness for himself, in-
> deed, even an eschatological self-consciousness. (Gadamer [1967] 1976,
> 231)

123. Compare Anderson's conclusion that, if Heidegger "has not succeeded, he
has not yet failed, either" (Anderson 1968, 60). This motive of "saving the
Heideggerian way," as it might be called, raises a question of conflictual relation
to Heidegger himself: insofar as a defense of Heidegger's way requires willing,
entrance to that way (and to the requisite "mood" of *Gelassenheit*) is blocked,
for the will-lessness required by *Gelassenheit* cannot be willed.

mind that Kaufmann judged, in his editorial introduction to Nietzsche's *Genealogy,* that "Heidegger is always on the way toward the point from which it may be possible some day to ask a question."[124]

Heidegger evinced deep concern for the condition of the world—a world that has "fallen into darkness," threatens self-destruction in the hands of a being who fashioned plunder into a system of ethics. Nearly every one of his published writings speaks such caring, and the speaking sometimes peals with a rush of indignation:

> Man has already begun to overwhelm the entire earth and its atmosphere, to arrogate to himself in forms of energy the concealed powers of nature, and to submit future history to the planning and ordering of a world government. This same defiant man is utterly at a loss simply to say what *is*; to say *what* this *is*—that a thing *is*. (Heidegger [1954c] 1975, 57)

But for all that, Heidegger's thinking is terribly remote from the living situations in which man, woman, and child must concretely decide and act. Whereas we may surmise from a reading of his essays on technology, the "turning," the "danger," and so on, that he was (in some sense) "opposed" to certain conditions—or at least that he was regretful of them, if not willfully against them—there is in his thinking of those conditions and their possibilities nothing in the manner of an aggressive *oughtness,* a struggle for the "otherwise"; instead, there is continuous suggestion of a quietude, a calmness of "letting-be" through rethinking.

Curiously, one of the hallmarks of Heidegger's care-full thinking in regard to the modern world condition takes its shape within the conceptual terrain of an early Greek word that was only rarely uttered by Heidegger— I recall seeing it only once in all of his published work: ὕβρις (*hubris*). This one appearance is in his commentary on Heraclitus's Fragment B 43: "Ὕβριν χρὴ σβεννύναι μᾶλλον ἢ πυρκαϊήν, which, in the English rendering of Heidegger's German translation, reads, "measureless pride needs to be extinguished sooner than a raging fire." Or, as Heidegger stated his message by way of expansion of the fragment, "Before you play with fire, whether it be to kindle or extinguish it, put out first the flames of presumption, which overestimates itself and takes poor measure because it forgets the essence of Λέγειν [*Legein:* in Heideggerian translation, "gathered-letting-lie-before"]" (Heidegger [1951b] 1975, 75–76). *Hubris*—that ex-

---

124. The sentence appears on p. 441 of Kaufmann's Modern Library edition of *Basic Writings of Nietzsche* (see Nietzsche [1887] 1968).

cessive pride and arrogance of will, the presumptuousness of Prometheus and Icarus:[125] such is the fallen mood of a dark world.

Heidegger's "project," his "proposal" (to the extent that his thinking *was* a *pro*-posal), is suffused with a "grace" of irenics rather than the deliberative thrust of polemics. In his own historical contingency in the mundane circumstances of this fallen-into-darkness world, he had no advice to give—only the invitation to join in a rethinking that would allow the "letting-presence of presencing." One of his last public statements expresses this position in somber tones; it is *Der Spiegel*'s interview of 1966, granted under the stipulation that it would not be published until after Heidegger's death.

> As I see it, no single person can take sufficient survey of the world to be able to give practical advice, especially in face of the task of having first to find a new basis for thinking itself. Thought is over-taxing itself, so long as it takes itself seriously in the great tradition, if it undertakes the mission of providing direction at this point. On what authority could it do so? In the realm of thought there are no definitive utterances. The only standard for thought comes from the matter thought of itself. But that very matter is what is above all questionable. (Heidegger [1976] 1977, 25–26)

Whereas Nietzsche's speaking of "beyond good and evil" was forcefully pronounced from his confrontation with the evil of a morality that devalued all values, in Heidegger's speaking of "the task of/for thinking" we must strain to find even a hint of evil and good, or of a "beyond." And when we do detect what appears to be a hint, and then attempt to follow it back to the core of his thinking, we lose our way in the mystery of a Being of beings that is itself neither good nor evil but that purports to be entirely prior to any *axios*—much like the Unmoved Mover of an earlier epoch.

5. WITTGENSTEIN: "LANGUAGE GAMES" AND "FORMS OF LIFE"

According to Heidegger, "Language is not a tool at [our] disposal, rather it is that event which disposes of the supreme possibility of human existence" (Heidegger [1936] 1949, 276–79). Without language, there is no world; without world, no history. "The being of men is founded in lan-

---

125. The mention of Icarus brings to mind another debate, this between Haldane (1924), with his promotion of the powers and promise of modern science, and Russell (1924), who replied with a more "pessimistic" view based on the claim that "man" is insufficiently "rational" to subdue his "passions" and reckless fancies.

guage. But this only becomes actual in *conversation*"—that is, in a "process of coming together," not as a *consequence* of the actualization of language but "contemporaneous with it." Deliberations on language were central to Heidegger's quest. Whether in the outer context of reflections of a Hölderlin sketch, a fragment from Anaximander, or talk of "human resources" for a clinic, the speaking-hearing, *belonging*-togetherness of the actuality of language was a consistent and fundamental concern. Yet Heidegger's work has not been accorded much attention in the Anglo-American academy, partly because of the widespread view that his writings too often degenerated into a language-mongering. As the *"Denker"* of Freiburg and the Black Forest was committing his labors of rethinking, reactions against "specialization" of philosophical vocabulary were elsewhere in the brew; Heidegger came to be seen by many as the chief offender.

The twentieth-century revolt against obscurantism and the esoterica of philosophers' special vocabularies has some roots, no doubt, in the work of G. E. Moore, particularly in his "defense of common sense" (e.g., 1925).[126] But the major theoretical thrust of that revolt originated in the nexus formed by the later writings of Ludwig Wittgenstein (1889–1951) and their reception at the hands of several scholars who then developed what has loosely been called "ordinary-language analysis." Until recently this movement has been an almost wholly Anglo-American event—a circumstance due in part, perhaps, to Moore's preliminary tillage and Wittgenstein's presence at Cambridge rather than, say, Heidelberg or Frankfurt. While some commentators have drawn early connections between Wittgensteinian ordinary-language analysis and the hermeneutic branch of German philosophy (see, e.g., Albert 1971),[127] the first outstanding example of a work that attempted to articulate the two discourses as an integrated foundation of social theory was authored by a British scholar (Winch 1958). Among German philosophers the intersection of hermeneutics with Wittgenstein's later work, and that of the ordinary-language analysts inspired by it, has been typically one of fundamental critique of the latter by the former, as exemplified most importantly by Gadamer's *Truth and Method* ([1965] 1967)—although more recently some scholars, Habermas (e.g., 1970a; 1970b) being the most visible, have attempted to adapt certain

126. For a discussion of Moore's "common sense" from a Wittgensteinian point of view, see Malcolm [1949] 1969.

127. Albert argued the case of similarities with regard to hermeneutics' "linguistic orientation" and concomitant "emphasis on the problem of linguistic meaning," together with its philosophical tendency toward transcendentalism, that is, its use of "ontological arguments in the direction of an apriorism in which language is elevated to an unmistakable transcendental factor" (Albert 1971, 110).

features both of the hermeneutic and the ordinary-language analysts' constructions to their own work (cf. Apel 1965).

Wittgenstein's writings, early or late, do not contain what would be considered an explicitly formulated theory of knowledge.[128] In fact, he was of the stated opinion that *Erkenntnistheorie* is a fruitless endeavor (see, e.g., [1922] 1961, §4.1121). Nevertheless, his discussions of language and meaning hold profound implications for any theory of knowledge. Relative to the then-existing theories in Anglo-American philosophy, it could be said, as von Wright did, that Wittgenstein's later philosophy is "entirely outside any philosophical tradition and without literary sources of influence," or that his *Investigations* stood as "a new chapter in the history of philosophy . . . something wholly original" (Hartnack [1962] 1965, 63).[129] From beginning to end, his central concern was with the question: How do language and reality, the word and the world, relate? What is the meaning of "meaning"? Following the early formulations by Moore and Russell, this had become a major issue—some have said *the* major issue—of most Anglo-American academic philosophy. Ryle, for example—himself a noted figure in the broadly labeled ordinary-language movement—observed at midcentury that "answers to this highly abstract question, What are meanings? have in recent decades bulked large in philosophical and logical discussions. Preoccupation with the theory of meaning could be described as the occupational disease of twentieth-century Anglo-Saxon and Austrian philosophy" (Ryle 1957, 239).

128. Only two of Wittgenstein's philosophical works were published before his death: the *Tractatus* in 1922 and a paper on "logical form" which he repudiated soon after (see Wittgenstein 1933; also Moore 1954). Posthumously published works include the *Investigations* (1953), of which part 1 was composed during 1936–45 and part 2 during 1947–49; materials concerning the foundation of mathematics (1956), written during the same period as part 1 of the *Investigations*; manuscripts on *Philosophical Grammar* (1974a), written during 1932–34; the preliminary studies generally known as *The Blue and Brown Books* (1958), notes dictated to his students in 1933–34 and 1934–35, respectively; and his notes on doubt and certainty (1969), written during the last year and a half of his life. Some of his correspondence has been published (e.g., 1974b; Engelmann 1967). *N.B.*: As with most of Wittgenstein's published works, part 1 of the *Investigations* was organized in sections (paragraphs and sets of paragraphs) and will be cited in that manner; the one major exception is part 2 of the *Investigations*, and citations of that material will therefore be by page number.

129. Useful exegetical treatments of Wittgenstein's writings have been given by Malcolm (1954), Pole (1958), Hartnack (1962), and Fann (1969), each of which contains more detailed descriptions that I shall undertake here. There is also Pitkin's (1972) fine appreciation of Wittgenstein's later philosophy and its implications for social-science theory.

During the first third of the century, the dominant view (best exemplified by the early Russell and by Wittgenstein's own *Tractatus*) held that the meaning of a word consisted foremost in its representational function of "naming," that is to say, in the denotational linking of a discriminant phonetic unit to some nonlinguistic entity, palpable or not. It was, as is sometimes said, a "picture theory" of language: through the device of language we "make to ourselves pictures of facts" (Wittgenstein [1922] 1961, §§2.1, 3.203). The entire argument of the *Tractatus* is dominated by an atomistic notion of "the one formal logic"—a uniform and nondistorting medium through which the "disguising" tendencies of "colloquial languages and differing social rules and conceptions of reality could be consistently related and evaluated" (§§4.002–4.003, 3.325)—and by a strong "antipsychological" stance in opposition to any sort of "mentalist" or "state-of-mind" explanation, as a result of which Wittgenstein said very little about "problems of consciousness" except in a most abstract way. The *Tractatus* proposed a language-transcendentalism that was in some ways similar to the transcendentalism of the Kantian philosophy of consciousness, insofar as its object of pursuit was conceived as a "world-representational" language that would determine a priori the limits and the mode of empirically meaningful statements about events and states of affairs in the world (e.g., Wittgenstein [1922] 1961, §§5.4, 5.552; cf. Apel [1965] 1967).

Although the divergence between his early and his later work is not so great as is sometimes imagined,[130] after Wittgenstein's return to Cambridge in 1929 his expressed views on the problem of meaning underwent considerable modification. By the end of the next decade his statements had taken on a very different character. Gone was the surety of "the one formal logic," that sturdy framework of a universal master language through which such perplexing matters as the problem of synonymity would be resolved. In contrast to the sharp and confident cadences of the *Tractatus*, Wittgenstein was now saying:

130. On the one hand, Wittgenstein's later work has roots in his original concern with abstractions of formal logic (see, e.g., 1974a, part 2). On the other hand, the *Tractatus* manifests a fateful ambivalence in his position: in his stress on the tautological character of logic there was a profound threat to the supposed promise of logic—namely, that it was simultaneously the most elemental and the supreme language of the universe. It was during the period of Wittgenstein's reformulation, it may be noted, that Gödel (1931) published his famous demonstration of the formal undecidability of *Principia Mathematica* (and related systems) in its own terms: that decisions of proof regarding truth claims derived from premises of this and similar formalized systems cannot be rendered without recourse to principles more general than the given system itself.

When I talk about language . . . I must speak the language of every day. Is this language somehow too coarse and material for what we want to say? *Then how is another one to be constructed?* . . .
Philosophy may in no way interfere with the actual use of language; it can in the end only describe it.
For it cannot give it any foundation either.
It leaves everything as it is. (Wittgenstein [1953] 1968, §§120, 124)

The false rigors of a positivist language analysis had been thrown over the side (although not entirely, as we will see), as a result of intensive self-critique.[131] "Colloquial language," the language of every day, was now considered to be completely ordered and justified within itself. Ordinary language was now appreciated very differently; so, too, were the constitution of meaning and the proper task of philosophy.

By the time he completed the first part of his *Investigations,* Wittgenstein had replaced his earlier emphasis on formal logic (as giving the measure of correct standards) with an emphasis on the pragmatics of language: not the entity "denoted" or "referred to," not the "picture" of the logical structure of facts, but the *use* of a word constitutes its meaning; even the meaning of "naming," even the naming of palpable objects, consists in the use of the naming-word.[132] Meaning is never "the word itself," nor images or feelings, nor "the thing" to which the word "attaches" or "refers"; in order to know the name of a "thing" (whether palpable or, as in "pain," not), for example, one must already have facility in the language activity of which it is a part. The key sentence from the *Investigations* is characteristically short: "For a *large* class of cases—though not for all—in which we employ the word 'meaning' it can be defined [*erklären*] thus: the meaning of a word is its use in language" (Wittgenstein [1953] 1968, §43).[133]

131. In Gadamer's view, "The really astounding thing is that Wittgenstein's self-critique moves in a direction" within the Vienna Circle and Anglo-American approach to the problem of language "similar to" the self-critique of phenomenology by Heidegger (Gadamer [1963] 1976, 174).

132. Even an ostensive definition presupposes some practical knowledge of the given language (see, e.g., Wittgenstein [1953] 1968, §§30–32).

133. There has been the usual abundance of mostly infertile argumentation of "what the master really meant"—in this case, especially what he meant by "meaning as use." I shall not attempt even to survey all of those arguments. While Wittgenstein's writings may be somewhat "enigmatic" at times (as several commentators have claimed), the main outline of his thesis is clear enough. (It is not at all clear, of course, what criteria of "enigmatic writing" those commentators had in mind.)

The meaningful use of a word is never the use of a merely formal "word-in-general," so to speak; rather, it always takes place within a specific context and under specific conditions. Wittgenstein asserted over and over that we must think of a word as a tool, as that which acquires significance of effect in its employment for some end or purpose. In making that point, he frequently drew upon the metaphor of "idling"—as in a wheel turning idly, seemingly on its own, unconnected to any larger mechanism and therefore doing no work. So it is, he argued, with a word that is not engaged, that is "hanging in the air," having no place in accepted practice[134]—as in the sentence, "Is the radius of this circle too hot?" or "The palm of my left hand kicked him in the shin." We may speak of "violations of rules" in those sentences, to be sure, but "what the rules *are*" is determined by the actual conduct of linguistic activity within some community of speakers: "It is our *acting* which lies at the bottom of the language-game" (Wittgenstein [1969] 1972, §204). In other words, meanings are constituted in and are relative to complexes of linguistic activity, or "language-games," for it is the use of a word within a particular language-game—a use determined and regulated by the grammar of that language-game—that establishes its meaning. Moreover, this relativity of meaning constitution is enforced by the circumstance that each language-game is completely ordered within itself; while there may be "family resemblances" among language-games (but *only* that; see Wittgenstein [1953] 1968, §§65–67), each must be grasped in its own setting and in terms of its own pattern of relations.

Wittgenstein's conception of meaning and ruledness in relativistic pragmatic terms stemmed from his conviction that the meaning and therefore the force of words are anchored in the ordinary practice of life. The entirety of his later philosophy is characterized by the tension of this duality of language and life-being-in-the-world, a duality which he attempted to articulate, without eventual success, through a weakly dialectical construction involving concepts of "grammar," "forms of life," and "criteria." The first of these, "grammar," consists of the rules that regulate our language-games. It is not, however, merely the surface grammar written in a teacher's casebook; rather, it includes all actual, contextual uses of words. For example, it "is part of the grammar of the word 'chair' that *this* is what we call 'to sit on a chair,' and it is part of the grammar of the word 'meaning' that *this* is what we call 'explanation of meaning' " (1958, 24). In other words, the grammar of a word includes not only the general qualification— in the case of *chair*, "that upon which one can sit"—but also, to continue

---

134. Thus: "The confusions which occupy us arise when language is like an engine idling, not when it is doing work" (Wittgenstein [1953] 1968, §132).

the same example, the specification of which activities qualify as instances of "sitting on a chair." These actual specifications are always historically contextual, in the sense that they are activities of our life-in-the-world and are dependent upon already established qualifications. Thus, grammar regulates "the '*possibilities*' of phenomena," because it controls "*the kind of statement* that we make about phenomena" (Wittgenstein [1953] 1968, §90).

Wittgenstein did not provide an explicit definition of his concept "form of life"—it appears only five times in the whole of the *Investigations* (Wittgenstein [1953] 1968, §§19, 23, 241; pp. 174, 226)—but its general sense is evident from its direct and indirect uses.[135] A "form of life" is simultaneously the foundation and the context of particular language-games and the regularities of their grammars. More than mere "conventions" or deliberate contrivances and agreements of opinion, they are patterns of living "which no one has doubted, but which have escaped remark only because they are always before our eyes" (§415). The regularities of the forms of life make possible the regularities of our language-games: the "formation of concepts can be explained . . . by very general facts of nature. (Such facts as mostly do not strike us because of their generality)" (§230).[136] Forms of life are of the "*natural history*" of human beings; they simply *are*, and must be accepted as given—they cannot be justified.[137] Once we have explained the grammar of a word and the language-game in which it exists, we "have reached bedrock" and can go no further (§217). In arriving at such bedrock we may have gained some added sentience of regard for the

135. For a discussion of four somewhat different interpretations of "form of life," see Hunter [1968] 1971, who preferred what he called the "organic" conception. Other commentators have noted resemblances of Wittgenstein's *Lebensformen* to Husserl's *Lebenswelt*; but the closer comparison is to the post-Husserlian notion of an "everyday, taken-for-granted world"—as formulated by Alfred Schutz (1953b), for example.

136. Thus, in instances of "a complete irregularity" (as opposed to the irregularity of a "mistake"—"for which, as it were, a place is prepared in the game"), theretofore relevant concepts are no longer useful, at least for the duration of the "complete irregularity" (see Wittgenstein [1953] 1968, §80; Wittgenstein [1969] 1972, §647).

137. Pitkin (1972, 102) has argued that Wittgenstein's seeming naïveté with regard to culture and "human nature" is just that—merely apparent—and cited as evidence of his "cultural sensitivity" his (1967) review of Frazer's *Golden Bough*. However, the passages cited show only that Wittgenstein could be offended by Frazer's ethnocentrism, that is, his violation of liberalist principles of relativism. It is abundantly evident from Wittgenstein's discussions that his conception of "human nature" (and "forms of life") was a fundamentally naturalistic conception.

given form of life; we may even be able to imagine a different form of life in which the particular language-game would be unworkable; but we cannot explain or justify the form of life itself. "What has to be accepted, the given, is—so one could say—*forms of life*" (p. 226).

There is a sense in which Wittgenstein conceived "grammar" in its depth as constituting the interpenetration of "form of life" and the meaning-as-use of words in a language game; that is, the depth regularities of grammar are regularities of "natural-historical" forms of life. However, the vehicle of interpenetration, so to speak, was provided by the concept of "criteria," which we have encountered already in the example of "sitting on a chair." In general, a "criterion" is that which qualifies particular cases as instances of a specific grammar. Thus, Wittgenstein said of the grammar of "a state"—examples of which are "being of an opinion, hoping for something, knowing something, being able to do something," but also states "of hardness, of weight, of fitting," and so on—"in order to understand the grammar of these states it is necessary to ask: 'What counts as a criterion for anyone's being in such a state?' " (§572).[138] Unfortunately, Wittgenstein offered little more in the way of definition or comments that would aid our understanding of what criteria *are* (as opposed to what they are not), and in consequence there is some confusion attending the concept. The confusion is partly due also to the circumstance that, in addition to the features noted above, Wittgenstein stipulated on more than one occasion that criteria enter the game only when a state is not experienced directly: "What is the criterion for the redness of an image? For me, when it is someone else's image: what he says and does. For myself, when it is my image: nothing" (§377, also §290). Yet, if "criteria" are what establish the qualifying use of a word, and thus its meaning, what does so for *me*, when "the redness of an image . . . is my image"? Given Wittgenstein's denial of the possibility of "private rules" and "private language" (about which, more below), such establishment must be, for me, too, it would seem, by a "criterion" that I learned as part of a language-game and, once learned, employ as a priority to the experience or state of "seeing red." Consider one of Wittgenstein's own examples: "it makes sense to say about other people that they doubt whether I am in pain; but not to say it about myself" (§246); and consider Pitkin's argument, made in her discussion of Wittgenstein's apparent inconsistency of treatment of "criteria," that "one cannot imagine . . . a situation in which we would be moved to say, 'I have this

---

138. This does not mean that a criterion is a "symptom." Whereas a "symptom" is "a phenomenon of which experience has taught us that it coincided, in some way or other, with the phenomenon which is our defining criterion," the criterion of a word or concept is tautological rather than correlative to it (Wittgenstein 1958, pp. 24–25).

peculiar painlike feeling even though there is no occasion for pain.' " (Pitkin 1972, 132). But of course one *can and does* say just those words. I may say exactly that to a physician, for example, who inquires as to why I am sitting in *this* examination room: I experience this "state," this "feeling," this "sensation," and I do not *know* if it does qualify as "pain" in the particular language-game (see Wittgenstein 1974a, 105).

In any event (for I do not pretend to have solved therewith the riddle "what Wittgenstein really meant by the concept 'criteria' "), the core of his argument remains undisturbed. The meaning of words is constituted in their use according to the grammar of a language-game embedded in a "natural-historical" form of life. The word "language" does not name a single phenomenon or even a class of phenomena all of which are rigorously interrelated by aprioristically established categories of a formal logic. To talk about "language in general" as a singular feature of human reality is to talk gibberish. There are, on the contrary, innumerable language-games—those that exist now or that have existed and those that could exist or might yet exist—all of which are distinctly different games, even though we may notice certain "family resemblances" crisscrossing among them.[139] Moreover, because the meaning of a word is determined not simply by the "contents of mind" of the speaker/thinker but by the circumstances of the practice of a language-game, there can be no private rules or private language. "It might be said," said Wittgenstein, that "if you can give yourself a private definition of a word, then you must inwardly *undertake* to use the word in such-and-such a way" (Wittgenstein [1953] 1968, §262). But: "How do you undertake that? Is it to be assumed that you invent the technique of using the word; or that you found it ready-made?" His argument against the possibility of a private language turns on the general stipulation that a language, or a language-game, is a social process of uses: "I could not apply any rules to a private transition from what is seen to words. Here the rules really would hang in the air; for the institution of their use is lacking" (§380). The use of a word requires the possibility that practice can be checked now and again so as to determine whether the practice is correct practice.[140] The figure of a hermit sitting on a mountain-

---

139. Not only language-games but other sorts of games as well are highly varied in their practiced rules, Wittgenstein argued. Furthermore, a given game "is not everywhere circumscribed by rules," even though it does have regularity. There are, for example, no rules governing "how high one throws the ball in tennis; yet tennis is a game for all that and has rules too" (Wittgenstein [1953] 1968, §68).

140. As Malcolm pointed out, the "conception of private language that Wittgenstein attacks is not the conception of a language that only the speaker does understand, but of a language that no other person *can* understand" (Malcolm [1954] 1963, 124; cf. Wittgenstein [1953] 1968, §243).

top and speaking his unique language illustrates the limit. He had no one to tell him whether his speaking is regular and sensible—indeed, whether his speaking follows the same rules today as yesterday. His own "private memory," to continue the figure, can be no judge of the matter, for if he *were* speaking by different rules today, his remembering the past would also be by those different rules and therefore could not detect the difference. As Wittgenstein put it, "Don't clutch at the idea of our always being able to bring red before our mind's eye even when there is nothing red anymore. . . . For suppose you cannot remember the colour anymore?" (Wittgenstein [1953] 1968, §57; see also Wittgenstein 1974a, 84–85). If nothing "red" remains, and if you have forgotten what "red" means—what the color "looks like"—the word "red" may not cease to have meaning entirely (e.g., if under those circumstances someone said to you, "I once saw a red house"—or "red tree," or whatever—it would have the meaning of a "puzzle," a "curiosity"); but if nothing "red" remains, and you do have a memory of what "red" "looks like," how do you know that this memory is correct? To what do you refer for judgment when you say, "I once saw a red tree," and then wonder if you are remembering it "as it really was"?

Wittgenstein's argument, I am aware, has been the object of very considerable debate in recent years, as challenges and counter-arguments have been offered from various quarters with the aim of showing that private language *is* possible (e.g., the claim that a sole surviving member of a linguistically unique society would then be a private-language speaker).[141] But one wonders why the tedious finery that has characterized this debate. The use of a language is to *communicate*, which implies "exchange" and is cognate with *community* and *communion*. Admittedly, Wittgenstein's argument rests partly in an "epistemically invidious distinction between private and public memory judgments," as Stocker put it (1966, 47). However, the "invidiousness" stems from assumptions about the "private-meaning" side, not the public "side"; acts of verification (e.g., of the "proper ruledness" of a speech-act) are inherently social. When reading some of the claims of antagonists (even some of those of protagonists) in this debate, one suspects that they often try to put too fine a point on Wittgenstein's argument, relative to the central thrust of his work.

The serious inadequacies of Wittgenstein's general project in the *Investigations* and related writings lie elsewhere than in the minutiae so carefully winnowed in the private-language debate. The inadequacies pertain to the variable fit between what people say and what they do, and to the conditions that make that fit so often a very poor one indeed. Pole was

141. For a summary of the controversy, see Smerud (1970); also the papers in Jones (1969). Dewey (1925, 185) had earlier rejected the possibility.

onto this basic inadequacy from one point of view, when he remarked that the

> notion of normativity in Wittgenstein is explained solely in terms of reference to standards, and these standards he finds in existing practice. The doctrine necessarily raises doubts as to the status of Wittgenstein's own activity, for evidently he can have no standards to appeal to. Within existing language-games we can sensibly talk of right and wrong; and yet Wittgenstein's own activity takes us outside this monadism of language-games. It stands over and collates them. Indeed it claims to do no more than describe them, but the description, we find, is not a merely impartial or neutral one. (Pole 1958, 84)

While we must not expect that Wittgenstein should have stood somehow *behind* language in order properly to address the constitution of "language-games" (as he attempted in the *Tractatus,* for example), it is the case that his location of all possible "standards" strictly within existing practice denied him any to which he could appeal self-consistently while "describing and collating" language-games. It is, as Pole remarked, "hard not to ask what sort of linguistic activity Wittgenstein himself is engaged in" and how he learned it; "what game is this, and where are we to look for its rules? . . . His own activity goes beyond all existing practice" (1958, 97).

Certainly Wittgenstein acknowledged that language-speaking is not the whole of life (e.g., Wittgenstein [1953] 1968, §23). So, one must ask, what of actions that do not correspond with the saying of them? Most activities require understanding not only in terms of the given language-game but also in terms of conditions and consequences of actual behaviors that do not correspond with "the concepts used in that game for public interpretation of the behavior" (Apel [1965] 1967, 56).[142] Consider the implications for Wittgenstein's notion of "truth," a property of propositional utterances in language-games. In his unfinished excursion into the question of doubt and certitude, written shortly before his death, he remarked that "what we can ask is whether it makes sense to doubt" a proposition: e.g., "such a proposition as 'I know I have a brain'? Can I doubt it? Grounds for *doubt* are lacking! Everything speaks in its favour, nothing against it. Nevertheless it is imaginable that my skull should turn out empty when it was operated on" (Wittgenstein [1969] 1972, §§2, 4, 80, 82). "The *truth* of my statements," he wrote, "is the test of my *under-*

---

142. One need not entertain any sort of "conspiracy" theory in order to raise that question. It is sufficient merely to observe that "language-games" are internally structured in relations of domination and control, and that the "not-said" is often more important than the "said."

standing of these statements. . . . What counts as an adequate test of a statement belongs to logic, . . . to the description of the language-game." The Wittgensteinian monadology of language-games is such that, by his contention, that which one would otherwise call the ambiguity of ordinary speaking—namely, the imprecision of rules—is only apparent. That is, the ordinary language-game is completely ordered in its own relations and thus can serve somehow as its own standard for analysis. But here we see revealed the silent continuation of a principled standpoint of "formal language" (despite Wittgenstein's assumption to the contrary) and, necessarily relatedly, the persistent *ahistorical* character of his conception of ordinary language (this, not despite but in conformity to his thinking of language-games vis-à-vis a "natural history" of human beings).[143] His language-games are ossified forms that cannot allow for the circumstance that one's language-learning—even a "native" or "primary" language-learning—is never at any moment a complete and unambiguous, once-and-for-all mastery of model rules. The rules themselves, the grammars of speaking/thinking, are of historical process; they require, but also they *provide for*, their own ongoing development and, as Gadamer (1965) argued, "interpretation" throughout the life-activity of the speaker.[144]

Wittgenstein attempted to insulate his own investigations through his notion of the proper task of philosophy: to engage in "a battle against bewitchment of our intelligence by means of language" (Wittgenstein [1953] 1968, §109). In his view the traditional philosophical problems have

143. A contrary view has been argued by Cavell (1969, 47–52), in his criticism of Pole's (1958) account.

144. Pole pointed to an aspect of this ossification of words in Wittgenstein's program, when he referred to the latter's

> characteristic anxiety to pin language down within the limits of its origins. He asks us to consider the situations in which words were first learnt; and clearly he wishes their career to end in the same circle in which it began. He is successful enough; if we are never to take account of our feelings as to what further applications the existing pattern demands, what further steps are necessary; if, too, we are never to use pictures or metaphors drawn from old fields of thought in tackling new ones, then creative thinking will certainly come to a stop—not only in Philosophy but generally. Wittgenstein's whole treatment of language takes no account of the necessity or possibility of its growth; one may go further, it comes near to prohibiting it. (Pole 1958, 91–92)

One need not accept the positivistic atomism that seems to lurk behind Pole's charge (e.g., in the recommended simple transfer, as it were, from old to new fields of thought); but it *is* the case that, by Wittgenstein's argument, our knowledge of our own and other's activities and their effects would be restricted to a virtual repetition of our "native language-learning" through which we were socialized vis-à-vis the existing "form of life" (cf. Habermas 1970c, 255–56).

a sort of artificial and illicit quality about them. They occur when language "goes on holiday," when language or words are idling. It stands to reason by this view, then, that the traditional problems of philosophy can be properly addressed only when we "bring words back from their metaphysical to their every day use" (§116). His own efforts were conceived accordingly as varied "therapies," that is, as therapeutic descriptions of various language-games undertaken not so much as refutations as clarifications. He was "interested in language as a procedure according to explicit rules, because philosophical problems are misunderstandings which must be removed by clarification of the rules according to which we are inclined to use words" (1974a, 68). It is the business of philosophy to remove misunderstandings through elucidation of the correct language-games within which particular words are used. Once a "philosophical problem" has been completely clarified, it simply has disappeared. With that definition of the philosopher's mission in mind, Wittgenstein characterized his own work as primarily "descriptive" rather than "normative"; yet while his effort may have been at one level simply to *describe* the constitution and relations of language-games, there is much in his writing to indicate that at another level he sought to *alter* linguistic usage, and thereby meaning, in the direction of his own doctrine. However—and this is the great rub—it was only linguistic usage, and the linguistic usage of philosophers only, that was the object of his program of improvement. By the terms of his relativism, we must be content with the usages and meanings of common-sense talk in the common-sense world, whatever the form of life, for we are faced finally and simply with the naturalistic givenness of language-games and their conditions in the natural-historical forms of life: "What has to be accepted, the given, is . . . *forms of life*" (Wittgenstein [1953] 1968, 226).

Again, we must be careful not to ask too much of Wittgenstein—specifically, that he should have laid out for us a blueprint detailing the means and process of a radical reconstruction of the world. He was very far from doing that. The task, as he saw it, was merely to understand existing practice clearly through clarified language-games, not to change practice (save for the philosopher's language practice). The predominant image was of philosophy leaving "everything as it is" (Wittgenstein [1953] 1968, §124). Thus, Wittgenstein made no theoretical claims for his "therapeutic" activities, beyond the return of words from their metaphysical to their common-sense uses.[145] He offered no grounds by which to assert a theoretical project.

145. Wittgenstein's position may be contrasted with that of John Austin (1911–60)—along with Wittgenstein, one of the early leading figures in the "ordinary-language" movement. Whereas Wittgenstein saw philosophy as a "therapeutic activity" that only alleviates "confusions," Austin saw it as an enterprise that *may* accumulate a body of verified knowledge. Wittgenstein understood "truth" as

Moreover, it is instructive to consider Winch's attempt to develop from Wittgenstein's discussions a social theory that, as Winch (1958, 102) recognized, would be radically relativistic ("connected with the realisation that intelligibility takes many and varied forms is the realisation that reality has no key"). But he could only pretend to occupy a sort of free-floating locality from which to move in and out of the grammar of existing language-games without the restrictions of any dogmatic language of his own. As Habermas remarked, Winch relied "as naively as [Alfred] Schutz on the possibility of pure theory" (Habermas 1970c, 244). In terms of the practical potential or capacity of his program (if not the actual limits of his practice; see Pole 1958, 97), Wittgenstein was dependent on much the same fiction.

6. QUINE: "EPISTEMOLOGY NATURALIZED"

Earlier in this century, one of the broad marks of success in epistemology was considered by many philosophers to be the reducibility of theoretical propositions to an "observation language" of formal-logical and sensory terms. Despite the implications of Hume's predicament, it was believed that such translation was not only possible but indeed practiced, at least in the more "advanced" areas of natural science—in other words, that "theoretical" and "observation" languages are fundamentally distinct from one another and that the former can be reduced to the latter in order to yield an empirically verified knowledge of the truths of "the world as it is." The initial linguistic program in Anglo-American philosophy held that since any fact of the world consists of a definite ontic structure, if a sentence uttered in description of some component or aspect of the world does assert a fact of the world, then the grammatical structure of that sentence must be consonant with the ontic structure of the fact; therefore, truths of the world can be discovered by studying the structure of sentences. Apropos was Russell's view that "partly by means of the study of syntax, we can arrive at considerable knowledge concerning the structure of the world" (1940, 438). More recently, however, the constitutive notion of reducibility has been met in many quarters with a greater degree of pessimism, and with a

---

dependent on a situation of "human nature," but Austin apparently rejected such a notion (see 1950). Austin agreed that traditional philosophy had mostly yielded confused or wrongheaded conclusions, but the reason for it was nothing more fundamental than premature closure. Moreover, Austin disputed the claim that one can have certain knowledge only of one's *own* feelings, sensations, etc.; the distinction on which that claim rests is, he argued, "the 'original sin' by which the philosopher cast himself out from the garden of the world we live in" (1953, 136). Rather, one cannot always be certain of one's own feelings, etc., since one may misname them, have inadequate experience by which to judge them, and so forth (1953, 135–37).

renewed memory of Humean conclusions regarding empiricist doctrines of truth. In the words of Willard van Orman Quine (b. 1908), a member of the Anglo-American academy whose views have gained in prominence since midcentury:

> Philosophers have rightly despaired of translating everything into observational and logico-mathematical terms. They have despaired of this even when they have not recognized, as the reason for this irreducibility, that the statements largely do not have their private bundles of empirical consequences. And some philosophers have seen in this irreducibility the bankruptcy of epistemology. Carnap and the other logical positivists of the Vienna Circle had already pressed the term "metaphysics" into pejorative use, as connoting meaninglessness; and the term "epistemology" was next. Wittgenstein and his followers, mainly at Oxford, found a residual philosophical vocation in therapy: in curing philosophers of the delusion that there were philosophical problems. (Quine 1969a, 82)

Quine has not been so willing to join in the surrender of "epistemology" to some realm of meaninglessness (wherever that might be), however. A major aspect of his work has consisted in efforts to rescue epistemology from the threat of expatriation. Before examining those efforts, it will be useful to survey his argument against reducibility.

The "crucial consideration" on which Quine's argument rests, according to his account of it, is that "a statement about the world does not always or usually have a separable fund of empirical consequences that it can call its own" (1969a, 82). This consideration stands behind the claim of "the impossibility of an epistemological reduction of the sort where every sentence is equated to a sentence in observational and logico-mathematical terms," and in the same way it stands behind the Quinean claim of "the indeterminacy of translation" generally, which has been argued in several of Quine's publications (e.g., Quine [1958] 1969; Quine 1959; Quine 1960, chap. 2; Quine [1968] 1969, 29–40).

Typically, Quine has argued the "indeterminacy of translation" claim in the manner of the following scenario of "radical translation." Suppose that a renowned linguist has just come upon a heretofore totally isolated people "whose language is without known affinities." Mustering the wherewithal for another assault on the unknown, our linguist sets out "to learn the language directly by observing what the natives say under observed circumstances, encountered or contrived." By compiling a fund of empirical observations of the native language in use, it should be possible to formulate falsifiable hypotheses regarding basic lexicon, rules of syntax, and so forth, which hypotheses would then be tested against further instances of the language in use, perhaps contrived as well as "naturally encountered." Eventually a manual of translation could be prepared. Now, assume that at first observation our linguist hears a native speaker utter the sound "Gavagai" and correlatively sees the speaker point toward a scene describable by the linguist as "a rabbit scurrying by." According to Quine, the linguist may conclude that "Gavagai" was prompted by a stimulation (i.e., that the utterance resulted from something in the "external world") and may *conjecture* that the stimulation had something to do with the scene described as "a rabbit scurrying by." On the basis of subsequent episodes judged by our linguist to be cases of "a rabbit in motion," Quine would be prepared to "grant that the linguist may establish inductively, *beyond reasonable doubt*, that a certain heathen expression is one to which natives can be prompted to assent by the presence of a rabbit, or a reasonable *facsimile*, and not otherwise" (first emphasis added).[146] Although the nemesis of inductive conclusions—namely, the uncertainty of the next observation—is not sundered in this grant, the Quinean linguist may be content with pragmatic justification: thus the decisive, if not quite definitive, "beyond reasonable doubt."

Based on some quantity of inductive evidence, then, Quine's linguist is

> warranted in according the native expression ["Gavagai"] the cautious translation "There's a rabbit," "There we have a rabbit," "Lo! a rabbit," "Lo! rabbithood again," insofar as the differences among these English sentences are counted irrelevant. This much translation can be objective, however exotic the tribe. It recognizes the native expression as in effect a rabbit-heralding sentence. But the linguist's bold further step, in which he imposes his own object-positing pattern without special warrant, is taken when he equates the native expression or any part of it with the *term* "rabbit." (Quine [1958] 1969, 2)

Clearly our linguist has not gotten very far. The fund of correlated experiences of seeing a rabbit and hearing "Gavagai" may constitute a sufficient basis for warranting translation of the native expression into a particular heralding sentence of the linguist's own language; but it is not sufficient to warrant an object nomination: "Appeal to an object category is unwarranted."

What is the reason for this limitation? In the first place, even if we

---

146. It is because a "reasonable facsimile" can elicit the same response ("Gavagai," in this case) that we must "think of what prompts the native's assent to 'Gavagai?' as stimulations and not rabbits" (Quine 1960, 31).

assume that the native expression does in fact herald the presence of something, an X, it is not demonstrated that X is "rabbit." The presence of X could instead be "all the various temporal segments of rabbits" or "all the integral or undetached parts of rabbits," and in order to discriminate among such possibilities more must be known about and of the native language (e.g., identity, quantification) than is yet available to this novitiate. Moreover—and this contradicts the above-tendered assumption of heralding—it is by no means established from the fund of correlative experiences that the native expression actually has the form "presence of an X." Conceivably, the expression should be rendered "with an abstract singular term," as Quine phrased it—that is, not that "*a* rabbit is present" but that "rabbithood is locally manifested." Or, to take the matter further, it is conceivable that "Gavagai" is uttered always and only when a rabbit is present to our linguist, and yet that the native expression means to the native speaker nothing at all like a category of our zoological tables but, instead, a category of foodstuffs or of ancestral spiritualization or of meteorological prognostication, or, as Steiner has pointed out, a joke or derisive hoax contrived for the benefit of the linguist-intruder (Steiner 1975, 355). The possibilities may not be endless, but they are sufficiently numerous to defy the naive empiricism of unambiguous translation (Quine [1958] 1969, 1–3; Quine 1960, 29–33, 45–46, 51–53).

Any linguist who would insist on being "as cagey as all this," Quine acknowledged, would succeed at most in offering us an inventory of uncertain and "simple-minded announcements of observable current events"—which is a good deal less than we have come to expect from our linguist-translators (cf. Wittgenstein [1953] 1968, §§206–7). When Matthiae and his associates unearthed thousands of clay tablets from the remains of palace archives of Ebla, and concluded that the tablet inscriptions were in a language known by no living person (see Matthiae 1976), linguistic authorities looked upon the find with an excitement born partly of the confident expectation that their cryptographic efforts would be successful. With a little time and much colligation, their efforts would yield a manageable table of rules and equivalences by which the plenitude of an unfamiliar otherness would be distilled into familiar sameness. We expect of the linguist-translator, as Quine put it, "a manual of instructions for custom-building a native sentence to roughly the purpose of any newly composed English sentence, within reason, and vice versa." And that is what a "proficient" translator accomplishes.

Yet: just what *is* it that the translator does accomplish? Once our proficient linguist-translator has completed the "necessary job of lexicography, forwards and backwards," how may we characterize the resulting table and manual of instruction? Whatever else we may say about them, Quine warned, we cannot avoid their origin in our linguist's historical cultural modality—that is, the circumstance that our linguist has "read our ontological point of view into the native language. He has decided what expressions to treat as referring to objects, and, within limits, what sorts of objects to treat them as referring to. He has had to decide, however arbitrarily, how to accommodate English idioms of identity and quantification in native translation." The constructed table of rules and equivalences is never a neutral third that stands midway between the "this side" of our linguist and the "other side" of the native speaker—at least it is never knowably so, not even if the result of protracted negotiations between linguist and one or many native speakers. True, if our linguist measured up to our expectations of proficiency, he would have tested provisional versions of the table against additional data before certifying it as an accurate representation of the native language. This procedure may be "good scientific method," Quine allowed, "but it opens up no new kind of data." For it remains the case that "English general and singular terms, identity, quantification, and the whole bag of ontological tricks may be correlated with elements of the native language in any of various mutually incompatible ways, each compatible with all possible linguistic data, and none preferable to another save as favored by a rationalization of the *native* language that is simple and natural to *us*" (Quine [1958] 1969, 3–6; Quine 1960, 72).

Quine's argument of indeterminacy is wide-ranging in its application. For instance, it challenges the strict notion of "synonymy": just as the quantity and variety of possible candidates of meaning for any given native expression are large enough that the probability that any two languages will contain words having precisely identical meanings is very low, so too with the model category of synonymic translation within a single language: two words (or sentences) may share some definitive properties—of denotation, connotative association, affective response, etc.—but it is highly improbable that they equivalently share all properties.

The indeterminacy argument also applies to translations attempted between diachronically removed languages as well as to intercultural synchronic translations. The controversies of classicists—among themselves and with regard to Heideggerian readings (as noted above in section 4)— about the proper meaning of a sentence purportedly authorized by Parmenides, for example, provide us with suitable illustrative material. Here, as in the case of Quine's "heathen" language, "the obstacle to correlating conceptual schemes is not that there is anything ineffable about language or culture, near or remote." To the contrary: as the example of a Parmenidean sentence demonstrates, there is much that can be uttered in description of any language or culture. "The obstacle is only that any one intercultural correlation of words and phrases, and hence of theories, will be just one among various empirically admissible correlations, whether it is suggested by historical gradations or by unaided analogy; there is nothing for such a correlation to be uniquely right or wrong about" (Quine 1953, 20–46; Quine [1958] 1969, 25; Quine 1960, 46–56).[147]

The foundation of Quine's indeterminacy argument consists in a fundamental attack on the concept of analyticity, first fully presented in his famous essay "Two Dogmas of Empiricism" (Quine [1951] 1953, 20–46). By conventional definition from the tradition of classical empiricism, an analytic statement is true or false solely by virtue of logico-linguistic grounds; analytic truths are necessary truths, truths that hold independently of worldly events and states of affairs, whatever these may be. A synthetic statement, on the other hand, is true or false not only by virtue of its logico-linguistic properties (i.e., a synthetic statement cannot be true if it violates one or another rule of logic) but also with reference to worldly circumstances of facticity. This distinction between the analytic and the synthetic (the necessary and the contingent, "relations of ideas" and "matters of fact," etc.) has long served as a mainstay of empiricism—and of the positivist's judgment that metaphysics deals in meaningless claims insofar as metaphysical statements are purportedly both factually representative of the world *and* necessary.[148] In other words, while the truth of any synthetic statement is dependent on factual conditions of the world as well as logico-linguistic canon, a statement that claims to announce a logical truth cannot be contingent on worldly conditions. However, because of the futility of efforts to explicate all classes of analyticity without surreptitiously invoking analyticity itself,[149] Quine was prompted to argue that "belief in some fundamental cleavage between truths that are *analytic*, or grounded in

147. Quine acknowledged that in "saying this I philosophize from the vantage point only of our own provincial conceptual scheme and scientific epoch, true; but I know no better" (Quine [1958] 1969, 25).

148. Many philosophers, the early Wittgenstein included, were led to conclude that, metaphysics being meaningless, the proper business of philosophy is to clarify the logico-linguistic conditions of truth (i.e., analyticity) and that synthetic statements, because they are contingent on worldly conditions, should be left to science. By this account, philosophy becomes logic and certain aspects of language (plus ethics and aesthetics, to the extent that these are recognized); all else that is meaningful in a worldly way becomes the matter of science. As will be seen below, Quine's argument extends this reallocation between philosophy and science.

149. Quine (1953) recognized two classes of analytic statements: those that are true or false by virtue solely of their logical form (e.g., "No unmarried man is married") and those that are true or false by virtue of their meaning (e.g., "No bachelor is married"). Statements of the first class are straightforward; that is, a purely "logical truth" is true regardless of any systematic substitution of its nonlogical terms (e.g., "No unemployed person is employed"). But statements of the second class resist equally definitive explication.

meanings independently of matters of fact, and truths that are *synthetic*, or grounded in fact," is an "ill-founded" belief and "the root of much nonsense." One simply cannot isolate the truth claim of any individual statement and cleanly divide it into two piles of components, one labeled "logico-linguistic" and the other "factual." Moreover, this ill-founded and misleading dogma of radical separation is "intimately connected" with another—indeed, is "at root identical" to it—namely, "reductionism," or the belief that each synthetic statement can be linked with "a unique range of possible sensory events such that the occurrence of any of them" tends to confirm the truth claim of the statement, and, as well, "another unique range of possible sensory events," the occurrence of which would tend to falsify the claim. As already indicated, the Quinean position is that unique correlations or translations from individual statements of theory to exclusively applicable packages of "sensory events" are extremely improbable (Quine 1953, 20–23, 40–42).[150]

It is to be expected that an attack on a principle of empiricism as fundamental as the analytic/synthetic distinction would not go unanswered. The issue was quickly joined, beginning most notably with Grice and Strawson's (1956) well-known, and ultimately unsuccessful, response (see also Dolan 1967). Of course, it must be recognized that Quine did not reject empiricism *in toto*. Nor did he assert that the analytic-synthetic distinction is without use, or that it does not exist in the world of philosophical discourse, or that philosophers do not agree in its usage. In my own writing, here and elsewhere in this chapter, for example, I frequently make use of published works that are conventionally termed "translated editions"; likewise, I frequently deploy the locution "in other words" (or "i.e.," "that is," "to put it otherwise," and so on) with the aim of restating "the same meaning" through the vehicle of "a different sentence." From Quine's point of view, there is indeterminacy in all of this. From Quine's point of view, I agree. Still, the uses are there for all to see. We rely on translations, and we deploy those locutions, usually with some expectation of being understood "just so" or "more or less so" (and in the case of the "in other words" sort of locution, even with expectation of enhancing the probability of being understood "just so"). If the notion of complete determinacy of translation is illusory, if the claimed fundamental distinction between the analytic and the synthetic is illusory, what warrant can we invoke? For Quine, it must be an empirical pragmatic warrant. "As an

150. Another challenge to the analytic/synthetic distinction, inspired by a reading of Dewey, was presented by Morton White (1950) before the publication of Quine's famous attack. Their arguments have much in common, White's paper having been formulated in the context of discussions with Quine and Nelson Goodman.

empiricist I continue to think of the conceptual scheme of science as a tool, ultimately, for predicting future experience in the light of past experience." But the situation is such that the scientist must import "irreducible posits" of various kinds—"physical objects," "forces," etc.—when weaving a fabric of explanatory/predictive statements. These posits are inescapably cultural, that is, relative to a particular cultural matrix; we may even call them "myths," if we choose, just as Homeric gods are myths. Nevertheless, such posits are integral to the web of statements that, as a web, constitute scientific explanation/prediction. Of course, relative to a given cultural matrix, some posits are better than others: for example, the "myth of physical objects is epistemologically superior to most in that it has proved more efficacious than other myths," such as those of the Homeric gods, "as a device for working a manageable structure into the flux of experience." And therein lies the familiar thread of Quine's warrant: efficacy of means to successful explanation/prediction of our sense experiences. Each of us, according to Quine, "is given a scientific heritage plus a continuing barrage of sensory stimulation." As we process this "input," we maintain an asymmetry of authority between the received heritage, on the one hand, and the sensory stimulation on the other; we mold the former to the shape of the latter. And "the considerations which guide [us] in warping [our] scientific heritage to fit [our] continuing sensory promptings are, where rational, pragmatic" (Quine 1953, 44–46).[151]

In Quine's reconstruction of an "empiricism without the dogmas," any statement depends for its empirical meaning on its position within a particular field of statements, and any attempt to utter or to address "the empirical content of an individual statement" as such will perforce be misleading.

> The totality of our so-called knowledge or beliefs, from the most casual matters of geography and history to the profoundest laws of atomic physics or even of pure mathematics and logic, is a man-made fabric which impinges on experience only along the edges. . . . A conflict with experience at the periphery occasions readjustments in the interior of the field. Truth values have to be redistributed over some of our statements. Re-evaluation of some statements entails re-evaluation of others, because of their logical interconnections—the

151. This separation of "components" of the "input" is perhaps more sharply made than Quine intended. He would probably agree, for example, that the "scientific heritage" which we are "given" counts as part of the "continuing sensory promptings" (i.e., we hear it, read it, etc.). However, he would no doubt insist that the rule of judgment, as conceived within his pragmatic empiricism, must be in terms of "sensory stimulations," especially those of physical objects.

logical laws being in turn simply certain further statements of the system. . . . But the total field is so undetermined by its boundary conditions, experience, that there is much latitude of choice as to what statements to re-evaluate in the light of any single contrary experience. No particular experiences are linked with any particular statements in the interior of the field, except indirectly through considerations of equilibrium affecting the field as a whole. (Quine 1953, 42)

Not merely any statement or any translation but, more, any "irreducible posit" and any object or force or state of affairs so posited are always inescapably relative to a web of statements and to the "background language" from which the web of statements gains its possibility. The dimensions of a background language, of the cultural matrix that pulses through it, constitute the "coordinate system" within which, and only within which, we can sensibly ask about the references of our terms. Thus, it "is meaningless to ask whether, in general, our terms 'rabbit,' 'rabbit part,' 'number,' etc., really refer respectively to rabbits, rabbit parts, numbers, etc., rather than to some ingeniously permuted denotations." We cannot ask such a question meaningfully by any absolute standard; "we can meaningfully ask it only relative to some background language." Each thing acquires its thingness and its difference or identity vis-à-vis another thing only by virtue of a background language. True, any given background language is itself meaningful only in relation to still another background language, and with that recognition we enter a regress. In principle, the regress is unending; but "in practice we end the regress of background languages, in discussions of reference, by acquiescing in our mother tongue and taking its words at face value" (Quine 1953, 42–43; Quine [1968] 1969, 48–49).[152]

What, then, of epistemology? Given the Quinean argument of irreducibility and indeterminacy of translation, is there any point in retaining the philosopher's enterprise of epistemological inquiry? Evidently so: "Epistemology still goes on, though in a new setting and a clarified status."

Epistemology, or something like it, simply falls into place as a chapter of psychology and hence of natural science. It studies a natural phenomenon, viz., a physical human subject. This human subject is accorded a certain experimentally controlled input—certain patterns of

152. This "ontological relativity" does not imply that we cannot speak of "natural kinds" of things: "Surely there is nothing more basic to thought and language than our sense of similarity; our sorting of things into kinds." Quine has contended, however, that "it is a mark of maturity of a branch of science that the notion of similarity or kind finally dissolves, so far as it is relevant to that branch of science" (1969b, 116, 121).

irradiation in assorted frequencies, for instance—and in the fullness of time the subject delivers as output a description of the three-dimensional external world and its history. The relation between the meager input and the torrential output is a relation that we are prompted to study for somewhat the same reasons that always prompted epistemology; namely, in order to see how evidence relates to theory, and in what way one's theory of nature transcends any available evidence. (Quine 1969a, 82–83)

Whereas traditionally the epistemologist has been appreciated as combined architect and custodian of the house of knowledge—responsible for a founding enterprise that would "contain, in a sense, natural science," that is, that would "construct it somehow from sense data"—Quine's epistemologist has become a naturalized citizen of the abode called natural science, the only house of knowledge worthy of the name at least in this corner of the universe. An epistemologist now is that resident who studies how other residents perform the building of the house in which they all live. There is nothing fundamentally special about epistemological enterprise; like that of the natural science of psychology of which it is a component, it is simply "our own construction or projection from stimulations like those" which the epistemologist metes out to the "epistemological subject."

Standards of judgment admitted in this psychological study of the process of knowledge are the very same standards employed in natural science generally. They take their measure in the authority of observation sentences—not, however, the "observation sentence" as conceived by classical empiricism, since the notion of a theory-free language of facts is ill-founded. Rather, "an observation sentence is one on which all speakers of the language give the same verdict when given the same concurrent stimulation," that is, "one that is not sensitive to differences in past experience within the speech community." Questions of what will qualify as "same concurrent stimulation," of what determines "membership in the same community," of what defines the limiting "beyond reasonable doubt" (as invoked by Quine himself, for example, in his case of the linguist-translator of "Gavagai")—all these and related questions are settled in the same manner and by the same force of authority: negotiations of convention among members of the given speech community, a convention in the sense of what "the community sees eye-to-eye on."[153] Epistemological judgments

---

153. Compare Wittgenstein [1953] 1968, §241: " 'So you are saying that human agreement decides what is true and what is false?'—It is what human beings *say* that is true and false; and they agree in the *language* they use. That is not agreement in opinions but in form of life."

have no privileged status relative to other judgments undertaken in the community of scientists; they are all cut from the same bolt, by the same shears, along the same internal measuring stick. While this view may seem to invite the old charge of circularity, the charge no longer really applies, according to Quine, now that we no longer dream the old dreams "of deducing science from sense data." In our more enlightened condition we are instead "after an understanding of science as an institution or process in the world, and we do not intend that understanding to be any better than the science which is its object" (1969a, 83–84, 86–87).

Quine's project may be described as a kind of pragmatic empiricism which, while attempting to tread between physicalism and phenomenalism without collapsing into either, calmly announces a relativism triumphant. That epistemological judgments are contingent on the conditions of a community of speakers and can claim no priority vis-à-vis the traditional business of natural science is no longer a "problem" or "dilemma"; it is merely a fact of life from which none can escape. Knowing can be thought of as a game—a game that may differ in degree but not in kind from other games. In this game, as in any other, determinations of successful outcome, of what is more and what is less efficacious as a means to successful outcome, and of what counts as proof of efficacy and of success, are all made by the historical community of players of the game itself. It could be argued that, on the surface, Quine's view provides us with a useful beginning, insofar as it sketches the existent "is" of the process of knowing. However, it is grievously eviscerated because it sketches just that and nothing more. No doubt the older tradition of epistemology has been wrapped up in some foolish dreams, including, as Quine said, the dream of deducing science from sense data. But the older tradition prized another dream that Quine's rescued epistemology does not, and this one we would be foolish to relinquish: the dream of a basis of critical judgment that in some manner stands as otherness to the existent "is." Such absence makes the Quinean sketch faulty, even as a beginning.

Much of the development of Quine's argument has been informed by contrast to the sort of position exemplified in Carnap's work (e.g., Carnap [1950] 1952; Carnap 1956). Whereas Carnap's position relies on a premise of basic differentiation between "theoretical language" and "observation language," and attempts to adjudicate problematic cases of the one through linguistic-pragmatic efforts and of the other through scientific-methodical observation, Quine's argument asserts that *both* receive pragmatic adjudication. "Physical objects are conceptually imported into the situation as convenient intermediaries," and they are "comparable, epistemologically, to the gods of Homer"; that is, with respect to "epistemological footing" any physical object differs "only in degree and not in kind" from Homer's gods (Quine 1953, 44). But of course the statement there enunciated is incompletely revealing of the Quinean argument, which also takes for granted a certain naturalistic knowledge acquired by physical science. Quine himself has acknowledged his affinity for naturalism—in particular the naturalism propounded by Dewey (see, e.g., Dewey 1925, 185), with whom he has shared the view "that knowledge, mind, and meaning are part of the same world that they have to do with, and that they are to be studied in the same empirical spirit that animates natural science. There is no place for a prior philosophy" (Quine [1968] 1969, 26). He chose to begin the opening chapter of *Word and Object,* entitled "Language and Truth," with presumptive assertions about his "familiar desk": that it "manifests its presence by resisting my pressures and by deflecting light to my eyes. Physical things generally, however remote, become known to us only through the effects which they help to induce at our sensory surfaces" (1960, 1). And, although he has generally treated "mental entities" as unnecessary baggage (see, e.g., 1953, 10, 48, 72), his nomination of objects that qualify as pragmatically justifiable objects—"ordinary physical objects," plus the microscopic, atomic, and subatomic objects of science, plus mathematical objects (see 1953, 44)—indicates further the extent of his subjection to received constructions of a natural science.[154]

His (1969b, 126–27) treatment of "the problem of induction" is equally instructive. On the one hand, one part of the problem can be dismissed straightaway: "*That* there are or have been regularities, for whatever reason, is an established fact of science; and we cannot ask better than that. *Why* there have been regularities is an obscure question, for it is hard to see what would count as an answer." (Apparently the conventions of a community of speakers do not count here.) On the other hand, in answer to the question "Why does our innate subjective spacing of qualities accord so well with the functionally relevant groupings in nature as to make our inductions tend to come out right?" Quine suggested Darwinian evolutionism: "If people's innate spacing of qualities is a gene-linked trait, then the

---

154. Why Quine's "special deference to physical theory as a world version, and to the physical world as the world"? His own answer, recently stated in his review of Goodman's *Ways of Worldmaking* (1978), is as follows:

> Nothing happens in the world, not the flutter of an eyelid, not the flicker of a thought, without some redistribution of microphysical states. It is usually hopeless and pointless to determine just what microphysical states lapsed and what ones supervened in the event, but some reshuffling at that level there had to be; physics can settle for no less (Quine 1978, 25).

Because it settles for no less, physics offers a complete world theory. (No doubt Quine would reverse that sentence: Because physics offers a complete world theory, it can settle for no less.) Thus, against Goodman's postulation of many worlds Quine asserted his preference of one world, "*the* physical world," of which there may be several versions.

spacing that has made for the most successful inductions will have tended to predominate through natural selection." Here again, Quine protested the likely objection of circularity (using inductive generalizations as justification of induction), arguing that he "shall not be impressed by this" charge because his "position is a naturalistic one; I see philosophy not as an *a priori* propaedeutic or groundwork for science, but as continuous with science." Yet, if possibilities of knowledge and meaning "are to be studied in the same empirical spirit that animates natural science," are we not allowed the query, *Which* "natural science"? *Whose* "natural science"? Why *this* rather than *that* historical cultural formation of "natural science"? Or are these questions meaningless to him?

Quine's pragmatic empiricism accepts the triumph of relativism on pain of subjugation to the dominant historical formation of natural science. It cannot undertake critical investigation of the foundation of the dominant formation because it claims that dominance as its *own* foundation. The effect is at root identical to Sartre's response to his own experience of nausea. As recounted by a recent commentator:

> Finding life meaningless—drifting in a pointless and sickening universe, perceiving himself to be a brute "existent" without "essence"— Sartre sorted through his own life for pattern, any pattern, found certain causal structures there, and, having nothing else at hand, affirmed them as the purpose of his existence, later elaborating them into what amounts almost to a metaphysic. Sartre's program was undeniably a courageous and, in the ordinary sense, intelligent one. But the example of Bluebeard should give us pause. For years he has been, for one reason or another, killing off his wives. Now, finding his life disgusting, devoid of sense, he searches his experience for pattern, sees that he has regularly murdered his wives, and asserts that next time he will do it on purpose. (Gardner 1977, 33)

Such failure to grasp the dialectic of *poiesis* means that our knowledge always comes after the world of which it is about is already there, "cut and dried," and that our consciously drawn futures are successive linear recapitulations of "naturally embedded forces," about which we are condemned always to know too little.

It may seem paradoxical, but it is not, that Quine's pragmatic-empiricist view, with its partial acceptance of both correspondence and coherence notions of truth, does not sufficiently appreciate the potentiality and creativity of falseness. Insofar as "the false" is merely "untruth"—the formal opposite of "what the community sees eye-to-eye on"—the category of falsity is more or less manageable (if also nearly useless) by Quine's pragmatism. But falsity is a good deal more complex than that: consider the consequentiality in human life of the lie and the joke, hyperbole, apocrypha, and Socratic irony, the potentiality of "that which is not." In both Quine's and Nietzsche's writings we read passages to the effect that our knowledge is an invention, "a man-made fabric." But Nietzsche, who was surely not a pragmatist, also spoke of the life-giving power of the lie. We must not lose sight of the importance of his meaning.

4

*A*rchimedean Pivots
and Privileged Speaking

I. INTRODUCTION

IT MAY WELL BE THE CASE, as Berkeley suggested in the introduction to his
treatise on human knowledge (1710), that philosophers very often "have
first raised a dust and then complain [they] cannot see." But surely they
have a wealth of company. Practicing members of the so-called human or
social sciences have raised a great quantity of dust of our own, and if we
are ourselves less likely to ask whether we then see clearly, our spectacles
may be just as dust-covered nonetheless. It is to questions of "seeing"
clearly and truly in the realm of social science that this and the following
chapter are addressed, with particular reference to the works of a selected
series of twentieth-century social theorists. There is, I must admit, cause
for embarrassment in speaking of these works as "social theory," as distinct
from the works of scholars whom we name "philosophers." Even from the
point of view of a conventional "history of thought," one would be hard
put not to admit within the circle of social theory Hegel's studies of bureaucracy, for example, or Nietzsche's penetrating look at *ressentiment* and
domination—although it is undeniably the case that neither of these examples, nor others that are equally germane, now command much attention
in the halls of social science. In making the distinction, as it appears in this
sequence of chapters, I am simply reproducing the perspective of a science
that seeks constantly to distance itself from the mere speculations of philosophy. Whether the one cloud of dust is thicker than the other remains
to be seen.

The first principal to be considered in this chapter is Max Weber,
long regarded in Anglo-American social theory as the preeminent theorist

of this century. Before turning to an examination of Weber's epistemological foundation, however, I want to establish a point of contrast by describing briefly the perspective of a contemporary, Georges Sorel (1847–1922).[1] Like Nietzsche, though not to the same fervent pitch, Sorel wrote in disgust of the morality of decadence and resignation that characterized modern life. And much as with Durkheim and his series of attempted solutions of the moral "crisis of civilization,"[2] Sorel sought the believable grounds of a moral knowledge that would constitute the underpinnings of a moral policy, against the "disorder [that] has become as great as it was after the Renaissance." Having eschewed the positions of "philosophers who want to save the idea of certitude at any price [by injecting] the superhuman into the theory of knowledge as was done before Kant," Sorel accepted the insurmountability of the dilemma of epistemological relativism but never the frustrations ensuing from it (Sorel [1921] 1976, 259). If Kant and his successors were no longer adequate to the task of justifying certain criteria of human knowledge, nevertheless the kernel of the Kantian dilemma remained, and it demanded continued obedience. Sorel could respond with only a pragmatism:

> The Kantian theory of knowledge has become outdated since it has entirely lost the historical basis that once gave it such great value. Science indeed no longer appears to us as a definitively constituted system whose formulas would be decreed by the absolute experts of an *Ecclesia docens*; it springs forth in the midst of the agitations of a *Cité savante* ["scholarly community"] which works unceasingly to recast its constructions with the aim of rendering them more useful. The philosopher who wants to reduce science to a human level no longer turns to Kantianism, but to pragmatism. (Sorel [1921] 1976, 260)

Sorel's stance of relativistic pluralism—within which only pragmatic criteria of truth were practicable and from which he formulated his method of "diremption"[3]—provided him with a lifelong platform from which to

1. Here, as before, the focus of my examination is (to put the matter loosely) not so much on what the several social theorists had to say about bureaucracy or plebiscitarian relations or the correlates and consequences of heterogamy, for example, as it is the explicit and/or implicit grounding and warrant for *saying*, that is, for asserting their claims of knowledge.

2. See the useful discussions by Marks (1974) and Lukes (1972).

3. Contrary to the conjecture of the translator of *Reflections on Violence*, Sorel did not coin the term *"diremption,"* although it is probably true that the word had fallen from general usage. Deriving from the Latin *dirimere* (*dir* + *emere*:

hurl his morally inspired iconoclastic arrows. But the destructiveness of his stance toward his own moral impulse led Sorel through the despair of overturning, one after another, the various policy claims allowable by pragmatic pluralism—from those of the various socialisms, including the Kautskian and then the Bernsteinian versions of Marxism, to those of monarchism. It is in this context that the frequent labeling of Sorel as "anarchist" must be understood. Because of the self-annihilative dilemma of epistemological relativism, Sorel could not escape what were but different guises of the object of his intendedly moral critique.

Sorel's epistemological stance did not differ fundamentally from that of Max Weber. But if we remember Weber's "methodological" contributions to social science better than Sorel's—and surely Max Weber has been much more of a name to reckon with—it is partly because the "anarchist" was in a sense more "honest" about the moral energy of his search for an acceptable ground of knowledge. Given Weber's disquisitions on such matters, Sorel's overt "mixture" of the moral and the scientific may strike those of us who were nurtured on the doctrine of "ethical neutrality" as being simply another confirmation of the preeminence of Weber in the establishment of a truly scientific discipline of social studies.

2. MAX WEBER (1864–1920)

Already by the time of Max Weber's major contribution to the problem of knowledge—a set of critical essays on the work of Roscher, Knies, and a number of other late nineteenth-century scholars embroiled in the issues of the famous *Methodenstreit* (Weber [1903] 1975; Weber [1905–6] 1975; Weber 1907)—the separation of "theoretical knowledge" (epistemology) and "practical knowledge" (ethics) was virtually complete in social science. Weber was no exception in regard to acceptance of this separation. Early in the first installment of "Knies and the Problem of Irrationality," for example, Weber writes, with a measure of emphasis, that his essay was intended as "an inquiry into knowledge of logical relations *for its own sake*" and that he would "*not* take up" questions of practical knowledge

---

"apart" + "to take"), it has been defined in general usage as "a forcible separation or severance." Hobbes so used the word in his *Decameron Physiologicum* (Hobbes [1678] 1839–45, iii.25), and it can be found in the English translation of Hegel's *Encyclopedia* (Hegel [1830b] 1970, §249 *Zusatz*). As for Sorel's method, it was formulated in opposition to "holistic" approaches, which he deemed unacceptable, and as the investigation of parts without attending to their connections in the whole of which they are parts (see Sorel [1913] 1961, 259). Perhaps the best example of his application of this method is his investigation in *The Illusions of Progress* (Sorel [1908] 1969).

(Weber [1905–6] 1975, 98n). Moreover, the problem of "theoretical knowledge" when separated from the practical was conceived already in terms no wider than those of a "philosophy of science"; here, too, Weber was no exception, as he acknowledged his own preference to speak of "methodological," not "epistemological," questions. He conceived his resolution of the "methods controversy" as if it rested not in any theory of knowledge but only in the axiological relations that define the historical "theoretical interest" of a scientific activity.

Before proceeding with a sketch of the major arguments of Weber's contribution, one additional preliminary remark may be tolerated. I cannot accept the opinion of Oakes that Weber's "theses constitute a novel contribution" to the *Methodenstreit* (Oakes 1975, 35), except in the very limited sense of weighing Weber's contribution against only those of other direct participants in this often heated debate. A curious (though not inexplicable) feature of Weber's essays is that, even though the objects of his critical commentary date from the 1840s (e.g., Roscher's Outline of *Lectures on Political Economy according to the Historical Method*, published in 1843) to the years of his own writing, Weber did not discuss, not even cursorily, Marx's epistemological critique and "reconstruction." How such an undertaking as Weber's could have been conceived and conducted without serious discussion of the enormous contribution of Marx is an even greater "oddity" than that the central issues of the "methods controversy" could have been formulated after Marx in the first place.

When Weber began his undertaking, following his return from an extended period of convalescence in Italy, two general versions of a solution to the controversy about methods in social science were the topic of debate: the positivist and the intuitionist. Weber rejected both. Against the positivist proposal he argued that sociocultural science must use a method fundamentally different from that treated as the "logical idea" of the natural sciences: "It obviously does not make sense to suppose that the ultimate *purpose* of concept formation in the historical sciences could be the deductive arrangement of concepts and laws . . . under other concepts and laws of increasingly general validity and abstract content," for, as careful consideration of our interest in studying the sociocultural shows, "it is obvious that historical reality, including those 'world-historical' events and cultural phenomena which we find so significant, could never be deduced from [the natural-science ideal of] formulae of absolutely general validity" (Weber [1903] 1975, 65–66, 64). At the same time, Weber rejected the various "intuitionist" assertions of the distinctiveness of sociocultural knowledge. Throughout the second and longer of his two essays, Weber argued that the distinction of sociocultural science cannot reside in any "intuitive," "sympathetic," or "empathetic" participation or in any other sort of "re-creation of the immediate experience" of a phenomenon.[4] Oakes's well-constructed inventory (1975, 31) serves nicely as a summary of this side of Weber's critical stance: the definitive property of sociocultural science is not constituted by any allegedly peculiar or unique kind of part-whole relationship, complexity, irrationality, or indeterminacy of sociocultural phenomena, nor by any allegedly unique variety of "mental causality" or criteria of "validity," "certainty," or "imagination" (Weber [1905–6] 1975, 106–8, 120–24, 156, 160–63, 174–76, 196–98).

The thrust of Weber's argument against not only intuitionism but also aspects of the positivist "resolution" can be appreciated in the following passage:

> Consider any given piece of knowledge. Neither the "substantive" qualities of its "object" nor the "ontological" peculiarities of the "existence" of this "object" nor, finally, the kind of *"psychological"* conditions required for its acquisition are of any consequence as regards its *logical* content and the presuppositions on which its "validity" is based. *Empirical* knowledge in the domain of the "mental" and in the domain of "external nature," knowledge of processes "within" us and of those "without" us, is invariably tied to the instrument of "concept formation." From a logical point of view, the nature of a "concept" in these two substantive "domains" is the same. The *logical* peculiarity of "historical" knowledge in contrast to "natural-scientific" knowledge—in the logical sense of this expression—has nothing at all to do with the distinction between the "psychical" and the "physical," the "personality" and "action," on the one hand, and the dead "natural object" and the "mechanical process of nature," on the other. To identify the "self-evidence" of "empathy" in the actual or potential "conscious" inner "experience"—an exclusively phenomenological quality of "interpretation"—with a unique empirical "certainty" of processes "susceptible to interpretation" is an even more serious mistake. Physical and psychical "reality," or an aspect of "reality" comprehending both physical and psychical components, constitutes an "historical entity" because and insofar as it can "mean" something to us. (Weber [1905–6] 1975, 184–85)

In the Weberian architecture, Solomon's house contains not one but many rooms, and activities performed in certain of the rooms are very different

---

4. It is debatable whether Weber did in fact succeed in distancing himself from the play of "empathic experience" in his subsequent studies; my own view is that he did not, but the question is not of importance here.

from those performed in others but not because of any logical difference in the "instrument of 'concept formation' " or in the "objects" of the pursuits of natural and sociocultural sciences and not because of those "methodologically dangerous" (Weber [1905–6] 1975, 179–81) differences proposed by the intuitionists.

In what, then, does the distinctiveness of the "historical and related sociocultural sciences" consist? Weber's answer to this question of (as he chose to view it) the logic of scientific "method" was simply that such distinctiveness is constituted in our "theoretical interest" or "purpose" of "understanding" "subjectively meaningful" phenomena. Adopting the neo-Kantian position that intelligibility of any "fact" or "empirical proposition," whether in knowledge of the sociocultural or of the "dead 'natural object,' " presupposes a conceptual apparatus that constitutes the criteria of that intelligibility—that is, that there is no theory-free observation language—Weber held that from "a logical point of view" neither the "nature" of the formation of nor the "objects" referred to by a conceptual apparatus distinguish the two "realms" of scientific knowledge. Rather the conceptual apparatus manifests historically the "cultural values" of the "*theoretical interest*" of knowing; and in the realm of the sociocultural that interest is to understand "subjectively meaningful" behavior.

The "theoretical interest" of the nomological natural sciences is to explain by recourse to universal-general concepts and propositions or "laws"; but because the "success" of this method of knowing corresponds to the "validity" of increasingly general concepts and propositions, each layer having increasingly diminished content, the nomological method is incommensurate axiologically with our interest to understand those phenomena of "*variations in meaning* that arouse our historical interest to the greatest extent." To Weber the difference was clear: "The specific historical task of the cultural sciences is profoundly antithetical to the aims of all disciplines which attempt to reduce phenomena to causal equivalences. The conception of *differences* in causal status as differences in axiological status is the definitive category of the cultural sciences" (Weber [1905–6] 1975, 104). Whenever it "is possible in principle" to construct a "meaningful" understanding, there is the historical task of sociocultural science, for "in the interpretation of 'action' " (i.e., subjectively meaningful behavior),

we are not satisfied by merely establishing a relation between the action and a purely empirical *generalization*, regardless of how strict this generalization may be. . . . [The] formulation of such a generalization—even if it had the character of strict nomological regularity—could never *replace* by a simple reference to a law that which is achieved by a "meaningful" interpretation. Moreover, such "laws" are *intrinsically* of absolutely no "significance" for the interpretation of "action." Suppose that somehow an empirical-statistical demonstration of the strictest sort is produced, showing that all men everywhere who have ever been placed in a certain situation have invariably reacted in the same way and to the same extent. . . . Suppose that this reaction is, in the most literal sense of the word, "calculable." Such a demonstration would not bring us a single step closer to the "interpretation" of this reaction. By itself, such a demonstration would contribute absolutely nothing to the project of "understanding" "why" this reaction ever occurred and, moreover, "why" it invariably occurs in the same way. As long as the "inner," imaginative *reproduction* of the motivation responsible for this reaction remains impossible, we will be unable to acquire this understanding.[5] *As long as* this is not possible, it follows that even an ideally comprehensive empirical-statistical demonstration of the regular recurrence of a reaction will still *fail* to satisfy the criteria concerning the *kind* of knowledge which we expect from history and those "sociocultural sciences" which are related to history in this respect. (Weber [1905–6] 1975, 128–29)

Thus, Weber's "thesis" can be stated in the following manner: we understand and expect the historical-sociocultural sciences to be distinctive because of our own historical, axiological "theoretical interest" in understanding or interpreting the "meaningfulness" of that which is, axiologically, interesting to us and about which we want to know—namely, phenomena of subjectively meaningful behavior. The *factum* is constituted as such "because and insofar as it can 'mean' something to us," that is, be a "meaningful thing" to us. Contrary to the position of the late nineteenth-century positivists, sociocultural phenomena *are* distinguishable from those of natural science, not because of any difference of ontological properties (as the intuitionists argued) and not because of any difference ensuing from a theory of the "knowing subject," but because of the axiological difference in "theoretical purpose." By virtue of this—the basic—difference of the two "realms," according to Weber, a different method of inquiry is called for: the method of *verstehen*, that is, to "stand under" or "within" the subjectively meaningful and therein attempt to comprehend the conditions of its existence by building an account of the motives that will provide a

5. Weber here noted that "it is possible to speak of 'reproduction' only in a very figurative sense. However, in this context—which is concerned with the phenomenological distinction between the 'interpretable' and the 'uninterpretable'—the force of the expression is unmistakable."

satisfactory explanation of, which is to say a sufficient ground for, the subjectively meaningful.

This proposed solution of the *Methodenstreit* forms the background of Weber's later substantive investigations in sociology (a term Weber never comfortably accepted, due to its previous association with "system-building" works), which he defined as "a science concerning itself with the interpretive understanding of social action and thereby with a causal explanation of its course and consequences." The subject matter of his discipline, "social action," was defined explicitly: it is " 'action' insofar as the acting individual attaches a subjective meaning to his behavior—be it overt or covert, omission or acquiescence"—and it is " 'social' insofar as its subjective meaning takes account of the behavior of others and is thereby oriented in its course."

The key term of this latter definition, *meaning*, must be restricted to two senses: on the one hand, "the actual existing meaning in the given concrete case of a particular actor, or to the average or approximate meaning attributable to a given plurality of actors"; on the other, "the theoretically conceived *pure type* ["ideal type"] of subjective meaning attributed to the hypothetical actor or actors in a given type of action." Weber explicitly rejected any reference to "an objectively 'correct' meaning or one which is 'true' in some metaphysical sense," arguing once again that "it is this which distinguishes the empirical sciences of action, such as sociology and history, from the dogmatic disciplines in that area, such as jurisprudence, logic, ethics, and esthetics, which seek to ascertain the 'true' and 'valid' meanings associated with the objects of their investigation" (Weber [1922] 1968, 1:4; see also Weber [1907] 1977, 106–15).

Weber's response to the debate of method has had a very considerable "influence" on twentieth-century social science, especially on academic sociology in the United States. The center of this manifold influence is both epistemological and ethical; it informs the thinking of scholars otherwise as "divergent" as Parsons and Dahrendorf, Schutz and Geiger, Merton and O. D. Duncan. And so we must now ask, what *was* Weber's epistemology? Of course, Weber disavowed an epistemological grounding of his conception of "history and the related sociocultural sciences"; yet he did have a "theory of knowledge," no matter how unwittingly or weakly formulated, no matter how implicit and inconsistent. We must be careful to grasp clearly what he *did* and what he did *not* say about the grounds of knowledge and about the axiological distinctiveness of his discipline.

In the first place, it is of crucial importance that Weber, like many other scholars then and now, insisted on a separation of knowledge (or "scientific knowledge") and ethics. As further testimony to this insistence, consider the last sentence of the above-quoted passage from *Economy and Society*. In what respect are disciplines "such as jurisprudence, logic, ethics," and the rest "dogmatic"? In the respect that they (or their practitioners) seek and, to the measure of their success, assert the truth of certain values. Weber's interpretive science, however, because of its historical *axiological* purpose or "theoretical interest," has as its subject matter the "subjectively meaningful" phenomena, which involve values, although not exclusively. Given an epistemology (or interpretive knowledge) that must be separated from ethics, and ethics from epistemology, the sociocultural scientist— although subject to the axiological foundation of the "theoretical interest" of knowing the sociocultural in a specifically constrained way—must strive for the ideal of "ethical neutrality." This ideal that the sociocultural scientist "wishes to realize" (i.e., itself a "cultural value" by Weber's definition; see Weber [1904] 1949, 57) consists in "the intrinsically simple demand that the investigator and the teacher should keep unconditionally separate the establishment of empirical facts (including the 'value-oriented' conduct of the empirical individual whom he is investigating) and *his* own practical evaluations, i.e., his evaluation of these facts as satisfactory or unsatisfactory (including among these facts evaluations made by the empirical persons who are the objects of investigation)" (Weber [1917–18] 1949, 11). This "intrinsically simple demand," Weber acknowledged, grows complicated in the extrinsic circumstances of the course of its realization. Such complications notwithstanding, however, there is a practicable "ethic of responsibility" to be rigorously "ethically neutral"; only thereby, can one be intellectually honest. In that vein, Weber argued that

> the standpoint that the distinction between purely logically deducible and empirical factual assertions on the one hand, and practical, ethical or philosophical value-judgments on the other, is correct, but that, nevertheless (or perhaps, precisely because of this), both classes of problems properly belong within the area of instruction . . . is acceptable . . . only when the teacher sets as his unconditional duty . . . to make relentlessly clear to his audience, and especially to himself, which of his statements are statements of logically deduced or empirically observed facts and which are statements of practical evaluations. Once one has acknowledged the logical disjunction between the two spheres, it seems to me that the assumption of this attitude is an imperative requirement of intellectual honesty. (Weber [1917–18] 1949, 1–2)

Most objectionable to Weber is the contention that both assertions of empirical facts and assertions of value-judgments ought to be made "with the same cool dispassionateness"; this, he cautioned, is a "narrow-minded, bureaucratic opinion" (Weber [1917–18] 1949, 2).

But what, one must ask, of the values (or "value-judgments") that are embedded "dispassionately" in, that are presupposed by, "statements of logically deduced or empirically observed facts"? Several times, Weber as much as acknowledged the grounds of this question—for example, in the following opinion stated against those who were tolerant toward socialists, Jews, and any others but anarchists: "An anarchist can surely be a good legal scholar. And if he is such, then indeed the Archimedean point of his convictions, which is outside the conventions and presuppositions which are so self-evident to us, can equip him to perceive problems in the fundamental postulates of legal theory which escape those who take them for granted" (Weber [1917–18] 1949, 7). Here and elsewhere, Weber was trying to exercise the greatest care, commensurate with the stance of liberalist tolerance, in formulating the subtle and often ambiguous concretions of his logical disjuncturing of fact and value, and, further, of value and ethic (the latter being an asserted normative principle of policy, based in a value or a set or congeries of values). Certainly "the problems of the social sciences are selected by the value-relevance of the phenomena treated," Weber ([1917–18] 1949, 21) argued, but, as problems of "empirical disciplines," they are "not problems of evaluations" and cannot be solved evaluatively. But if, on the one hand, the investigator and the teacher ought to be "ethically neutral" and refrain from value-judgments insofar as empirical knowledge is concerned, yet, on the other hand, empirical knowledge of the sociocultural is constituted as such axiologically in the historical "*Erkenntnisinteresse*," then the investigator and the teacher *are*, Weber must admit, advocating values. Moreover, (1) insofar as they engage their empirical knowledge with "cool dispassionateness," they advocate values with the same "cool dispassionateness" and therefore are walking enactments of that dreaded "narrow-minded bureaucratic opinion"; (2) even though *they* may not (according to Weber, must not) derive any ethical principles from the demonstrated empirical facts, insofar as the "facts-as-ideas" are materialized in policy, *someone* makes such derivation; and (3) the values being advocated are most likely—though not, in all cases, necessarily—those that are dominant, which is to say the values constituted in the historical, concrete conditions of those who are dominant in society.

The other side of Weber's attempted separation of the "is" and the "ought" was his candid desire, clearly expressed as early as his Freiburg inaugural lecture (1895), to relieve science of intrinsic value-judgments so as to make it serviceable to values externally formulated, particularly those of *Realpolitik* (and, for Weber, those of German national policy). Always Weber insisted that he did not "underestimate Ought questions" simply by virtue of arguing "on every occasion so sharply and perhaps even pedantically against the fusion of Is [*Seienden*] and Ought [*Seinsollen*]"; rather, he insisted that he chose to protect those questions—especially those that are, "in a certain sense, the highest problems that can move a human breast"—from the technical-practical demands of science (Weber [1909] 1924, 419). Certainly Weber's many critics are quite correct in pointing out the resulting implicit value infusion and "handmaiden" character of science. But we must comprehend in his insistence on the fact-value disjuncture also the skeptical attitude with which he regarded scientific knowledge.

To many members of that remarkably productive "generation of the 1890s," the dilemma of relativism must have seemed to proclaim that the final offer of epistemological inquiry was at the very best a pervasive skepticism. Although Weber kept mostly on the high wire of ambivalence, he keenly felt the Nietzschean pessimism of a "nihilistic escape." In some ways concerned with such fundamental problems of the human conditions of capitalism that had previously drawn Marx's attention (as Löwith [1932] 1969 attempted to show; but see also Kocka 1966), Weber's solution tended in a very different direction: in order to be free in this disenchanted world, we must take over completely and apply in day-to-day life the principles of formal rationality.[6] This pessimistic side of Weber's ambivalence, the hopelessness that has its roots in the desire to disjoin (a trivialized) epistemology and ethics, startles us brutally in the prophecy of the "iron cage": "In combination with the dead machine," he warned, bureaucracy "is at work to set up the iron cage of that bondage of the future to which perhaps some day men like the fellaheen in ancient Egypt will helplessly be forced to submit" (Weber [1917] 1968, 337). That this liberal-individualistic pessimism regarding the relentless formal rationalization of the world was not peculiar to a "stage" of his thinking can be appreciated from a dreadful pronouncement uttered in his inaugural lecture at Freiburg:

> The somber seriousness of the population problem in itself keeps us from being eudaemonists, from believing that peace and human happiness lie concealed in the womb of time and that elbowroom in earthly life can be gained in any other way but in a hard struggle of men against men.
>
> As for the dream of peace and human happiness, *Lasciate ogni speranza* is written over the gate to the unknown future of human history. (Weber [1895] 1968, 18)[7]

---

6. Weber's deployment, with resignation to its certainty, of the Schillerian romanticist "*Entzauberung der Welt*" can be seen nowhere better than in the concluding passages of his famous lecture on the "calling" of politics: "Not summer's bloom lies ahead of us, but rather a polar night of icy darkness and hardness. . . . When this night shall have slowly receded, who of those for whom spring apparently has bloomed so luxuriously will be alive?" (Weber [1919a] 1946, 128).

7. "*Lasciate ogni speranza, voi ch'entrate!*"—"All hope abandon, ye who enter here!" (Dante's *Inferno*, III, 9; the inscription over the gate to Hell). Weber is reputed to have said of his inaugural lecture that it "aroused horror at the brutality of my views" (quoted by Marianne Weber [1926] 1975, 216).

And in a more particular context, Weber described an aspect of bureaucracy that, by his own prognosticative reckoning of the course of formal rationalization, must be applied to the organization of science itself—namely, the

> superiority of the professional insider [that] every bureaucracy seeks further to increase through the means of *keeping secret* its knowledge and intentions. Bureaucratic administration always tends to exclude the public, to hide its knowledge and action from criticism as well as it can. . . . This tendency toward secrecy is in certain administrative fields a consequence of their objective nature: namely, wherever power interests of the given structure of domination *toward the outside* are at stake. (Weber [1922] 1968, 992)

If the more hopeful side of Weber's ambivalence could be described by a single word, perhaps the most fitting choice would be *pragmatic*, in its nonspecific sense, although Weber did not incorporate philosophical pragmatism into a deliberate, systematically wrought theory of knowledge, as Sorel did, for example.[8] But in a looser than doctrinal sense of the term, one can see in Weber's activity aspects of the pragmatic response of *adapting to* rather than deliberately shaping a given, preexisting environment—in particular, of shifting from the seemingly insoluble problem of relativism in gnoseological inquiry to the seemingly tractable problems of methodology in a "philosophy of science."

Indeed, Weber's "solution" to the larger problem was to ignore it. Epistemology was held apart as a realm of different questions—questions that perhaps could *never* be answered satisfactorily, questions that at least would not be the focus of his own scientific concern to explicate the definitiveness of, and the proper method of, historical, sociocultural knowledge. In consequence of this oscitance by design, Weber consigned himself to acceptance of, and thus captivity within, the relativist dilemma; in consequence, all effective effort to surmount the dilemma was precluded. He could work only and wholly within the domain of the unchallenged rela-

---

8. Nor did Weber's position offer any of the simple confidence of positivistic objectivity. As Jameson has described it, "Weber's *Wertfreiheit* is a passionate refusal of the illusions of meaning itself, a repudiation of all philosophies which . . . seek to persuade us that some teleological movement is imminent in the otherwise chaotic and random agitation of empirical life" (Jameson 1974, 60–61). Weber's relativistic pluralism was that of a heroic battle among "different gods [who] struggle with one another, now and for all times to come. . . . Fate, and certainly not 'science,' holds sway over these gods and their struggles. One can only understand what the godhead is in the one or in the other order" or realm of our "shattered modern world" (Weber [1919b] 1946, 148).

tivism on problems of what then became merely a "philosophy of science." Necessarily, it was a philosophy of science thoroughly stained with the gray uncertainties of the relativist dilemma.

So captured, Weber could never surmount the present of the existent "is"; he could never construct a critique of the ills of current human conditions that did not succumb to itself, could never take seriously potentiality. The accuracy of his descriptions of the observable "is" always carried the same inscription: *Lasciate ogni speranza*!

Consider the following passage, taken from Weber's essay "Knies and the Problem of Irrationality":

Suppose that in English history the bubonic plague is not conceived as an event which has an explanation within the domain of bacteriology. Suppose it is treated as an event which is, as it were, "extrahistorical," as an "accident." For the most part, a conception of this sort is simply based on those "constitutive principles" which underpin every science. To this extent, therefore, it is not *epistemologically* grounded. Of course, a "history of the bubonic plague" that carefully analyzed the course of the epidemic and the specific conditions under which it occurred is obviously quite within the realm of possibility. However, such an account would qualify as "history" in the genuine sense *only* if it were governed by those cultural values which dominate—or, in any case, can dominate—our view of a history of England during the period concerned. That is to say, such an account qualifies as "history" only if its theoretical purpose is not the discovery of laws, e.g., bacteriological laws, but rather the causal explanation of the cultural-historical "facts." Because of the content of the concept of "culture," this *invariably* means that such an account is complete only when we have knowledge of a nexus into which *understandable* human action—or, more generally, "behavior"—fits, a nexus which is conceived as a determinant of behavior. Why is this the case? Because the "historical" *interest* is anchored in this theoretical purpose. (Weber [1905–6] 1975, 141–42; see also 157–58)

This passage, as well as numerous other passages, exemplifies Weber's strongly dystopian affinities. In eschewing confrontation with epistemological relativism and, instead, accepting the apparent inevitability of its dilemma, Weber could go no farther than to acknowledge an axiologic constitution of knowledge. He could justify the designation of a particular "method of knowing" or "item of knowledge" as distinctively "sociocultural-scientific" *only* on the basis that, and only to the extent that, a "*theoretical* purpose" of the activity of "knowing the sociocultural" is specified in the given "historical interestedness," as delineated by the given "cultural values" (i.e., ideals that we "wish to realize"). The "practical purpose" of knowing, according to Weber, is entirely another matter: "Theoretical knowledge"—knowledge *"for its own sake"*—"has value . . . regardless of whether it produces 'prescriptions' for 'praxis' " (Weber [1905–6] 1975, 98n; see also 99n). (As to the determination and consequences of *that* "theoretical value," the value of knowledge "for its own sake," Weber was silent.) In short, Weber's case for the distinctiveness of sociocultural knowledge, and, it is clear, his *general* case for the validity of *any* scientific knowledge, rests finally on the analytic presentments of passive, disembodied *"theoretical* interests" and *theoretical* "values." There is no place in Weber's architectural redesign of Solomon's house at which Weber the scientist can stand in deliberate otherness to the givenness of cultural values. There is none of that *ethical impulse toward the Other* that makes the utopian different from the dystopian. There is only that "cultural relativity" of *facts in relation to values,* of "some values" in relation to "other values," and thus of "some facts" in relation to "other facts."[9] Weber's analytic formalism (within which the concrete human being is lost completely behind such divisions as the "theoretical" versus the "practical" and "fact" versus "value") turns back upon Weber's own activity and sterilizes it.

W *eber's* knowledge, the knowledge that he wrought *about* knowledge of the sociocultural in his engagement with the "methodological" issues of the *Methodenstreit,* was that knowledge is constituted relative to the cultural values that "make" it meaningful to the knower. But the passivity or neutrality of *his* knowing about knowing forces *his* knowledge to collapse into its object; in other words, both *his* knowledge and the knowledge *about* which he knows share the topological space of a three-dimensional involute. Content merely to offer description and internal, analytic explanation of the existent "is" of scientific knowledge, Weber would not take the totality of *this level* of the relations of knowledge as an object of inquiry to be conducted from the grounds afforded by a deeper level of epistemic space. Presumably he would not—or could not—because the dilemma of relativism seemed to deny the very *possibility* of such depth to epistemic

---

9. Of Weber's agnosticism toward a world governed by different gods in eternal struggle, Lukács observed: "What lies behind this is that Max Weber, in the society he was faced with, could not possibly arrive at an unambiguous concept of 'if-then' *ratio,* but remained fixated to the struggle of those different ethical principles which he did not want to reduce further. Such a reduction would have led to consequences that he could not integrate, and so he took refuge, so to speak, in the mythological conception of gods struggling against one another" (Lukács [1967] 1975, 47–48; see also Lukács 1953, 484–89).

space.[10] It seemed rather that every attempted metatheory stood in the same relation to *its* object as the outside stood in relation to the inside of Fortunata's purse—that is, a relation of simultaneity, by virtue of which that famous "little" purse held all the wealth of the world.

To say that Weber self-consciously averted his gaze from basic epistemological issues (that, indeed, he never seriously entertained the question, what *is* "knowledge"?) does not imply that his formulations about his own discipline were devoid of epistemology.[11] Likewise, to say that his implicit epistemology was basically that of a neo-Kantian relativism, abnegational in and to its very core, does not imply that his position was inconsequential. On the contrary, his position has extremely grave consequences.

Weber's attempt to know the subject matter of his discipline—both to have knowledge *about* the constitution of knowledge of the "subjectively meaningful" and to have knowledge *of* the "subjectively meaningful"— was intended (presumably) in self-conscious relation not to values external to the knowledge activity but to one central internal value, which was considered to be (formally) the most rational orientation of the knowledge activity: the value of *Wertfreiheit*. To the extent that such an internality could be maintained, that is, that the knowledge activity could be free of values external to it, the knowledge activity would result in understandings that were *only* efficient descriptions of an existent "is" (efficient "for its own sake"). But of course the internality cannot be maintained in its purity,

10. There are notable parallels between this epistemological aspect of Weber's thinking and particular features of his "historical sociocultural" studies. In *The Protestant Ethic and the Spirit of Capitalism* (1905), for example, he demonstrated a measure of perceptiveness insofar as he resisted definitive statements of causal direction in explanation of the relationships of observables of "religious" doctrines and actions to observables of "economic" doctrines and actions, preferring instead to state the matter in terms of mutual interdependencies and affinities (though it must be said that his mode of concept formation belies the *real* ground of that perceptiveness). But Weber was unwilling (unable) to go deeper and to see in those interdependencies and affinities among observables that the *same* structure ran throughout that production of the social world in its entirety.

11. In a critical commentary on Weber's argument, Strauss noted the "striking fact" that "Weber, who wrote thousands of pages, devoted hardly more than thirty of them to a thematic discussion of the basis of his whole position" regarding the relationship between "ultimate values" and "human reason" (1953, 64). Strauss understood this (rightly, so far as he went, I think) as indicating that Weber's thesis seemed self-evident to him because it was "only the generalized version of an older and more common view, namely, that the conflict between ethics and politics is insoluble."

as Weber himself had to admit, somewhat surreptitiously, through the device of "theoretical interest"; values "external" to the activity of knowledge-for-its-own-sake do "enter" (i.e., the logical distinction upon which Weber insists in one place is, he is forced to acknowledge in another, untenable), and the stance of "ethical neutrality" is therefore *not* the "ethic of responsibility" that Weber imagined it to be but is instead, in the concreteness of the real knowledge activity, an *abdication* of responsibility. Though perhaps unfair as a testament to Weber's self-conscious intentionality, one must be willing to appreciate the structure of descendence that relates Weber's conception of the knowledge activity (and its expression in its treatment of capitalist organization) and Luhmann's postulation of "mechanisms of mutual indifference" (Luhmann 1969, esp. 191 ff., 225, 234–35, 250), which, in the face of crises of authority, must be made more efficient in their mandate to "regulate and diffuse dissatisfaction," to increase the predictability of individual behavior, to abolish "dysfunctional" motivations through a "restructuring of expectations" so as to conform to demands of the political-administrative apparatus—all of which, Luhmann insisted, is, because of the interiority of the singularly justifiable interest, "system maintenance," *free* of the imprint of political domination! (Luhmann 1969, 225).

3. MAX SCHELER (1874–1928)

Whereas Weber tried to guide the carriage of his thought very lightly over a smooth "methodological" surface of what, with the warmth of human touch, would melt like the tundra into a sticky, seemingly bottomless mire, his slightly junior compatriot, Max Scheler, rode more deeply in search of a "Ground of Being" that would make truth discoverable. Of course, in the broad sense of certain virtually inescapable complexes of "influence," the works of the two scholars shared in the variety of resources from which they were drawn: on the "intellectual" side, for example, the idealist frames of German philosophy; their respective readings of the so-called philosophers of life, of the "naturalism" of Darwin and others, and of the "Marxisms" so popular at the turn of the century; and—though more generously in the case of Scheler, who unlike Weber has been called a disciple of the founding master—the early phenomenology of Husserl. But, even though it may be said that Weber and Scheler experienced with equal intensity the drifting malaise of the human condition, including the condition of human knowledge, their reactions differed; for it was Scheler and not Weber who forged with passionate self-consciousness the total corpus of his work—his sociology as much as his ethics and his (never finished) philosophical anthropology—from that central feeling of malaise. Certainly much less disposed than Weber to a doctrine of "ethical neutrality," and, judging from the flavor of his written works, evidently somewhat less pessimistic, Scheler's questing was not simply for a methodical science of the human world (like others of that generation, he rejected completely the positivist notion of a single, unified science) but for a secure and securely intelligible human world. "In approximately ten centuries of history," he wrote shortly before death, "this is the first in which man finds himself completely and utterly 'problematical,' in which he no longer knows what he is and simultaneously *knows that* he does not have the answer" (Scheler [1926a] 1958, 65). The destruction of medieval society was at base a shattering of awareness of the objective hierarchy of values and thus a loss of human capacity to stand in accordance with such an order. As Scheler expressed it in one of his early treatises,

> With the development of modern civilization, *nature* (which man has tried to reduce to a mechanism for the purpose of ruling it) and *objects* have become man's *lord* and *master*. The *machine* has come to dominate *life*. The "objects" have progressively grown in vigor and intelligence, size, and beauty, whereas man, who created them, has become increasingly no more than a cog in his own machine. (Scheler [1912] 1961, 172)

This subversion of the hierarchy of true and eternal values, a subversion springing from the "self-poison" of *ressentiment* (that "victory of the value judgments of those who are vitally inferior, of the lowest, the pariahs of the human race!"), can be overcome only by wiping the canvas clean of all traditional solutions, so as to be able to gaze upon the human in complete alienation and astonishment, and thereby resolve that utter uncertainty through the reconstitution of valid insights into the "place of man" in the order of things (Scheler [1912] 1961, 45, 48, 172; Scheler [1926a] 1958, 65–66).

Although the skein of Scheler's work may twist and turn (some readers have seen in it more or less clearly demarcated "stages"), consistently throughout he reasserted the warrant of metaphysical inquiry and of a metaphysically based epistemology and ethics. "Man is not free to choose whether or not he wants to develop a metaphysical idea and a metaphysical awareness," argued Scheler. "Man, *necessarily* and always, consciously or unconsciously, *has* such an idea, such a feeling acquired by himself or inherited from tradition. All he can choose for himself is a good and reasonable or a poor and unreasonable idea of the absolute." Neither positivism (as in the works of E. Mach or R. Avenarius), which concluded "that not only metaphysical solutions but even *investigations* of this kind were meaningless," nor neo-Kantianism, which "did recognize metaphysical questions as eternal problems of reason, but considered them theoret-

ically insoluble,"[12] nor historicism, which "saw in all views of the world
. . . only changeable expressions of varying and historical and social conditions," could demolish the actuality of metaphysical awareness. Not only
is metaphysics "always real." Every man, woman, and child, "by right,
also possesses the *means to know*" and is always "capable of *three-fold
knowledge*—knowledge of *control* and achievement, knowledge of *essence*
or culture, knowledge of *metaphysical reality* or salvation." That is, knowledge never exists for its own sake but instead for what might be called
"adaptational functions" (biological and sociohistorical), of which Scheler
designated three categories:

1. *Herrschaftswissen* or *Leistungswissen*—pertaining to functions of mastery, domination, control, technical accomplishment;
2. *Wesenswissen or Bildungswissen*—pertaining to functions of education,
   personal formation, "culture";
3. *Heilswissen* or *Erlösungswissen*—pertaining to functions of salvation,
   redemption, realization.

Whereas animals are to some extent capable of knowledge of the first
category (a knowledge of particulars), according to Scheler, the second (a
knowledge of universals and essences) marks the specific difference of being
human. The third and highest category, which can be attained only on the
basis of a synthesis of the preceding categories, signifies realization of true
human potentiality (Scheler [1928] 1958; Scheler [1926b] 1960; see also
Scheler [1913–16] 1973).[13]

At the core of his own contribution to a "resolution" of the "utter
uncertainty of man," Scheler constructed an inherently asymmetrical, im-

12. At one period of the development of his thinking, Scheler espoused a predominantly neo-Kantian view of "problems of reason," a view partly inspired by one
of his teachers, the *Lebensphilosoph* Rudolf Eucken (1846–1926), at Jena. With
the awakening to Husserl and to his phenomenology as an intended alternative
both to empiricism and to rationalism, Scheler moved away from the neo-Kantian
relativism of Eucken. Another student of Eucken, Hermann Schmalenbach (1885–
1950), also turned in the direction of Husserl, and at about the same time, although
he rejected the transcendentalism of Husserl's phenomenology. On Eucken, see
Jones (1912); to appreciate Schmalenbach, see his 1922 essay "The Sociological
Category of *Bund*" and his 1926 study of the concept and meaning of the Middle
Ages.

13. Compare Habermas's triadic grouping of possible knowledge: that of technical control (the empirical-analytic sciences), that of the understanding of meaning (the hermeneutical-historical sciences), and that of emancipated consciousness
(the critical science) (Habermas [1965] 1971).

mutable, and eternal hierarchy of being, the levels of which range from the energetics of the "vital impulse" or drive of "life" (the lower forms) to the originally impotent but directing and guiding information of "spirit" (the higher forms).[14] The opposition of "life" and "spirit" is asymmetric inasmuch as the lower forms can exist without the higher but realization of the higher forms (as in the human) is dependent on the lower. Whereas the "higher forms of being may determine the essence or the essential regions of the world, . . . these essences are realized only through another principle ["vital impulse"] that belongs to Ground of Being as intimately as the spiritual principle" (Scheler [1927] 1974, 66). In his reproduction of this post-Hegelian antagonism of "spirit" and "life"—where the "life" or "life-urge" (Lebensdrang) concept serves as the philosopher's vehicle for purported movement from the abstract concept of the rational being to the concrete human being—Scheler rejected the "classical theory of spirit" which had been "a basic conception of a large segment of bourgeois thought in the Western world"; although "spirit" is the "special and unique quality" of being human, that which makes the human one who can be a "nay-sayer" (der Neinsagenkönner), the "spirit as such is in its 'pure' form originally without any 'power', 'energy,' and 'activity'." At the same time Scheler rejected the naturalistic view of the human as nothing but a creature differing only in degree (e.g., of intellect), not in kind from any other creature (Scheler [1926a] 1958, 76–82). Even though without original power, the "will" of this autonomous spirit, through a process of "direction," (somehow) "withdraws from the opposing vital impulses the images necessary for action." The spirit is dependent; it "can only call upon energy complexes" of the life-urge, "which will then act through the organism in order to accomplish what the spirit 'wills' " in a process of "guidance" (Scheler [1927] 1974, 62–63).

The crux of Scheler's theory of knowledge—that which he projected as an epistemology, not that which he realized in his own acts of projection—consists in this attempted integration of "spirit" with "life" that constitutes the all-of-that-which-is in such a way that its essential relations are supposedly revealed.[15] "Man alone—insofar as he is a person [i.e.,

---

14. There is a notable resemblance to Parsons's more recent formulation of a hierarchy of "being" described in terms of those factors that are high in "information" and functionally "controlling" and those factors that are high in "energy" and functionally "conditioning" (Parsons 1966, 8–28).

15. See Landgrebe's discussion of the final, teleological character of Scheler's ontic view, which, as Landgrebe put it, "was designed to alleviate [the] disquietude" of noticing that the "I think"—supposedly the " 'absolute' starting point of philosophic reflection—is nothing but the ego of actual man, embedded in his actual historical situation" (Landgrebe [1957] 1966, 42–43).

"person" as the centering of spirit in its resistance to life-urge]—is able to go beyond himself as an organism and to transform, from a center beyond the spatiotemporal world, everything (including himself) into an object of knowledge."

That Archimedean point, according to Scheler, "cannot itself be part of this world . . . but can only be located in the highest Ground of Being." Because of the capacitation that is autonomous spirit—"the basic presupposition for the idea of truth and the possibility of discovering the truth"— the human person can "de-actualize" or "de-realize" the world in an act of pure ideation, by means of which a knowledge of "the essential modes" of the world may be grasped. It is this knowledge of essential conditions that proves the sensibility of questions of the following sort: "What must be the nature of things that such a thing as 'pain itself' is possible?" In "de-actualizing" the world, the spirit steals energy from the drives of life ("cancels" the primitive natural reality), harnesses the energy of its own "higher will," and thereby moves the person toward the goal of veridical knowledge of absolute being (Scheler [1927] 1974, 46–55).

By this oppositional linkage of processes of "pure ideation" and those of sublimation and repression, Scheler sought to boost us out of the morass of a radically problematic condition—to give us firm anchorage outside the "this world" of our being, in the "highest Ground of Being." The accomplishment of that reanchoring requires two actions, Scheler contended: first, becoming aware that in our very denial of the absolute we engage in the fetishism of substituting "a *finite* content" for the true content of the realm of "absolute being and good"; second, smashing the idols by putting "the overly loved object back into its *relative* position in the finite world" (Scheler [1928] 1958, 3). Just such an idol is the epistemology allegedly "free of value judgments," which itself is conditioned "by the 'vital' value that is embodied in a world view—a world view which comprises exclusively those elements of natural phenomena which are important for world domination" (Scheler [1926b] 1960, 139).[16] *Any* grasping of existing entities, Scheler argued, is founded in an axiological experience that has its own origin in emotional experience. The fetishism of the modern, ultimately nihilistic condition consists in the absolutization of the merely "vital" or "life-urge" (i.e., lower) emotional experience and valuation, which is technical control or mastery of the world. In order to abolish this and all other idols, to replace them into their relative positions in the finite world, we must acknowledge the spiritualization of life that is the truly absolute

16. Yet, in an earlier essay (Scheler 1922), he could also defend Weber's views on the "ethical neutrality" of science and recommend a compartmentalization of science, religion, and philosophy.

hierarchy of value, emotion, being. This means the adoption of a non-aggressive attitude wherein knowledge is "participation of one entity in the pure essential being (*Sosein*) of another entity, . . . a self-transcending participation in the pure essence of being" that stems ultimately from what "may be formally characterized as 'love' " (as stated by Landgrebe [1957] 1966, 156; see also Scheler [1926b] 1960, 245).

Against the several versions of *Weltanschauungsphilosophie*, Scheler attempted to escape the self-devolving abyss of phenomenal relativism by arguing that even while all of the historical mental creations of a particular society are manifestations of one or another "relatively natural *Weltanschauung*," there exists behind the entire range of the latter an "absolutely natural *Weltanschauung*." It was in terms of this constant, "absolutely natural" formation, constituted in the pregivenness of values and being, that Scheler formulated his sociological theory of the "order of historical causal factors (the 'real' and the 'ideal' ones)" and his analysis of the "forms of knowledge and . . . the measures of cognition (knowledge of work [control and achievement], education [essence and culture], and salvation)" (Scheler [1913–16] 1973, preface to the third edition; Scheler [1926b] 1960, 61, 40). All human thought, he argued, is "codetermined simultaneously" by both ideal and material factors (*Idealfaktoren* and *Realfaktoren*). However, the social determination of thought "refers *only* to the *selection* of objects of knowledge," that is, only to "the *forms* of the mental processes by means of which knowledge is acquired." Both the "content and the validity of knowledge" are constituted in a "supratemporal metaphysical sphere of truth in which the individual incarnations of truth participate" (Scheler [1926b] 1960, 20, 29, 40, 58).

Nevertheless, these constitutive "eternal essences"—autonomous in their own realm but powerless in themselves—can be actualized in the human world only through human apprehension of them, and such apprehension is always governed by the *Realfaktoren* of the "perspective of ruling interests," that is, the interests of a ruling group. Because spirit is in itself impotent, the truth of the absolutely natural *Weltanschauung* can become manifest in historical-cultural formations only by virtue of the energy of the life-urge ("vital impulse," "drives," etc.; the power of blood relationships, the heroic will-to-power drive characteristic of feudalism, the economic-profit drive of capitalism, etc.). This infusion of power occurs through a process of "functionalization." Because the drives, the *Realfaktoren*, are heterogeneous in spatiotemporal existence, functionalization is selective; at any moment only selected aspects of the truth of the absolutely natural *Weltanschauung* are shaved off, as it were, to become the relative truths of relatively natural *Weltanschauungen* (Scheler [1926b] 1960, 26, 44–45, 51, 258–59; Scheler [1913–16] 1960, 97–100). Thus, according to Scheler,

The human mind is not only differently filled in different epochs; it is differently constituted. In this respect there are many different truths. They all spring from the perception of the same ontic realm of ideas and value orderings, however. Hence behind all the apparently exclusive universes of validity there lies the one real dimension that imparts true validity and ultimate unity to all of them. Thus, we give up as wholly relative, as historically and sociologically dependent on the particular standpoints, all orderings of *goods, goals* and *norms* in human societies, . . . and retain nothing but the idea of the eternal logos, whose transcendent secrets cannot be explored, in the form of a metaphysical *history*, by any one nation, any one civilization or even all cultural epochs that have emerged so far, but only by *all together*, including all future ones—by temporal and spatial cooperation of irreplaceable (because individual) unique cultural entities working together in complete mutual solidarity. (Scheler [1926b] 1960, 26)

Heidegger pointed out in his several appreciations of Scheler's work that Scheler's proposed resolution of what was widely believed to be not merely crises in human knowledge and existence but their crisis *as* human knowledge and existence—this veridical, emancipatory knowledge of the "transcendent secrets" to be gained through the spatiotemporal cooperation of "working together in complete mutual solidarity"—was a once-again (after Kant) integrated epistemology-ethic grounded in a metaphysics of "love" (*agapē*, not *erōs*).[17] The "knowledge of salvation" was simultaneously an ethic neither of transforming nor of mastering but of surrendering in receptivity of the cognized being.

In a number of respects Scheler's work can be held up for admiration, not because it attained a successful finality but because of features of the impulse behind it: an insistent broadening of the bounds of human knowledge past those defined in science, the consideration of "desire" and other "categories" of emotion as relevant to knowledge constitution, an attempted reunion of ethics in epistemology—features that no doubt partly account for the neglect of Scheler's work by academicians of social science. Nevertheless, when he (following Husserl) postulated eternal, a priori, absolute values in a realm of ideal objects having the same objectivity,

17. "Nietzsche ignored the fact that love in the Christian sense is always primarily directed at man's ideal spiritual self. . . . Therefore he equated the Christian idea of love with a completely different idea . . . ," the fetish-love of idols (Scheler [1912] 1961, 114). Scheler, it is clear, did not fully appreciate the depth of Nietzsche's critique.

autonomy, and independence vis-à-vis the knowing subject as material objects or sensory qualities,[18] he cast into the state of heavenly dictatorship "objects" that are humanly created just as much as the "machine" against which he directed his charge. Scheler set out to construct a "mediation" of the *Realfaktoren* and the *Idealfaktoren*.[19] His construction broke, even in its own terms; but the basic fault was with the very conception of the necessity, indeed the possibility, of "mediation" itself, for that meant he was proceeding from the abstract to the concrete, from reified abstractions as the real objects to the concrete human world. In conceiving that such *real objects* as the ideal and the material require *mediation*, Scheler was already caught up in the one-sidedness of an idealist construction of the world. One manifestation of this is his reservation of the ideal in its purity as the ultimate standard. When he said that ideas "are completely ineffectual in history" unless and until they gain material expression in "objective forces, interests, passions and drives," he was thereby also forced to the neo-Kantian position (as was Weber) that these pure existences of spirit, these "higher" and "nobler" truths, in order to become effective must suffer debasement.[20] Once again, then, a construction of relativism is made (though in this instance quite unwillingly), and we are at the border of skepticism and nihilism.

18. This postulation appeared in Scheler's *Ethics* (1913–16), in his sociology of knowledge (1926b), and in his last work toward a comprehensive philosophical anthropology (1927).

19. This notion of "mediation," prevalent in German philosophy and art (e.g., Wagner's *Parsifal*), has strong connections with the concept of "mediator" in Christianity, especially the mediating Church as in Catholicism (see Paul Kluck-hohn 1925, 7). Quasi-secular versions had been embedded in political ideology long before Scheler. Müller, for example, in *Elements of Statecraft* used the concept to link the general ideal and the concrete particular—for example, the judge as mediator between a general law and a particular case, as opposed to the bureaucratic administrator who subsumes particular cases under the impress of the general law (Müller [1809] 1922, 1:143, 148, 179; see also Mannheim [1927] 204ff., for a discussion of Müller).

20. The elitism of his stance was manifested also of course in his views of the polity and the "expansion of democracy":

> The type of democracy which condemned Socrates and Anaxagoras in Athens is slowly reappearing in the West and perhaps in North America too. Only the struggling, predominantly liberal democracy of relatively "small elites"—so the facts already teach us—is an ally of science and philosophy. The democracy now dominant, and finally extended to women and half-children, is not the friend but rather the enemy of reason and science. (Scheler [1926b] 1960, 89)

4. KARL MANNHEIM (1893–1947)

In the concluding pages of the original edition of his most famous work, *Ideology and Utopia*, Karl Mannheim wrote in a warning tone:

> While the decline of the ideological represents a crisis only for certain strata and while the objectivity that comes from the unveiling of ideologies brings self-clarification to the whole society, the complete disappearance of the utopian would transform the very shape of the whole process of becoming human. The disappearance of utopia brings about a static objectivity in which man himself becomes a thing. There would arise the greatest paradox imaginable, namely, that the man of the most rational mastery over things would become the man of impulses. (Mannheim [1929] 1936, 236)

Several characteristics of Mannheim's work are fairly captured by this passage—the celebration of "spirit" and "self-correcting thought," the strain toward transcendence (utopia) over immanence (ideology), the alienation that "allowed" him to issue such a warning, in 1929, in the future conditional (compare Weber [1905] 1930; and Marx [1844] 1975). Like his mentors and many of his contemporaries—those involved in the anti-positivist movement of *Geistesgeschichte* and *Geisteswissenschaft*, including Dilthey, Rickert, Max Weber, Alois Riegl (also Scheler and Lukács)— but with less clarity and sharpness of construction than some of them, Mannheim was greatly concerned to overcome the malaise of doubt that, as he saw it, *threatened* to wreck "the very shape of the whole process of becoming human" in the modern world. His answer, never worked out with full coherence, was a thesis of the "relational" constitution of knowledge, which revolved around the simple notion that everyone has a point of view from which the human world is seen and that these "perspectivic" understandings or interpretations can augment one another; that is, that "objectivity" as an impersonal standpointlessness is impossible. The stronghold of reason and truth in such augmentation was located in the manifold perspectives of a "socially unattached intelligentsia" (*freischwebende Intelligenz*, an expression taken from Alfred Weber; see Mannheim [1927] 1971, 183 n. 1). Mannheim's search for the reliable ground of reason—a search undertaken within an orienting framework not so different from that of Scheler as sometimes suggested—proceeded in an intense awareness (especially after 1933) of what (following the Jungian doctrine of archetypes or images that crystallize the "impulses" of the "irrational drives") he considered to be the basic and powerful irrational components of human nature (see, e.g., the papers compiled in his *Diagnosis of Our Time*, 1943). The tension of the irrational and the rational was never resolved. Whereas

Scheler found (or so he believed, some of the time) his Kundry, his vehicle of mediation through which the un-meaning of life-urge entered the realm of spirit, found conscience and therewith confronted the choice of good spirit (rationality) versus evil spirit (irrationality) and chose the former, Mannheim was never successful in efforts to integrate into his formulation of a theory of knowledge this "dark side" of human nature, which thus remained a residue—powers from the primeval well of the pre-civilized beast (un-meaning) harnessed as historical but nonetheless dangerously demonic meaning—and which therefore was addressable only through piecemeal extensions of his formulation in a kind of "sociological psychology" and in various programmatic writings about educational reform, the creation of a civilizing elite, incremental planning, and the like. It has been suggested that Mannheim may not have been cognizant of that failure.[21] On the contrary, I believe he was very much aware of it, and faced it in an attitude of resignation. Max Weber turned away from the so-called problem of knowledge early on, adopted an attitude of agnosticism, and pretended indifference to the warrant of his own scientific activity; concomitantly, his practical ideology was a more or less consistently practiced one (nationalist liberalism). Scheler, although remaining essentially unchanged in the fundamental terms of his problematic and hence of his solution, formulated a series of expressions of that solution, always with belief in its efficacy and yet always too with the occasional suspicion that this problem was of greater complexity than his solution admitted. Concomitantly, Scheler's ideological subscription ranged through a series of practical statements, from the political "left" to the political "right." Mannheim's self-reaction was somewhere between that of Weber and that of Scheler—never in agreement with agnosticism but never really comfortable with the thought that his own solution was adequate, yet also, especially after the early 1930s, unwilling to defer diagnoses and curative efforts with regard to the "practical problems" of *Realpolitik*.

Mannheim's formulations began in his earliest writings with logic and psychology as "epistemological tools," soon moved to the perspective of historicism (which he counterposed not only to the currently recognized positivist doctrines but also to Scheler's modern phenomenology), and by the late 1920s became a "sociology of knowledge" (or of "thought," or of "mind"—all three terms were used, apparently interchangeably). It was this last-named discipline, described in his introduction to the English edition of *Ideology and Utopia* as "the *systematization* of the doubt which is to be found in social life as a vague insecurity and uncertainty" (Mann-

21. See, e.g., Wolff's comments in his editorial introduction to a collection of Mannheim's works (*From Karl Mannheim*, pp. xl–xlii, lxviii).

heim [1929] 1936, 45), that constituted the final quasi-systematic expression of Mannheim's solution, although we can read much of the basic argument in essays written during his Weimar period.

It was Mannheim's contention that the "self-relationization of thought" was not in itself new but that it had combined with three other factors to create a new configuration or "systematization" of human thinking. First, an "unmasking turn of mind," based on the premise that public meaning hides the true meaning of ideas. This attitude toward thought is not one merely of testing and approving or refuting ideas but is "rather to *disintegrate* them," to reveal their "*extra-theoretical function*" as ideologies, to show them up to inspection as mere stories having no connection, or at best a dubious connection, to truth. In our unmasking of ideologies, moreover, "we seek to bring to light an unconscious process, not in order to annihilate the moral existence of persons making certain statements," as we do, for example, in the case of the "liar," an immoral person; instead we seek amorally "to destroy the social efficacy of certain ideas by unmasking the function they serve." We rob thought of its purity, its innocent morality, by showing inevitable connections to the mundane and the selfish. It is not just that ideas, in order to gain effectiveness in the material world, must be soiled; they have their origin there. The unmasking of lies has been a perpetual feature of human discourse (cf. Montaigne [1580–88] 1952, 1:9); the unmasking of ideologies, according to Mannheim, "seems to be an exclusively modern phenomenon." And whereas revealing the lie disputes the morality of the liar, with disintegration of an ideology "the whole world outlook of a social stratum becomes disintegrated at the same time" (Mannheim [1925] 1952, 137–41).

Second, the relativization of thought and the unmasking of ideologies are anchored not in religious or ecstatic experience but in the findings of empirical science and particularly in the reality of the sociological experience. The "being" to which all thought is relative is sociological being, and with that difference the relativizing and the unmasking take their reference from the factual rather than from the ethical or the aesthetic.[22] In the words of Thomas Gradgrind, speaking of correct preparation for life, "Now, what I want is, Facts. Teach these boys and girls nothing but Facts. Facts alone are wanted in life. Plant nothing else and root out everything else" (Dickens [1854] 1908, 1).

Finally, in connection with his own typology of interpretation (Mannheim [1922b] 1953, 39; Mannheim [1926] 1971), Mannheim argued that

---

22. "We arrive at this level when we no longer make individuals personally responsible for the deceptions which we detect in their utterances, and when we no longer attribute the evil that they do to their malicious cunning" (Mannheim [1929] 1936, 54).

in this problem constellation of the presuppositions of knowing (of "transcendental" as opposed to "immanent knowledge"), the relativization and the unmasking are no longer partial exercises limited to the bounds of one or another particular idea or amalgam of ideas (the "particular conception of ideology," Mannheim [1929] 1936, 50–52) but have undergone a totalization in the demonstration of "the existentially determined nature of an entire system of *Weltanschauung*. . . . That one could not, in this connection, consider ideas and beliefs in isolation, but had to grasp them instead as mutually interdependent parts of a systematic totality, this was the lesson we learned from modern historicism" (Mannheim [1925] 1952, 142–43; Mannheim [1924] 1952).

The new problem constellation of modern thinking, Mannheim concluded, is constituted by these several factors (Mannheim [1925] 1952, 144–46; Mannheim [1929] 1936, 49–62). Not simply as an additive nexus, however: the constellation "arose as a result of the interplay" among those factors, that is, from a "systematization" of spheres of thinking, through which the original emphases are altered. Unmasking, for instance, once we become "aware of the fact that *all* thinking of a social group is determined by its existence, . . . undergoes a process of sublimation which turns it into a mere operation of determining the functional role of any thought whatever."[23] All thought becomes instrumentalized (the coinage of interests), and the purpose of "the critical operation" is simply a matter-of-fact specification that "the 'locus' of the idea which is to be combated belongs to an 'obsolete' theoretical system, and, further, to an existential whole which evolution has left behind." Similarly, totalization expands to include as socially determined not only the entire world view of one's opponent (the "special" form of the "total conception of ideology") but one's own world view as well (the "general form of the total conception of ideology," Mannheim [1929] 1936, 68–69): "the choice of the social sphere as a system of reference"—which "was first erected" by the "oppositional science" of sociology, bourgeois in provenience— "gradually became more or less a common possession of all camps . . . , a new type of historical interpretation which has to be added to the earlier ones" (cf. Mannheim [1926] 1971). Finally, and very importantly for Mannheim's theory, the self-relativization of thought is itself dynamic, by virtue of the fact that the "thatness" to which thought is relative is dynamic Being.

---

23. Why a "process of *sublimation*"? The implicit argument (which Mannheim developed only partially) is that by raising "the critical operation" to a higher level, into an ethically neutral level, the continued *oppositional* stance of concretely dominant groups in unmasking the ideas of subordinate groups as falsity and deception enjoys the force of a matter-of-fact legitimacy (cf., e.g., Mannheim [1929] 1936, 51).

This poses the task of satisfying the urge toward totality in a more radical fashion. It is not enough to see that the "ideas" of an antagonistic class are dictated by its "existence," it is not enough to recognize that our own "ideas" are dictated by our own existence; what we have to grasp is that both our "ideas" and our "existence" are components of a comprehensive evolutionary process in which we are engaged. This overall process, then, is posited as our ultimate "absolute" (albeit a changing and evolving one). . . . [The] present problem constellation necessarily implies this radical following through of these ideas to their last consequences. (Mannheim [1925] 1952, 146)

This premise of the absolute (hardly original to Mannheim) permitted him to speak of the "stubbornness of facts," as we will see below, and of a truthful knowledge contained within the world as it is dynamically evolving. Given the premise, his task was to show how human thinking could have a dependable and responsible relation to that absolute. Where Scheler sought to overcome the whole of relativism, Mannheim attempted to split this problem of knowledge along a supposed line between central factual conclusion and practical implication. Factually, thought is always "existentially related," Mannheim conceded,[24] but that relatedness does not imply the necessity of the skeptic's lament. "Knowledge, as seen in the light of the total conception of ideology"—that is, as "relational"—"is by no means an illusory experience, for ideology in its relational concept is not at all identical with illusion" (Mannheim [1929] 1936, 76).

Having assayed the major features of his problem constellation, Mannheim examined what he took to be a cross section of the most important contemporary "standpoints from which reality is being interpreted today" and which were asserting their own solutions to the problem (see Mannheim [1925] 1952, 149ff). Of the four standpoints considered, he attended most to the "debate" between "material apriorism," or, in particular, the modern phenomenology propounded by Scheler, and historicism, including especially his own approach. Positivism he dealt with rather quickly: both in its "bourgeois positivist" variant (naming Durkheim, Lévy-Bruhl, and Je-

---

24. Mannheim qualified this general assertion about the "existential relatedness" of thought. He exempted the world of "natural objects" (e.g., Mannheim [1924] 1952, 115; Mannheim [1926] 1971, 117–18; Mannheim [1929] 1936, 170). But also, it seems, he was prepared to exempt, "in large measure," aspects or components of the "social world": "There are, doubtless, areas of political-historical knowledge in which there is an autonomous regularity which may be formulated, in large measure, independently of one's *Weltanschauung* and political position" (Mannheim [1929] 1936, 166).

rusalem as exemplary figures) and in the "proletarian 'nuance' " of materialist positivism (vulgar Marxism), positivism had made important contributions to the formation of the problem constellation, Mannheim believed, but with its rejection of metaphysics (i.e., its metaphysics of antimetaphysics, wherein it "hypostatizes one particular conception of empiricism . . . as absolutely valid [which] thereby becomes a metaphysics itself"), the positivists proposed a false monism by disregarding meaning, or by driving it wholly into an external and independent "naturalistic being," and therefore they "did not rise above a relatively primitive level." On the other hand, whereas "the positivist attitude is necessarily blind [to] the phenomenological difference between 'being' and 'meaning,' " formal apriorism (the fourth of the standpoints inspected by Mannheim) "depreciates Being, as against thought," and hypostatizes meaning as a supratemporal absolute. Because "all *material* propositions are given up as purely relative and existentially determined, but autonomy and supratemporality is claimed for the *formal* elements of thought, such as the categories or—in newer variants of this philosophy—formal values," formal apriorism is unable to account for "the most essential problems of a sociology of knowledge," inasmuch as all cultural products are assigned the same timeless validity (Mannheim [1925] 1952, 152–53).

As for material apriorism, Mannheim indicted Scheler's theory as a misguided pursuit of "timeless characteristics of man," as an effort "to explain any concrete historical situation as a complex of such characteristics" by examining "in a 'generalizing' fashion the interaction of the 'real' and 'cultural' factors [*Real* and *Idealfaktoren*]—taking it to exhibit a general law of succession, rather than a sequence of concrete, unique temporal phases." But, Mannheim warned, "it is clear that such 'laws' can result only from the application of the generalizing categories of natural science," i.e., the application of categories of the "un-meaning" to the realm of thought (Mannheim [1925] 1952, 157). Thus, for example, Scheler erroneously treated the category of "drives" (the essential "real factors") "as a supratemporal, unchanging entity, in terms of which the historical process is to be explained in part" (Mannheim [1925] 1952, 164).[25] And his insistence on the "idealistic dualism" of an ultimate separation of being and meaning was mistaken. For Mannheim, too, there

> is a phenomenological separation between Being and Meaning; but this phenomenological duality can no longer be considered as fun-

---

25. However, it is clear that Scheler *did* intend the "drives" as having a historical distribution insofar as their concrete manifestation is concerned (see, e.g., Scheler [1926b] 1960, 44–51).

damental when we come to examine both terms as parts of a dynamic genetic *totality*. . . . For any philosophy or theory of culture or sociology . . . which seeks to transcend the abstract immanence of the various cultural products and to analyze them as part and parcel of an overall life process, the phenomenological duality cannot be more than a provisional device. One should not object at this point that the historian engaged in positive research is not interested in these metaphysical questions, since he [allegedly] need not go beyond the phenomenological separation of the spheres of "Being" and "Meaning" when he tries to give a historical account of the immanent evolution of ideas. This objection merely arises from a positivistic delusion which prevents us from realizing how deeply the supposedly pure scientist is engaged in metaphysics whenever he gives interpretations, establishes historical relationships, ascertains historic "trends," or puts "real" factors in correlation with "ideal" ones. (Mannheim [1925] 1952, 161)

Moreover, to classify a factor as "real," Mannheim continued, does not necessarily imply that it is "completely devoid of meaning and purely 'material' " (Mannheim [1925] 1952, 162–63). As an illustration of his claim (from which, by the way, we can see an aspect of Mannheim's own conception of the "real" vis-à-vis "nature"), he pointed to the "economic factor" of the "hunger drive": "Only the physiology of the hunger drive belongs to mere 'nature' [un-meaning], but . . . this physiological substratum constitutes an element of the historic process only insofar as it enters into mental configurations, for example by assuming the form of an economic order or some other institutional form."

At this juncture in his critical analysis, Mannheim introduced the vague outlines of a concept formation of great potential import, when he proposed to speak of the mutual relationship of "real" and "ideal" as one of "mind-in-the-substructure" and "mind-in-the-superstructure":

If the two spheres of the "mental" are distinguished in this fashion, then we are of the opinion that the mind-in-the-substructure—involving primarily the conditions of production, *together with all concomitant social relationships*—does in part shape and determine mind-in-the-superstructure. For we should not forget that mind-in-the-substructure is the more "massive" factor, if for no other reason, then because it is the components of this substructure which create the enduring framework of the continuous existence of human beings—that which is generally called *milieu*. (Mannheim [1925] 1952, 163)

But the formation was abortive, owing to Mannheim's projection of it from the continued claim of a "being-meaning" duality and as a matter of two "mental spheres" discernible if "we constantly lower the limit of the 'natural' by refining our distinctions." He did not take notice, apparently, that if "mind-in-the-substructure" does in fact involve "the conditions of production, together with all concomitant social relationships," then it *necessarily simultaneously* "involves" the "mind-in-superstructure," inasmuch as production is production of *human life*.[26]

While Mannheim's critical account of Scheler's theoretical proffer is not, in my opinion, entirely adequate or fair, he was correct in attributing to Scheler's argument "a logical immanence of the ideal sphere," an absolutization of an independently given and separate realm of the ideal, and a fundamental incapacity to make sensible certain aspects of the "problem constellation" of human knowledge. For his own part, Mannheim chose what he took to be a different and (need it be said?) correct absolutization as the solution to relativism: the "knowing subject" is placed in relation to an absolutized "object of knowledge," the absolute historical process. Repeatedly, from his early writings on the classification of the sciences (1922a) and his "structural analysis" of epistemology (1922b) to his study of conservative thought (1927), *Ideology and Utopia* (1929), and beyond, Mannheim insisted on the bedrock of a world the essential dynamic structure of which is objective, absolute, and, in a sense, unchangeable in its evolution. By 1924, with his essay on "Historicism," he had worked out a relativization of the human knower vis-à-vis the unchangeable yet dynamic object of knowledge through a conception of the historicity of perspective. Already (e.g., 1922b) he had insisted that proper understanding of historical phenomena must be conducted in terms of "systematization" of thought, rather than in terms of isolated ideas; and already there too he had emphasized the object of knowledge as a nonrelative existent on which different historical perspectives are possible (Mannheim [1922b] 1953, 40n). Now, in "Historicism," he argued further:

> The historical subject-matter (the historical content, so to speak, of an epoch) remains identical "in itself," but it belongs to the essential

---

26. Of course, Mannheim intended by "production" something different and less comprehensive—namely, "economism," which from the point of view of historicism appears "as something merely corresponding to one particular phase of the historical process—inasmuch as the 'vital centre' of man moves into different spheres of activity in different epochs, and each epoch understands historical reality most clearly in connection with the sphere in which it lives most intensely" (Mannheim [1925] 1952, 163n. 1).

conditions of its cognizability that it can be grasped only from differing intellectual-historical standpoints—or, in other words, that we can view only various "aspects" of it. By analogy with the discovery of Husserl [1913, §41]—that it is a characteristic of the spatial object that we can view it only in different "profiles" [*Abschattungen*], i.e., from definite local positions and in definite perspectives—one could, it seems to us, venture the thesis that it is part of the essence of a historico-cultural, but also of a psychic object, that it is penetrable only in "mental and psychic profiles," that is, by way of certain cross-sections and dimensions of depth the nature of which is dependent on the mental-psychic perspectivic location of the observing, interpreting subject. (Mannheim [1924] 1952, 105)

The following year, in "The Problem of a Sociology of Knowledge," Mannheim again located the absolute in an objective world that can be known by the human subject only partially and from the particular perspective of his or her social location in a historical context (Mannheim [1925] 1952; see also Mannheim [1931] 1936, 256). While this understanding of knowledge may seem to be corrupted by "a theoretical *circulus vitiosus*," it actually is not—or it need not be—according to Mannheim: "What we mean by [the self-relativization of thought] is by no means epistemological 'relativism' but merely the opposite of 'autonomy.' One may very well assert that thought is 'relative to being,' 'dependent on being,' 'non-autonomous,' 'part of a whole reaching beyond it,' without professing any 'relativism' concerning the truth value of its findings" (Mannheim [1925] 1952, 137–38). Knowledge of the social (though not of the natural) is constituted partly in intellectual competition, involving interests of power and prestige, to gain an acknowledged right to publicize the "correct" interpretation, or paradigm, of the world (Mannheim [1928] 1952, 191–95); but to say that does not imply more than that "certain (qualitative) truths cannot even be grasped, or formulated, except in the framework of an existential correlation between subject and object." Mannheim proposed to escape the vicious circle "by conceiving thought as a mere partial phenomenon belonging to a more comprehensive factor within the totality of the world process, and particularly by devaluing, as it were, the sphere of theoretical communication in which this self-contradiction arises." With added conviction, Mannheim repeated in more specific terms the argument already percolating in his "structural analysis" of epistemology (1922b) and the study of historicism (1924):

If one maintains that the sphere of thought . . . is merely one of *expression* rather than of the ultimate cognitive *constitution of objects*, the contradiction, otherwise insurmountable, becomes devalued. . . . We have to do here with an act of breaking through the immanence of thought—with an attempt to comprehend thought as a partial phenomenon within the broader field of existence, and to determine it, as it were, starting from existential data. (Mannheim [1925] 1952, 138)

This "existential thinker"—standing at an alleged point outside thought—believes that "thought neither constitutes objects nor grasps ultimately real matters of fact but merely expresses extra-theoretically constituted and warranted beliefs." When we devalue thought in this manner, Mannheim concluded, "inner contradictions . . . and paradoxes can no longer be considered as symptoms of defective thinking"; on the contrary, we are indirectly grasping aspects of the historically real, and the "symptoms" are actually "manifestations of some extra-theoretical phenomenon being truly grasped in existence" (Mannheim [1925] 1952, 138).

This true if indirect grasping of the absolute object of knowledge, Mannheim acknowledged, rests on the metaphysical assumption "that the global process within which the various intellectual standpoints emerge is a meaningful one" (Mannheim [1925] 1952, 177). Given that the historical process houses meaning, the "entire problem of 'absolute' truth" becomes tractable, for it coincides with the problem of the "unitary meaning of the process as a whole." The relevant question, then, "is how far we are able to grasp the evolutionary goal that *can* be seen at a given moment." This is a matter of understanding in the "completed *Gestalt*," or systematization of a historical epoch, "the functional role of thought patterns relative to the goal at which the evolutionary process had been aiming." Of course, Mannheim was quick to add, history is always "in process," and we as the knowing subjects "are wholly *in statu nascendi.*" Consequently our perceptions are only of "the clash of antagonistic aspirations." Since our own standpoint falls within one or another of these competing frames, we can gain "only a partial and perspectivic view of what is unfolding" as the historical process. Moreover, the same is true of our understanding of "the past," insofar as it "depends on the interpretation of the ongoing process."

Yet, Mannheim insisted, the existentially necessary partiality of the knowing subject's understanding need not entail an artificial valorization of thought, an arbitrary fixing of the "market worth" of a given view; it need not lead to an epistemological conclusion of relativism or illusionism, or to "a negation of the reality of the historic process." Rather there is an operative possibility, enactable through a specific cooperative method, of veridical knowledge in the community of views on and aspects of the historically real. While the historicist approach may *start* with a position of relativism, "eventually it achieves an absoluteness of view, because in its final form it posits history itself as the Absolute." It is "this alone" that "makes it possible that the various standpoints, which at first appear to be anarchic, can be ordered as component parts of a meaningful overall process" (Mannheim [1925] 1952, 172–73). The possibility of such meaningful ordering exists not as some vague chance, that is, not as one of a random assortment of orderings, but by virtue of the governance of the "stubborn facts" of that objective, absolute object of knowledge, namely the real historical process. Simply because any system of thought must belong essentially to one or another standpoint does not mean, Mannheim stressed,

> that the whole concreteness, "stubborn-factness" of the data and essential meanings is dissolved into a number of various perspectives. Every one of us refers to the same data and essences. To be sure, . . . a given movement can discover only a limited range of facts . . . but once these facts have been made visible, every one is obliged to take them into account. Moreover, we understand, looking at things from our perspective, the possibility and necessity of other perspectives; and no matter what our perspective is, we all experience the controlling "stubbornness" of the data; thus, we all have every reason to assume that we move in the medium of reality, so that we can disclaim all illusionism. (Mannheim [1925] 1952, 173)

Certainly there is in Mannheim's construction a vain celebration of "thinking," which, at this juncture, has the (shallow) appearance of an egalitarianism. One could formulate a sense of his argument to the effect that veridical knowledge can be *put together* only in a community of open exchange among cooperative, representative persons and their dually representative perspectives.[27] There is indeed in Mannheim's work the strong conviction of the powers of thinking by reasonable persons engaged in reasonable discourse.[28] But it would be mistaken to read Mannheim's proposal as one of radical positivism, that is, that we have merely to record and summate "unmediated" and "stubborn facts." Mannheim himself ventured a defense against such a reading, by cautioning that he meant that facts are "stubborn" only "in the sense that they constitute a control we

27. In other words, representative on the one side of the array of social positions and perspectives from which the knowers gain their understandings; on the other side, representative of the numerous aspects of the historical process. There is, of course, the question of the means by which every aspect of the absolute object of knowledge is surveyed from a corresponding perspective and social position.

28. Compare the similar faith in Scheler's statement about the necessity of the "temporal and spatial cooperation of irreplaceable (because individual) unique cultural entities working together in complete mutual solidarity" (Scheler [1926b] 1960, 26).

may use in ruling out arbitrary constructions" and expressly not in the sense "that they can be grasped outside any system, in isolation, without reference to meanings" (Mannheim [1925] 1952, 173). The "facts" are always knowable only from one or another perspective; but it is this quality of "stubbornness" that enables us to distinguish between the faithful, existentially related facts on the one side and, on the other, the lie or deliberate dissimulation and those existentially related "facts" that, because of some indeliberate failing on the part of the knower, are *not* faithful to the purported aspect of the object of knowledge.

It is in regard to the question of who are the bearers of that knowledge which transcends partial knowledge, and how they discriminate faithful from unfaithful facts—that is, the question of the composition and warrant of a transcendental intellectual community—that we see the culmination of Mannheim's liberal elitist celebration of thinking (cf. Eichhorn et al. 1972). Arguing that "a valid synthesis" of the manifold perspectives and partialities of knowing "must be based on a political position which will constitute a progressive development," a position which "calls for a peculiar alertness toward the historical reality of the present" (Mannheim [1929] 1936, 137), he adopted the image of a "socially unattached intelligentsia" as a social category capable collectively of surmounting the fragmentation of perspectives and constituting a "dynamic mediation" of the multiplicities (144). Mannheim developed his characterization of this mediative category most expansively in the context of deciding the possibility and nature of a "science of politics" (136–146), but already in the essay on conservative thought he had described, in rather melodramatic words, the heavy burden assigned to these "unattached" people:

> The fate of the world of thought is in the care of a socially unattached, or barely attached, stratum whose class affinities and status in society cannot be precisely defined; a stratum which does not find the aims it pursues within itself but in the interests of strata with a more definite place in the social order. . . . If . . . there were no such stratum [of these "advocate-philosophers, *ideologues* who can find arguments in favor of any political cause they may happen to serve," (Mannheim [1927] 1971, 185)], it might easily happen that all spiritual content would disappear from our increasingly capitalistic society and leave nothing but naked interests. (Mannheim [1927] 1971, 186)

By Mannheim's accounting, the one common trait that gives this stratum of unattached intellectuals their singular capacity, and that "binds them together in a striking way," is their participation in a lengthy educational process that tends to suppress "differences of birth, status, profession, and wealth" yet by the same token preserves in synthesis the variety of "opposing tendencies in social reality." Although they do not participate directly in production, according to Mannheim, they can "develop the social sensibility . . . essential for becoming attuned to the dynamically conflicting forces" of a given historical situation, and of the course of historical epochs. As a matter of actual practice, the intellectuals historically either have aligned themselves with this or that particular class and party[29]—which affiliation "shows a tendency, even though it is unconscious, toward a dynamic synthesis" of perspectives—or have become "aware of their own social position and the mission implicit in it," namely the mission of supplying the "needed" dynamic synthesis of perspectivic, partial thought. Clearly Mannheim was of the opinion, expressed in his continual "diagnosis of our time," that if ever there was a time for the stratum of unattached intellectuals to experience self-enlightenment, to develop a self-consciousness of mission and take charge of interpreting the world, his was it. The polarization of thinking he had described previously (e.g., 1926, 1927; and again in the context of "ideological" and "utopian" thought)[30] now had its instrument of mediation—that is, an agency that could forge the *total* perspective, that would properly integrate all competing interests and aspirations and partial understandings. Although not "absolute truth" in the older sense, this total perspective would be the closest approximation that humans can accomplish; it would *be* truth, the only truth possible.

According to one of his students, Paul Kecskemeti (editorial introduction to Mannheim 1952, 1), "Mannheim's sociology of knowledge was often misunderstood as a variant of scepticism and illusionism," whereas actually "his purpose was not to demonstrate the inescapability of relativism and scepticism, but rather the thesis that in spite of the inescapability of certain relativist conclusions, genuine knowledge of historical and social phenomena was possible, . . . [that] participation in the social process, which renders one's perspective partial and biased, also enables one to discover truth of deep human import." No doubt Kecskemeti's comment ushers us to a reasonably accurate image-screen of Mannheim's projected intent and commitment; I feel quite as much when I read Mannheim's works. Nevertheless—and with more than a little irony—Mannheim was thoroughly subject to his own dictum that "no antithesis escapes conditioning by the thesis it sets out to oppose" (Mannheim [1927] 1971, 147).

---

29. "It was usually the class *in need of* intellectual development which received their support" (Mannheim [1929] 1936, 142; emphasis added).

30. I have here said nothing directly of Mannheim's 1929 analysis of utopist, in contrast to ideological, thinking. Although not crucial to our understanding of his operative epistemology, it has been a resource of some importance in subsequent treatment of utopist thought and of sociological theory (see, e.g., Polak [1955] 1973; Strasser 1976, 4–27, especially p. 6 n. 28).

And in consequence, as many commentators hitherto have made clear (e.g., Schaff [1971] 1976; Lukács 1953, 500–507; Grünwald 1934, 74–84, 229–32),[31] the actualization of Mannheim's purpose amounted finally to a revitalized skepticism, centered within the more acceptable (because less metaphysical sounding) domain of a "sociology of knowledge," inasmuch as his solution to the self-annihilative status of relativism rested in an absolutization of progressive truth-in-History, the absolutism of which contradicts his own position. Mannheim attempted to insulate his stance with a semantic nuance—"relationalism"—but on that effort there is no escaping Lukács's cold verdict: "The difference between relativism and

31. This is an appropriate occasion for remarks about the extensive analysis of the sociology of knowledge of Ernst Grünwald (1912–33). His own position, tied to the then-current disjuncture of "social" and "cultural," was a kind of agnosticism: it *may* be that knowledge is socially connected or determined, but science cannot prove as much because it has no capability of choosing among possible interpretations (Grünwald 1934, 56–60). So, with conviction that knowledge of "ultimate reality" is doubtful, Grünwald concluded that a sociology of knowledge can never touch matters of epistemology (86–88, 230–4). But it must be seen that Grünwald conceived truth as a property of absolutized Logos. Thus, after concluding that "the external view" of knowledge "interprets the relation between the *ens realissimum* and the cultural phenomenon as an emanatist relation," in which "the absolute emits from itself the other layers, which are ontically less real, and the proposition, too, is an entirely passive emanation," he then asked, "Is the proposition really the vehicle of the manifestational meaning and the object of the specific mode of understanding from the external view?" (71, 72). His answer was "No" (73–74). Because a proposition's claim of validity, he reasoned, is an *essential constituent* of the proposition, and because the "immanent sense" of a proposition "is the exclusive 'privilege' of the internal view [which] alone . . . can say anything about the validity, . . . the external view, which *per definitionem* does not do justice to the immanent sense . . . but on principle goes behind it, *a limine* does not get the representative function and thus the claim of validity into sight." In order justly to consider a proposition, Grünwald argued, I must "take some position" regarding its validity claim; but that "can be done only so long as I am viewing the significatory or representative aspect of a proposition, since the concept of validity, or truth, is meaningful only in that dimension." By definition, that view is the internal or intrinsic view.

But it is clear that Grünwald's argument can succeed only in the measure of our acquiescence to his insistence that, if we are to speak justly about a statement of knowledge, we must do so *within its own terms* of validity claim—that is, whether we decide in favor of or against the claim, we must accept its terms of the possibility of validity or truth. To the extent that we do so, of course, we have, as he contended, no capability of choosing among possible interpretations. Were it not for his own absolutization of basic categories of thought and the rules of formal logic, Grünwald would have found himself in a most radically relativist conclusion.

relationalism is approximately the difference (as in Lenin's letter to Gorki [November 14, 1913]) between the yellow and the green devil" (Lukács 1953, 500).

Mannheim persistently urged the claim of a non-relative, humanly knowable, external world. The natural world, the world of mere "unmeaning," was not problematic with respect to that claim. Rather it was knowledge of the human world that had lost anchorage, and Mannheim's project was to find it a new one, the *real* and *necessary* anchorage. His question was, at what point does one pass historical relativity and reach that absolute world? His frustration was that the longer he searched, the more that elusive point receded from his grasp. But his celebration of thinking would not be stilled, and so he argued the semantic trick of "relationalism" and a privileged group of thinkers who collectively are able to condense the kaleidoscope of existentially related views into truth.

In a way, Mannheim's conception of a "socially unattached intelligentsia" was fitting, given his glorification of disembodied thinking, for these intellectuals constitute individually and severally a kind of socially disembodied thinker. Despite the fact that they produce books, paintings, and plays, progeny, disciples, and epigone, devils yellow or green, and any number of other creations, somehow they manage to avoid participating directly in production (Mannheim [1929] 1936, 140). But that absurdity is quite appropriate, since the socially unattached intelligentsia were not expected to *make* truth about the absolute world, only to *interpret* it, to apprehend and tell the meaning of the truth of the absolute world.[32]

There is a variation of the Homeric vision of tragedy here: each character in the play of life is always both right and wrong, always telling understandings that are simultaneously valid and invalid, for truth resides in the epic as a whole and not in the individual players. In our world of mortals—as in the funeral games for Patroclus when Achilles sought futilely to banish conflict once and for all—that is the tragic vision. Truth, justice, the good flatly refuse to be contained by the individual. This spell of Homer's has had a tenacious grip through the ages—in philosophy, in histories and in myths, in belletristic literatures of all sorts—and so it is hardly surprising to read its reproduction in, for example, Max Weber (whose fascination with Dostoyevsky was hardly incidental to his sociolog-

---

32. One cannot escape noticing Mannheim's vulnerability to the most obvious critique, as etched with a trace of acid by Adorno: "The answer to Mannheim's reverence for the intelligentsia as 'free-floating' is to be found not in the reactionary postulate of its 'rootedness in Being' but rather in the reminder that the very intelligentsia that pretends to float freely is fundamentally rooted in the very being that must be changed and which it merely pretends to criticize" (Adorno [1955] 1967, 48).

ical thinking about bureaucracy and the charismatic), in Max Scheler, or in Karl Mannheim. But in Mannheim's variation, the socially unattached intelligentsia would accomplish what Achilles could not: they would become *playing spectators* whose unique excellence would consist in apprehension of the total perspective. What Mannheim failed to appreciate of the Greek sense of tragedy was the essential identity of unique excellence and fatal flaw.

Mannheim's attitude regarding the truth of the absolute world is told by his choice of words, especially those choices most likely unweighed and thus all the more reflective—for example, "We can *extract* objectified meanings out of a given reality only to the extent that we are able to ask intelligent and *revealing* questions" (Mannheim [1929] 1936, 79n.2; emphases added). The linchpin of Mannheim's elusive "dynamically absolute world" consists in the secret meanings of that world, and, as we are so often told, more than half of the victory in our battle of discovery is in asking the right question.

I have spoken of Mannheim's elitist celebration of thinking. Perhaps its most obvious hallmark is the privileged cognitive space of his intelligentsia, but its image can be located also in broader and earlier constructions. For instance, consider the previously cited passage about the "self-relativization of thought," wherein he asserted that "the attempt to relativize any other sphere [than the sphere of thought], such as art, religion, [ethics, etc.], encounters no such obstacle" of self-invalidation (Mannheim [1925] 1952, 137–38). Note his abstraction of "thought" vis-à-vis art, religion, ethics, and so forth (cf. also Mannheim [1921–22] 1952, 40): What can possibly remain of these "other spheres" if one removes from them the human thinking, the projected and the realized meanings that are integral to their production and consumption? This separation of the "sphere of thought" connects, too, with Mannheim's notions of the "atheoretical" and "systematization." Regarding the latter, he argued that thinking is "an effort to find the logical place of a concept in the total framework of the mental spheres," that is, "in the currently accepted orders, series, and the levels" (Mannheim [1922b] 1953). To speak of "a completely and finally isolated, self-sufficient mental creation" is to speak of an impossibility. "Even an action, let alone a concept, displays the structure of a systematization; it is this structure which gives it meaning and consistency, which in fact makes it what it is." But while Mannheim was prepared to argue as much in the case of the "meaning of thought," even that of "action"—stimulated, no doubt, by similar statements by Gestaltism, Weber's interpretive sociology, and Dvorák's (1918) parallelism in art (cf. Mannheim [1921–22] 1952)—he was *not* willing to undertake the same argument in regard to the being of "objects," or the "world of being" generally. Despite his saying the contrary (e.g., [1925] 1952, 161), Mannheim reserved a separation of "being" and "meaning"—one that permitted him to speak, for example, of the "un-meaning being" of a natural world— and somehow it is "meaning" that has the greater stature. Mannheim's "solution" to the problem of relativism failed not simply because of the impotence of a semantic nuance ("relationalism") nor simply because of the hollowness of his "socially unattached intelligentsia." The failure was given by his assumption, as by Scheler's, of an ultimate disjuncture of "being" and "meaning," of the "material" and the "ideal," of "existence" and "thought."

5. GEORG LUKÁCS (1885–1971)

Perhaps the one understanding of Georg Lukács we learn most often from readings of social-science texts is that he published in 1923 a set of essays under the title, *History and Class Consciousness*, a few years later was "forced" (in rather a Galilean fashion, it may be said) to recant his her-meneutical errors as these were "demonstrated" by the hierarchy of ortho-dox Communism, and thereafter turned his pen to matters mostly "tangen-tial" to the substance of a science of society—for example, aesthetics, literary criticism, etc. If one were to indulge a certain attitude of disdain, such observation could be recast into scathing comment on the orthodoxies of both the academicians and the party hierarchs. But pretermission here conserves energy for expenditures later, and I shall instead answer only that such a view of Lukács's work does serious injustice to its richness of critique and to its essential unity. From the standpoint of theory of knowl-edge, the position formulated in the 1923 essays was reformulated without fundamental emendation in Lukács's study *The Young Hegel* (1954; orig-inal edition completed in 1938), in his extended essay *The Destruction of Reason* (1953), and again in his *Aesthetics* (1963). In his preface to the 1967 edition of *History and Class Consciousness*, Lukács himself asserted that, while he may have committed such errors of thinking as affirming the Hegelian identity of "alienation" and "objectification," nevertheless in many respects the position he had argued in 1923 he still held to be accurate and valid.

Consider, for example, *The Destruction of Reason*, which on the surface appears as a kind of intellectual history of nineteenth- and twentieth-century philosophic and scientific systems understood in their relations to the social-structural conditions of their creation. In sequence, he examined the works of Schelling, Schopenhauer, and Nietzsche; the members of the *Lebensphilosophie* school of social science, notably Dilthey, to whom he was critically sympathetic, and Simmel and Scheler; the "parasitic subjec-tivism" of Heidegger and Jaspers; neo-Hegelianism; followed by German sociologists of the imperial period, especially Tönnies, Max Weber, and

Mannheim; and social Darwinism, race theory, and fascism. His criticisms were often devastating and they grew increasingly virulent as he turned to what he considered the immorality of Heidegger and Jaspers and the superficiality of Scheler, Weber, and Mannheim, among others. But Lukács's "history" of philosophy is in fact a very long text, extending from *History and Class Consciousness*, where the principal target of criticism is Kant, to *The Young Hegel*, *The Destruction of Reason*, and beyond. Throughout, one reads both an indictment of the increasing "irrationalist relativism," the skepticism and agnosticism that have gnawed at the foundations of effective knowledge and value, leaving a consciousness of despair, *and* a genuine passion-filled desire to repour those foundations. If the desire's claim stands forth more clearly in the earlier set of essays and the indictment more clearly in his later work, that may be taken as the measure of Lukács's "recantation" before the eye of perversity (cf. Lukács [1967] 1975, 73–74).

Lukács's critique is often brilliant. In making his *own* claim to transcend critique, however, Lukács failed. But if his solution proved finally to be no solution, we can nevertheless appreciate that it was no solution to a problematic better apprehended than by most, and never apprehended by many. Here I shall attend not to the substance of his critique (some of which is reproduced in my own) but to an examination of his positive claim. In order to do this, it is necessary that we start with the awareness that his goal was to overcome rampant skepticism, to offer a solution firmer than Weberian agnosticism and Mannheimian "relationalism," by demonstrating an identity of subject-object in history. In this he relied heavily on his readings of Hegel and Marx, though to an extent he also incorporated certain constructions of neo-Kantian idealism (including some from Weber). His relation to Marx, and thus to Hegel, was complicated by the circumstances that already by the turn of the century Marx's work had been vulgarized in a mechanistic, "economic determinist" direction and that important parts of Marx's work (e.g., the Paris manuscripts of 1844; the *Grundrisse*) were either unknown or neglected. Lukács sought to correct both by reading Marx in the light of Hegel. The success of his effort was quite remarkable insofar as he retrieved to view Marx's early investigation of the grounds of consciousness and the alienation of life; but the failure of his effort was finally decisive for the adequacy of his own proffered solution.

Lukács sought to demonstrate subject-object identity by taking over the Hegelian concepts of "totality" and "mediation." In the idea of totality, he argued, we have "the presupposition necessary to comprehend reality," the dialectical relation between subject and object in the historical process (Lukács [1923] 1971, 21–22). "Facts," "elements," and so on can never be truly known in isolation but only in their relations to the whole, for the true objectivity of objects (including the subject as object) is constituted only in the dynamic relation of the objects to the dynamic totality. Moreover, "knowledge of the real, objective nature of a phenomenon, the knowledge of its historical character and the knowledge of its actual function in the totality of society form . . . a single, undivided act of cognition" (14). In contrast to the Kantian principle—where, by definition, the knowing subject can never be an object—the " 'subject' here is not a detached spectator" of history; rather, "the rise and evolution of its knowledge and its actual rise and evolution in the course of history are just the two different sides of the same real process" (21). Thus, one's knowledge depends upon one's place in the totality of the historical process.

Lukács developed his thinking of the category of "totality" most expansively in his *Ästhetik*, and so it is to this difficult work as well as to *History and Class Consciousness* that we must turn. Consider any product of human being or activity in the totality of the world (Lukács 1963, 2:229–34). This product is not a "mere" object or collation of objects but an extension of the production in the self-evolution and self-preservation of reality, and, as such, it expresses the historical *hic et nunc* of its origin, its being made. This circumstance means that the product can be understood neither in terms of the category of the "universal" (*das Allgemeine* or *Allgemeinheit*), since it contains the conditions of *its historical* origins, nor in terms of the strictly "individual" (*das Einzelne* or *Einzelheit*), since the object as such is not "in-itself" but is generalized through its being-in-relation, that is, its relation to a dynamic totality. In short, the object as human product is neither a matter of universal law nor a matter of isolated individuality. A third objective category, or category of objective reality, is required for our understanding—namely, the category of "speciality" (*das Besondere* or *Besonderheit*)—because it is through the special that the universal and the individual are incorporated into the totality of an object as it "reflects" the dynamic totality of reality.[33] Therefore, the process of knowing consists in a movement back and forth from the individual to the universal or from the universal to the individual. Everyone immediately perceives reality in the same way, as sense-contacts with the individual or with congeries of individuals. But the mere individual can never be understood or expressed. Rather, to say what the "this" of individuality is, one must express its *relations*, which is to say "specify" its thisness, in a movement between individuality and universality. Such movement consists of

---

33. "Reflection," in the literature of German idealism, it may be recalled, is a process in which the knowing subject, when "reflecting" *on* an object of consciousness, forces that object of reflection to "bend back" in such a way that its constitution as an object of consciousness is revealed.

numerous "relative generalizations," which mediate between the extreme categories and create the totality of the object. These "mediations" (*Vermittlungen*) constitute a "field of mediations" referred to by Lukács as the category of "speciality" (2:196–99, 205).

It is crucial to bear in mind that these three categories—the individual, the special, and the universal—were treated not as categories simply of "mind," not as impositions by "mind" on objective reality, but as categories of the real. Moreover, the categories must be understood as dynamic; they change into one another in a process that is objectively real. The categories are contained by the dialectical movement of the world as historical totality (cf. e.g., Lukács 1963, 2:196, 202–4, 207, 225).

Given that the connections of objects in the world rest on mediations, in order to know something—for instance, to know what being human is—we must know about species of humanness and about individuals; no one of these alone is intelligible. But mediations differ in consequentiality according to their locations relative to the totality. Thus, asserted Lukács, there is the objective possibility of a mediation characterized by its "objective superiority" (*sachliches Übergewicht*) over the extremes; this mediation is an organizing "mean" (*Mitte*), which is rational and higher than the ends that it serves (Lukács 1963, 2:209; Lukács [1923] 1971, 163–64). This objective possibility is an integral characteristic of the world; accordingly, we find it expressed by Lukács in his ethics as well as in his theory of knowledge. Ethical conduct is a "mediating mean," in the network of human activity, between the universality of purely objective law (*Recht*)— that is, the idea of law as a set of general rules—and the individuality of purely subjective conscience (*Moralität*)—that is, the idea of individual morality—both of which are sublated and transcended (the dialectic of *Aufhebung*) in the "mean" (Lukács 1963, 2:213). As with knowledge so with ethics, the extremes of universal and individual are not chimera but are justified existences as "moments" or aspects of the dynamic totality of human life. Only when either is abstracted as an isolated thing-in-itself, a reified abstraction from actuality, does it become false—erroneous, immoral, unreal (2:213–216).

Now, let us recall that for Lukács reality is known from the position of the knower relative to the totality—that is, from the position of the knower's class as a relation in the production of the world, through the mediation of socially determined categories of conceptual framework. *All* thought is class-determined. Thus, two possibilities are objectively presented: either the "contents" of thought, the product of knowing, correspond with the actuality of the world, or they do not. This discrimination, Lukács contended—and it is the essential discrimination of veridical, necessary knowledge from false knowledge—is wholly determined by the integration of objective reality and the objective possibility of effective knowledge (and effective ethics) in moments of the dynamic totality. Class position as a relation to the totality describes simultaneously one's being and the possibility of one's knowledge.

Bourgeois thought (e.g., the false objectivity of positivist science) is both inherent in the being of that class relation and inherently false because it is a *reification* (Lukács 1923, 83–92, 110–21, et passim) of immediately given perceptions of the world, that is, perceptions *un*mediated by conceptual categories that reveal the entirety of the structure and development of society. This inaccessibility of reality to bourgeois thought is unitary to bourgeois knowledge, ethics, and being, because of the objective circumstances of the position and therefore the interest of the bourgeoisie:

> It is true that the bourgeoisie acts as a class in the objective evolution of society. But it understands the process (which it is itself investigating) as something external which is subject to objective laws which it can only experience passively. (Lukács 1923, 63)

The ahistoricity of bourgeois thought shows clearly in bourgeois science, which is incapable of completion, and equally clearly in bourgeois modernist literary expression, where the "negation of history takes two different forms," according to Lukács:

> First, the hero is strictly confined within the limits of his own experience. There is not for him—and apparently not for his creator—any pre-existent reality beyond his own self, acting upon him or being acted upon by him. Secondly, the hero himself is without personal history. He is "thrown-into-the-world": meaninglessly, unfathomably. He does not develop through contact with the world; he neither forms nor is formed by it. (Lukács [1958] 1964, 21)[34]

On the other hand, whereas bourgeois knowledge of the world sloshes about in "the mire of immediacy" and accepts the immediately given world as its comprehension of (what must therefore be a nonhistorical) reality, proletarian knowledge sees through the immediately given to the objective historical situation. The "objects of the empirical world are . . . aspects of a total social situation caught up in the process of historical change." Because Lukács's proletariat is constituted simultaneously as the subject and the object of that process—"the essence of the method of historical materialism is inseparable from the 'practical' and 'critical' activity of the

---

34. The phrase quoted herein by Lukács was undoubtedly a reference to the Heideggerian notion.

proletariat: both are aspects of the same process of social evolution"—the "immanent meanings" of the historical process are "objectively effective" in the consciousness of the proletariat. In comparison with other knowledge, proletarian knowledge stands on "a higher scientific plane objectively" (i.e., it is the objective possibility of that superior mediation or organizing "mean"), inasmuch as the proletariat, by virtue of its position as a class in relation to the total structure of society, "is far more powerfully affected by the dialectical character of the historical process in which the mediated character of every factor receives the imprint of truth and authentic objectivity only in the mediated totality." Even in its momentary condition of false consciousness, the fact of the expropriation of labor means the development of true self-knowledge of society (Lukács [1923] 1971, 20–23, 156, 162–64).

Thus, Lukács hypothesizes two kinds of knowledge in accordance with the opposition of class position in the historical totality of society. In the one case,

> man in capitalist society confronts a reality "made" by himself (as a class) which appears to him to be a natural phenomenon alien to himself; he is wholly at the mercy of its "laws," his activity is confined to the exploitation of the inexorable fulfillment of certain individual laws for his own (egoistic) interests. But even while "acting" he remains, in the nature of the case, the object and not the subject of events. (Lukács [1923] 1971, 135)

Here knowledge is necessarily of a reified existence, and therefore false. In the other case, the human knower comes upon

> authentic humanity, the true essence of man liberated from the false, mechanizing forms of society: man as a perfected whole who has inwardly overcome, or is in the process of overcoming, the dichotomies of theory and practice, reason and the senses, form and content; man whose tendency to create his own forms does not imply an abstract rationalism which ignores concrete content; man for whom freedom and necessity are identical. (Lukács [1923] 1971, 136–37)

This difference between false and effective knowledge, in Lukács's view, resides in the fact that the immediately given world, while common to bourgeoisie and proletariat alike, has fundamentally different implications through their respective class positions (Lukács [1923] 1971, 164, 165). Given its class interest, the bourgeoisie cannot escape from its reified world of immediacy; it can only work out its objective historical consequences. In contrast, "the social existence of the proletariat is far more powerfully affected by the dialectical character of the historical process": the proletariat becomes the *Mitte*, the mediating, organizing "mean" of this historical process—not through an impassive search for the truth of universal *ratio* (which Lukács rejected), not that of an allegedly superior "intuitive" knowledge (he also rejected as meaningless the distinction of "intuitive" and "non-intuitive" knowledge), but as "a matter of life and death." For every time "the individual worker imagines himself to be the subject of his own life he finds this to be an illusion that is destroyed by the immediacy of his existence." The accumulation of shattered illusions eventually is forged into an awareness of the *commodity* of labor power, and through realization of this self-knowledge the object of knowledge undergoes an objective structural change. Lukács's proletariat stands as embodiment of the objective possibility of this genuine consciousness, the dialectial necessity of historical development. When the proletariat puts this transforming consciousness into practice, "it can only breathe life into the things which the dialectics of history have forced to a crisis. . . . For it is itself nothing but the contradictions of history that have become conscious" (Lukács [1923] 1971, 177–78).

Despite the trenchant, often brilliant, force of his critique of other theories of knowledge, Lukács's way out of the problem of relativism finally dissolves completely into a hypostatization of an abstract concept (à la the Weberian ideal-typification) of proletarian thought. That much is clearly evident already—his investiture of "historical reason" and the concrete dynamics of human life in a hypostatized abstraction—and the irony of it is nearly overwhelming. But, although this oft-stated charge is accurate and certainly very serious, we cannot let it go at that. The earth-line of a fissure does not always represent in true proportions the magnitude of the fault beneath.

How are we to understand the juxtaposition of Lukács's introduction of a reified conception of proletarian through—that is, as the embodiment of the historically rational—with his own extensive criticism and analysis of the problem of reification? The answer, I believe, must be formulated at the level of his practical conception of "mediation," of which the proletariat was reputed to be the foremost current historical realization. Lukács attempted to solve the dilemma of relativism through an objective idealism that identifies "object" and "content" of thought by assimilating the former to the latter. It is this "content" of thought that constitutes the possibility of mediation, mediation between the formal and the material, between the merely theoretical and the merely practical, ultimately between "object" and "subject." The content is rational (mediative) if it "agrees with our experience in labour and our mastery of reality" (Lukács [1967] 1975, 46–47); otherwise, it is irrational (nonmediative; unmediated thought). Because of the proletariat's position relative to the historical totality, its thought or consciousness becomes the realm of the objective possibility of such agreement, and the proletariat therefore stands as the vehicle of the dialectic of historical rationality.

But to speak of the necessity of mediation is to grant the stature of ready existence to a "thisness" and a "thatness" which are in some purported sense "in need of" mediation. There is the implication of "things to be mediated"—particularly, in Lukács's construction, "subject" and "object." Yet the imputed prior separation of "things" now requiring mediation was fundamentally a separation only within a false consciousness of the world. Certainly the false consciousness was and is consequential, inasmuch as it issues its own reproduction through false practice. But no one actually produces life, even alienated life, in the capacity of mere "subject" or mere "object." The duality behind the dilemma of relativism against which Lukács so strongly fought was a duality within the materialized thought systems of those (e.g., Kant) against whom Lukács directed his attacks, and its falseness was shown as such by the very constitution of the activity of its producers, which constitution was necessarily simultaneously that of subject and object (albeit *alienated* subject and object).

In other words, the paradox of Lukács's formulation can be understood only on the basis of this diagnosis: he conceded much too much to the recipients of his critique and in consequence was captivated by them—subtlely, to be sure, but captivated nonetheless, and surely enough that he undermined his own critique. Of the many demonstrations of this, I shall mention only two. Recall his central argument regarding the three categories of reality, understood by him as dynamic and objective (as against static, subjective features of "mind")—in particular his contention of the necessity of the objective category termed "speciality." Any product of human creation cannot fit the category of the "universal," inasmuch as it contains the conditions of its own *origin* in human life, and those conditions are *historical*. Nor can it fit the category of the "individual," for the being of a product is never that of an isolated entity, a "thing-in-itself," but always is constituted as a *relation* to the "dynamic totality" (as Lukács called it). Consequently, it must be said that those two categories, the "universal" and the "individual," are *empty* categories—except insofar as they are assigned a content or meaning by false consciousness. But it was in relation to such categories that Lukács formulated his third, *mediative* category of "speciality," that is, that which enables the sublation-transcendence of the irrationality of relative knowledge. When Lukács accepted the problem of relativism as a meaningful problem to be addressed and solved, he quite correctly appreciated that "it is only meaningful to speak of relativism where an 'absolute' is in some sense assumed" (Lukács [1923] 1971, 185–89). And yet when he hypostatized the "consciousness of the proletariat" as the "objectively superior mediation"—as that which can "point out the road along which dialectics of history is *objectively impelled*" and as that which "*only then*" will "*become* the identical subject-object of history" (197; emphases added)—he relegitimated, through the back door as it were, the "meaningfulness" of relativism.

A second instance of the self-undermining concerns his repeated efforts to demonstrate the falsity of "naturalism." In places, his critique seems to proceed from what can only be taken properly as the fundamental starting point, namely, that "nature" is a human reality. But that appearance is belied by his reversion to the naturalistic postulation of a world of nature anterior to, antecedent to, and abaxial to, the human. As he stated the matter most recently, "Production as it occurs in labour consists of course in the labourer setting himself a teleological aim that he plans to realize. In this way something completely new can come into being." Given his own project regarding naturalistic thinking, one would have expected Lukács to fulfill the promise by incorporating in his laborer's teleological project the production of nature. Instead, he argued that the laborer's project "is such that, with the help of the knowledge of causal series, it allows these precise causal series in nature to act on one another in a different combination than would have occurred without the teleological project." And what of those "precise causal series in nature"? They are thoroughly external givens: "The existing causal relationships can only be known and applied; they can never be altered." Consequently, production "involves an identity of identity and non-identity, insofar as the wheel [for example] is certainly something newly produced by man, but yet there is *nothing in the wheel that does not correspond exactly to the prevailing causal series in nature that are independent of men*" (Lukács [1967] 1975, 74–75; emphasis added). Lukács was unmistakably clear about the logical priority of nature. Not only can there be nothing in a human product that fails to correspond to independently existing natural laws, "men can only have a transforming effect on nature in the context of human praxis," and, moreover, nature "evidently develops completely independently of men."[35] To say that human life is nonexistent on Venus or Mars, Lukács reasoned, does not imply the nonexistence of Venus or Mars. Indeed not. But to deny that Venus and Mars are human productions, and *only* that, is to import the entirety of human life into the realm of naturalistic thinking of naturalistic laws.

35. Similarly, in speaking of Solzhenitsyn's Ivan Denisovich and his circumstances, Lukács said: "However 'natural,' inexorable, cruel, senseless, inhuman its effects may appear, they *are* consequences of human acts, and a person defending himself against them must behave quite differently toward them than toward real nature." And: "Nature is really independent of us humans; it can be subordinated to practical human knowledge, but its essence is necessarily immutable" (Lukács [1969] 1971, 21, 22).

6. GEORGE HERBERT MEAD (1863–1931)

With the shift in attention from Lukács to George Herbert Mead, we move not only from one continent to another but also from the epistemologically severe terrain of German idealism to the more matter-of-fact optimism of American pragmatism. Widely regarded as one of the few truly important social theorists to have sprung from the cultural matrix of the United States, Mead is often hagiolatrized as "the father of social psychology" and of the "symbolic interactionist" point of view regarding "the social." Certainly a very large number of social scientists have claimed a basic affinity to the Meadian view, and many more can trace a line of substantial indebtedness to Mead's essays on social consciousness and the constitution of selfhood. One must hasten to add, however, that much of his work has been neglected. Most social scientists now read only the posthumously arranged volume entitled *Mind, Self, and Society* (1934), even though that volume is not fully indicative of Mead's basic endeavors and becomes secondary once his earlier essays and the other volumes of his transcribed thinking have been carefully read.

There is a measure of irony in the neglect of Mead's basic work, for the larger part of it was collected after Mead's death, in volumes entitled *The Philosophy of the Present* (1932) and *The Philosophy of the Act* (1938), together with *Movements of Thought in the Nineteenth Century* (1936), yet one of the most widely received messages of Mead's proclaimed doctrine of knowledge stated that philosophical discourses, save for a scientized philosophy of science itself, were anachronistic to the tasks of knowledge-seeking in the modern world. Indeed, I believe the case can be made for Mead's singular stature among the small number of social theorists native to the United States, not because of the significance of his "symbolic inter-actionism" and its following, nor because of his unusual attention to certain aspects of "the social" (how many theorists have taken seriously the spatiotemporal laminations of social intercourse?) but rather because of the exemplary role that his pragmatic view of science, and of knowledge generally, came quickly to play. The unmitigated optimism that incremental accretions of useful techniques of the act in "concrete" situations prove the warrant of claims to genuine knowledge was hardly peculiar to Mead, but one cannot find a more persistent or less-doubted conviction that pragmatic science faithfully "answered to" the human needs of knowing.

On numerous occasions Mead spoke impatiently of "the hopeless epistemological problem" in which philosophy had long been ensnarled. The kernel of the problem, as he saw it, lay

in the assumption that the immediate object of knowledge is in such a sense an effect produced in the percipient individual that he is after all unable to know the world that he guesses to produce these effects in him, but he can know only the effects themselves. He can only pass by an unverifiable inference from what must be called his own experience to the world external to that experience, but which he assumes is the condition of the experience from which he is unable to escape. (Mead 1938, 27)

Yet, it seemed to Mead, the particular business of science was especially impressive by virtue jointly of its disregard of any "general problem of knowledge" and its record of success in pursuing useful knowledge. There was much to be appreciated in the observation that, for all the obviously futile story-making and ideational gymnastics of philosophy, "epistemology, the problem of knowledge, has excited not the slightest interest among scientists, whose profession is that of discovering what has been unknown" (26). If the epistemological problem were either truly unsolved or as fundamental as had been claimed, surely the scientists could not have been so effective in the conduct of their enterprise. Indeed, did such a dilemma of knowledge even *exist*? Mead thought it did not. Of course, he granted, there was the *appearance* of a fundamental problem still wanting of solution (27). But that "hopeless problem" philosophy had made for itself, and in the process had made itself helpless. What better proof of the chimerical status of this "problem" could one request than the clear and present fact that "the knower par excellence [the scientist] has not had it obtruded upon him among the other research problems with which he is occupied" (26)?[36] Philosophy had gone astray by mythologizing certain "discarded attitudes toward nature"—namely, rationalized presentations of the world "in the guise of men's sensations and ideas, . . . in his states of consciousness" (Mead, 1929, 66–68). The locus of this philosophical misfeasance was fixed by Mead in the character of Renaissance thinking about the relation of nature to art and to mind, and in particular in the attitude that the *raison d'être* of the natural world "was its being the habitat of man." In philosophy's endeavor to account for the world, it got caught up in a "rationalization of the medieval cult," that is, in a persistent compulsion to explain old habits that had "outlived" their situations.

36. Compare Kant's proclamation of the "sure march of science" and his reference, in the preface to his *Critique of Pure Reason* (1787), to the activities of physicists as a prototypical characterization of true knowledge.

  Although Mead's attribution to the scientist of such lack of interest in epistemological problems was without question a generally accurate one, we may wonder about his apprehension of Einstein's 1905 paper on the special theory of relativity (which was in many ways of great import to Mead), inasmuch as the first third of that famous paper was devoted to an intensive epistemological analysis and, as a whole, the paper diverged remarkably from the accepted style of a scientific article.

The Newtonian mechanical universe in a considerable measure removed the situations which called out naturally the responses due to
man's central position in the world. Philosophy in rationalizing this
new situation sought so to restate the world which science did not
call in question that human experience would remain central. Philosophy had then to restate the world which for science was unshaken,
and the success of science compelled it to use the results of scientific
analysis. When it sought for its own ποῦστω, that world within which
its problem lay, it could find it only in the mind of the individual—
cogito ergo sum. (Mead 1929, 68)

Having so found that domain, philosophy then faced "the task of getting
back to external things from a world described in states of mind."

Mead agreed with Whitehead (1925) that the medieval doctrine had
been adequately expository of its own omnifarious world, insofar as it gave
proof that everything, be it of Earth, Heaven, or Hell, had its place in the
great order. But what Whitehead did not appreciate sufficiently was that
"this perfect fit between doctrine and the course of events in the world
reflected rather the nice adjustment of the cult of men's needs." It was a
historic moment of perfection, and inevitably it was subject to instability
from its dependence on the flow of externalities, the proof of which was
experienced when finally the natural world rose from slumber and shook
the blanket of dust from its back. Yet, when the situation of the "world
that was simply there" did change, and even though the nascent Renaissance
science "set about the discovery of new things," philosophy merely ritualized its old ways and created rationalizations of "old things" such that it
"forced the new into the same dress."[37] Whereas the scientist "is ready to
find a problem at any point in the structure of scientific doctrine, a problem
which may invalidate any theory," and indeed "welcomes such outbreaks"
and lives his "exciting life in their midst,"

What arrests the philosopher's attention is that this attitude carries
with it no sense of insecurity. The philosopher still has the Medieval-
ist's yearning to rest in the arms of finality. Whether idealist or realist
or neo-Kantian phenomenalist, he seeks repose for his perturbed spirit
in the everlasting arms of an absolute of one sort or another. His
philosophic mind is attuned to the present French political mind; it

---

37. Mead's charge that philosophy insisted on explaining the new by the old, a
thesis strongly exemplified in the work of Emile Meyerson (1921), was very much
like that of Mead's near-contemporary Gaston Bachelard—e.g., consider Bachelard's (1928) argument that philosophy uses such concepts as "time" and "space"
as though science had had nothing of importance to say about them since Newton.
Compare Nietzsche [1901] 1967, §551.

cannot conceive of security of method, it must have security of structure. (Mead 1929, 69)

And so philosophy has drifted off on a mission of oneiromancy, blind to the error that it "has not given to the thing its value of a thing before the problem arose and after the solution, but has kept it in terms of logical and metaphysical speculation."

Mead's view of knowledge centered on the thesis of a naturalism that tried to disavow all dualisms of spirit and nature and that strove to push a falsely separated spirit ("mind," "meaning," "thought") entirely back into nature. Thus, one finds a level of consistency in Mead's positive apprehension of Wundtian psychophysical parallelism and his equivalent rejections of Watsonian behaviorism and numerous varieties of mentalism (cf. Mead 1909; 1910a; 1910b; 1913; 1934). Following the argument set out in Peirce's essay on "The Fixation of Belief" (Peirce [1877] 1960, paras. 375–76), Mead disputed the possibility of Cartesian radical doubt: we cannot doubt everything at once even if everything is susceptible of doubt. While the beginning of knowledge rests in the attitude of doubt, the possibility of doubt can occur in the first instance only within the confines of that which is undoubted or "simply there."[38] Thus, the process of knowing is always a process of partialities, consisting in acts of doubting and repairing *seriatum*: "To gain the whole world epistemologically is to lose the import and character of the experiences that constitute the self." A problematic is always furnished with limits, which are "the world that is there," that is, a "world of common reality" that contains individual experiences, the experiencing self, and any apparatus integral to the acts of experience. If that common world should somehow disappear (as in the alleged imagination of total doubt), individual experiences as such would likewise vanish. The "shattered fragments of things" that appear in the experiences of individuals are "the building materials first of the mind and second of the repaired world, but they would have as little value without a world *independent of*

---

38. Compare, e.g., Mannheim's (1925) juxtaposition of meaning against "unmeaning" being, as well as his conception of the partiality of perspective. The similarities of Mead's argument regarding the contingency of doubt (contingent on provisionally nonproblematic suppositions) may be extended beyond Peirce's theory of "fallibilism," as well as beyond Dewey's contemporary work. For instance, Karl Leonhard Reinhold (1758–1823), a major philosopher of the Kantian school, asserted that one must begin inquiry with provisionally nonproblematic suppositions in order to doubt other suppositions (cf. Reinhold 1791; 1816). Reinhold's method did not escape the epistemologically self-incriminating circularity of pretending to address the being of all knowledge, including itself, as if it were foundationless.

them as would a million bricks and a carload of Portland cement at some unoccupied point in starry space" (Mead 1938, 34, 37; emphasis added).

In sum, Mead was identifying the proper attitude of philosophy, and the pursuit of knowledge in general, with a particular conception of the methods of science. The real object of science plainly consists in the discovery of knowledge about the real world, wherein the test of truthfulness rests in "the accord of . . . hypothetical construction with the world within which the problem has appeared." Equally plainly to be seen, science had been very successful in accomplishing its object. The scientist's conduct, understood by Mead within his general formulation of "the stages of the act" (cf. Dewey 1938), begins with apprehension of a problem, which comes about from "the checking or inhibition of some more or less habitual form of conduct, way of thinking, or feeling . . . an obstacle in overt action, or an exception to an accepted rule or manner of thought, or some object that calls out opposing emotions." There follows a description of the problem "in terms of the conditions of its possible solution" and, to the measure of available intelligence, "in the form that invites solution"; the formation of a "reconstruction of the situation, in which the data or facts will no longer inhibit action, thought, or feeling," together with a "mental testing" of the plausibility of that reconstruction. Finally, the scientist undertakes a practical test, that is, finds or constructs "an actual situation answering to the hypothesis" and then discovers "whether action, thought, or feeling can continue unimpeded." Always the scientist must work within an accepted world that is simply there, although any part of that world may have once been and/or may later become problematical. Given this limit, the scientist's data (i.e., "exceptional experiences" in the world) can never have the logical form of final meanings, nor can they be equated with "the building material of the world within which the problem [to which they are relevant] appears." The data, being integral to the statement of the problem and thence to its solution, "pass in new forms into the reconstructed meanings which experiment shows to fit into the world, insofar as it was not involved" in the particular problem. By Mead's conception, then, knowledge (i.e., scientific knowledge as the paladin of truth) consists exclusively in "the discovery through the implication of things and events of some thing or things which enable us to carry on where a problem has held us up. It is the fact that we can carry on that guarantees our knowledge" (Mead 1929, 70, 73; Mead 1938, 28–29, 81, 94–95).

As the linchpin of his attempt to bridge rationalism and empiricism, the Meadian world-that-is-there was conceived as having a precognitive status, that is, as existing independently of cognition, knowledge, mind. It is not created by mind, but neither is mind merely a passive spectator of it. Because mind is a part of nature, mind creates in conjunction with other parts of nature an *evolution* of meanings. The world-that-is-there and all it contains, including reflective experience, "exist in the form of situations [which] are fundamentally characterized by the relation of an organic individual to his environment or world." Differences or peculiarities of "situations" are objectively real, not mere "appearances or phenomena which inadequately reflect an absolute reality. These situations *are* the reality" (Mead 1938, 215; emphasis added).

Mead attempted to discriminate his view of the grounds of knowing in and of the world from those of the unacceptable doctrines of phenomenalism and positivism. On the one side, he contended that the world-that-is-there is both more than and prior to sensation, hence the object of knowledge cannot be assimilated to the content: in a laboratory experiment, for example, the finding of data presupposes the "organic conditions . . . of the nervous system, and the apparatus and happenings of the laboratory," all of which "are there in advance of the sensation and ideas, and . . . will be there when these have passed." On the other side, Mead rejected the positivist attitude of constancy of fact—the attitude that "what is observed is . . . there in a sense in which it can never be false"—for one must consider not only the possibility of drawing false inferences from fact (which, Mead acknowledged, positivists recognized) but more fundamentally the circumstance that the "fact of immediate experience" is itself always open to question: "The scientist's observation always carries a content or character in what is observed that may conceivably be shown under other conditions to be erroneous, though the probability of this be very slight" (Mead 1938, 41, 47). In short, an adequate solution to a problematic constitutes a repairing of the world, and the action (meaning) in which it is constituted *as* meaning is real; but there can be no assurance of final meaning, inasmuch as what was once undoubted and then a problematic resolved may again become a focal point of doubt. If knowledge cannot be gained without the stimulus of doubt, it is also the case that knowledge persistently calls out the possibility of its own negation.

Indeed, Mead's world-that-is-there exhibits a perpetual shimmer. Mind, as part of the natural, is an active principle incessantly reconstructing the world-that-is-there, though always by increments. These restructurings—fittings of now-solved problematics—are constructive of new meanings, which is to say new ways of acting-on-objects-in-the-world, and so "the world is ceaselessly becoming what it means" (Mead 1938, 515). The justification of a given restructuring—that is, the truth—consists solely in its enabling of effective practice in the *hic et nunc* of the world-that-is-there; but the situation within which conduct proves in the instance to be effective or not is unstoppably dynamic, and in the next instance a once-effective way of acting on objects may find the conditions of its impotence. The problem solution which the world-that-is-there "answered to" yesterday may fail tomorrow, in which case the knowledge constituting those earlier ways of acting will be kicked into a suspension of belief. It is an inexorable process, within which the knowing subject necessarily lives as part of the world-that-is-there. Because the natural world is a continuous evolution, new problems in the relation of self to environment forever emerge; knowledge is the intercalation of emergence and novelty with adjustment and restructuring.[39] In Mead's words:

> Cognition, and thought as a part of the cognitive process, is reconstructive, because reconstruction is essential to the conduct of an intelligent being in the universe. This is but part of the more general proposition that changes are going on in the universe, and that as a consequence of these changes the universe is becoming a different universe. Intelligence is but one aspect of this change. It is a change that is part of an ongoing living process that tends to maintain itself. What is peculiar to intelligence is that it is a change that involves a mutual reorganization, an adjustment in the organism and a reconstitution of the environment. (Mead 1932, 3–4)[40]

Organisms meet the problematic of a situation with adjustment and restructuring, with the "creation of new forms" to which the environment may or may not respond in ways that allow the organism "effective" conduct

39. This "stimulus-response" theme, with its pernicious adumbration of the relation of "the human" and "nature," has a wide dispersion. Toynbee, for example, built a human history from sequences of "challenge and response"—in terms of which he once gave this account of novelty: "However methodically Nature may have stacked the cards in this psycho-somatic pack [the human organism], and however successful a student of human nature may be in discovering what Nature's method here is, any attempt to make infallible predictions of a person's future actions on this basis will be invalidated by the presence in the pack of a 'joker' that cannot be eliminated and cannot be counted on to behave in the future invariably as it has usually behaved in the past. This intractable 'joker' is the apparent freedom of a human will to vary its response to an identical challenge when this identical challenge is presented to it on different occasions" (Toynbee 1966, 7).

40. Compare Mead's (1913, 1934; also 1912, and 1924–25) discussion of intelligence within the context of his account of the social self. For example, as defined in a section on "Meaning," "intelligence on the human level" is "the adjustment to one another of the acts of different human individuals within the human social process. This adjustment takes place through communication—by gestures on the lower planes of human evolution and by significant symbols (gestures which possess meanings and are hence more than mere substitute stimuli) on the higher planes of human evolution" (Mead 1934, 75). In its more general sense, intelligence is "a function of the relation of the form and its environment," implicated in "the action of the form in its commerce with the environment" (328).

(Mead 1936, 360–85). Intelligence is the measure of selection and guidance of restructurings and adjustments that will elicit desired responses; that is, there is in the nature of the situation a variety of logically possible reformations and adjustments, with a variety of implicated meanings as possible consequences, and intelligence is a matter of selecting and enacting the "proper" one (i.e., taking the "perspective" that will allow actions previously inhibited).[41]

Mead formulated the central dynamic of this process as consisting in a manipulative action in "contact experience," which first of all makes possible the meaning of the object. Materiality is known within the spatiotemporal distance of a situation only insofar as there are experiences of contact with the Whiteheadian property of "pushiness" of objects. That is to say, in Mead's view our awareness of objects of the world-that-is-there comes about as a consequence of their resistance to, or inhibition of, habitual conduct and desired responses.[42] This frustration of effective practice which makes one cognizant of features of one's environment—that is, of problematics—is constituted by a mutuality of stimulus-response and manipulation. Taking the Newtonian third law of motion as a fundamental attitude, Mead argued that "the thing stimulates the organism to act as the

41. For Mead, "perspectives" are objective realities in nature that express the mutual interdependence of organism and environment, and of object and object's field: "The perspective of the individual exists in nature, not in the individual. Physical science has recently discovered this and enunciated it in the doctrine of relativity" (Mead 1938, 515). Mead argued that the "conception of a world . . . independent of any organism is one that [would be] without perspectives. There would be no environments. There would be no objects except physical particles." (Apparently Mead did not appreciate the inconsistency told by his exception.) According to "the principle of perspective, . . . the object exists in its relation to the aspects of the world to which it is related—the form and its environment" (163–65).

42. Cf. Nietzsche ([1901] 1967, §§533–34, 618–39). Regarding the Meadian notion of "taking the role of the other," the following passage may be compared:
    To understand another, i.e., *to reproduce his feeling in us*, we certainly do frequently go back to the *reason* for his . . . feeling and ask, for example: *why* is he sad?—in order then to become sad for the same reason; but it is much more usual not to do this and to generate the feeling in us through the *effects* which it . . . manifests in the other person: we reproduce the expression of his eyes, his voice, his gait, his posture. . . . Then a similar feeling originates in us as a consequence of an old association of movement and feeling which is drilled to run forward and backward (Nietzsche 1881, §142; quoted in revised translation by Kaufmann 1968, 269).
Perhaps someone will undertake a critical, intensive comparative study of Nietzsche, Whitehead, and Mead with respect to their treatments of "object" constitution/apprehension.

thing acts upon the organism, and . . . the action of the thing is the organism's resistance to pressure such as arises when a hard object is firmly grasped in the hand" (Mead 1932, 121–22; see also 1934, 248–49). It is by virtue of this "formula" of haptic experience that we are justified in believing the meaningful existence of objects as objects existentially independent of the believing subject and as objects the meanings of which are nonassimilable to ideas or to sense-data.[43] The quality of "pushiness," originally a property only of the organism, is "transferred to the object":

> The organism in grasping and pushing things is identifying its own effort with the contact experiences of the thing. It increases that experience by its own efforts. To take hold of a hard object is to stimulate oneself to exert that inner effort. One arouses in himself an action which comes also from the inside of the thing. It comes from the inside of the thing because the experience is increased by the action of bodies upon organisms and upon other things in the perceptual world. The organism's object arouses in the organism the action of the object upon the organism, and so becomes endowed with that inner nature of pressure which constitutes the inside of the physical thing. It is only insofar as the organism thus takes the attitude of the thing that the thing acquires such an inside. (Mead 1932, 121–22)

As to the experience of objects-at-a-distance, Mead argued similarly that through experiences of manipulation we anticipate resisting responses of the distant object, responses that we expect will be completed when distance shrinks to contact (Mead 1932, 123–24). Mead explained:

> What I wish to emphasize is that the physical thing in contact pressures, and at a distance in awakening anticipatory manipulatory responses, calls out in the organism what is continuous with its own inner nature, so that the action of the thing where it is, is identified with the response of the organism. It is this that makes it possible for the organism to place itself and its manipulatory area at any distant object, and to extend the space of the manipulatory area indefinitely, thus reaching out of dissonant perspectives a homogeneous space. (Mead 1932, 124).

43. Compare Piaget's account of the "haptics" of tactile perception and visual imagination in the development of the child's conception of "representational space" (Piaget and Inhelder [1948] 1956, 4–5, 17–23). (Piaget's original term was "*stereognostique*," referring to the apprehension of forms of solid objects by way of touch, which is approximately the meaning also of "haptic".)

In respect to distant objects and the continuity of time, the event at a distance ("past" or "future") is always constituted in the manipulatory responses of the here and now. As one commentator has put it, for Mead the world-that-is-there is always "there" in an undifferentiated present, "the world within which we act when our action is unreflective" (Lee 1963, 53). But disruptions of that world—that is, the problematic experience within the present, "the occasion of the *reflective* act"—imply a differentiation of the now (the exceptional experience), the before-now (awareness of the exceptional experience against a background of nonexceptionality), and an after-now (projection of the desired response of a repaired world "answering to" an anticipated solution). By Mead's accounting, in other words, our cognition of "a past" is predicated in doubt regarding the origin of that which is exceptional, namely, the event of a disrupted naive reality. And integral to the solution of a problematic is the creation of a new past—just as there is creation of a new space—that will account for the novelty and repair the experience to the world-that-is-there. Thus, "the past" has no finality, only a fluidity in the course of problematics. "That which has happened is beyond recall" and is irrevocable; but that quality is of little significance. "It is the 'what it was' that changes," and *this* quality is crucial. The irrevocability of "that which has happened" is attached "to the 'what it was,' and the 'what it was' is what is not irrevocable"—precisely because it is a formulation in the present. "It is the import of what is going on in action or appreciation [i.e., in the present] which requires illumination and direction, because of the constant appearance of the novel from whose standpoint our experience calls for a reconstruction which includes the past" (Mead 1932, 3, 27). The past always stands relative to the present, as does the future—not as a subjectivity or fiction but as an objective reality of the world of the present.

Mead devoted the bulk of his scholarship to an explication of the complexities of the social act in this world of the present. Indeed, it has been said that these two concepts, the "social act" and the "present," form the central stanchions of the Meadian construction of social reality. Whether or not we agree with that appraisal, I think we can agree in the observation of certain curiosities of the construction. One of the more arresting features of his formulation of the process of knowledge, for example, is the poverty of attention to questions of the social formations in which such interests are embedded. In fashioning what he wanted to be a distinctive argument vis-à-vis contemporary doctrines, especially the varieties of idealism and Watsonian behaviorism, Mead insisted that the foundations of knowledge are social-behavioral, consisting in the matrix of habitual and self-conscious activities of social individuals (here there are obvious similarities to Max Weber's *Kategorienlehre*) and explicable in terms of the evolution of the social behavior of the human animal. The veracity of knowledge, according to Mead, can never be written in the large, inasmuch as it is inherently relative to the situation from which it was extracted and within which it is putatively practiced. But in the spread of his naturalistic social-evolutionary scheme, Mead universalized and homogenized those foundations to such an extent that they could have resembled little that was real and consequential of the concrete relations of knowledge in the structures of domination essential to Mead's own world. It is instructive in this regard to consider one of the apparently few discussions of conflict offered by Mead (1934, 303–11);[44] the discussion touches on his conception of the relation of nature and society, about which I shall have more to say before concluding this look at Mead. In this passage, Mead asserted his "behavioral view" of "conflict" as denoting one of the two main categories of the "fundamental socio-physiological impulses or behavior tendencies . . . which constitute the ultimate basis" of human society—the other category being "cooperation" (303). Now one need not be practiced in unusual feats of percipience in order to appreciate in the supposition of that passage a universalistic conception of "basic human nature": it is a latter-day variation of the Hobbesian portrait, albeit fitted with an evolutionary frame. To be sure, Mead stated his exception to the "contract" theory of society, namely its genetic assumption of a "deliberate coming-together" of spontaneously generated rational minds: "the self could not antedate the social organism" (233). There *is* that difference between Mead's view and those of the classic contract theorists.

Nevertheless, the distance of that difference is not so great, inasmuch as Mead simply removed the locus of the resolution of dualist human nature from a rationalistic mind to a naturalistic evolution, the governance of which is lawful and knowable by its own emergent properties, "human mind." According to Mead, the durability of social organization is contingent on harnessing these "destructive impulses," which, "if anything, are more easily and immediately aroused" than are their opposites; that is, even though these destructive behavior tendencies are, "in the broadest and strictest non-ethical sense," as fully social, and as common or universal, as the "friendly" tendencies, the perseverance of social organization depends nonetheless upon their being "combined and fused with, and organized by means of the 'friendly' human impulses," such that they are "made to enter as integral elements into the foundations of that organization, . . . [and are] utilized by that organization as fundamental impulsive forces in its own further development," or to "serve as a basis for social progress within its relational framework" (Mead 1934, 304–5).

Relative to these two "fundamental impulses" that constitute "the

<hr />

44. I say "apparently," because much of what we have of Mead's thinking was written not by his own hand but by the transcribing hands of editor-disciples from allegedly verbatim notes compiled by Mead's classroom pupils.

ultimate basis" of human society, Mead's history of the domestication of the beast evokes an evolutionary gradient extending through the "relatively loose and disintegrated social organization" of feudal civilization to "the national civilization of modern times, with its relatively tight and integrated social organization . . . , [which] exhibits the constant evolution of human social organization in the direction of greater and greater relational unity and complexity, [and in a] more and more closely knit interlocking and integrated unifying of all the social relations of interdependence which constitute it and which hold among the individuals involved in it" (Mead 1934, 310–11).

As I have indicated already, Mead did not begin his study of the process of knowledge with an undertaking of fundamental epistemological inquiry but with a sense of science and what scientists do, as if the epistemic warrant of science had been established completely and indisputably. For Mead, as for many others then and now, the test of experience showed that such warrant surely was in force, inasmuch as the practitioners of science were undeniably succeeding in their proper endeavors of "discovering new things." Indeed, it would be most odd if they were not, for "the scientific method is, after all, only the evolutionary process grown self-conscious" (Mead 1936, 364; see also 258–59, 264–91).

One could hardly imagine a more optimistic post-Baconian celebrant of the powers of science and its "practical attitude" than George Herbert Mead, who advocated the application of the scientific method to every aspect of human life. Consider his position regarding ethics. Having rejected (and rightly so) the postulate of an ideal order independent of and serving as a beacon for the natural world—there could be no humanly knowable evidence of such an order, and belief in such an order obviates human moral responsibility (Mead [1908a] 1964, 90)—he proposed as the only sound basis of ethical determination the application of science. Moral or ethical problems must be approached with the scientific method and its practical attitude.[45] What that approach entailed is illuminated clearly enough by Mead's commentary on the Social Settlement experiment conducted by Addams and others: "The settlement is practical in its attitude,

---

45. An instance of the vacuity of Mead's account of "ethical problems" can be read in the notes from his discussion of "Obstacles and Promises in the Development of the Ideal Society" (Mead 1934, 319–23); ethical and unethical behavior are associated respectively with integration and disruption, i.e., with "the social and the asocial . . . sides or aspects of the individual self."

Mead's position was not that of a Spencerian ethics, to be sure, but it *was* within the realm of what Moore called "naturalistic ethics" (Moore 1903, 39), that is, an ethics the conclusions of which are presumably to be established "by means of empirical observation and induction."

but inquiring and scientific in its method. If it did nothing else it illustrates concretely how the community ought to form a new moral judgment" (Mead 1908b, 110). By "practical attitude," one must add, Mead intended a specific mode of ethical decision: *"There is no other test of moral and intellectual hypotheses except that they work"* (Mead [1930] 1964, 391; emphasis added). Jaded though our sensibilities may be, we can hardly conclude that the Meadian commendation of science amounted to no more than a harmless puffery.

This pragmatic formula of truth—that truth is only what has been shown by scientifically controlled inquiry "to work" in a given situation, that is, to facilitate previously thwarted conduct—was a relativist position generally propounded by the founders of pragmatic naturalism. It was in the particular case of Mead's construction ("objective relativism," as he called it), however, that the formula was most alluring for social science, especially in the United States. This corrupt view of the constitution of veridical knowledge has been reproduced to an enormous extent (albeit often as a corruption of corruption) in the instrumental rationality of the activity of social science. It is endemic both to the technology of science and to the science of technology. It pervades not only the hollow enterprise of empiricist research but also the terrain of what passes as theory. Consider, for example, the illustrative case of a recent book by R. Collins, wherein the author proposed to move sociology "toward an explanatory science." In his working toward a general "conflict theory of society," Collins (1975) gave special emphasis to a social-constructionist understanding of the putatively central conflict for status advantage. But, like the "social constructionism" of Berger and Luckmann (1966), there is an arbitrariness to Collins's constructionism that turns back upon his own activity of thinking, proposing, and writing. Collins saw this self-denial and therewith attempted to insert an insulating distance between the arbitrariness implied as a property of the object of knowledge and his own activity of knowing, by appealing to a pragmatic privilege of "useful ideas" and of proceeding with the proper business of social science. Only so long as one refuses to examine the epistemological anchorage of his "isolated" constructionism, of course, does the annihilative contradiction escape one's attention.

Mead's optimism concerning the pragmatic formula and its incremental fruits was sometimes expressed in pronouncements about the character of early twentieth-century industrial society that, some fifty years later, strike us as naive and even ludicrous—for example, the appraisal that "the development of a human society on a larger scale has led to a very complete control of its environment" (Mead 1934, 249). But his failure to look for the underside of that which seemed obvious was nowhere more sharply or more seriously evident than in the test of experience he so approvingly applied to science: scientists obviously progressing in the work of "discovering new things." Mead never considered whether there might have been an underside to that "self-evident fact," whether the experiences and consciousness constituting this test might have been false. Granted, it would be an exaggeration to say that he was oblivious to aspects of the negation of human life. One of his students has recited his essay on aesthetic experience (1925–26) in this way:[46]

> Through the factory means of producing goods there are a great number of different kinds of acts, each performed by separate individuals who need not, and in many instances do not, understand the relationship between their particular roles and the roles of others. Nor, in many instances, does the factory worker know what his performance has to do with any finished product. . . . In such cases the laborer cannot "put himself into his work," and his work is called drudgery. (Miller 1973, 220–21)

But the point is, the laborer *does* put something of "himself into his work." This "drudgery" ("the opposite of the aesthetic experience") was considered by Mead to apply "more to the attitude of the laborer, to the cognitive side of his experience, than to the actual effort expended." Quoting Dewey (presumably from *Experience and Nature*), Mead (Mead [1925–26] 1964, 300) agreed that "shared experience is the greatest of human goods"—a statement that would identify "the good" with "the *least* good for the greatest number" as readily as with its opposite—and then continued by saying that "if out of the drudgery that men put through together there arises a social end in which they are interested, achieving this end will have its delight, and insofar as this end can involve the tasks themselves, the dignity and delight of the social realization will suffuse the tasks." Mead had too little appreciation that alienation lies in the structure of social relations, whether cognized by the laborer or not, and he neglected to understand that the actuality of modern science itself, whether in the scientist's laboratory, the engineer's workshop, or in the latest factory, is integral to that structure.

If drudgery is the antipode of the aesthetic, it is also a symptom of more than what one finds in the conventionally delimited realm of "the aesthetic experience." All pretensions to a critical stance notwithstanding, the Meadian view was quietistic and conformist to existing structures,

---

46. A portion of this essay on the aesthetic experience was included in part 4 of *The Philosophy of the Act* (Mead 1938, 454–57), to which were appended some student notes wherein Mead was recorded as having said, "There is no science in the statement of value." One must wonder if that verdict applied to Mead's statement of the value of *science* and its practical attitude.

owing to a failure to appreciate the possibility that thoughts or meanings deemed "useless" in or contradictory of a present reality may not be false meanings. The anodyne of Mead's gazing upon the human world, manifested in tone (always irenic, never polemical) as well as in the substance of his words, was that redundantly described "practical attitude" of carrying-on-in-the-world: "It is the fact that we can carry on that guarantees our knowledge" (Mead 1938, 95). It was an "attitude" *and an activity* that have become all too familiar in our fetishistically technological age, where the "obstacles" resulting from one yield of "technical mastery" are conceived as simply the "problems" to be solved by the next (and both of which come ultimately to be summed in the GNP, our principal measure of collective health).[47]

Mead dismissed inquiry into the possibility of necessary and truthful knowledge vis-à-vis the contemporary dilemma of epistemological relativism as an antiquated, ritualistic exercise akin to the fabled scholasticism of an era long dead and supplanted through the efforts of science. Yet, that dismissal notwithstanding, there was in Mead's work an implicit, but fatally flawed, epistemic argument. Like any epistemological argument unconnected to a theory of society, as his was, it was purely formal and abstract. It was a scientism striving to assimilate philosophy, the very same sort of scientism that Lukács (1923) was indicting as an alienation that deprives us of the human and substitutes the self-dominating, self-negating object. Mead did attempt to relocate truth into human activity, and, insofar as unconsummated efforts can be judged, that was a promising beginning. But in the final analysis it proved to be a simplistic, mechanical relocation.

Let's examine the core of Mead's argument, according to which problems of knowledge are only local problematics perceived within a world the other localities of which are "simply there," that is, nonproblematic, and make the local problematics possible. The scientist's findings about a local problematic "are from reality, and . . . are simply certain happenings, determined within the limit of the error of observation, in a world which is not involved in the problems which engage the intense interest of science." There can be no merger of "the problem that engages thought with a larger problem which denies validity to the conditions that

---

47. It is appropriate to repeat here a trenchant and admonitory passage from Husserl:

> The exclusiveness with which the total world-view of modern man, in the second half of the nineteenth century, let itself be determined by the positive sciences and be blinded by the "prosperity" they produced, meant an indifferent turning-away from the questions which are decisive for a genuine humanity. Merely fact-minded sciences make merely fact-minded people. (Husserl [1936] 1970, 5–6)

are the necessary tests of the solution which thought is seeking" (Mead 1929, 78). The validity of the solution of a local problematic, in other words, is wholly dependent on the taken-for-granted frame that is the "simply-there" world. But, if that frame is dubitable, if Mead cannot demonstrate the veritable existence of his world-that-is-there (in the double sense of basis and content of *his* knowing), then any solution to any local problematic is also dubitably valid. What, we must ask, was *Mead's* entitlement to a privileged ground as knower? By his own terms, his conception of world-that-is-there proposed a dilemma: in order to know that this world-that-is-there has a palpable and reliable existence necessary to the very constitution of local problematics and their tested solutions, Mead must have once doubted that existence; but that doubt would have been the total doubt that Mead had already denied possible. As a minding self in search of knowledge, Mead was *in* his world-that-is-there, which *as such* was simultaneously asserted by Mead as a presupposition of knowledge. He postulated its existence, but he could not prove its existence inasmuch as he granted it immunity from doubt; and so it remained that which, by his own statement, it could not be, a dubitable existence.

Mead, as well as Dewey and other fellow travelers on the road of pragmatism, was confronted with a failure totally destructive of his own epistemological stance and thus of his account of the veracity of scientific knowledge. From the shambles of that account, human knowledge takes on the look of an unattached game of internally logical but externally arbitrary moves. Mead's final criterion, "effective conduct," is merely an instance of *petitio principii* (but a particularly dangerous instance): How do we *know* what is *"effective* conduct"? What are the foundation and criteria of *that* knowledge? And what are "the necessary tests of the solution which thought is seeking"? More to the point, *who decides* what is a necessary test, what is fact and what fiction, and *who decides* which conduct is effective? Again we encounter the disaster of the unconnectedness to a theory of society of Mead's implicit epistemological position. We see the ugliness of its pseudocritical, conformist implication. That which is, is effective (for if it were not effective, it would not be). Appearance is the real, the essentially real. There is no potentiality beyond that which is already implicated in an incremental projection of a present reality (Mead's discussion of "novelty" notwithstanding).

Before terminating this commentary on Mead, I shall argue one other crucial aspect of his work—his conception of the "natural" vis-à-vis the "social"—for it looms greatly (though not originally) in the Meadian corpus and has been reproduced over and over in the activities of social scientists who have adopted Mead as their most luminous ancestor.

You may recall from *Mind, Self, and Society* (as well as from other sources) the famous description of "meaning" as a part of the ubiquitous process of adjustment: "Within any given social act, an adjustment is effected, by means of gestures, of the actions of one organism involved in the actions of another; the gestures are movements of the first organism which act as specific stimuli calling forth the (socially) appropriate responses of the second organism" (Mead 1934, 13 n. 9). *Consciousness* of meaning, we were told, is "not necessary to the presence of meaning in the process of social experience" (activities may entail unseen but very meaningful consequences) inasmuch as "meaning" exists as an objective feature of social structures, and humans are unique in that they alone have the necessary capacity for, which is not to say the necessary enactment of, consciousness of meaning (78–81). Symbol and referenced meaning are distinguishable, according to Mead, and whereas nature "has meaning and implication," it does not exhibit "indication by symbols." "Meanings are in nature, but symbols are the heritage of man." This passage is a bit cryptic, nevertheless Mead's argument becomes clear once we remember that in rejecting idealist doctrines he strove to identify such concepts as "mind" and "meaning" and indeed the origins of human activity *in* "nature," that is, as the effluence of a "nature-in-evolution." Mead's repairing of what he had diagnosed as "bifurcated nature" (1938, 18) involved the postulation of an integral, uniform, systematic nature, the existence of which both prefaced and issued in the human. It is within the boundaries of that conception that we must understand his search for the anteriority not merely of "the social individual" (see e.g., Mead 1934, 347–53) but of the species being of *homo sapiens*. Such is the context of his frequent comparisons of the human creature with lesser animals and of his important concept of the "gesture," which was posited as the basic nexus of a jointly implicated "meaning" and "being" that, in the evolutionary course of nature, antedated the human creature (42–75)—and which implies accordingly that the origins of human meaning are to be found in events and processes created other than by human activity.

Conceived from a sense of the Darwinian construction, Mead's "nature," in all aspects of its extensionality, was a hypostatized nature. Consider again the following statement, which already we have confronted through different words from another of the volumes of his collected works: "The method which nature has followed, if we may speak so anthropomorphically, has been the production of variations until finally some one variation has arisen which has survived. Well, what science is doing is making this method of trial and error a conscious method" (Mead 1936, 367). The defensive anticipation of being accused of "anthropomorphization of nature" is deeply telling. One has only to notice that it was his own hypostatization of a historical conceptual entity that enabled him not only to speak so sanguinely of "the method of nature," and of "nature," with the universalizing definite article affixed (explicitly or implicitly)—and without thought of arousing ambiguity in his audience's hearing—but also to speak of "the method of nature," and of "nature," as a prior and necessary existence of which *anthrōpos* later became aware. So, too, one must notice that by virtue of his hypostatization, Mead's optimistic pronouncement regarding science and the "domination of nature" ("what we learn about nature enables us to control nature"; "the mechanical science of this period has not mechanized human conduct" but has "given freedom"; and so on; Mead 1936, 261) translates into an affirmation of what it obscures—namely, the human domination of human beings.

7. ALFRED SCHUTZ (1899–1959)

There is very little of an overt formulation of a theory of knowledge by Alfred Schutz, despite (perhaps because of) his ever-present reach for authorization through invocation of the proper name "Edmund Husserl." Schutz's constructions tend *away from* rather than toward the root questions of gnosiologic possibility. His writing was conducted almost from the first within his construction of a puppet-populated "world of common sense" and the "everyday life," wherein knowledge is already given as an everyday nonproblematic occurrence, and wherein the possibility of a false consciousness is restricted to the perspectivism of an inaccessible subjective meaning. Nonetheless I include him in this series of expositions and critiques because of my sense of the consequentiality that has been accorded his work in the historical moment.[48]

Schutz's major writing, *The Meaningful Construction of the Social World*, was published in 1932, although it did not appear fully in English translation until 1967 (as *The Phenomenology of the Social World*). Following the original publication, Schutz, having migrated from a doomed Austria in 1938, first to Paris and then to New York, authored a series of essays that, while mostly reweaving and elaborating the 1932 volume, served to present his thinking to an English-reading audience. Death in 1959 precluded his final preparation of what some have said was to have been the definitive systematic account of his theoretical enterprise, *Structures of the Life-World* (Schutz and Luckmann 1973).[49]

48. One has only to think of the popular reception among students of social science accorded such writings as Berger's *Invitation to Sociology* (1963; see especially pp. 122–50 and 182) and Berger and Luckmann's *The Social Construction of Reality* (1966).

49. Luckmann, a student of Schutz, completed the preparation after Schutz's death (to date, only part of the work has been published in an English edition). For this reason of posthumous collaboration, I have not relied on *Structures of the Life-world* as a Schutzian resource, even though it does correspond quite closely to works published at Schutz's own direction.

To the extent that one can speak of Schutz's epistemological effort, it must be read first and foremost against the background of Max Weber and the idealist-individualist tradition of *Geisteswissenschaft-Geistesgeschichte*—for that is where his project began—and only then in terms of certain "borrowings" from Husserlian (and Bergsonian) phenomenology, plus stimulations from William James, G. H. Mead, John Dewey, and, no doubt, others. Indeed, two decades after publication of *Der sinnhafte Aufbau der sozialen Welt*, Schutz was yet of the opinion that the "attempts of Simmel, Max Weber, Scheler to reduce social collectivities to the social interaction of individuals is [are], so it seems, much closer to the spirit of phenomenology than the pertinent statements of its founder [i.e., Husserl]" (Schutz [1953a] 1966, 39). It was in Weber's approach to "the roots of the problems of the social sciences," which was that of examining "the fundamental facts of conscious life," that Schutz saw an approach both correct in direction and determining "conclusively the proper starting point of the philosophy of the social sciences" (Schutz [1932] 1967, xxxi–xxxii).[50] Weber had appreciated the still unanswered basic question: "How is it possible to form objective concepts and an objectively verifiable theory of subjective meaning structures?" And "never before" had an answering formulation "been so radically carried out as it was in Max Weber's initial statement of the goal of interpretive sociology."[51] Even so, Schutz concluded, he failed, due to an insufficient depth of pursuit: Weber arrived "at what he assumes to be the basic and irreducible elements of social phenomena," namely his "key idea" of the "meaningful act of the individual," but in fact that was "a mere label for a highly complex and ramified area that calls for much further study" (Schutz [1932] 1967, 5–9; Schutz [1953b] 1962, 1:34; Schutz [1954] 1962, 1:62–63).

The basic task, which Schutz set out to complete, consisted in "the project of reducing the 'world of objective mind' to the behavior of individuals." It was at this point, with a problematic devised principally from a consideration of Weber's work, that Schutz imported his reading of Husserl's phenomenology. The importation was limited. Schutz proposed

---

50. This assertion about the "proper starting point of the philosophy of the social sciences," presented in 1932 in Vienna, may be compared with Schutz's later description (1945, in New York), with reference to Husserl, of the "admitted refusal" of phenomenology "to accept uncritically the givenness of sensory perception, of biological data, of society and environment, as the unquestionable point of departure for philosophical investigation" (Schutz [1945a] 1962, 101).

51. Schutz was referring to essays in the compilation of Weber's *Wissenschaftslehre* and to the *Kategorienlehre* of the first edition of *Economy and Society*. His assessment of Weber followed partly from the critique made by von Mises (e.g., see von Mises [1933] 1960, 74–129; for the reception von Mises gave Schutz's just-published book, see p. 78 n. 27).

analyses "of the constituting process in internal time consciousness" that would be "carried out within the 'phenomenological reduction' " and that would therefore "presuppose the bracketing (disconnection) of the natural world and therewith the carrying into effect of a complete change of attitude (the epoché) toward the thesis of the 'world-given-to-me-as-being-there' [als daseiende gibt]"; yet the purpose of his work, "which is to analyze the phenomenon of meaning in ordinary [mundanen] social life, does not require the achievement of transcendental knowledge" beyond that of internal time consciousness, nor does it require "a further sojourn within the area of the transcendental-phenomenological reduction." In short, Schutz's concern was explicitly not with the "constituting phenomena as these are studied within the sphere of the phenomenological reduction"; rather it was directed toward those "phenomena corresponding to them in the natural attitude" (Schutz [1932] 1967, 6, 43–44, 97; see also Schutz [1953b] 1962; Schutz [1954] 1962; Schutz [1945b] 1962).

Having said that, Schutz proposed to conduct his analysis of the relation between "the world of objective mind" and individual behavior wholly within the dimensions of "the phenomenon of meaning in ordinary social life." But such analysis would require a particular method of scientific knowledge—a method of knowledge not merely of the life-world but simultaneously in the life-world—since the social scientist, who purportedly fashions objectively verifiable theories of subjective-meaning structures, is also an individual-in-the-life-world whose subjective meanings include those objectively verifiable theories. Accordingly, in order to show "the specific nature of the thought objects of social sciences," it is necessary first "to characterize some of the common-sense constructs used by men in everyday life. It is upon the latter that the former are based" (Schutz [1953b] 1962, 1:7; see also Schutz [1932] 1967, 9–10, 14, 220–24; Schutz [1954] 1962).

For Schutz the point of departure was always "the individual," a singular being who is born into a cognitively prestructured life-world and then goes about the building of a comprehension of his or her surroundings. This individual-in-the-world-as-given performs what Schutz termed the "Act of attention," that is, a conscious reflection by which one attends to one's living experience and apprehends from the "flow of duration" certain "objects of attention as constituted experiences."[52] If I "simply live immersed in the flow of duration," in the continuous "stream of conscious-

52. This "Act of attention to life" is a witting, "wide-awake" apperceptive orientation to an intended object in terms of one's "knowledge at hand" and with regard to assessment of object-uses vis-à-vis some "purpose at hand" (see Schutz [1932] 1967, 46–47, 53–57; Schutz [1945b] 1967, 212–13).

ness" that has no temporal or spatial locality, I "encounter only undifferentiated experiences that meld into one another in a flowing continuum." At this "level of consciousness," as Schutz called it, "each Now differs essentially from its predecessor in that within the Now the predecessor is contained in retentional modification"; but I can "know nothing of this while I am simply living in the flow of duration." Distinctions of Same-Other and Now-Thus exist profusely in the stream, as it were, but not to my knowledge. It is only at a second level of consciousness, that of the "Act of reflective attention," that I can "catch sight of the retentional modification and therewith of the earlier phase" of the stream. My experience in the world becomes to me a meaningful experience only by my having "turned back" against that which was there in the being of duration, such that what was originally there only as a "phase" of that duration, and as merely possibly knowable, has now become a distinguished "full-blown experience" (Schutz [1932] 1967, 51–52).

Such experiences are in and of a world that "existed before our birth" and that has been "experienced and interpreted by others, our predecessors, as an organized world. . . . All interpretation of this world is based on a stock of previous experiences of it," including not only the interpreter's own but also "those handed down . . . by parents or teacher." Each of us is characterized in a given moment by the "sediment" of a personal past, that is, by a "biographically determined situation," which is the "sedimentation of all of [an individual's] previous experiences, organized in the habitual possessions of his stock of knowledge, at hand, and as such [is] his unique possession, given to him and to him alone." This structured "stock of knowledge at hand," integral to localization of the individual, is continually "constituted in and by previous experiencing activities" and serves the individual "as a scheme of interpretation of his past and present experiences, and also determines his anticipations of things to come."[53]

53. A particular localization of "biographical situation" and "knowledge at hand" is determined by "because-of motives" rooted in the individual's actual past. These motives are never immediately known to the individual, inasmuch as they are not "attendable" in the moment of action; rather, one must "stop" and "reflect back" to a past and relate it to one's current purpose or goals (the "in-order-to motives"), which, existing in hierarchical arrangement in one's biographically determined situation, constitute the centralizing element of one's action (Schutz [1932] 1967, 86–96; Schutz [1951] 1962, 1:93–94; Schutz [1953b] 1962, 1:22; Schutz [1960] 1964, 2:11–13). Even so, the relationship between the "actually rooted" because-of motives and the construction of them made by the actor in "reflecting back" remains problematic. According to some posthumously published materials (1970, 68–74), it seems Schutz later attempted to take his account of individual action beyond the limits of these two motivation constructs, but the effort was unsuccessful.

One may doubt any or several parts of this "stock at hand" in a given instance but never simultaneously the whole (Schutz [1932] 1967, 78–84; Schutz [1953b] 1962, 1:7; Schutz [1959] 1964, 2:281–91; Schutz 1966). Included in this stock of knowledge is "our knowledge that the world we live in is a world of more or less well circumscribed objects with more or less definite qualities," objects that surround us and resist us, and that we manipulate. But we do not perceive these objects as insulated; from the outset each object is

> an object within a horizon of familiarity and pre-acquaintanceship which is, as such, just taken for granted until further notice as the unquestioned, though at any time questionable, stock of knowledge at hand. The unquestioned pre-experiences are, however, also from the outset, at hand as *typical*, that is, as carrying open horizons of anticipated similar experiences. For example, the outer world is not experienced as an arrangement of individual unique objects, dispersed in space and time, but as "mountains," "trees," "animals," "fellow-men." . . . In the more technical language of Husserl, . . . what is experienced in the actual perception of an object is apperceptively transferred to any other similar object, perceived merely as to its type. (Schutz [1953b] 1962, 1:7–8; see also Schutz [1932] 1967, 139–214)

These common-sense typifications, emerging in the everyday experience of the world-as-taken-for-granted, constitute a socially derived frame of reference within which interpretations are made. A given "purpose at hand" ("in-order-to motive") "defines those elements among all others" in a biographically determined situation that are "relevant" to that purpose, and the resulting "system of relevances in turn determines what elements have to be made a substratum of generalizing typification, what traits of these elements have to be selected as characteristically typical, and what others as unique and individual" (Schutz [1953b] 1962, 1:9–10; Schutz [1954] 1962, 1:61; Schutz [1959] 1964).

According to Schutz, the category of "meaningful experience" always refers to a "subjective meaning," constituted as an operation of intentionality (i.e., it is always a conscious experience *of something*) and a frame of interpretation applied to past experiences by the individual ego and necessarily relative to the biographically determined situation of that individual ego. Whereas "objective meaning" can be predicated only "of the already constituted meaning context of the thing produced, whose actual production we meanwhile disregard," and therefore can consist "only in a meaning context within the mind of the interpreter," the presence of "subjective meaning" always refers beyond the mind of the interpreter "to a meaning context in the mind of the producer." Moreover, Schutz added, "even under optimum conditions of interpretation" the subjective meaning of experience "remains a limiting concept"; ultimately it is impossible for Other to comprehend the subjective meaning of Actor. Thus, there is an inevitable duality of "inside-outside" to apprehensions of the world, a duality measured in the distance between Actor and Other (Schutz [1932] 1967, 133–36, 37–38, 98–100, 69–71; Schutz [1951] 1962, 1:95).

But if Other can never faithfully comprehend Actor's subjective meanings, then how is the Ego-Other, insider-outsider duality resolved in effective knowledge of and conduct in the world? How, in other words, do we get from the isolated individual–subjective meaning to a basis of knowledge of the Other? Schutz offered in response to that question the "general thesis of the reciprocity of perspectives," which consists of "two basic idealizations":

> The idealization of the interchangeability of the standpoints: I take it for granted—and assume my fellow-man does the same—that if I change places with him so that his "here" becomes mine, I shall be at the same distance from things and see them with the same typicality as he actually does; . . . The idealization of the congruency of the system of relevances: Until counterevidence I take it for granted— and assume my fellow-man does the same—that the differences in perspectives originating in our unique biographical situations are irrelevant for the purpose at hand of either of us and that he and I, that "We," assume both of us have selected and interpreted the actually or potentially common objects and their features in an identical manner or at least an "empirically identical" manner, i.e., one sufficient for all practical purposes. (Schutz [1953b] 1962, 1:11–12)

Thus we simply make certain common-sense assumptions that enable us to have a common world of cooperation for a given purpose at hand. Moreover, "This 'We' does not merely include you and me but 'everyone who is one of us,' i.e., everyone whose system of relevances is substantially (sufficiently) in conformity with yours and mine." This shared knowledge becomes anonymous and objective, insofar as it is detached from any particular biographically determined situation and, within certain social limits, stands available as "everyone's knowledge" (Schutz [1953b] 1962, 1:4–12, 20–34; Schutz [1932] 1967, 100–107, 113–16, 134–36, 174; Schutz [1955] 1962, 1:315–16).[54]

Now, whereas the ordinary actor in ordinary life proceeds in terms

---

54. However, stocks of knowledge are distinguished differentially among different groups within a society, such that the individual screens of relevance, through which experiences are interpreted meaningfully, are relative to group memberships and references (see, e.g., Schutz [1953b] 1962, 1:13–18; Schutz [1954] 1962, 1:55, 61; Schutz [1932] 1967, 81).

of more or less shared common-sense typifications—that is, socially derived and approved "recipes" for typical conduct in typical situations (e.g., Schutz [1954] 1962, 1:61)—Schutz's social scientist proceeds somewhat differently insofar as he or she builds second-order typifications in compliance with a formally rationalized architectural program. In the first place, the social scientist must proceed from "the postulate of subjective interpretation," which requires the adoption of "a general principle of constructing course-of-action types in common-sense experience" in order to carry out the programmatic task of analyzing "human conduct and its common-sense interpretation in the social reality" from the point of view of the actor. That is, in order to grasp that social reality, the social scientist's "thought objects" must be "founded upon the thought objects constructed by the common-sense thinking of men" as they live their daily lives "within their social world."[55] This means that the social scientist's "thought objects" are typifications of typifications, models of models, or, in Schutz's words, "constructs of the constructs made by the actors on the social scene, whose behavior the social scientist has to observe and to explain in accordance with the procedural rules of his science," which include that postulate of subjective interpretation. The scientist conjures "homunculi" or "puppets" (as Schutz called them) as models of actors to whom are ascribed "typical course-of-action patterns corresponding to the observed events." These homunculi have entire arrays of typical sets of because-of and in-order-to motives, stocks of knowledge, systems of relevance, and all of the other features designated by Schutz's conceptual apparatus. The point of it is that Schutz's scientist manipulates these puppets according to the terms and prospects of the scientific problem at hand (Schutz [1953b] 1962, 1:34, 40–42; Schutz [1954] 1962, 1:59; Schutz [1932] 1967, 62, 220–24; Schutz [1943] 1964).

Such puppet-making must be governed by a procedural rationality, of which Schutz nominated three rules that he deemed to be essential to a scientific method capable of dealing "in an objective way with the subjective meaning of human action." One of these rules has been mentioned already: the "postulate of subjective interpretation," according to which the "model of an individual mind" (and its "typical contents") must be constructed in such a manner that it can "explain the observed facts as the result of the activity of such a mind in an understandable relation." This postulate "warrants the possibility of referring all kinds of human action or their

---

55. In an earlier formulation, Schutz concluded that "the 'interpretive understanding' which is definitive of interpretive sociology cannot be observational understanding. Rather, the scientific method of establishing subjective meaning is motivational understanding, whereas the kind of understanding proper to everyday life is observational in character" (Schutz [1932] 1967, 31).

result to the subjective meaning such action or result . . . had for the actor." The second rule of scientific puppet-making stipulates internal "logical consistency," that is, the scientist must build his or her puppets with a conceptual framework that is clear and distinct, and thoroughly "compatible with the principles of formal logic." It is especially in terms of "their strictly logical character" that the scientist's constructs are different from those of the everyday actor—and thus that their "objective validity" is warranted. Finally, "the postulate of adequacy" requires that each puppet, and all of its elements, must be so built "that a human act performed within the life-world by an individual actor in the way indicated by the typical construct would be understandable for the actor himself as well as for his fellow-man in terms of common-sense interpretations of everyday life." It is this postulate that "warrants the consistency" of social-scientific vis-à-vis common-sense experiential constructs of social reality (Schutz [1953b] 1962, 1:43–44; see also Schutz [1932] 1967, 236, 241–42; Schutz [1943] 1964).

The question now arises, *how* must the social scientist proceed in order to comply with those formally rational stipulations of method? Surely the "ordinary actor," too, builds "constructs of constructs" in the course of daily living in the life-world; and surely the "social scientist" is also "in the life-world." So how, precisely, does the social-scientist-as-actor-in-the-life-world erect models that differ essentially (by those stated criteria) from the models fabricated by the nonscientific "ordinary actor"? Schutz's answer to this major question has all the luminosity but none of the density of those famous "Black Holes in Space":

> Let us briefly consider the particular attitude of the theoretical social scientist of the social world, in contradistinction to that of the actor on the social scene. The theoretical scientist—qua scientist, not qua human being (which he is, too)—is not involved in the observed situation, which is to him not of practical but merely of cognitive interest. The system of relevances governing common-sense interpretation in daily life originates in the biographical situation of the observer. By making up his mind to become a scientist, the social scientist has replaced his personal biographical situation by what I shall call, following Felix Kaufmann [1944], a scientific situation. (Schutz [1954] 1962, 1:63)

Whereas the ordinary actor's common-sense "constructs are formed from a 'Here' within the world which determines the presupposed reciprocity of perspectives," and simply take for granted "a stock of socially derived and socially approved knowledge," the Schutzian social scientist "has no 'Here' within the social world, or, more precisely, he considers his position within it and the system of relevances attached thereto as irrelevant for his scientific understanding." To be sure, the scientist, too, has a stock of knowledge that is derived and approved (from and in the scientific community), and the scientist takes this "corpus of scientific knowledge," which includes both "substantives" and "procedural rules," as a "for-granted" presence so long as it remains "scientifically ascertained." But this corpus of science "is of quite another structure than that which man in everyday life has at hand"; the structuration of scientific knowledge is dependent on "knowledge of problems solved, of their still hidden implications and open horizons of other still not formulated problems," but it is *independent* of "the beliefs accepted by an in-group in the world of everyday life."[56] The proper attitude of the social scientist is, according to Schutz, "that of a mere disinterested observer of the social world" (Schutz [1953b] 1962, 1:38–40, 36; Schutz [1932] 1967 220–24).[57]

Although I have neglected some of the detailed embroidery, the foregoing discussion provides a fair and accurate exposition of the basic figure of the Schutzian social scientist—of what might be designated, from a site within Schutz's own constructive boundaries, his puppet-typification of the scientific puppet maker of ordinary actors' less consistent but no less real or subjectively imbued puppet-making activities. Now, as I said at the outset, Schutz mostly skirted fundamental issues of epistemology, even as they were patently involved in the bindings and at the roots of his own formulations. He evaded major questions of self-consistency and enunciative warrant, which, it is difficult not to suppose, must have been naggingly salient to him. When he did address the presence of dilemma, it was usually through the prestidigital declaration of its absence. But we must not fail to take Schutz's enterprise seriously, even though it substituted neglect and obscurantism where certain preceding endeavors had offered at least a grappling view of crucial issues of human knowledge. The Schutzian account has been invoked often, especially in the romantic rebellion against forces of a remnant positivism, as the serious beginning of a humane yet rigorous science of the human world.

Schutz's central question—inherited, as he saw it, from Max Weber—

---

56. Schutz acknowledged that he "intentionally disregard[ed] the problems of the so-called sociology of knowledge here involved" (Schutz [1953b] 1962, 39 n. 51). That "disregard" never gave way to careful consideration of those "problems," at least not in his published writings.

57. Here, as in numerous other places, the similarities to the formulations of pragmatists (including those of Mead) are striking; see, in that regard, Schutz's comment on "the similarity of certain themes" from (his account of) "the mainstream of Husserl's argument" to themes of "William James, Santayana, Dewey, George H. Mead, Cooley, and others" (Schutz [1953a] 1966, 3:36).

was seemingly straightforward enough: "How is it possible to form objective concepts and an objectively verifiable theory of subjective meaning structures?" The breadth and depth of his answer consisted totally in his proposal of a project of "reducing the 'world of objective mind' to the behavior of individuals." That project remained simply *as project*; it was not questioned, it was not demonstrably warranted, its realization was not consummated; it was simply and baldly "there," as if the presence of a magical solution. The Schutzian project-to-be-realized consisted of objectively verifiable knowledge of subjective-meaning structures in the everyday life-world. Accomplishment of that knowledge, he said, required a particular method of scientific knowing, a method capable of attending faithfully to the subjective meanings of the actor's point of view; but, Schutz continued, before he himself could demonstrate the possibility of that method of social-scientific knowledge, he had to characterize the everyday life-world in which the scientist as well as the scientist's actor (and the "real" ordinary actor) lived—that is, a *characterization of that which Schutz's still undemonstrated method of knowing takes as its assigned object, and context, of knowledge*, the subjective-meaning structures of the everyday life-world. The unmistakable result was a self-annihilative relativism that extended not only to Schutz's social-scientific puppet maker but, as well, to Schutz's *own* activity of knowing.

Without question, Schutz had reached toward the phenomenological investigations of Husserl for an authoritative warrant, for an anchorage that would annul the epistemological doubt once and for all. However, even independently of the question whether Husserl had accomplished such an anchoring solution (which he had not), the Schutzian project was hardly Husserlian. The master himself had clearly and forcefully stated that science, insofar as it is properly, self-responsibly conceived, can be only that which "unremittingly imposes on itself to accept no knowledge that cannot be accounted for by original first principles, . . . principles such that profounder inquiry makes no sense" (e.g., Husserl [1929] 1969, 4–9; see also Husserl [1936] 1970). It is necessary to the rightful claim of *any* project as scientific, Husserl continued, that that project be subjected to a "radical investigation of sense" in order "to convert the 'intensive sense' (*intendierenden Sinn*), the sense 'vaguely floating before us,' in our unclear aiming, into the fulfilled, the clear, sense, and thus to procure for it the evidence of its clear possibility." Schutz did none of this. He merely *assumed* the possibility of his project. Relative to Husserl's explicit prescription, his project was founded precisely in nothing other than that "vaguely-floating-before-us" sense, which was then glossed with an apparent Husserlian vocabulary.

Indeed, Schutz's "adoption" of Husserlian phenomenology must be judged a travesty. While I shall not undertake here to document all particulars of the burlesque—others already have given good witness[58]—at the very least it must be understood that Schutz confused a critical distinction in Husserl's analysis, the empirical psychological ego and the transcendental Ego. In Husserl's view (e.g., Husserl [1931] 1960, §§8–11, 30–41; see also Husserl [1913] 1967, §§149–53), it was the latter that was constituting: "The world that exists for me . . . derives its whole sense and its existential status . . . *from me as the transcendental Ego*, the Ego who comes to the fore only with the transcendental-phenomenological epoché."[59] As we have read, however, Schutz rejected that argument, preferring instead the very psychologism to which Husserl had objected as perversion of the essential question of phenomenology. The purpose of his own study, Schutz said, was "to analyze the phenomenon of meaning in ordinary [*mundanen*] social life," and the project "*does not require the achievement of a transcendental knowledge*" beyond the sphere of "a clear understanding of the internal time-consciousness" (Schutz [1932] 1967, 44; emphases added). With regard to "ordinary social life we are *no longer concerned* with the constituting phenomena as these are studied within the sphere of the phenomenological reduction" but instead "are concerned only with the phenomena corresponding to them within the natural attitude," that is, phenomena of the psychological ego (see also Schutz [1932] 1967, 97–98). With this psychologism in mind, it is not surprising that Schutz could judge the "reductive" efforts of Simmel or Max Weber to be "much closer to the spirit of phenomenology" than statements by Husserl himself.

Granted that Schutz's theoretical proffer was not Husserlian except by falsified vocabulary, in what did its actual, implicit, epistemological foundations consist? Insofar as consistent foundations can be reproduced, I believe they correspond rather closely to those of the naturalistic positivist sciences against which Schutz directed this imprecations. The correspondence is ethical as well as epistemological.

To begin with, Schutz accepted as given the premise of radical duality of perspective in regard to the knowing subject's attitude toward that which is to be known—the duality that had been described in Weber's circle, for instance, as issuing in a "social sociology" and a "cultural sociology."

---

58. For example, see Hindess (1972), who has made valuable exposure of Schutz's allegedly Husserlian resources and, as well, of the basic similarities of Schutz's science with that of positivistic empiricism. My own discussion parallels Hindess's in several respects. Other relevant but less incisive commentaries include Heap and Roth (1973) and Gorman (1976).

59. I am aware that Schutz's *Der sinnhafte Aufbau* was completed before he had read the *Cartesian Meditations* (see Schutz [1932] 1967, 43, n. 82); but Husserl's position on this question was well established before 1929, the date of the original text of the *Meditations*, which was published in French translation in 1931.

Schutz expressed the matter in no uncertain terms (or so he apparently thought) in a paper written in 1940: The "basic postulate of the methodology of social science," he asserted, requires the scientist to choose either an "objective or [a] subjective frame of reference," in accordance with the scientific problem at hand, and then to "consider its limits and possibilities, make its terms compatible and consistent with one another, and having once accepted it, stick to it!" (Schutz [1960] 1964, 2:8).[60]

For Schutz, of course, the proper perspective was the subjective—lest "the world of social reality . . . be replaced by a fictional nonexisting world constructed by the scientific observer." But, lest *his* scientist construct an equally "fictional nonexisting world," it was incumbent on Schutz not merely to assume but to demonstrate the possibility and the actuality of truthful knowledge of another's subjective meanings. Otherwise, his scientist's interpretation of subjective-meaning structures could be nothing more than a fiction, even though it might be a conventional or "agreed-upon" fiction. Yet nowhere did Schutz actually demonstrate the possibility of anything more than a radically relativistic, self-annihilative knowledge. Inasmuch as his category of "subjective meaning" was always (for Schutz or anyone else) "a limiting concept even under optimum conditions of interpretation" and could never be comprehended as subject's "intended meaning" (since that would presuppose that the interpreter had "lived through all the conscious states and intentional Acts" of the other), Schutz explicitly denied the possibility of a necessary and veridical knowledge of others' subjective meanings. In his scheme, the space between two egos is abysmal. Despite Schutz's effort to soften the finality of that verdict—as, for example, when he reminded us to his "point . . . that the meaning I give to your experiences cannot be *precisely* the same as the meaning you give to them when you proceed to interpret them" (Schutz [1932] 1967, 99; emphasis added)—the verdict is inescapable; for, if we absolutely cannot

---

60. This article was written in 1940 as the last part of a larger essay, the first two-thirds of which consisted of critical commentary on Parsons's *The Structure of Social Action* (1937). See Schutz (1978) for his review of Parsons's work and their ensuing correspondence.

In Schutz's opinion, most "of the fallacies in the social sciences can be reduced" to a failure to observe this "so often misunderstood postulate of 'purity of method.' " As for the importance of consistency, Schutz's advice to the scientist was to adopt and observe stringently a particular writing habit, which was cultivated by Korzybski (1933), among others at the time: "See to it that the 'subscript' of all the terms and concepts you use is the same!" However, whereas Korzybski, Bachelard (e.g., Bachelard [1940] 1968, 108–14), and others spoke of the practice in recognition of the historicity of words and concepts, Schutz apparently meant it only as a device for consistency in "subjectivist" or "objectivist" point of view.

know interpretively the "precise," then we have no measure by which to judge the interpretationally "approximate" or "adequate."

Schutz as much as acknowledged his dilemma, though in a removed manner, in one of his discussions of "foundations of a theory of inter- subjective understanding." It is not often that we read in a work its author's explicit denial of the possibility of that which he or she set out to accomplish by the work. Here we do, and I cannot pass by the opportunity to quote it at length:

> As we proceed to our study of the social world, we abandon the strictly phenomenological method. We shall start out by simply ac- cepting the existence of the social world as it is always accepted in the attitude of the natural standpoint, whether in everyday life or in sociological observation. In so doing, we shall avoid any attempt to deal with the problem from the point of view of transcendental phenomenology. . . .
> We must, then, leave unsolved the notoriously difficult problems which surround the constitution of the Thou within the subjectivity of private experience. We are not going to be asking, therefore, how the Thou is constituted in an Ego, whether the concept of "human being" presupposes a transcendental ego in which the transcendental alter ego is already constituted, or how universally valid intersubjec- tive knowledge is possible. As important as these questions may be for epistemology and, therefore, for the social sciences, we may safely leave them aside in the present work. (Schutz [1932] 1967, 97–98)

Having said that, Schutz admitted relativism—indeed, a radical, psycho- logistic relativism—with a vengeance. Given his failure to demonstrate the clear possibility of knowledge fundamentally, he could not succeed in his self-assigned task of showing a necessary connection, or "reduction," of "the world of objective mind" to the "behavior of individuals." He had denied himself the warranted ground of a speaking subject who can de- monstrably speak more than fairy tales and puppet plays.

Yet, Schutz continued undeterred, as if none of the consequences of his admission of relativism among radically isolated egos really applied to him. A particular example of that continuance was his effort to defend certain social scientists' formulations against the attack of some logical- positivist philosophers of science, wherein he urged his reader to understand that his own "main concern" was not with what those "social scientists *said* but what they *meant*" (Schutz [1954] 1962, 1:50). One must wonder on what basis he warranted this privileged position, from which he could possibly determine the "meant" from the "said." Especially we must won- der, when in the very same essay we read him alluding "to a statement Kant made in another context" and suggesting thereby "that it is a 'scandal of philosophy' that so far a satisfactory solution to the problem of our knowledge of other minds . . . has not been found and that, until rather recent times, this problem has even escaped the attention of philosophers." Quickly our wonder is spoiled, however, for in nearly the same move of the pen Schutz displayed his solace in the observation that "the solution of this most difficult problem of philosophical interpretation is one of the first things taken for granted in our common-sense thinking," and it is "practically solved without difficulty in each of our everyday actions" (Schutz [1954] 1962, 1:57).[61] *There*, in that "practical solution," then, lay the boundaries of the actual project of Schutz's scientific inquiry: to explicate the secret of the ordinary actor's everyday practical solution so that the social scientist could perform the same feat, but more rationally, consistently, and adequately.

But without first a clear and consistent answer to those fundamental questions of epistemology that he so matter-of-factly brushed aside, Schutz denied himself the necessary ground on which to stand in order to explicate that practical solution enacted "without difficulty" by the ordinary actor. Consequently, even his seemingly formal rules of scientific model-building collapse into the rubble of his project. Consider, for instance, his "postulate of adequacy": it was offered as the full provision of consistency between the scientist's puppets and the everyday life-world common-sense constructs of the ordinary actor; yet Schutz proved no means by which the scientist or "the actor himself" (or "his fellow-men") can engage the other in a necessary relation of veridical knowledge that would judge such a claim of consistency. The best that either can do is to negotiate with the other a settlement of adequacy, a settlement necessarily devoid of any assurance, other than the assurance constituted by the structure of domination, of the actual approximation between scientist's model and ordinary-actor's understanding of it (or, between ordinary-actor's model and scientist's understanding of it). Indeed, remembering that Schutz himself, because he could not warrant his implicit claim to a privileged epistemic platform, must be counted as one of the radically isolated egos caught in psychologistic relativism, we must doubt the status of *his* allegedly scientific understanding of the typifications of ordinary actors in the life-world—of the very understanding in which he proposed to anchor those "foundations of a theory of intersubjective understanding."

---

61. Schutz continued with the quaint argument of *fait accompli*: "Since human beings are born of mothers and not concocted in [philosophical] retorts, the experience of the existence of other human beings and of the meanings of their actions is certainly the first and most original empirical observation man makes."

At one level of response, we can regard Schutz's science as impotent, even empty. Consider his description of the proper "scientific observer" as a case in point. This observer was cast in the fictive stance of the scrupulously impartial fact-finding accountant of precisely that which is observed; that is, an observer was believed to be uninvolved in the "observed situation," as if merely a passive receptor of phenomena, having no practical interest in the situation. Schutz much admired Weber's "great achievement"—"he was one of the first to proclaim that the social sciences must abstain from value judgments" (Schutz [1932] 1967, 5)[62]—and accordingly his own model of the proper scientist had considerable stress on the value of "value neutrality." Simply by "making up his mind to become" a scientist, this puppet-scientist of puppets would divest himself or herself of all original biographic situation or sediment and, as if exchanging some mundane suit of clothing for that special suit worn by the scientist, become the "disinterested observer" who is capable of questioning to the core that which is taken for granted by ordinary folk.[63] To be sure, Schutz did say that he recognized that "in his daily life the social scientist remains a human being, a man living among his fellow-men, with whom he is interrelated in many ways," and that, "surely, scientific activity itself occurs within the tradition of socially derived knowledge, is based upon co-operation with other scientists, requires mutual corroboration and criticism and can only be communicated by social interaction" (Schutz [1953b] 1962, 1:36–37). But such a fairy-tale picture of social interaction it is! Schutz's scientists not only have no practical interest or involvement in their "objects of study," they also live the pristine life of reasoned conversation, free of any of the so-called baser motives. Moreover, somehow Schutz figured a disarticulation of "the world of the social scientist" from "the world of social science" that he apparently thought would allow him to speak sensibly of

62. Schutz continued his expression of admiration for Weber by saying that "he defined the task of sociology not as metaphysical speculation but as the simple and accurate description of life in society." As further testimony, he quoted with agreement the opinion of Jaspers that, with Weber, "sociology is no longer the philosophy of human existence. It is the particular science of human behavior and its consequences" (Jaspers [1931] 1951, 151, quoted in Schutz [1932] 1967, 5).

63. As Hindess (1972, 2–5) has pointed out, Schutz's "puppets" are fundamentally similar to Lazarsfeld's (1954) famous "monsters." Whether the one or the other, Schutz's disquisition reminds me of a judgment rendered by Samuel Johnson of the author of an eighteenth-century *Free Inquiry into the Nature and Origin of Evil*: "The only end of writing is to enable the readers better to enjoy life, or better to endure it: and how will either of those be put more in our power by him who tells us, that we are puppets, of which some creature not much wiser than ourselves manages the wires" (Johnson 1757, 302).

that special category of the "disinterested attitude" (Schutz [1932] 1967, 221; Schutz [1953b] 1962, 1:3⁷, 39). Somehow, dealing "with science and scientific matters within the social world is one thing," while that "special attitude which the scientist has to adopt toward his object is another"; and somehow it is by adopting this "disinterested attitude of a scientific ob-server" that the nascent social scientist "detaches himself from his biograph-ical situation within the social world" and thereafter becomes free to un-dertake works "governed by the disinterested quest for truth in accordance with preestablished rules, called the scientific method," and a stock of knowledge having "quite another structure than that which man in every-day life has at hand."

To say merely that such formulations as the foregoing are impotent or empty is grossly inadequate, however. For it is not simply a matter of failed formulations or of undemonstrated claims of privileged grounds. The claims made were simultaneously epistemological and ethical, even though implicitly so in some instances, and they had positive implications.

On numerous occasions in recent years, as Schutz's name has come to be one to reckon with, various participants in the academic enterprises of social science have spoken of great impressions formed from their read-ings of Schutz's supposedly profound insights; some have been indulged in the curiosity of a "marriage" of Schutz with Karl Marx. It is perhaps not so surprising that many intellectuals and pupils of the academy of social science have experienced a certain resonance of views when reading Schutz, by or through which the seeming "relevance" of Schutz's science stands in an imagined relation of exposure of and opposition to the stale "irrelevan-cies" of "conventional social science." It is not surprising, because Schutz's account of the life-world rather well describes the liberalist consciousness of society.

But there can be no mistake regarding the actual implications of the Schutzian view; they are covertly elitist, apologetic of the prevailing order, and quietistic. Schutz's puppet-making scientist must set about the construc-tion of accounts of the subjective-meaning structures of ordinary actors from observations that are simply taken for granted, for which the criteria of objective validity include, in addition to a formal rationality of internal logical consistency, the requirement that the stories be at least plausible if not entirely credible to those actors about whom they are fashioned. Neither the scientist nor the ordinary actor has a definitive ground from which to propound a *nonrelative* judgment of veracity, either of the observations or of the account; yet the scientist has only to invoke the ready-made mask of "disinterested, impartial observer."

But what of the structure of that criterion of plausibility or credibility? That which is plausible or credible to the ordinary actor (as to the scientist) is necessarily situated, by Schutz's own argument, as relative to the given biographically sedimented subjective-meaning structures of the actor. Now, unless we assume that (somehow) the ordinary actor's subjective-meaning structures are always constituted as veridical knowledge, those structures may be in a given case constituted as *false* consciousness, in which event the scientist's criterion of "plausibility" is governed by false consciousness. The same conclusion applies, of course, to the scientist's own subjective-meaning structures.

Relatedly, Schutz's radical individualist stance consisted only of empiricist speculations about the surfaces of social formations; historical-social structure was present only as a given, never as an active principle of inquiry. His actor was conceived as one who "freely" constructs a course-of-action pattern based on the stock of knowledge at hand—though this stock of knowledge at hand consists of socially derived and validated recipes of action, in consequence of which the actor typically "merely" discerns the recipe that is deemed to be appropriate to a given situation. Not incidentally, when characterizing his "ordinary actor" (puppet) in relation to group membership, Schutz displayed a predilection for such words as "habituality," "automatism," and "half-consciousness" (e.g., Schutz [1944] 1964, 2:101–2; Schutz [1953b] 1962, 1:19, 32–33). Thus, despite his effort to rescue "freedom" for his individual actor—to "save" the unique actor as a "free agency" by locking it away in an unknowable, totally private "ego"—his analysis left the knowable actor (including the *self*-knowable actor) in a condition of naive, humble acceptance of the existent "is" resulting from those objective forces of "because-of motivation" (see, e.g., Schutz [1932] 1967, 189–91, 229–32, 241–42; Schutz [1951] 1962, 69–78, 84–88). Consequently—and despite his insistence on the "postulate of subjective interpretation"—his analysis differs from that of the strictest objectivist-empiricist science, against which he hurled his displeasure, only by its *pretense* of empowering subjective meaning as an instrument of veridical knowledge.

Schutz's conception of social science—which was, we must remember, not just a description of the existent "is" of science but a positive profession of the "ought"—constitutes a program the epistemological and ethical implications of which leave us with only two "choices": the ahistoric inevitability of the "iron cage," or that "affirmative culture" doctrine of unconditional belief in a "universally obligatory, externally better, and more valuable world . . . , a world essentially different from the factual world of the daily struggle for existence, yet realizable by every individual for himself 'from within,' without any transformation of the state of fact" (Marcuse [1965] 1968, 95).

5

K_lein_ Bottles
and Generalized Irony

1. LEO STRAUSS (1899–1973)

THE PRECEDING CHAPTER ENDED with considerations of theorists whose approaches to the problem of knowledge, including the problem of the warrant of their own positive claims, were similar insofar as they sought to allow historical-cultural contingency of the *object* of social-science knowledge without acknowledging the vulnerability of the *process* of such knowledge to the very same contingency. Even as they denied that their science rested on privileged claims, they assumed a privileged position from which to render judgments. I shall begin this chapter, a continuation of the series of case studies of twentieth-century social theory, with consideration of a theorist who well recognized the inconsistency and final dilemma of that exercise of privilege, and who responded to the problem of relativism frontally.

Although nominally affiliated most often with departments of political science, Leo Strauss was usually described, by himself as by others, as a "political philosopher" rather than as a "social-science theorist."[1] The choice of appellations signified both a vertical and a horizontal remove

---

1. The referential context is, of course, the social-science academy in the United States. Strauss left his native Germany in 1932, having received his doctorate at Hamburg in 1921, followed by a post at the Berlin Academy of Jewish Research and service as coeditor of the Jubilee Edition of the works of Moses Mendelssohn. Living first in France and then in England, Strauss resettled permanently in the United States in 1938.

from the increasingly behavioralist consciousness of the social sciences. For one thing, Strauss and his nominal colleagues resided in different textual worlds. There was overlap, to be sure—Strauss's world included Max Weber, Tönnies, Tawney, Beard, and other scholars still located within the bibliographic space of social science—but much more conspicuously the Straussian text encompassed also such "distant" figures as Hobbes, and his relation to Machiavelli in one direction and Locke in the other; Rousseau, Burke, and Madison; Spinoza and Maimonides; and, most importantly, Socrates, Plato, and Aristotle. Moreover, the extraordinary breadth of this consciously held text was unified and centered in a no-longer-popular thematic purpose: the defense of a classical doctrine of "natural law." It was on the basis of such doctrine that Strauss persistently strove to demonstrate the availability of an epistemology of *universal objective* knowledge of the good, the right, and the true, an epistemology immune to the enervative infections of relativism. The natural-law thesis began with a value judgment, however, and that made it wholly anathematic to the dominant self-understanding of modern science. In consequence, the thesis has been "rejected in our time by almost all students of society who are not Roman Catholics." It is "today primarily a historical subject," a topic for the historian of philosophy (Strauss 1968, 80).[2]

The basic thesis of "natural law" (and, as Strauss approached it, its primary question of "natural right") consists in the claim that there are discoverable *natural* principles, principles that do not originate merely as human conventions. They are founding principles, without which no rule whatever, whether epistemic or ethical, could possibly be justified. Because they are constituted entirely outside or behind any and all historical circumstance, these natural principles are universal. They are "natural" in the sense, for example, that Plato considered "the naturally right" to be the "idea" of justice, that is, "justice itself, justice pure and simple" (*Republic*, 501B; Strauss 1968, 81). It is "natural law" not in the sense of *nomos* but in that of *physis*, for *nomos* (νομός) means "anything *assigned*," that is, "convention" or "usage"; and the "natural principles" in question are of the order and power of *physis*.[3]

---

2. Rather peculiar constructions have often been made from this opposition by defenders of a natural-law thesis. For example, consider Burhoe's recent effort to respond to "the crisis of human purpose" in scientific civilization by anchoring a theory of value and an ethic within a natural-law context. Burhoe put it this way: "There are scientific grounds for supposing that values, goals, attitudes, and preferences are factual, objective, scientifically investigatable processes or patterns of living systems, developed under nature's laws" (Burhoe 1971, 231).

3. It is worth noting that *nomos* (νομός) designated in the Homeric lexicon "a feeding-place for cattle"; later it was used to refer more generally to "one's assigned or allotted place," and thence still more generally to "anything assigned."

In the contrasting view of positivist science, which Strauss recognized as "externally the most powerful in the present-day West," such principles simply do not exist—or, if they do exist, it is an "existence" that cannot be demonstrated scientifically (Strauss 1961, 148).[4] Rules defining and governing "the good" and "the right," for instance, have their genesis solely as conventions, according to positivism; and although in the past these conventions may have arisen indeliberately or by indirection, it is in the possibility of a conscious devising of conventional rules based on scientifically validated factual knowledge that the prospects of human betterment lie. Between these contrasting views, it is clear, much of the difference has to do with the relation of "fact" to "value." The positivist argument insists on contingency and the intrinsic presence of axiological interest as properties only of its object. With regard to its own position as knowing subject in relation to its object, it believes that it successfully evades the dilemma of self-relativization through use of "the same device by which it frees itself from Hume's or any other psychology: through the Kantian distinction between validity and genesis." However, the crux of Kant's transcendence of psychology actually consisted in a "device" that positivism denies, namely the a priori. An a priori "does not have a genesis, at least not an empirical genesis," and precisely because of its nonempirical status, positivism rejects it as an unnecessary prop fabricated in metaphysical speculation. Hence, Strauss argued, positivism is caught in an argumentation that necessarily involves questions of psychology, in particular "the question of the empirical genesis of science out of what precedes science" (Strauss 1961, 149). Given its definition of its object and, by implication, of its own circumstances, positivism cannot stop at simply trying to answer the question "What is science?" but must also raise the question *why* there is science and what its meaning is. "Since positivism denies that there is a 'pure reason' or a 'pure mind,' it can answer the question, Why science? only in terms of 'the human organism' " and its putative "needs."[5]

Just as positivism became ensnared in the self-denying circularity of its own constituting argument, so also did the historicist doctrine of "human studies." Historicism, Strauss acknowledged, has often stood in attempted

---

Thus, as Strauss (1968, 80) pointed out, the phrase "natural law" (νομός τῆς φύσεος) is a contradiction in terms, inasmuch as *nomos* originates as human agreement concerning assignments to categories (i.e., "law" as *human* law), whereas the "natural" refers to that which is aboriginally of nature, i.e., *physis*.

4. For an exposition of a moderate version of the positivist view and its relation to natural-law arguments, see Hart (1961).

5. An instructive case study in this regard comes to us in the form of work published by the philosopher of science, Karl Popper (e.g., 1972), who seemingly thought of science as answering a human "need" in somewhat the way that a spiderweb answers a spider's. See chapter 2, section 3, above.

critique of positivism because of the latter's insufficient attention to historical-cultural particularities in its efforts to discover empirical generalizations. Nevertheless, historicism has shared with positivism a rejection of the "metaphysics" of natural law. According to the historicist argument, "all human thought is dependent on unique historical contexts that are preceded by more or less different contexts and that emerge out of their antecedents in a fundamentally unpredictable way: the foundations of human thought are laid by unpredictable experiences or decisions." Yet the circularity is plain to be seen: if valid thought is indeed strictly dependent on the unique historical context of its provenience, then no thinker in the here and now can possibly judge the "valid thoughts" of an earlier contingent situation in order to know that there *is no* common principle underlying the "valid thoughts" of the two historical contexts. There may be no basis for judgment of sameness; but then neither is there any basis for judgment of *difference*. The historicist argument rests at best on an assumption that it cannot demonstrate. Moreover, Strauss concluded, historicism "thrives on the fact that it inconsistently exempts itself from its own verdict about all human thought. . . . We cannot see the historical character of 'all' thought—that is, of all thought with the exception of the historicist insight and its implications—without transcending history, without grasping something trans-historical." Not that Strauss considered situation-specific standards of judgment, as these are accepted and enacted by situated actors, to be dispensable; on the contrary, he gave great emphasis to the exegetical principle that, in order to understand an author's text properly, one must first take care to understand it just as the author did. In this, he partly agreed with the interpretive stance outlined by Max Weber. But he diverged sharply from all notions of the "value neutrality" of interpretation, and he rejected the conclusion that interpretation or understanding is finally and unavoidably relative to the factually contingent situation. The pursuit of knowledge, he asserted, must yield something more than "pieces which behave as if they were parts of a worm" (Strauss 1953, 19, 25, 50–59; Strauss 1936, 129–70; Strauss [1955] 1959, 17).

That Strauss was very much aware of the nihilist conclusion of epistemological relativism is abundantly evident in many of his essays.[6] That he appreciated Nietzsche's "first step" toward a solution to the problem is also evident—not merely from the circumstance of a "shared" enjoyment of the Greek classics but more significantly from the following passage, in which Strauss observed with reference to Nietzsche that the solution might seem to be

6. Among the numerous instances, see his 1961 rebuttal of Brecht's 1959 criticisms of some of his earlier publications.

that one turn one's back on this lesson of history [i.e., the lesson of historical contingency and skepticism], that one voluntarily choose life-giving delusion instead of deadly truth, that one fabricate a myth. But this is patently impossible for men of intellectual probity. The true situation comes to sight once one realizes the essential limitation of objective history or of objective knowledge in general. Objective history suffices for destroying the delusion of the objective validity of any principles of thought and action; it does not suffice for opening up a genuine understanding of history. The objective historian cannot grasp the substance of the past because he is a mere spectator, not dedicated or committed to substantive principles of thought and action, and this is the consequence of his having realized that such principles have no objective validity. But an entirely different conclusion may and must be drawn from the realization of this objective truth. The different values respected in different epochs had no objective support, i.e., they were human creations; they owed their being to a free human project that formed the horizon within which a culture was possible. What man did in the past unconsciously and under the delusion of submitting to what is independent of his creative act, he must now do consciously. This radically new project—the revaluation of all values—entails the rejection of all earlier values, for they have become baseless by the realization of the baseless character of their claim, by which they stand or fall, to objective validity. But precisely the realization of the origin of all such principles makes possible a new creation that presupposes this realization and is in agreement with it, yet is not deducible from it; for otherwise it would not be due to a creative act performed with intellectual probity. (Strauss 1961, 152–53)

No doubt Strauss found a certain resonance between that "first step" by Nietzsche and his own commitment. Yet he was also aware of the ambivalence of Nietzsche's doctrine of "the will to power"—whether it was itself "the final truth" or simply a project that could be "superseded by other such projects in the future"—and he was inclined to decide the ambivalence on Nietzsche's behalf by concluding (though as acknowledged speculation) that Nietzsche probably decided to "deny the possibility of theory proper and so [conceived] of thought as essentially subservient to, or dependent on, life or fate" (Strauss 1961, 153; Strauss 1953, 26).[7] From Strauss's

7. It must be noted here that, for all his appreciation of Nietzsche's "first step," Strauss tended to misidentify Nietzsche as a *Lebensphilosoph* in sympathy with "the historical school." Apparently this was due, at least in part, to Strauss's

point of view, that sort of conclusion was totally unacceptable. It was unacceptable because it denied the necessity that any project of consciously creating new values (and hence new facts) must have as its foundation some governing principle or set of principles that is itself axiologically primary and free of the contingency of historical circumstance. In other words, such a project would be constituted as "political action," in the full sense of the term, and that constitution implies the necessity of a guiding principle.

> All political action aims at either preservation or change. When desiring to change, we wish to bring about something better. All political action is then guided by some thought of better or worse. But thought of better or worse implies thought of the good. The awareness of the good which guides all our actions has the character of opinion: it is no longer questioned but, on reflection, it proves to be questionable. The very fact that we can question it directs us towards such a thought of the good as is no longer questionable—towards a thought which is no longer opinion but knowledge. All political action has then in itself a directedness towards knowledge of the good: of the good life, or of the good society. For the good society is the complete political good. (Strauss [1955] 1959, 10)

But what can be that guiding principle? If derived from historical facticities, it would suffer the same contingency as those facticities: it would not be able to justify self-consistently its claim to universal objective knowledge of the good, as opposed to mere opinion about the good or about what it *might* be.

The conditions of the Straussian answer to that question of a founding principle are given in Strauss's project of a return to "the classical form of political philosophy." To begin with, he called upon us to recognize that "the mere fact that we can raise the question of the worth of the ideal of our society shows that there is something in man that is not altogether in slavery to his society." Evidently there does exist some sort of "standard with reference to which we can judge the ideals of our own as well as of any other society." Evidently, too, however, such a standard cannot be sought in "the needs of the various societies," that is, in the particulars of historical circumstance, because "the societies and their parts have many

---

reliance on Nietzsche's earlier writings (see, e.g., Strauss 1953, 26 n. 9). Contrary to Strauss's speculative conclusion that he leaned toward an unprincipled solution to the ambivalence, Nietzsche's resolution of the status of "the will to power" (to the extent that the question *was* resolved) is actually not so far removed from Strauss's own foundational argument (see Nietzsche [1883–85] 1954; Nietzsche [1889] 1954).

needs that conflict with one another." The standard must be constituted in such a way that it will enable us to judge the difference between "genuine needs and fancied needs" and, concomitantly, to know "the hierarchy of the various types of genuine needs." Knowledge of the good, in short, requires that we investigate the natural conditions of human action— "natural" in the sense that the actions are "guided by nature rather than by convention, or by inherited opinion, or by tradition, to say nothing of mere whims." The requisite epistemological relationship is therefore one of immediacy to the natural order of things, a relation that is not moderated or already interpreted by a screen of received opinion that has been interposed between knowing subject and that which is to be known.[8] To say that it must be a relation of immediacy is not to call upon the positivist's notion of direct sensory experience, however, for that notion carries in itself the supposition of a pure, value-free factuality—all of which is itself a convention. Rather, that to which there must be an immediate relation is constituted unhistorically as the inherent power and validity of principles of *physis* (Strauss 1953, 3; Strauss [1955] 1959, 27).

Thus it is, Strauss argued, that we must look to a time when thought had, on the one hand, recognized the distinction of *physis* and *nomos* but, on the other, had not yet become laden with the contaminations of "tradition" or "inherited opinion" or "mere whim." The situation of "classical philosophy" was, by Strauss's account, just such a time: the screen of mediation by received opinion did not exist, yet already "man [had] embarked on the quest for the first things in the light of the fundamental distinctions between hearsay and seeing with one's own eyes . . . and between things made by man and things not made by man." Previously, the entirety of that which emerged from chaos had been experienced as an undifferentiated presence ("custom"). In the classical situation, however, nature had been discovered as a *distinction*, as a contrast to the conventional. It was a "fertile moment when all political traditions were shaken, and there was not yet in existence a tradition of political philosophy." Every subsequent situation of thought had behind itself a heritage that it could not forget. Whether one agreed or disagreed with this or that received interpretation, this or that understanding of "the meaning of the past," the fact remained that *some* interpretation of "the past" was always already there as something to be taken into account, and the resulting formation of political thought was always derivative. By contrast, the classical phi-

---

8. There are loose similarities here to aspects of Husserl's critique, but they are on the level of problematics rather than of projected consequences of critique. Strauss's understanding of Husserl can be judged from an essay published shortly before his death (Strauss 1972). See also his discussion of Heidegger and "the ontological problem," in his memorial to Kurt Riezler (Strauss [1956] 1959).

losophers saw "the political things with a freshness and a directness which has never been equalled." Not that they had no predecessors; they did, of course, but they acknowledged whatever opinions their predecessors may have handed down as *contemporary* opinion, not as historically different tradition. There was no consciousness of a necessary contingency or relativity of judgment; classical thought was "unhistorical" (Strauss 1953, 88–90; Strauss [1955] 1959, 27; Strauss [1949] 1959, 67–69).

With that construction as background, Strauss proposed that by means of investigations of classical philosophical texts we can acquire knowledge of a *natural* standard of the good and the right, by which to guide judgments of "the ideals of our own as well as of any other society"— that is, the founding of a universal objective knowledge—and by which to guide our political actions: "Reading old books is today indispensable as an antidote to the ruling dogma that the very notion of a final and true account of the whole is absurd." We must exercise proper care in our reading of those texts, however, in order to understand them just as their authors understood them. This means not only to avoid the conceit that we can understand the authors *better* than they themselves did—a conceit that has come to roost in the lofty domain of historicism[9]—but also it means to be watchful for hidden relations in those texts, that is to say, relations that qualify as "between-the-lines" writing. The exigencies of historical circumstance are frequently such that seekers of truth must camouflage "proper meanings" in order not to exacerbate the inherent tension between the quest for truth and society, to the detriment certainly of the former and possibly of both. We must be alert to the existence of these hidden confessions, told only to those who can read the shadows of words.

> Philosophy or science, the highest activity of man, is the attempt to replace opinion about "all things" by knowledge of "all things"; but opinion is the element of society; philosophy or science is therefore the attempt to dissolve the element in which society breathes, and thus it endangers society. Hence philosophy or science must remain the preserve of a small minority, and philosophers or scientists must respect the opinions on which society rests. (Strauss [1954] 1959, 221–22)

Philosophers or scientists need not accept any of those opinions as the truth, of course. But when disputing those opinions or some portion of them, they may—if they hold to "this view about the relation of philosophy or

---

9. Strauss was here responding in part to Dilthey, who proposed as the "final goal of the hermeneutic procedure" an interpretive criterion of understanding "the author better than he understood himself" (Dilthey [1900] 1976, 259–60).

science and society"—dispute them in "a peculiar manner of writing which would enable them to reveal what they regard as the truth to the few, without endangering the unqualified commitment of the many to the opinions on which society rests" (Strauss [1954] 1959, 221–22, 228; see also Strauss 1952, passim).[10]

Strauss's central concern was to return philosophy, and the philosophical basis of science, to its original Socratic interest. As Strauss read the record, philosophy had been originally "the humanizing quest for the eternal order, and hence it had been a pure source of humane inspiration and aspiration." With the crisis and eventual breakdown of the modern version of the natural-law thesis (focused by Strauss in the contrast between Rousseau and Burke), the "historical school" emerged as inheritor, with the consequence that, since "the seventeenth century, philosophy has become a weapon, and hence an instrument," serving the interests of this or that particular formation of the historical moment.[11] "It was this politicization of philosophy that was discerned as the root of our troubles by an intellectual who denounced the treason of the intellectuals," although he himself—the reference is to Benda (1927)—was a "dupe of the delusion he denounced," inasmuch as he fell into "the fatal mistake" of equating intellectuals and philosophers. "For the politicization of philosophy consists precisely in this, that the difference between intellectuals and philosophers—a difference formerly known as the difference between gentlemen and philosophers, on the one hand, and the difference between sophists or rhetoricians and philosophers, on the other, becomes blurred and finally disappears."[12] Strauss wished to reinstate that "essential difference," to

10. Strauss noted that he was led to this "way of conceiving the relation between the quest for truth (philosophy or science) and society" by his study of "certain earlier thinkers," including Maimonides, Halevy, and Spinoza (Strauss [1954] 1959, 221).

11. Strauss once remarked, presumably with reference to the politics of the U.S. academy, that "what Machiavelli did apparently, our social science would actually do if it did not prefer—only God knows why—generous liberalism to consistency: namely, to give advice with equal competence and alacrity to tyrants as well as free peoples" (Strauss 1953, 4; regarding Machiavelli, see also Strauss 1953, 161–62; Strauss 1958).

12. With Machiavelli, for instance, one takes one's "bearings by the extreme situations in which the demands of justice are reduced to the requirements of necessity, and not by the normal situations in which the demands of justice in the strict sense are the highest law." With the Aristotelian preference, by contrast, one takes one's "bearings by the normal situation and by what is normally right"; only with reluctance does one deviate "from what is normally right," and then "only in order to save the cause of justice and humanity itself." This difference has become blurred, through the combination of the "two opposite extremes, which at present are called 'cynicism' and 'idealism' " (Strauss 1953, 162).

return philosophy from its destruction in the politics of sectional interest and the contingency of situation to its classical seat, from which then to limn the naturally founded principles of human life (Strauss 1953, 34, 120–23, 252–55, 294–95).

Was Strauss's wish only a vacant hope? Did he, that is, demonstrate the possibility, if not the exact procedures, of this return, and thereby the possibility of his naturally founded universal and objective knowledge? To this last question the answer is unmistakably "no." To begin with, it must be said that "the historical approach" which comprised part of the object of his critique was a rather naive version, constructed mainly around the notion that we in the present understand the thought of past thinkers not only differently but that we understand it intrinsically better than they did. However, rejection of that claim (whether by the delusion of empirical evidence or on other grounds) does not automatically entail rejection of the argument of historical consciousness. And, as Gadamer has cautioned, "Simply to show that the classical philosophers thought differently, i.e., unhistorically, says nothing about the possibility of thinking unhistorically today" (Gadamer [1965] 1975, 483). If the latter has not been demonstrated, not simply as possibility but (in Strauss's activity) as actuality, how can one know (how did Strauss know) the self-understanding of classical philosophers *as such*? How does a reader who is historically situated in the here and now, embedded in materializations of historical consciousness, achieve access to the classical text *as it was two millennia ago*? Strauss did not, and indeed could not, demonstrate his assumed ability to achieve such access; who could have stood in Socrates' place and, *as Socrates*, judged the quality of reading?

The point is, Strauss failed to appreciate the dialectical conditions of textuality: the objectness of "a text" is never pure objectness, immune to history and given eternally in self-vocalization; it is always objectness to and by a historical subject who produces/reproduces it as objectness, and standards of judgment that qualify "correct reading" or "correct interpretation" come not from the (imaginary) "original-text-in-itself" but from the historical conditions of that production/reproduction. Thus, when Strauss spoke of the "hidden relations" of a "peculiar manner of writing" (as adopted by Spinoza, say, in order to avoid persecution), he ignored his own presence in the decision of what was deliberate "writing between the lines" and what was not. The qualification of confession, whether it be confession through some "peculiar manner of writing" or through a speaking to an unseen other, is determined no less by the authority of the hearer/reader than by the one who is speaking or writing. Here again, Gadamer made the point, although with a somewhat deflected emphasis, when he asked whether "conscious distortion, camouflage, and concealment of the proper meaning" are not "in fact the extreme case of a frequent, even a normal situation?—just as persecution . . . is only an extreme case when compared with the intentional or unintentional pressure that society and public opinion exercise on human thought" (Gadamer [1965] 1975, 484).[13]

This "hermeneutic" issue is not merely a matter of disputation over some scholastic propriety or decorum of interpretive reading. Given Strauss's purpose in seeking a return to the attention of classical philosophy, the issue is integral to the whole of what may be called the problem of societal reconstruction. It is, for example, one side of Hegel's question of political action (see Hegel [1802] 1968).[14] According to Strauss, a basic principle of classical philosophy by which thought and action ought to be oriented is that of "the best regime," that is, the "order" or "form" which would give society its best "character"; and although the underlying "that-ness" of human "nature is enslaved in so many ways that it is almost a miracle if an individual achieves the highest" (therefore, "what can one expect of society!"), nevertheless the orienting goal of "best regime" can be projected in knowledge on the basis of a natural principle of "general virtue." Thus, "only in the best regime [are] the good of the regime and the good of the good man identical, that goal being virtue" (Strauss [1955] 1959, 34–35). On the other hand, given the admitted existence of historicity in postclassical thought, Strauss faced a rather different order of question (whatever the "correct reading" of "the classical situation" might be). The contingency of thought and action is constituted not merely as an imma-terial "historical consciousness"; it is embedded in the historical differen-tiations of actual conditions of life. Consequently, postulation of a return to "unhistorical" thinking of "natural principles" requires more than a demonstration of the possibility of breaching the mediating "screen" of accumulated "tradition" and "received opinion." If thought and action are contingent on particularities of situation, then one may ask (as evidently many members of modern society *have* asked, in effect if not in vocaliza-tion): should not the interests of one's thought and action be particularis-tically instrumental? The circumstances of an affirmative answer to that question have led to widespread privatization of interests and to a relative neglect of "the public good," the standing of the commonweal, conceived as a principle in itself. As Hegel saw it, there was no possibility of sur-

13. Strauss's position rests also on the questionable assumption that that which has been propelled by confession, as it were, through a thicket of concealment is somehow more truthful, more trustworthy, precisely because it *is* confession.

14. See also the lucid discussion by Avineri (1972, 82–86). The "question" was not Hegel's alone, of course; it occupied the attention of Hobbes, Rousseau, Madison, Marx, Durkheim, and many others. For an analysis of the current conditions of privatization and public legitimacy, see Habermas 1962; Habermas [1973c] 1975.

mounting or repairing this fragmentation into individualistic privacy by trying to resurrect the classical natural-law thesis of "virtue"; existing differentiations could not be abrogated (although they might be integrated in the universalizing state). For Strauss, there was no acceptable alternative to the natural-law thesis in its classical form; yet he failed to demonstrate the conditions of its possibility even for himself. While we may be sympathetic with Strauss in his rejection of theory that has become "understanding of what practice has produced or of the actual," to the exclusion of being "the quest for what ought to be" (Strauss 1953, 320), we surely are not mistaken in expecting that he should have clarified how he or any other historical subject could achieve an *un*historical access to the *un*historical conditions of a universal, objective, naturally founded knowledge of the good.

2. JEAN PIAGET (1896–1980)

Whereas the political scientist/philosopher Strauss sought to answer basic epistemological questions through a "return" to classical philosophy, the psychologist/philosopher Jean Piaget sought rather to answer such questions by "liberating" epistemology from philosophy and making of it a strictly scientific enterprise—not in the sense that Husserl wished to make philosophy a "strict science" but, to the contrary, in the manner that psychology, a "genetic psychology," is scientific. In this, Piaget has stood closer to the pulse of contemporary social science, and indeed of contemporary philosophy of science (see, e.g., Quine 1969a).

Trained as a paleontologist, and having written a dissertation on the distribution of Jurassic gastropods in the Valaisian Alps of southern Switzerland, Piaget soon turned to the greater attraction of questions pertaining to the cognitive development of children. Beginning with his first major work, *The Language and Thought of the Child* ([1923] 1924), he became a widely renowned and prolific author of studies commonly classified as "the psychology of child development," studies ranging from the origin of the child's conceptions of number, space, time, and causality, to the origin of moral judgment (e.g., Piaget [1927] 1960; Piaget and Inhelder [1948] 1956; Piaget with Garcia [1971] 1974; Piaget [1974a] 1976; Piaget [1974b] 1978). Throughout this large collection of experimental investigations, a chief concern has been to explicate the ontogenic process of the cognitive functions, especially the development of what might be called logical pragmatics. At the same time, however, his work can be seen—as in fact some have described it (e.g., Mays 1953–54)—as an effort to investigate "the Kantian categories" experimentally. Increasingly, since the 1930s, Piaget has stood as a champion of the passage of epistemology from being a merely philosophical-speculative activity to the "mature" status of a science of knowledge. Although the main features of his epistemological position can be read in his earliest writings on language and thought, it was especially in recent decades, in such works as *Biology and Knowledge* ([1967] 1971), *Genetic Epistemology* (1970a), and his introduction to a UNESCO report of research trends in "the social and human sciences" ([1970b] 1974), that he promoted his view of a systematic, scientific "genetic epistemology."

On the "central question" of the origin and development of logical thought, Piaget tried to steer a middle course between his construction of the two extremes of "blank-slate" empiricism, on the one hand, and the hereditarian view of complete innate endowment, on the other. The latter view cannot be accepted, according to Piaget, because it implies that even the youngest child can engage in logical operations, yet scientific experiments show that logical operations develop gradually through several stages of formation (see, e.g., Piaget [1967] 1971, 313–17). Likewise, the rationalistic "preformationist" conception of language—that language is "based on reason, which is thought to be innate in man"[15]—must be rejected. On the other hand, this does not mean that we can accept "the linguistic view of the positivists," who consider logic to be "simply a linguistic convention." Rather, between these extreme positions there exists "a whole selection of possible solutions"; and whatever their competing merits may be, "the choice among these solutions must be made on the basis of fact, that is, on the basis of psychological research. The problems cannot be resolved by speculation." But already Piaget has drawn certain conclusions in the direction, if not the culmination, of a solution, based on the experiments he and his associates conducted: "The roots of logic are to be found on the sensori-motor level" of human activity; "prior to language and on the level of its substructures, there is a logic of coordinations of action including the fundamental structures of order and interrelation."[16] In other words, the genesis of logical thought has been located by Piaget in the prelinguistic, sensori-motor level of actions taken by the child in response to the child's surroundings. It is in the child's acting on the environment that the basic relations and categories of logic, indeed of thought in general, develop, and thus all questions of the genesis of knowledge must be approached through a genetic psychology of the knowing subject as an active, manipulative

15. Here and elsewhere, Piaget made specific reference to Chomsky's work—and, it must be said, overdrew the difference vis-à-vis his own position (see, e.g., Piaget 1970a, 47).

16. "The truth, in short, lies half-way between empiricism and apriorism: intellectual evolution requires that both mind and environment should make their contribution" (Piaget [1927] 1960, 258). It is doubtful that Piaget meant us to take that "half-way" quite literally, in the manner of recent efforts by Jensen (1969) or Jencks and associates (1972) to achieve an algebraic partition of "endowment" and "achievement." But, as one commentator has remarked, "Precision and clarity are not Piagetian hallmarks" (Gould 1977, 144).

principal in the construction of knowledge (Piaget 1970a, 9–10, 47; Piaget [1970c] 1977, 112–16, 140; Piaget [1936] 1963, 18–19).

According to Piaget's diagnosis, "All epistemologists refer to psychological factors in their analysis"—psychological data being "indispensable" in the nature of the case—but by and large their references to psychology either have been "speculative" (i.e., "not based on psychological research") or, as in the instance of logical positivism, have not been acknowledged. This circumstance can be attributed partly to the failure to continue the historical appropriation of philosophical discourse: psychology itself was the last discursive region to be removed from philosophical speculation and revitalized as a scientific enterprise; the time has come to complete the next step, which is the appropriation of epistemology. "So long as we continue to discuss the global question 'what is truth?' even specifying that it is a question of knowledge or of scientific Truth, it is evident that we will be unable to avoid interference of such discussions with fundamental metaphysical debates on the reality of the outer world, on the nature of mind, and so forth." A proper theory of knowledge, at least of scientific knowledge, is itself scientific, in the sense that the knowing subject must be investigated scientifically within a restricted scope of problematicity. Such theory is convened as a "posing of problems in such a manner that they can be solved in the same way by various research teams independent of their personal philosophy." In answer to the rhetorical question how that is possible, Piaget averred that "we merely have to ask ourselves not what is definitely scientific knowledge envisaged as a whole, statically, but 'how knowledge increases' considered in its multiplicity and above all in the diversity of its respective developments." In short, it is the question not of the possibility of an apodictic knowledge as such but of the increase and development of that which is accorded the designation of "knowledge," especially "scientific knowledge," within the historical moment (Piaget 1970a, 7–8; Piaget [1970c] 1977, 26, 97–98; also see Piaget [1970c] 1977, 135–36; Piaget [1967] 1971, 361–62).

Already, however, Piaget discerned that "contemporary epistemology is more and more the work of scientists." In part, of course, he was referring to the enterprise of his own "genetic epistemology," which "attempts to explain knowledge, and in particular scientific knowledge, on the basis of its history, its sociogenesis, and especially the psychological origins of the notions and operations upon which it is based."[17] This epistemological domain had been prepared by the research of genetic psychology, and it

17. When Piaget wrote these words about epistemology being "more and more the work of scientists," he was no doubt aware of the similarities between his general position and the stated views of numerous other social scientists and philosophers of science, including most probably G. H. Mead, Karl Popper, and R. K. Merton.

was conceived as differing from the older, speculative epistemological domain in the same way that science and philosophy differ, namely by "but one distinctive criterion": whereas science "is concerned with particular questions," philosophy "would tend toward total knowledge" in a quest that is, "perhaps forever, an affair of provisional synthesis and of partly subjective synthesis, because it is in fact dominated by value judgments which are nonuniversal but peculiar to certain collectivities and even to certain individuals."[18] From that basic difference, Piaget reckoned, there follow two cardinal distinctions of procedure. First, the scientist will try to take one problem at a time, rather than presume to talk "about everything all at once"; second, the scientist will not proceed with efforts to solve any problem "until agreement is reached among all researchers on facts or deductions." As a result of these procedural rules (pragmatic conventions, one might say), "science advances, whereas philosophy either keeps harping on itself or benefits from the progress of particular solutions" that have been provided by science (Piaget [1970c] 1977, 26, 93–95; Piaget [1967] 1971, 362).[19]

All of the sciences, including the nomothetic members of the "human and social sciences," benefit from the advantages of the same standardized methodical procedures for investigating particularized problems—experimentation, systematic observation, "algorithmic deduction," and so forth—which sharing, in fact, constitutes a major part of the unity of science. Not that we should advocate or accept the "false unity" proposed by the logical-positivist reduction, Piaget cautioned. Nevertheless, there is a unity among the sciences (or at least among those that are nomothetic), not only because of shared methods but also because of the way they intersect with each other in relations of interdependency. They form a "circle of science," the closure of this circle being finally achieved with the insertion of a scientific epistemology between mathematics on the one side and psychology on the other. The systematic unity of the sciences "is to be

18. It may be noted that this statement is *not* consonant with the statement given by quotations in the preceding paragraph. In fact, whereas Piaget would attempt to restrict the question of knowledge to that which is accepted as knowledge in the particular moment of a scientific "community," he would also insist on a universal, nonprovisional, nonsubjective, and value-neutral scientific knowledge. I shall return to this matter shortly.

19. In turn, philosophy can sometimes provide scientists with lessons of "the benefits of 'critical' reflection, which was given new life by Kant's Copernican revolution" (Piaget [1970c] 1977, 91). This enunciation exemplifies a general feature of Piaget's writing about issues epistemological—namely, the paucity of reference to post-Kantian philosophical argument other than varieties of positivism and logical empiricism, most of which he rejected. There is no more than passing reference to Hegel, Nietzsche, Husserl, Heidegger, or the late Wittgenstein.

conceived as a cyclic order," and this ordering represents the achievement of the epistemological integration of subject and object: a circumscription defined by the sequence of domains from mathematics to physics to biology to sociology (and related disciplines) to psychology, and finally to "genetic epistemology," which connects with the mathematical, closes the circle, and relates the cognitive-behavioral process of the knowing subject, as psychosocial, biophysical subject, to the structures of the formative processes of the mathematical, physical, biological (etc.), objects of knowledge (Piaget [1970c] 1977, 90–94, 116–20, 128; see also Piaget 1970a and Piaget [1970b] 1974).

By his own account, Piaget's "fundamental hypothesis" has been the existence of a basic parallelism according to which integration of subject and object is achieved (and the circle of science made sensible). In *Biology and Knowledge* he asked: "Does the human child, during its period of mental growth, only manifest characteristics that are transmitted to it by language, its family, and its school, or does the child itself provide spontaneous productions which may have had some influence, if generalized, on more primitive societies than our own?" (Piaget [1967] 1971, 83). His answer—an answer he sometimes treated as conjecture but other times as assumptive principle—was affirmative. The "fundamental hypothesis" of his epistemological project, for which the numerous experiments conducted under his auspices presumably supply confirmatory evidence, proposes that "there is a parallelism between the progress made in the logical and rational organization of knowledge," which is a sociohistorical dimension, "and the corresponding formative psychological processes" of child development, which constitute a biographic or ontogenic dimension. Such hypothesis, he acknowledged, calls for the "biogenetic" approach of "reconstituting human history," including "the history of human thinking in prehistoric man"; but the "field of biogenesis is not available to us," hence we must "do as the biologists do and turn to ontogenesis." Thus, stimulated in part by a common conception of the impact that embryology had had on general morphology and the thesis of evolution in biological science, Piaget invoked a supposition of the relation between "ontogenic" and "phylogenic" processes: if not that ontogeny recapitulates phylogeny, as Haeckel had wrongly argued, then that ontogenic and phylogenic sequences move in parallel (Piaget 1970a, 13; Piaget [1970c] 1977, 23–25, 105–6; Piaget [1936] 1963, 407).[20]

20. Occasionally, it is true, Piaget admitted that "in detail" this parallelism "remains far from exact" and that he may have tended to exaggerate it (see, e.g., Piaget [1970c] 1977, 25). But in the substance of his own argumentation of "genetic epistemology," for which the parallelism is a major stanchion, he offered no qualifications of consequence.

With the foregoing as framework, Piaget's account of the genesis and development of knowledge unfolds in a seemingly simple and straightforward way. As mentioned already, he rejected the passivity of the empiricist view, which he described as "the myth of the sensorial origin of knowledge." Rather, "we only know an object by acting on it and transforming it," which is accomplished through certain cognitive operations. To begin with, Piaget argued, it is necessary to distinguish between two different but complementary "aspects of thinking." One is "the figurative aspect," that is, "an imitation of states taken as momentary and static"; these are, "above all, perception, imitation, and mental imagery" (or "interiorized imitation"). The other aspect of thinking is "the operative aspect," which results in "transformations from one state to another" and includes both "actions themselves" and "the intellectual operations." The operative aspect is always dominant: "Any state can be understood only as the result of certain transformations or as the point of departure for other transformations." Perception issues in no new knowledge unless some operation is performed on that which is perceived. Thus, knowing is an "essentially active" process that involves one of two sorts of action (and frequently both).[21] The object to be known can be transformed by "physical action," that is, by "modifying its positions, its movements, or its characteristics in order to explore its nature"; and it can be transformed through "logico-mathematical action," which consists of processes of "enriching the object with characteristics or new relationships which retain its characteristics or previous relationships, yet completing them by systems of classification, numerical order, measure, and so forth." The "cognitive functions," according to Piaget, are simultaneously "the outcome of organic autoregulation, reflecting its essential mechanisms, and the most highly differentiated organs of this regulation at the core of interactions with the environment." Thus:

> Knowing reality means constructing systems of transformations that correspond, more or less adequately, to reality. They are more or less isomorphic to transformations of reality. The transformational structures of which knowledge consists are not copies of the transformations in reality; they are simply possible isomorphic models among which experience can enable us to choose. Knowledge, then, is a system of transformations that become progressively adequate. (Piaget 1970a, 15)

---

21. Piaget rejected the "copy theory of knowledge" because "the only way to know the model is by copying it," and very quickly "we are caught in a circle, unable ever to know whether our copy of the model is like the model or not" (Piaget 1970a, 15; Piaget [1967] 1971, 6–8, 361–62; Piaget [1936] 1963, 375).

Or, as Piaget stated the matter in *Biology and Knowledge*, knowledge is "a system of real interactions reflecting the autoregulatory organization of life just as much as the things themselves do" (Piaget [1970c] 1977, 67; Piaget 1970a, 14–15; Piaget [1967] 1971, 26–27).

In many respects Piaget's argument suffers from an astounding lapse of precision. Perhaps some part of this looseness can be attributed to inconcinnities of enunciation. Yet there are questions of underlying formulation that require careful, mutually congruent answers. For example, if, as proposed by Piaget, "to know" is an "outcome of organic autoregulation," then how to know independently that set of conditions *is* "organic autoregulation"? Where does one stand epistemologically? Or, consider the longer passage quoted above: the two "transformational structures," one as knowledge and the other as reality, supposedly exist in parallel and are related as *possible* isomorphs; but how to judge "correspondence"? And from what site can one judge the hypothesis of "progressive adequacy" proposed in the characterization of knowledge as "a system of transformations that become progressively adequate"?[22] How did Piaget escape, or suppose that he had escaped, his own criticism of the so-called copy theory of knowledge? Questions such as these are, in a sense, "nonquestions" within the Piagetian framework, for that framework refers at its foundation to a naturalistic presupposition. To an extent, Piaget has acknowledged as much. Thus, while he has described his project as "attempting to interpret knowledge in terms of its own construction, which is no longer an absurd method [as it was before epistemology became scientific] since knowledge is *essentially construction*" (Piaget [1967] 1971, 362), he has also remarked—in response to his own query "Do relations have objective independent existence?"—that "it is nearly impossible to understand and justify the validity of our knowledge without presupposing the existence of relations" (Piaget [1970c] 1977, 23). A naturalistic standard is presumed by his ability to distinguish "rational systems" from "myths and ideologies" (139); likewise, such a standard informs the assertion that "the true is not egocentric and must not remain anthropocentric," but is simply "organization of the real" (Piaget [1967] 1971, 362). Further evidence is provided

---

22. In another passage already quoted, it may be remembered, Piaget spoke without qualification of "the progress made in the logical and rational organization of knowledge" (Piaget 1970a, 13). Nearly in the same breath, however, he also denied that his psychological-epistemological framework had anything to do with determining "whether or not a certain state of knowledge is superior to another state" (12–13). Such determination "is one for logicians or for specialists" within their own "realm of science."

by his general prescription, "What we must try to do . . . is not to get away from nature, for no one can escape nature, but to penetrate it gradually with the aid of science," since, "despite all that philosophers say, nature is still very far from having yielded up all of her secrets" (362). And again:

> Explaining a phenomenon by means of a set of conditions considered as causal amounts to showing, on the one hand, through what transformations it was produced and, on the other, how the new aspects of the result correspond to certain transmissions from the initial stages. This dual aspect of production and conservation is characteristic of operational [i.e., knowing subject] as well as causal [i.e., object] transformations, and is evident in both by the fact that the construction in question seems necessary. Seen genetically, the operations transform the real and thus correspond to what the subject can do to the objects in his deductive or deductible manipulations, which are at first material but susceptible of progressively formal refinement. Causality, on the other hand, expresses what the objects do as they act on one another and on the subject. There must, therefore, be an intimate relationship between these two kinds of actions; otherwise the logico-mathematical constructions of the subject would never meet with reality, while reality would modify the subject's operations without his knowing it. (Piaget with Garcia [1971] 1974; 1–2)

(But how do we know, one might ask, that "reality" does *not* "modify the subject's operations without his knowing it"?)

This naturalistic premise is also the source of Piaget's "protection" against relativism. He has acknowledged that his work is "characterized by a certain culture, a certain language, and so forth"—hence, that it "remains essentially conjectural until we have furnished comparative material for control purposes" (Piaget [1970c] 1977, 61). This amounts to admission of at least the possibility of cultural, linguistic, and other contingencies of his research product; but the proposed solution to that limitation consists in the husbanding of cross-cultural, cross-linguistic, and other "comparative material." Presumably, the Piagetian "genetic epistemologist" will serve as the grand translator across those materials and will extricate valid conclusions from them. Once again, then, we are confronted with a formulation in which a claim of privilege is quietly asserted: a certain contingency is permitted in regard to the intricacies of the object of knowledge, but not, ultimately, in regard to the place and practice of the Piagetian knower. Piaget's epistemology is purportedly nothing less than "the theory of valid knowledge," and, although knowledge "always forms a process" and is never final, this "process" is nonetheless "essentially the passage of a lesser to a greater validity" (Piaget [1970c] 1977, 7–8).[23] That itself is unquestioned by his "genetic epistemologist."

The pedagogic lesson would seem to be the by-now-familiar admonition that one must not ask about the warrant of basic framework and central claims of science *qua* scientific activity in the here and now; rather, one proceeds with the business of science within that framework and because of those claims. As to axiological implications of that commitment, especially in regard to an ethic, the prescribed conclusion was given in Piaget's suggestion concerning the definition or selection of values to be invoked as standards in decision-making and policy execution: "It is uncertain whether the present dominating tendencies of philosophy would prove of great assistance in this respect"; but "if in ideologies and metaphysics we wish to achieve the common denominators of human values, it would be better to turn to comparative sociology than to philosophy necessarily tainted by a more or less important subjective coefficient" (Piaget [1970c] 1977, 125).

Approached in its own terms, Piaget's naturalistic account of the process of knowledge relies heavily on the hypothesis of parallelism between "ontogenic" and "phylogenic" sequences—that is, between the sequence of knowledge-constituting acts performed by the child in ontogenic or biographic development and the sequence of "progressively adequate" constructions and organizations of knowledge as such in human history. Ironically, as Gould has told us, "Piaget's contemporary explanation of parallels between ontogeny and phylogeny harks back to the earliest theory of all— the Meckel-Serres law of early nineteenth-century *Naturphilosophie* and transcendental morphology," according to which the parallels are attributed "not to any interaction of one sequence with another (as Haeckel was later to require), but to a common constraint—the single direction of all development—acting separately on two independent sequences" (Gould 1977, 147).[24] For Piaget the historical and the biographical are related

---

23. The argument is similar to Popper's (see chapter 2, section 3, above), and of course Popper and Piaget face the same quandary: how to know what is "lesser" and what is "greater validity" (or "verisimilitude")? What, and who, constitutes the standard according to which the alleged "passage" *can be* passage (i.e., in the first instance a traversing that marks simple "difference," and in the second instance one that marks nonrandom "difference")? This is the criticism, it may be noted, that Piaget himself leveled against the "copy theory of knowledge" (see, e.g., Piaget 1970a, 15; Piaget [1967] 1971, 6–8, 361–62; Piaget [1936] 1963, 375).

24. This was the form of explanation preferred also by the Gestalt psychologist Koffka (e.g., [1924] 1928, 46–51), whose "correspondence" theory was presented in studies of child development a few years before the appearance of Piaget's

neither by the asymmetry of an analytic reduction nor by that of a recapitulative process; rather, the existence of parallel sequences of development is understood as a consequence of the basic orderedness and uniformity of nature: parallel sequences obeying the same law, as if they were "double aspects" of a common underlying order.[25] However, his deployment of this argument of parallelism does not withstand careful scrutiny. On the issue of the priority of "language" or "logic," for example, he has steadfastly championed the view that logic (i.e., a rudimentary or "semi-logic") develops prior to language; results of his experimental studies of child development allegedly evidence this view.

Yet one cannot fail to witness a curious disjuncture in the meaning of the phrase "prior to language." On the one hand, in his child-development studies the phrase means "prior to the child's acquisition or learning of language," in the sense of a hearing/speaking performance. On the other hand, Piaget also sought to render the epistemological implication of that phrase as "prior to the development of language *as such*," that is, to extend it to the genetic dimension in the "phylogenic" or historical sense. Such extension, it may be recalled, is the constitution of that which he designated the "fundamental hypothesis" of his epistemological project: that "there is a parallelism between the progress made in the logical and rational organization of knowledge" in the historical or "phylogenic" dimension and "the corresponding formative psychological processes" of the development of the child (Piaget 1970a, 13). But since the evidentiary basis of his position derived only from the "ontogenic" dimension, this "hypothesis" could achieve "validation" only in the guise of a transformation to the status of presupposition—namely, the naturalistic presupposition that both sequences develop "in parallel" because both are a function of a singular developmental force operating within common constraints.

Moreover, even in regard to the "ontogenic" or biographic dimension, Piaget's evidentiary foundation is suspect. In order to answer the question of "logic-language" priority, according to his design, we must "look to see whether there is any logical behavior in children before language develops"—in other words, "whether the coordinations of their actions reveal a logic of classes, reveal an ordered system, reveal correspondence structures," and so forth. If we do "find logical structures in the coordinations

Language and Thought of the Child. No doubt Piaget was aware of Koffka's work, but to what extent the latter's "correspondence" theory was taken explicitly as a model I do not know.

25. Cf. Piaget's discussions of the formations of "intelligence" (Piaget [1936] 1963, 407–19) and "the evolution of reasoning power" (Piaget [1967] 1971, 77–80).

of actions in small children even before the development of language, we are not in a position to say that the logical structures are derived from language" (Piaget 1970a, 8–9). But there are some obvious queries to be asked here. *Whose* "logic," as such, would be "revealed" in those observations of "logical behavior in children," the child's or the observer's? When observing "logical behavior" *as* a manifestation of logic, is not the observer a linguistic observer? And is there no language already embedded in the structured world within and by which the infant is cast? Where, in short, is the language-free site of "child development" and "psychological observation"? Piaget rightly argued against the qualification of "intelligence" or "reasoning faculty" as a one-sided mentalist symboling function; but he failed to appreciate the other half of this criticism—namely, that the world of human activity even in its nonconscious structures of the unsaid is not devoid of language.[26]

Piaget said that "the major objection" which philosophers have raised against his "discipline of genetic epistemology" consists in the assertion

---

26. In support of his argument that "well-developed logical thinking" develops "even without thinking," Piaget (1970a, 46) has cited the work of Hans Furth (1966) with children who are "deaf and dumb," the contention being that such children experience (in Piaget's words) "a certain delay in the development of logical structures"—which is "not surprising since the social stimulation" of those children is "so limited"—but otherwise "the development of the logical structures is similar." Again one must remember the *parole-langue* distinction, and raise questions about the embeddedness of language in the world into which any child enters. Indeed, what sense does it make to say "thinking without language"? Is language only the written word we see, the spoken word we hear? In fairness to Furth, it should be noted that he himself usually qualified his argument as pertaining only to a "verbal language" of speaking/hearing. Thus, for example: "The phenomenon of deaf children and adolescents without a verbal language should be a source of constant wonderment at the inventive power of the human intellect. We hearing persons have been exposed to the verbal language of our society and can be considered fortunate that ready symbols are supplied to us" (Furth 1966, 198). In this sense of "verbal language" Furth concluded that "deaf people's intelligence can obviously not be explained as due to language" but must be due to such "nonverbal symbolism" as "visual, kinesthetic, and gestural symbols." Nevertheless, there is confusion in Furth's formulation, too, as evidenced by his ultimate conclusion: "Thinking develops through living contact with the environment regardless of the *presence or absence* of a ready-made linguistic symbol system"; and "most deaf children grow up without a ready-made symbol system for communication and hence without that abstract system of symbols by which we refer to concepts. They are *largely left to their own devices* for communication with others and for internal thinking" (198–99; emphases added). (The issues adumbrated here, it may be noted, intersect with the "private-language" debate; see, e.g., the papers collected in Jones 1969).

that its central project of "tracing the development of ideas or the development of operations" is a proper activity for the historian and the psychologist but is of "no direct concern to epistemologists" (Piaget 1970a, 1). Perhaps some philosophers have objected in that fashion. So stated, however, it is hardly the major objection. There are numerous flaws in Piaget's construction of a scientific epistemology, many of which appear as inconsistencies at various levels of his argumentation. The *fundamental* inconsistency is located in his failure to address the problem of his own epistemological site from which he made *his* claim to know, in a straightforward way, that which constitutes the formation of scientific knowledge. It is here that one encounters the central objection to his "genetic epistemology": his construction supposes that the *basic* questions of the possibility and the warranting of a true or valid knowledge have been answered *already*, and that the text of this answer has been preserved in the methodical form of science itself. It was the presupposition of an already founded naturalistic psychologism that served him as putative insulation against the threat of relativism, for example, and it afforded insulation only insofar as he refused to allow it to be subjected to the doubt even of a clarifying inquiry. Piaget relied on what the logicians call the fallacy of *hysteron proteron* ("the later earlier"), that is, the fallacy of adopting an implication or consequence of that which is to be demonstrated as a premise of the demonstration itself. Clearly such a "solution" is specious (though not uncommon in contemporary philosophy of science). In the words of a well-known critic—not of Piaget alone but of his general form of "solution"—the "idea of an epistemology based on a science, on psychology in particular, is revoltingly absurd," because to "believe in a psychological epistemology amounts to believing that we are allowed to accept the results of one particular science in order to legitimate the claims of any science to objectivity or to endow with meaning all sciences, and this obviously involves a vicious circle" (Kolakowski 1975, 6–7).[27]

3. CLAUDE LÉVI-STRAUSS (b. 1908)

To say of Claude Lévi-Strauss that he is an anthropologist, even the most celebrated and controversial anthropologist, is to offer a paltry description, if by that appellation one means simply the specialist of a department of social science. Lévi-Strauss has been no ordinary anthropologist, though

---

27. Kolakowski was here speaking for Husserl, as well as for himself, and referring to no one psychologistic claimant in particular. In a subsequent passage, however, he remarked, quite rightly, that Piaget's construction harbors a "generic relativism" despite Piaget's efforts of insulation (Kolakowski 1975, 26–28).

clearly he has been a student of *anthrōpos*. There are many among his nominal colleagues, no doubt, who would prefer to say of Lévi-Strauss (as others would say analogously of Leo Strauss) that he has been other than a social scientist; for it must seem to them that in his work the lines separating philosopher, artist, bricoleur, critic, and scientist have been uncomfortably blurred or even made nonexistent. His work has posed certain challenges to the self-understandings of anthropology—indeed, of social science in general. From the viewpoint of his critics, the Lévi-Straussian project fails to measure up to expected and proper standards of social science. To begin with, he has conveyed himself by a prose that is hardly concordant with the usual tenets of scientific writing. The magisterial *Tristes Tropiques* (1955a) contrasted markedly with the earlier *Elementary Structures of Kinship* (1949a), and subsequent works such as the *Mythologiques* have continued the "unorthodox style." Lévi-Strauss's writing is at once playful and serious. It is replete with subtle configuration and indirection, double entendre and pun, evocation and allusion; it is carefully orchestrated; it conveys the common root of poetics and poietics. This "style" is intended not as embellishment, nor as still another lame attempt to "bridge the gap" between "science" and "culture," but as a deliberate communication of meaning integrally and inseparably "form" as well as "content." To many of his nominal colleagues in social science, however, the communication is unacceptable: his "style" is as mystifying as his "substance" is mystical.

The Lévi-Straussian challenge goes to the core of the activity of science. At one level, his work can be read as an attack on biologistic assumptions of the social, whereby "primitive" and "civilized," "mythic" and "scientific" thought are posited as stations on an ascending road of human evolution. By the same token, Lévi-Strauss has attacked relativistic doctrine in a most vigorous and, for some, appealing way; as Bauman has said of Lévi-Strauss's program, the "pledge to get rid once and for ever of the troublesome ghost of relativism was only one, though the most obvious, of its advantages" (Bauman 1973, 67). In short, his work addresses a variety of disputes with particular themes and views in social-science theory, all of them interrelated in terms of "the place of the human in the natural order." But his challenge extends beneath those disputes, to the terrain of prevailing conceptions of the constitution of scientific theory. Is theory simply the description, the so-called parametric description, of associations and correlations among existent observables synchronically and diachronically arranged, that is, "explanatory" accountings of how much entity Y (or property Y of entity Q) changes when entity X (or property X) changes by a certain quantity? In answering negatively, Lévi-Strauss has referred us to a lesson of one of *"mes trois maitresses"*: If the appearance and the essence of reality are one and the same, then what is the point of a science? It is this rhetorical question, more than any other apprehended "component" or "aspect" of Lévi-Strauss's work, that has provoked charges of mysticism, chicanery, and antiscientism. The bias to which this question is a direct challenge is deeply seated (witness theory-poor enterprises defending steadfastly their impoverishment), and no doubt many of those who were at one time or another enticed by the celebrity of "anthropologist as hero" are adhering once again to their earlier views of the constitution of theory.[28] But it must be said that if, from the point of view of anthropological research, some or all of Lévi-Strauss's work has been "a splendid failure" (as Edmund Leach once said of *The Elementary Structure*), though a failure nonetheless, it has been so within an enterprise where successes generally have been measured by the criteria of an expeditionary force.

The bulk of Lévi-Strauss's writing consists of detailed investigations of mythic thought (e.g., 1962a; 1962b; 1964a; 1966; 1968; 1971). His object in this massive undertaking has been the demonstration of a rather bold hypothesis. As he argued in the second volume of *Mythologiques:*

> The demarcative features exploited by the myths do not consist so much of things themselves as of a body of common properties, expressible in geometrical terms and transformable one into another by means of operations which constitute a sort of algebra. If this tendency towards abstraction can be attributed to mythic thought itself, instead of being . . . wholly imputable to the theorizing of the mythologist, it will be agreed that we have reached a point where mythic thought transcends itself and, going beyond images retaining some relationship with concrete experience, operates in a world of concepts which have been released from any such obligation, and combine with each other in free association: by this I mean that they combine not with reference to any external reality but according to the affinities or incompatibilities existing between them in the architecture of the mind. (Lévi-Strauss [1966] 1973, 473)

This is to say, he has reasoned that if one could demonstrate conclusively that "human mind" is "bound and determined in all its operations" in this

---

28. I do not mean to discount those few who have attempted to respond constructively to Lévi-Strauss. Legessee (1973) is one who, though not a disciple of the one-time French guru, has taken him seriously in a study of the "Gada system" of the Borana. Another example is Kelly's *Etoro Social Structure*, a study of a society in which the "structural form which the lineage presents to us at any given point in time is . . . an explicit denial of the processes by which it emerges as a distinct, bounded unit" (Kelly 1977, 71).

realm called "mythic thought," then, "a fortiori, it must be so everywhere" (Lévi-Strauss 1963, 630).

I shall not attend to the details of Lévi-Strauss's studies of the hundreds of myths that he has catalogued. Rather, I shall direct attention to his mode of concept formation, to his concept of structure and its implications, and to the epistemological stance wherefrom he can allegedly know the reality of human thought ("scientific" as well as "mythic"), and indeed all of human culture, as a network of exchanges of information, without suffering the self-annihilations of the relativist dilemma.

Throughout his work, Lévi-Strauss has propounded a distinctive view of the constitution of reality. It is a view that he has understood from his famous "three mistresses"—geology ("the mother and wet-nurse of history"), Marx, and Freud—and from developments in the study of language beginning with Saussure's 1916 critique of atomistic conceptions of language. Of the trio, Lévi-Strauss has said that each showed him that "understanding consists in the reduction of one type of reality to another," that that which is most obvious is never the true, and that the nature of the true "is already apparent in the care which it takes to evade our detection." The pertinent issues, of course, are those of rationalism and empiricism— the problem of "the relation . . . between reason and sense-perception"— and Lévi-Strauss has sought to reinstate within the world of a heavily empiricist social science the ratio of *Vernunft*. His goal, purportedly of the same cloth as the goals of geology, Marx, and Freud, has been the construction of "a sort of *super-rationalism* in which sense-perceptions will be integrated into reasoning and yet lose none of their properties" (Lévi-Strauss [1955a] 1963, 59–62).

The crucible of Lévi-Strauss's attempted resolution of the "sense-experience" versus "reason" duality consists of a particular mode of concept formation, the exemplary product of which is his concept of "structure" (see, e.g., Lévi-Strauss [1953] 1967; Lévi-Strauss [1956] 1967; Lévi-Strauss [1958] 1967; Lévi-Strauss [1962b] 1966). This mode of concept formation may be referred to as "relational," as opposed to the "atomistic" conception of discrete entities having discrete particle-properties.[29] That is, reality is conceived not in terms of entities having discrete and independent identities, each of which bear upon one another positively or negatively in greater or smaller magnitude of intensity, duration, and consequence, but rather in terms of relations that constitute, in a relational field or region,

---

29. Leach has depicted the atomistic concept of "society" or "culture" (depending on the social scientist's predilection) as "a totality made up of a number of discrete, empirical 'things,' of rather diverse kinds, e.g., groups of people, 'institutions,' customs," and so forth (Leach 1961, 6).

the specific identities of entities-in-the-world. The quiddity of a thisness or a thatness is always constituted within and by a relational field. Thus, it was with such constitutionality in mind that Lévi-Strauss argued, in a previously quoted passage, that "the demarcative features exploited by the myths do not consist so much of things themselves as a body of common properties, expressible in geometrical terms and transformable one into another by means of operations which constitute a sort of algebra."[30] In Lévi-Strauss's view, the fundament of reality is "ordering"—sets of basic codes and their transformations—and the basic fabric of human thought, whether "primitive" or "scientific," is one of classifying and naming, that is, the construction of classes, which is to say relations, that articulate the mutual demarcations (connections) of all events and objects in the world *as* demarcated (connected) events and objects. Quoting a turn-of-the-century ethnographer's account of a Pawnee's "penetrating comment that 'All sacred things must have their place,' " Lévi-Strauss remarked further:

> It could even be said that being in their place is what makes them sacred for if they were taken out of their place, even in thought, the entire order of the universe would be destroyed. Sacred objects therefore contribute to the maintenance of order in the universe by occupying the places allocated to them. Examined superficially and from the outside, the refinements of ritual can appear pointless. They are explicable by a concern for what one might call "micro-adjustment"—the concern to assign every single creature, object or feature to a place within a class. (Lévi-Strauss [1962b] 1963, 10)[31]

Such remarks must not be misunderstood as founded in a solipsistic charade, by any means. As I shall try to make clear later, Lévi-Strauss's epistemological position hardly countenances an idealist devolution of all to an "individual self." For the moment, however, it will suffice to note simply that his remark is about the "order of the universe" in human thought, as indeed the bulk of his project concerns human thought and especially the relation of "the cultural" to "the natural" in human thought. In the words

---

30. This invocation of mathematics is not gratuitous (although Lévi-Strauss has done little to develop the connections). I shall argue later the appropriate uses of certain varieties (e.g., topological) of mathematical representations of theoretical statements developed on the basis of this "relational" mode of concept formation.

31. Thus, at one level of comparison, mythic thought demands a total determination of events and objects, whereas scientific thought "allows" in its "micro-adjustments" a reverse of indeterminacy and random occurrences. This comparison is sometimes called upon as testimony to the advancement of scientific over primitive thought.

of his own depiction of his project, he does not question "the undoubted primacy of infrastructures" but leaves the study of them to disciplines other than ethnology, which is "first of all psychology" and is not principally concerned with "infrastructures." The reality of the human world is jointly determined by "techno-economic-demographic" factors, on the one hand, and by activities of human thinking, on the other; his concern is principally with the latter, as they intersect with the former. The infrastructures may be of "undoubted primacy," he has averred, nevertheless events in the world—human practices, behaviors—do not follow directly from those infrastructures but are mediated by a "conceptual scheme by the operation of which matter and form, neither with any independent existence, are realized as structures, that is as entities which are both empirical and intelligible." By his studies of "mythic thought," Lévi-Strauss has intended to contribute "to this theory of superstructures, scarcely touched on by Marx" (Lévi-Strauss [1962b] 1963, 130, 66; Lévi-Strauss [1972] 1978; Lévi-Strauss [1955b] 1967).

Human practices and events—phenomenal reality—are constituted relationally; that is, relations demarcate the features of phenomenal reality *as* particularized events, practices, and objects in the world. However, the bases of the constitution of these relations exist not at the level of phenomena as such but at an underlying, nonobservable level of structuration as logical relations that define theoretical possibilities of events, practices, and objects in the world. This proposal, which reproduces the premise of the nonidentity of appearance and essence, underwrites Lévi-Strauss's method of investigation, which "consists in the following operations":

1. define the phenomenon under study as a relation between two or more terms, real or supposed;
2. construct a table of possible permutations between these terms;
3. take this table as the general object of analysis which, at this level only, can yield necessary connections. The empirical phenomenon considered at the beginning being only one possible combination among others, the complete system of which must be reconstructed beforehand. (Lévi-Strauss [1962a] 1963, 16; see also Lévi-Strauss [1955b] 1967, 207–9)

The *table of relations,* completed by permutational elaboration, and not the original phenomenon, becomes "the general object of analysis." The phenomenon exists as a "surface structure," an observable relational field, that manifests an underlying or "deep structure." Indeed, this deep structure, composed of a basic code together with rules of transformation, constitutes the *very possibility* not simply of the given phenomenon but of a large though finite permutational range of phenomena, of which the given case is an instance (a member of the table), and it is that deep structure, the entire table of relations, that is to be understood. Any one of the possible phenomena of a deep structure may or may not be manifested as an observable event or object in the world, for the event is a specific spatio-temporal localization, a historically contingent occurrence.

> No doubt, the factors which determine the formation and the respective growth rates of the different parts of a plant are present in the seed. But the "dormancy" of the seed, that is, the unforeseeable time which will elapse before the mechanism begins operating, does not depend upon its structure, but on an infinitely complex pattern of conditions relating to the individual history of each seed and all kinds of external influences. (Lévi-Strauss [1966] 1973, 474)

In short, the presence of the concrete event, the "lived event," is the historically contingent outcome of complex interactions between the deep structure that "enables" a range of possible events and the determining factors (techno-economic-demographic, etc.) of the existing environmental conditions. Analysis of the "table of possible permutations," that is, investigation at the level of deep structure, and "at this level only, can yield *necessary* connections" (Lévi-Strauss [1962a] 1963, 16; emphasis added).

Eventuality is dependent on deep structure, but in its historical contingency it differs from deep structure as *parole* differs from *langue* (Saussure [1916] 1959), as "message" differs from "code" (Jakobson and Halle 1956), as "usage" differs from "schema" (Hjelmslev [1943] 1961), as diachrony differs from synchrony.[32] The reality of "myth" consists in the "tale" and the structure that is beneath it (and beneath all other tales of the same "kind"): as tale (*parole*) its time is irreversible, it "tells what happened"; as deep structure (*langue*) its time is reversible, it is brought to light again and again with each telling. Whereas each telling of the tale is an unrepeatable utterance, historically contingent and concrete, the structure undergirding it is repeated in each telling (and repeatable in each possible telling), and the myth as both *parole* and *langue* is timeless.[33] At a

32. This is not to say, certainly, that Lévi-Strauss's formulations are equivalent to those of Saussure, Jakobson, or Hjelmslev (or that the latter are equivalent among themselves).

33. Lévi-Strauss has attempted clarification of this "timelessness" by the example of "a comparison between myth and what appears to have largely replaced it in modern societies, namely, politics":

fundamental level of inquiry, therefore, the huge diversity of myths-as-tales that appears to our ears is in fact illusory. The communications of the tales (or of any phenomena of culture, all of which exist as information exchange) seem to be saying an enormous diversity of often confused messages; but what we witness in that welter of appearance is simply the extensionality of topological orderings—the metaphoricality, the metonymy, and so forth, of a rather small number of underlying structurations of basic codes.[34]

"The distinctive character of myths," according to Lévi-Strauss, "is precisely emphasis," the emphasis that results from "the multiplication of one level by one or several others, and which, as in language, has as its function to signify signification." Myths are textual governors of meaning. Like kinship and other cultural texts, they simultaneously differentiate and interrelate experience. They classify and reclassify, construct and recon-

> When the historian refers to the French Revolution, it is always as a sequence of past happenings, a non-reversible series of events the remote consequences of which may still be felt at present. But to the French politician, as well as to his followers, the French Revolution is both a sequence belonging to the past—as to the historian—and a timeless pattern which can be detected in the contemporary French social structure and which provides a clue for its interpretation, a lead from which to infer future developments. (Lévi-Strauss [1955b] 1967, 205; cf. Schaff [1971] 1976, 3–42)

34. The study of myths "confronts the student with a situation which at first appears contradictory. On the one hand it would seem that in the course of a myth anything is likely to happen. There is no logic, no continuity. Any characteristic can be attributed to any subject; every conceivable relation can be found. With myth, everything becomes possible. But on the other hand, this apparent arbitrariness is belied by the astounding similarity between myths collected in widely different regions" (Lévi-Strauss [1955b] 1967, 203–4). A related statement was made by Santillana and von Dechend, who, in discussing the prevalent tales of "Deluge" as references "to an old astronomical image, based on an abstract geometry," chide their reader as follows: "That this is not an 'easy picture' is not to be wondered at, considering the objective difficulty of the science of astronomy. But although a modern reader does not expect a text on celestial mechanics to read like a lullaby, he insists on his capacity to understand mythical 'images' instantly, because he can respect as 'scientific' only page-long approximation formulas, and the like. He does not think of the possibility that equally relevant knowledge might once have been expressed in everyday language. He never suspects such a possibility, although the visible accomplishments of ancient cultures—to mention only the pyramids, or metallurgy—should be a cogent reason for concluding that serious and intelligent men were at work behind the stage, men who were bound to have used a technical terminology" (Santillana and von Dechend 1969, 57–58).

struct.[35] As such, "mythical thought always progresses from the awareness of oppositions toward their resolution," but the oppositions are never "solved" in any final sense, rather they are transformed and relocalized with the consequence that more expansive significations are made available. Totemic myths, for example, "no doubt explain nothing and merely shift the difficulty elsewhere, but at least in so doing, appear to attenuate its crying illogicality" (Lévi-Strauss [1964a] 1969, 4–6; Lévi-Strauss [1955b] 1967, 204–6, 221, 226).[36]

That which constitutes the unity of "a myth" is not simply a particular tale but includes *all* variants commonly articulated at the level of a deep structure. The celebrated "problem of totemism," seen as the fetishistic association of a clan or tribe with one or another botanic or zoologic species

35. It is appropriate to speak of "cultural texts" in regard to Lévi-Strauss, but the suitability has its limits. Already far too much of the fetishism of catchphrases has been wrapped around the notion of "culture as text"—and not from a single source or with uniform meaning but from varieties of hermeneutic and linguistic arguments. As an example of what I mean, consider Ricoeur's (1971) comparatively careful study of the "model of the text" in relation to "meaningful action." In discussing the spoken and written word (compare William Chase Greene 1951), Ricoeur emphasized that with "written discourse, the author's intention and the meaning of the text cease to coincide. ... [T]he text's career escapes the finite horizon lived by its author." Properly formulated, that could be taken as an important insight into the process of inscription. But Ricoeur held further: "What the text says now [i.e., after escape] matters more than what the author meant to say," and writing, that is, "inscription in 'external marks,' which first appeared to alienate discourse, marks the actual spirituality of discourse." All of this is constructed from the point of view of "text" as the agent rather than from the points of view of the "writer" and the "reader" as active producer/reproducer. The latter, the true agent, has been dissolved into a reified isolated abstraction. The "meaning of a text" after it "escapes" the author's control (after it is published, for example) is in its *uses*. Writing or reading a text cannot alone accomplish the concrete reality of whatever projected differences (e.g., "a new world") the writer or reader may intend; the concrete conditions of textual reproduction (*not* "interpretation," which implies the revelation of that which is already present), which is to say *the concrete conditions of life*, must have been altered in accordance with the imaginations of that project. Notions of the written text spiritually transcending that "materializing alienation" of inscription in "external marks" are plain rubbish.

36. The last of these quotations is itself a quotation of Durkheim's *Elementary Forms*. On this matter of displacement, Greimas's remark is appropriate: "Signification is therefore nothing but such transposition from one level of language to another, from one language to a different language, and meaning is nothing but the possibility of such *transcoding*" (Greimas 1970, 13).

(e.g., see Lippert [1886–87] 1931, 560–63; Goldenweiser 1910), was in fact, according to Lévi-Strauss, an illusory problematic created from a failure to understand the structural character of myth:

> The heterogeneous beliefs and customs arbitrarily collected together under the heading of totemism do not rest on the idea of a relationship of substance between one or more social groups and one or more natural domains. They are allied to other beliefs and practices, directly or indirectly linked to classificatory schemes which allow the natural and social universe to be grasped as an organized whole. (Lévi-Strauss [1962b] 1966, 135)

The homologies are not between the entities depicted in one or another tale (the clans and the species); they are between the relations constituting those entities. That is to say, rather than "Clan A is like Species A, and Clan B is like Species B," the homology is stated correctly as "the relation 'Clan A: Clan B' is like the relation 'Species A:Species B.' " The mythic structure encompasses a range of common relational fields, or "bundles" of relations, whether these relations are seemingly definitive of "totemic" phenomena or of some other phenomenon.

I do not wish to delve very far into the intricacies of Lévi-Strauss's analyses of particular myths (some of which are less convincing than others); my object here, as in other sections of this and the previous chapter, is to examine explicit and/or implicit espistemological positions, and I must assume of the reader some familiarity with the works in question. However, a brief illustration may be usefully interjected at this point.

The illustration involves related tales recited by the Bella Bella and by the Chilcotin, neighboring peoples located in the northwestern part of North America (Kwakiutl and Salish language groups, respectively).[37] According to the Bella Bella tale, in its most developed version, a girl-child who cried too much was kidnapped one day by a cannibalistic ogress, a supernatural being who was greatly feared. The girl was treated very badly until one day she was told by a supernatural helper to gather clam siphuncles and place one on each of her fingertips. This she did and then proceeded to wave these clawlike projections at the ogress, who promptly fell down the side of a steep mountain and died. Now free from her tormentor, the girl acquired all of the ogress's property, which consisted of copper plates, furs, dressed skins, dried meats, and the like, and went off to distribute the wealth to her people. Thus was the origin of potlatch.

---

37. My recitation is based on Lévi-Strauss's own illustrative discussion in his Gildersleeve Lecture [1972] 1978.

According to the Chilcotin tale, on the other hand, a boy-child who cried too much was kidnapped by an owl-sorcerer, a benevolent supernatural being who treated his captive well. But one day the parents of this now-grown boy found him and convinced him to flee with them. The owl gave chase, so the young man placed on his fingertips some mountain-goat horns and waved these clawlike projections at his pursuer, intending to frighten him away. The startled owl fell into some water, though he did not drown, and the young man made good his escape—taking with him all of the owl's dentalia shells, previously the exclusive property of this supernatural being. Thus the origin of the Chilcotin's most precious possession, dentalia shells.

Now, the oppositions and inversions between these two tales are rather obvious: for example, a crying girl versus a crying boy; a humanlike malevolent female being versus a birdlike benevolent male being; soft, harmless, seaside clam siphuncles versus hard, harmful, landside mountain-goat horns; the ogress killed on the mountain versus the owl surviving the water; the captured treasures of landside objects versus those of seaside objects. Moreover, we can easily note the alternations in the list of oppositions: for example, the soft (female) ogress (bad) dies on a hard landside object (mountain) when threatened by a soft and harmless seaside weapon (clam siphuncles), and loses her landside treasure (copper plates, etc.); the hard (male) sorcerer (good) survives a soft seaside object (water) when threatened by a hard and harmful landside weapon (mountain-goat horns), and loses his seaside treasure (dentalia shells). Through such analyses of the relational fields manifested in these tales, Lévi-Strauss concluded that the two tales are of the same mythic structure; they share the same underlying necessary connections of basic code and rules by which one tale can be transformed into the other and indeed into numerous others. In short, two seemingly different tales—accounts of practices and objects in the world: in one case, the origin of potlatch; in the other, the origin of dentalia shells among a mountain people—are in fact constituted by the same set of codes and rules of formation/transformation.

The question why the different tales exist as such, why the different accounts of treasure, must be answered in terms of historically contingent conditions, not in terms of necessary connections (as in the mythic structure itself). To take this illustrative case of the Bella Bella and the Chilcotin that additional step, we would ask with Lévi-Strauss why the Chilcotin people

need to explain the origin of dentalia shells and why should they do it in such a devious way, by giving them a terrestrial instead of an oceanic origin? And if for some reason or another, the Bella Bella require an inverted image of mountain goat horns used as claws, why should they pick up clam siphons when their natural surroundings did provide them with a great many empirical items which could fulfill the same function? Why, too, were the Bella Bella uninterested in the origin of dentalia shells and more preoccupied with a different kind of treasure? (Lévi-Strauss [1972] 1978, 229)

The answer rests, according to Lévi-Strauss, in the historical circumstances of their respective ecological-economic matrices of life conditions. In regard to the first of those questions, for example, it is necessary to note that, whereas the Bella Bella were a coastal people (the Milbank Sound region of British Columbia) and were reluctant to venture into the Coast Mountains, the Chilcotin resided on the inland side of the mountain divide and maintained trade routes to the coastal region. Still to the east of the Chilcotin, as it happened, there resided some neighboring peoples (also Salish-speaking—e.g., the Thompson and the Coeur d'Alene) who valued dentalia shells and got them in trade from the Chilcotin. The Chilcotin, of course, relied on trading expeditions to the Bella Bella for their supply of the shells. Relative to their eastern neighbors, therefore, and "in order to protect their monopoly and to give it glamour in foreigners' eyes, the Chilcotin had a capital interest to make a fiction hold, according to which their seemingly inexhaustible supply of dentalia originated in their own land as a result of supernatural events." Inverted relationships obtain in the case of the Bella Bella situation. In each case, then, a "naturally local" object (mountain-goat horns; clam siphuncles) acts as means to the acquisition of a valued object that is not "naturally local" (dentalia shells; copper plates, furs, etc.) in a supernatural event—all of which is sensibly articulated in a structurally common though phenomenally variant explanation (Lévi-Strauss [1972] 1978, 229–30).[38]

Characterizations of Lévi-Strauss's project often designate as its central theme the "nature-culture" opposition in human thought: the question how people distinguish between, and therewith also connect, "nature" and "culture" as categories of reality. The various binary oppositions, such as "raw-cooked," "container-contained," "hot-cold," "hard-soft," and so on, are all seen to be tropological (*"figuratif"*) transformations of the "nature-culture" opposition. That theme is present, to be sure. But epistemologically

---

38. See Lévi-Strauss [1972] 1978 for additional discussion of these illustrative cases. Raymond C. Kelly incorporated a similar framework: "The organization of contradictions [in this case, the phenomenal level of the lineage being "an explicit denial of the processes by which it emerges as a distinct, bounded unit"] is the essence of social structure and . . . cultural perception of the social order expresses an ideological denial of its dialectical basis," a consequence of which is maintenance of existing relations of agnatic solidarity (Kelly 1977, 3, 71, 84, 298).

it is not the center of the Lévi-Straussian enterprise. Octavio Paz stated the matter correctly when he said that Lévi-Strauss's work purports to be "a bridge suspended between two opposite landscapes: nature and culture. Within the latter, the opposition is repeated" (Paz [1967] 1970, 81). It is at the level of this *contained* opposition—interior to the cultural antipode of that opposition that defines its space—that the structural analyses of "mythic" thought are located. It is there that one looks with Lévi-Strauss for the basic structures of (phenomenally) culturally variant conceptions of "the place of humankind" in (phenomenally) culturally variant conceptions of "the natural order." It is there, in that space of permutable oppositions that is itself one side of a parent opposition (the other side of which is noncultural nature), that the Lévi-Straussian project envisions a kind of Mendeleevian table:

> The ensemble of a people's customs has always its particular style; they form into systems. I am convinced that the number of these systems is not unlimited and that human societies, like individual beings (at play, in their dreams, or in moments of delirium), never create *absolutely*: all they can do is to choose certain combinations from a repertory of ideas which it should be possible to reconstitute. For this one must make an inventory of all the customs which have been observed by oneself or others, the customs pictured in mythology, and the customs evoked by both children and grown-ups in their games. The dreams of individuals, whether healthy or sick, and psycho-pathological behavior should also be taken into account. With all this one could eventually establish a sort of periodical chart of chemical elements, analogous to that devised by Mendeleev. In this, all customs, whether real or merely possible, would be grouped by families, and all that would remain for us to do would be to recognize those which societies had, in point of fact, adopted. (Lévi-Strauss [1955a] 1963, 160)

Within the cultural antipode of the opposition *ab origine*, in other words, one collects a wide range of observations of peoples' mental accounts and customs—"knowledge of social facts must be based on induction from individualized and concrete knowledge of social groups localized in time and space" (Lévi-Strauss [1949b] 1967, 9); these phenomenal relations comprise the data to be analyzed in terms of underlying structural relations of codifications and transformations that constitute the possibility of those phenomenal relations plus all phenomenal relations structurally akin to them.

Lévi-Strauss's project as such, however—that is, *his* mythology of human thought, *his* construction of knowledge *about* cultural knowledges of the relation of "culture" and "nature"—is situated epistemologically at that anterior level of the parent opposition between "nature" and "culture," which is the "gap" his project purportedly bridges. His concern with cultural accounts or depictions of "culture" and "nature" as categories of reality is constituted in terms of the relationship between that reality of which "nature" and "culture" are depicted as categories by one or another people and the reality that stands behind, and is presupposed by, *any* people's depiction.

Here the importance of Rousseau figures greatly. Indeed, when all is said and done about Lévi-Strauss's claimed "mistresses," there is still his "matrimony" with Rousseau (1755; 1781) in a vision of that instantaneous creation of the state of society: a threefold transition—from nature to culture, from animality to humanity, from emotion to intellect—constituted in the practice of language. It was his reading of Rousseau, he has acknowledged, that suggested to him the proper method of inquiry and, with that, a response to the "inescapable dilemma" of relativism.[39] As he remembered in his autobiographical poetic,

> I went to the ends of the earth in search of what Rousseau [1755, preface] called "the barely perceptible advances of the earliest times." Beneath and beyond the veil of the all-too-learned laws of the Bororo and the Caduveo I had gone in search of a state which, to quote once again from Rousseau, "no longer exists, perhaps may never have existed, and probably will never exist." "And yet," he goes on, "without an accurate idea of that state we cannot judge properly of our present situation." Myself luckier than he, I thought that I had come upon that state in a society then nearing its end. It would have been pointless for me to wonder whether or not it was a vestigial version of what Rousseau had in mind; whether traditional or degenerate, it brought me into contact with one of the most indigent of all conceivable forms of social and political organization. I had no need to go into its past history to discover what had maintained it at its rudimentary level—or what, as was more likely, had brought it thus far down. I had merely to focus my attention on the experiment in

---

39. "The dilemma is inescapable: either the anthropologist clings to the norms of his own group, in which case the others can only inspire in him an ephemeral curiosity in which there is always an element of disapproval; or he makes himself over completely to the objects of his studies, in which case he can never be perfectly objective, because in giving himself to all societies he cannot but refuse himself, willingly or not, to one among them" (Lévi-Strauss [1955a] 1963, 382).

sociology which was being carried out under my nose. (Lévi-Strauss [1955a] 1963, 310)[40]

This "state of Society," as a general condition (i.e., regardless of its "level"), is "inherent in mankind," according to Lévi-Strauss. But we are faced with the undeniable conclusion that "it brings evil with it," and so we must strive to answer the question "whether or not these evils are themselves inherent in that state." The answer can be gained only if we "go beyond the evidence of the injustices or abuses to which the social order gives rise and *discover the unshakeable basis of human society*." It has been Lévi-Strauss's conviction that we can best find that "unshakeable basis" through the study of "untamed" societies. Through such studies we can "construct a theoretical model of a society which corresponds to none that can be observed in reality" but which will nevertheless "help us to disentangle 'what in the present nature of Man is original, and what is artificial' " (Lévi-Strauss [1955a] 1963, 389–90; emphasis added).

It has also been Lévi-Strauss's contention that such a model will provide an effective point of reference by which the dilemma of relativism can be converted from "a danger ever present on the anthropologist's path" to the "constructive" attitude of two, only "apparently contradictory," practices: "respect for societies very different from ours, and active participation in the transformation of our own society" (Lévi-Strauss [1955a] 1963, 387–89, 391; Lévi-Strauss [1958] 1967, 330–31). But what, we may be so bold to ask, is the anchorage by which Lévi-Strauss can evade the duplication problem of relativism in his construction of such a model? If it is in terms of the projected actuality of a still-hypothetical model that the anthropologist is to apprehend "the unshakeable basis of human society," allegedly in a manner and with consequences free of the taint of self-annihilative suppositions of knowledge, then what constitutes the immunity of the process by which that model is thought in the first place? In what

---

40. Lévi-Strauss went on to say that his expected "experiment" proved to be elusive: "I had been looking for a society reduced to its simplest expression. The society of the Nambikwara had been reduced to the point at which I found nothing but human beings" (Lévi-Strauss [1955a] 1963, 310). The phrase may convey the intended pathos of a people dissolving in the juices of "civilization," nevertheless "nothing but human beings" has a rather slippery referencing. Presumably "nothing but human beings" was imagined as a state opposed to "human beings in society"—an opposition that raises the question, when does "a society of human beings" cease to exist as such and become a collection of "nothing but human beings"? Turnbull's 1972 study of the Ik both illustrates and suffers from that question.

manner has Lévi-Strauss attempted to warrant his assertions of knowledge of "deep structures"—that is to say, knowledge of the nonobvious—as true and necessary knowledge? By his own account, of course, his constructions comprise not only a "mythology" but also a "myth of mythology"; we may be sure, however, that such accounting is not a confession of the surreptitious entry of epistemological relativism.

The process by which Lévi-Strauss has proposed to anchor his knowledge constructions is one of assimilating "mind" to "nature." If we can trust his recollections over the span of three decades (e.g., Lévi-Strauss [1955a] 1963, 59–62), this epistemological preference was in place already in his youth. Having rejected the increasingly popular phenomenological doctrine, "insofar as it postulated a continuity between experience and reality" (i.e., "there is no continuity in the passage between the two"), and having rejected the also increasingly popular existentialism, because of its "indulgent attitude toward the illusions of subjectivity," he formulated a kind of monistic position, not as in the classical doctrine of singularism (the postulation of a single "level" of reality) nor in the sense of a numerical identity of real objects and sense-data of them, but as a postulation of the basic constitution both of the knowing subject's capacity of knowing and of the susceptibility of the object-to-be-known to knowledge. Speaking of his meditations during the 1920s, he remembered that he

> became convinced that . . . people and things could be apprehended in essence without losing that sharpness of outline that serves to distinguish one from the other and gives to each a decipherable structure. Knowledge was not founded upon sacrifice or barter: it consisted in the choice of those aspects of a subject which were *true*—which coincided, that is to say, with the properties of my own thought. Not at all, as the neo-Kantians claim, because my thought inevitably exerted a certain constraint on the object under study: but rather because my thought was itself such an object. Being "of this world," it partook of the same nature as that world. (Lévi-Strauss [1955a] 1963, 59)

With regard to the contrasted doctrines of "idealism" and "materialism"—and therein the question whether his notion of "*esprit*" is one or the other (a question debated both ways)—Lévi-Strauss has wanted to abandon those categories as inappropriate to his activity. His "super-rationalism" allegedly integrates, in both directions, the "sensory" with the "intellectual" (see, e.g., Lévi-Strauss [1955a] 1963, 61). The postulation of an integrity that dissolves the notion of a fundamental duality of "mind" and "matter"— the integrity of a determinative order consisting of structurations informing *all possibilities* of phenomena, thought as well as the thought-about—

supposedly affords Lévi-Strauss the security of knowing truly the "deep structures" of phenomenally variant cultural statements of "the place of culture in nature," because *his* thought, "being 'of this world,' . . . partook of the same nature as that world." Dissolution of the merely apparent gap between *his* thought and the thoughts that are the "objects" of his thinking is effected at levels beneath the "observable text," that is, at the levels of those deep structurations that commonly constitute the range of possibilities of others' (phenomenal) cultural statements and Lévi-Strauss's statements about those statements. To be sure, the destination of a Lévi-Straussian journey into the laminations of structure is a receding one; his analysis translates or transforms one text into another, *seriatum*. However, what is crucial about the journey is not "the final text," as it were, but rather the rules of operation: "It is not a question of sailing toward other lands, the whereabouts of which may be unknown and their very existence hypothetical. . . . [The] journey alone is real, not the landfall, and sea routes are replaced by the rules of navigation" (Lévi-Strauss [1964a] 1969, 25; see also Lévi-Strauss [1962b] 1966, 250).

Thus, the passage between the poles of that primary opposition that defines the limits and the connections of Lévi-Strauss's work is conducted through the basic structure of "mind"—a structure allegedly universal to human thought, and according to which Lévi-Strauss has supposed an absolute rooting beneath the relativistic surface of his knowledge statements. In other words, the putative surety of those knowledge statements turns on acceptance of his claim to have deciphered the code, the rules and relations, constituting a "periodic chart" of all human thought, both the already manifested and the possible but not yet manifested. The site of that universality and that rooting is not "mind" in the sense of an ephemeral Cartesian "mental substance," however; in Lévi-Strauss's words, the "original logic" of codification and transformation is a "direct expression of the structure of the mind (and behind the mind, probably, of the brain)" (Lévi-Strauss [1962a] 1963, 90). While the phrasing of that conjunction of "mind" and "brain" is not altogether unambiguous, it is clear from the tendency of his formulation that his monism is not, strictly speaking, a "neutral monism"—certainly not of the variety that rests on the posited existence of "*sensibilia*" as that of which "mind" and "body" are logical constructions (e.g., Russell 1921, chap. 1)—although at first glance one can read resemblances to the variety sometimes called "double-aspect theory."[41] Instead it may be described as a "super-rationalist realism" (epistemologically essentialist) in which "mind" and "body," as phenomenal existences relationally interdependent, are mutually assimilated to a universal "nature of reality." The monism consists not in a commonality of atomistic "things," of which "mind" and "body" are different complexes or arrangements, but in an essential integrity of underlying "rules of operation," an "original" and "elementary logic," by which the relational constitution of "things" and "thoughts" can occur. It is in terms of this sort of monistic framework that one might properly characterize the Lévi-Straussian project as a search for "the code of a universal brain," or for the rules of an "unconscious silence of neurological determination" (cf. Burke 1953, 46).

Within that framework, the word "nature" is meant to appear twice, and a careless reading of Lévi-Strauss can confuse that appearance of the word for a double placement of one concept (see Charbonnier [1961] 1969, 151–55). On the one hand, Lévi-Strauss has argued that "it is independently of ourselves that the great phenomena of astronomy or meteorology have their effect—an effect as discreet as it is ineluctable—in every part of the globe" (Lévi-Strauss [1955a] 1963, 126). And this:

> if it were true, as biologists hold, that the anatomical, physiological, and ethnological diversity of some two million living species may be analyzed in terms of variations of the chromosomes which are reducible to a periodicity in the distribution of four distinct groups on the molecular chain, then we could perhaps grasp the deeper reason for the special significance man has seen in the notion of species. We should understand how this idea can furnish a mode of sensory apprehension of a combination objectively given in nature, and that the activity of the mind, and social life itself, do no more than borrow it to apply to the creation of new taxonomies. (Lévi-Strauss [1962b] 1966, 137)

And, in the same vein, he has referred to a still imagined time "when we do finally succeed in understanding life as a function of inert matter" (but with the prediction that "it will be to discover that the latter has properties very different from those previously attributed to it") (247–48). But there are also passages such as the following:

> Natural conditions are not just passively accepted. What is more, they do not exist in their own right, for they are a function of the techniques and way of life of the people who define and give them a meaning by developing them in a particular direction. Nature is not in itself contradictory. It can become so only in terms of some specific human activity which takes part in it; and the characteristics of the

environment take on a different meaning according to the particular historical and technical form assumed in it by this or that type of activity. (94–95)

One might conclude from this conjunction of arguments that a serious inconsistency in the Lévi-Straussian enterprise has been brought to light. Whereas the first of those longer passages, involving reference to chromosomes and "a combination objectively given in nature," would seem to be an advocation of an objective naturalism, the last passage would seem to indicate rejection of such doctrines. (Even in this latter indication, however, the position is not clearly drawn, inasmuch as his remarks about "developing" natural conditions could be read as an implicit naturalism.) But we must take care to observe the difference in his argument between his gazing upon his subjects (Amerindian or otherwise), which is the gaze about which he reports most in his writings, and his gazing upon the conditions of his knowledge (and, indeed, his being), which is the gaze set simultaneously as presupposition and confirmational end of the entire Lévi-Straussian project. Lévi-Strauss has described, for example, a nature-culture opposition wherein a gourd is both a natural container of culture (as a ceremonial rattle, the gourd is "an instrument of sacred music . . . seen . . . as an inclusion of culture in nature") and a cultural container of nature ("as a receptacle for food and water," the gourd is a "non-sacred cooking utensil, a container intended to hold natural products, and therefore an appropriate illustration of the inclusion of nature in culture") (Lévi-Strauss [1966] 1973, 472–73). For the people among whom that construction was current, we may surmise with Lévi-Strauss that "raw food" and "water" were members of the logical space "of nature" as opposed to that "of culture." For Lévi-Strauss, on the other hand, gourd-as-natural-container-of-culture and gourd-as-cultural-container-of-nature were *both* located in the space "of culture," not in the space "of nature." However, in the symmetry of his own construction, in the space wherein *he* stands as observer/thinker of the cultural presence of such nature-culture oppositions and displacements, there is for Lévi-Strauss himself a nature-culture opposition—namely, that anterior opposition within one side of which the opposition is repeated but at a different level—and it is *this* opposition that Lévi-Strauss's project seeks to displace (resolve) through a mythic construction that *simultaneously demonstrates and partakes of* a universalist essential "nature" existent beneath all phenomenal nature-and-culture. This "nature" is, vis-à-vis Lévi-Strauss's theory of mythic construction (i.e., "myth of mythology," theory of knowledge), hypological in the sense of being beneath, and underwriting the possibility of, Lévi-Strauss's knowledge assertions.

The integrative connections between those telescoped levels of nature-culture opposition, the elucidation of which is the task of Lévi-Strauss's method of analysis from "event" to "deep structure," are established in the production of phenomena (events) of human thought and practice according to "two kinds of determinism." One kind, consisting of necessary relations, is the determinism of "mental laws," which, "not unlike those operating in the physical world, compel ideological constructs such as myths to become organized and . . . transformed in accordance with recurring patterns." The other kind consists of historically contingent relations and stems "from the ecology on the one hand, and on the other, from the techno-economic activities as well as the socio-political conditions" (Lévi-Strauss [1972] 1978, 229). From the point of view of the world of "lived events," it is difficult to sort out these two determinisms, for they are "simultaneously at work in social life."

> Behind every ideological construct, previous constructs stand out, and they echo each other back in time, not indefinitely but at least back to the fictive stage when . . . an incipient mankind thought out and expressed its first ideology. But it is equally true that at each stage of this complex process, each ideological construct becomes inflected by techno-economic conditions and is, so to speak, first attracted and then warped by it. Even if a common mechanism should exist underlying the various ways according to which the human mind operates, in each particular society and at each stage of its historical development, those mental cogwheels must lend themselves to being put in gear with other mechanisms. Observation never reveals the isolated performance of one type of wheel-work or of the other: we can only witness the results of their mutual adjustment. (Lévi-Strauss [1972] 1978, 228).[42]

But in order to comprehend "the coherence of each system of classification" that is performed in human thought and practice, we must sort through the complications of historical contingency and search for "another type of explanation, namely, constraints specific to the human mind," which are discernible as rules of codification and transformation operative of the

---

42. Lévi-Strauss was not here suggesting that "mind" is a passive reflector of "techno-economic conditions." Following the passage just quoted, he noted that when

> confronted with a given ecological and techno-economic situation, the mind does not stay inactive. It does not merely reflect it, it reacts to it and works it out into a system. Furthermore, the mind does not react only to the particular environment which it perceives through the senses. It also keeps aware of environments which are not experienced in a direct way, and it keeps aware of the ways in which other peoples react to them. (Lévi-Strauss [1972] 1978, 230).

relations of a finite set of basic codes. These rules are noncontingent; "we do not invent" them, rather "they are, so to speak, imbedded" in the myths that we analyze, and when "formulated by the analyst, they become overt manifestations of inner laws governing the minds" of listeners and tellers, readers and writers (Lévi-Strauss [1972] 1978, 227, 229).

To say that there are two kinds of determinism in the constitution of events or practices in the world is not, Lévi-Strauss has cautioned, to fall "back toward some kind of philosophical dualism" in which "ecology on the one hand and the mind on the other" are thought of "as mutually irreducible entities." Mind and the "mental constraints ever-recurring in mankind" necessarily have "natural foundations," which is to say that they "can be linked, even indirectly, to conditions prevailing in man's anatomy and physiology." The linkages are present inasmuch as "these biological aspects are also part of the environment in which mankind develops, works and thinks; and even more so as it is through his anatomy and physiology that man perceives the world outside." Consequently, according to Lévi-Strauss, it follows that the "world outside . . . can only be apprehended through sensory perception and through the processing of sensory data which takes place in the brain. *All these phenomena must share something in common* which might explain their collusion" (Lévi-Strauss [1972] 1978, 231–32; emphasis added).

As this last sentence makes clear, Lévi-Strauss was not speaking revisionally of a classical materialist or epiphenomenalist or biologistic-naturalist assimilation of "mind" to "body." The assimilative logic pertains instead to a mind-body linkage and to the intersection of those "two kinds of determinism," one necessary and one contingent, in that super-rationalist universalist "nature" that hypologically establishes the possibility *both* of Lévi-Strauss's fundamentally structured objects, events, and practices in the world *and* of his commonly fundamentally structured knowledge of them. In other words, that to which the mind-body linkage is assimilated is, if you will, a "hypo-language"—the language of that "nature" to which Lévi-Strauss refers when he speaks of "the inner nature of reality itself." So the "linguistic metaphor" is silently extended back to the point of universality, whereupon it ceases to be metaphor and *all else* becomes tropological transformation of *it,* that is, of that "original logic" that is the meaning of meaning. Thus, it is in terms of this siting of what I have been calling "assimilation" that we must comprehend the thrust of Lévi-Strauss's effort to "reduce" the level of the "etic" to the level of the "emic."

[It] is the "etic" level, too long taken for granted by mechanistic materialism and sensualist philosophy, which we should consider as an artefact. . . . [The] "emic" level is the one where the material operation of the senses and the more intellectual activities of the mind can meet, and altogether match with the inner nature of reality itself.

. . . Ideal and real, abstract and concrete, "emic" and "etic" can no longer be opposed to each other. What is immediately "given" to us is neither the one nor the other, but something which lies betwixt and between, that is, already encoded by the sense organs as well as by the brain, *a text* which, like any text, must be first decoded to translate it into the language of other texts. Furthermore, the physico-chemical processes according to which this original text was primitively encoded are not substantially different from the analytical procedures which the mind uses in order to decode it. And even more so, . . . since the ways and means of the understanding are not quartered within a restricted field. They do not exclusively pertain to the higher intellectual activities of the mind. Rather, the understanding takes over and develops intellectual processes already operating in the sensory organs themselves. . . . [Nature] appears more and more made up of structural properties undoubtedly richer although not different in kind from the structural codes in which the nervous system translates them, and from the structural properties elaborated by the understanding in order to go back, as much as it can do so, to the original structures of reality. It is not being mentalist or idealist to acknowledge that the mind is only able to understand the world around us because the mind is itself part and product of this same world. Therefore the mind, when trying to understand it, only applies operations which do not differ in kind from those going on in the natural world itself. (Lévi-Strauss [1972] 1978, 232–33)[43]

The fulcrum of this displacement of the opposition of "emic" and "etic" (levels that "can no longer be opposed to each other") consists in that underlying or inner nature of reality, about which Lévi-Strauss remarked that "the nature of things is 'emic,' not 'etic' " (Lévi-Strauss [1972] 1978, 232). This is the "emic" not of *Verstand*—it is not the subjective meaning of a historicist-hermeneutic or Herskovitsian cultural-relativist view of phenomenally variant "nature-culture" oppositions, conducted from within a culture that is sited in opposition to nature—but it is instead the "emic" of *Vernunft*, the "meaning of meaning," which (somehow) constitutes the essential siting of that nature-and-culture which is self-contained and therefore all-containing.[44] It *is* "the inner nature of reality itself."

Epistemologically, one might say of Lévi-Strauss's project that it is

43. See also Lévi-Strauss's discussion of "cybernetic" functions in his conversation with Georges Charbonnier (Charbonnier [1961] 1969, 153–54).

44. In the same way, "the historical" (i.e., Western historical thinking) and "the ahistorical" are subsumed by that same fundamental structure that is the "inner nature of reality itself."

"anachronistic" (whatever precisely one intends by that deceptive notion) because it references a metaphysics that seemingly was put aside once we became enlightened to the condition subsequently problematized as the self-relativization of thought. Also, and not necessarily inconsistently, one might say, as Lacroix did, that Lévi-Strauss has been "carrying out a rigorous and strictly scientific work," all the while "reflecting on this work, examining the method of it, extracting philosophic elements from it, and remaining throughout a kind of Rousseau, both misanthropic and a friend of mankind, who sometimes dreams of reconciling East and West by completing the economic liberation inherent in Marxism with a spiritual liberation of Buddhist origin" (Lacroix 1966, 222; see, e.g., Lévi-Strauss [1955a] 1963, 393–98). True, there has been much debate whether Lévi-Strauss's work is indeed "rigorous and strictly scientific," but by and large that debate has been distinguished by its vacuity. According to any conventional standard of social science, as applied to a Weber or a Durkheim, for example, Lévi-Strauss's work can surely be considered "scientific"—for what that is worth.

Likewise, we cannot fairly deny the self-conscious axiological deliberations undertaken in struggles with issues of enslavement/liberation and the relation of evil to an "unshakeable basis of human society." His writings are laden with despairing attention to the gravity with which "scientific civilization" presses upon the smaller worlds of human life (e.g., Lévi-Strauss [1955a] 1963; Lévi-Strauss [1960] 1967; Lévi-Strauss [1949b] 1967; Lévi-Strauss [1964b] 1976). He would implore us to appreciate the "palpable significance" of finding "our image of [human brotherhood] confirmed in the poorest of tribes" and not to duplicate "the zealots of progress," who "run the risk of underestimating, and thus of knowing too little about, the immense riches which our race has accumulated to one side and the other of the narrow furrow on which [the zealots] keep their eyes fixed" (Lévi-Strauss [1955a] 1963, 392). There is in Lévi-Strauss some sense of fusion of the epistemological and the ethical, and he attempts to instruct us about the constitution of that fusion. Thus, we are told that if "our race has concentrated on one task, and one alone—that of building a society in which Man can live—then the sources of strength on which our remote ancestors drew are present also in ourselves. All the stakes are still on the board, and we can take them up at any time we please. Whatever was done, and done badly, can be begun all over again" (392). But there is a terrible naiveté recessed among the dark spaces of these sympathies and platitudinous lessons, for at the bottom (epistemically, ethically) of his own constructions Lévi-Strauss has in fact invoked the same conditions of "the true" and "the good" that had been invoked previously by those who rendered the enslavements and the destructions to which he referred when advising us of a central lesson of "our adventurings into the heart of the New World," namely, "that the New World was not ours to destroy, and yet we destroyed it; and that no other will be vouchsafed to us" (392). They are the conditions purportedly constituted as the "inner nature of reality," of which we are "an ephemeral efflorescence," finally extraneous, yet a presence "whose activity hastens the disintegration of an initial order and precipitates a powerfully organized Matter towards a condition of inertia which grows ever greater and will one day prove definitive" (397).

It is the case, of course, that Lévi-Strauss's effort to formulate a self-warranting epistemological position, by which to evade the dilemma of relativism, including relativist ethics of one sort or another, culminated in a peculiar resurrection of what Bourdieu called "the old entelechies of the metaphysics of nature" (Bourdieu [1972] 1977, 27). The claimed affinity of Lévi-Strauss to Marx, and all of the ostensible similarities at the surfaces of their respective formations (e.g., the relational mode of concept formation), melt away once this fundamental divergence of warranting is comprehended.[45] Lévi-Strauss merely reproduces the duality of "infrastructure" and "superstructure" when, forgetting that thinking is materialized already in whatever "infrastructures" exist and, vice versa, that "infrastructures" are idealized in thinking, he attempts to develop a "theory of superstructure" separately from matters of "infrastructure," even though this latter is always of "undoubted primacy" (Lévi-Strauss [1962b] 1966, 130). His presumed warrant for this feat—i.e., his conception of that which provides anchorage for "infrastructure" and "superstructure" alike—consists in the notion of a "praxis" existing behind thought (not just false consciousness but *all* thought) under the guise of an objective structure of the psyche and of the brain. This "praxis" is a kind of cybernetic emission, as it were, from the stark order of an original cryptogram. For Lévi-Strauss, "the human spirit" is not of the historical labor of men, women, and children; it is "of nature."

Here, "nature" is intended not in any sense of the "socialized nature" that appears within cultural accounts of "the relation of culture to nature." When Lévi-Strauss thinks the priority of this all-embedding "nature of reality," he thinks as a twentieth-century Prolixenes, arguing that

> nature is made better by no mean
> But nature makes that mean: so, over that art,
> Which you say adds to nature, is an art
> That nature makes. You see, sweet maid, we marry
> A gentler scion to a bark of baser kind

---

45. I am here reminded of Richard Macksey's remark on this very question: "In the traditional academic slaughter of the father, one of the most popular, if confusing, variations seems to be the adoption of one or more surrogate 'fathers' whose chastity in the alleged paternity seems beyond doubt" (Macksey and Donato 1970, 246).

By bud of nobler race. This is an art
Which does not mend nature—change it rather—but
The art itself is nature.

(The Winter's Tale, IV. iv. 89–97)

Nature communicates with itself, through (as) human activity and otherwise; Prolixenes and Lévi-Strauss know this, even if the unenlightened
Perdita and Lévi-Strauss's naive subjects do not.[46] In some respects, it is
indeed accurate to say, as several commentators have, that the Lévi-Straussian enterprise is "a replay of the Kantian dilemma of the unknowability
of the thing-in-itself" (Jameson 1972, 109).[47] But that comparison must
not be carried too far. Lévi-Strauss has sought to displace the knowing
subject by identifying that constitution with the constitutiveness of "the
inner nature of reality." He postulates unchanging, universalist categories
and rules of codification/transformation, and a valorization of "thought"
(despite his occasional glance toward the "undoubted primacy" of "infrastructures"), which ironically undercuts the implicit claim of abolition of
the poetics-poietics separation and indeed reproduces it with a vengeance.
But most importantly there is that total assimilation to the super-rationalist
Vernunft, not simply of an allegedly species-common neurological apparatus but of a universal, hyperabstract order-as-such—an ordering that is
simply given as the fundament of reality, that is dynamic only in the
repetitions of its "original logic," and that is the meaning by which all
phenomenal meanings-to-be-known can be known. It is the common foundation that establishes the very possibility that "subject" and "object" exist
in a mutual relation of univocity—that they can be "speaking the same
language," one beneath the various "languages of culture" and the various
"languages of nature"—because they are constituted of the same codes and
rules of communication.

Accordingly, we can appreciate the intended significance of Lévi-

---

46. Lévi-Strauss has stated that he does "not aim to show how men think in
myths, but how myths think themselves in men, and without their knowing it"
(Lévi-Strauss [1964a] 1969, 12). There is an ambiguity in that description, which
Paz has exposed in his juxtaposition of the following renditions: "myths communicate with each other by means of men and without men knowing it"; and
the "social group which elaborates the myth does not know its meaning; he who
tells a myth does not know what he is saying" (Paz [1967] 1970, 39). The latter
is a sensible if partial account of a frequently actualized condition and situation.
The former, on the other hand, asserts that myths make use of their human tellers
rather than that some people make use of others through the telling of myths.

47. Ricoeur has referred to Lévi-Strauss's project as a "Kantianism without a
transcendental subject" (Ricoeur [1969] 1974, 52; see Lévi-Strauss [1964a] 1969,
11). Compare Kant's remark that his "schematism" is hidden deep within the
soul, and otherwise is of unknown origin (Kant [1787] 1952, 62).

Straussian passages that might otherwise be read as advocacy of some "biologistic determinism." For example, in speaking of the "origins and functions of power," he has observed that "if there are chiefs, it is because there are, in every group of human beings, men who, unlike their companions, love importance for its own sake, take a delight in its responsibilities, and find rewards enough in those very burdens of public life from which their fellows shrink" (Lévi-Strauss [1955a] 1963, 310). No doubt, he continued, "these individual differences" vary from culture to culture in development and expression. "But the fact that they exist in a society so largely uncompetitive as that of the Nambikwara would suggest that their origin is not entirely social," rather that they are "a part of that raw material of psychology in which every society somewhere finds its foundations." It should be clear, now, that such "raw material" of which Lévi-Strauss spoke was conceived as being not of a socialized or phenomenal cultural "nature" and that it was conceived not in the terms of reference of a biological science but instead within that postulated space of "the inner nature of reality" that undergirds the possibility of *any* human practice.[48] It is the same referencing according to which he argued that

> language does not consist in the analytical reason of the old-style grammarians nor in the dialectic constituted by structural linguistics nor in the constitutive dialects of individual *praxis* facing the practico-inert, since all three presuppose it. Linguistics thus presents us with a dialectical and totalizing entity but one outside (or beneath) consciousness and will. Language, an unreflecting totalization, is human reason which has its reasons and of which man knows nothing. (Lévi-Strauss [1962b] 1966, 252)

To recall a distant metaphor, it is the language of *liber naturae*.[49]

---

48. It is in the same vein that we are to understand what may be called Lévi-Strauss's "theory of anticipations" (see, e.g., Lévi-Strauss [1962b] 1966, 11–12), according to which the "type" of knowledge-construction referred to as "magic" has often anticipated the results of "a science yet to be born," even to the extent of *de facto* applications of procedures that science had not yet incorporated. "In this history of scientific thought this 'anticipation-effect' has . . . occurred repeatedly. . . . [It] is due to the fact that, since scientific explanation is always the discovery of an 'arrangement,' any attempt of this type, even one inspired by non-scientific principles, can hit on true arrangements." In other words: the "arrangement" or "order" *is*; it can be *discovered* by any method attuned to the possibilities of orderings. (One may be excused to wonder what "method" is *not*, by Lévi-Strauss's implicit depiction of "discovery," so attuned.)

49. An interesting discussion of developments of this metaphoric figure has been given by Curtius in regard to "preparations" of seventeenth-century activities of "the new science" and arguments of the relation between "the immediately given"

Epistemologically, then, while Lévi-Strauss has argued *within* his enterprise that "nature" must be considered not as an aprioristic existence but as the social phenomenality of various cultural statements made in solution of the central question, "What is the order of things?" (i.e., "What is the proper nomenclature?"), he has also tried to argue, *from within his enterprise outward, to the anteriority of his own argument*, that there exists a common and universal funding which constitutes the underlying integrity of all those cultural statements (the possible as well as the manifest), including his own, and by virtue of which it is possible that human knowledge can escape those dreaded involutions of self-relativized thought. When Lévi-Strauss thinks "an image of the world which is already inherent in the structure of the mind" ([1964a] 1969, 341), he presumes his own subsumptive location in that space of reality that is neither "world" nor "mind" but the foundation of both. And there he presumes to stand when he passes judgment, as in this reference to matters totemic: "Anthropologists of former times were the prey to an illusion" (Lévi-Strauss [1962b] 1966, xi). However, he became trapped in the oscillations of his effort to connect the interior and the anterior of his own enterprise. The manner of his bridging was promised from a model of signification in which the signifier signifies doubly, that is, its own existence and that which it means: should it be "asked to what final meaning these mutually significant meanings are referring—since in the last resort and in their totality they must refer to something—the only reply to emerge from [Lévi-Strauss's analysis] is that myths signify the mind that evolves them by making use of the world of which it is itself a part" (Lévi-Strauss [1964a] 1969, 341). That "inner nature of reality," then, is *as* a language speaking of itself.

This notion of the double constitution of "the nature of reality," here contrived after a linguistic model, has undoubtedly for many academicians of social science the look of a peculiar mysticism. But in its general resemblances, at the very least, it is peculiar neither to Lévi-Strauss nor to so-called French structuralism. Of course, presumptions of the power of a "language model" to generate insights transcendent of nature-spirit, actual-imaginary, mind-cosmos dualities can be reconstructed in activities as "removed" from Lévi-Strauss as those of Emerson, Whitman, or the early Melville (of *Moby-Dick* rather than *Billy Budd* or *Israel Potter*), that is, adherents of what has been called the "American Renaissance" faith in the power of language to create alternative worlds. But there are also the recent formulations of theoretical physicists such as Bohm (1971; 1973; see also Bohm and Hiley, 1975), who asserts that beneath what he calls the "explicate" or *un*folded level of reality (phenomenal) there is an "implicate" or

and that which can be known through "the immediately given" (Curtius [1948] 1963, 319–47; cf. Duerr 1978).

*en*folded order that is the primary nature of reality, each region of which reproduces the whole (that is, the whole of this founding reality is without localization—localities, i.e., entities *within* space-time regions, beings of phenomenal existence).[50] From the viewpoint of a conventional history of ideas, one can see in Bohm's theory of the foundation of reality, as in Lévi-Strauss's argument, certain perdurable themes that are repetitive of the Stoic doctrine of *physis* (ontologically and epistemologically)—that the essential, unchanging properties of all reality consist in, are determined by, the power of a universal reason—and the correlative Stoic doctrine of, in the Roman version, *honestas* (epistemologically and ethically)—that wisdom, freedom, and justice (in general the Stoicist condition of *eudaimonia*) follow from discovery of an obedience to that underlying order of *physis*.[51] In Lévi-Strauss's "inner nature of reality," as in Bohm's hologrammatic "enfolded order," it is the macrocosm-microcosm relation, the reproduction of the fundamental order of the whole in each of its phenomenally conceivable regions, that underwrites the essential connection between the contingent level of particular events and that founding level by virtue of which *any* events are at all possible.[52] But indeed Lévi-Strauss (and Bohm, with his different discipline of constructs) has not proposed to await the intervention of a divine revelation; rather he has himself proposed to be (not uniquely) the active agent of cryptography and to bring out of shadows the rules of navigation for passage from the interior to the anterior. The

50. It is perhaps not accidental that Bohm has employed usages frequently a part of seventeenth-century (and earlier) discourse but now considered "archaic"; his adjectival terms "implicate" and "explicate" once were rendered lexically in English as they are etymologically in Latin: respectively, *implicatus* ("enfolded") and *explicatus* ("unfolded"), past participles of *implicare* ("to enfold") and *explicare* ("to unfold").

51. Burkhardt (1941, 73–96) and Loemeker (1972) offer relevant discussions of reconstructions of the doctrine of *honestas* during the seventeenth century. For Lévi-Strauss the crucial nexus of issues and responses in Rousseau followed from those debates between *honestas* and the skepticism of the "freed man," *libertus*: for example, Montesquieu's "law of laws," or the necessary relations constituted in/by the nature of things; Montaigne's doubts toward the certitude of reason as opposed to revelation. And, of course, much of Shakespeare's writing (e.g., *The Winter's Tale*) can be read as a discourse on the epistemological and ethical conflicts of those manifold oppositions. Unfortunately, an adequate treatise on this complex of productions, one that avoids the pitfalls of the usual "history of ideas," has yet to be constructed.

52. One may also note the similarity between Lévi-Strauss's treatment of the concept of time (e.g., [1962b] 1966, 231–69) and the Stoic view of time as not a vessel within which events or things "happen" but as a dimension of things (or relations).

potency of his enterprise as a knowledge-claiming enterprise must depend on the connectedness of his activity to that anterior "nature of reality" at least to the degree that he can know the real as opposed to the apparent (i.e., an apparent "nature of reality") when he confronts it; this he has tried to establish by assimilating the interior to the anterior—the locality as a reproduction of the basic order of "the inner nature of reality"; that is, *he, too*, is *of* that basic order—but this displacement cannot stop the shimmer (except by way of an "intervening" divine revelation). If, as he acknowledges, his subjects in Amazonia (and elsewhere) as well as he himself are equally *of* that universal "nature of reality," then what is the essential criterion, and how can he discriminate it a true apprehension, by which his claims of knowledge differ from and are to be accepted as replacements for those of, say, Julius Lippert or Alexander Goldenweiser? What made Lévi-Strauss special—the "speciality" mediative of "the particular" and "the universal"—within the macrocosmic fundament?

Lévi-Strauss's ethic and his epistemology are founded in the recessive captivity of reified abstractions against which the concrete being of the artificer can stand only as human *creature*, who merely translates or "metaphorizes" the elementary logic of a universal and therefore critically inaccessible createdness. Consequently, Lévi-Strauss's appeals for a global responsibility announce their own ludicrous pretense; they are as a trumpeting in the imagination of a perfect vacuum, for their own formulation is simultaneously call and response in a silent language. In this radically quietistic "ethic," there is no original responsibility of the concrete man or woman or child. There is but a poor eclecticism of displaced abstractions, in which Lévi-Strauss imagines, among other quaint conjunctions, a potent conciliation of Marx and Buddha, whereby the "partiality" of the former is somehow rectified in a Buddhistically inspired attitude of cosmic resignation.

4. MICHEL FOUCAULT (1926–1984)

It has become virtually a matter of custom to introduce the written enterprise of Michel Foucault through the telescoped lenses of quotations: to quote this sagacious scholar quoting Jorge Borges quoting a passage from "a certain Chinese encyclopaedia," the palpable existence of which we delightedly take for granted. So I, too, shall begin by recounting the categories of this fabulous table, simultaneously proportionate and disproportionate, in which "animals are divided into: (a) belonging to the Emperor, (b) embalmed, (c) tame, (d) sucking pigs, (e) sirens, (f) fabulous, (g) stray dogs, (h) included in the present classification, (i) frenzied, (j) innumerable, (k) drawn with a very fine camelhair brush, (l) *et cetera*, (m) having just broken the water pitcher, (n) that from a long way off look like flies."

That passage cannot but strike our fancy, as it did Foucault's, for its quaintness, its nonsensicality, its outlandish mocking of reality—and yet also, and here is the catch of doubt, for its continued presence in the shifting layers of our reflexivity as a purported record of a certain people's sensibility. It has all the majesty of the relation of a child's fable to the child: that which makes it so "outlandish" makes it a real place, and one that questions *this* place. When reading of the ordered bestiary, we must wonder, as Foucault said he wondered, how anyone could think *that* ordering, and thus how such thoughts can possibly relate to our own discrimination of that which is "Same" versus that which is "Other" (Foucault [1966] 1970, xv). "In the wonderment of this taxonomy, the thing we apprehend in one great leap, the thing that, by means of the fable, is demonstrated as the exotic charm of another system of thought, is the limitation of our own, the stark impossibility of thinking *that*."

But might we ask instead about the conditions that make it possible to think and to say and to write *that*—and, by the same stroke, impossible to think and to say and to write a different "that"; the conditions which render to our apperceptive eye and ear a site in which certain things may come together while others must be kept apart, just as we discern in the passage from Borges an impossibility not merely of "the propinquity of the things listed" but of "the very site on which their propinquity would be possible" (Foucault [1966] 1970, xvi)? What, indeed, *are* the structure and the conditions of existence of any given discourse, a particular discourse-as-practice? It is toward such questions that Foucault has oriented his "attempt to practise a quite different history of what men have said," that is, his enterprise of an "archaeological" description/analysis of discourse (Foucault [1969a] 1972, 138). By his own account, the Foucauldian enterprise is a new one: neither a traditional history of ideas nor a sociology of knowledge, it is a project of looking at what people have said, of comprehending not only how it was said, and why *that* rather than the *not-that* was said, but also how and why that was *sayable* to begin with (see also Foucault [1971a] 1972; Foucault [1971b] 1977).

In the preface to his study of the conditions and rules of discourses that, during the small compass of years around 1800, emerged as clinical medicine, Foucault posed in a preliminary way the question of the possibility and possible siting of his enterprise. Although the enterprise has since changed in some important respects,[53] I believe this discussion retains an accuracy of positioning that justifies a recitation at length:

---

53. Some of these changes have been acknowledged by Foucault (see, e.g., [1969a] 1972; [1975] 1977; [1976] 1978).

It may well be that we belong to an age of criticism whose lack of a primary philosophy reminds us at every moment of its reign and its fatality: an age of intelligence that keeps us irremediably at a distance from an original language. For Kant, the possibility and necessity of a critique were linked, through certain scientific contents, to the fact that there is such a thing as knowledge. In our time—and Nietzsche the philologist testifies to it—they are linked to the fact that language exists and that, in the innumerable words spoken by men—whether they are reasonable or senseless, demonstrative or poetic—a meaning has taken shape that hangs over us, leading us forward in our blindness, but awaiting in the darkness for us to attain awareness before emerging into the light of day and speaking. We are doomed historically to history, to the patient construction of discourses about discourses, and to the task of hearing what has already been said.

But is it inevitable that we should know of no other function for speech (*parole*) than that of commentary? *Commentary* questions discourse as to what it says and intended to say; it tries to uncover that deeper meaning of speech that enables it to achieve an identity with itself, supposedly nearer to its essential truth. . . . In this activity known as commentary . . . is concealed a strange attitude toward language: to comment is to admit by definition an excess of the signified over the signifier; a necessary, unformulated remainder of thought that language has left in the shade—a remainder that is the very essence of that thought, driven outside its secret—but to comment also presupposes that this unspoken element slumbers within speech (*parole*), and that, by a superabundance proper to the signifier, one may, in questioning it, give voice to a content that was not explicitly signified. By opening up the possibility of commentary, this double plethora dooms us to an endless task that nothing can limit: there is always a certain amount of signified remaining that must be allowed to speak, while the signifier is always offered to us in an abundance that questions us, in spite of ourselves, as to what it "means" (*veut dire*). . . .

To speak about the thoughts of others, to try to say what they have said has, by tradition, been to analyze the signified. But must the things said, elsewhere and by others, be treated exclusively in accordance with the play of signifier and signified, as a series of themes present more or less implicitly to one another? Is it not possible to make a structural analysis of discourses that would evade the fate of commentary by supposing no remainder, nothing in excess of what has been said, but only the fact of its historical appearance? The facts of discourse would then have to be treated not as autonomous nuclei of multiple significations, but as events and functional segments gradually coming together to form a system. The meaning of a statement would be defined not by the treasure of intentions that it might contain, revealing and concealing it at the same time, but by the difference that articulates it upon the other real or possible statements, which are contemporary to it or to which it is opposed in the linear series of time. A systematic history of discourses would then become possible. (Foucault [1963a] 1973, xv–xvi, xvii)

In short, in our time all the conventional approaches to the archives of consciousness are doubly bound on a single-surfaced plane of thinking and seeing, on the curvature of a Möbius strip, by our awareness of language as simultaneously externality and interior propinquity of saying the said. The absence of that "original language" that would restore the dimensionality of an Archimedean sheet-anchor to that unisurface, and abolish at once all remainder of the signified and all superabundance of the signifier, is also the presence of an infinite regress of commentary on commentary. The situation of knowledge is that of a chess match having no endgame, that of a play with no final act and consequently only presumptuous curtain calls. Foucault has asked whether there may be a way of circumventing the dilemma of that "double plethora" that is admitted by, that is the substance of, commentary. His enterprise is the design of an armory of devices that will both constitute and traverse such a way, which he has called the "archaeological" way (see, e.g., [1963b] 1977; [1971b] 1977).

It bears repeating that this archaeology is not a traditional history of ideas; rather, it is "a systematic rejection of [the] postulates and procedures" of the traditional history of ideas. Whereas the latter focuses on discourse as a sign or a "document" of something else, the former treats the discourse "in its own volume," in the measure of its own existence—or, to invoke Foucault's borrowing from Canguilhem, "as a *monument.*" Whereas traditional history tries to transform monuments of the past into documents that tell about that past (to "lend speech to those traces which, in themselves, are often not verbal" or speak only in silence), archaeological description works from within, in an "intrinsic description" of the document-as-monument. The document is treated not as "an inert material" through which one may attempt a reconstruction of "what men have done or said, the events of which only the trace remains," but as heterogeneous materials that must be divided, distributed, and organized in levels and series and defined unities. Whereas the traditional history of ideas strives to reduce "the tangled mess of discontinuities" that are the events of the past to the continuity of the plane of unnoticed transition, whereupon all is interrelated in one or a few great unities, the Foucauldian archaeology breaks received continuities—those of the "book" and of "tradition" itself, for example—into their elemental dispersions and seeks to discern from within the regularities of discursive practice, even as they cut across or through individual traditions, *œuvres*, and the like. Most importantly, whereas traditional history peers into "that elusive nucleus in which the author and the *œuvre* exchange identities" and struggles to restore the original, concealed-revealed meaning of the author, this archaeological enterprise disavows such "anthropological justification" and establishes itself as "nothing more than a rewriting: that is, in the preserved form of exteriority, a regulated transformation of what has already been written"; not the futile effort of "a return to the innermost secret of the origin" but the "systematic description of a discourse-object" (Foucault [1969a] 1972, 6–7, 138–40, 189–92; Foucault [1966] 1970, x–xi, xxi–xxiv; Foucault [1969b] 1977).[54]

This archaeological project promises "to reveal a *positive unconscious* of knowledge," to show in discursive formations that which such received categories as "discipline" and "tradition" distort (Foucault [1966] 1970, xi; see also Foucault [1963b] 1977). Let us take Foucault's own example of this distortion and his promise:

> The linch-pin of *Madness and Civilization* was the appearance at the beginning of the nineteenth century of a psychiatric discipline. This discipline had neither the same content, nor the same internal organization, nor the same place in medicine, nor the same practical function, nor the same methods as the traditional chapter on "diseases of the head" or "nervous diseases" to be found in eighteenth-century medical treatises. But on examining this new discipline, we discovered two things: what made it possible at the time it appeared, what brought about this great change in the economy of concepts, analyses, and demonstrations, was a whole set of relations between hospitalization, internment, the conditions and procedures of social exclusion, the rules of jurisprudence, the norms of industrial labour and bourgeois morality, in short a whole group of relations that characterized for this discursive practice the formation of its statements; but this practice is not only manifested in a discipline possessing a scientific status and scientific pretensions; it is also found in operation in legal texts, in literature, in philosophy, in political decisions, and in the statements made and the opinions expressed in daily life. The discursive formation whose existence was mapped by the psychiatric dis-

---

54. Compare the intersecting statement by Furet (1971), one of the leading members of the Annales group. One wonders what conditions of discourse were "linked" with Furet's omission of citations of Foucault.

cipline was not coextensive with it, far from it: it went well beyond the boundaries of psychiatry. Moreover, by going back in time and trying to discover what, in the seventeenth and eighteenth centuries, could have preceded the establishment of psychiatry, we realized that there was no such prior discipline: what had been said on the subject of mania, delirium, melancholia, and nervous diseases by the doctors of the Classical period in no way constituted an autonomous discipline, but at most a commentary on the analysis of fevers, of alterations in the humours, or of affections of the brain. However, despite the absence of any established discipline, a discursive practice, with its own regularity and consistency, was in operation. The discursive practice was certainly present in medicine, but it was also to be found in administrative regulations, in literary or philosophical texts, in casuistics, in the theories or projects of obligatory labour or assistance to the poor. In the Classical period, therefore, there were a discursive formation and a positivity perfectly accessible to description, to which corresponded no definite discipline that could be compared with psychiatry. (Foucault [1969a] 1972, 179)

Foucault's archaeology was conceived in an effort to formulate a history of the sciences and the nonsciences (or "false sciences") that would be free of the dilemma of a "continuity-discontinuity" opposition, that would describe the articulations within the field of knowledge among ideologies, the pretensional sciences, and the sciences, without entering into any subjectivism. While affirming that the Bachelardian epistemology of "the rupture" and "the obstacle" had shown up to view the falsity of all "continuist" histories of science,[55] Foucault has also contended (correctly) that Bachelard's psychologistic construction remained inadequate, for (taking the case just displayed in quotation as example) to explain the relation between psychiatry and the earlier discourse on madness and diseases of the head as that of a "rupture" is finally to explain nothing. Foucault's impulse has been to dissolve the opposition of the image of continuity, with its valorization of "subject," to that of discontinuity, with its valorization of "object." His point of departure consists in the groupings that a conventional history of ideas brings to us—but "only to subject them at once to inter-

55. Among other works composed by this distant "teacher" of Foucault, see Bachelard's essay on "the new scientific spirit" (Bachelard 1934; also Bachelard [1940] 1968), his preface to Jacques Brosse's book, The Order of Things (1958), and his "Fragment of a Diary of Man" (1952), (both in The Right to Dream, ed. Underwood, 1971). The historicity of epistemologies and the problem of "the problem of representation" were at the core of Bachelard's "philosophie du non" (see, e.g., Bachelard [1940] 1968).

rogation," to sunder the bindings that they are and to study the dispersions thus released. Once the "immediate forms of continuity"—the "book," the "œuvre," "traditions," "schools," etc.—have been suspended, "an entire field is set free": a field vast but nonetheless definable, "made up of the totality of all effective statements (whether spoken or written), in their dispersion as events and in the occurrence that is proper to them." In this field, with these properly occurring events, where a trust has been restored beneath the forms of continuity, the materials with which the archaeologist deals are, in their "raw, neutral state, a population of events in the space of discourse in general." The task, then, is to undertake "a *pure description of discursive events* as the horizon for the search for the unities that form within it" (Foucault [1969a] 1972, 26–27; Foucault [1970] 1977, 179–81).

Enough stage-setting: it is time to deploy, albeit in rather small compass, the concentrated and seemingly exotic stuff of the Foucauldian corpus, so as to grasp the main features of it as an "archaeology." Of course, my intention is also to grasp his construction at the level of gnosiological claims. I shall work principally with his own lean presentation of the archaeological method (1969a; also 1969b; 1971a; 1971b), leaving to the reader's initiative most of the pleasures of Foucault's thick excursions into the discourses of psychiatry (1961; also 1973), clinical medicine (1963a), prisons and confinement (1975), sexuality (e.g., 1976), and the human sciences (1966).[56]

I shall begin with two words in which Foucault has invested a special load. Among the many pleonastic offerings of a definition of this "archaeological description," for instance, we encounter the following: such description attempts to analyze discursive formations, or groups of "verbal performances at the level of the *statements* and of the form of *positivity* that characterize them; or, more briefly, it is to define the type of positivity of a discourse" (Foucault [1969a] 1972, 125; emphasis added). Now, those two italicized words have particular significances about which we must be clear at the outset. As we know from a good dictionary, the term "positiv-

<hr>

56. These sharp prisms of the archaeologist's eye refract many of the tropic appearances of *connaissance* in modern life, but none more centrally than those of the relations of power (see, e.g., Foucault [1976] 1978, 81–96; Foucault [1972] 1977, 212–17; Foucault [1971c] 1977; Foucault 1978; see also Guédon 1977). And, while there is no doubt that the ordered disorder of his prismatic dispersions are often first appreciated in a revelatory confrontation of "voilà!"—an abrupt shift in the literality of *voir dire*, analogous to the psychologist's "perceptual illusion"—it is with regard to the substance and support of relations of power in discourse that his archaeologic endeavors confess their weakness. For a discussion of Foucault's tropologic sense, see White [1973a] 1978, 251–55.

ity" generally designates that which can be affirmed or is susceptible of affirmation, that is, a nonfictitious "being." For Foucault it designates not merely the surface of the affirmable but also the conditions of possibility, and thus the conditions of reality, of "statements" (the meaning of this latter term being undecided for the moment) (Foucault [1969a] 1972, 126–28). This notion of the "positivity of a discourse" allocates space for the dispersions and the specificities of "statements"—their "flaws of non-coherence," their "overlapping and mutual replacement," their nonunifiable simultaneities and nondeducible successions. It is concerned not with a "rediscovering [of] what might legitimize an assertion" but with the existence of the statement and a "freeing of the conditions of emergence of statements," that is, with rules that govern the mutuality of statements, their "mode[s] of being," their survival, transformation, and disappearance, rules that exist beneath or behind the level of the speaker/writer's consciousness in speaking/writing. In short, the positivity of a discourse is "the group of rules that characterize a discursive practice," that enable the possibility and the actuality of it, that inscribe its frontiers. This concept orients one to "the fact that discourse has not only a meaning or a truth, but a history, and a specific history that does not refer it back to the laws of an alien development" (e.g., commentarial accounts of a linear course of science). Yet the positivity itself, while a group of nonobvious rules that accredit a discourse with a specific history, "does not elude historicity." The rules of which a positivity consist have not the fixity of an imposition from without; they do "not constitute, above events, and in an unmoving heaven, an atemporal structure"; a positivity is not, and it does not refer to, "a great, unmoving, empty figure that irrupted one day on the surface of time, that exercised over men's thought a tyranny that none could escape, and which then suddenly disappeared in a totally unexpected, totally unprecedented eclipse." To the contrary, these rules have all the fluidity of "the very things that they connect" and in which they are bound.

Granted that this word *positivity*—a *"historical a priori,"* in Foucault's phrase, though not that of truths which might never be spoken or actually presented to experience but that of "a history that is given, since it is that of things actually said"—granted that this word is an encapsulated admonition to attend to "statements" (still undefined) in all their dispersion and discontinuity. To what end? Already I have recited Foucault's answer, his program, but another recounting may be helpful:

> The positivity of a discourse—like that of Natural History, political economy, or clinical medicine—characterizes its unity throughout time, and well beyond individual *œuvres*, books, and texts. This unity certainly does not enable us to say of Linnaeus or Buffon, Quesnay or Turgot, Broussais or Bichat, who told the truth,

who reasoned with rigour, who most conformed to his own postulates; nor does it enable us to say which of these *œuvres* was closest
to a primary, or ultimate, destination, which would formulate most
radically the general project of a science. *But what it does reveal is
the extent to which Buffon and Linnaeus* (or Turgot and Quesnay,
Broussais and Bichot) *were talking about "the same thing,"* by placing
themselves at "the same level" or at "the same distance," by deploying
"the same conceptual field," by opposing one another on "the same
field of battle"; and it reveals, on the other hand, why one cannot say
that Darwin is talking about the same thing as Diderot, that Laennec
continues the work of Van Swieten, or that Jevons answers the Phy-
siocrats. It defines a limited space of communication. (Foucault
[1969a] 1972, 126; emphases added)

So far I have left undefined the terminological significance of *statement*,
even while writing about *positivity* and using the word (and silently the
significance) in so writing. The statement, as Foucault has remarked, "is
certainly a strange event," for while it has to do with "the gesture of writing"
and the "articulation of speech," it also has to do with "the field of a
memory," whether in the materiality of a brain or in the materiality of a
book; while unique, it is also "subject to repetition, transformation, and
reactivation"; while it has connections with the situations and consequences
of its presence, it also relates, "in accordance with a quite different modality,
to the statements that precede and follow it" (Foucault [1969a] 1973, 28).
The statement is not a structure but a *function*, "a sort of vertical dimension" that cuts across the horizontal planes of sentences, propositions,
formulations, verbal performances, etc.; it is not visible, the way a stencil
or a linotype creates the visibility of a printed page or the way the logical
structure of a proposition has a visibility, but neither is it hidden behind or
below the apparent surface of a verbal performance, like some "secret
meaning that lies buried" within or beneath the verbal performance. The
statement is an enunciative function that gives to a group or series of signs
its specific existence, that is, "the modality of existence proper"—an "existence that reveals such a series as more than a mere trace, but rather a
relation to a domain of objects; as more than the result of an action or an
individual operation, but rather a set of possible positions for a subject; as
more than an organic, autonomous whole, closed in upon itself and capable
of forming meaning of its own accord, but rather an element in a field of
coexistence; as more than a passing event or an inert object, but rather a
repeatable materiality" (Foucault [1969a] 1973, 107, 108–9, 110–11, 26–
27).

    "Statement," then, refers to the existence but also to the forming and
to the conditions of the forming of the existence of sequences of signs.

These sequences, "insofar as they are statements, that is, insofar as they can be assigned particular modalities of existence," constitute discourse. The regularity of a series is a *discursive formation,* that is, "the principle of dispersion and redistribution . . . of statements," and insofar as a group of statements belongs "to a single system of formation" it is constitutive of a particular discourse (Foucault [1969a] 1972, 107). Neither sentence nor proposition, neither formulation nor performative act, the statement is a function that provides by one or another modality a specific "substance" and "support," and from that "rule of materiality" a site and a date,[57] to groups of signs or verbal performances. While the statement "exists in" a regime of materiality and is linked to the materiality of speaking/writing, the focus is precisely that of speaking/writing—that is, to *verbal performances.* A skyscraper or a mud hut, a formal garden, a jail or a gallows, a church steeple or an ICBM: none is in itself a statement. In a passage to which I shall return later for further study, Foucault has made explicit a coupling/opposition that pervades the entirety of his archaeological enterprise, namely his contrast of "statements and groups of statements" to "events of a quite different kind (technical, economic, social, political)" (Foucault [1969a] 1972, 29).[58]

The archaeological task of describing/analyzing statements, in a way that avoids employment of hermeneutics, is to describe/analyze "discursive practice" or the practice of a discursive formation, that is, "a body of anonymous, historical rules, always determined in the time and space that have defined a given period, and for a given social, economic, geographical, or linguistic area, the conditions of operation of the enunciative function" (Foucault [1969a] 1972, 109, 116–17; Foucault [1969b] 1977). This enunciative function operates with certain, and ascertainable, regularities in four "domains" or "levels" of discourse, in correspondence with which the archaeologist must undertake four "directions" of analysis: analysis of the formation of objects of discourse, analysis of the formation of enunciative modalities or "subjective positions," analysis of the formation of concepts, and analysis of the formation of strategic or thematic choices.[59]

---

57. "The rule of materiality that statements necessarily obey is therefore of the order of the institution rather than of the spatio-temporal localization" (Foucault [1969a] 1973, 103).

58. If it is understood that the logic of a formation tends toward its full expression and therefore toward exhaustion of the formation, then Foucault has contributed toward the exhaustion of a certain analytic formation by incising a line between that which is discursive and that which is social, political, technical, or economic; thus, by moving closer to the point at which that which is analyzed is nullified in its own analytic dispersion.

59. More will be said about these four "levels" of discourse and "directions" of analysis shortly.

As mentioned previously, this undertaking must be enacted relative to a suspension of all received and accepted unities of discourse, as offered by traditional "continuist" histories of ideas: for example, notions of "tradition" itself, of "influence" (as an apparent process of effective causation), "development," "evolution"; such "divisions or . . . forms or genres as science, literature, philosophy, religion, history, fiction, etc." (i.e., accepted divisions of *connaissances* and associated *langages*), since they themselves are "facts of discourse" (i.e., "reflexive categories, principles of classification, normative rules, institutionalized types") and surely "deserve to be analyzed beside others"; especially the notions of "book" and "*œuvre*"; and the "linked, but opposite themes" of, first, the always secret origin of the "irruption of a real event" (i.e., an ever-receding origin hidden behind each and every "apparent beginning") and, second, the secret foundation of all manifest discourse on a level of an "already-said" that is simultaneously a "never-said" (i.e., "an incorporeal discourse" that supplies to discourse in general the mark of "infinite continuity").

These and other conventions must be put in abeyance, according to Foucault, so that the archaeologist may, first, "restore to the statement the specificity of its occurrence"; second, free it of any "synthesizing operations of a purely psychological kind" (authorial intentionality, etc.) and thereby "be able to grasp other forms of regularity"; and third, describe unities other than those suspended, "this time by means of a group of controlled decisions"—i.e., consciously, deliberately—and by means not of a hermeneutic interpretation of statements (an endless cycle of commentary) but of "the analysis of their existence, their succession, their mutual functioning, their reciprocal determination, and their independent or correlative transformation" (Foucault [1969a] 1972, 21–25, 28–29).

Therefore, an archaeological description does not seek the unities of discourse according to the conventional system of references invoked in the traditional history of ideas: not by reference to "same object" or "different object," for "object" is not or need not be a unitary constancy, a "single object formed once and for all";[60] not by reference to an assumption that

---

60. Among the several beautifully crafted if yet unfinished pieces in Foucault's workshop, one of the most significant is his enforcement of the historicity of objects of discourse:

> What we are concerned with here is not to neutralize discourse, to make it the sign of something else, and to pierce through its density in order to reach what remains silently anterior to it, but on the contrary to maintain it in its consistency, to make it emerge in its own complexity. What, in short, we wish to do is to dispense with "things." To "depresentify" them. To conjure up their rich, heavy, immediate plenitude, which we usually regard as the primitive law of a discourse that has become divorced from it through error, oblivion, illusion, ignorance, or the inertia of beliefs and

words keep their meaning, that desires always point "in a single direction," that ideas retain their logic, that "the world of speech and desires" is somehow immune to "invasions, struggles, plundering, disguises, ploys"; not by reference to the "style" or a "certain constant manner" of statements; not by reference to a "system of permanent and coherent concepts," for these, like matters of "style," change in subtle and misleading ways; not by reference to "the identity and persistence of themes" or theoretical strategies, for the "same" theme may be "articulated on the basis of two sets of concepts, two types of analysis," etc., and different opinions and conclusions may rest "exactly on the same system of concepts." All of these frames of reference must be set aside, for, "if there really is a unity, it does not lie in the visible, horizontal coherence of the elements formed; it resides, well anterior to their formation, in the system that makes possible and governs that formation." This system (a system of dispersions) and its rules of discursive practice must be the point of attack.

The rules—"distinct groups of relations"—are articulated at four levels of formation, to which correspond the four "directions" of analysis that were mentioned previously: the *formation of objects*, where reference is to "the space in which various objects emerge and are continuously transformed," and to the interlinked authorities of emergence, delimitation, and specification of objects; the *formation of enunciative modalities*, or subjective positions, where reference is to the coexistence of statements that are dispersed and heterogeneous in style or form; the *formation of concepts*, where reference is to the simultaneity or succession of concepts, to "the interplay of their appearances and dispersions"; and the *formation of strategies*, or thematic choices, where reference is to "the dispersion of the points of choice" and to the fields of "strategic possibilities" that lie behind any option or "any thematic preference." These regularities are those of a discursive practice; as such, they constitute a "system of formation" for a given discourse and belong to that discourse. They are interrelated among themselves in a hierarchy of dependencies that is at once conditioning and controlling. On the one hand, "not all the positions of the subject, all the types of coexistence between statements [i.e., concepts], all the discursive strategies, are equally possible, but only those authorized by anterior lev-

traditions, or even the perhaps unconscious desire not to see and not to speak. To substitute for the enigmatic treasure of "things" anterior to discourse, the regular formation of objects that emerge only in discourse. To define these *objects* without reference to the *ground*, the *foundation of things*, but by relating them to the body of rules that enable them to form as objects of a discourse and thus constitute the conditions of their historical appearance. (Foucault [1969a] 1972, 47–48; see also Foucault [1970] 1977; Foucault [1971b] 1977.

els"; on the other hand, once certain strategic choices (for example) are made, those choices "exclude or imply, in the statements in which they are made," the formation of certain concepts, certain enunciative modalities, certain objects. Not that this vertical coherence of a discursive formation is "a stranger to time," however: the regularities of discursive practice, as the discourse they constitute, are historical. In Foucault's words, the temporal "mobility of the system of formation" occurs when "the elements that are being related to one another . . . undergo a number of intrinsic mutations that are integrated into discursive practice without the general form of its regularity being altered," and when "the discursive practices modify the domains that they relate to one another" (Foucault [1969a] 1972, 32–39, 72–75; Foucault [1971b] 1977, 139–40).

So Foucault's project is the construction of a new table of organization for the description/analysis of the frontiers of particular discourse. It is a project in which "*words* are as deliberately absent as *things* themselves" (Foucault [1969a] 1972, 48); i.e., his archaeologist challenges both "words" and "things" as words said and things represented without effective consciousness of the conditions and regularities of the saying and the representing. Because his faith urges that the unities of a discourse actually reside not in the visible layer that we divide in tables of "books," "*œuvres*," "schools of thought," and the like, nor in the hidden layers of the "authors' intentions" or the hermeneuts' texts, but in the anteriority that conditions the formation of discourse, Foucault has his archaeologist look among those anterior and "heterogeneous elements (institutions, techniques, social groups, perceptual organizations, relations between various discourses)," and in terms of the vertical levels or domains or distinct groups of relations (i.e., the formation of objects, enunciative modalities or positions of speaking subjects, concepts, and strategic choices), for "the relation that is established between them—and in a well determined form—by discursive practice" (Foucault [1969a] 1972, 72).

But what of those conditions and that anteriority? What of those complex twinings—"between institutions, economic and social processes, behavioral patterns, systems of norms, techniques, types of classification, modes of characterization" (certainly a wild congeries, is it not?)—that weave up and down in Foucault's own writing, relations that are not *in* discourse yet enable discourse to appear? The Foucauldian mapping of this space, in which possible discourses are articulated, delineates three "systems of relations," the discriminations of which are partly analogous to that division between referent and representation, between Schelerian *Realfaktoren* and *Idealfaktoren*, between a that-which-is and a that-said-about-that-which-is. In Foucault's archaeologic stratigraphy there are first of all *primary* or *real relations*, relations that exist "between institutions, techniques, social forms, etc.," and that may be described "independently of all discourse or all object of discourse" (Foucault [1969a] 1972, 45–46); that is, they are anterior to the anteriority proper to discursive surfaces. And there are *secondary* or *reflexive relations*, which emerge from discourse itself and which consist of the that-said-about the primary or real relations, that is, the discursive surface. But the relation of each of these two systems of relations to that of discursive formation is problematic, according to Foucault: on the one side, "the relations of dependence that may be assigned to this primary level are not necessarily expressed in the formation of relations that makes discursive objects possible";[61] on the other side, the relations constituting the reflexivity of this secondary level need not—and, by Foucault's argument, typically do not—duplicate the formation of discursive relations. Accordingly (and this is the flywheel of his enterprise), Foucault has inserted another system of relations, the *discursive relations*, which, being neither internal nor external to discourse but at its limit or frontier, "interplay" with the primary and the secondary relations and "determine the group of relations that discourse must establish in order to speak of this or that object, in order to deal with them, name them, analyze them, classify them, explain them, etc." Discursive relations characterize neither the "natural language" (i.e., "ordinary language," whether French, German, English, etc.) employed in discourse nor "the circumstance in which it is deployed, but discourse itself as a practice." *As a practice*: that bears repeating, for Foucault's effort has been to attempt to establish what might be called "the regime of discursive practice," and throughout this effort there surges the energy of the opposition between "discursive" and "nondiscursive practice." The Foucauldian search is for much more than some new category or exotic view of "discourse"; it is for the rugged

61. Regarding this phrase "are not necessarily expressed" ["*ne s'expriment pas forcément*"]: did Foucault intend the categorical "not necessarily expressed *at all, in any fashion*"? Or was he thinking a qualitative modifier (such as "exactly" or "faithfully") that did not pass through the ink of his pen? Elsewhere, in a response to queries about *The Order of Things*, he has spoken of transformations in the conditions of the existence of a discourse as being "neither 'reflected' nor 'translated' nor 'expressed' " in the concepts, etc., of the discourse; rather those transformations modify its rules of formation (Foucault [1968] 1972). I shall assume some qualitative modifier *was* thought, that he was disputing any so-called reflectionist theory of consciousness. To argue that "consciousness" does not duplicate its "object" (as a compass-corrected mirror would duplicate its), or that the formation of discursive relations does not duplicate in that fashion the relations of dependence at the primary level, is *not* to argue that the relations constituting that dependence are not at all expressed, in any fashion or however "unfaithfully," in those discursive relations or in that consciousness. To assert the latter would be to assert the case of independence.

articulations—still masked by the softness of such words as "interplay"—between those two "kinds" of practice: between "real relations" on the one side and "discursive" (and thence, "reflexive") relations on the other. The search is for a route by which to skirt the flank of "the problem of representation." As of this writing (1978), the direction of search is well enough marked; recall his stipulation, previously cited, that statements "necessarily obey" the rule of materiality collectively designated by Foucault as that of "institutions" (Foucault [1969a] 1972, 103–4). Yet the velocity of search has shown signs of waning.

At this juncture I must register the occurrence of a significant change between *The Order of Things* and *The Archaeology of Knowledge*. In the former volume, Foucault asked about the actual constitution of the "human sciences"; they consist, he argued, not in an analysis of "what man is by nature" but rather in "an analysis that extends from what man is in his positivity"—i.e., a living, laboring, speaking being—"to what enables this same being to know (or seek to know) what life is, in what the process of labor and its laws consist, and in what way he is able to speak. The human sciences thus occupy the distance that separates (though not without connecting them) biology, economics, and philology from that which gives them possibility in the very being of man." It is not their orientation to a certain object ("that singular object, the human being") which definitively characterizes the human sciences; rather it is the simple yet complicating circumstance that, in relation to economics and to philology (wherein, in each case, the human being is given as exclusive object) and to biology (wherein the human being is given as one of several objects), the human sciences "are in a position of duplication, and . . . this duplication can serve *a fortiori* for themselves." That is, the human sciences duplicate the sciences of life, labor, and language, and at their limit they can duplicate even themselves. In the one level of duplication, they "treat man's life, labour, and language . . . in that stratum of conduct, behavior, attitudes, gestures already made, sentences already pronounced or written, within which they have already been given once to those who act, behave, exchange, work, and speak." In the other level of duplication, in which are arrayed the regressive possibilities of a "sociology of sociology," an "anthropology of anthropology," and so forth, the human sciences are attuned to their own presence in the mirror but still preserve the distance of a gaze—as in the observation "that for certain individuals or certain societies there is something like a speculative knowledge of life, production, and language—at most, a biology, an economics, and a philology." In these activities, as the human sciences perform their duplications, "man" recedes through a hole in the space of analysis; the human sciences "thrust man, whom they take as their object in the area of *finitude, relativity,* and *perspective,* down into the area of the *endless erosion of time*" (Foucault [1966] 1970, 353–55; emphases added).

By Foucault's assessment, then, the relation of the "human sciences" to those of life, labor, and language is defined by the edges of the possibility of representation: the spaces where the living being, the laboring being, and the speaking being offer themselves representations of the regions (of life, of society, of language) within which those activities take place. Two features of that epistemological space must be noted here. First, the human sciences have had to borrow their constituent models from the domains of biology, economics, and philology-linguistics; they have none that is original to themselves. Their specific positivities, "the concepts around which they are organized, the type of rationality to which they refer and by means of which they seek to constitute themselves as knowledge," are locked in the place defined by relations of the biologic, the economic, and the philologic-linguistic—that is, by the particular arrangement of the epistemological space. This siting of the human sciences is not simply a "limited episode" in their history (an episode of immaturity, a prepuberal stage of still undeveloped powers of technique); *it is their very constitution*, their necessary confrontation with the space of possibility that is left to them. It has been only on the basis of their borrowed "constituent models" that the human sciences have been able "to create groups of phenomena as so many 'objects' for a possible branch of knowledge." Indeed, it has been only on such basis that they have been able to constitute the prime object of their realm, "*man*," a being who did not exist in Natural History, in the Analysis of Wealth, or in General Grammar.[62] In short, the human sciences emerged from "a general redistribution of the *episteme*" (Foucault [1966] 1970, 356–57, 345).

Second, in that same moment of redistribution the classical theory of representation dissolved, and thus the human sciences were constituted precisely within the field of an enormous problematic: on the one hand, they reside within representation, inasmuch as they *are* representation of their prime object, "man"; on the other hand, they have located representation as an activity *of* man, be it conscious or unconscious activity. Given their constitution in the space of the redistributed *episteme*, the human

---

62. "The epistemological field traversed by the human sciences was not laid down in advance: no philosophy, no political or moral option, no empirical science of any kind, no observation of the human body, no analysis of sensation, imagination, or the passions, had ever encountered, in the seventeenth or eighteenth century, anything like man; for man did not exist (any more than life, or language, or labour)" (Foucault [1966] 1970, 344).

sciences are simply incapable of solving or even circumventing the problem of representation:

> When dealing with what is representation (in either conscious or unconscious form), [the human sciences] find themselves treating as their object what is in fact their condition of possibility. They are always animated, therefore, by a sort of transcendental mobility. They never cease to exercise a critical examination of themselves. They proceed from that which is given to representation to that which renders representation possible, but which is still representation. (Foucault [1966] 1970, 364)

Foucault's critique of the place (the possibility and the capacity) of the "human sciences," though hardly the first to mark their dilemma, is surely a keenly wrought negation: the epistemological configuration that provides them "with a site, summons them, and establishes them" also denies them the status of what they pretend to be, sciences. They lack the "characteristics of objectivity and systematicity" that would "make it possible to define them as sciences." They belong to the modern *episteme*: they are charades of the mythic philosopher who presumes to "inhabit the whole of his language like a secret and perfectly fluent god" (Foucault [1966] 1970, 364–65; Foucault [1963b] 1977, 41–42).

As the foregoing passages show, in the earlier construction of his critique Foucault relied heavily on a notion of *episteme* as a definition of the space of dispersion within which possibilities of discourse and of particular knowledges are given—the space within which terrains of "thought" (thinking and object) can be etched by the relations of what is said to the multiplicities of silence.[63] Between the writing of *The Order of Things* and that of *The Archaeology of Knowledge*, however, he passed from a notion of *episteme* to one of *savoir*. The change is of considerable significance.

---

63. "Silence itself—the things one declines to say, or is forbidden to name, the discretion that is required between different speakers—is less the absolute limit of discourse, the other side from which it is separated by a strict boundary, than an element that functions alongside the things said, with them and in relation to them within over-all strategies. There is no binary division to be made between what one says and what one does not say; we must try to determine the different ways of not saying such things, how those who can and those who cannot speak of them are distributed, which type of discourse is authorized, or which form of discretion is required in either case. There is not one but many silences, and they are an integral part of the strategies that underlie and permeate discourses" (Foucault [1976] 1978, 27).

Foucault might well argue that the change was simply a tactical substitution and that everything encompassed within the orbit of *savoir* had been already a complete and apprehended presence in his thinking *episteme*.[64] In any case, at some juncture of his enterprise he undoubtedly remarked to himself on this troublesome circumstance of the actual practice of the *episteme* notion: that the materiality of the regulated manner by which discursive practice is formed escapes the fold of epistemology. The inadequacy of the *episteme* concept consists in its obdurate voicing of the classical promise of "pure theory"; and increasingly in his archaeologic critique Foucault has urged a passage to the materiality of discursive formation—to those material relations that, in their embodiment as "institutions," lend structure and support in discursive practice.[65] Thus the concept of "savoir" was formulated, though not as the customary lexical sense of "all knowledge" or "knowledge in general" but, to the contrary, as the sense of that which is ("literally") the necessary hypostasis of a particular knowledge or of any knowledge. Relative to *episteme* and its typically idealist practice, *savoir* may be thought of as Foucault's attempt to inscribe in our apprehending of activities of knowing, in our sense of the procession and object of thought, the furrow of a rupture. The place of *savoir* is anterior to that of *episteme*; it is that which gives rise to one or another *episteme*, and the absence of others; it is that which makes possible the "epistemologization" of discourse. "Epistemology" must be left where in fact it has been conducted, in the realm of a history of ideas already articulated (though not necessarily as sciences). The conduct of *savoir* is therefore not a replacement, not a substitution within a shared space, not an activity postulated from within the epistemological trihedron formed by the relations of the sciences of biology, economics, and philology-linguistics; Foucault's formulation of *savoir* as that to which his *recherche archeologique* is addressed is integral to the project of an enterprise that would not be encumbered by the problem of representation.

Savoir is a complex formation. To begin with, it has been described as "a field of co-ordination and subordination of statements in which

64. But for silly deliberations about the qualification of "genius," or at least "sagacious thinker," this matter of reconstructed intentionality (i.e., "Foucault's intention") is really much less important than the actual presentation of *savoir* as a concept formation distinguished from *episteme*.

65. Compare his (1968) caution, uttered even before the appearance of *The Archaeology of Knowledge*, that "*episteme*," as deployed in *The Order of Things*, must not be read as *Weltanschauung*, nor as some "grand underlying theory," nor as a stage or cycle of reason (see also 1969a:191; 1970; 1971b). It is, of course, very understandable that many of his critics were convinced of the promotion of yet another idealist program.

concepts appear, and are defined, applied and transformed." It is also "that of which one can speak in a discursive practice, which is thereby specified: the domain constituted by the different objects that will or will not acquire a scientific status"—that is, the field of the sciences but also the fields of ideologies and of those discourses that pretend to a scientific status, the field of whatever one can think. Moreover, *savoir* "refers to the conditions that are necessary in a particular period for this or that type of object to be given to *connaissance* and for this or that enunciation to be formulated." *Savoir*, in short, encompasses the conditions of the constitution of any discourse, the domain of discursive practices actually constituted, and the that-which-is-thought in discursive practice. *Connaissance*, on the other hand, refers to a particular body of knowledge, its language (*langage*), and its activity—thus to a particular "relation of the subject to the object and the formal rules that govern it," all of which is given to it by *savoir*. It is in the element of *connaissance* that the traditional history of ideas "finds the point of balance of its analysis" and therein is compelled, "against its will, to encounter the transcendental interrogation." Foucault's archaeology, rather than traversing the horizontal axis of "consciousness/*connaissance*/ science" (an axis that "cannot escape subjectivity"), follows the different axis of "discursive practice/*savoir*/science" and explores the various ar- chaeological territories in which there is formed, "in a regular manner by a discursive practice," a structure (a *savoir*) that is "indispensable to the constitution of a science," even though it is "not necessarily destined to give rise to one." These territories are not themselves scientific domains; they are organized differently and they are more extensive—for example, they may include texts differentiated by the scientist as "literary" or "phil- osophical" or "ideological." In other words, the instance of *savoir* is present not only in the syllogistic and experimental demonstrations of science but also in "fiction, reflexion, narrative accounts, institutional regulations, and political decisions." It is more than just science that appears "in the element of a discursive formation and against the background of *savoir*" (Foucault [1969a] 1972, 15 n. 2, 182–84).

So, *savoir* is constituted as a set of practices, discursive and nondis- cursive. But what are the relations formed within and between those prac- tices, such that a science emerges as a localization within a field that is occupied also by persisting themes of ideology and pseudosciences? It is with questions of this sort that Foucault struggled in the penultimate chapter of *The Archaeology of Knowledge*, as he sought to demonstrate the relations of materiality of discursive practice. The responses broached in this discus- sion evidence his confrontation with the basic perplexities of his own enterprise.

During the span of his public works from *Madness and Civilization* to *The Archaeology of Knowledge*, Foucault has made increasingly visible the primacy of the task of defining the "regime of materiality that statements necessarily obey." The regime of materiality is "of the order of the institution rather than of the spatio-temporal localization," that is, the site and the date of a statement are deducible from the material existence of the relations that constitute the substance and the support of the statement (Foucault [1969a] 1972, 103, 101). "What archaeology wishes to uncover is primarily—in the specificity and distance maintained in various discursive formations—the play of analogies and differences as they appear at the level of rules of formation" (160). But it also seeks to reveal

> relations between discursive formations and non-discursive domains (institutions, political events, economic practices and processes). These *rapprochements* are not intended to uncover great cultural continuities, nor to isolate mechanisms of causality. Before a set of enunciative facts, archaeology does not ask what could have motivated them (the search for contexts of formulation); nor does it seek to rediscover what is expressed in them (the task of hermeneutics); it tries to determine how the rules of formation that govern it—and which characterize the positivity to which it belongs—may be linked to non-discursive systems: it seeks to define specific forms of articulation. (Foucault [1969a] 1972, 162)

The Foucauldian context within which the regime of materiality of discourse is to be defined circumscribes knowledge as *savoir*, within which are formed the differences of "science proper," those discourses that pretend to that status, and "ideology." Although closely linked at a given moment, the regions of the tripartite division are not related reductively or as mutual inversions: the emergence of a science proper, for example, does not terminate ideology, nor does it drain the field of the pretending sciences; a science functions nonexclusively within knowledge (*savoir*). It is a task of archaeology to "show positively how a science functions in the element of knowledge"—how it emerges as a discursive formation against the background of *savoir*, how it articulates its *connaissance*, how it relates to those discourses that falsely claim equivalent status. Here the Foucauldian deployment of "ideology" is met: "It is probably . . . in that space of interplay" between science and *savoir* "that the relations of ideology to the sciences are established."

> The hold of ideology over scientific discourse and the ideological functioning of the sciences are . . . articulated where science is articulated upon knowledge. If the question of ideology may be asked of science, it is insofar as science, without being identified with knowledge, but without either effacing or excluding it, is localized in it,

structures certain of its objects, systematizes certain of its enunciations, formalizes certain of its concepts and strategies; it is insofar as
this development articulates knowledge, modifies it, and redistributes
it on the one hand, and confirms it and gives it validity on the other;
it is insofar as science finds its place in a discursive regularity, in
which, by that very fact, it is or is not deployed, functions or does not
function, in a whole field of discursive practices. In short, the question
of ideology that is asked of science is not the question of situations
or practices that it reflects more or less consciously; nor is it the
question of the possible use or misuse to which it could be put; it is
the question of its existence as a discursive practice and of its functioning among other practices. (Foucault [1969a] 1972, 185)

In other words, ideological formations—for example, the religious, moral,
and political ideologies subsisting within a *savoir*, but neither as sciences
proper nor as pretended sciences—exert a hold over the discursive practice
of a science at the point of its constitution within the field of *savoir*. With
that emergence, those formations articulate the role, its place and relative
importance, of a particular scientific knowledge (*connaissance*) within *savoir*. And it is through the "interlocking" between such ideological formations, on the one hand, and the "institutions, economic practices and
processes," and so on, on the other, that the relations of the regime of
materiality, the "linkage" between discursive and nondiscursive practices,
are constituted (Foucault [1969a] 1972, 181–86).

But, as Foucault is surely aware (see, e.g., [1969a] 1972, 184), this
construction is woefully inadequate: it does not even begin to answer the
question of the so-called regime of materiality of discourse, that is, the
structure of "articulation" of discursive and nondiscursive practices; it
merely reproduces the question, behind the veil of an "interlockage" or
"linkage."[66] There is, of course, no mistaking Foucault's *own* "authorial
intent," the effective achievement *he* wishes to authorize between, on the
one side, the crude "correspondent/representation" epistemological figure
of a unilateral reductive causality from the materiality of "real relations"
of institutions to the ideality of "reflexive relations" of interpretive consciousness and, on the other side, the "construction/interpretation" figure
of a subjectivist accounting of "real relations" through "reflexive relations."
It is clear that Foucault will choose neither but instead will seek the measure
of a third structure of "discursive relations" into which the elements of that
crude opposition collapse and are redeployed (see Foucault [1969a] 1972,

66. Similar criticisms have been made by Lecourt though without noticeable
conclusion (Lecourt [1972] 1975, 208–9; see also Guédon 1977, 261).

45–46). However, whereas he has succeeded quite well in demonstrating that the reflexive relations (i.e., the relations composing the surface of that-which-is-said) often do not duplicate the discursive relations (i.e., the relations composing the possibility of the said and the not-said), he has not at all succeeded in demonstrating what precisely *is* the "linkage" or the "interplay" between discursive relations and what is anterior to them and independent of them, namely the "primary" or "real relations" of institutions. We are told, for example, that discursive practices "are embodied in technical processes, in institutions, in patterns for general behavior, in forms for transmission and diffusion, and in pedagogical forms which, at once, impose and maintain them"; we are told that the "transformation of a discursive practice is linked to a whole range of usually complex modifications that can occur outside of its domain (in the forms of production, in social relationships, in political institutions)"—as well as inside its own domain and "to the side of it (in other discursive practices)"—and that "it is linked to these modifications not as a simple result but as an effect that retains both its proper autonomy and the full range of its precise functions in relation to that which determines it" (Foucault [1970–71] 1977, 200). We are told—in a discussion of the conditions of the formation of particular theoretical choices or themes in discursive practice—of the importance of that authorization constituted "by the *function* that the discourse . . . must carry out *in a field of non-discursive practices.*" Analysis of this authority upon which the theoretical choices of a discursive formation depend "must show that neither the relation of discourse to desire, nor the processes of its appropriation" by one or another group of people, "nor its role among non-discursive practices is extrinsic to its unity, its characterization, and the laws of its formation"—that is, that desire, the relation of discourse to it, and so forth, "are not disturbing elements which, superposing themselves upon its pure, neutral, atemporal, silent form, suppress its true voice and emit in its place a travestied discourse, but, on the contrary, its formative elements" (Foucault [1969a] 1972, 67–68). In all of this instruction, a multifaceted duality has been reproduced and preserved—"ideology" and "institutions"; "statements and groups of statements" and "events of a quite different kind (technical, economic, social, political)" (29); the discursive and the nondiscursive—and with a remarkable absence of theorization of the relations that differentiate/connect the one with the other.

The biblical injunction of the Word required that each and every thing be given its proper name. Thus, the activity of Linnaeus as well as Adam: wording is different from doing, and the conjunction of words and things is that of a representation rather than that of a production. Things belong to Nature (or to God); words belong to Man; and the former can be truly re-presented through the latter. But the problem of representation is a beggar's crossroads; in all directions it leads to disaster. Foucault has sought to avoid this fetish of the word. In his enterprise, "*Words* are as deliberately absent as *things* themselves" (Foucault [1969a] 1972, 48). Foucault has sought to nullify the problem of representation, to decenter the speaking subject, to survive without the gray matter of authorial intentionality and interpretive retrospections. Yet there is, as he has acknowledged, a question that "embarrasses"; what is the "status" of *his* discourse? Is it "history or philosophy?" Between the beginning and the end of *The Archaeology of Knowledge*, we are told that Foucault "tried to define the blank space from which I speak," but the space seemingly would not yield to definition: "for the moment, and as far ahead as I can see, my discourse, far from determining the locus in which it speaks, is avoiding the ground on which it could find support" (17, 205).

According to Foucault's several self-descriptions, his "aim" has been "to reveal a *positive unconscious* of knowledge: a level that eludes the consciousness of the scientist and yet is part of scientific discourse" (Foucault [1966] 1970, xi); "to uncover the principles and consequences of an autochthonous transformation that is taking place in the field of historical knowledge" (Foucault [1969a] 1972, 15); to make an "analysis purged of all anthropomorphisms" and free of all impositions of "the categories of cultural totalities (whether world-views, ideal types, the particular spirit of an age)" (Foucault [1969a] 1972, 15–16); to overcome the problem of representation, the dilemma of epistemological relativism, the conclusion of nihilism. His aim has been to reveal a nonconsciousness—and thereby also a false consciousness—in the fields of that-which-has-been-said (as *connaissances* of sciences and of pseudosciences), and to do so if not exactly as a presuppositionless inquiry then at least by a method that shatters in advance the constraints of received orderings and that enables him to access the "raw, neutral state" of events (the dispersed "population of events," now to be etched in "*a pure description*"). It is correct to say, as Foucault has said, that his enterprise has been neither philosophy nor history, in the traditional self-understandings of those disciplines: it has been neither a "memory or a return of the origin" nor a "giving life to half-effaced figures" (Foucault [1969a] 1972, 206).

But where, in all of this archaeological enterprise, has Foucault stood?—not as "psychological individuality," to be sure, but as (social-historical) producer? His utterances are inescapably deictic in the fullness of their concrete conditions and actuality. What is the ground from which *he* can speak and describe (if not "things," then that "*raw, neutral state*" of "events"), without suffering the handicaps of those whose methods he has rejected? Surely he would not have us believe that he has been the totally effaced instrument of a discourse that is his, yet not *really* his. But it is here, in this reflectedness of producer and object produced, that the dilemma of epistemological relativism, with its anthropomorphisms, the problem of representation, and so on, is most pointedly present. If Foucault cannot demonstrate the warrant of *his* saying, then he has "surmounted" the problem of representation and associated puzzlements only through the false consciousness of a determinism of discursive facticities in which he supposedly has no effectivity.

Thus, in perusing his accounts of the aims of his project, one is led to ask: "Even so, what is the purpose of such archaeological reconstruction? What value does Foucault intend to realize by it?" That purpose would appear to be to arrive at the truth—or at *a* truth?[67]—of what has taken place in discursive practices and (necessarily) in the "regimes of materiality" that constitute their support and substance. We must take care here to appreciate the manner of his attempt to slice through what might be called "the problem of Foucault and his double." A previously quoted passage will serve to illustrate: while the archaeologically determined unity of a discourse "does not allow us to say of Linnaeus or Buffon," for example, "who told the truth," it does nevertheless "reveal . . . the extent to which Buffon and Linnaeus . . . were talking about 'the same thing,' by placing themselves at 'the same level' or at 'the same distance,' by deploying 'the same conceptual field,' by opposing one another on 'the same field of battle' " (Foucault [1969a] 1972, 126). Now in the first instance, we cannot say of Linnaeus or Buffon "who told the truth" not simply because their "authorial intentions" are irretrievable but because the attempt to do so would transport us directly into the constraints of *their* problems of representation, into *their* representing "the natural givenness of things" through "the artifice of words." But in the second instance, Foucault himself has made tropologic constructions/comparisons of Linnaeus and Buffon whereby he knows whether they "were talking about 'the same thing,' " and so forth, whether they were in/of the same discursive practice. His knowing *that*, his limning the measure of "same/other," was an enactment of judgmental standards—be they called "truth" (of coherence if not of correspondence), "correctness," or what have you. Yet the ground on which such "truth" or "correctness" *can be such*, the ground from which Foucault's claims of archaeological knowing can be warranted, has not been demonstrated by his archaeological enterprise.

5. JÜRGEN HABERMAS (b. 1929)

At first glance one might imagine that to attempt to construct a critical exposition of the writings of an author still in the fifth decade of life is to

---

67. Among Foucault's disclaimers of privileged position, there is this description of *The Archaeology of Knowledge*: "It is not a way of saying that everyone else is wrong"; it does not try "to reduce others to silence, by claiming that what they say is worthless" (Foucault [1969a] 1972, 17, 205).

invite quick obsolescence—especially so, if, as in the case of Jürgen Habermas, the already elapsed years of that decade have been a time of mounting prolificacy and elaboration of argument. After all, the author has the prerogative of changing course and radically recasting the measures of earlier work, although the likelihood of that happening is actually rather less than first glance would suggest. Once an author has committed to a foundational stance—once, that is, the basic stamp of a project has been impressed and publicly revealed—the major features of the impression typically persist through whatever additions, unfoldings, or reticules may be made. This resilience we might credit to a certain authorial vanity, to a deep reluctance to undertake the self-criticism of admitting fundamental error in the thinking of one's project. Alternatively, if we pause to consider that the project exists as an externalized embodiment of the project-maker's historical being-in-the-world, we might prefer to conclude that the resilience is a manifestation of something more profoundly human than opprobrious vanity. But, whatever explanation one prefers, fundamental alterations come neither easily nor often. With regard to Habermas, who most surely may be expected to continue his deliberations at a vigorous pace, I should be only slightly less surprised by a basic change in the stamp of his project than by an equivalent change in that of, say, Lévi-Strauss's project.[68]

Since the late 1960s Habermas has attained wide notice as one of the most productive (and controversial) second-generation members of the so-called Frankfurt School.[69] Inasmuch as Habermas came of age within that circle of scholars identified with the Frankfurter *Institut für Sozialforschung*, it is in relation to their central project that one must begin an understanding of Habermas's work. That project consisted in the instauration of criticism in social theory by combating the prevalent trivializations of Marx's theory as a one-sided materialistic, even positivistic, economic determinism (and a "nothing-but-mere-reflection" thesis of superstructure) and by restoring/developing an integral theory of society. According to Max Horkheimer, the current crisis of humanity—"a new kind of barbarism," he and Adorno called it in their *Dialectic of Enlightenment* (Horkheimer and Adorno [1947] 1972, xi)—was fundamentally a crisis of reason.[70] At a certain point in history, "thinking either became incapable of

68. Subsequent to the writing of this section on Habermas the generally excellent study of his work by McCarthy (1978) has appeared. Although there are some differences between our respective critiques, McCarthy's treatment is a more nearly complete description of the Habermasian project.

69. As is by now generally recognized, this reference to a "school" of thinking suggests more unity of view than was actually present among the founding "members," to say nothing of the later figures.

70. In focusing on Max Horkheimer (1895–1973) as "representative" of the Frankfurter group, I do not intend a depreciation of the works of other members,

conceiving" the objectivity of reason as "ultimately beyond, though related to, the faculty of thinking" or, in what amounts to the same effect, "began to negate it as a delusion." The result was a relativistic doctrine, a subjectivization of reason. The reason of *Vernunft* was either abolished outright or subordinated to that of *Verstand*. The negativity of critique was lost, and traditional theory became essentially apologetic of existing conditions, as it had no basis for standards that could transcend those conditions. Reason became an instrumentality, whereby "thought serves any particular endeavor, good or bad"—surely a mere tool, and "a tool of all actions of society," but one that "must not try to set the patterns of social and individual life, which are assumed to be set by other forces." This crisis of reason is simultaneously, then, a redoubled crisis of freedom: "Reason has never really directed social reality, but now reason has been so thoroughly purged of any specific trend or preference that it has finally renounced even the task of passing judgment on man's actions and way of life" (Horkheimer [1947] 1974, 7–9, 19).

The project of critical theory was intended as one of reinvigorating the negativity of critique and of restoring reason as objectivity in a mediation of the duality of subject-object, ideality-materiality, spirit-nature. "The assumption of an ultimate duality is inadmissible," Horkheimer argued, "not only because the traditional and highly questionable requirement of an ultimate principle is logically incompatible with a dualistic construction, but because of the content of the concepts in question. The two poles cannot be reduced to a monistic principle, yet their duality too must be largely understood as a product" (Horkheimer [1947] 1974, 171). Hegelian identity theory was rejected (especially by Horkheimer, less steadfastly by some of his colleagues), on the grounds that it meant enslavement of the concrete subject to the reified abstraction of a universalized thought. Not "thought" as such, nor "spirit" as such, but only concretely historical spirits or thoughts can be accorded the status of creditable reality, as opposed to that of a false consciousness.

This rejection of identity theory, however, did not have as a corollary a straightforward acceptance of Marxian theory (in any of its current versions) as a putative integration or mediation of the remaining duality. Certainly an important aim of the restoration of negativity included demolition of the view of Marx's theory as simply an antonymic answer to idealism (see, e.g., Horkheimer 1933). But Horkheimer in particular, while preferring to see his own efforts as those of a properly conceived materialist theory of society, nonetheless rejected Marx's centrally important concep-

---

especially the rather chaotic but insightful legacy of T. W. Adorno (1903–1969). This is not the place for a systematic and detailed study of their varied contributions.

tion of labor, arguing that to "make labor into a transcendent category of human activity is an ascetic ideology" (Horkheimer 1934, 181).[71] The contention was that Marx had mislocated the dynamics of reification and alienation, that his conception of essential human activity was one-sided, and that the very processes he had envisioned as leading to emancipation were in fact reproducing the alienated conditions of human existence at a new and intensified level. Accordingly, not only did the negativity of critique have to be recovered from the blindly optimistic palp of "affirmative culture"; the very siting of critique needed to be changed. The critique of political economy had to become a critique of instrumental reason and of the technical civilization, inasmuch as the crucial nexus had shifted to the dominion of politics and culture, where the seemingly invincible grasp of instrumentalism held sway over the possibility of freedom. It was for all to see that the reputedly dauntless powers of the "revolution of the proletariat" had proved to be ineffectual. Prior to their seizure of control, Horkheimer observed in his renewed tribute to Schopenhauer, "the aim of Lenin and most of his friends was a society of freedom and justice, yet in reality they opened the way to a terroristic totalitarian bureaucracy that certainly does not come closer to freedom than the empire of the Czar" (Horkheimer [1962] 1967, 69). Clearly the source of emancipation lay not in the conditions of human labor but deeper, in the conditions of reason (cf. Horkheimer 1933; Horkheimer [1937] 1972; Horkheimer [1947] 1974; Horkheimer [1967] 1974).

Throughout the development of this argument, emphasis was always on the sanctity of reason—not the reason of mere appearances and understanding but that of underlying reality, synthetic reason. The defense of reason meant negation of those attacks that were designed to banish it as metaphysical contemplation irrelevant to conduct in the real world. But defense also meant the formation of a correct practice that would preserve the possibility of freedom and eventually realize it. The effort to achieve the necessary integration of these concerns of reason and practice never succeeded, however. Horkheimer, for example, simply took over from Hegelianism the view of reason and freedom as fundamental copresences, thereby importing, despite his general rejection of idealism, what amounted to an idealist construction. His insistence on the historicity of thought— that truth is not an eternal constant to be set against the course of history— meant that truth is relative; yet, having at the same time rejected relativism as an abdication of reason, he faced the task of grounding the possibility

71. This theme recurred throughout the works of various *Institut* members. Adorno is reputed to have said that if Marx had gotten his way, he would have converted the whole world into one "giant workhouse." Aspects of the theme have been repeated by Habermas, as we will see.

of truth of his own critical theory. This he failed to accomplish, with the consequence that his critical theory reproduced the duality that he rightfully held to be inadmissible (cf. Horkheimer 1935; Horkheimer [1937] 1972; Horkheimer [1947] 1974). Although Horkheimer and his colleagues succeeded to the extent of fabricating a remarkable series of studies of symptoms—studies that, if nothing else, helped to preserve the vital impulse of negation—their critiques were nevertheless fundamentally constrained in an unsurmounted negativity and were therefore unable to escape the dilemma of self-incrimination.

In the conception of his own project, Habermas treated the works of the Frankfurt School as one point of departure in the double sense of beginning with elements of their problematic and yet parting from the constrictions of their critique. A central theme of his early writing was of course the necessity to continue the Frankfurter critique of "scientism,"[72] that is, the prevailing analytic-philosophic orientation according to which "a scientific philosophy, just like science itself, must proceed *intentione recta*, i.e., it must have its object before itself (and is not allowed to approach it reflexively)." But the previous level of critique was only partially adequate at best, even in relation to previous circumstances of society. The banishment of self-reflection had combined with the movement of science and technology into the central region of productive forces, resulting in the substantially altered conditions and consequences of "late capitalism." Under the new circumstances certainly new and more powerful critiques must be made.[73] The prevailing scientistic orientation, to the extent that it has entertained concerns of the problem of knowledge, has steered analysis away from matters of "constitution" and toward those of "representation," that is, "in the direction of methodology of science based on linguistic analysis, which down to the time of the late Wittgenstein's new insights excluded the *pragmatics* of natural and scientific languages from logical analysis" (1973a, 158; emphasis added).[74] Habermas has joined Apel and others in rejecting this "abstractive fallacy," as Apel has termed it:

72. I would include in this category of "early writing" works of the period 1962–1970, from publication of his essay on structural change of "publicness" to that of his most famous work to date, *Knowledge and Human Interests*.

73. The view that science has become an increasingly central force in general processes of production is not unique to Habermas or to his predecessors at Frankfurt, of course; compare, for example, the perspectives of Russell (1952), Ziman (1976), and Turchin (1977, especially 323).

74. "Pragmatics (*pragma*: "deed," "things done") concerns the relation of sign-maker to sign, as distinct from the relation of sign to its referent, for example. The distinctions of "syntax," "semantics," and "pragmatics" are generally credited to Morris (1938). Carnap (1942), among others, adopted the scheme. An

If we abstract from the pragmatic dimension of symbols, there can be no human subject of the reasoning process. Accordingly, there can be no reflexion upon the predetermined conditions of why reasoning is possible. What we do get is an infinite hierarchy of meta-languages, meta-theories, etc., containing (and concealing) the reflexive competence of man as a reasoning subject. (Apel 1973, 2:406)

The circumstances of this nonreflective scientism are found in the disjuncture of that fact/value, empiricity/normativity duality that earlier members of the Frankfurt School had attempted to resolve but actually had only reproduced. In Habermas's vocabulary, it is the separation of "empirical-analytic" and "historical-hermeneutic" sciences.

These separate sciences are constituted as different and partial objectifications of reality: in the one case, instrumentally constituted objects of the type that we experience as "things, events, and conditions which are, in principle, capable of being manipulated"; in the other, interactionally constituted objects of the type that we experience as "persons, utterances, and conditions which in principle are structured and [are] to be understood symbolically." That we daily undertake our objectifications of reality "always from the viewpoint" of one or another of these "knowledge-constitutive" and "knowledge-guiding" interests is, according to Habermas, "revealed by a methodological comparison of the fundamental theoretical concepts, the logical construction of the theorems, the relationship of theory to the object domain, the criteria of verification, the testing procedures, and so forth." But most striking of all is that "difference in the pragmatic function which the information produced by the different sciences can have"—in other words, that very difference of technical control and domination versus intersubjective communication and understanding.

In the empirical-analytic sciences, the pragmatic function is predominantly one of nomothetic explanation, conditional prediction, and mastery of the objectified reality of "observed phenomena"; in the historical-hermeneutic sciences, it is predominantly one of interpretation, understanding, and facility with reference to the objectified reality of "traditional complexes of meaning." This easily detectable difference of viewpoint and orientation is anchored in the duality of deep-seated, "invariant," "quasi-transcendental," and "abstract" rather than "concrete" "biologically based" interests (those of technical control and intersubjective communication) that "result from the imperatives of a sociocultural life-form dependent on labor and language" (Habermas [1971a] 1973, 8–9; Habermas [1965] 1971; Habermas [1968b] 1970).

effort to formulate a pragmatics of communication based on cybernetic and psychoanalytic conceptions can be found in Watzlawick et al. (1968).

As simultaneous critique and rectification, Habermas has proposed development of a "critical science" constituted and guided by what he presumes to be a deep, underlying impulse toward "emancipation." Against the obfuscations and repressions that accord disinterested science the full extent of knowledge, his synthetic-integrative category would reclaim and preserve the no longer hidden self-reflection of science as epistemological critique. It would surmount the Hegelian idealism yet, unlike the actual though presumably unintended outcome of Marx's effort (as Habermas has constructed it; [1968a] 1971, 25–63), maintain the depth and density of Hegel's insight. Habermas has taken what he considers to be appropriate theoretical steps toward the complete realization of emancipatory critical science, partly by way of a linguistic-philosophic reformulation of certain problematics of "historical materialism." His rationale for this reformulation is that today, allegedly, the problem of language and communicative structure has "replaced the traditional problem of consciousness" and, correspondingly, "the transcendental critique of language supersedes that of consciousness." From the beginning, however, Habermas has expressed awareness of the contingency of "theory of knowledge" in general and theoretical formulations of adequate science in particular on the self-understanding as well as the concrete conditions of historical society as such. In a passage of his Frankfurt inaugural address, Habermas adumbrated a view of his project that would be continually unfolded and elaborated in subsequent writings:

Only in an emancipated society, whose members' autonomy and responsibility had been realized, would communication have developed into the non-authoritarian and universally practiced dialogue from which both our model of reciprocally constituted ego identity and our idea of true consensus are always implicitly derived. To this extent the truth of statements is based on anticipating the realization of the good life. The ontological illusion of pure theory behind which knowledge-constitutive interests become invisible promotes the fiction that Socratic dialogue is possible everywhere and at any time. From the beginning philosophy has presumed that the autonomy and responsibility posited with the structure of language are not only anticipated but real. It is pure theory, wanting to derive everything from itself, that succumbs to unacknowledged external conditions and becomes ideological. Only when philosophy discovers in the dialectical course of history the traces of violence that deform repeated attempts at dialogue and recurrently close off the path to unconstrained communication does it further the process whose suspension it otherwise legitimates: mankind's evolution toward autonomy and responsibility. (Habermas [1965] 1971, 314–15)

"Critical science" must strive (albeit necessarily imperfectly) to enact that discovery of the sources and conditions of deformity, so as to further that process of evolution toward "autonomy and responsibility," whether they are merely approachable, historically contingent, directive values or finitely attainable goals (Habermas [1965] 1971; Habermas [1968a] 1971, 1–63; Habermas 1970c, 220; Habermas 1975a; Habermas 1975b).

Thus, the Habermasian enterprise is oriented in part by the relations among three knowledge-constitutive interests and three varieties of science: technical control (empiricities of the empirical-analytic sciences), intersubjective understanding (normativities of the historical-hermeneutic sciences), and emancipation (self-reflexivity of critical science). If this triad arouses a sense of familiarity, it is no doubt because of similarities to the constructions of various predecessors. The seventeenth-century Spinozan hierarchy— "confused ideas," which are empiricist experiences deriving from causal associations in which we bodily engage; "adequate ideas," or rationalist general notions that form cumulatively from corrections of "confused ideas," are common to all members of the community, and pertain characteristically to all bodies; and the synthetic-integrative category of "intuitive ideas," which are emancipative in the extent of their approach (necessarily asymptotic) to Spinoza's God-Nature equation—offers us an intriguing if distant juxtaposition from the annals of academic philosophy (Spinoza [1677] 1927). A less distant juxtaposition is available in the case of Scheler's triad, as I have mentioned already, which differentiated the interestedness of adaptive functionalities of knowledge in terms of mastery and domination (knowledge of specific achievements), personal development and culture (knowledge of essences), and salvation (Scheler's "emancipatory" synthetic-integrative category of knowledge of the Absolute) (Scheler [1926b] 1960, 20, 40, 61).[75] I do not, of course, mean to suggest that Habermas's product can be identified with Scheler's (much less Spinoza's) or that there exists some singularly special relationship between them (though certainly none of the differences correspond with any claim of Habermas's having surmounted idealism). Nevertheless, at the site of their respective grapplings with the post-Hegelian opposition of materiality and spirituality (Spinoza's assumed unification no longer standing), the similarities between Scheler's and Habermas's triads are evidence not merely of a sharing in what might be seen as the common store of theoretical problematics and resources but also, at the level of thinking the project,

---

75. Scheler considered "knowledge of specific achievements" (for the sake of mastery and domination) a kind of knowledge of which animals have in some sense at least a limited capability. As we will see below, Habermas's formulation includes a similar construction, which he relates to alleged inadequacies of Marx's theory.

common apprehensions of the opposition itself and of the possibility of its resolution or synthesis. In this regard it is not at all far-fetched to consider seriously the relations of mutuality between Habermas and Talcott Parsons as well as Scheler—altogether, a seemingly odd company of theorists.[76]

For Habermas, a consistently central resource has been Hegel's so-called Jena *Philosophy of Mind* (1803–4; 1805–6) which, he has reckoned, "offered a distinctive, systematic," though later abandoned, "basis for the formative process of the spirit." In contrast to the Kantian effort, Hegel did not attempt to "link the constitution of the 'I' to the reflection of the solitary 'I' on itself"; rather he understood it "in terms of formative processes, namely the communicative agreement [*Einigung*] of opposing subjects." Therefore, Habermas has argued, for Hegel it was "not reflection as such which is decisive" but "the medium in which the identity of the universal and the individual is formed." That medium consisted of the distinctive categories of "language, tools, and family," categories that "designated three equally significant patterns of dialectical relation: symbolic representation, the labor process, and interaction on the basis of reciprocity." These fundamental, distinctive, equally significant categories "are each developed as a specific configuration of mediation" of a subject and object.[77] It is not "the spirit in the absolute movement of reflecting on itself which manifests itself in, among other things, language, labor, and moral relationships"; rather it is "the dialectical interconnections between linguistic symbolization, labor, and interaction which determine the concept of spirit" (Habermas [1967] 1973, 142–44, 152; see also Habermas [1968a] 1971, 19–24, 43–63; Habermas 1973a).

Inspired by his reading of that Hegelian construction, Habermas postulated in the framework of his critical inquiry a set of linkages of the knowledge-constitutive interests and corresponding sciences to the "universal media" within which the social life of the human species evolves. "Technical interests" are those of object-instrumentalities in the medium of *labor* or *work*; "practical interests" are those of intersubjective understandings of traditional complexes of meaning in the medium of *language* or "communicative action"; "emancipatory interests" are those of self-reflective constitution in the medium of "discourse" wherein the crucial process is *domination*. This compound triad of analytical categories—of the universal media of human life, of knowledge-constitutive and guiding

---

76. Therborn (1971), among others, has pointed to some similarities between Habermas and Parsons, in his rather weak examination of Habermas's early writings.

77. Compare the treatment by Lukács [1954] 1976, especially parts 3 and 4; see also Lukács 1963.

interests, and of sciences—comprises the principal order of Habermas's investigations.

The categorization informs not only the series of writings dating from his Frankfurt inaugural address (1965) but also, *in statu nascendi*, some of his earliest publications. In an entry for the popular *Fischer-Lexicon* of philosophy, for example, Habermas set out his claim to knowledge-critique by reminding that to "speak, act, and produce means not only to make use of certain bodily organs but also to disclose a meaning" (Habermas 1958, 19–21, 32–33). The human is a creature of biological existence and of cultural significance whose "existence denotes a peculiar combination of environmental confinement and purposive openness." Either of these combined aspects would be singularly "applicable to animals or to angels; but man is placed between both." To localize the human within the one or the other, that is, within a naturalistically fixed environment or within a pure spirit, would be to propose a static, dogmatically inclined ontology: "When clinging to a substantive (ontologic) procedure by focusing on the unchanging or permanent features of human life, anthropology is uncritical and encourages in the end a dogmatism with political implications (which are the more dangerous because they are purportedly scientific)." Habermas's affirmative claim is, as he later put it, that "knowledge-constitutive interests mediate the natural history of the human species with the logic of its self-formative process" (Habermas [1968a] 1971, 196–97); these interests are not meant "to reduce this logic" to a naturalistic dimension. Although the connection between knowledge and interest is usually indirect and complexly fashioned, it is nonetheless the case that, in the depth of self-reflection, thought can penetrate the distortions of communicative action and merge with the experiential base.

> Knowledge-constitutive interests can be defined exclusively as a function of the objectively constituted problems of the preservation of life that have been solved by the cultural form of existence as such. Work and interaction by nature include processes of learning and arriving at mutual understanding. Starting at a specific stage of evolution, these processes have to be maintained in a form of methodical inquiry if the self-formative process of the species is not to be endangered. On the human level, the reproduction of life is determined culturally by work and interaction. That is why the knowledge-constitutive interests rooted in the conditions of the existence of work and interaction cannot be comprehended in the biological frame of reference of production and the preservation of species. The reproduction of social life absolutely cannot be characterized adequately without recourse to the cultural conditions of reproduction, that is, to a self-formative process that *already implies* knowledge in both forms. (Habermas [1968a] 1971, 196–97)

The preceding passage manifests the fact that Habermas's return to the Hegelian *Philosophy of Mind*, and its categories of work, language, and domination, incorporated a major critique of Marx's theory as a "historical materialism" that neglected the vital nexuses of communicative action, nexuses that must be comprehended in the institutional framework of a relation of force that "usually appears in *political form*."[78] In Habermas's view, Marx unwittingly reduced his promised critical science to the level of a "materialist scientism," modeled after the existent natural science and wholly eliminating "epistemology in favor of unchained universal 'scientific knowledge'—but this time of scientific materialism instead of absolute knowledge" (Habermas [1968a] 1971, 25–63). At the level of his categorical construction, Marx amalgamated that which must be distinguished in correspondence with the difference between the external world of nature and the intersubjective world of role structures:

> While *instrumental action* corresponds to the constraint of external nature and the level of forces of production determines the extent of technical control over natural forces, *communicative action* stands in correspondence to the suppression of man's own nature. The institutional framework determines the extent of repression by the unreflected, "natural" force of social dependence and political power, which is rooted in prior history and tradition. (Habermas [1968a] 1971, 53)

Marx's central concept of "labor" was intended as a wholly adequate basis for distinguishing the human species and thus for formulating an understanding of the history of one species. But this concept does not "sufficiently determine the form of reproduction of human life," according to Habermas. "If we consider this [question] in the light of recent anthropological

> findings, it appears that the concept of social labor extends too deeply into the scale of evolution: not only *homo sapiens* but even the hominids are distinguished from other primates in that they reproduce themselves through social labor and develop an economy. [Whereas the] Marxist concept of social labor is . . . suitable for distinguishing the mode of life of the hominids from that of the primates, . . . it does

---

78. A similar critique and programmatic conclusion have been made by Wellmer (e.g., [1969] 1971), another of the "critical theory" proponents of the Frankfurt School; to date, however, Wellmer's work has been both less intensive and briefer in scope than Habermas's work. Compare also the critique by Baudrillard (e.g., [1973] 1975).

not hold for the specifically *human* mode of reproduction of life. What is specific for human beings is that they are the first to break up the social structure which had emerged from the vertebrates; only they break up that one-dimensional status order in which each animal has a single status in the hierarchy. As far as we know, the hominid societies based on social labor had not yet been organized in kinship relationships. Only a family system allows status in the adult male's system of the hunting group to be linked (via the father's role) to status in the system of the female-and-young, thus integrating functions of social labor with functions of nurture of the young. (Habermas 1975b, 288)

Whereas emancipation from "the external forces of nature" comes about through labor processes, emancipation from "the compulsion of inner nature" and from the repressions of the institutional process can be achieved only "to the degree that institutions based on force are replaced by an organization of social relations that is bound only to communication free from domination." But, in the philosophical foundation of his critique of Hegel, Marx allegedly comprehended the self-constitution of the species as merely a "materialist activity" (social labor), and thus " 'production' seems to him the movement in which instrumental action and the institutional framework, or 'productive activity' and 'relations of production,' appear merely as different aspects of the same process." He left no place for a transcendental-philosophical grounding of ideology or critique of ideology. Although Marx was correct in asserting that a theory of knowledge is concretely possible only as a theory of society, his restriction of synthesis to the materialist category of labor aborted both his criticism and the promise of a transcendental framework of species self-constitution. This "latent positivism" was subsequently extended, in different ways, by the positivist abolition (or re-abolition) of epistemology and by the formulations of naturalistic pragmatism.

For Habermas, it is clear, Marx's concrete "sensuous human activity" must be fractured into the analytically distinct, mutually irreducible, yet interdependent categories of labor as instrumental action and intersubjectivity as communicative action. Only on the basis of that distinction, we are told, can the interrelations of "economic base" and "political-sociocultural superstructure" be fathomed without slipping on the one side into economism or on the other into idealism. Only with the distinction between labor, which is common to hominids as well as *homo sapiens*, and symbolically mediated interaction, which is singularly human, can we adequately reconstruct the evolution of the human species as a historical process of interdependencies between the level of technical-instrumental developments of productive forces (labor as the appropriation of external nature) and the level of institutional-interaction complexes of meanings and normative formations.[79] Only on the basis of that distinction between the knowledge-constitutive interests of technical control and of intersubjective understanding—in both cases, interests that are universal, irrevocable, "quasi-transcendental," and of the logic of the species' self-formative process—can we comprehend the third category of interest, that is, emancipation through processes of self-reflection, prototypical activations of which can be found in the efforts of psychoanalysis and ideology critique to break through distortion and repression (Habermas [1968a] 1971, 50–54, 62–63; Habermas [1971a] 1973, 1–40; Habermas 1971d; Habermas 1971e; Habermas 1973a; Habermas 1975a).

Thus, in his conviction of the conceptual inadequacies of Marx's theory Habermas sought to recover the lost depth of insight manifested in those Hegelian categories of labor and interaction. For purposes of his own theory of world-constitution, however, certain reformulations were deemed necessary, particularly in regard to the second of the categories. As previously conceived, the category of interaction was inadequate inasmuch as it offered only radically relativistic grounds for discriminating between symbolically mediated interactions that are free of distortions or repressions and those that are not. Only on a most arbitrary basis could one declare the presence of the impulse toward emancipatory world-constitution in this or that communicative action. In short, the emancipatory interest could not be warrantably located "within" the category of interaction as such but had to be imported from some "external," and undecided, source. As rectification of that conceptual inadequacy, Habermas turned toward certain apprehended "lessons" of ordinary-language philosophy and linguistic analysis, in relation to which he has striven to build a theory of "communicative competence" around the key premise that the emancipatory impulse (the impulse to undistorted self-reflection) must be located within language structure (cf. Horkheimer [1947] 1974, 179). As one commentator has described this important turn, Habermas has presumed that "a scientific study of the pragmatic universals of speech acts shows that the

---

79. On this matter of "species history," Habermas has argued that a reformulated historical materialism distinguishes "criteria of historical progress"—namely, "the development of productive forces" and "the maturation of forms of social integration that enable increased participation in politically relevant decision-making processes"—that are susceptible of "systematic justification. In any case, I assume that the idea of the history of the species can be reformulated to meet the objections against the idea of one-dimensional necessary and irreversible social evolution of a reified species subject" (Habermas 1975b, 291).

use of language logically accords better with some forms of institutionalized intersubjectivity than with others" (Lenhardt 1972, 243).[80]

I shall not attend here to all the details of this theory of communicative competence, nor shall I attempt to reconstruct the subjective intentionalities behind the evident shifts in emphasis of terminology and level of analysis (shifts that have contributed, no doubt, to the charges of Habermasian "eclecticism"). In this latter regard, it is apparent that Habermas altered some of the dimensions of his project shortly after (perhaps during) its manifestation as *Knowledge and Human Interests*; the self-critical statements in his new introduction to the revised, fourth edition of *Theory and Practice* (Habermas [1971a] 1973, 1–40), as well as the character of his arguments in the debates with Luhmann (Habermas 1971c; 1971d; 1970a; 1970b) and Gadamer (e.g., Habermas 1971b), are testimony to that. Nevertheless, while I shall necessarily take into account these alterations (which, it seems to me, were not as unexpected as some have believed), I have no magical scope with which to probe the "inner meanings" of Habermas's now distant rethinking of his project.

With his theory of communicative competence, Habermas has maintained a critical attitude toward approaches that have assimilated *praktikōs* to *technē* (i.e., the empirical-analytic sciences) and toward those that have tried to retrieve *praktikōs* as *praxis* but have failed to escape self-incrimination for want of a self-warranting epistemology (i.e., the historical-hermeneutic sciences). Rather than locating the emancipatory interest of species self-constitution in an undifferentiated "practical action" or "interaction" (i.e., a practical interest in the establishment and continuance of distortion-free symbolically mediated interaction), as before, however, he has distinguished from the general category of "communicative action" a notion of "discourse." It is within *discourse*, according to Habermas, that we can become critically self-conscious and collectively self-reflective of world-constitution. Thus, "the constitution theory of experience" must be "integrated in a communication theory of society" that distinguishes clearly not only between the "rules according to which we constitute the world of experience" and "the rules determining social intercourse as a process of communication" but also between the level of the latter as ordinary symbolically mediated interaction (a taken-for-granted world of normativities) and the level of discursive communication *about* the possibilities of normativity, truth, and other claims of validity:

---

80. Lenhardt's commentary remains one of the most insightful of Habermas's developing framework of analysis. My own exposition parallels his in several respects.

In attempting to make knowledge that we command in practice an explicit and conscious knowledge, we are reconstructing rules—rules that are anthropological and deeply entrenched, and upon which the reproduction of individual lives in society is necessarily dependent. As we gain insight into these invariant structures, the possibility of criticism increases; that is, we learn to distinguish between norms of thinking and acting that are negatable in principle and those quasi-transcendental rules that make possible cognition and purposive-rational action, communicative understanding and interaction in a sociocultural world. To the extent that we become conscious of this critical distinction, we can also subject to collective self-reflection what until now has been a natural process of accepting or redefining cultural traditions and definitions of life. (1971d, 208, 281)

For the analysis of those sets of rules and their interrelations, Habermas has undertaken construction of the "universal pragmatics" of the general structure of communication. In his judgment, the approaches of ordinary-language analysis, semantical and syntactical investigations, as well as hermeneutics (excepting aspects of Gadamer's hermeneutics), have been fundamentally inadequate due to failures to grasp the crucial unique structure of communication. They neglect the pragmatic subject, even while they make use, though only *implicitly*, of "the non-analyzed communicative competence of a native speaker"; by their neglect of the pragmatic dimension and thus the human subject as such, they cannot critically engage the very conditions of argumentation, which are of course their own presuppositions (Habermas 1970a, 217; Habermas 1971b; cf. Apel 1973, 2:406).

In contrast to those approaches, including the empirical pragmatics of sociolinguistics, for instance, Habermas's universal pragmatics proposes "to establish in the first place the form of intersubjectivity between any competent speakers capable of mutual understanding," by exposing the general structures of communication that exist in all possible speech situations (Habermas 1970b, 369; Habermas 1971c, 102).[81] This analysis of pragmatic, or "dialogue-constitutive," universals focuses on the basis of *all* communicative actions, on the conditions of the possibility of any communication, including systematically distorted communication. The aim of universal pragmatics is nothing less than "a reconstruction of the rule system over which adult speakers must have mastery in order to use sen-

---

81. The terms *competent speaker* and *communicative competence* refer to "the ideal speaker's mastery of the dialogue-constitutive universals, irrespective of actual restrictions under empirical conditions" (Habermas 1970b, 369). The significance of *ideal speaker*, or the *ideal speech situation*, will be treated shortly.

tences in utterances at all, regardless of the specific natural language to which the sentence belongs or the context in which it happens to be embedded" (Habermas 1976a, 156).

Habermas adopted for his formulation the frequently noted concept of the "dual structure" of the speech act. On the one hand, there is the "illocutionary force" of the speech act ("doing something," as opposed to the locutionary level of "saying something"; cf. Austin [1962b] 1975), or that component that urges the auditor to base "his own actions on the assumption that the speaker is making a serious offer," and which takes the form, whether explicitly uttered or not, of "a sentence characterized by a performative verb in the first-person present tense" (e.g., "I assert . . ."). On the other hand, the "propositional component," or that which proclaims or mentions the abstracted experience of a signifier-referent representation, is "a dependent clause of propositional content." Corresponding to this dual structure of the speech act is an equally important distinction between two "levels of communication": that "level of intersubjectivity" which is the establishment, through the illocutionary force, of the communicative roles or interpersonal relationships of speaker and auditor in mutual understanding; and that "level of objects in the world or states of affairs" which is the establishment, through the propositional component, of a consensus regarding the propositional content, a consensus governed by rules of truth. Every successful speech act is contingent on fulfillment of the double structure of speech and on the execution of communication at both levels simultaneously. The speech act must "unite the communication of a [propositional] content [about objects in the world or states of affairs] with a meta-communication about the role in which the communicated content is to be taken" (Habermas 1976a, 156–57; see also Habermas 1971c; Habermas [1976b] 1979).[82]

More specifically, a "smoothly functioning language game" depends on consensus among participants regarding four general "claims of validity" implicated in the interaction: *comprehensibility*, or agreement that a given utterance is understandable; *truth*, or agreement that the propositional content of the utterance is true; *sincerity*, or agreement that the

---

82. Although both levels are always necessarily involved, according to Habermas, the focus may be on one or the other: an "interactive use of language," wherein "the type of relationship entered into by a speaker and hearer" is focalized, the propositional content being "only mentioned"; or a "cognitive use of language," wherein the focus is on "the content of the utterance as a proposition about something which happens (or could happen) in the world," the level of communicative roles being expressed only implicitly (Habermas 1976a). As we will see below, Habermas's distinction between the two levels of communication is important to his effort to formulate a unified theory of the true and the good.

speaker utters sincerely; *legitimacy*, or agreement that the speaker utters the speech act rightfully or appropriately. These claims of validity are integral to the pragmatics of communication. For example, speech focalized at the level of propositional content (i.e., a cognitive use of language) implies an "unmistakable validity claim: namely, a truth claim, . . . a clearly demarcated and universally acknowledged claim" of the truth of a proposition; the pragmatic situation of the propositional content proclaims the truthfulness of the proposed relation of signifier to its referent, the signified. In a "normal speech situation" the four validity claims are enacted implicitly by the participants; that is, as naively accepted and enacted claims, they constitute the normality of the smoothly functioning language game. When one or more of the claims is doubted, on the other hand, the situation becomes problematic (Habermas 1971c, 116–20; Habermas 1976a, 158; Habermas 1970b).[83]

Disputed claims and the resulting problematics of interaction are approached through the discursive performances of the metalinguistic structure of ordinary language. The speech situation of discourse differs from that of ordinary communicative action in that (ideally) discourse is "purged of action and experience" in order that all activity can be given over to redemption of the doubted claim and restoration of normal interaction. Put differently, in the "substantial arguments" of discourse, that "strange suspension or virtualization typifying hypothetical thought" extends to those validity claims that were "uncritically accepted in the practical realms of communicative and instrumental action."[84] The structure of discourse

assures us: that the bracketed validity claims of assertions, recommendations, or warnings are the exclusive object of discussion; that participants, themes and contributions are not restricted except with reference to the goal of testing the validity claims in question; that no force except that of the better argument is exercised; and that, as a

83. Compare Searle's 1969 discussion of illocutionary conditions, Fillmore's "somewhat rambling" discussion of pragmatic conditions (1974), and Traugott's 1973 discussion of contextualities of literary discourse. Traugott's nomination of "genre" as a major contextual condition may be subjected to the sort of criticisms Foucault made in regard to "traditions," "schools," and so forth (Foucault [1966] 1970; Foucault [1969a] 1972).

84. This concept of "substantial argument" comes from Toulmin's study of argumentation, from which Habermas has drawn much of his own formulation (see Toulmin 1958, 125–27). I shall defer definition of the concept—together with its counterpart, "analytic argument"—until additional aspects of Toulmin's investigation have been brought into account.

result, all motives except that of the cooperative search for truth are excluded. (Habermas [1973c] 1975, 107–8)[85]

Depending on the type of claim that is in doubt, discourse follows one or another form of argumentation. In the case of a disputed claim of comprehensibility, language itself becomes the objectified focus of discourse, and the claim can be redeemed through further interaction leading to the negotiation of some convention about linguistic usage. When sincerity is challenged, the intentionality of "inner nature" becomes the objectified focus, and further interaction involving "tests" or clarification of the speaker's sincerity (or pretense) may redeem the disputed claim. If truth is in doubt, the focus is on the facts of objectified external nature, and here the dubious claim can be revalidated only by entering into "theoretical discourse," that is, discourse regarding the proposal of signifier-referent relationships. Finally, if normativity is the site of disputation, the objectified focus concerns society, specifically the role structure of actual and potential participants in the language game; and the disputed claim can be redeemed only through a "practical discourse" concerning proprieties of participation. In Habermas's view, the ability to engage effectively in these several discursive performances is crucial to personal development as a competent speaker-auditor.[86] Only when one has attained the capability of "stepping

---

85. Habermas's notion of "the force of the better argument" will be discussed below.

86. Here I shall merely mention Habermas's classification of performative verbs, which he has related to the claims of validity. By his accounting, there are five classes of pragmatic or dialogue-constitutive universals (personal pronouns and their derivatives; forms of address and speech introduction, which correlate with the role structure of language games; deictic expressions, such as demonstratives and directives of place and time, the pragmatic logic of which Habermas has proposed to demonstrate within the context of a theory of experience; performatives; and a category of nonperformative intentional verbs plus some modal verbs, which correlate with the speaker's intentions and attitudes. So far Habermas has attended mainly to the performatives. These in turn are divided into four classes, which, inasmuch as every speech act involves a performative, are also classes of speech acts: "communicatives," which express the pragmatic meaning of utterances *as* utterances; "constatives," which explicate the meaning of statements as such and make it possible to distinguish between that-which-really-is (public world) from that-which-appears-to-be (private world); "representatives," which are used with propositional components containing intentional verbs to explicate the meaning of the speaker's representation of self to the auditor and thus to differentiate the speaking self from the utterances and actions within which the self is presented; and "regulatives," which explicate the normativity of the speaker-auditor role structure and undergird the distinction of "is" from "ought" (Habermas 1971c, 109–13; Habermas 1970b, 369–70; Habermas 1971d, 186–95, 202–20; cf. Searle 1969; Searle 1975; Searle 1976).

outside the contexts of communicative action [i.e., normal speech situation] from time to time," and appreciating thereby the place from which to "negate not only propositions and speech acts but also validity claims as such (i.e., think hypothetically)" has one learned "to master the modalities of being"—that is, "to distinguish being from appearance, is from ought, essence [Wesen] from existence [Erscheinung], and sign from meaning" (Habermas 1971c, 113–17; Habermas 1976a, 165; Habermas [1971a] 1973, 18–20; Habermas 1973a, 168).

Discourse is always available as an implicit presence in the normal context of interaction; indeed, to put it the other way around, normal interaction necessarily presupposes the possibility that discursive resources can be invoked at any time. In the normal speech situation we take for granted that the speaker not only utters deliberately, sincerely, appropriately, and with self-confidence but also could discursively justify the implicit claims of the utterance if challenged to do so. This tacit dimension of smoothly functioning language games is an essential feature of interaction; without its presence, interactions would unravel in an endless series of metalinguistic reflections.

Yet, paradoxical though it may seem, our granting undoubted (or at least unchallenged) authority to the speaker is more often than not counterfactual: "We know that institutionalized actions do not as a rule fit this *model of pure communicative action*, although we cannot avoid proceeding counterfactually as if the models were really the case—on this unavoidable fiction rests the humanity of intercourse among men who are still men."[87] Given the prevalence of this "unavoidable fiction," two questions are presented. First, what accounts for the persistence of such counterfactual beliefs as viable expectations regarding normal interaction? Where is the source of stability? Habermas's answer calls upon his notions of domination and systematically distorted communication: stability can be achieved

> only through legitimation of the ruling systems of norms and through the anchoring of the belief in legitimacy in systematic barriers to will-forming communication. The claim that our norms can be grounded is redeemed through legitimizing world views. The validity of these world views is in turn secured in a communication structure that excludes discursive will-formation. . . . [The] barriers to communication which make a fiction precisely of the reciprocal imputation of accountability, support at the same time the belief in legitimacy that

---

87. Here one readily thinks of the engaging descriptions provided by Garfinkel of the tacit agreements of language use (Garfinkel 1967); needless to say, awareness of that dimension has underwritten one genre of comedy for a very long time.

sustains the fiction and prevents its being found out. That is the paradoxical achievement of ideologies, whose prototype is the neurotic disturbance. (Habermas 1971c, 120)

Simply put, the conditions resulting in systematically distorted communication, which are at one and the same time the conditions that make the beliefs and expectations counterfactual, also legitimate and sustain the fiction in the guise of a factual situation. This "ideological justification" of validity consists of systematic chains of argument that simultaneously express a matter-of-fact truth and legitimacy and, surreptitiously, preclude the thematization and testing of those matter-of-fact claims (Habermas 1970a; Habermas 1970b; Habermas 1971b; Habermas 1971c; Habermas 1973b; Habermas 1976c; cf. Bourdieu and Passeron [1970] 1977; Bourdieu [1972] 1977).

This brings us to the second question: What *are* those conditions of "systematically distorted" or, conversely, "undistorted" communication? Habermas's answer again refers to the pragmatic structure of communication. Free or undistorted communication can occur only within a context of "pure interaction," that is, interaction free of all constraints of domination, whether these result from conscious strategic behavior or from barriers secured in ideological or neurotic formations. Such absence of constraint is conceived in terms of the "general requirement of symmetry," that is, a symmetrical distribution of chances to select and to employ speech acts. Symmetry must obtain for each of the four classes of Habermas's classification of speech acts.[88] As specific requirements for the possibility of discourse—that is, the creation of "pure communicative action" as a context of discourse—there must be a symmetry with respect to representative speech acts, such that all participants are completely sincere in revealing their "inner natures," and with respect to regulative speech acts, such that there are no privileged normative positions or conditions that would entail a merely formal equality of role assumption and performance. Similarly, as requirements directly of discourse itself, all participants must have the same chance to employ communicative speech acts, such that discourse can be initiated and continued by anyone at any time, and constative speech acts, such that all opinions and propositions can be argued openly and completely. These specific conditions of speech acts are considered by Habermas to be "a linguistic conceptualization of what are traditionally known as the ideas of truth [symmetries of constative speech acts], freedom [symmetries of representative speech acts], and justice [symmetries

---

88. This classification, it will be remembered, is simultaneously one of performatives.

of regulative speech acts]" (Habermas 1971c, 114–22; Habermas 1970b, 372; Habermas 1973b).[89]

Of course, the conditions of actual speech situations rarely if ever correspond to those just outlined. Rather, the situation defined by symmetries as stipulated in the general requirement is itself an idealization, referred to by Habermas as "the supposition of the ideal speech situation." In his view, it is an ideal that unites the conditions of "ideal discourse" with those of "ideal interaction" or, more generally, an "ideal life form." But, as an ideal, empirically "we can only anticipate it."

> A speech situation determined by pure intersubjectivity is an idealization. The mastery of dialogue-constitutive universals does not itself amount to a capacity actually to establish the ideal speech situation. But communicative competence does mean the mastery of the means of construction necessary for the establishment of an ideal speech situation. No matter how the intersubjectivity of mutual understanding may be deformed, the *design* of an ideal speech situation is necessarily implied in the structure of potential speech, since all speech, even of intentional deception, is oriented towards the idea of truth. This idea can only be analyzed with regard to a consensus achieved in unrestrained and universal discourse. Insofar as we master the means for the construction of an ideal speech situation, we can conceive the ideas of truth, freedom, and justice, which interpret each other—although of course only as ideas. On the strength of communicative competence alone, however, and independent of the empirical structures of the social system to which we belong, we are quite unable to realize the ideal speech situation, we can only anticipate it. (Habermas 1970b, 372)

Habermas's preference to treat the matter as "an *anticipation* of the ideal speech situation" signifies not only that the ideal may be used as a guide for constructions of a critique of systematically distorted communication, and a determination to institutionalize free discourse, but also that the "fundamental norms of rational speech that are built into universal pragmatics contain . . . a practical hypothesis." That is, the test of an anticipated situation, which is imagined in discourse, must be executed on practical grounds, namely whether or to what extent a now realized anticipated

---

89. It is worth noting that there are parallels between Habermas's discussion of "emancipated" or "domination-free" discourse and Hegel's discussions of the dangers especially of the privatization of interests and discourse that confront his "absolute *Sittlichkeit*" or "ethical life" (see, e.g., Hegel [1802] 1968, 450–57).

situation corresponds to the ideal (Habermas 1970b, 371–73; Habermas 1973b, 258; Habermas 1976c).

At this point a third question is well upon us; Habermas's answer to it is in fact implicated in the preceding discussion. Granted that the counterfactuality of the model of pure communicative action is stabilized by the ideological mode of justification, with the result that the conditions of counterfactuality can continue to serve as expectations of normal interaction. We must still ask the following: given the first instance of a successfully challenged claim of validity that is thematized as such at the level of the empirically limited structure of communication, from what matrix of reality constitution can there be derived an argumentative conclusion that is not merely redemptive but also certified and installed as an *unquestioned* claim of normal interaction? On what grounds can we (as the participants of a discourse) distinguish between alternative consensual conclusions of a discourse concerning disputed validity claims, between a consensus that is correct and a consensus that merely appears to be so? How can we ascertain the validity of a consensual redemption of disputed validity claims without succumbing to an infinite regression of discursive arguments and justifications, on the one hand, or to the importation of some external and unclarified "decisional force" on the other? In order to demonstrate Habermas's answer, we must consider further his concept of the ideal speech situation and in particular his so-called consensual theories of truth (facticity) and of justice (normativity). These latter, of course, reveal his theory of knowledge and his theory of ethics, which, he has asserted consistently, intersect in the "insight that the truth of statements is linked in the last analysis to the intention of the good and true life" (Habermas [1965] 1971, 317; Habermas [1971a] 1973; Habermas 1971c; Habermas 1973c; Habermas 1976c).

To begin with, it must be understood that the Habermasian theory shares with others the principle that "truth" relates linguistic formulations *about* the world, though Habermas's emphasis is upon the pragmatic rather than the semantic or syntactical dimension: "I may ascribe to an object a predicate if and only if *every other person who could* enter into a dialogue with me *would* ascribe the same predicate to the same object. . . . The condition of the truth of statements is the potential agreement of all others" (Habermas 1973b, 219).[90] Specifically, "truth" is a validity claim consti-

---

90. This formulation is close to that of Peirce—"The opinion which is fated to be ultimately agreed to by all who investigate, is what we mean by the truth . . ." (Peirce [1878] 1960, ¶407)—and it suffers some of the same difficulties. In the terms of Habermas's definition, for example, there is the regressive question of what truthful standard serves to discriminate "same predicate" from "different predicate" and "same object" from "different object."

tuted in the pragmatic universals of constative speech acts—which is to say, the cognitive use of language—and pertains to the propositional content of a statement. We can properly understand that constitution, according to Habermas, only on the basis of a fundamental distinction between the "constitution of objects" and the "constitution of facticities" (which corresponds to the difference between semantics of a propositional content and pragmatics of the performative part of a statement). The "categorical meaning" (semantic relation of sign to referent) is determined by and constituted with "the objects of possible experience." As such, it is "the material *a priori* premise of experience," from which we can then access reality "by objectivating it."

> The categorical meaning of propositions is connected with the species of objects of experience of which we predicate something. By contrast, the meaning of a discursive truth claim embodied in statements is connected with the existence of states of affairs [*Sachverhalten*] which we render in those statements. In every speech act, categorical meaning is contained in the propositional content, whereas the truth claim is contained in the performative part. For the categorical meaning always reflects the way in which we experience *something in the world*—as a thing or event, as a person or as that person's utterance. The truth claim, on the other hand, reflects the intersubjective validity, on the basis of which something may be predicated of objects of experience, i.e., that a state of affairs is indeed a fact. (Habermas 1973a, 166–67)

In the communicative action of normal interaction the categorical meaning of the propositional content and the *implicit* truth claim or facticity of the performative component are enacted nonproblematically. However, when the truth claim is challenged, the claim itself becomes objectified and focalized; the discursive argumentations that ensue focus on the question of facticity as such, not on the experienced "objects" or "states of affairs in the world." The site of dubiety is pragmatic rather than semantic, and the intendedly redemptive or resolutive arguments (enacting metalinguistic structures) consist of nonredundant utterances *about* the truth of (disputed) truth claims or facticities. Thus, Habermas's conception of "truth" in part emphasizes the important point that any determination of the relation between reality and knowledge of/about reality is achievable *only* through language and that the "correspondence theory of truth" is a pragmatic-logical impossibility, as it "attempts in vain to break out of the sphere of language" (Habermas 1973b, 214–19; Habermas 1971c, 123–36; Habermas 1970a, 206; Habermas 1973a; Habermas 1976c).

While experiences "*support* the truth claim of assertions" of propositional content, "a truth claim can be redeemed only through argumentation," in particular the argumentation of theoretical discourse. That is, a "claim *founded* [*fundiert*] on experience is by no means a *warranted* or *justified* [*begründet*] claim," according to Habermas's analysis. "Truth qua justification of the truth claim inherent in a proposition does not reveal itself, like the objectivity of experience, in feed-back controlled action but only in a process of successful reasoning by which the truth claim is first rendered problematic and then redeemed." Since this discursive warranting or justification of doubted truth claims is itself a normative process, and since the "rightfulness" of doubted claims of rightful action (i.e., norma-tivities) is established through the argumentation of practical discourse, the pragmatic logic of discourse must serve for both theory of knowledge ("the true") and theory of ethics ("the just" and "the good"). In both respects, as we have seen already, it is a unified "consensus theory"; "truth claim" is identified in terms of a resolutive process of "making the claim good," which means convincing the participants: "the condition for the truth of statements is the potential agreement of all others" (Habermas 1973b, 219, 242; Habermas 1973a, 169; Habermas 1971c, 124; Habermas 1976c).

However, mere consensus or "agreement of all others" cannot in itself be identified with "truth," for that would admit the possibility of an un-clarified, merely empirical constitution of truth, in which case there would be no rational grounds for the discrimination of genuine from apparent but false consensus. Truth cannot be simply

> the fact that a consensus is realized but rather that, at all times and in any place, if we enter into discourse a consensus can be realized under conditions that identify it as a warranted consensus. Truth means "warranted assertability." (Habermas 1973b, 239–40).[91]

The question is (still), what *are* those conditions by which we can know a warranted as opposed to an unwarranted or false consensus? If it is the case, as Habermas has insisted throughout (e.g., 1971c, 134), that "the truth of statements cannot be decided without reference to the competence of those who might possibly judge" (i.e., reference to a role), and that "this competence cannot be decided without an evaluation of the veracity of their expressions and the correctness of their actions"—all of which goes to say that determination of a warranted consensus cannot escape society (normativity) and subjective intentionality (questions of sincerity) any more than it can escape language—nevertheless there are still to be clarified the conditions of that "warranted assertability."

Here Habermas has introduced a notion of "the force of the better

---

91. Cf. Dewey's notion of knowledge as "warranted assertion" (see, e.g., Dewey 1929; Dewey 1938).

argument." Pragmatically one imagines in theoretical discourse an ideal speech situation, characterized by the absence of systematically distorted communication and by the conviction that a *genuine* consensus is indeed possible and will come about as the result of, and *only* as the result of, the force of the better argument.[92]

> Peirce and Toulmin have both seen the rationally motivating force of argumentation in the fact that the progress of knowledge takes place through substantial arguments. The latter are based on logical inferences, but they are not exhausted in deductive systems of statements. Substantial arguments serve to redeem or to criticize validity claims, whether the claims to truth implicit in assertions or the claims to correctness connected with norms (of action and evaluation) or implied in recommendations and warnings. They have the force to convince the participants in a discourse of a validity claim, that is, to *provide rational grounds for* the recognition of validity claims. (Habermas [1973c] 1975, 107)

This pragmatic force is centrally characterizable as a "cogency" of argumentation that creates the "rational motivation" of participants' agreement. "Cogency," in turn, has been explicated by Habermas with reference to Toulmin's 1958 analysis of argumentation, specifically his discrimination of the hierarchical structure or "layout" of argumentation. In contradistinction to the standard syllogistic account, Toulmin proposed a more sensitive and practically adequate construction of arguments, the terms of which are summarized as follows:

• the *claim*, or the "conclusion whose merits we are seeking to establish";

• the *data*, or "the facts we appeal to as a foundation for the claim" (in Habermas's terms, the "experiences" that may "support the truth claim" but that "by no means" can "warrant" or "justify" the claim);

• the *warrant*, or "general, hypothetical statements, which can act as bridges, and authorize the sort of step [from data to claim] to which our particular argument commits us";[93] as such, the "general, hypothetical

---

92. This force of the better argument is not the *argumentum ad baculum* of the logicians; the "force" in question rather has to do with the "persuasiveness" of talk. Yet, in saying that, one raises the question of where (how) precisely to draw the line between "reason" and "rod."

93. The warrant may be present only implicitly, until the relevance or propriety of the cited data vis-à-vis the conclusion is challenged, in which case the warrant will be invoked in order "to register explicitly the legitimacy of the step involved and to refer it back to the larger class of steps whose legitimacy is being presupposed" (Toulmin 1958, 100).

statements" must be differentiated according to the "different degrees of force" with which they "justify" the claim, that is, some warrants authorize unequivocally but others do not and thereby require the presence of both a *qualifier*, which stipulates (more or less precisely) the magnitude of the warranting force (i.e., the claim must be understood as a qualified conclusion of the data, in virtue of the given warrant), and the *conditions of rebuttal*, or "a specification of the circumstances in which the general authority of the warrant" does not apply;

- the *backing of the warrant*, or statements establishing the applicability or relevance not merely of the particular instance of the warrant but of the general class of warrants of which this instance is a member; such statements (which take a variety of forms, e.g., taxonomic regularities, legal provisions, statistical distribution of observations) are always categorical statements of facticities but, unlike the data of an argument, are at least initially nonexplicitly present; they consist of basic agreements of regularity or order of reality (see Toulmin 1958, 97–105).

Habermas's use of this construction focuses on the four major categories or levels of the structure of argumentation: claim, data, warrant, and backing of warrant. The conditions of cogency are considered to be those that allow movement of discourse to more and more radical levels, that is, from the surface level of claim and cited data to the level of warrant and then to the backing of the warrant. At the most radical level, the backing statements, discourse is focused on possible systematic changes of basic conceptual framework, which amounts to consideration of what will count as "knowledge" and what will not. Given that such consideration necessarily involves attention to knowledge-constitutive interests (i.e., what will count as "knowledge" for what purpose?), need structures are brought explicitly into play, and the distinction between facticities and normativities loses its sharp lines. In Habermas's terms, one can no longer clearly distinguish "theoretical discourse" from "practical discourse" (Habermas 1973b, 211–12, 241–46, 251–58).

Thus, we know that the constitution of a "rationally motivated consensus" depends on the degree of freedom with which discursive performers can shift from consideration of the face of the claim and its supporting data of experience to consideration of the underlying warrant and then to the statements backing that warrant. Given such freedom, disputed claims can be redeemed (or replaced) consensually by the force of the better argument rather than as a consequence of discursively extrinsic forces and constraints. To the question "What pragmatic properties of discourse make that freedom possible?" the answer is, of course, "Those defined as the ideal speech situation." Indeed, according to Habermas, the very enactment of any discursive performance concerning "the true" or "the just" and "the good" immediately evinces the performer's conviction that rationally grounded consensus can be achieved in principle and that it can be achieved through argumentation. Empirically, in the given situation, that may prove not to be the case:

> The ideal speech situation is neither an empirical phenomenon nor simply a construct but a reciprocal supposition which is unavoidable in discourse. This supposition can, though need not be, counterfactual; but even when it is counterfactual, it is a fiction operatively effective in communication. I would prefer therefore to speak of an anticipation of an ideal speech situation. . . . This anticipation alone is the warrant that permits us to join to an actually attained consensus the claim of a rational consensus. At the same time, it is a critical standard against which every actually realized consensus can be disputed and tested. (Habermas 1973b, 258)

Whether an "actually attained consensus" does indeed qualify as rationally motivated or grounded is an empirical question. Likewise, whether the anticipated ideal speech situation is realizable under existent conditions is and can only be a practical hypothesis, that is, a projected realization the sole effective test for which can be found in human practice.

Some aspects of the Habermasian theory of veridical knowledge might be acknowledged as fundamentally correct constructions—if one could discriminably accept analytically isolated "aspects" or "elements" of a formation. I should include in that hypothetical acknowledgment, for example, the assertions that a theory of knowledge must be a theory of society, that truth is integral with values, interests, and normativities, that truth determination is inherently a matter of human "agreements" formulated within the dynamic context of domination and force. Cast in the fantasy of context-free or analytically isolated "elements" or "aspects-in-themselves," we might agree there is much to be said for those assertions. However, taken *eo ipso* as a theory of knowledge, Habermas's so-called consensus theory (or "discourse theory") displays the substantial inadequacies of a one-sided, idealist formulation, wherein truth is held to derive from a relativistic process of serious talk ("discourse") about ideas. The grounding of arguments "has nothing to do with the relation between individual sentences and reality"; rather it is concerned "above all with the coherence between sentences within systems of speech" (Habermas 1973b, 245; but see p. 247, where he suggested the possible rejuvenation of correspondence theory).

Veridical knowledge is conceived as a direct matter of discursive practices, that is, of ideation, thinking, reason (albeit "reason" not as mere *Verstand*). Specific truths and the standards by which real and false consensuses can be distinguished are established relative to the conditions of thinking/talking—the conditions of communicative action or "language games" and in particular the conditions of the metacommunication of discourse. Now, it is granted that these conditions analytically correspond to the material conditions of the actuality of domination in society. "We have reason to assume," as Habermas has phrased it in one passage,

> that social action is not only—and perhaps not even primarily—controlled by motives which coincide with the intentions of the actor-speaker, but rather by motives excluded from public communication and fixed to a pre-linguistic symbol organization [i.e., nonconscious structures]. The greater the share of pre-linguistically fixed motivations which cannot be freely converted in public communication, the greater the deviance from the model of pure communicative action. I would propose to make the empirical assumptions, first, that these deviations increase in proportion to the degree of repression which characterizes the institutional system within a given society; and secondly that the degree of repression depends in turn on the developmental stage of the productive forces and on the organization of authority, that is, of the institutionalization of political and economic power. (Habermas 1970b, 373–74)

This declaration of the problematic would seem to imply, even to demand, that inquiry should begin not with the abstraction of a "discourse" and "discourse-constitutive universals" but with the concrete reality of domination and productive forces.

For Habermas, however, the problem of domination still remains. Because of his radical separations of "labor," "action," and "language," any concern for concrete relations of domination—supposedly central to his endeavor—slips through his fingers. He has often been in the position of treating reflexive apprehension of the concrete conditions of life as equivalent to a concrete capability of overturning those conditions (though there has been some effort in later works, such as *Legitimation Crisis in Late Capitalism* [1973c] 1975, to retrieve the centrality of domination).[94] He has proposed a theory of knowledge articulated in idealist terms on the supposition of an idealization of material conditions. Truths—always conditional-contingent truths—are arrived at in discursive agreements, but the emancipatory interest or constitutiveness of any of those truths depends upon the presence or absence of repressions and distortions—that is, on whether or not the conditions of discourse were actually those of the

---

94. Though in general both parties to the Habermas-Gadamer debate have gone astray, Gadamer was correct in his reservation: "I cannot share the claims of critical theory that one can master the impasse of our civilization by emancipatory reflection" (Gadamer 1975, 315).

idealized discursive situation. To be sure, Habermas has contended that the possibility of emancipation is given to us in and because of language:

> The human interest in autonomy and responsibility is not mere fancy, for it can be apprehended a priori. What raises us out of nature is the only thing whose nature we can know: *language*. Through its structure, autonomy and responsibility are posited for us. Our first sentence expresses unequivocally the intention of universal and unconstrained consensus. Taken together, autonomy and responsibility constitute the only idea that we possess a priori in the sense of the philosophical tradition. (Habermas [1965] 1971, 314)

But of course Habermas also has acknowledged that language, even as means and vehicle of the *expression* of that alleged aprioristic universal intention of emancipation, is itself historically contingent—in the terms of his analytics, contingent on action and on labor. In unemancipated society (Habermas's society, our society) action and labor are marked by repressions and distortions, which make language—his language, our language, language through which "autonomy and responsibility *are posited for us*"—susceptible of ideological deformity.

How, then, if the *idea* of emancipation, the ideal of distortion-free discourse, is itself susceptible of distortion and the suspicion of ideological deformity, can that *idea as such* possibly initiate a *critical practice* of the *realization* of the emancipatory intention? Habermas is obligated to demonstrate the possibility of breaking out of the dilemma of proposing an allegedly effective *idea of emancipation* within conditions of an *unemancipated* society. Unless and until he can demonstrate the possibility of distortion-free, repression-free conditions of discourse (i.e., conditions of action and labor, in his terms), and not merely for some elite category of scientists, he cannot demonstrate the possibility of distortion-free knowledge. The value in which his theory of truth and ethics is predicated, namely emancipation from alienating domination, refers to a practice that is not, and cannot be, merely ideal practice; it must be simultaneously material practice. Without that fundamental integrity, he reproduces the philosophic duality of a truth-capable mind and a toil-ridden body, and his proposed theory of truth degenerates from the level of whatever aprioristic ideal of human autonomy and responsibility he may have imagined to a level only marginally different from the liberalist paean of "seeking truth through reasoned conversation." Without the material grounding of a substantiated possibility of nonrepressed, nondistorted action and labor, Habermas's truth, the putative truth of his theory of truth, cannot be concretely discriminated from any other claim.

Habermas has surely been aware of the necessity of material grounding, or at least a material "linkage." To that end, he has proposed that his theory of communicative competence, at the level of its metatheoretical framework, must be "linked convincingly with the precisely rendered fundamental assumptions of historical materialism," from which may result an adequate theory of social evolution. Such theory must proceed in three dimensions: the development of the forces of production, the development of organizational forms and techniques that enhance the "guidance" or "steering capacities" of societies, and the development and critical dissolution of legitimating interpretive systems. In other words, an adequate theory of social evolution, which must be formulated in terms of the analytically separate dimensions of labor, action, and discourse, would provide linkages of ideal and material practices by virtue of the integrative metatheoretical structure of his theory of communicative competence (Habermas [1971a] 1973, 12; Habermas 1971d, 270–90; Habermas [1973c] 1975, 1–31; Habermas 1975a; Habermas 1975b). Habermas's typology of knowledge-constitutive interests (and of the sciences), one must recall, has as its direct counterpart at the level of that-about-which-knowledge-is-constituted a typology of "media" of world constitution—that is, labor, action, and language (discourse)[95]—and, it is clear, the proposed relation among these media is hierarchical: from labor to action to discourse, one of necessary conditioning; from discourse to action and labor, one of intendedly self-reflexive but empirically problematic control. In his recent analytics (e.g., Habermas [1973c] 1975, 4–17, and passim; Habermas 1975a; Habermas 1975b), he has addressed relations of these media in terms of the so-called systems-theoretic perspective (with particular reference to Niklas Luhmann and Talcott Parsons), in accordance with his continuing effort to realign and synthetically transcend the diverging "system" and "life-world" perspectives.[96] The relevant categories here are designated as the separable economic, political, and sociocultural systems or subsystems;[97] and in this vocabulary we are told, for example, that social

95. Object-constitution results from "the systematic interplay of sense reception, action, and linguistic representation" (Habermas 1971d, 206).

96. "If we comprehend a social system as a life-world, then the steering aspect is screened out. If we understand a society as a system, then the fact that social reality consists in the facticity of recognized, often counter-factual, validity claims is not taken into consideration" (Habermas [1973c] 1975, 5). (If "social reality" indeed consists only in "validity claims" that are "often *counter*factual," then "social reality" is identified with a sometimes *false* consciousness! One must wonder, what is the constitution of that "reality" *behind* the "social reality" on which basis one can discriminate the counterfactual from the factual, the false consciousness from the true? I shall return to this momentarily.)

97. "Sociocultural system" includes "the cultural tradition (cultural value systems), as well as the institutions that give these traditions normative power through processes of socialization and professionalization" (Habermas [1973c] 1975, 5 n. 15).

evolution takes place in the separate dimensions named "development of productive forces," "increase in system autonomy—power," and "change in normative structures"; that "crisis," as an experienced threat to social identity and normative structures, is explicable in terms of problems of "steering" or guidance (the political system), of which "the subjects are not generally conscious"; that "steering problems can have crisis effects if (and only if) they cannot be resolved within the range of possibility that is circumscribed by the organizational principle of the society," that is, by the "highly abstract regulations arising as emergent properties in improbable evolutionary steps and characterizing, at each stage, a new level of development"; that a given "principle of organization" determines "firstly, the learning mechanism on which the development of productive forces depends, . . . secondly, the range of variation for the interpretive systems that secure identity, and finally . . . the institutional boundaries for the possible expansion of steering capacity." The hierarchical relations among "possible developments" in these "spheres of productive forces, steering capacity, and world-views (or moral systems)" seem to Habermas to be characterized empirically by "a conspicuous asymmetry" at the level of the "reproduction of sociocultural life":

> While the development of productive forces always extends the scope of contingency of the social system, evolutionary advances in the structures of interpretive systems by no means always offer advantages of selection. . . . Because the mechanisms which cause developmental advances in the normative structures are independent of the *logic* of their development, there exists *a fortiori* no guarantee that a development of the forces of production and an increase in steering capacity will release exactly those normative alternatives that correspond to the steering imperatives of the social system. (Habermas [1973c] 1975, 12–13)

Thus it is that with such considerations in mind Habermas has set out "to look for organizational principles that determine the learning capacity, and thus the level of development, of a society—above all in regard to its forces of production and its identity-securing interpretive systems—and which thereby limit the possible growth in steering capacities as well" (Habermas [1973c] 1975, 16).

Before judging the mettle of these formulations of "media of world constitution," developmental "spheres," and a grounding of his consensus theory, we must try to be clear about Habermas's meaning of the nature-society distinction, inasmuch as it is a major site of reference for those formulations. In his recent disquisitions about "problems of legitimation" and the "reconstruction of historical materialism" (e.g., Habermas [1973c]

1975; Habermas 1973d; Habermas 1975a; Habermas 1975b), wherein he has taken steps toward that "linkage" of the analysis of communicative competence with processes of labor and productive forces from the standpoint of a projected synthesis of "system" and "life-world," one could easily conclude that he has lapsed into hypostatized imaginations of some analyzable, comprehendible presocial "natural state"—an "outer nature" that is "appropriated in production processes" and an "inner nature" that is appropriated in "socialization processes," both processes being accretive in appetite as the "steering capacity" of the "social system" develops. For instance, Habermas says:

> Production processes extract natural resources and transform the energies set free into use values. Socialization processes shape the members of the system into subjects capable of speaking and acting. The embryo enters this formative process, and the individual is not released from it until his death. (Habermas [1973c] 1975, 9)

This and other passages are not free of ambiguity. Are we to understand that those "natural resources" and their untransformed energies were thinkable as "not-yet" use values, that is, as not appropriate to, not a part of, society? That "members" and "embryo" were thinkable as a "not-yet" state, relative to the social? One might conclude, when Habermas wrote "the embryo *enters* this formative process" of socialization, that he was not thinking simply the specific historical contingency of the formation of a concrete woman or man—i.e., that persons of a particular society are produced and reproduced socially within and of *that* society—but rather that he was imagining an apprehensible passage from "embryo" as presocial "inner nature" to appropriate or socialized individual. Yet such conclusions seem indefensible in view of the pertinent argument set forth earlier in the first part of *Knowledge and Human Interests*. There he put forward the important point of the assumption of "something like a nature in itself"— that is to say, of what such an assumption can mean:

> It is prior to the world of mankind. It is at the root of laboring subjects as natural beings and also enters into their labor processes. *But as the subjective nature of man and the objective nature of their environment, it is already part of a system of social labor that is divided up into two aspects of the same "process of material exchange."* While epistemologically we must presuppose nature as existing in itself, we ourselves have access to nature *only within* the historical dimension disclosed by labor process. . . . "Nature in itself" is therefore an abstraction, which is a requisite of our thought [and, we must beware, an abstraction notoriously present as *reified* abstraction]: but we

always encounter nature within the horizon of the world-historical self-formative process of mankind. (Habermas [1968a] 1971, 34; emphases added)

This simple but fundamental point has the "epistemological function," Habermas then argued, of "pointing to the contingency of nature as a whole." It battles the nonsensical yet immensely dangerous idealist construction of a nature-in-itself, that is, the reductive view that posits "nature" as a mere externalization of mind; "it preserves nature's immovable facticity despite nature's historical embeddedness in the universal structure of mediation constituted by laboring subjects." In this discussion Habermas has reminded us of the unmitigated absurdity of all those "nature-in-itself" viewpoints—those reifications of an abstraction that can be *only* an abstraction, *our* abstraction—which would have us dance the fantasy of stepping behind our being in order to discover the meaning of our beingness. Far from positing a thinkable, speakable, describable—indeed, *positable*— nature as some presocial state, Habermas's discussion here places nature (even that very abstraction of nature "prior to the world of mankind") in precisely the only location we can think/make: not the location of a mere externalization of mind but that of "historical embeddedness" in the "world-historical self-formative process of mankind."

Still, there is in the Habermasian formulation an ambiguity that will not go away: on the one hand, "nature in itself" is only an abstraction; on the other hand, it is allegedly "a requisite of our thought," that is, "epistemologically we *must* presuppose nature as existing in itself." This purported necessity of the *in-itself*, "a nature preceding human history," reveals in Habermas's construction a tendency to try to retain that which he has also sought to abolish—namely, as Theunissen put it, "an unquestionably objectivistic nature-ontology, or at least . . . a mode of thought that grants nature priority over history and raises it to the status of the absolute origin" (Theunissen 1969, 13). It is a tendency to retain the illusion of the quest for ultimate origins (*Ursprung*), imagined as that which was prior to and at the root of human history, and yet somehow humanly accessible. Further indication of this tendency is given in a previously quoted passage, wherein Habermas evinced a willingness to rely on "recent anthropological findings," according to which "it appears that the concept of social labor extends too deeply into the scale of evolution" for it "sufficiently [to] determine the form or reproduction of human life"; indeed, "not only *homo sapiens* but even the hominids are distinguished from other primates in that they reproduce themselves through social labor and develop an economy" (Habermas 1975b, 288). Apparently he has not found it at all problematic to presuppose the validity of knowledge claims offered by this particular science ("anthropology") as part of the framework both of his critique of the "scientistic" character of modern science generally and of his effort to create a "critical-emancipatory" science.[98]

Habermas has reopened to our attention this crucial aspect of Marx's work (see also Schmidt [1962] 1971), and in doing so he has sought to combat certain perversions of it. Nevertheless, while purportedly working toward a revitalization of that aspect of Marx, he has become ensnared in the web of fictions of an original nature from which there improbably emerged an improbable creature, *homo sapiens*: such constructions are neither necessary nor innocent. Habermas has also read Marx as having proposed primarily a historical-materialist inversion of Kant, and with that construction, too, I cannot agree.[99] Let me quickly appeal, once again, that I do not intend to wander into the tiresome activity of divining intentions of dead authors; by opposing my construction to Habermas's I intend primarily to challenge certain of his formulations *as such*.

By Habermas's account, the "characteristic difference" distinguishing the works of Kant and Marx consists in their respective locations of the subject-object synthesis: whereas for Kant the "synthesis of the material of intuition by the imagination receives its necessary unity through categories of the understanding," which are themselves constituted as "transcendental rules of synthesis," for Marx the "synthesis of the material of labor by labor power receives its actual unity through categories of man's manipulations," that is, through categories that are constituted as instrumental or "technical rules of synthesis" belonging to the "historically alterable inventory of societies." In other words, Marx differed from Kant insofar as he anchored his conception of synthesis in a "historical-materialist" complex—in "empirically mediated rules of synthesis that are objectified as productive forces and [that] historically transform the subjects' relation to

98. The "anthropological findings" to which Habermas referred may well have been informed also by constructions from recent "ethological" and "sociobiological" studies—perhaps of the same textual network as referenced in Piaget's evolutionist argument. This juxtaposition with Piaget is not accidental: although the foundations of Habermasian and Piagetian theory are hardly identical, there are nevertheless some conventionally definable similarities between them. What is more, Habermas has acknowledged a favorable reception of "Piaget's *genetic* structuralism" and "developmental logic" (see, e.g., Habermas [1976d] 1979, 124–25).

99. In addition to the discussion in the first part of *Knowledge and Human Interests*, Habermas's early writings on Marx include the essay, "Between Philosophy and Science: Marxism as Critique" (1971a, 195–252), first published in 1963.

their natural environment" (Habermas [1968a] 1971, 34–37). Nonetheless, according to Habermas, there remained in Marx a major Kantian "component":

> What is Kantian about Marx's conception of knowledge is the invariant relation of the species to its natural environment, which is established by the behavioral system of instrumental action—for labor processes are the "perpetual natural necessity of human life." The conditions of instrumental action arose contingently in the natural evolution of the human species. At the same time, however, they bind our knowledge of nature to the interest of possible technical control over natural processes. (Habermas [1968a] 1971, 35)

It is in this component, Habermas claimed, that one finds the nurtured seeds of a modern "instrumental theory of knowledge." Quoting a passage from Marx—"Natural science will eventually subsume the science of man just as the science of man will subsume natural science: there will be a *single* science"—Habermas found this "demand for a natural science of man, with its positivist overtones" (Habermas [1968a] 1971, 46) (though elaborated not so much by Marx as later by the "naturalistic pragmatists," especially Peirce and Dewey; see Habermas [1968a] 1971, 113–39), to be an "astonishing" proposal by Marx.

Habermas's objection is that the instrumentalist construction—a framework "posited within the behavioral system of instrumental action"—is fundamentally inadequate precisely because of its restrictive instrumentalism: the "philosophical foundation of this materialism" that proposes synthesis exclusively through labor is clearly unable to found "an unconditional phenomenological self-reflection of knowledge and thus prevent the positivist atrophy of epistemology" (Habermas [1968a] 1971, 41–44). It is therein impotent because it is silent about that dimension of practice within which "phenomenological experience moves"—a dimension allegedly *noncoincidental* "with that of instrumental action," namely the symbolic interactions and cultural-institutional structures that constitute power, domination, and ideology. In sum, Habermas has indicted Marx's argument as being a "reduction of the self-generative act of the human species to labor," to labor conceived as the merely instrumental act of constituting material objects of "external nature":

> Marx deludes himself about the nature of reflection when he reduces it to labor. He identifies "transformative abolition (*Aufheben*), as objective movement which reabsorbs externalization," with the appropriation of essential powers that have been externalized in working on material. . . . *Marx conceives of reflection according to the model*

of production, [and therefore] he does not distinguish between the logical status of the natural sciences and of critique. (Habermas [1968a] 1971, 44)

What can be said of Habermas's judgment here? Above all else, this: it rests on a trivialization of Marx's theory. Undoubtedly there are various inconsistencies quite apparent on the surface of Marx's text, but it is wildly wrong-headed to argue that the underlying structure, the basic logic of the text, urges such a restricted conception of "labor" (or of "production") as Habermas has assumed. Nor is it accurate to say that Marx equated his theory with the existent natural science. When Habermas quoted with astonishment Marx's proposal regarding "a single science"—allegedly a positivist-like "demand for a natural science of man"—he was apparently confused in the (truly astonishing) impression that Marx had been referring to the existent, which is to say *alienated*, natural science! But my concern here is not with questions of "what Marx *really* meant"—which, after all, can be asked *and* answered only as constructions of the here and now. The primary matter is Habermas's formulation of "labor" and "production," on the one side, and "action" (communicative action, symbolically mediated interaction), on the other, as distinctive, noncoincidental dimensions or domains of the self-constitution of men and women. However, it is important to grasp the conditions of Habermas's own formulations, and one of the most central consists in his particular thesis of "the two versions of Marx."

By Habermas's reading, Marx's work evinces a perplexing disjuncture between the general categorical adequacy of his "material investigations" and sketch of appropriate methodological presuppositions, on the one hand, and, on the other, the wholly inadequate level of his "philosophical self-understanding" (Habermas [1968a] 1971, 52–63). Specifically, we are told, the "two versions" that have been set in relief by Habermas "make visible an indecision" in the development of critical theory, an indecisiveness "that has its foundation in Marx's theoretical approach":

> For the analysis of the development of economic formations of society [Marx] adopts a concept of the system of social labor that contains more elements than are admitted to in the idea of a species that produces itself through social labor. Self-constitution through social labor is conceived *at the categorical level* as a process of production, and instrumental action, labor in the sense of material activity or work, designates the dimension in which natural history moves. *At the level of his material investigations*, on the other hand, Marx always takes account of social practice that encompasses both work and interaction. The processes of natural history are mediated by the

productive activity of individuals and the organization of their inter-relations. These relations are subject to norms that decide, with the force of institutions, how responsibilities and rewards, obligations and charges to the social budget are distributed among members. The medium in which these relations of subjects and of groups are nor-matively regulated is cultural tradition. It forms the linguistic com-munication structure on the basis of which subjects interpret both nature and themselves in their environment. (Habermas [1968a] 1971, 52–53)

Habermas, it is plain to see, would make Marx's case analogous to that of the sixteenth-century Bruno, who, in his dialogues on *Cause, Principle, and Unity* (1584a) and *The Expulsion of the Triumphant Beast* (1584b), pow-erfully articulated a rejection of prevailing metaphysics in a theory of contradiction and dialectical unity, but then, in his failure of "philosophical self-understanding," unwittingly retained the dualism of positing that real-ity within a static, absolutist universe. The fundamental failure of Haber-mas's judgment rests in his analytic fracturing of the integrity of the labor concept in Marx's work. It may well be that Habermas, like Horkheimer before him, rejected the various turn-of-the-century (and later) revisions that made of Marx's work a vulgar materialism reductive of "superstruc-tural" processes to epiphenomena of matter; but, if so, he was seduced by what he rejected, for he has explicitly repudiated Marx's determination of "different social formations in terms of the command of the means of production" as being insufficiently abstract[100] and because it "suggests a narrow economistic interpretation" (Habermas [1973c] 1975, 16–17). Contrary to Habermas, for Marx "labor" constituted the activity of pro-ducing human life—*concrete, sensuous human life in its entirety*. Now, perhaps Habermas can explain to us the trick of how such production, as process and as consequence, could be devoid of intersubjectivities, com-municative action, discourse, claimed validities, normativities, and any other of those "elements" that purportedly are not "admitted to in the idea of a species that produces itself through social labor" (Habermas [1968a] 1971, 52); but to date he has not done so.

Habermas assumes that Marx's concept of labor was "adopted" specifically for purposes of "the analysis of the development of economic formations of society" (Habermas [1968a] 1971, 52), the presupposition being that "the economic" had been essentially discriminated from other "spheres" in the production of society. Not surprisingly, the burden of that presupposition reappears in Habermas's own project, as he treats as sepa-

---

100. "Organizational principles are highly abstract regulations that define ranges of possibility" (Habermas [1973c] 1975, 16–17).

rate dimensions of world constitution the economic ("work," "instrumen-tal-technical rules," etc.), the political ("steering capacity," "orienting ac-tion," etc.), and the sociocultural ("legitimating interpretive schemes," etc.). Whether given to us in the more conventional social-science vocabulary, as above, or in the Hegelian-inspired triad of "labor," "action" or "symbol-ically mediated interaction," and "discourse," the analytics are accorded foundational status throughout his project. Unfortunately, he has taken these separate dimensions to be concretely real formations in their analytic separation; that is, he has reified distinctions that are integral to the false consciousness, the repression and distortion of "actions," "world views," and "moral systems" that his critical science would oppose. Habermas has presumed to conceptualize separately and independently "labor," "action," and "discourse," or "the economic," "the political," and "the sociocul-tural," and then to raise and answer questions about their "involved *inter-dependencies*" (Habermas 1973a, 12; emphasis added). But the task surely is not to interrelate or put together what was only falsely separated to begin with—even though that false separation was apparently real and therefore consequential. The task is rather to demonstrate that the separation *was and is false*, to demonstrate why and with what consequences the separation was made, and simultaneously to demonstrate the real, concrete relations of "world constitution." When Habermas argued that the "function [of] regulating access to the means of production and indirectly the distribution of social wealth . . . is assumed in primitive societies by kinship systems and in traditional societies by political institutions," but that it "is not until the market, in addition to its cybernetic function, also takes over the function of stabilizing class relations that the relations of production assume a purely economic form" (Habermas 1975b, 292), he spoke fantasy—the fantasy of an "economic form" that is *not* at once "political-institutional" and that is devoid of the relations of kinship, the fantasy of a "kinship system" that is not also "economic" and "political."[101] Likewise, when he

---

101. Relatedly, his contention that "emancipation from the external forces of nature" is achieved through labor processes but that emancipation from "the compulsion of inner nature" is achieved only "to the degree that institutions based on force are replaced by an organization of social relations that is bound only to communication free from domination" manifests his confusion in his own abstrac-tions (Habermas [1968a] 1971, 53). Inasmuch as those "external forces of nature" are themselves *human* forces—humanly produced as much as are "the compulsion of inner nature" and the institutional repressions of domination—one emanci-pation cannot proceed independently of the other. Indeed, they must be one and the same process, for "emancipation from the external forces of nature" *means* emancipation from human domination. This is because the production of an "objectified nature," whether it be one from which we are emancipated or not, cannot possibly be free of the presence of communicative action. The "external forces of nature" exist as concretely human forces; such is their constitution.

argued against the singularly fundamental import of the labor concept that, "in the light of recent anthropological findings, it appears that the concept of social labor extends too deeply into the scale of evolution" (that is, "even the hominids are distinguished from other primates in that they develop an economy") (Habermas 1975b, 288), he again spoke fantasy—here, fantasy based in reification of anthropomorphisms. Anthropomorphic constructions are indispensable—indeed, one cannot think "hominids" or "primates" or "evolution" and so on other than in human terms—but the reality of those constructions must not be misassigned, as Habermas has done. We must not reify our abstractions as having a separate and independent reality against which we then set ourselves for measure and validation. Habermas's notion that the phylogenic extensivity of "social labor" goes "too deeply into the scale of evolution" is and can only be a *human* concept, predicated on certain values of human use.

Habermas suffers the not uncommon affliction of wanting to begin not at the beginning but at the end; not with the concrete reality of the production of human life but with the emptiness of abstractions (the "universal intention of emancipation," "abstract organizational principles," etc.) from whence he tries to proceed piece by piece toward a now elusive "real life." His search for those highly abstract organizational principles of society has so far resulted mainly in the conclusion that "the concept of the mode of production is not abstract enough to encompass the universals of developmental levels" (Habermas 1975b, 300), and in the related assertion that the sciences, as creators of technical and hermeneutic knowledges, have moved onto center stage in the play of world constitution. This assertion is significant, of course, for it emphasizes modes of cognition and cognitive interests as primary to the processes of world constitution: hence, the immense gravity that Habermas has assigned to the ideal of nondistorted discourse, because it is what makes possible the cognitive interest of emancipation. But inasmuch as he has conceived his foundation in terms of distinct "media" of world constitution (labor, action, and discourse), the "reintegration" of which he has not accomplished, that ideal and thus the possibility of the realization remain mere ideal. In the words of the author whose concept of labor is allegedly "too narrow" and insufficiently abstract: "The dispute over the reality or nonreality of thinking which is isolated from practice is a purely *scholastic* question."

The fracturing of the human production of the world into distinct "media" and cognitive interests creates certain limitations of the concept of truth. We may recall Habermas's differentiation of the "constitution of truth" and the "constitution of object" (e.g., Habermas 1973a, 166–67; see also Habermas 1973b; Habermas 1976c). Between "objectivated reality," or the "material *a priori* premise of experience," and human knowledge there is allegedly an essential difference that is manifested throughout world constitution but that is conceptualized primarily (if not exclusively) in terms of linguistic structure. In contrast to that premise of experience that gives to us "objects of possible experience," knowledge consists not in "things" or "objects" but in human statements about objects and events or states of affairs. Truth is constituted in the pragmatic relations, but it is *about* the propositional content, that is, the facticity of the purported sign-referent connection. Objects and states of affairs are produced by humans merely *as* "objects of experience," about which potentially or hypothetically true statements are made. Objects of experience are therefore neither true nor false, according to his reckoning; they simply "are." This absurdity of an essential split in world constitution between that which is constituted merely as material premise of experience, objects that simply exist, and that which is thought/spoken about them reveals the peculiar elitism of idealist abstraction. The production of objects, events, and states of affairs necessarily involves language, necessarily involves thinking/speaking, knowledge, "statements having propositional content"; if truth concerns such "contents," as Habermas says it does, then it must also concern those objects (etc.) *as such*. The concrete production of the world proceeds as a unitary constitution involving problematic realizations of necessarily value-laden statements of knowledge or "propositional contents"; accordingly, human knowledge exists not merely as a one-sided idealist construction but also as a materialized object. Habermas has neglected to consider the integral presence of language (thinking/speaking, knowing): it is to be seen not only in "utterances," whether public or not, but also in books, buildings, guns, roadways, traffic patterns, handshakes, and all other "physical" objects or states of affairs—in short, in the entirety of the human world. Just as it is a reproduction of false consciousness of human self-constitution to imagine "labor," "action," or "discourse" independently of the others, so the constitution of objects and the constitution of knowledges go hand in hand. Objects as well as utterances (or "propositional contents") are either true or false.

Karl Leonard Reinhold, a Kantian philosopher of some renown during his days, urged realization of the Enlightenment project of conditions under which the individual can seek and assert truth without external constraints and according to his or her own critical reason and moral principles (Reinhold 1784; Reinhold 1816). One could say as much for Habermas. But, like Reinhold before him, he cannot materially ground his idealist construction in a unitary formation. He has reproduced the duality. A theory of knowledge must indeed be constructed as a theory of society, and Habermas has confused this postulate as meaning that the production of knowledge *as mere cognition* is the controlling impulse in the production of society. Cognition isolated from practice—"discourse" isolated from "labor" and "action"—is pure scholasticism, the equivalent of counting angels on the head of a pin.

6

V*iewing Las Meninas*

I. LAS MENINAS AND THE BURNING BUSH

IN AN ANCIENT LEGEND remembered from Jainism, each of seven blind men, upon encountering an elephant, touched a different part of the elephant's anatomy, and each named a different object as that which he felt; none named an elephant. One of the "morals" of this familiar story has to do with a notion of perspectivism—in Jaina doctrine, called *naya*—namely, that perception is always partial, always undertaken from a particular standpoint toward multifaceted reality, and therefore that our claims to knowledge must be regarded as always partial, always tentative. Of course, if the seven blind men should collect their diverse contributions of perceptual information and order them just so, they might come to the cooperative conclusion of "an elephant"—thereby illustrating another lesson, the superiority of communal effort. But the feature of this legend that is here of greater interest consists in its relation of the said and the not-said. I mean the relation that gives the legend its particular force and expected effect.

Question: how do we know that the object felt by each and all of the seven blind men *was* an elephant? How do we know that "the object" was in fact a single entity, *an elephant*, and not seven different objects just as the men named them to be? And even if the men subsequently collected their experiences and ordered them into the conclusion "an elephant," how do we know that they would order correctly and that the agreed-upon singleness of object *would be* "an elephant"? We know—or to the extent that we *do* know, we know—that they apprehended "an elephant" because of that peculiar silence of speaking by the storyteller: the unseen storyteller—positioned behind an invisible screen as if totally effaced, a presence occulted in the telling of the story—told us that the object was in fact a single entity, an elephant. In telling that to us, to our credulity, the storyteller

450

was exercising a silence: the silence of the not-said constitutive of the said, which authorized an elephant. That is, the storyteller spoke from a position of privilege that was denied to the seven blind men. The storyteller knew unequivocally that the object was in fact an elephant; they did not. *How* the storyteller could assert such claims of knowledge when they could not is not said. That is the silence of the storyteller's authority.

But now let's modify the story just a bit: let's place the storyteller *inside* the story; let's assume the storyteller is one of the seven blind men. What happens? The entire structure of the story changes. The storyteller, now denied the privilege of position, now without that private law of rulership and moral lesson, can no longer say what blind men cannot say unequivocally. And if the storyteller tries to speak from a position both inside and outside the story, either simultaneously or sequentially, he accomplishes nothing so much as inducement of an eventually fatal shimmer in the authority of representation (cf. Goffman 1974).

Judith Shklar has said of the professional or academic historian, "If he comes to doubt the possibility of recreating the past accurately, he also loses his social purpose. Skepticism thus undoes the historian doubly" (Shklar 1980, 54). The same can be said of the social theorist generally, for the question of evidence is not confined to the historian's re-creation or representation of that which is called "the past." And when the fundamental conditions of the theorist's claim to knowledge come into doubt, what will be said of the utility or purpose of the "social role" of "theorist"? It is no longer convincing of the theorist to argue that skepticism is merely an instrument of the method of science, an instrument directed only toward propositions of the representation of an external world. Such an argument can no longer bestow the insulations that once shielded the crucial silence in authoritative representational speaking/writing. Such an argument will not now convince—not in the face of an ironization that has dissolved the containment of "inside" by "outside"; not when it has been decided that the determinative conditions, activities, and consequences of scientific knowing are ineluctably integral to that which *had* been regarded as "the external world"—from some Archimedean pivot the exact location of which no one ever succeeded in defining. And it is not adequate to say of this condition of the theorist or the historian (as Shklar said of the latter) that "philosophy is an unsettling presence for history," or that "philosophical difficulties—such as, what is evidence at all—do not go away simply because working historians do not encounter them day in, day out." Historians, theorists, all of us, *do* encounter them, day in and day out, albeit often in the occultation of their conventional apparel. And the issues that are difficulties do not materialize as importations from a domain ("philosophy") that now and again confronts the historian or theorist as an unsettling presence, a policing agency that irregularly checks credentials and the warrant of claims; rather, these issues are integral to the domain-defining activities and claims—socially, historically constituted activities and claims—of the historian and theorist themselves.

I mean, of course, issues such as those that have been attended in preceding chapters, among which the following may be named in a conventional manner:[1]

• the question of relations of epistemology, ethics, and aesthetics— including relations of thinking, doing, and making; truth/falsity, good/evil, and beauty/ugliness; reason, will, and passion; etc.

• the question of relations of fact and value—including relations of thingness, of anthropomorphism, of utopia; etc.

• the question of relations of meaning and being—including relations of representation: signifier and signified, the fit of words to world, theoretical and observational language, the literal and the figurative, the analytic and the synthetic, translation and commensurability; etc.

• the question of relations of time, space, and history—including relations of the past, the present, and the future; origin and end; discovery, anticipation, and memory; rupture and continuity; temporality and spatiality as that which gives measure to datings and sitings; etc.

• the question of the relations of nature and society—including relations of container and contained; the natural and the artificial; human nature and human freedom; etc.

I will not say that the issue of relativism—radical epistemological relativism, as it is sometimes denoted—is central to each of the relations nominated above, for it is no longer clear that any of them *has* "a center." Nonetheless, each of those relations could be constructed differently, that is, composed in different commentary, depending on one's answer to the question of "truth and contingency." Is history itself historical, "the lie commonly agreed upon," as Voltaire said? Is any claim of true knowledge of "the social world," though perhaps not of "the natural world," ineluctably contingent on the situated and partial perspective of the claimant, as Mannheim said? Such questions still elicit a diversity of answers, to be sure. But the balance of answers today is unlike that of a few generations ago, and with that shift the constitutions of those other relations—"meaning-being," "fact-value," and so on—have also changed. So long as the privilege of authorial silence was occulted in the very functioning of that privilege, its

---

1. In listing these conventional namings my aim is not to reconfirm them but first to draw attention to the separations inscribed by the namings—and later to question them. I shall return to this matter in volume 2.

enunciative force did not appear as a force but as a *natural expression* of that-which-is (or was). As with the storyteller of the Jain legend, the silent narrator—a "central intelligence or observer," in Booth's apt phrasing (Booth 1961, 273)—stood outside the scene of that which was represented in narration and, as self-effaced instrument of objectivities, expressed through neutral medium the literality of world-fitting words. But the crucial distinctions on which that self-occulting functioning depended have succumbed to the radically ironizing, destabilizing presence of a relativism that is constituted in remembrance of the old promises of absolutism (just as atheism is contingent on that which it denies), and the powers of that peculiar silence of authoritative speaking/writing have all but drained away.

The argument of relativism has slowly unfolded through all the regions of judgment that are conventionally distinguished in human consciousness: "the aesthetic," "the ethical," "the epistemological." Contentions of relativism in manners of "the aesthetic," or the "aesthetic experience," are surely not of recent dating, for there is a long tradition of emphasis on "subjective judgments of taste," that is, judgments not of "factual properties" of an external "objectivity" ("thingness") but of personal reaction to an "aesthetic object." Likewise, the view that ethical judgments are properly considered to be resolutions of axiologic and (sometimes) teleologic preference made by the given actor—a view associated with Hobbes as well as the Epicureans—is a view that can be constructed in terms of a more or less radicalized relativism. Such incorporations of relativistic formulation within the regions of aesthetic and ethical judgment were long held apart from the foundational circumstances of epistemology as a matter of principle, chiefly through the insulations afforded by such radical separations as that between "fact" and "value" and through the privileges afforded by such special relations as that between external "being" and representational "meaning." However, when "classical discourse, in which being and representation found their common locus, is eclipsed, then, in the profound upheaval man appears in his ambiguous position as an object of knowledge and as a subject that knows: enslaved sovereign, observed spectator" (Foucault [1966] 1970, 312).

Long before the Foucauldian replay, this verdict—which can also be read as a commentary on William Blake's "Truth can never be told so as to be understood and not be believ'd"—began gradually to invade the epistemological self-consciousness of theorists of knowledge, including more recently the scientific theorists of scientific knowledge. In some quarters, responses to this invasion have ranged from an equanimity born of misplaced confidence, to the phlegmatic response of unregard (clearly it is possible to continue one's daily activities of *scientia* much as before, relativism or no). But in other quarters, and perhaps especially among those stationmasters who are most acutely aware of the threat to that privileged speaking which is the seat of power for *scientia*, the insinuation of relativism into epistemological self-consciousness has been met with staunch resistance.[2] Some theorists have acknowledged the impeccable logic of the relativist argument of skepticism but then have sought to shunt the whole burden aside by observing that the "victory" won through flawless logic is Pyrrhic as well as Pyrrhonistic. A few (e.g., the logical positivist Ayer) have acknowledged further that, while the "victory" may well be Pyrrhic, as measured by one or another scale of costs, it nevertheless remains to be overturned by the antagonists of relativism. There have been numerous sallies, designed with intent at least to evade or, better, to sunder "the dilemma of relativism," as it has come to be named, but none has succeeded in the sense of a self-consistent demonstration of warrant for its own *nonrelativist* position.

Most efforts to confront the problem of relativism seriously, with the aim of overcoming it, have foundered on an insularity of logical ground. One manifestation of this failure can be exemplified well enough by means of a recent essay comparing "the contributions of Mannheim, Mills, and Merton," in which the author posed the "decisive question" thusly: "Can one maintain the relativist viewpoint, and, at the same time, defend one's own standpoint as rational?" (Phillips 1974, 86, 72). Certainly we may agree with the author's attribution that Mannheim, Mills, and many others have nervously contemplated this "relativist's dilemma," wherein "either the relativist's own assertions are themselves relative, and, therefore, lacking truth value; or his argument is unconditionally true, and, consequently,

---

2. Here as elsewhere, a passive resistance can sometimes be the more effective. For example, although I had been aware of the importance and strength of this perception of threat in other respects, I was rather slow to notice it specifically in connection with Foucault's *The Order of Things*. During a period of several months, I found myself now and again noting that many acquaintances had begun to read the book only to put it aside very soon thereafter as "too inaccessible." This was both puzzling and slightly irritating to me, because it seemed clear that these would-be readers simply were not being patient enough. Granted, Foucault's "style" of writing, which has been described as an instance of "the French poetic style" (whatever that means), can be rather foreign to the English eye and ear. Even so, it seemed to me, once an acclimation to this "style" had been effected— hardly a difficult feat—Foucault's book would be quite understandable by any social scientist, and surely by any scientist of science, who was willing to study it. Of course, what I neglected to consider, during these moments of puzzlement, was the level of perceived threat: no doubt many of those who began a reading understood Foucault's argument well enough—well enough, that is, to categorize it as "ideology," "metaphysical speculation," or simply "bad history." I suppose my acquaintances (at least the closer ones) were simply being kind in neglecting to tell me that a book I had recommended so highly they thought to be nonsense.

relativism is self-contradictory." But need we accept this conclusion? Indeed, can we? Note the equation from which that "decisive question" and that "dilemma" were made to issue: if a claim of knowledge is relative to the conditions of its production, it must be void of "truth value"; or, if a claim of knowledge is relative to the conditions of its production, it must be other than "rational." Such equation is sensible only on pain of accepting certain premises about the human knower, and these premises belie the real question.

The "dilemma" (or "contradiction") that appears to be so bothersome to these querists is a "dilemma" (or "contradiction") only insofar as an *extra*historical standard of "truth value" and "rationality" lingers in the foundation of their understanding of the possibility and conditions of human knowledge. To assert that an epistemological stance is "relativistic" and to intend thereby anything other than the historical, social contingency of knowledge production is to assert a proposition that can be meaningful only insofar as one believes oneself to be somehow standing outside the spectacle of history and yet fully comprehending of it. Claims of detachment from the spectacle are very often made, no doubt. Our schoolbook treatments of "the scientific method" counsel us to strive mightily to achieve and maintain a detached, disinterested attitude toward the world that is science's object. But any such project of detachment is always an effort to attain some goal or fulfill some purpose *within* the world (cf. Barrett 1978, 127). Contrary to the understanding formulated by Phillips as the "relativist's dilemma," the problem posed by epistemological relativism does not consist in the absence of rationality and truth-valued assertions but in the multiplicity of truth claims and rationalities that are generated in the differentiated contingencies of the production of claims of knowledge.

Relativism denies the applicability of any extrahistorical standard of judgment, and this denial means that the traditional expectation of a single truth and rationality—that is, the expectation that, among alternative claims of knowledge of a given object of knowledge, only one claim *can be* true—is confronted with the possibility of multiple and incommensurable truth claims. That is, the dilemma of relativism consists in nothing so definitive as self-contradiction, but in the instabilities and nihilistic incapacitation of an incommensurability of competing claims.

Given the deeply embedded traditional understanding of the production of knowledge, there appears to be *no* basis, no table of relations, by which to discriminate among competing claims in epistemologically self-consistent terms. Relativism dissolves the traditional authority of epistemological subject; and, with that, the pivot and center that was "man" swirls away in a vortex of lost finitude, as "man" becomes, in Barthes's elegant phrase, "a metaphor without brakes" (Barthes 1966, 82). Claims of knowledge are told from no common origin of authorization, no ultimate center of centerings, but always as "nomadic centers" (Deleuze 1968, 89–90), wandering, contending, provisional forces.

In the course of considering early reactions of Anglo-American social scientists to Mannheim's *Ideology and Utopia* (e.g., von Schelting 1936; Merton [1938b] 1973, 260n.20; Becker 1939), Phillips asked the question, "Why did they fear *relativism?*"—to which he gave a sensible answer: Relativism beckoned them to examine the conditions and prospects of nihilism, as Nietzsche had done; but diagnoses of nihilism had already become too palpable, as frighteningly palpable as the Nazi machine, to permit address of such matters from any point of view but one of complete noncontingency, in which God and the Eternal Verities were *unquestionably* on "our side" (Phillips 1974, 75–76). Note that Phillips did not ask *how* they could fear relativism—that is, by what chain of thinking they could arrive at the conclusion that Mannheim's argument culminated in an unacceptable thesis of relativism. Nevertheless, Phillips answered this question too, implicitly, when he quoted Merton's observation that the Mannheimian argument "leads at once . . . to radical relativism with its familiar vicious circle in which the very propositions asserting such relativism are *ipso facto* invalid" (Merton [1941] 1968, 557). And here again we must wonder, by what criterion are those propositions rendered *invalid?* Where is the "naturing principle" according to which the propositions are invalid *ipso facto*, that is, by the very nature of the case? It can only be in the concealment of an *extra*historical standard of validity. Even so, however, the theme of Merton's observation has become a common response of many of our "scientists of science" to the imperiling dilemma of relativism. A thoroughly exposed epistemological relativism, it is said, cannot survive a *reductio ad absurdum*: if any claim of knowledge is contingent, then the "metaclaim" about "any claim of knowledge" must also be contingent; therefore, the "metaclaim" is unsound.[3] Recently a philosopher of science, Yehuda Elkana (1978), implicitly adopted this theme as a point of departure in his project to domesticate the relativist peril by means of a dualistic

---

3. Presumably this argument is intended as an invocation of the Whitehead-Russell principle of *reductio ad absurdum*: [p ⊃ ~p] ⊃ ~p. By this principle, however, negation of a proposition is achieved insofar as a contradiction can be deduced from the proposition itself, *together with one or more additional propositions the truth of which has been at least granted if not already proven.* Again, then, we must query the concealed presence. (The more "relaxed" use of *reductio ad absurdum* as a means of countering relativism—that if all judgments are relative, it would be impossible to say anything about anything—has a very long textual history. One of the earliest recorded uses can be read in Socrates' attempted refutation of the Protagorean and Heraclitean views; see Plato's *Theaetetus*, 151–84.)

construction of "historical relativism" and "philosophical realism." The "realism" in question is reminiscent of G. E. Moore's (1939) rather curious exercise of his two hands, by which he sought to prove the existence of an "external world." (Moore stood before an audience at the British Academy and proclaimed: "Here is one hand," which he raised to view, "and here is another"; ergo, "there are at least two objects external to our minds, and you know it and I know it." Surely we must assume a great deal, if we are to accept that exercise as a "proof": e.g., if "external world" had actually been in doubt for Moore, on what grounds could he have presumed that any member of his audience was externally real, and not an illusion of his mind?)[4] In Elkana's construction, "realism" is conceived as neither an instrumentalism nor a conventionalism: "The evidence which makes us accept a law or theory is also evidence for its *truth*," where "truth" means correspondence to a "natural world that does not change at the behest of our theories" (Elkana 1978, 313, quoting Hesse 1974, 290). Relativism, on the other hand, "is the view that truth and logic are always formulated in the framework of, and are relative to, a given thought-world with its own language." Between these two views, Elkana proposed the following relationship:

> It is commonly held that one is either a realist or a relativist, and if one attempted to hold both views simultaneously one would be courting paradox. Is this true? In my view, it is not. . . . I claim that the two positions (realism and relativism) are not inconsistent. This polarization is not only unnecessary but dangerously misleading, and the solution to the apparent inconsistency is simply to hold them both simultaneously. This is what I mean by *two-tier-thinking*. (Elkana 1978, 313)[5]

4. Such "proofs," in other words, would require that one stand outside the frame of that which is to be judged—i.e., a position from which the hypothetical "object" can be judged as to the dubiety/certainty of its external existence (or of claims thereof); otherwise, as judge one could be unknowingly a victim of the same illusoriness as that which is considered to be possibly illusory. (In fairness to Moore, it should be noted that the "hand exercises" were not the only method of proof he offered; see, in this regard, Ambrose 1952 and Moore 1952.)

5. In the passage deleted from this quotation, Elkana asked whether it is true, as is commonly held, that one cannot be both a "realist" and a "conventionalist." He concluded that it *is* true, but that it is "trivially true." The more important question, he believed, is whether a relativist is "necessarily a conventionalist," that is, a proponent of the view "that the truth-value of a statement [is] not a question of fact but a matter of convention." To this question he answered in the negative: "To say that the truth-value of a statement is a convention is a signifi-

In this "two-tier-thinking," Elkana meant to construct a nesting of statements in such a way that one could subscribe simultaneously to two arguments: first, "the impossibility of objectively ordering different conceptual frameworks according to their degree of rationality or their degree of approximation to a context-independent Truth" (i.e., his "historical relativism"); second, "once a framework is given we can define criteria of rationality and truth relative to that framework, and order the world inside that framework according to those criteria" (i.e., his "realism"). To put the thesis more simply, Elkana's "realism"—which he considered to be, in one variety or another, "indispensable" for the scientist—is nested within a relativist "tier" that encompasses all defensible varieties of "realism." Relativism is incontestable, inasmuch as any claim of knowledge is necessarily dependent on the context of some "conceptual framework," and the classical doctrine of a correspondence theory of truth does not survive. But, once a particular "conceptual framework" has been accepted as a "reasonable" context, the scientist and the philosopher can proceed with a "realistic" view of the world that is defined by that context. And within that context, the truth value of propositions can be determined by something like a "coherence-criterioned" correspondence theory of truth (Elkana 1978, 310–18).[6]

There is a connection between the sort of response to relativism that is exemplified in Elkana's essay and Russell's famed "theory of types," inasmuch as Elkana's notion of "two-tiers" can be read as a diluted application of Russell's theory. Russell's theory of types was formulated partly in response to paradoxes of the Epimenidean class, the nominal instance of which is: "Epimenides, a Cretan, said, 'Cretans always lie.' " There are many instances of this class, of course. Another is: "What I tell you three times is true" (with credit to Lewis Carroll's *The Hunting of the Snark*). All instances of the class seem to be vulnerable to *reductio ad absurdum*. Or, as Russell characterized it, the class has the general form: "It is not true for all propositions p that if I affirm p, p is true" (Russell [1908b] 1956, 61–62, 75). Thus, whatever we take as a "totality of propositions"—

cantly different thing from saying that a fact is only relative to a given conceptual framework, and that, relative to another one, it may turn out to be a complex theoretical entity (or even a non-fact)." In other words, according to this muddle, relativism does not imply that a proposition is only conventionally true or false, rather than factually true or false—even though the qualification of what can count as "fact" is determined in terms of the convention of a particular "conceptual framework."

6. Similar attempts to solve "the relativist's dilemma" have been offered by others: e.g., see Suppe's effort in terms of the so-called *K-K thesis* (Suppe 1977, 716–27).

i.e., the composition of "all"—"statements about this totality generate new propositions which, on pain of contradiction, must lie outside the totality." We may seek to evade the dilemma by expanding the totality; but that action will fail, for it "equally enlarges the scope of statements about the totality." The lesson to be drawn, according to Russell, is that "no totality can contain members defined in terms of itself"; or, "Whatever contains an apparent variable must not be a possible value of that variable." In other words, the "container" ("context," "nest," etc.) of the given variable must be of a higher "type" (the second of Elkana's "tiers") than the possible values of that variable.

Now, Russell's theory of types is indisputably a useful tool of formal logic; its applicability extends to many different topical matters. Consider, for example, the distinction between the "locutionary" and the "illocutionary" components of a "speech act," as this distinction has been described by Austin ([1962b] 1975), Searle (e.g., 1976), and other analysts of language use. The nominal case of the Epimenidean class of paradoxes can itself be treated in those terms: the proposition "Cretans always lie" is the locutionary component; the phrase "Epimenides, a Cretan, said" is the illocutionary component or "force."[7] Clearly, the speech-act theorists such as Austin and Searle have intended these two components as being of different logical typing: a given illocutionary component can serve as the context or nesting for a variety of locutionary components or propositions. Russell's theory relates as well to numerous other substantive matters, such as the "problem of scale" or "levels of analysis" (e.g., the so-called ecological fallacy), the issue of "insiders vs. outsiders" (e.g., Merton [1972] 1973), and so on. But, as useful as the theory of types is, it is essentially a diagnostic tool. As Russell himself came to realize, his theory does not solve the Epimenidean and related classes of paradox; rather, it elucidates some of the conditions of paradox and to that extent may serve as an aid to the detection of paradoxical constructions. Neither the theory of types nor any of the diluted applications of it will solve the problem of relativism, simply because the essential means to the solution of relativism do not lie within the scope or power of logical devices. Indeed, it is precisely this conclusion that must be drawn from the Russellian theory itself, together with Gödel's incompleteness theorem: if it is possible to construct within any formal system a proposition the truth or falsity of which cannot be formally decided within that system—which possibility entails logical incompleteness *ad*

---

7. By Austin's taxonomy of illocutionary acts, it is an "expositive" (Austin [1962b] 1975, 151–52); by Searle's, it is a "representative," the function of which is "to commit the speaker . . . to the truth of the expressed proposition," that is, to state a particular "fit of words to world" (Searle 1976, 10).

infinitum, as in the painting *Las Meninas* by Velazquez[8]—then determinative criteria other than those of formal logic must be brought to bear as means to the solution of relativism. I am hardly the first to have arrived at this conclusion. Nor was Nietzsche, although he sustained the argument longer than most.

A few years ago, Richard Harvey Brown published a delightfully intelligent book entitled *A Poetic for Sociology*, in which he proposed some determinative criteria for an "aesthetic approach" to the relativistic problem of commensurability in comparative understandings of social theory. According to this construction, the theory and practice of social theory are to be seen as Wittgensteinian "games" and, as such, are to be evaluated as more or less adequate constructions of tropic (especially metaphoric) models. In this way, Brown tried to bridge competing claims of truth offered by two or more theories. For all the charm of his presentation, however, Brown's approach does not solve the problem of relativism. Instead, it reproduces and accepts the problem fundamentally in its own terms, for the problem of relativism is no less present in the conduct of aesthetic experience and judgment than it is in the conduct of epistemological experience and judgment. This much surely was held in mind by a journal reviewer of Brown's argument, when, among his favorable remarks, he included the warning, "When ideals are replaced by notions of the relativity of judgment, evaluation of social science, as of art, becomes highly problematic, making sound art criticism and sound sociological criticism extremely difficult, if not impossible" (Goldfarb 1978, 465)—though he did not instruct us as to what the "otherwise" of noncontingent judgment could be.[9]

Surely the failure of criticism may be considered an endemic condition, not only of literatures of science and philosophy of science but also of those literatures once satisfactorily described as belletristic. But here too there is suspicion of a double failure—that is, a failure of criticism of "the failure of criticism." Consider, for example, Goodheart's *The Failure of Criticism*, in which he argues that "the inherent instability of language, which modern imaginative literature reveals or betrays with a vengeance and which is as unchecked in Derrida's book [*Glas*] as it is in *Finnegans Wake*, becomes

---

8. The visual lesson of *Las Meninas* by Velazquez (1656)—a painting that includes the painter and the canvas on which he is painting—was fruitfully deployed by Foucault in *The Order of Things*.

9. Brown urged that his "poetic for sociology" not only "sees formal thought as a game, but it also recognizes that the toy soldiers have real guns" (Brown 1977, 230)—to which Goldfarb replied, "How does one decide upon the reality of the guns?"

the energizing principle of what purports to be criticism" (Goodheart 1978, 3, 5). Goodheart's chief *bête noire* was the "school" of "French structuralist" critics (which he miscast to the extent of citing Derrida and Barthes as exemplars). "By radically weakening if not destroying the privileged point of view, modern literature has sanctioned . . . the *de*moralization of criticism," according to Goodheart, with the result that its "evaluative function is now seen as an arbitrary exercise of taste." Aside from the question of the ground from which *these* critics speak, however, Goodheart has missed the point by giving them too much credit. Although these critics may well have tried to play the part of a latter-day Nietzsche—namely, to show up the *im*morality of those privileged points of view—it is much too wide of the mark to say that *they* have radically weakened or destroyed such points of view.[10]

The reflexivity of incapacitation is not unique to Brown's effort, nor does it spring from any peculiarity of an "aesthetic approach" to the constitution of knowledge. Other efforts, frequently much less imaginative than Brown's, have suffered the same incapacitation, and they have most often *not* been deliberately conceived projects of an aesthetic approach to the comparative judgment of claims of theory and practice in the "human sciences," much less in the "natural sciences." The record of assaults against the "Pyrrhic victory" of relativism has not been favorably impressive *generally*—especially when it is viewed from the standpoint of a tradition that places great pride of stock in an ability of human intellect to account for its own activities in a coherent, self-consistently principled, original discourse. In consideration of such record and tradition, one might well be tempted to concur with Needham's conclusion:

The phantasmagoric variegation of the collective forms of significance, in grammar and classificatory concepts and styles of thought, reflects the essential relativity that marks all ideas about the meaning and determination of human experience.

10. Certainly we may agree with Goodheart that claims such as Sollers'—namely, that in "the final analysis we are nothing other than our system of reading and writing" (Sollers 1968, 248)—*are* perverse. But the bankruptcy is not merely of an authority of characters or of an anonymous storyteller in "belletristic" or "artful" literatures. Muecke's comment is more nearly to the point: "We ought to be suspicious of the general charge that irony is rocking the boat. It is the function of irony to point out that it is the waves that are doing the rocking and that this is only to be expected when one is at sea and not on dry land. It is the function of irony to ask whether we have any reason to suppose we inhabit a world whose meaningfulness irony could destroy rather than a world whose meaninglessness irony might make clear (Muecke 1969, 245–46).

I am not saying that human life is senseless, but that we cannot make sense of it. If only it were at least a tale told by an idiot, we might arrive at some coherent meaning, but the metaphor presupposes criteria of intelligibility and sanity that we do not possess except by convention. Once outside a given form of life, man is lost in a "wilderness of formes." (Needham 1972, 244)[11]

Or one might concur with Gregory Bateson, who, in his last testament, offered this two-fold observation: first, "What has to be investigated and described is a vast network or matrix of interlocking message material and abstract tautologies, premises, and exemplifications"; but, second, "as of 1979, there is no conventional method of describing such a tangle. We do not know even where to begin" (Bateson 1979, 20).

Some authorities, I am aware, will seek to argue that all the issues of relativism are as vaporous as human breath in a cold wind—in this case, the cold wind of "the real world." They will raise questions of utility, "realistic" and "pragmatic."[12] For example, given conclusions that the epistemological positions held (explicitly or implicitly) by the several theorists considered in preceding chapters are not self-consistently warrantably founded, and thus that those theorists' claims of speaking true or valid knowledge are not demonstrable, are we then to conclude that any and all of the "substantive" works authored by those theorists—Weber's *Economy and Society*, Piaget's studies of child development, and so on—are totally and uniformly *useless*? If such conclusion is indeed accepted, then were all those treatises and essays and research reports to be consumed in an orgy of fire, nothing would be lost. Perhaps we could ceremonialize such depletion of uselessness in our world as an act of cleansing—a removal of some printed stain from our essential being—in the manner of other book-burnings notarized in our annals. But *are* those "substantive" studies of this or that state of affairs completely bootless? It would seem so, inasmuch

11. The phrase quoted by Needham is from Browne [1643] 1955, 62. Note, however, that Needham also claimed that he did not mean "to assert a complete relativity in the representation of human existence, but to underline the methodological precept that we should begin our inquiries *as though* everything *were* relative (Needham 1972, 210; emphases added).

12. Thus, an argument currently favored by many philosophers of science with regard to the collapsed distinction between "language of theory" and "language of observation" attempts to reconstitute an authorizing silence by quietly invoking the insulation of consensual presuppositions about the *fait accompli* of scientific successes: that experimental psychologists do agree about the composition and theory-relevance of the facts of rat behavior on a test track, for example, is taken as proof of the availability of theory-neutral facts.

as none of their authors succeeded in demonstrating a self-consistent epistemological grounding by which the profferred statements of and about the affairs of "the real world" could be warranted as true knowledge, factual and firmly rooted in the ground of that externally real world, rather than as merely contingent opinion. Yet those many "substantive" studies persist in our attention, and in the shadows cast by their imitators and successors. So, let us ask once again: *Are* all those treatises and essays and reports useless? Evidently not. And we need not lapse into a corrupt "functionalism" in order to see that they are not, or to appreciate the absurdity of the contrary conclusion; for "uselessness" can be thought and acted only relative to value and its capacitation of passion—however "unexposed" the value or lacerated the capacitation may be (witness, e.g., the Eiffel Tower handled by Barthes 1964b). Is *The Golden Bough* useless? or Wells's *The Time Machine*? or Margot Austin's *Peter Churchmouse*? How, then, could we conclude that any of those "scholarly" treatises and essays and reports are useless, simply because their authors failed in the fundamentals of making good the epistemological grounds of their knowledge claims? Each of the works in question weaves a story of the reality of this or that state of affairs—perhaps some stories are more to one's fancy than others, but epistemologically they are equivalently dubitable (or indubitable)—and the uses of these stories, or, if you prefer, these scholarly accounts, analyses, and explanations, are as evident to view as anything can be in our situation of epistemological uncertainty. Consider, for instance, Weber's famed essay, *The Protestant Ethic and the Spirit of Capitalism*: for how many thousands of people has it been useful during the past half-century and more? To some, it has been useful as a "refutation" of Marx's "crass economic determinism" and "one-sided materialism." To some, including some of those just mentioned, it has been useful in its telling that the "acquisitive drive" of capitalist accumulation has roots in religion. To some, it has been useful as a foil for the showing of what *really* happened during the dawn of capitalism. To some, it has been useful as an income-bearing property. No doubt it has had many other uses. And consider Dewey's *The School and Society*, which was published shortly before the turn of this century: it has been enormously useful, first as an authority for revamping primary and secondary education in the United States—for example, the development of new curricula, new schemes of order and discipline, new laboratory schools in teacher-training colleges and universities—and then, when it was decided that schools were not adequately training youth in obedience to the "role requirements" of the social order, as a locus of blameworthiness for such failures. Merton's studies of "the ethos of science," Piaget's studies of child development, Foucault's studies of the prison, the clinic, the asylum—each has had its particular uses. All of the "substantive" works referred to above have been useful, though perhaps in varying degree, as resources to be drawn upon (perhaps as Heidegger's "standing-reserve") in careers and livelihoods of academic production (publications, reputations, students, etc.) and as commodities in the commerce of publishing, printing, paper, advertising, computers, libraries, universities, building construction, and on and on.[13]

So, if the classical "knowing subject" has been sucked into the vanishing hole of relativistic regress, that does not mean that we can no longer have characters for our plays, short stories, and novels (though Little Nell and Billy Budd they will not be), or celebrated discoverers and didacts for our treatises of science. It does mean, on the other hand, that without a speaking subject "I simply write or talk around a void" (Said 1975, 293). And in this immensely dangerous world we have made for ourselves, Paul Valéry's question "Can the human mind master what the human mind has made?" becomes ever more insistent. Or, in writing and talking around a void, will we accomplish nothing so successfully as writing and talking ourselves *into* a void?

The issues of relativism are anything but vaporous precisely because (in part) they deny the presence of a self-consistently warranted foundation from which to judge, control, and change the uses and understandings and things that are evidently *here* in the concrete existences of men, women, and children. The issues of relativism are consequential in numerous specific ways—too numerous even to be named and enumerated. I shall mention by way of excursus only two, which have to do directly with the sorts of judgments that we do make in the here and now of concrete existence.

Excursus: Given the presence of epistemological relativism, what becomes of the proscription of *argumentum ad hominem*? Where is the measure that will discriminate self-consistently between it and *argumentum ad rem* ("argument to the point")?

By long convention, *argumentum ad hominem*—defined in the OED as an argument founded on the preferences or principles of a particular person, rather than on abstract truth or logical cogency—is fallacious and disallowed in proper discourse. To say that it is formally disallowed, by the convention, does not mean that it has not been employed, of course, even to great effect. With a sympathetic audience in hand, subtle techniques of locution have been used on many occasions, we may suspect, to cloud arguments that otherwise would not have passed inspection on ground of "abstract truth" or "logical cogency." And sheer volume of utterance may aid the camouflage: "a Fallacy which when stated barely . . . would not

---

13. No doubt the production/consumption of any of these uses *could* be regarded as the sort of "wastefulness of resources" described by Lindblom and Cohen (1979, 86–88).

deceive a child, may deceive half the world, if *diluted* in a quarto volume" (Whately 1834, 162). But the proscription has nonetheless remained in place in our table of fallacies. Especially among those throne-sitters who like to emphasize "disinterestedness" and "universality" as definitive features of "the ethos of science," violations of this proscription count among the most serious of offenses. The practice may be tolerable in our legislative assemblies and in discursive relations across nation-state boundaries, but never within the halls of science (*pace* Velikovsky).

The range of practices that will disqualify an argument as *ad hominem*, by the convention, is somewhat broader than you might suspect. The phrase "malicious attacks on the person" loosely describes one sort of banned practice. I may not, for instance, credit or discredit your proposition of the economic consequences of heterogamy among early eighteenth-century New Englanders on the grounds that you are an obnoxious boor, that you own thousands of shares in a South African gold-mining company, or that you mistreat your children; nor may I appeal to my attributes in an effort to win acceptance of my own claims about heterogamy. But the *ad hominem* label has also been applied to a rather different sort of practice (exemplified in the work of Popper-Lynkeus 1910): suppose I come upon a person who proposes adoption of a policy the implementation of which would entail, along with its intended benefits (or perhaps as one of them), certain death for one or a hundred thousand innocent people; suppose further that I countered this proposal by winning from its author the two-fold admission that all innocent persons share equally in "the right to live" and that the proposed policy would not be justified if its author were included among the innocent victims; by the convention, I would have constructed an *ad hominem*.[14] Appeals to the preferences or principles of a particular person are inappropriate.

Yet, in the words of a popular textbook, *Fallacy, the Counterfeit of Argument*, how can we "take account of the character and motives of parties to an argument without falling into fallacy? Personal considerations are certainly relevant for judging the reliability" of a claimant, even "his willingness to tell the truth" (Fearnside and Holther 1959, 99–101). In the days when "abstract truths" could be absolute (because enacted by God or Nature) and "everyone" knew them, when the demarcation between *scientia* and *opinio* was crystalline to all who cared, it may have been less difficult to decide such matters. Today, even though some remnants of that older scheme remain, the qualifying criteria of judgment are fundamentally uncertain. If claims of knowledge are relative to conditions of the claimant,

14. I have borrowed this example from Edwards's 1967 biographic account of Popper-Lynkeus.

what is the measure by which we are to discriminate "the preferences or principles of a particular person" (who never develops such preferences and principles in hermetic isolation, and whose perspective may indeed be generally affected, or indicated, by his or her ownership of South African gold-mining stocks, mistreatment of children, or boorishness) from "abstract truth or logical cogency"? By what stick, other than a relativistic one, can we differentiate "abstract truth" from "mere ideology," and know that our differentiation is itself not "ideological" but "truthful"? The sort of understanding that has been promoted as "sociology of knowledge"—Mannheim's "perspectivism" and "relationism," for instance—enjoins us to consider the philosopher with the philosophy, the knowledge-giver with the knowledge given. But where then do we draw the line separating "relevant" considerations for an *argumentum ad rem* from those "irrelevant" considerations that would result in an *argumentum ad hominem*? And, given the self-relativization implicit in that understanding, how can we determine whether any line drawn by any person was itself determined by "relevant" rather than by "irrelevant" considerations of preference or principle?

Excursus: Given the presence of epistemological relativism, what happens to such qualities as "hypocrisy" and its opposite, "sincerity"? Where now is the measure that will discriminate the two?

By long convention, we have counted upon "hypocrisy"—defined in the *OED* as the assumption of false appearances of virtue or conviction, a dissimulation of true character, inclination, or intent—to assist in anchoring the baser side of our taxonomy of qualities of human discourse. Surely it has long served as one of the more useful charges to hurl at a tough adversary, one of the finer distinctions to draw between ourselves and the disreputably successful, one of the main emblems for those negative models that we use in our portrayals of proper character development. No one seeks to be known as a "hypocrite"; everyone strives to be "sincere." And yet some very intelligent people have claimed that "hypocrisy" suffers an undeserved reputation, that the pure "anti-hypocrite" (such as Molière's Alceste) is the true misanthrope, because cut off from an embedded appreciation of the stuff of human life. One can think of numerous situations that, by the convention, illustrate the point these "very intelligent people" want to make. Consider, for instance, the growing proportion of young women who have entered the faculty ranks of the academy in recent years. When a young woman, fresh from her years as a student, joins a college department that has had a predominantly male faculty, she no doubt faces a challenge of integration. I can imagine that on occasion, under such circumstances, she may choose to seem less critically intelligent, less assertive of opinion, more demure and diffident and even docile, than she "really" is, or than she allows herself to be with her female colleagues. Is that "hypocrisy"? Perhaps so, by the convention; but it can be a most useful approach to some of the challenges of her situation—just as the word "hypocrisy" itself recalls etymologically the playing of a role on stage. Yet, as Shklar has remarked in her fine essay on the convention, "hypocrisy" is the one "character flaw" almost certainly to be held in harsh regard: it "remains the only unforgivable sin even, perhaps especially, among those who can overlook and explain away almost every other vice. However much suffering it may cause, and however many social and religious rules it may violate, evil is to be understood after due analysis. But not hypocrisy, which alone is now inexcusable" (Shklar 1979, 1). The key presumption has been that, whereas no one is wittingly evil, the "hypocrite" deliberately manipulates through the instruments of false appearance and veiled practice. Heroic models, as well as the less exceptional of our emulable designs of rectitude of character, have traditionally assigned high importance to the opposite of "hypocrisy"—namely, that unshakable "sincerity" of utterance and deed that purportedly issues from strength of "inner self." Habermas's assignation of "sincerity" as one of the four crucial dimensions of an "ideal speech situation," and as the dimension according with the resource of "inner nature," continues this tradition.

Today we think we understand better than did Hawthorne and his fellow nineteenth-century theorists of the supreme "inner self"—at least we do understand differently—the complexities of selfhood. We understand, for example, à la G. H. Mead and his successors, that "the self" is not so much that bedrock of attributes which, once formed, perseveres, for good or ill and more or less successfully, through the demands and the temptations of a lifetime of associations. Rather, we think of "selfhood" as a continually modifiable composition that varies in accordance with relational context: there are as many facets of "the organized self" as there are significant differentiations within "the community" of "the generalized other" (Mead 1934, 154, 260–62).[15] But in a world of contextually contingent selfhood, in a world of none but relativistic claims of knowledge,

---

15. I do not mean to suggest that Mead was the first to formulate this contrast. In his *Letter to M. d'Alembert*, for instance, Rousseau stated his concern for what he diagnosed as the eclipse of an independent, transcendent "selfhood" in favor of a "selfhood" that was variably and malleably formed in the mutual dependencies of social matrix or association, where "the principal object is to please" and the ultimate fulfillment is "that the people enjoy themselves" (Rousseau [1758], 18). Locke's disquisition on "self" and "personal identity," in book 2, chapter 27, of *Human Understanding*, struggles with much the same issues: for example, is "self," once formed, a permanent and constant presence? Or is it modified as the circumstances of consciousness, on which it depends, are modified? Among recent discussions, compare Adorno [1964] 1973 and Trilling 1972.

what remains in the shimmering field of judgment to lend credence to our discriminations between "false appearances of virtue or conviction" and "true character"? What possibilities are left for the "anti-hypocrite," so that he does not slip on the banana peel of his own "sincerity"? Remembering Nietzsche's revelation of the lie, and of the immorality of morality, one thinks of power: relations of power and domination, and their conditions. Perhaps, in this, we may remember too that the convention of "hypocrisy" encouraged the substitution of judgments of "hypocrisy/sincerity" for judgments of the morality of those situations that often elicit "hypocrisy" as response—indeed, that constitute the material of "hypocrite" and "anti-hypocrite" alike. (Have we, for instance, more quickly taken offense at those conditions of the academy to which a young woman might choose to respond with "dissimulation," than at the unmasked "hypocrisy" itself?) Perhaps too, in this remembrance of Nietzsche, we may ask whether we have become so proficient in adjusting to situations that we no longer bother to think questions of "evil/good" in our morality (which evidently has not succumbed to the "revaluation of all values")—that we now are synaptically immune to horrification, and acquiesce to each situation as merely another demand for increments of adjustment in that contextually contingent and modifiable composition called "the organized self."

The absence of self-consistent, incontrovertible demonstration that our truth claims of predicative judgment are epistemologically grounded is no guarantee that those claims and their conveyances will be useless. (Our toy soldiers' weapons may not be epistemologically certifiable as "real," yet they do seem to result in plunder and death.) The explanation of *why* those uses exist, of why science has produced *just these* and not other understandings and things, cannot be found in the tradition of epistemology as such, however. The tradition of epistemology—and this includes the self-consciousness of science itself, which, in its subjugated philosophy-of-science depiction of itself, has proclaimed itself to be a sovereignly autonomous, almost autochthonous, evolutionary force that guides humankind from error to truth—this tradition can neither warrant the knowledge that is supposedly behind those uses, understandings, and things, nor explain why they are nevertheless here. Yet, is it not vital to us that we have, as truthfully effective reflexive consciousness, a self-consistently warranted foundation from which to judge, control, and change those uses and understandings and things? Is it not vital to us that we finally negate the false consciousness that proclaims "knowledge for its own sake"—that perverse self-deception that Nietzsche aptly described as "the last snare of morality: with that one becomes completely entangled in it once more" (Nietzsche [1886] 1968, §64)—and acknowledge the historically embedded faces of our own will, including the face of "destruction for its own sake"? Is it not vital to us that we answer the sages who counsel us to ignore these very questions of the possible grounding of true judgment, because (as our counselors tell it) "the whole matter is a witch's puzzle that can only transfix you in confusion and enfeeble you, but that otherwise is of no consequence to the real world"?[16]

There *is* a failure of criticism, a double failure of criticism, as I described it before, and it is pervasive. Because it is pervasive, in depth as well as breadth, it can hide behind its own occulting presence and reproduce its conditions of existence under other banners—for a widespread failure easily takes the name of success. Our pursuit of "objective knowledge" of a that-which-is-already masks our avoidance of responsibility for the project we make. And in the continuing play of that wager, we adjust to fit the changing odds as they are reconstituted by each of our collective rolls of the dice. More than half a century ago the famed British biologist J. B. S. Haldane, grasping at his optimism in the wake of a Great War, pleafully argued that "the tendency of applied science is to magnify injustices until they become too intolerable to be borne" (1924, 85)—at which point, presumably, the injustices are erased, or at least reduced. Now, more than half a century later, we have tested many new magnifying appliances of science, pronounced some of them to be especially effective, and, so it appears, settled upon our eventual solution to the problem of injustice. We shall erase ourselves.

Once, in an age that we usually think as being much less complex than our own, it was announced that "criticism has torn the imaginary flowers from the chain not so that man shall wear the unadorned, bleak chain but so that he will shake off the chain and pluck the living flower" (Marx [1844] 1975, 176). How far removed are we now, from the fundament of *that* potentiality?

2. BEGINNINGS AND CONSEQUENCES

The expositive field of the preceding chapters has been constructed in repeated traversings of numerous issues of "theory and practice," issues which, in their apparent discriminations, establish the coordinations and densities of commentary in those chapters. Because those chapters *are* commentary—indistinguishably expositive and negationally critical commentary—there is much more that could be said within the created field,

---

16. Such are the wisdoms of our counselors who, as Barrett depicted them, seek "to drag out the death rattle of philosophy as a series of annotations upon science" (Barrett 1978, 199). The characterization is fitting. But it is not the tradition of philosophy that is chiefly in peril—which is one of the major concerns (as I shall develop in volume 2) by which the argument I attempt differs from Rorty's brilliant critique of "foundationalism" (Rorty 1979).

both *as* such commentary and as commentary *about* the already said. The presumption that "scientific discourse" occupies a space of possibility of finally definitive statements, statements exhaustive of given facticities and different in kind from the "poetic" or "rhetorical" or "essayist" language of the potentially interminable discourse of commentary, has been one of the notable victims of the radicalized discovery of language, so-called, and self-relativization of thought.

But while there is much more that *could* be said within, or as expansion of, the created field of those chapters, I shall soon interrupt the commentary, and I shall do so in full awareness that the basis from which to make the interruption, to decide its *hic et nunc*, will have been left more to the not-said than to the said. Indeed, the unexplicated basis is of much more than interruption; if of that, then it must also be of the very *beginning* of my critical argument. Strange though this circumstance may initially seem, it has been unavoidable: the terms and thematizations by which the beginning (and thus the interruption) can be explicated cannot be explicated as part of the beginning itself. In these last paragraphs of this volume, I shall try to clarify some of the conditions of my critical argument as beginning.

Interruption has been a challenging presence throughout the commentary of preceding chapters. Of course, it has been present first of all explicitly—that is, each time I interrupted a claim in order to interrogate its foundation. But interruption has also been a challenging presence throughout the husbanding of the not-said of commentary, like a shadow seeking to mask its own sun. For the question that has asked to be asked a thousand times over would constitute an interrogation not *in* the explicit of that commentary but *of* it: how to construct, here and now, an effective criticism of received claims and traditions, precisely when there appears to be no warranted foundation for this or any other criticism? If the impeccable logic of epistemological relativism vanquishes every claim of noncontingent judgment, every assertion of an absolute zero-point; if the yield of representation is never more than an implication of its presupposition of correspondence, an enactment of its prejudgment of coherence; if the field of critical judgment cannot be said to be "*a* field," nor even yet a "babel," because there is no common table of relations by which to found the differences/connections that would make up either; then what gives the possibility of *this* criticism? In an absence of warranting foundation for criticism, this interruptive challenge postpones its own silence long enough to recommend cessation: "Put down the pen," it repeats; "all entitlements to criticism have been exhausted. Only yesterday's charlatan still appeals to a 'curse of writing'—that privileged affliction about which Mann's Tonio Kröger said that it 'begins by your feeling yourself set apart, in a curious sort of opposition to the nice, regular people; there is a gulf of ironic sensibility, of knowledge, skepticism, disagreement, between you and others' (Mann [1903] 1928, 153–54). The whole world has become a schooling in irony, and habits of skepticism and ironic displacement have lost their old exclusivity. Who now does not see that writing is about nothing but writing, and that one claim of criticism generates nothing but material for a next claim of criticism, and that arguments revolve around each other in the centerless finitude of an endless assortment of incommensurable claims? But then this *was* the message of 'knowledge for its own sake,' wasn't it? The place of *eutopos* has been emptied, its human time taken over by daydreaming and somnambulance. So, put down the pen."

Not to cease, in that absence of warranted foundation, must surely be the epitome of arrogance—that is, an act of arrogation, an asserting of claim without warrant. Yet I did refuse to cease. And in that refusal there is assertion of a claim the warranting foundation of which has not been unfolded as its beginning. The beginning I *have* constructed, a beginning that has pointed away from the not-said of its own warrant, was decided for me, in a manner of speaking, by the structure of domination manifested in/as discourse. I mean nothing mystical or mystifying by this manner of speaking, nothing surreptitious or pretersensuous or absolutizing, nothing like a "cunning of discourse" or a "metaphysical necessity." The constraint is one that we have interrogated over and over again in preceding chapters: a claim of knowledge, whether advertised as "purely expository," as "critically exegetical," or otherwise, is historically embedded and historically contingent. If I had attempted to construct, as my beginning, the warranting foundation of my claim of destructive criticism, the attempt would have dissolved in its own presumption of an ahistoricity of language-use. That is, the attempt would have been defeated in the presumption that language-use ("my" language-use, i.e., the language-use constituted in relations of "your reading my writing in a discursive field") would somehow have been free of the very claims that later I would have sought to criticize, on the basis of that warranting foundation, as claims having no self-consistent demonstrable warrant. This presumption of neutrality or freedom, of a "blank slate" on which writing can originate each time anew, is a tempting device, to be sure; it answers so many troublesome questions in advance of any particular question. But its yield can therefore be no more than a begging of questions. There is no Origin, only the historicity of beginnings. Consider: even though not self-consistently demonstrably warranted, those claims, to the extent they were accredited, were not merely claims of knowledge "expressed" in language-use. They were claims *on* language-use, *of* language-use. To that same extent, accordingly, the language-use that would have been most insinuatingly present to "my" ("our") construction of a beginning, had I attempted to construct it by formulating first the warranting foundation of my own claim of criticism, would have been the language-use integral to claims that *do not have* a self-consistent demonstrable warrant. Once again, then, criticism would have been undone in its beginning: its project would have been enslaved in that which it was to have criticized.[17] Thus, if in the very beginning there could be no escape from the historicity of a discourse, and if fundamental claims in that discourse (claims *on* and *of*, as well as in, language-use) were claims I sought to reject as unwarranted and, indeed, as unwarrantable, then I could construct a beginning of effective criticism only within that historical structure and only as *a display* of that absence of warranting foundation—even though I could therefore also only display the absence of any explication of the warranting foundation of my own claim of destructive criticism.

In consequence, the critical argument sustained throughout the many pages of this volume has completed nothing. At most it has begun the requisite clearing of a place for construction. While a careful reading of the structure of that critical argument will yield perhaps more than a glimmer of its project—that is, the construction for which the clearing is designed— an "explicit unfolding" has yet to be made. It will not be made here. Even though the failure of theory has been manifested as a failure of answers to questions that we regard as fundamental questions—questions such as those I named in conventional manner early in this chapter: the question of relations of "nature and society," the question of relations of "fact and

---

17. This "enslavement" is the process I have described in preceding chapters by the locution "being captured by the object of one's criticism." In many of the examples observed in those chapters, the failure can be accounted as an insufficiency of radical formulation of critique. But it can come about in other ways, too. Goldmann's citation of the case of the Jesuit defense of "faith" vis-à-vis "reason" provides an example (Goldmann [1968] 1973, 60). During the Enlightenment controversy over "the nature of God," the Jesuits sought to define a suitable defense of religious consciousness and action in relation both to their secular opponents, who had declared already that God was in very poor health if not actually dead, and to their Jansenist brethren, who staunchly defended the Augustinian tradition of faith and rejected outright the Enlightenment argument of reason (including its image of God-the-master-clockmaker whose works can be known through reason). Seeking to come to terms with the argument of reason, the Jesuits accused the Jansenists of promoting a repugnant doctrine of a tyrannical God. A Jesuit sermon of the time (quoted by Groethuysen 1927, 1:142–43), for example, spoke of the Jansenist God as being "neither holy nor just nor merciful" and as "nothing less than a merciless and barbarous tyrant who deserves all my hatred." But, in turning away from the Jansenist position of defense, and in attempting instead to come to terms with the secular movement, the Jesuits found themselves deliberating over the place of faith within natural reason, not the place of reason within faith. Contrary to their historical mission, they had adapted their own discourse to the terms of the very arguments against which they had thought to defend religious consciousness by way of dialogue.

value," and so on—the failure is not simply of answers. It is more radical, deeper, than that. It is a failure of the roots of our claim to knowledge, of our formations of the quiddity of knowledge. The conditions of failure announce their own destiny in the questions themselves. Not simply in the answers—but in the formations that determine limits of what can qualify as possible answer. Not simply in the agreement of the questions—but in the conventions by which those questions are produced and reproduced as domain-constituting claims, language-uses, activities. Or, to adapt a famous statement of criticism from the previous century: Not only in the answers, but even in the questions, there is mystification.[18]

Because the critical argument begun in this volume has completed nothing, I cannot write a conclusion for the volume. Only an adjournment. Etymologically, adjournment depends on an assumption that is itself not merely etymological. Nor will failure of that assumption be merely etymological.

The act of adjourning must remind us of the opening chapter and of the warning that runs epigraphically throughout: "Man would rather will *nothingness* than *not* will." This "will" is the potentiality of *poiēsis*. It is neither arbitrary nor original but arises historically from the conditions of its own production. In the interest of adjournment, therefore, this dialogue:[19]

I suddenly beheld the figure of a man, at some distance, advancing towards me with superhuman speed. He bounded over the crevices in the ice, among which I had walked with caution; his stature, also, as he approached, seemed to exceed that of man. I was troubled; a mist came over my eyes, and I felt a faintness seize me; but I was quickly restored by the cold gale of the mountains. I perceived, as the shape came nearer (sight tremendous and abhorred!) that it was the wretch whom I had created. I trembled with rage and horror, resolving to wait his approach and then close with him in mortal combat. He approached; his countenance bespoke bitter anguish, combined with disdain and malignity, while its unearthly ugliness rendered it almost too horrible for human eyes. But I scarcely observed this; rage and hatred had at first deprived me of utterance, and I recovered only to

18. The statement is from an alternative sheet of the opening of *The German Ideology*, written in 1845–46 (see Marx and Engels [1932] 1976, 28).

19. The dialogue is from Mary W. Shelley's *Frankenstein, or The Modern Prometheus* (Shelley [1831] 1968, 362–63), first published in 1818 and long since trivialized in cinematic consciousness.

overwhelm him with words expressive of furious detestation and contempt.

"Devil," I exclaimed, "do you dare approach me? And do not you fear the fierce vengeance of my arm wreaked on your miserable head? Begone, vile insect! Or rather, stay, that I may trample you to dust! And, oh! That I could with the extinction of your miserable existence, restore those victims whom you have so diabolically murdered!"

"I expected this reception," said the demon. "All men hate the wretched; how, then, must I be hated, who am miserable beyond all living things! Yet you, my creator, detest and spurn me, thy creature, to whom thou art bound by ties only dissoluble by the annihilation of one of us. You purpose to kill me. How dare you sport thus with life? Do your duty towards me, and I will do mine towards you and the rest of mankind. If you will comply with my conditions, I will leave them and you at peace; but if you refuse, I will glut the maw of death, until it be satiated with the blood of your remaining friends."

References

Aberle, David F., Albert K. Cohen, A. K. Davis, M. J. Levy, Jr., and F. X. Sutton. 1950. "The Functional Prerequisites of a Society." *Ethics* 60:100–111.

Achinstein, Peter. 1965. "The Problem of Theoretical Terms." *American Philosophical Quarterly* 2:193–203.

———. 1968. *Concepts of Science.* Baltimore: Johns Hopkins University Press.

Adorno, Theodor W. [1955] 1967. *Prisms.* Translated by S. Weber and S. Weber. London: Neville Spearman.

———. [1964] 1973. *The Jargon of Authenticity.* Translated by K. Tarnowski and F. Will. Evanston: Northwestern University Press.

Albert, Hans. 1971. *Plädoyer für kritischen Rationalismus.* Munich: R. Piper.

Alston, William P. 1964. *Philosophy of Language.* Englewood Cliffs, N.J.: Prentice-Hall.

Ambrose, Alice. 1952. "Moore's 'Proof of an External World.' " In *The Philosophy of G. E. Moore,* 2d ed., edited by P. A. Schilpp, 397–417. New York: Tudor.

Anderson, John M. 1968. "Truth, Process, and Creature in Heidegger's Thought." In *Heidegger and the Quest for Truth,* edited by M. S. Frings, 28–61. Chicago: Quadrangle.

Anderson, Perry. 1976. *Considerations on Western Marxism.* London: New Left Books.

Anscombe, G. E. M. [1958] 1969. "Modern Moral Philosophy." In *The Is/Ought Question,* edited by W. D. Hudson, 175–95. London: Macmillan.

Apel, Karl-Otto. 1955. "Das Verstehen (eine Problemgeschichte als Begriffsgeschichte)." *Archiv für Begriffsgeschichte* 1:142–99.

———. [1965] 1967. *Analytic Philosophy of Language and the Geisteswissenschaften.* Translated by H. Holstelilie. Dordrecht: D. Reidel.

———. 1973. *Transformation der Philosophie.* 2 vols. Frankfurt am Main: Suhrkamp.

Arendt, Hannah. 1978. *The Life of the Mind: Willing.* New York: Harcourt Brace Jovanovich.

Arnheim, Rudolf. 1954. *Art and Visual Perception.* Berkeley: University of California Press.

475

Austin, John L. 1950. "Truth." *Proceedings of the Aristotelian Society, Supplement* 24:111–28.

———. 1953. "Other Minds." In *Logic and Language*, 2d series, edited by A. G. N. Flew, 123–58. Oxford: Basil Blackwell.

———. 1961. *Philosophical Papers*. Edited by J. O. Urmson. Oxford: Oxford University Press.

———. 1962a. *Sense and Sensibilia*. Edited by G. J. Warnock. Oxford: Clarendon.

———. [1962b] 1975. *How To Do Things with Words*. 2d ed. Edited by J. O. Urmson and M. Sbisà. Cambridge: Harvard University Press.

Avineri, Shlomo. 1972. *Hegel's Theory of the Modern State*. Cambridge: Cambridge University Press.

Ayer, Alfred J. 1940. *The Foundation of Empirical Knowledge*. London: Macmillan.

———. 1946. *Language, Truth, and Logic*. 2d ed. London: Victor Gollanz.

———. 1956. *The Problem of Knowledge*. Harmondsworth: Penguin.

———. [1962] 1970. "Philosophy and Science." In *Metaphysics and Common Sense*, 82–93. San Francisco: Freeman, Cooper.

———. [1964a] 1970. "Knowledge, Belief, and Evidence." In *Metaphysics and Common Sense*, 115–25. San Francisco: Freeman, Cooper.

———. [1964b] 1970. "Man as a Subject for Science." In *Metaphysics and Common Sense*, 219–39. San Francisco: Freeman, Cooper.

———. [1967] 1970. "Has Austin Refuted the Sense-Datum Theory?" In *Metaphysics and Common Sense*, 126–48. San Francisco: Freeman, Cooper.

———. [1968] 1970. "What Must There Be?" In *Metaphysics and Common Sense*, 47–63. San Francisco: Freeman, Cooper.

———. 1977. *Part of My Life*. London: William Collins Sons.

Ayres, Russell W. 1975. "Policing Plutonium: The Civil Liberties Fallout." *Harvard Civil Rights–Civil Liberties Review* 10.

Bachelard, Gaston. 1928. *Essai sur la connaissance approchée*. Paris: J. Vrin.

———. 1934. *Le Nouvel Ésprit scientifique*. Paris: Presses Universitaires de France.

———. [1940] 1968. *The Philosophy of No: A Philosophy of the New Scientific Mind*. Translated by G. C. Waterston. New York: Orion.

———. [1952] 1971. "Fragment of a Diary of Man." In *The Right to Dream*, translated and edited by J. A. Underwood, 203–13. New York: Orion.

———. [1958] 1971. "Preface to Jacques Brosse, *The Order of Things*." In *The Right to Dream*, translated and edited by J. A. Underwood, 162–67. New York: Orion.

Bachelard, Suzanne. [1957] 1968. *A Study of Husserl's Formal and Transcendental Logic*. Translated by L. E. Embree. Evanston: Northwestern University Press.

Bacon, Francis [1605] 1952. *Of the Proficience and Advancement of Learning Divine and Human*. Chicago: Encyclopedia Britannica (Great Books, 30).

———. [1620] 1952. *Novum Organum: Aphorisms concerning the Interpretation of Nature and the Kingdom of Man*. Chicago: Encyclopedia Britannica (Great Books, 30).

———. [1622] 1870–82. "The Natural and Experimental History for the Foundation of Philosophy." In *The Works of Francis Bacon*, edited by J. Spedding, R. L. Ellis, and D. D. Heath, 9:369–75. Boston: Houghton Mifflin.

Ballard, E. G. 1953. "In Defense of Semiotic Aesthetics." *Journal of Aesthetics and Art Criticism* 12:38–43.

Barnes, S. Barry. 1977. *Interests and the Growth of Knowledge*. London: Routledge & Kegan Paul.

Barnett, H. G. 1948. "On Science and Human Rights." *American Anthropologist* 50:352–55.

Barrett, William. 1978. *The Illusion of Technique*. New York: Doubleday/Anchor.

Barth, Hans. [1961] 1976. *Truth and Ideology*, 2d ed. Translated by F. Lilge. Berkeley: University of California Press.

Barthes, Roland. [1957] 1979. "Shock-Photos." In *The Eiffel Tower and Other Mythologies*, translated by R. Howard, 71–73. New York: Hill and Wang.

———. [1961] 1977. "The Photographic Image." In *Image-Music-Text*, translated by S. Heath, 15–31. New York: Hill and Wang.

———. [1964a] 1977. "Rhetoric of the Image." In *Image-Music-Text*, translated by S. Heath. New York: Hill and Wang.

———. 1964b. *La Tour Eiffel*. Lausanne: Delpire.

———. 1966. *Critique et vérité*. Paris: Seuil.

Bateson, Gregory. 1979. *Mind and Nature: A Necessary Unity*. New York: E. P. Dutton.

Baudrillard, Jean. [1973] 1975. *The Mirror of Production*. Translated by M. Poster. St. Louis: Telos.

Bauman, Zygmunt. 1973. "'The Structuralist Promise." *British Journal of Sociology* 24:67–83.

Becker, Howard. 1939. Review of K. Mannheim's *Ideology and Utopia*. *American Sociological Review* 3:260–62.

Benda, Julien. [1927] 1955. *The Betrayal of the Intellectuals*. Translated by H. R. Aldington. Boston: Beacon.

Benjamin, Walter. [1950] 1968. "Theses on the Philosophy of History." In *Illuminations*, translated by H. Zohn, edited by H. Arendt, 255–66. New York: Harcourt, Brace and World.

Ben-David, Joseph. 1971. *The Scientist's Role in Society*. Englewood Cliffs, N. J.: Prentice-Hall.

Berger, Peter. 1963. *Invitation to Sociology*. New York: Doubleday.

Berger, Peter, and Thomas Luckmann. 1966. *The Social Construction of Reality*. New York: Doubleday.

Bergson, Henri. [1903] 1912. *An Introduction to Metaphysics*. Translated by T. E. Hulme. New York: G. P. Putnam.

Berkeley, George. [1710] 1952. *Treatise concerning the Principles of Human Knowledge*. Chicago: Encyclopedia Britannica (Great Books, 35).

Bernstein, Richard J. 1976. *The Restructuring of Social and Political Theory*. New York: Harcourt Brace Jovanovich.

Black, Max. 1964. "The Gap between 'Is' and 'Should.' " In *The Is/Ought Question*, edited by W. D. Hudson, 99–119. London: Macmillan, 1969.

Bloch, Ernst. [1918] 1964. *Vom Geist der Utopie*. Frankfurt am Main: Suhrkamp.

———. 1954–59. *Das Prinzip Hoffnung*. 3 vols. Frankfurt am Main: Suhrkamp.

Bohm, David. 1965. *The Special Theory of Relativity*. New York: Benjamin.

———. 1971. "Quantum Theory as an Indication of a New Order in Physics. Part A: The Development of New Orders as Shown through the History of Physics." *Foundations of Physics* 1:359–81.

———. 1973. "Quantum Theory as an Indication of a New Order in Physics. Part

B: Implicate and Explicate Order in Physical Law." *Foundations of Physics* 3:139–68.

Bohm, David, and B. J. Hiley. 1975. "On the Intuitive Understanding of Nonlocality as Implied by Quantum Theory." *Foundations of Physics* 5:93–109.

Booth, Wayne C. 1961. *The Rhetoric of Fiction*. Chicago: University of Chicago Press.

Botero, Giovanni. [1588] 1956. *Treatise concerning the Causes of the Magnificencie and Greatness of Cities*. Translated by R. Peterson. New Haven: Yale University Press.

———. [1589] 1956. *The Reason of State*. Translated by P. J. Waley and D. P. Waley. New Haven: Yale University Press.

Bourdieu, Pierre. [1972] 1977. *Outline of a Theory of Practice*. Translated by R. Nice. Cambridge: Cambridge University Press.

Bourdieu, Pierre, and Jean-Claude Passeron. [1970] 1977. *Reproduction*. Translated by R. Nice. London: Sage.

Brecht, Arnold. 1959. *Political Theory*. Princeton: Princeton University Press.

Brecht, Bertolt. [1943] 1966. *Galileo*. New York: Grove.

Bridgman, Percy W. 1948. *The Logic of Modern Physics*. 2d ed. New York: Macmillan.

Brown, Richard Harvey. 1977. *A Poetic for Sociology: Toward a Logic of Discovery for the Human Sciences*. Cambridge: Cambridge University Press.

Browne, Thomas. [1643] 1955. *Religio Medici*. Edited by J.-J. Denonain. Cambridge: Cambridge University Press.

Bruno, Giordano. [1584a] 1964. *Cause, Principle, and Unity*. Translated by J. Lindsay. New York: International.

———. [1584b] 1964. *The Expulsion of the Triumphant Beast*. Translated by A. D. Imerti. New Brunswick: Rutgers University Press.

Burhoe, Ralph Wendell. 1971. "What Specifies the Values of the Man-made Man?" *Zygon* 6:224–46.

Burke, Edmund. [1756] 1757. *A Vindication of Natural Society*. London: R. & J. Dodsley.

Burke, Kenneth. 1953. *Counter-Statement*. 2d ed. Berkeley: University of California Press.

Burkhardt, Carl J. 1941. *Gestalten und Machte*. Zurich: Fretz und Wasmuth.

Burnet, John. [1892] 1957. *Early Greek Philosophy*. New York: Meridian.

Campbell, Donald T. 1975. "On the Conflicts between Biological and Social Evolution and between Psychology and Moral Tradition." *American Psychologist* 30:1103–26.

Carnap, Rudolf. [1932] 1959. "The Elimination of Metaphysics through Logical Analysis of Language." Translated by A. Pap. In *Logical Positivism*, edited by A. J. Ayer, 60–81. Glencoe, Ill.: Free Press.

———. 1936–37. "Testability and Meaning." *Philosophy of Science* 3:419–71; and 4:1–40.

———. 1942. *Introduction to Semantics*. Cambridge: Harvard University Press.

———. [1950] 1952. "Empiricism, Semantics and Ontology." In *Semantics and the Philosophy of Language*, edited by L. Linsky, 208–28. Urbana: University of Illinois Press.

————. 1956. "The Methodological Character of Theoretical Concepts." In *Minnesota Studies in the Philosophy of Science,* edited by H. Feigl, et al. 1:38–76. Minneapolis: University of Minnesota Press.

Carroll, Lewis. 1876. *The Hunting of the Snark.* London: Macmillan.

Cassirer, Ernst. [1923–29] 1957. *Philosophy of Symbolic Form.* Translated by R. Manheim. New York: Oxford University Press.

————. 1944. *An Essay on Man.* New Haven: Yale University Press.

Cavell, Stanley. 1969. *Must We Mean What We Say?* New York: Charles Scribner's Sons.

————. 1979a. "Epistemology and Tragedy: A Reading of Othello (together with a cover letter)." *Daedalus* 108:27–43.

————. 1979b. *The Claim of Reason.* New York: Oxford University Press.

Charbonnier, Georges. [1961] 1969. *Conversations with Claude Lévi-Strauss* Translated by J. Weightman and D. Weightman. London: Jonathan Cape.

Chase, Richard X. 1978. "Production Theory." In *A Guide to Post-Keynesian Economics,* edited by A. S. Eichner, 71–86. New York: M. E. Sharpe.

Chisholm, Roderick M. 1957. *Perceiving.* Ithaca: Cornell University Press.

————. 1961. "Evidence as Justification." *Journal of Philosophy* 58:739–48.

Cioran, Emile M. [1964] 1970. *The Fall into Time.* Translated by R. Howard. Chicago: Quadrangle.

————. [1969] 1974. *The New Gods.* Translated by R. Howard. New York: Quadrangle/New York Times Books.

Cohen, Hermann. 1914. *Logik der reinen Erkenntnis.* Berlin: B. Cassirer.

Cohen, Morris R. 1931. *Reason and Nature: An Essay on the Meaning of the Scientific Method.* New York: Harcourt, Brace.

Collins, Randall. 1975. *Conflict Sociology: Toward an Explanatory Science.* New York: Academic.

Curtius, Ernst Robert. [1948] 1963. *European Literature and the Latin Middle Ages.* Translated by W. R. Trask. New York: Harper Torchbooks.

Dahrendorf, Ralf. 1968. *Essays in the Theory of Society.* Stanford: Stanford University Press.

Danto, Arthur C. 1965. *Nietzsche as Philosopher.* New York: Macmillan.

Deleuze, Gilles. 1968. *Différence et répétition.* Paris: Presses Universitaires de France.

Derrida, Jacques. 1972. *La Dissémination.* Paris: Seuil.

————. 1974. *Glas.* Paris: Éditions Galilée.

Descartes René. [1637] 1952. *Discourse on the Method of Rightly Conducting the Reason and Seeking for Truth in the Sciences.* Translated by E. S. Haldane and G. R. T. Ross. Chicago: Encyclopedia Britannica (Great Books, 31).

————. [1641] 1952. *Meditations on First Philosophy.* Translated by E. S. Haldane and G. R. T. Ross. Chicago: Encyclopedia Britannica (Great Books, 31).

Dewey, John. 1903. *Studies in Logical Theory.* Chicago: University of Chicago Press.

————. [1910] 1965. *The Influence of Darwin on Philosophy, and Other Essays in Contemporary Thought.* Bloomington: Indiana University Press.

————. 1916. *Essays in Experimental Logic.* Chicago: University of Chicago Press.

————. [1922] 1930. *Human Nature and Conduct*. New York: Modern Library.

————. 1925. *Experience and Nature*. LaSalle, Ill.: Open Court.

————. 1929. *The Quest for Certainty*. New York: Minton, Balch.

————. 1934. *Art as Experience*. New York: Minton, Balch.

————. 1938. *Logic: The Theory of Inquiry*. New York: Henry Holt.

————. 1946. *The Problems of Men*. New York: Philosophical Library.

Dewey, John, and Arthur F. Bentley. 1949. *Knowing and the Known*. Boston: Beacon.

Dickens, Charles. [1854] 1908. *Hard Times*. London: Dent.

Diels, Hermann, and Walther Kranz. 1960. *Die Fragmente der Vorsokratiker*, 3 vols. 9th ed. Berlin: Weidmann.

Dilthey, Wilhelm. [1883] 1959. *Einleitung in die Geisteswissenschaften*. 4th ed. Edited by B. Groethuysen. Vol. 1 of *Gesammelte Schriften*. 17 vols. Göttingen: Vandenhoeck & Ruprecht.

————. [1900] 1976. "The Development of Hermeneutics." In *Selected Writings*, translated and edited by H. P. Rickman. Cambridge: Cambridge University Press.

Dirac, Paul A. M. 1947. *The Principles of Quantum Mechanics*. 3d ed. London: Oxford University Press.

Dodds, Eric R. 1951. *The Greeks and the Irrational*. Berkeley: University of California Press.

Dolan, John M. 1967. "A Note on Quine's Theory of Radical Translation." *Mechanical Translation and Computer Linguistics*, vol. 10.

Donzelot, Jacques. [1977] 1979. *The Policing of Families*. Translated by R. Hurley. New York: Pantheon.

Dostoyevsky, Fyodor. [1866] 1956. *Crime and Punishment*. Translated by C. Garnett. New York: Random House.

Drell, Sidney D. 1980. "Arms Control: Is There Still Hope?" *Daedalus* 109:177–88.

Duerr, Hans Peter. 1978. *Traumzeit: Über die Grenze zwischen Wildnis und Zivilisation*. Frankfurt am Main: Syndikat Autoren- und Verlagsgesellschaft.

Duhem, Pierre M. M. [1914] 1954. *The Aim and Structure of Physical Theory*. 2d ed. Translated by P. P. Wiener. Princeton: Princeton University Press.

Dumas, Charles-Louis. 1804. *Discours sur la progrès futurs de la science de l'homme*. Montpellier: Tournel.

Dunn, John. 1979. *Western Political Theory in the Face of the Future*. Cambridge: Cambridge University Press.

Durkheim, Emile. [1895] 1964. *The Rules of Sociological Method*. Translated by S. A. Solovay and J. H. Mueller; edited by G. E. G. Catlin. New York: Free Press.

————. 1912a. Review of *Le Conflit de la morale et de la sociologie*, by Simon Deploige. *Année sociologique* 12:326–28.

————. [1912b] 1965. *The Elementary Forms of the Religious Life*. Translated by J. W. Swain. New York: Free Press.

Dvořák, Max. [1918] 1967. *Idealism and Naturalism in Gothic Art*. Translated by R. J. Klawiter. Notre Dame: University of Notre Dame Press.

Eddington, Arthur. [1939] 1958. *The Philosophy of Physical Science*. Ann Arbor: University of Michigan Press.

Edwards, Paul. 1967. "Joseph Popper-Lynkeus." In *The Encyclopedia of Philosophy*, edited by P. Edwards, 6:401–7. New York: Macmillan.

Eichhorn, Wolfgang et al., eds. 1972. *Istoricheskii materialism kak teoriya sotsial'nago poznaniya. Sbornik statei*. Moscow.

Einstein, Albert. [1905] 1923. "On the Electrodynamics of Moving Bodies." In *The Principle of Relativity*, edited by H. A. Lorentz, A. Einstein, H. Minkowski, and H. Weyl, translated by W. Perrett and G. B. Jeffery, 35–65. London: Methuen.

Eisenstein, Elizabeth L. 1966. "Clio and Chronos: An Essay on the Making and Breaking of History-Book Time." *History and Theory* 6:36–65.

Eley, Lothar. 1973. "Afterword to Husserl, *Experience and Judgment:* Phenomenology and Philosophy of Language." Translated by K. Ameriks. In *Experience and Judgment*, by E. Husserl, 399–429. Evanston: Northwestern University Press.

Elias, Norbert. [1939] 1976. *Über den Prozess der Zivilization: Soziogenetische und psychogenetische Untersuchungen*. 2 vols. Frankfurt am Main: Suhrkamp.

Elkana, Yehuda. 1978. "Two-Tier-Thinking: Philosophical Realism and Historical Relativism." *Social Studies of Science* 8:309–26.

Ellis, John M. 1974. *The Theory of Literary Criticism*. Berkeley: University of California Press.

Engelmann, Paul. 1967. *Letters from Ludwig Wittgenstein, with a Memoir*. New York: Horizon.

Fann, K. T. 1969. *Wittgenstein's Conception of Philosophy*. Berkeley: University of California Press.

Fearnside, W. Ward, and William B. Holther. 1959. *Fallacy, the Counterfeit of Argument*. Englewood Cliffs, N.J.: Prentice Hall.

Fechner, Gustav Theodor. 1876. *Vorschule der Ästhetik*. Leipzig: Breitkopf und Härtel.

Feyerabend, Paul K. 1970a. "Classical Empiricism." In *The Methodological Heritage of Newton*, edited by R. E. Butts and J. W. Davis, 150–70. Toronto: University of Toronto Press.

———. 1970b. "Consolations for the Specialist." In *Criticism and the Growth of Knowledge*, edited by I. Lakatos and A. Musgrove, 197–230. Cambridge: Cambridge University Press.

———. 1975. *Against Method: Outline of an Anarchistic Theory of Knowledge*. London: New Left Books.

———. 1978. "From Incompetent Professionalism to Professional Incompetence— The Rise of a New Breed of Intellectuals." *Philosophy of the Social Sciences* 8:37–53.

Fichte, Johann Gottlieb. [1808] 1922. *Addresses to the German Nation*. Translated by R. F. Jones and G. H. Turnbull. Chicago: Open Court.

Fillmore, Charles. 1974. "Pragmatics and the Description of Discourse." In *Berkeley Studies in Syntax and Semantics, I*. edited by C. Filmore, G. Lakoff, and R. Lakoff, 1:V1–V21. Berkeley: University of California, Department of Linguistics and the Institute of Human Learning.

Fleck, Ludwig. 1935. *Entstehung und Entwicklung einer wissenschaftlichen Tatsache: Einführung in die Lehre vom Denkstil und Denkkollektiv*. Basel: Schwab.

Foucault, Michel. [1961] 1965. *Madness and Civilization: A History of Insanity in the Age of Reason.* Abridged by Foucault. Translated by R. Howard. New York: Random House.

———. [1963a] 1973. *The Birth of the Clinic.* Translated by A. M. S. Smith. New York: Pantheon.

———. [1963b] 1977. "A Preface to Transgression." In *Language, Counter-Memory, Practice,* translated by D. F. Bouchard and S. Simon, edited by D. F. Bouchard, 29–52. Ithaca: Cornell University Press.

———. [1966] 1970. *The Order of Things: An Archaeology of the Human Sciences.* Translated by A. M. Sheridan Smith. New York: Pantheon.

———. [1968] 1972. "Réponse à une question." Translated by A. M. Nazzaro, as "History, Discourse, and Discontinuity." *Salmagundi* 20:225–48.

———. [1969a] 1972. *The Archaeology of Knowledge.* Translated by A. M. Sheridan Smith. New York: Pantheon.

———. [1969b] 1977. "What Is an Author?" In *Language, Counter-Memory, Practice,* translated by D. F. Bouchard and S. Simon, edited by D. F. Bouchard, 113–38. Ithaca: Cornell University Press.

———. [1970] 1977. "Theatrum Philosophicum." In *Language, Counter-Memory, Practice,* translated by D. F. Bouchard and S. Simon, edited by D. F. Bouchard, 165–96. Ithaca: Cornell University Press.

———. [1970–71] 1977. "History of Systems of Thought." In *Language, Counter-Memory, Practice,* translated by D. F. Bouchard and S. Simon, edited by D. F. Bouchard, 199–204. Ithaca: Cornell University Press.

———. [1971a] 1972. *The Discourse on Language.* Translated by R. Swyer. Appendix to *The Archaeology of Knowledge.* New York: Pantheon.

———. [1971b] 1977. "Nietzsche, Genealogy, History." In *Language, Counter-Memory, Practice,* translated by D. F. Bouchard and S. Simon, edited by D. F. Bouchard, 139–64. Ithaca: Cornell University Press.

———. [1971c] 1977. "Revolutionary Action: 'Until Now.' " In *Language, Counter-Memory, Practice,* translated by D. F. Bouchard and S. Simon, edited by D. F. Bouchard, 218–33. Ithaca: Cornell University Press.

———. [1972] 1977. "Intellectuals and Power." In *Language, Counter-Memory, Practice,* translated by D. F. Bouchard and S. Simon, edited by D. F. Bouchard, 205–17. Ithaca: Cornell University Press.

———, ed. [1973] 1975. *I, Pierre Rivière . . . : A Case of Parricide in the Nineteenth Century,* translated by F. Jellinek. New York: Pantheon.

———. [1975] 1977. *Discipline and Punish: The Birth of the Prison.* Translated by A. Sheridan. New York: Pantheon.

———. [1976] 1978. *The History of Sexuality,* vol. 1. Translated by R. Hurley. New York: Pantheon.

———. 1978. "Politics and the Study of Discourse." *Ideology and Consciousness.* 3:7–26.

Freeman, Kathleen. 1946. *Ancilla to the Pre-Socratic Philosophers.* Oxford: Basil Blackwell.

Frings, Manfred S., ed. 1968. *Heidegger and the Quest for Truth.* Chicago: Quadrangle.

Frye, Northrop. 1970. *The Stubborn Structure: Essays on Criticism and Society.* Ithaca: Cornell University Press.

Furet, François. 1971. "Quantitative History." Translated by B. Bray. *Daedalus* 100:151–67.

Furth, Hans. 1966. *Thinking without Language.* New York: Free Press.

Gadamer, Hans-Georg. [1963] 1976. "The Phenomenological Movement." In *Philosophical Hermeneutics,* translated and edited by D. E. Linge, 130–81. Berkeley: University of California Press.

———. [1965] 1975. *Truth and Method.* 2d ed. Translator not listed. New York: Seabury.

———. [1967] 1976. "Heidegger and the Language of Metaphysics." In *Philosophical Hermeneutics,* translated and edited by D. E. Linge, 229–40. Berkeley: University of California Press.

———. 1975. "Hermeneutics and Social Science." *Cultural Hermeneutics* 2:307–16.

———. 1977. "Sein, Geist, Gott." In *Heidegger: Freiburger Universitätsvorträge zu seinem Gedenken,* by H.-G. Gadamer, W. Marx, and C. F. von Weizsäcker, 43–62. Munich: Karl Alber.

Galilei, Galileo. [1632] 1967. *Dialogue concerning the Two Chief World Systems.* Translated by S. Drake. 2d ed. Berkeley: University of California Press.

———. [1638] 1914. *Dialogues concerning Two New Sciences.* Translated by H. Crew and A. de Salvio. New York: Macmillan.

Gardner, John. 1977. *On Moral Fiction.* New York: Basic Books.

Garfinkel, Harold. 1967. *Studies in Ethnomethodology.* Englewood Cliffs, N.J.: Prentice-Hall.

Gavre, Mark. 1974. "Hobbes and His Audience." *American Political Science Review* 68:1542–56.

Geertz, Clifford. 1980. "Blurred Genres: The Refiguration of Social Thought." *The American Scholar* 49:165–79.

Geoffroy Saint-Hilare, Étienne, and Isidore Geoffroy Saint-Hilare. 1836. *Traité de tératologie.* 3 vols. Paris: J.-B. Baillière.

Georgescu-Roegen, Nicholas. 1971. *The Entropy Law and the Economic Process.* Cambridge: Harvard University Press.

Gibbs, Jack P. 1979. "The Elites Can Do Without Us." *The American Sociologist* 14:79–85.

Giddens, Anthony, ed. 1974. *Positivism and Sociology.* London: Heinemann.

Giedymin, Jerzy. 1970. "The Paradox of Meaning Variance." *British Journal for the Philosophy of Science* 21:257–68.

Gilson, Étienne. 1930. *Études sur le rôle de la pensée médiévale dans la formation du système cartésien.* Paris: Vrin.

Glasstone, Samuel, and Philip Dolan, eds. 1977. *The Effects of Nuclear Weapons.* Washington, D.C.: Government Printing Office.

Glucksmann, André. [1977] 1980. *The Master Thinkers.* Translated by B. Pearce. New York: Harper & Row.

Gödel, Kurt. [1931] 1967. "On Formally Undecidable Propositions of *Principia Mathematica* and Related Systems. I." Translated by J. van Heijenoort. In *From Frege to Gödel: A Sourcebook in Mathematical Logic, 1879–1931,* edited by Jean van Heijenoort, 596–616. Cambridge: Harvard University Press.

Goethe, Johann Wolfgang von. [1832] 1952. *Faust.* Translated by G. M. Priest. Chicago: Encyclopedia Britannica (Great Books, 47).

Goffman, Erving. 1974. *Frame Analysis.* Cambridge: Harvard University Press.

Goldenweiser, Alexander A. 1910. "Totemism, an Analytical Study." *Journal of American Folklore* 23:179–293.

Goldfarb, Jeffrey C. 1978. Review of *A Poetic for Sociology,* by R. H. Brown. *American Journal of Sociology* 84:464–66.

Goldmann, Lucien. [1968] 1973. *The Philosophy of the Enlightenment.* Translated by H. Maas. Cambridge: MIT Press.

———. [1973] 1977. *Lukács and Heidegger: Towards a New Philosophy.* Translated by W. Q. Boelhower. London: Routledge & Kegan Paul.

Gombrich, Ernst H. 1959. *Art and Illusion.* Princeton: Princeton University Press.

Goodheart, Eugene. 1978. *The Failure of Criticism.* Cambridge: Harvard University Press.

Goodman, Nelson. 1978. *Ways of Worldmaking.* Indianapolis: Hackett.

Gorman, Robert A. 1976. *The Dual Vision: Alfred Schutz and the Myth of Phenomenological Social Science.* London: Routledge & Kegan Paul.

Gould, Stephen Jay. 1977. *Ontogeny and Phylogeny.* Cambridge: Belknap.

Gouldner, Alvin. 1970. *The Coming Crisis of Western Sociology.* New York: Basic Books.

———. 1976. *The Dialectic of Ideology and Technology.* New York: Seabury.

Graff, Gerald. 1979. *Literature against Itself.* Chicago: University of Chicago Press.

Grazia, Alfred de. 1966. *The Velikovsky Affair.* New York: University.

Green, Martin. 1972. *Cities of Light and Sons of the Morning.* Boston: Little, Brown.

Greene, William Chase. 1951. "The Spoken and the Written Word." *Harvard Studies in Classical Philology* 60:23–59.

Greimas, Algirdas J. 1970. *Du sens: essais sémiotiques.* Paris: Seuil.

Grice, H. P., and Peter F. Strawson. 1956. "In Defense of Dogma." *The Philosophical Review* 65:141–58.

Groethuysen, Bernard. 1927. *Entstehung der bürgerlichen Welt- und Lebensanschauung in Frankreich.* 2 vols. Halle/Saale: M. Niemeyer.

Grünwald, Ernst. 1934. *Das Problem der Soziologie des Wissens.* Edited by W. Eckstein. Wien: Wilhelm Braumüller.

Guédon, Jean-Claude. 1977. "Michel Foucault: The Knowledge of Power and the Power of Knowledge." *Bulletin of the History of Medicine* 51:245–77.

Habermas, Jürgen. 1958. "Anthropologie." *Fischer-Lexicon: Philosophie,* edited by A. Diemer and I. Frenzel. Frankfurt am Main: Fischer.

———. 1962. *Strukturwandel der Öffentlichkeit.* Neuwied: Luchterhand.

———. 1963. "Analytische Wissenschaftstheorie und Dialektik. Ein Nachtrag zur Kontroverse zwischen Popper und Adorno." In *Zeugnisse. Theodor W. Adorno zum sechzigsten Geburtstag,* edited by M. Horkheimer, 473–501. Frankfurt am Main: Europäische Verlagsanstalt.

———. 1964. "Gegen einen positivistisch halbierten Rationalismus. Erwiderung eines Pamphlets." *Kölner Zeitschrift für Soziologie und Sozialpsychologie* 16:635–59.

———. [1965] 1971. "Knowledge and Human Interests: A General Perspective." In *Knowledge and Human Interests,* translated by J. J. Shapiro, 301–17. Boston: Beacon.

———. [1967] 1973. "Labor and Interaction: Remarks on Hegel's Jena *Philosophy of Mind.*" In *Theory and Practice*, 4th ed., abridged and translated by J. Viertel, 142–69. Boston: Beacon.

———. [1968a] 1971. *Knowledge and Human Interests.* Translated by J. J. Shapiro. Boston: Beacon.

———. [1968b] 1970. "Technology and Science as 'Ideology.' " In *Toward A Rational Society*, translated by J. J. Shapiro, 81–122. Boston: Beacon.

———. [1968c] 1970. "Technical Progress and the Social Life-World." In *Toward a Rational Society*, translated by J. J. Shapiro, 50–61. Boston: Beacon.

———. [1968d] 1970. "The Scientization of Politics and Public Opinion." In *Toward a Rational Society*, translated by J. J. Shapiro, 62–80. Boston: Beacon.

———. 1970a. "On Systematically Distorted Communication." *Inquiry* 13:205–18.

———. 1970b. "Towards a Theory of Communicative Competence." *Inquiry* 13: 360–75.

———. 1970c. *Zur Logik der Sozialwissenschaften: Materialen.* 2d ed. Frankfurt am Main: Suhrkamp.

———. [1971a] 1973. *Theory and Practice.* 4th ed. Translated and abridged by J. Viertel. Boston: Beacon.

———. 1971b. "Der Universalitätsanspruch der Hermeneutik." In *Hermeneutik und Ideologiekritik*, by K.-O. Apel et al., 120–59. Frankfurt am Main: Suhrkamp.

———. 1971c. "Vorbereitende Bemerkungen zu einer Theorie der kommunikativen Kompetenz." In *Theorie der Gesellschaft oder Sozialtechnologie—Was leistet die Systemforschung?* by J. Habermas and N. Luhmann, 101–41. Frankfurt am Main: Suhrkamp.

———. 1971d. "Theorie der Gesellschaft oder Sozialtechnologie? Eine Auseinandersetzung mit Niklas Luhmann." In *Theorie der Gesellschaft oder Sozialtechnologie—Was leistet die Systemforschung?* by J. Habermas and N. Luhmann, 142–290. Frankfurt am Main: Suhrkamp.

———. 1971e. "Why More Philosophy?" Translated by E. B. Ashton. *Social Research* 38:633–54.

———. [1971f] 1977. "Martin Heidegger: On the Publication of Lectures from the Year 1935." Translated by D. Ponikvar. *Graduate Faculty Philosophy Journal*, 6:155–80.

———. 1973a. "Postscript to *Knowledge and Human Interests.*" Translated by C. Lenhardt. *Philosophy of the Social Sciences* 3:157–89.

———. 1973b. "Wahrheitstheorien." In *Wirklichkeit und Reflexion: Festschrift für Walter Schulz*, edited by H. Fahrenbach, 211–65. Pfullingen: Neske.

———. [1973c] 1975. *Legitimation Crisis.* Translated by T. M. McCarthy. Boston: Beacon.

———. [1973d] 1974. "What Does a Crisis Mean Today?" *Social Research* 40: 643–67.

———. 1975a. *Zur Rekonstruktion des historischen Materialismus.* Frankfurt am Main: Suhrkamp.

———. 1975b. "Towards a Reconstruction of Historical Materialism." Abridged and translated by R. Strauss. *Theory and Society* 2:287–300.

486   REFERENCES

———. 1976a. "Some Distinctions in Universal Pragmatics." Translated by P. Pekelharing and C. Disco. *Theory and Society* 3:155–67.

———. 1976b. "Was heisst Universalpragmatik?" In *Sprachpragmatik und Philosophie*, edited by K.-O. Apel, 174–273. Frankfurt am Main: Suhrkamp.

———. 1976c. *Wahrheit und Diskurs.* Frankfurt am Main: Suhrkamp.

———. [1976d] 1979. "Historical Materialism and the Development of Normative Structures." In *Communication and the Evolution of Society*, translated by T. M. McCarthy, 95–129. Boston: Beacon.

Haldane, John B. S. 1924. *Daedalus, or Science and the Future.* London: Kegan Paul.

Hamburger, Michael. 1957. *Reason and Energy: Studies in German Literature.* New York: Grove.

Handlin, Oscar. 1971. "History: A Discipline in Crisis?" *The American Scholar* 40:447–65.

———. 1979. *Truth in History.* Cambridge: Harvard University Press.

Hanson, Norwood R. 1958. *Patterns of Discovery.* Cambridge: Cambridge University Press.

Hardin, Garrett. 1979. "Political Requirements for Preserving Our Common Heritage." In *Wildlife and America*, 310–16. Washington, D. C.: Council on Environmental Quality.

Hare, Richard M. 1952. *The Language of Morals.* Oxford: Clarendon Press.

———. [1964] 1969. "The Promising Game." In *The Is/Ought Question*, edited by W. D. Hudson, 144–56. London: Macmillan.

Harré, Romano. 1972. *The Philosophies of Science.* London: Oxford University Press.

Hart, Herbert L. A. 1961. *The Concept of Law.* Oxford: Clarendon.

Hartnack, Justus. [1962] 1965. *Wittgenstein and Modern Philosophy.* Translated by M. Cranston. New York: Doubleday/Anchor.

Hauser, Arnold. [1958] 1963. *Philosophy of Art History.* New York: Meridian Books.

Heap, James L., and Phillip A. Roth. 1973. "On Phenomenological Sociology." *American Sociological Review* 38:354–67.

Hegel, G. W. F. [1802] 1968. "Über die wissenschaftlichen Behandlungsarten des Naturrechts." In *Gesammelte Werke*, edited by H. Buchner and O. Pöggeler, 4:417–85. Hamburg: Felix Meiner.

———. [1803–4] 1932. *Jenaer Realphilosophie I: Die Vorlesungen von 1803/04.* Edited by J. Hoffmeister. Leipzig: Felix Meiner.

———. [1805–6] 1967. *Jenaer Realphilosophie II: Vorlesungsmanuskripte zur Philosophie der Natur und des Geistes von 1805/06.* Edited by J. Hoffmeister. Hamburg: Felix Meiner.

———. [1807] 1977. *Phenomenology of Spirit.* 5th ed. Edited by J. Hoffmeister. Translated by A. V. Miller. Oxford: Clarendon.

———. [1821] 1952. *The Philosophy of Right.* Translated by T. M. Knox. Chicago: Encyclopedia Britannica (Great Books, 46).

———. [1830a] 1974. *Hegel's Logic: Being Part One of the Encyclopaedia of the Philosophical Sciences.* 3d ed. Translated by W. Wallace. Oxford: Oxford University Press.

————. [1830b] 1970. *Hegel's Philosophy of Nature: Being Part Two of the Encyclopaedia of the Philosophical Sciences.* 3d ed. With Michelet's *Zusätze.* Translated by A. V. Miller. Oxford: Clarendon.

————. [1830c] 1971. *Hegel's Philosophy of Mind: Being Part Three of the Encyclopaedia of the Philosophical Sciences.* 3d ed. With Boumann's *Zusätze.* Translated by W. Wallace and A. V. Miller. Oxford: Clarendon.

Heidegger, Martin. [1927] 1962. *Being and Time.* Translated by J. Macquarrie and E. Robinson. New York: Harper & Row.

————. [1929] 1949. "What Is Metaphysics?" Translated by R. F. C. Hull and A. Crick. In *Existence and Being,* 325–61. Chicago: Henry Regnery.

————. [1936] 1949. "Hölderlin and the Essence of Poetry." Translated by D. Scott. In *Existence and Being,* 270–91. Chicago: Henry Regnery.

————. [1943] 1949. "On the Essence of Truth." Translated by R. F. C. Hull and A. Crick. In *Existence and Being,* 292–324. Chicago: Henry Regnery.

————. [1947] 1962. "Letter on Humanism." Translated by E. Lohner. In *Philosophy in the Twentieth Century,* edited by W. Barrett and H. D. Aiken, 3:270–302. New York: Random House.

————. [1949] 1956. "The Way Back into the Ground of Metaphysics." Translated by W. Kaufmann. In *Existentialism from Dostoevsky to Sartre,* edited by W. Kaufmann, 207–21. Cleveland: Meridian.

————. [1950a] 1971. "The Origin of the Work of Art." Translated by A. Hofstadter. In *Poetry, Language, Thought,* 15–87. New York: Harper & Row.

————. [1950b] 1975. "The Anaximander Fragment." Translated by D. F. Krell. In *Early Greek Thinking,* 13–58. New York: Harper & Row.

————. [1950c] 1971. "What Are Poets For?" Translated by A. Hofstadter. In *Poetry, Language, Thought,* 91–142. New York: Harper & Row.

————. [1950d] 1970. *Hegel's Concept of Experience.* Translator not listed. New York: Harper & Row.

————. [1951a] 1962. *Kant and the Problem of Metaphysics.* 2d ed. Translated by J. S. Churchill. Bloomington: Indiana University Press.

————. [1951b] 1975. "Logos (Heraclitus, Fragment B 50)." Translated by D . F. Krell. In *Early Greek Thinking,* 59–78. New York: Harper & Row.

————. [1952a] 1977. "The Word of Nietzsche: 'God is Dead.' " Translated by W. Lovitt. In *The Question concerning Technology and Other Essays,* 53–112. New York: Harper & Row.

————. [1952b] 1977. "The Age of the World Picture." Translated by W. Lovitt. In *The Question concerning Technology and Other Essays,* 115–54. New York: Harper & Row.

————. [1952c] 1971. "Building Dwelling Thinking." Translated by A. Hofstadter. In *Poetry, Language, Thought,* 143–61. New York: Harper & Row.

————. [1953] 1959. *Introduction to Metaphysics.* Translated by R. Manheim. New Haven: Yale University Press.

————. [1954a] 1973. "Overcoming Metaphysics." Translated by J. Stambaugh. In *The End of Philosophy,* 84–110. New York: Harper & Row.

————. [1954b] 1977. "The Question concerning Technology." Translated by W. Lovitt. In *The Question concerning Technology and Other Essays,* 3–35. New York: Harper & Row.

———. [1954c] 1975. "Aletheia (Heraclitus, Fragment B 16)." Translated by F. Capuzzi. In *Early Greek Thinking*, 102–23. New York: Harper & Row.

———. [1954d] 1975. "Moira (Parmenides VIII, 34–41)." Translated by F. Capuzzi. In *Early Greek Thinking*, 79–101. New York: Harper & Row.

———. [1956] 1958. *What Is Philosophy?* Translated by W. Kluback and J. T. Wilde. New York: Twayne.

———. [1957] 1969. *Identity and Difference*. Translated by J. Stambaugh. New York: Harper & Row.

———. [1959a] 1966. *Discourse on Thinking*. Translated by J. M. Anderson and E. H. Freund. New York: Harper & Row.

———. [1959b] 1971. "Words." Translated by J. Stambaugh. In *On the Way to Language*, 139–56. New York: Harper & Row.

———. [1959c] 1971. "A Dialogue on Language." Translated by P. D. Hertz. In *On the Way to Language*, 1–54. New York: Harper & Row.

———. [1959d] 1971. "The Nature of Language." Translated by P. D. Hertz. In *On the Way to Language*, 57–108. New York: Harper & Row.

———. 1961a. *Nietzsche*. 2 vols. Pfulligen: Neske.

———. [1961b] 1973. "Metaphysics as History of Being." (*Nietzsche*, vol. 2, chap. 5; translated by J. Stambaugh.) In *The End of Philosophy*, 1–54. New York: Harper & Row.

———. [1961c] 1973. "Sketches for a History of Being as Metaphysics." (*Nietzsche*, vol. 2, chap. 6; translated by J. Stambaugh.) In *The End of Philosophy*, 55–74. New York: Harper & Row.

———. [1961d] 1973. "Recollection in Metaphysics." (*Nietzsche*, vol. 2, chap. 7; translated by J. Stambaugh.) In *The End of Philosophy*, 75–83. New York: Harper & Row.

———. [1962a] 1967. *What Is a Thing?* Translated by W. B. Barton, Jr., and V. Deutsch. South Bend, Ind.: Gateway Editions.

———. [1962b] 1977. "The Turning." Translated by W. Lovitt. In *The Question concerning Technology and Other Essays*, 36–49. New York: Harper & Row.

———. [1963] 1972. "My Way to Phenomenology." Translated by J. Stambaugh. In *On Time and Being*, 74–82. New York: Harper & Row.

———. [1964] 1972. "The End of Philosophy and the Task of Thinking." Translated by J. Stambaugh. In *On Time and Being*, 55–73. New York: Harper & Row.

———. [1968] 1972. "Time and Being." Translated by J. Stambaugh. In *On Time and Being*, 1–24. New York: Harper & Row.

———. [1969] 1972. "Summary of a Seminar on the Lecture 'Time and Being.'" Translated by J. Stambaugh. In *On Time and Being*, 25–54. New York: Harper & Row.

———. [1976] 1977. "Only a God Can Save Us Now." *Der Spiegel* interview of 1966. Translated by D. Schendler. *Graduate Faculty Philosophy Journal* 6:5–27.

Heidel, William A. 1912–13. "On Certain Fragments of the Pre-Socratics: Critical Notes and Elucidations." *Proceedings of the American Academy of Arts and Sciences* 48:681–734.

Heisenberg, Werner. [1954] 1958. *The Physicists's Conception of Nature*. Translated by A. J. Pomerans. New York: Harcourt, Brace.

Herskovits, Melville J. [1942] 1972. "On the Values in Culture." In *Cultural Relativism: Perspectives in Cultural Pluralism*, edited by F. Herskovits, 3–10. New York: Vintage.

Hesse, Hermann. [1927] 1963. *Steppenwolf*. Translated by B. Creighton and W. Sorell. New York: Modern Library.

Hesse, Mary. 1974. *The Structure of Scientific Inference*. Berkeley: University of California Press.

Hindess, Barry. 1972. "The 'Phenomenological' Sociology of Alfred Schutz." *Economy and Society* 1:1–27.

Hjelmslev, Louis. [1943] 1961. *Prolegomena to a Theory of Language*. Translated by F. J. Whitfield. Madison: University of Wisconsin Press.

Hobbes, Thomas. [1651] 1952. *Leviathan*. Edited by N. Fuller. Chicago: Encyclopedia Britannica (Great Books, 23).

———. [1678] 1839–45. *Decameron Physiologicum*. Vol. 7 of *The English Works of Thomas Hobbes of Malmesbury*, edited by W. Molesworth. London: J. Bohn.

Horkheimer, Max. 1933. "Materialismus und Metaphysik." *Zeitschrift für Sozialforschung* 2:1–33.

———. 1934. *Dämmerung*. Zurich: Oprecht & Helbling.

———. 1935. "Zur Problem der Wahrheit." *Zeitschrift für Sozialforschung* 4:321–63.

———. [1937] 1972. "Traditional and Critical Theory." In *Critical Theory*, translated by M. J. O'Connell et al., 188–243. New York: Seabury.

———. [1947] 1974. *Eclipse of Reason*. New York: Seabury.

———. [1962] 1967. "Schopenhauer Today." Translated by R. Kolben. In *The Critical Spirit: Essays in Honor of Herbert Marcuse*, edited by K. H. Wolff and B. Moore, Jr., 55–71. Boston: Beacon.

———. [1967] 1974. *Critique of Instrumental Reason*. Translated by M. J. O'Connell. New York: Seabury.

Horkheimer, Max, and Theodor W. Adorno. [1947] 1972. *Dialectic of Enlightenment*. Translated by J. Cumming. New York: Herder and Herder.

Hume, David. [1739–40] 1964. *A Treatise of Human Nature*. Edited by L. A. Selby Bigge. Oxford: Oxford University Press.

Hunter, J. F. M. [1968] 1971. " 'Forms of Life' in Wittgenstein's *Philosophical Investigations*." In *Essays on Wittgenstein*, edited by E. D. Klemke, 273–97. Urbana: University of Illinois Press.

Husserl, Edmund. 1891. *Philosophie der Arithmetik*. Vol. 1. Halle: Pfeffer.

———. [1910–11] 1965. "Philosophy as Rigorous Science." Translated by Q. Lauer. In *Phenomenology and the Crisis of Philosophy*, edited by Q. Lauer, 71–147. New York: Harper & Row.

———. [1913] 1967. *Ideas: General Introduction to Pure Phenomenology, I*. Translated by W. R. Boyce Gibson. New York: Humanities.

———. [1913–21] 1970. *Logical Investigations*. 2d ed. Translated by J. N. Findlay. London: Routledge & Kegan Paul.

―――. [1928] 1964. *The Phenomenology of Internal Time-Consciousness.* Edited by M. Heidegger. Translated by J. S. Churchill. Bloomington: Indiana University Press.

―――. [1929] 1969. *Formal and Transcendental Logic: Toward a Critique of Logical Reason.* Translated by D. Cairns. The Hague: Martinus Nijhoff.

―――. [1931] 1960. *Cartesian Meditations.* Edited by S. Strasser. Translated by D. Cairns. The Hague: Martinus Nijhoff.

―――. [1936] 1970. *The Crisis of the European Sciences and Transcendental Phenomenology. Husserliana,* Vol. 6. Edited by W. Biemel. Translated by D. Carr. Evanston: Northwestern University Press.

―――. [1948] 1973. *Experience and Judgment: Investigations in a Genealogy of Logic.* Edited by L. Landgrebe. Translated by J. S. Churchill and K. Ameriks. Evanston: Northwestern University Press.

Hutchison, Terence W. 1977. *Knowledge and Ignorance in Economics.* Chicago: University of Chicago Press.

Hymes, Dell, ed. 1972. *Reinventing Anthropology.* New York: Pantheon.

Iserloh, Erwin. 1956. *Gnade und Euchariste in der philosophischen Theologie des Wilhelm von Ockham, ihre Bedeutung für die Ursachen der Reformations.* Wiesbaden: F. Steiner.

Jacob, François. [1970] 1973. *The Logic of Life: A History of Heredity.* Translated by B. E. Spillmann. New York: Pantheon.

Jacoby, Henry. [1969] 1973. *The Bureaucratization of the World.* Translated by E. L. Kanes. Berkeley: University of California Press.

Jakobson, Roman, and Morris Halle. 1956. *Fundamentals of Language.* The Hague: Mouton.

James, William. 1907. *Pragmatism, a New Name for Some Old Ways of Thinking.* New York: Longmans, Green.

Jameson, Fredric. 1972. *The Prison-House of Language.* Princeton: Princeton University Press.

―――. 1974. "The Vanishing Mediator." *New German Critique* 1:52–89.

Jaspers, Karl. [1931] 1951. *Man in the Modern Age.* Translated by E. Paul and C. Paul. London: Routledge & Kegan Paul.

―――. [1935] 1965. *Nietzsche: An Introduction to the Understanding of His Philosophical Activity.* Translated by C. F. Wallraff and F. J. Schmitz. Tucson: University of Arizona Press.

Jencks, Christopher, and associates. 1972. *Inequality: A Reassessment of the Effect of Family and Schooling in America.* New York: Basic Books.

Jensen, Arthur R. 1969. "How Much Can We Boost I.Q. and Scholastic Achievement?" *Harvard Educational Review* 39:1–123.

Johnson, Samuel. 1757. Review of *A Free Inquiry into the Nature and Origin of Evil,* part 3, by Soame Jenyns. *Literary Magazine* 15:301–6.

Jonas Hans. 1963. *The Gnostic Religion.* 2d ed. Boston: Beacon.

Jones, O. K., ed. 1969. *The Private Language Argument.* London: Macmillan.

Jones, Richard F. [1936] 1965. *Ancients and Moderns.* Berkeley: University of California Press.

Jones, William T. 1912. *An Interpretation of Rudolf Eucken's Philosophy.* London: Williams & Norgate.

Joravsky, David. 1979. "Scientists as Servants." *New York Review of Books* 26 (June 28): 34–39.

Kahn, Herman, and Anthony J. Wiener. 1967. *The Year 2000.* New York: Macmillan.

Kant, Immanuel. [1755] 1968. *Universal Natural History and Theory of the Heavens.* Translated by W. Hastie. New York: Greenwood.

———. [1785] 1952. *Fundamental Principles of the Metaphysic of Morals.* Translated by T. K. Abbott. Chicago: Encyclopedia Britannica (Great Books, 42).

———. [1786] 1970. *Metaphysical First Principles of Natural Science.* Translated by J. Ellington. Indianapolis: Bobbs-Merrill.

———. [1787] 1952. *The Critique of Pure Reason.* 2d ed. Translated by J. M. D. Meiklejohn. Chicago: Encyclopedia Britannica (Great Books, 42).

———. [1788] 1952. *The Critique of Practical Reason.* Translated by T. K. Abbott. Chicago: Encyclopedia Britannica (Great Books, 42).

———. [1798a] 1947. *Der Streit der Fakultäten.* Edited by K. Rossmann. Heidelberg: A. Rausch.

———. [1798b] 1974. *Anthropology from a Pragmatic Point of View.* Translated by M. J. Gregor. The Hague: Martinus Nijhoff.

Kateb, George. 1963. *Utopia and Its Enemies.* New York: Free Press.

Kaufmann, Felix. 1944. *Methodology of the Social Sciences.* New York: Oxford University Press.

Kaufmann, Walter. 1968. *Nietzsche: Philosopher, Psychologist, Antichrist.* 3d ed. New York: Vintage.

Kelly, Raymond C. 1977. *Etoro Social Structure.* Ann Arbor: University of Michigan Press.

Kevles, Daniel J. 1977. *The Physicists: The History of a Scientific Community in Modern America.* New York: A. A. Knopf.

Kierkegaard, Søren. [1843] 1946. *Repetition.* Translated by W. Lowrie. Princeton: Princeton University Press.

Kirk, Geoffrey S., and J. E. Raven. [1957] 1963. *The Presocratic Philosophers: A Critical History with a Selection of Texts.* Cambridge: Cambridge University Press.

Kluckhohn, Clyde. [1951] 1962. "Values and Value Orientations in the Theory of Action." In *Toward a General Theory of Action,* edited by T. Parsons and E. Shils, 388–433. New York: Harper Torchbooks.

Kluckhohn, Paul. 1925. *Persönlichkeit und Gemeinschaft. Studien zur Staatsauffassung der deutschen Romantik.* Halle: M. Niemeyer.

Kocka, Jürgen. 1966. "Karl Marx und Max Weber: Ein methodologischer Vergleich." *Zeitschrift für die gesammte Staatswissenschaft* 122:328–57.

Koffka, Kurt. [1924] 1928. *The Growth of the Mind.* 2d ed. Translated by R. M. Ogden. London: Kegan Paul, Trench, Trubner.

Kolakowski, Leszek. [1966] 1969. *The Alienation of Reason: A History of Positivist Thought.* Translated by N. Guterman. New York: Doubleday/Anchor.

———. 1975. *Husserl and the Search for Certitude.* New Haven: Yale University Press.

Korsch, Karl. 1938. *Karl Marx.* New York: John Wiley & Sons.

Korzybski, Alfred. 1933. *Science and Sanity: An Introduction to Non-Aristotelian*

Systems and General Semantics. New York: International Non-Aristotelian Library.

Kraft, Victor. [1950] 1953. *The Vienna Circle.* Translated by A. Pap. New York: Philosophical Library.

Kreckel, Reinhard. 1972. *Soziologische Erkenntnis und Geschichte: Über Möglichkeit und Grenzen einer empirisch-analytischen Orientierung in den Human-Wissenschaften.* Oplanden: Westdeutscher Verlag.

Kristeva, Julia. 1974. *La Révolution du langage poétique.* Paris: Seuil.

Kuhn, Thomas S. 1970a. *The Structure of Scientific Revolutions.* 2d ed. Chicago: University of Chicago Press.

————. 1970b. "The Essential Tension: Tradition and Innovation in Scientific Research." In *The Ecology of Human Intelligence,* edited by L. Hudson, 342–59. London: Penguin.

————. 1974. "Second Thoughts on Paradigms." In *The Structure of Scientific Theories,* edited by F. Suppe, 459–82, 500–517. Urbana: University of Illinois Press.

Kuznetsov, Boris. 1972. *Einstein and Dostoyevski: A Study of the Relation of Modern Physics to the Main Ethical and Aesthetic Problems of the Nineteenth Century.* Translated by V. Talmy. London: Hutchinson Educational.

Lacroix, Jean. 1966. *Panorama de la philosophie française contemporaine.* Paris: Presses Universitaires de France.

Lakatos, Imre. 1970. "Falsification and the Methodology of Scientific Research Programmes." In *Criticism and the Growth of Knowledge,* edited by I. Lakatos and A. Musgrove, 91–196. Cambridge: Cambridge University Press.

Landgrebe, Ludwig. [1957] 1966. *Major Problems in Contemporary European Philosophy.* Translated by K. F. Reinhardt. New York: Ungar.

————. 1962. "Husserls Abschied vom Cartesianismus." *Philosophische Rundschau* 9:133–77.

Langer, Lawrence L. 1978. *The Age of Atrocity: Death in Modern Literature.* Boston: Beacon.

Lazarsfeld, Paul F. 1954. "A Conceptual Introduction to Latent Structure Analysis." In *Mathematical Thinking in the Social Sciences,* 349–87. New York: Free Press.

Leach, Edmund R. 1961. *Rethinking Anthropology.* London: Athlone.

Lecourt, Dominique. [1972] 1975. *For a Critique of Epistemology.* Translated by B. Brewster, as *Marxism and Epistemology,* part 2. London: NLB.

Lee, Harold N. 1963. "Mead's Doctrine of the Past." *Tulane Studies in Philosophy* 12:52–75.

Legesse, Asmarom. 1973. *Gada: Three Approaches to the Study of African Society.* New York: Free Press.

Lekachman, Robert. 1976. *Economists at Bay.* New York: McGraw-Hill.

Lenhardt, Christian K. 1972. "Rise and Fall of Transcendental Anthropology." *Philosophy of the Social Sciences* 2:231–46.

Levinson, Charles. 1971. *Inflation and the Multinationals.* London: Allen & Unwin.

Lévi-Strauss, Claude. [1949a] 1969. *The Elementary Structure of Kinship.* Translated by J. H. Bell and J. R. von Sturmer. Edited by R. Needham. Boston: Beacon.

————. [1949b] 1967. "History and Ethnology." In *Structural Anthropology*, vol. 1, translated by C. Jacobson and B. G. Schoepf, 1–28. New York: Doubleday/ Anchor.

————. [1953] 1967. "Social Structure." In *Structural Anthropology*, vol. 1, translated by C. Jacobson and B. G. Schoepf, 269–319. New York: Doubleday/ Anchor.

————. [1955a] 1963. *Tristes Tropiques*. Abridged and translated by J. Russell. New York: Atheneum.

————. [1955b] 1967. "The Structural Study of Myth." In *Structural Anthropology*, vol. 1, translated by C. Jacobson and B. G. Schoepf, 202–28. New York: Doubleday/Anchor.

————. [1956] 1967. "Structure and Dialectics." In *Structural Anthropology*, vol. 1, translated by C. Jacobson and B. G. Schoepf, 229–38. New York: Doubleday/Anchor.

————. [1958] 1967. "Postscript to Chapter XV (Social Structure)." In *Structural Anthropology*, vol. 1, translated by C. Jacobson and B. G. Schoepf, 320–42. New York: Doubleday/Anchor.

————. [1960] 1967. *The Scope of Anthropology*. Translated by S. O. Paul and R. A. Paul. London: Jonathan Cape.

————. [1962a] 1963. *Totemism*. Translated by R. Needham. Boston: Beacon.

————. [1962b] 1966. *The Savage Mind*. Translator not listed. Chicago: University of Chicago Press.

————. 1963. "Réponses à quelques questions." *Esprit*, no. 322: 628–53.

————. [1964a] 1969. *Mythologiques, I: The Raw and the Cooked*. Translated by J. Weightman and D. Weightman. New York: Harper & Row.

————. [1964b] 1976. "Scientific Criteria in the Social and Human Disciplines." In *Structural Anthropology*, vol. 2, translated by M. Layton, 288–311. New York: Basic Books.

————. [1966] 1973. *Mythologiques, II: From Honey to Ashes*. Translated by J. Weightman and D. Weightman. New York: Harper & Row.

————. [1968] 1978. *Mythologiques, III: The Origin of Table Manners*. Translated by J. Weightman and D. Weightman. New York: Harper & Row.

————. [1971] 1981. *Mythologiques, IV: The Naked Man*. Translated by J. Weightman and D. Weightman. New York: Harper & Row.

————. [1972] 1978. "Structuralism and Ecology." *Graduate Faculty Philosophy Journal* 7:153–78.

Lévy, Bernard-Henri. [1977] 1979. *Barbarism with a Human Face*. Translated by G. Holoch. New York: Harper & Row.

————. 1979. *Le Testament du Dieu*. Paris: Grasset.

Lewis, Clarence I. 1929. *Mind and the World Order*. New York: Charles Scribner's Sons.

————. 1946. *An Analysis of Knowledge and Valuation*. La Salle, Ill.: Open Court.

Lindblom, Charles E., and David K. Cohen. 1979. *Usable Knowledge: Social Science and Social Problem Solving*. New Haven: Yale University Press.

Lippert, Julius. [1886–87] 1931. *The Evolution of Culture*. Abridged and translated by G. P. Murdock. New York: Macmillan.

Locke, John. [1690] 1952. *An Essay concerning Human Understanding.* Edited by A. C. Fraser. Chicago: Encyclopedia Britannica (Great Books, 35).

Loemeker, Leroy E. 1972. *Struggle for Synthesis.* Cambridge: Harvard University Press.

Löwith, Karl. [1932] 1969. "Max Weber and Karl Marx." In *Gesammelte Abhandlungen. Zur Kritik der geschichtlichen Existenz,* 1–67. Stuttgart: W. Kohlhammer.

———. [1941] 1967. *From Hegel to Nietzsche: The Revolution in Nineteenth-Century Thought.* Translated by D. E. Green. New York: Doubleday/Anchor.

———. [1950] 1966. "Man between Infinities." In *Nature, History, and Existentialism, and Other Essays in the Philosophy of History,* edited by A. Levison. Evanston: Northwestern University Press.

Lortz, Joseph. [1939–40] 1968. *The Reformation in Germany.* Translated by R. Walls. London: Darton, Longman & Todd.

Lu Hsün. [1934] 1960. "On Face." Translated by H. Yang and G. Yang. In *Selected Works of Lu Hsün,* 4:129–32. Peking: Foreign Language Press.

Luhmann, Niklas. 1969. *Legitimation durch Verfahren.* Neuwied: Luchterhand.

Lukács, Georg. [1910] 1974. *Soul and Form.* Translated by A. Bostock. Cambridge: MIT Press.

———. [1923] 1971. *History and Class Consciousness.* Translated by R. Livingstone. Cambridge: MIT Press.

———. 1953. *Die Zerstörung der Vernunft.* Berlin: Aufbau.

———. [1954] 1976. *The Young Hegel: Studies in the Relations between Dialectics and Economics.* Rev. ed. Translated by R. Livingstone. Cambridge: MIT Press.

———. [1958] 1964. *The Meaning of Contemporary Realism.* Translated by J. Mander and N. Mander. New York: Harper & Row.

———. 1963. *Ästhetik, Teil 1: Die Eigenart des Ästhetischen.* 2 vols. Neuwied: Luchterhand.

———. [1967] 1975. *Conversations with Lukács.* With H. H. Holz, L. Kofler, and W. Abendroth. Edited by T. Pinkus. Cambridge: MIT Press.

———. [1969] 1971. *Solzhenitsyn.* Translated by W. D. Graf. Cambridge: MIT Press.

Lukes, Steven. 1972. *Emile Durkheim: His Life and Work.* New York: Harper & Row.

Lyell, Charles. 1830–33. *Principles of Geology.* 1st ed. 3 vols. London: J. Murray.

McCarthy, Thomas. 1978. *The Critical Theory of Jürgen Habermas.* Cambridge: MIT Press.

Mach, Ernst. [1883] 1960. *The Science of Mechanics.* Translated by T. J. McCormick. LaSalle, Ill.: Open Court.

Machlup, Fritz. 1961. "Are the Social Sciences Really Inferior?" *The Southern Economic Journal* 27:173–84.

Macksey, Richard, and Eugenio Donato, eds. 1970. *The Languages of Criticism and the Sciences of Man.* Baltimore: Johns Hopkins University Press.

MacRae, Duncan, Jr. 1976. *The Social Function of Social Science.* New Haven: Yale University Press.

Makkreel, Rudolf. 1969. "Wilhelm Dilthey and the Neo-Kantians: The Distinction of the *Geisteswissenschaften* and the *Kulturwissenschaften.*" *Journal of the History of Philosophy* 7:423–40.

———. 1975. *Dilthey: Philosopher of the Human Studies.* Princeton: Princeton University Press.

Malcolm, Norman. [1949] 1969. "Defending Common Sense." In *Studies in the Philosophy of G. E. Moore,* edited by E. D. Klemke, 200–219. Chicago: Quadrangle.

———. [1954] 1963. "Wittgenstein's *Philosophical Investigations.*" In *Knowledge and Certainty,* 96–129. Englewood Cliffs, N.J.: Prentice-Hall.

Mann, Thomas. [1903] 1928. *Tonio Kröger.* Translated by H. T. Lowe-Porter. London: Martin Secker.

Mannheim, Karl. [1921–22] 1952. "On the Interpretation of *Weltanschauung.*" In *Essays on the Sociology of Knowledge,* translated and edited by P. Kecskemeti, 33–83. London: Routledge & Kegan Paul.

———. [1922a] 1964. "On the Problem of the Classification of the Sciences." In *Wissenssoziologie,* edited by K. H. Wolff, 155–65. Neuwied: Luchterhand.

———. [1922b] 1953. "Structural Analysis of Epistemology." In *Essays on Sociology and Social Psychology,* translated by E. Schwartzschild and P. Kecskemeti, edited by P. Kecskemeti, 15–73. London: Routledge & Kegan Paul.

———. [1924] 1952. "Historicism." In *Essays on the Sociology of Knowledge,* translated and edited by P. Kecskemeti, 84–133. London: Routledge & Kegan Paul.

———. [1925] 1952. "The Problem of a Sociology of Knowledge." In *Essays on the Sociology of Knowledge,* translated and edited by P. Kecskemeti, 134–90. London: Routledge & Kegan Paul.

———. [1926] 1971. "The Ideological and the Sociological Interpretation of Intellectual Phenomena." In *From Karl Mannheim,* translated by P. Kecskemeti and K. H. Wolff, edited by K. H. Wolff, 116–31. New York: Oxford University Press.

———. [1927] 1971. "Conservative Thought." In *From Karl Mannheim,* translated by P. Kecskemeti and K. H. Wolff, edited by K. H. Wolff, 132–222. New York: Oxford University Press.

———. [1928] 1952. "The Significance of Competition in the Area of Intellectual Phenomena." In *Essays on the Sociology of Knowledge,* translated and edited by P. Kecskemeti, 191–229. London: Routledge & Kegan Paul.

———. [1929] 1936. *Ideology and Utopia.* Enl. ed. Translated by L. Wirth and E. Shils. New York: Harcourt, Brace.

———. [1931] 1936. "The Sociology of Knowledge." In *Ideology and Utopia.* Enl. ed. Translated by L. Wirth and E. Shils. New York: Harcourt, Brace.

———. [1932] 1953. "American Sociology." In *Essays in Sociology and Social Psychology,* translated by E. Schwartzschild and P. Kecskemeti, edited by P. Kecskemeti, 185–94. London: Routledge & Kegan Paul.

———. 1943. *Diagnosis of Our Time.* London: Routledge & Kegan Paul.

———. 1952. *Essays on the Sociology of Knowledge.* Translated and edited by P. Kecskemeti. London: Routledge & Kegan Paul.

Manuel, Frank E. 1965. *Shapes of Philosophical History.* Stanford: Stanford University Press.

Marcuse, Herbert. [1965] 1968. *Negations: Essays in Critical Theory*. Translated by J. J. Shapiro. Boston: Beacon.

Marks, Stephen R. 1974. "Durkheim's Theory of Anomie." *American Journal of Sociology* 80:329–63.

Marx, Karl. [1843] 1975. *Contribution to the Critique of Hegel's Philosophy of Law*. In *Collected Works*, by K. Marx and F. Engels, translated by M. Milligan, B. Ruhemann, et al., 3:3–129. New York: International.

———. [1844] 1975. "Contribution to the Critique of Hegel's Philosophy of Law. Introduction." In *Collected Works*, by K. Marx and F. Engels, translated by M. Milligan, B. Ruhemann, et al., 3:175–87. New York: International.

———. [1852] 1979. *The Eighteenth Brumaire of Louis Bonaparte*. In *Collected Works*, by K. Marx and F. Engels, translated by C. Dutt, R. Livingstone, et al., 11:101–97. New York: International.

———. [1932] 1975. *Economic and Philosophic Manuscripts of 1844*. In *Collected Works*, by K. Marx and F. Engels, translated by M. Milligan, B. Ruhemann, et al., 3:229–346. New York: International.

Marx, Karl, and Friedrich Engels. [1932] 1976. *The German Ideology*. In *Collected Works*, translated by C. Dutt et al., 5:19–539. New York: International.

Matthiae, Paolo. 1976. "Ebla in the Late Early Syrian Period: The Royal Palace and the State Archives." *Biblical Archeologist* 39:94–113.

Mays, Wolfe. 1953–54. "The Epistemology of Professor Piaget." *Proceedings of the Aristotelian Society*, n.s., 54:49–76.

Mead, George Herbert. [1908a] 1964. "The Philosophical Basis of Ethics." In *Selected Writings*, edited by A. J. Reck, 82–93. Indianapolis: Bobbs-Merrill.

———. 1908b. "The Social Settlement: Its Basis and Function." *The University* [of Chicago] *Record* 12:108–10.

———. 1909. "Social Psychology as Counterpart to Physiological Psychology." *Psychological Bulletin* 6:401–8.

———. 1910a. "What Social Objects Must Psychology Presuppose?" *Journal of Philosophy, Psychology, and Scientific Method* 7:174–80.

———. 1910b. "Social Consciousness and the Consciousness of Meaning." *Psychological Bulletin* 7:397–405.

———. 1912. "The Mechanism of Social Consciousness." *Journal of Philosophy* 9:401–6.

———. 1913. "The Social Self." *Journal of Philosophy* 10:374–80.

———. 1917. "Scientific Method and the Individual Thinker." In *Creative Intelligence*, edited by J. Dewey et al., 176–227. New York: Henry Holt.

———. 1924–25. "The Genesis of the Self and Social Control." *International Journal of Ethics* 35:251–77.

———. [1925–26] 1964. "The Nature of Aesthetic Experience." In *Selected Writings*, edited by A. J. Reck, 294–305. Indianapolis: Bobbs-Merrill.

———. 1929. "A Pragmatic Theory of Truth." In *Studies in the Nature of Truth*, University of California Publications in Philosophy, vol. 11, edited by G. P. Adams, J. Loewenberg, and S. C. Pepper, 65–88. Berkeley: University of California Press.

———. [1930] 1964. "The Philosophies of Royce, James, and Dewey in Their American Setting." In *Selected Writings*, edited by A. J. Reck, 371–91. Indianapolis: Bobbs-Merrill.

————. 1932. *The Philosophy of the Present*. Edited by A. E. Murphy. Chicago: Open Court.

————. 1934. *Mind, Self, and Society: From the Standpoint of a Social Behaviorist*. Edited by C. W. Morris. Chicago: University of Chicago Press.

————. 1936. *Movements of Thought in the Nineteenth Century*. Edited by M. A. Moore. Chicago: University of Chicago Press.

————. 1938. *Philosophy of the Act*. Edited by C. Morris, with J. M. Brewster, A. M. Dunham, and D. L. Miller. Chicago: University of Chicago Press.

Meadows, Dennis L., et al. 1974. *The Dynamics of Growth in a Finite World*. Cambridge: Wright-Allen.

Mehta, Jarava L. 1971. *The Philosophy of Martin Heidegger*. Rev. ed. New York: Harper & Row.

Menger, Carl. [1883] 1963. *Problems of Economics and Sociology*. Translated by F. Nock. Edited by L. Schneider. Urbana: University of Illinois Press.

Merleau-Ponty, Maurice. [1961] 1964. *Sense and Non-Sense*. 3d ed. Translated by H. L. Dreyfus and P. A. Dreyfus. Evanston: Northwestern University Press.

Merton, Robert K. [1938a] 1970. *Science, Technology, and Society in Seventeenth-Century England*. New York: Harper & Row.

————. [1938b] 1973. "Science and the Social Order." In *The Sociology of Science*, edited by N. W. Storer, 254–66. Chicago: University of Chicago Press.

————. [1941] 1968. "Karl Mannheim and the Sociology of Knowledge." In *Social Theory and Social Structure*, enl. ed., 543–62. New York: Free Press.

————. [1942] 1973. "Science and Technology in a Democratic Order." In *The Sociology of Science*, edited by N. W. Storer, 267–78. Chicago: University of Chicago Press.

————. [1945a] 1973. "Sociology of Knowledge." In *The Sociology of Science*, edited by N. W. Storer, 7–40. Chicago: University of Chicago Press.

————. [1945b] 1968. "Sociological Theory." In *Social Theory and Social Structure*, enl. ed., 139–55. New York: Free Press.

————. [1949a] 1968. "Introduction to Part 3: The Sociology of Knowledge and Mass Communications." In *Social Theory and Social Structure*, enl. ed., 493–509. New York: Free Press.

————. [1949b] 1973. "The Role of Applied Social Science in the Formation of Policy." In *The Sociology of Science*, edited by N. W. Storer, 70–98. Chicago: University of Chicago Press.

————. [1961] 1973. "Social Conflict over Styles of Sociological Work." In *The Sociology of Science*, edited by N. W. Storer, 47–69. Chicago: University of Chicago Press.

————. [1963] 1973. "The Ambivalence of Scientists." In *The Sociology of Science*, edited by N. W. Storer, 383–412. Chicago: University of Chicago Press.

————. 1965. *On the Shoulders of Giants: A Shandean Postscript*. New York: Free Press.

————. [1967] 1968. "On the History and Systematics of Sociological Theory." In *Social Theory and Social Structure*, enl. ed., 1–38. New York: Free Press.

————. 1971. "The Precarious Foundations of Detachment in Sociology." In *The Phenomenon of Sociology*, edited by E. A. Tiryakian, 188–99. New York: Appleton-Century-Crofts.

————. [1972] 1973. "Insiders and Outsiders: A Chapter in the Sociology of

Knowledge" (3d ed.). In *The Sociology of Science*, edited by N. W. Storer, 99–136. Chicago: University of Chicago Press.

———. 1975. "Structural Analysis in Sociology." In *Approaches to the Study of Social Structure*, edited by P. M. Blau, 21–52. New York: Free Press.

Meyerson, Emile. 1921. *De l'explication dans les sciences*. Paris: Payot.

Michelet, Jules. [1836] 1861. *La Mer*. 2d ed. Paris: Hachette.

Miller, David L. 1973. *George Herbert Mead: Self, Language, and the World*. Austin: University of Texas Press.

Monod, Jacques. [1970] 1972. *Chance and Necessity: An Essay on the Natural Philosophy of Modern Biology*. Translated by A. Wainhouse. New York: Vintage.

Montaigne, Michel Eyquem de. [1580–88] 1952. *The Essays of Michel Eyquem de Montaigne*. Translated by C. Colton. Edited by W. C. Hazlitt. Chicago: Encyclopedia Britannica (Great Books, 25).

Moody, Ernest A. [1935] 1965. *The Logic of William of Ockham*. New York: Russell and Russell.

Moore, George Edward. 1903. *Principia Ethica*. Cambridge: Cambridge University Press.

———. 1925. "A Defense of Common Sense." In *Contemporary British Philosophy*, 2d series, edited by J. H. Muirhead, 192–223. London: Allen & Unwin.

———. [1939] 1959. "Proof of an External World." In *Philosophical Papers*, 127–50. London: Allen & Unwin.

———. 1952. "A Reply to My Critics." In *The Philosophy of G. E. Moore*, 2d ed., edited by P. A. Schilpp, 535–677. New York: Tudor.

———. 1954. "Wittgenstein's Lectures in 1930–33." *Mind* 63:289–316.

More, Thomas. [1516] 1972. *Utopia*. Translated by P. Turner. London: The Folio Society.

Morris, Charles W. 1938. *Foundations of the Theory of Signs*. Chicago: University of Chicago Press.

Muecke, Douglas C. 1969. *The Compass of Irony*. London: Methuen.

Müller, Adam H. [1809] 1922. *Die Elemente der Staatskunst*. 2 vols. Edited by J. Baxa. Vienna and Leipzig: Wiener Literarische Anstalt.

Munro, Thomas. 1928. *Scientific Method in Aesthetics*. New York: W. W. Norton.

———. 1970. *Form and Style in the Arts*. Cleveland: Press of Case Western Reserve University.

Nagel, Ernest. 1961. *The Structure of Science*. New York: Harcourt, Brace and World.

National Academy of Sciences. 1975. *Long-Term Worldwide Effects of Multiple Nuclear Detonations*. Washington, D.C.: National Academy of Sciences.

Needham, Rodney. 1972. *Belief, Language, and Experience*. Oxford: Basil Blackwell.

Neurath, Otto. 1931. "Physicalism." *Monist* 41:618–23.

Nietzsche, Friedrich. [1872] 1968. *The Birth of Tragedy*. Translated by W. Kaufmann. In *Basic Writings of Nietzsche*, edited by W. Kaufmann, 3–144. New York: Modern Library.

———. [1874a] 1957. *Untimely Meditations, II: Of the Use and Disadvantage of History for Life*. Translated by A. Collins. New York: Liberal Arts Press.

———. [1874b] 1965. *Untimely Meditations, III: Schopenhauer as Educator.* Translated by J. W. Hillesheim and M. R. Simpson. Chicago: Henry Regnery.

———. [1881] 1923–27. *The Dawn.* Translated by J. M. Kennedy. *The Complete Works of Friedrich Nietzsche,* edited by O. Levy, vol. 9. New York: Macmillan.

———. [1882] 1974. *The Gay Science.* Translated by W. Kaufmann. New York: Random House.

———. [1883–85] 1954. *Thus Spoke Zarathustra.* Translated by W. Kaufmann. In *The Portable Nietzsche,* edited by W. Kaufmann, 112–439. New York: Viking.

———. [1886] 1968. *Beyond Good and Evil.* Translated by W. Kaufmann. In *Basic Writings of Nietzsche,* edited by W. Kaufmann, 191–435. New York: Modern Library.

———. [1887] 1968. *On the Genealogy of Morals.* Translated by W. Kaufmann and R. J. Hollingdale. In *Basic Writings of Nietzsche,* edited by W. Kaufmann, 449–599. New York: Modern Library.

———. [1889] 1954. *Twilight of the Idols.* Translated by W. Kaufmann. In *The Portable Nietzsche,* edited by W. Kaufmann, 464–563. New York: Viking.

———. [1895] 1954. *Revaluation of All Values, I: The Antichrist.* Translated by W. Kaufmann. In *The Portable Nietzsche,* edited by W. Kaufmann, 568–656. New York: Viking.

———. [1901] 1967. *The Will to Power.* Translated by W. Kaufmann and R. J. Hollingdale. Edited by W. Kaufmann. New York: Random House.

———. [1908] 1968. *Ecce Homo.* Edited by W. Kaufmann. In *Basic Writings of Nietzsche,* edited by W. Kaufmann, 671–791. New York: Modern Library.

Oakes, Guy. 1975. "Introductory Essay." In Max Weber, *Roscher and Knies: The Logical Problems of Historical Economics,* translated by G. Oakes, 1–49. New York: Free Press.

Öhman, Susanne. 1951. *Wortinhalt und Weltbild.* Stockholm: P. A. Norstedt & Söner.

Ogden, Charles K., and Ivor. A. Richards. 1923. *The Meaning of Meaning.* New York: Harcourt, Brace.

Ophuls, William. 1977. *Ecology and the Politics of Scarcity.* San Francisco: W. H. Freeman.

Orr, Linda. 1976. *Jules Michelet: Nature, History, and Language.* Ithaca: Cornell University Press.

Overington, Michael A. 1977. "The Scientific Community as Audience: Toward a Rhetorical Analysis of Science." *Philosophy and Rhetoric* 10:143–64.

———. 1979. "Doing the What Comes Rationally: Some Developments in Metatheory." *The American Sociologist* 14:2–12.

Ozment, Steven, ed. 1971. *The Reformation in Medieval Philosophy.* Chicago: Quadrangle.

———. 1975. *The Reformation in the Cities.* New Haven: Yale University Press.

Palmer, Richard E. 1969. *Hermeneutics: Interpretation Theory in Schleiermacher, Dilthey, Heidegger, and Gadamer.* Evanston: Northwestern University Press.

Pap, Arthur. 1949. *Elements of Analytic Philosophy.* New York: Macmillan.

Parsons, Talcott. [1937] 1949. *The Structure of Social Action.* New York: Free Press.

——. 1951. *The Social System.* Glencoe, Ill.: Free Press.

——. 1966. *Societies: Evolutionary and Comparative Perspectives.* Englewood Cliffs, N.J.: Prentice-Hall.

Pascal, Blaise. [1670] 1960. *Pensées.* Translated by J. Warrington. London: J. M. Dent & Sons.

Paz, Octavio. [1967] 1970. *Claude Lévi-Strauss.* Translated by J. S. Bernstein and M. Bernstein. Ithaca: Cornell University Press.

Pears, David F. 1972. *Bertrand Russell and the British Tradition in Philosophy.* 2d ed. London: Collins/Fontana.

Peirce, Charles Sanders. [1877] 1960. "The Fixation of Belief." In *Collected Papers,* edited by C. Hartshorne and P. Weiss, 5:223–47. Cambridge: Belknap.

——. [1878] 1960. "How To Make Our Ideas Clear." In *Collected Papers,* edited by C. Hartshorne and P. Weiss, 5:248–71. Cambridge: Belknap.

——. [1901] 1960. "Definitions of Truth." In *Collected Papers,* edited by C. Hartshorne and P. Weiss, 5:394–98. Cambridge: Belknap.

Phillips, Derek L. 1974. "Epistemology and the Sociology of Knowledge: The Contributions of Mannheim, Mills, and Merton." *Theory and Society* 1:59–88.

Phillips, D. Z., and H. O. Mounce. 1965. "On Morality's Having a Point." In *The Is/Ought Question,* edited by W. D. Hudson, 228–39. London: Macmillan.

Piaget, Jean. [1923] 1926. *The Language and Thought of the Child.* Translated by M. Warden. New York: Harcourt, Brace.

——. [1927] 1960. *The Child's Conception of Physical Causality.* Translated by M. Gabain. Paterson, N.J.: Littlefield, Adams.

——. [1936] 1963. *The Origins of Intelligence in Children.* Translated by M. Cook. New York: W. W. Norton.

——. [1967] 1971. *Biology and Knowledge: An Essay on the Relations between Organic Regulations and Cognitive Processes.* Translated by B. Walsh. Chicago: University of Chicago Press.

——. 1970a. *Genetic Epistemology.* Translated by E. Duckworth. New York: Columbia University Press.

——. [1970b] 1974. *The Place of the Sciences of Man in the System of Sciences.* New York: Harper Torchbooks.

——. [1970c] 1977. *Psychology and Epistemology: Towards a Theory of Knowledge.* Translated by A. Rosin. Harmondsworth: Penguin.

——. [1974a] 1976. *The Grasp of Consciousness.* Translated by S. Wedgwood. Cambridge: Harvard University Press.

——. [1974b] 1978. *Success and Understanding.* Translated by A. J. Pomerans. Cambridge: Harvard University Press.

Piaget, Jean, with R. Garcia. [1971] 1974. *Understanding Causality.* Translated by D. Miles and M. Miles. New York: W. W. Norton.

Piaget, Jean, and Bärbel Inhelder. [1948] 1956. *The Child's Conception of Space.* Translated by F. J. Langdon and J. L. Lunzer. London: Rouledge & Kegan Paul.

Pinxten, Rik, ed. 1976. *Universalism versus Relativism in Language and Thought: Proceedings of a Colloquium on the Sapir-Whorf Hypothesis.* The Hague: Mouton.

Pitkin, Hanna Fenichel. 1972. *Wittgenstein and Justice.* Berkeley: University of California Press.

Planck, Max. [1928] 1949. *Scientific Autobiography, and Other Essays.* Translated by F. Gaynor. New York: Philosophical Library.

Pöggeler, Otto. 1959. "Sein als Ereignis." *Zeitschrift für philosophische Forschung* 13:597–632.

Poincaré, Henri. [1905] 1958. *The Value of Science.* Translated by G. B. Halsted. New York: Dover.

Polak, Frederik L. [1955] 1973. *The Image of the Future.* Abridged and translated by E. Boulding. Amsterdam: Elsevier.

Pole, David. 1958. *The Later Philosophy of Wittgenstein.* London: Athlone.

Pollard, Sidney. [1968] 1971. *The Idea of Progress.* Harmondsworth: Pelican.

Popper, Karl R. [1935] 1959. *The Logic of Scientific Discovery.* Translated by K. R. Popper, with J. Freed and L. Freed. New York: Basic Books.

———. [1958–59] 1965. "Back to the Presocratics." In *Conjectures and Refutations: The Growth of Scientific Knowledge,* 2d ed., 136–53 (plus Appendix). New York: Harper & Row.

———. 1962. *The Open Society and Its Enemies.* 2 vols. 4th ed. London: Routledge & Kegan Paul.

———. 1965. *Conjectures and Refutations.* 2d ed. New York: Harper & Row.

———. 1972. *Objective Knowledge: An Evolutionary Approach.* London: Oxford University Press.

Popper-Lynkeus, Joseph. 1910. *Das Individuum und die Bewertung menschlicher Existenz.* Dresden: C. Reissner.

Preus, James S. 1969. *From Shadow to Promise: Old Testament Interpretation from Augustine to the Young Luther.* Cambridge: Belknap.

Putnam, Hilary. [1962] 1975. "What Theories Are Not." In *Mathematics, Matter and Method: Philosophical Papers,* 1:215–27. Cambridge: Cambridge University Press.

Quine, Willard Van Orman. [1951] 1953. "Two Dogmas of Empiricism." In *From a Logical Point of View,* 20–46. Cambridge: Harvard University Press.

———. 1953. *From a Logical Point of View.* Cambridge: Harvard University Press.

———. [1958] 1969. "Speaking of Objects." In *Ontological Relativity and Other Essays,* 1–25. New York: Columbia University Press.

———. 1959. "Meaning and Translation." In *On Translation,* edited by R. A. Brower, 148–72. Cambridge: Harvard University Press.

———. 1960. *Word and Object.* Cambridge: MIT Press.

———. [1968] 1969. "Ontological Relativity." In *Ontological Relativity and Other Essays,* 26–68. New York: Columbia University Press.

———. 1969a. "Epistemology Naturalized." In *Ontological Relativity and Other Essays,* 69–90. New York: Columbia University Press.

———. 1969b. "Natural Kinds." In *Ontological Relativity and Other Essays,* 114–38. New York: Columbia University Press.

———. 1978. "Otherworldly." Review of *Ways of Worldmaking,* by N. Goodman. *New York Review of Books* 25 (November 23): 25.

Radnitsky, Gerard. 1968. *Contemporary Schools of Metascience.* 2 vols. Göteborg: Akademiförlaget.

Reinhold, Karl Leonard. 1784. "Gedanken über Aufklärung." *Teutscher Merkur.*

———. 1791. *Über das Fundament des philosophischen Wissens.* Jena: J. M. Mauke.

———. 1816. *Das menschliches Erkenntnisvermögen aus dem Gesichtspunkt der durch die Wortsprache vermittelten Zusammenhänge zwischen Sinnlichkeit und dem Denkvermögen.* Keil: Academische Buchhandlung.

Rickert, Heinrich. [1892] 1928. *Der Gegenstand der Erkenntnis.* Tübingen: J. C. B. Mohr.

———. [1896–1902] 1921. *Die Grenzen der naturwissenschaftlichen Begriffsbildung.* 4th ed. Tübingen: J. C. B. Mohr.

———. [1899] 1921. *Kulturwissenschaft und Naturwissenschaft.* 5th ed. Tübingen: J. C. B. Mohr.

Ricoeur, Paul. [1949] 1967. "Husserl and the Sense of History." In *Husserl: An Analysis of His Phenomenology,* translated by E. G. Ballard and L. E. Embree, 143–74. Evanston: Northwestern University Press.

———. [1951–52] 1967. "Husserl's *Ideas II*: Analyses and Problems." In *Husserl: An Analysis of His Phenomenology,* translated by E. G. Ballard and L. E. Embree, 35–81. Evanston: Northwestern University Press.

———. [1955] 1965. *History and Truth.* Translated by C. A. Kelbley. Evanston: Northwestern University Press.

———. 1967. "Husserl's Fifth Cartesian Meditation." In *Husserl: An Analysis of His Phenomenology,* translated by E. G. Ballard and L. E. Embree, 115–42. Evanston: Northwestern University Press.

———. [1969] 1974. *The Conflict of Interpretations: Essays in Hermeneutics.* Translated by K. McLaughlin et al. Evanston: Northwestern University Press.

———. 1971. "The Model of the Text." *Social Research* 38:529–55.

Rieff, Philip. 1959. *Freud: The Mind of the Moralist.* New York: Viking.

Rorty, Richard. 1979. *Philosophy and the Mirror of Nature.* Princeton: Princeton University Press.

Rosenberg, Alexander. 1980. *Sociobiology and the Preemption of Social Science.* Baltimore: Johns Hopkins University Press.

Rousseau, Jean-Jacques. [1755] 1964. *Discourse on the Origin and Foundation of Inequality.* In *The First and Second Discourses,* translated by R. D. Masters and J. R. Masters, edited by R. D. Masters, 77–228. New York: St. Martin's.

———. [1758] 1968. *The Letter to M. d'Alembert.* Translated by A. Bloom. Ithaca: Cornell University Press.

———. [1781] 1967. *Essay on the Origin of Languages.* Translated by J. H. Moran. In *On the Origin of Language: Jean-Jacques Rousseau and Johann Gottfried Herder,* edited by J. H. Moran and A. Gode, 1–74. New York: F. Ungar.

Rudner, Richard. 1951. "On Semiotic Aesthetics." *Journal of Aesthetics and Art Criticism,* 10:67–77.

———. 1966. *Philosophy of Social Science.* Englewood Cliffs, N.J.: Prentice-Hall.

Russell, Bertrand. [1903] 1910. "The Free Man's Worship." In *Philosophical Essays,* 59–70. London: Longmans, Green.

———. [1905] 1956. "On Denoting." In *Logic and Knowledge: Essays, 1901–1950,* edited by R. C. Marsh, 41–56. New York: Macmillan.

———. 1908a. "Pragmatism." *Edinburgh Review* 209:363–88.

———. [1908b] 1956. "Mathematical Logic as Based on the Theory of Types." In *Logic and Knowledge: Essays, 1901–1950*, edited by R. C. Marsh, 59–102. New York: Macmillan.

———. 1912. *The Problems of Philosophy.* New York: Henry Holt.

———. 1914. *Our Knowledge of the External World as a Field for Scientific Method in Philosophy.* London: Allen & Unwin.

———. [1918] 1956. "The Philosophy of Logical Atomism." In *Logic and Knowledge: Essays, 1901–1950*, edited by R. C. Marsh, 177–281. New York: Macmillan.

———. 1921. *The Analysis of Mind.* London: Allen & Unwin.

———. 1924. *Icarus, or the Future of Science.* London: Kegan Paul.

———. 1927. *The Analysis of Matter.* London: Allen & Unwin.

———. 1940. *An Inquiry into Meaning and Truth.* New York: W. W. Norton.

———. 1948. *Human Knowledge.* London: Allen & Unwin.

———. [1950] 1956. "Logical Positivism." In *Logic and Knowledge: Essays, 1901–1950*, edited by R. C. Marsh, 367–82. New York: Macmillan.

———. 1952. *The Impact of Science on Society.* London: Allen & Unwin.

———. 1957. *Why I Am Not a Christian.* New York: Simon & Schuster.

———. 1959. *My Philosophical Development.* London: Allen & Unwin.

Ryle, Gilbert. 1954. *Dilemmas.* Cambridge: Cambridge University Press.

———. 1957. "The Theory of Meaning." In *British Philosophy in the Mid-Century*, edited by C. A. Mace, 239–64. London: Allen & Unwin.

Said, Edward W. 1975. *Beginnings: Intention and Method.* New York: Basic Books.

Santillana, Giorgio de, and Hertha von Dechend. 1969. *Hamlet's Mill: An Essay on Myth and the Frame of Time.* Boston: Gambit.

Sapir, Edward. [1921] 1949. *Language.* New York: Harcourt, Brace and World.

Sassoon, Siegfried. 1936. *Sherston's Progress.* New York: Doubleday, Doran.

Saussure, Ferdinand de. [1916] 1959. *Course of General Linguistics.* Edited by C. Bally and A. Sechehaye. Translated by W. Baskin. New York: Philosophical Library.

Scattergood, V. J. 1971. *Politics and Poetry in the Fifteenth Century.* London: Blandford.

Schacht, Richard. 1973. "Nietzsche and Nihilism." *Journal of the History of Philosophy* 11:65–90.

Schaff, Adam. [1971] 1976. *History and Truth.* Translator not listed. Oxford: Pergamon.

Scheffler, Israel. 1967. *Science and Subjectivity.* Indianapolis: Bobbs-Merrill.

———. 1972. "Vision and Revolution: A Postscript on Kuhn." *Philosophy of Science* 39:366–74.

Scheler, Max. [1912] 1961. *Ressentiment.* Translated by W. Holdheim. Edited by L. Coser. New York: Free Press.

———. [1913–16] 1973. *Formalism in Ethics and Non-Formal Ethics of Values.* Translated by M. S. Frings and R. L. Funk. Evanston: Northwestern University Press.

———. 1922. "Weltanschauungslehre, Soziologie, und Weltanschauungssetzung." *Kölner Vierteljahrsheft für Soziologie und Sozialwissenschaft* 2:18–33.

504   REFERENCES

———. [1926a] 1958. "Man and History." In *Philosophical Perspectives*, translated by O. A. Haac, 65–93. Boston: Beacon.

———. [1926b] 1960. *Die Wissenformen und die Gesellschaft.* 2d ed. *Gesammelte Werke*, vol. 8. Bern: Francke.

———. [1927] 1974. *Man's Place in Nature.* Translated by H. Meyerhoff. New York: Noonday.

———. [1928] 1958. "Philosopher's Outlook." In *Philosophical Perspectives*, translated by O. A. Haac, 1–12. Boston: Beacon.

Schlegel, Richard. 1973. "Quantum Physics and Human Purpose." *Zygon* 8:200–220.

Schmalenbach, Hermann. [1922] 1977. "The Sociological Category of *Bund.*" In *On Society and Experience: Selected Papers*, translated and edited by G. Lüschen and G. P. Stone, 64–125. Chicago: University of Chicago Press.

———. 1926. *Das Mittelalter. Sein Begriff und Wesen.* Leipzig: Quelle und Meyer.

Schmidt, Alfred. [1962] 1971. *The Concept of Nature in Marx.* Translated by B. Fowkes. London: NLB.

Schöfer, Erasmus. 1962. *Die Sprache Heideggers.* Pfulligen: Neske.

Schopenhauer, Arthur. [1841] 1960. *Essay on the Freedom of the Will.* Translated by K. Kolenda. New York: Liberal Arts.

———. [1844] 1883–86. *The World as Will and Idea.* 3 vols. 2d ed. Translated by R. B. Haldane and J. Kemp. London: Trübner.

Schrödinger, Erwin. [1958] 1967. *Mind and Matter.* Cambridge: Cambridge University Press.

Schutz, Alfred. [1932] 1967. *The Phenomenology of the Social World.* Translated by G. Walsh and F. Lehnert. Evanston: Northwestern University Press.

———. [1940] 1962. "Phenomenology and the Social Sciences. In *Collected Papers*, vol. 1, edited by M. Natanson, 118–39. The Hague: Martinus Nijhoff.

———. [1943] 1964. "The Problem of Rationality in the Social World." In *Collected Papers*, vol. 2, edited by A. Brodersen, 64–88. The Hague: Martinus Nijhoff.

———. [1944] 1964. "The Stranger: An Essay in Social Psychology." In *Collected Papers*, vol. 2, edited by A. Brodersen, 91–105. The Hague: Martinus Nijhoff.

———. [1945a] 1962. "Some Leading Concepts of Phenomenology." In *Collected Papers*, vol. 1, edited by M. Natanson, 99–117. The Hague: Martinus Nijhoff.

———. [1945b] 1962. "On Multiple Realities." In *Collected Papers*, vol. 1, edited by M. Natanson, 207–59. The Hague: Martinus Nijhoff.

———. [1951] 1962. "Choosing among Projects of Action." In *Collected Papers*, vol. 1, edited by M. Natanson, 67–96. The Hague: Martinus Nijhoff.

———. [1953a] 1966. "Edmund Husserl's *Ideas*, Vol. 2." In *Collected Papers*, vol. 3, edited by I. Schutz, 15–39. The Hague: Martinus Nijhoff.

———. [1953b] 1962. "Common Sense and Scientific Interpretation of Human Action." In *Collected Papers*, vol. 1, edited by M. Natanson, 3–47. The Hague: Martinus Nijhoff.

———. [1954] 1962. "Concept and Theory Formation in the Social Sciences." In *Collected Papers*, vol. 1, edited by M. Natanson, 48–66. The Hague: Martinus Nijhoff, 1962.

———. [1955] 1962. "Symbol, Reality, and Society." In *Collected Papers*, vol. 1, edited by M. Natanson, 287–365. The Hague: Martinus Nijhoff.

———. [1959] 1964. "Tiresias, or Our Knowledge of Future Events." In *Collected Papers*, vol. 2, edited by A. Brodersen, 277–93. The Hague: Martinus Nijhoff.

———. [1960] 1964. "The Social World and the Theory of Social Action." In *Collected Papers*, vol. 2, edited by A. Brodersen, 3–19. The Hague: Martinus Nijhoff.

———. 1966. "Some Structures of the Life-World." Translated by A. Gurwitsch. In *Collected Papers*, vol. 3, edited by I. Schutz, 116–31. The Hague: Martinus Nijhoff.

———. 1970. *Reflections on the Problem of Relevance*. Edited by R. M. Zaner. New Haven: Yale University Press.

———. 1978. *The Theory of Social Action: The Correspondence of Alfred Schutz and Talcott Parsons*. Edited by R. Grathoff. Bloomington: Indiana University Press.

Schutz, Alfred and Thomas Luckmann. 1973. *Structures of the Life-World*. Vol. 1. Translated by R. M. Zaner and H. T. Engelhardt, Jr. Evanston: Northwestern University Press.

Searle, John R. 1964. "How to Derive 'Ought' from 'Is.' " *Philosophical Review* 73:43–58.

———. 1969. *Speech Acts: An Essay in the Philosophy of Language*. Cambridge: Cambridge University Press.

———. 1975. "A Taxonomy of Speech Acts." In *Language, Mind, and Knowledge*, Minnesota Studies in the Philosophy of Science, vol. 7, edited by K. Gunderson, 344–69. Minneapolis: University of Minnesota Press.

———. 1976. "A Classification of Illocutionary Acts." *Language in Society* 5:1–23.

Segerstedt, Torgny T. 1947. *Die Macht des Wortes*. Zurich: Pan.

Seward, Desmond. 1978. *The Hundred Years War*. New York: Atheneum.

Shelley, Mary Wollstonecraft. [1831] 1968. *Frankenstein; or, The Modern Prometheus*. Rev. ed. In *Three Gothic Novels*, edited by P. Fairclough, 257–497. Harmondsworth: Penguin.

Sherover, Charles W. 1971. *Heidegger, Kant, and Time*. Bloomington: Indiana University Press.

Shklar, Judith N. 1957. *After Utopia*. Princeton: Princeton University Press.

———. 1979. "Let Us Not Be Hypocritical." *Daedalus* 108:1–25.

———. 1980. "Learning without Knowing." *Daedalus* 109:53–72.

Simmel, Georg. 1907. *Schopenhauer und Nietzsche*. Leipzig: Duncker & Humblot.

———. [1918] 1968. *The Conflict in Modern Culture*. 2d ed. Translated by K. P. Etzkorn. In *The Conflict in Modern Culture and Other Essays*, edited by K. P. Etzkorn, 11–26. New York: Teachers College Press.

Singer, J. David, and Melvin Small. 1972. *The Wages of War, 1816–1965*. New York: John Wiley & Sons.

Sinsheimer, Robert L. 1976. "Recombinant DNA: A Critic Questions the Right to Free Inquiry." *Science* 194:303–6.

———. 1978. "The Presumptions of Science." *Daedalus* 107:23–35.

Skinner, Quentin. 1978. *The Foundations of Modern Political Thought*. 2 vols. Cambridge: Cambridge University Press.

Smerud, Warren B. 1970. *Can There Be a Private Language?* The Hague: Mouton.

Smirnov, V. A. [1964] 1970. "Levels of Knowledge and Stages in the Process of

Knowledge." In *Problems of the Logic of Scientific Knowledge*, edited by P. V. Tavenec, translated by T. J. Blakeley, 22–54. Dordrecht: D. Reidel.

Sneed, Joseph D. 1971. *The Logical Structure of Mathematical Physics*. Dordrecht: D. Reidel.

Sollers, Phillipe. 1968. *Logiques*. Paris: Seuil.

Sontag, Susan. [1963] 1965. "The Death of Tragedy." In *Against Interpretation and Other Essays*, 132–39. New York: Farrar, Straus & Giroux.

———. 1977. *On Photography*. New York: Farrar, Straus & Giroux.

Sorel, Georges. [1908] 1969. *The Illusions of Progress*. Translated by J. Stanley and C. Stanley. Edited by J. Stanley. Berkeley: University of California Press.

———. [1913] 1961. *Reflections on Violence*. 3d ed. Translated by T. E. Hulme and J. Roth. London: Macmillan.

———. [1921] 1976. *The Utility of Pragmatism*. Translated by J. Stanley and C. Stanley. In *From Georges Sorel*, edited by J. Stanley, 257–90. New York: Oxford University Press.

Spinoza, Benedict de. [1677] 1927. *Ethics*. Translated by W. H. White and A. H. Stirling. 4th ed. Oxford: Oxford University Press.

Stegmüller, Wolfgang. [1973] 1976. *The Structure and Dynamics of Theories*. Translated by W. Wohlhüter. New York: Springer.

Steiner, George. 1975. *After Babel: Aspects of Language and Translation*. New York: Oxford University Press.

Stocker, Michael A. G. 1966. "Memory and the Private Language Argument." *Philosophical Quarterly* 16:47–53.

Stolnitz, Jerome. 1960. *Aesthetics and the Philosophy of Art Criticism*. Boston: Houghton Mifflin.

Strasser, Hermann. 1976. *The Normative Structure of Sociology*. London: Routledge & Kegan Paul.

Strauss, Leo. 1936. *The Political Philosophy of Hobbes: Its Basis and Its Genesis*. Translated by E. M. Sinclair. Oxford: Clarendon.

———. 1947. "On the Intention of Rousseau." *Social Research* 14:455–87.

———. [1949] 1959. "Political Philosophy and History." In *What Is Political Philosophy? and Other Studies*, 56–77. New York: Free Press.

———. 1952. *Persecution and the Art of Writing*. Glencoe, Ill.: Free Press.

———. 1953. *Natural Right and History*. Chicago: University of Chicago Press.

———. [1954] 1959. "On a Forgotten Kind of Writing." In *What Is Political Philosophy? and Other Studies*, 221–32. New York: Free Press.

———. [1955] 1959. "What Is Political Philosophy?" In *What Is Political Philosophy? and Other Studies*, 9–55. New York: Free Press.

———. [1956] 1959. "Kurt Riezler (1882–1955)." In *What Is Political Philosophy? and Other Studies*, 233–60. New York: Free Press.

———. 1958. *Thoughts on Machiavelli*. Glencoe, Ill.: Free Press.

———. 1961. "Relativism." In *Relativism and the Study of Man*, edited by H. Schoeck and J. W. Wiggins, 135–57. Princeton: Van Nostrand.

———. 1968. "Natural Law." In *International Encyclopedia of the Social Sciences*, edited by D. L. Sills, 11:80–85. New York: Macmillan.

———. 1972. "Philosophy as Rigorous Science and Political Philosophy." *Interpretation* 2:1–9.

Strawson, Peter F. 1949. "Truth." *Analysis* 9:83–97.
———. [1950] 1971. "On Referring." In *Logico-Linguistic Papers*, 1–27. London: Methuen.
———. 1959. *Individuals*. London: Methuen.
Strohm, Paul. 1977. "Chaucer's Audience." *Literature and History* 5:26–41.
Suppe, Frederick. [1974] 1977. "The Search for Philosophic Understanding of Scientific Theories." In *The Structure of Scientific Theories*, 2d ed., edited by F. Suppe, 1–241. Urbana: University of Illinois Press.
———. 1977. "Afterword." In *The Structure of Scientific Theories*, 2d ed., edited by F. Suppe, 617–730. Urbana: University of Illinois Press.
Surkin, Marvin, and Alan Wolfe, eds. 1970. *An End to Political Science*. New York: Basic Books.
Tarski, Alfred. [1931] 1956. "The Concept of Truth in Formalized Languages." In *Logic, Semantics, Metamathematics*, translated and edited by J. H. Woodger, 153–278. Oxford: Clarendon.
———. 1944. "The Semantic Conception of Truth and the Foundation of Semantics." *Philosophy and Phenomenological Research* 4:341–76.
Tayler, Edward William. 1964. *Nature and Art in Renaissance Literature*. New York: Columbia University Press.
Therborn, Göran. 1971. Jürgen Habermas: A New Eclecticism." *New Left Review* no. 67: 69–83.
Theunissen, Michael. 1969. *Gesellschaft und Geschichte. Zur Kritik der kritischen Theorie*. Berlin: de Gruyter.
Thompson, Michael. 1979. *Rubbish Theory: The Creation and Destruction of Value*. Oxford: Oxford University Press.
Tocqueville, Alexis de. [1860] 1971. "A Fortnight in the Wilds." In *Journey to America*, rev. ed., translated by G. Lawrence, edited by J. P. Mayer, 350–403. New York: Doubleday/Anchor.
Toland, John. [1970] 1971. *The Rising Sun*. New York: Bantam.
Toulmin, Stephen E. 1958. *The Uses of Argument*. Cambridge: Cambridge University Press.
———. 1961. *Foresight and Understanding*. Bloomington: Indiana University Press.
———. 1970. "Does the Distinction between Normal and Revolutionary Science Hold Water?" In *Criticism and the Growth of Knowledge*, edited by I. Lakatos and A. Musgrove, 39–47. Cambridge: Cambridge University Press.
Toynbee, Arnold J. 1966. *Change and Habit*. New York: Oxford University Press.
Traugott, Elizabeth. 1973. "Generative Semantics and the Concept of Literary Discourse." *Journal of Literary Semantics* 2:5–22.
Trilling, Lionel. 1972. *Sincerity and Authenticity*. Cambridge: Harvard University Press.
Turchin, Valentin F. 1977. *The Phenomenon of Science*. Translated by B. Frentz. New York: Columbia University Press.
Turnbull, Colin M. 1972. *The Mountain People*. New York: Simon & Schuster.
Twain, Mark. [1880] 1977. *A Tramp Abroad*. Abridged and edited by C. Neider. New York: Harper & Row.
Ullmann, Walter. 1961. *Principles of Government and Politics in the Middle Ages*. London: Methuen.

————. 1966. *The Individual and Society in the Middle Ages*. Baltimore: Johns Hopkins University Press.

Unger, Roberto Mangabeira. 1975. *Knowledge and Power*. New York: Free Press.

U.S. Council on Environmental Quality and U.S. Department of State. 1980. *The Global 2000 Report to the President*. 3 vols. Washington, D.C.: Government Printing Office.

Urry, John. 1973. "Thomas S. Kuhn as Sociologist of Knowledge." *British Journal of Sociology* 24:462–73.

Vaihinger, Hans. [1911] 1935. *The Philosophy of "As If."* Translated by C. K. Ogden. London: Kegan Paul, Trench, Trubner.

Valentine, Charles W. 1913. *The Experimental Psychology of Beauty*. New York: Dodge.

von Humboldt, Wilhelm. 1880. *Über die Verschiedenheit des menschlichen Sprachbaues*. Edited by A. F. Pott. Berlin: S. Calvary.

von Mises, Ludwig. [1933] 1960. *Epistemological Problems of Economics*. Translated by G. Reisman. Princeton: Van Nostrand.

————. 1961. "Epistemological Relativism in the Sciences of Human Action." In *Relativism and the Study of Man*, edited by H. Schoeck and J. W. Wiggens. Princeton: Van Nostrand.

von Schelting, Alexander. 1936. Review of K. Mannheim's *Ideology and Utopia*. *American Sociological Review* 1:664–74.

von Wright, Georg H. 1963. *The Varieties of Goodness*. London: Routledge & Kegan Paul.

Watkins, John W. N. 1970. "Against 'Normal Science.'" In *Criticism and the Growth of Knowledge*, edited by I. Lakatos and A. Musgrove, 25–37. Cambridge: Cambridge University Press.

Watzlawick, Paul, Janet H. Beavin, and Don D. Jackson. 1968. *Pragmatics of Human Communication*. London: Faber and Faber.

Weber, Alfred. 1920. "Prinzipielles zur Kultursoziologie: Gesellschaftsprozess, Zivilizationsprozess, und Kulturbewegung." *Archiv für Sozialwissenschaft und Sozialpolitik* 47:1–49.

Weber, Marianne. [1926] 1975. *Max Weber: A Biography*. Translated and edited by H. Zohn. New York: John Wiley & Sons.

Weber, Max. [1895] 1968. "Der Nationalstaat und die Volkswirtschaftspolitik." In *Gesammelte politische Schriften*, edited by J. Winckelmann, 1–25. Tübingen: J. C. B. Mohr.

————. [1903] 1975. "Roscher's 'Historical Method.'" In *Roscher and Knies: The Logical Problems of Historical Economics*, translated by G. Oakes, 53–91. New York: Free Press.

————. [1904] 1949. "'Objectivity' in Social-Scientific and Social-Policy Knowledge." In *The Methodology of the Social Sciences*, translated and edited by E. A. Shils and H. A. Finch, 50–112. New York: Free Press.

————. [1905] 1930. *The Protestant Ethic and the Spirit of Capitalism*. Translated by T. Parsons. London: Allen & Unwin.

————. [1905–6] 1975. "Knies and the Problem of Irrationality." In *Roscher and Knies: The Logical Problems of Historical Economics*, translated by G. Oakes, 93–207. New York: Free Press.

———. [1906] 1949. "Critical Studies in the Logic of the Cultural Sciences." In *The Methodology of the Social Sciences*, translated and edited by E. A. Shils and H. A. Finch, 113–88. New York: Free Press.

———. [1907] 1977. *Critique of Stammler*. Translated by G. Oakes. New York: Free Press.

———. [1909] 1924. "Diskussionsreden auf den Tagungen des Vereins für Sozialpolitik (1905, 1907, 1909, 1911)." In *Gesammelte Aufsätze zur Soziologie und Sozialpolitik*, 394–430. Tübingen: J. C. B. Mohr.

———. [1913] 1964. "Gutachen zur Werturteilsdiskussion im Ausschuss der Vereins für Sozialpolitik." In *Max Weber: Werk und Person*, by E. Baumgarten, 102–39. Tübingen: J. C. B. Mohr.

———. [1917] 1968. "Parliament und Regierung im neugeordneten Deutschland." In *Gesammelte politische Schriften*, edited by J. Winckelmann, 294–431. Tübingen: J. C. B. Mohr.

———. [1917–18] 1949. "The Meaning of 'Ethical Neutrality' [*Wertfreiheit*] in Sociology and Economics." In *The Methodology of the Social Sciences*, translated and edited by E. A. Shils and H. A. Finch, 1–47. New York: Free Press.

———. [1919a] 1946. "Politics as a Vocation." In *From Max Weber*, translated and edited by H. H. Gerth and C. W. Mills, 77–128. New York: Oxford University Press.

———. [1919b] 1946. "Science as a Vocation." In *From Max Weber*, translated and edited by H. H. Gerth and C. W. Mills, 129–56. New York: Oxford University Press.

———. [1922] 1968. *Economy and Society: An Outline of Interpretive Sociology*. 2 vols. Translated by G. Roth et al. Edited by G. Roth and C. Wittich. New York: Bedminster Press.

Wellmer, Albrecht. [1969] 1971. *Critical Theory of Society*. Translated by J. Cumming. New York: Herder and Herder.

Whately, Richard. 1834. *Elements of Logic, comprising the Substance of the Article in the Encyclopaedia Metropolitana*. Rev. ed. New York: William Jackson.

White, Hayden. [1973a] 1978. "Foucault Decoded: Notes from Underground." In *Tropics of Discourse: Essays in Cultural Criticism*, 230–60. Baltimore: Johns Hopkins University Press.

———. 1973b. *Metahistory: The Historical Imagination in Nineteenth-Century Europe*. Baltimore: Johns Hopkins University Press.

White, Morton. 1950. "Analytic—Synthetic: An Untenable Dualism." In *John Dewey: Philosopher of Science and Freedom*, edited by Sidney Hook, 316–30. New York: Dial.

Whitehead, Alfred North. 1925. *Science and the Modern World*. New York: Macmillan.

Whorf, Benjamin L. [1956] 1967. *Language, Thought, and Reality: Selected Writings*. Edited by J. B. Carroll. Cambridge: MIT Press.

Wigner, Eugene P. 1967. *Symmetries and Reflections*. Edited by W. J. Moore and M. Scriven. Bloomington: Indiana University Press.

Winch, Peter. 1958. *The Idea of a Social Science and Its Relation to Philosophy*. London: Routledge & Kegan Paul.

Winner, Langdon. 1980. "Do Artifacts Have Politics?" *Daedalus* 109:121–36.

Wittgenstein, Ludwig. [1922] 1961. *Tractatus Logico-philosophicus*. Translated by D. F. Pears and B. F. McGuinness. London: Routledge & Kegan Paul.

———. 1933. "Letter." *Mind* 42:415–16.

———. [1953] 1968. *Philosophical Investigations*. Translated by G. E. M. Anscombe. Oxford: Basil Blackwell.

———. 1956. *Remarks on the Foundations of Mathematics*. Translated by G. E. M. Anscombe. Oxford: Basil Blackwell.

———. 1958. *The Blue and Brown Books*. Oxford: Basil Blackwell.

———. 1967. "Bemerkungen über Frazers *The Golden Bough*." *Synthese* 17:233–53.

———. [1969] 1972. *On Certainty*. Edited by G. E. M. Anscombe and G. H. von Wright. Translated by D. Paul and G. E. M. Anscombe. New York: Harper & Row.

———. 1974a. *Philosophical Grammar*. Edited by R. Rhees. Translated by A. Kenny. Oxford: Basil Blackwell.

———. 1974b. *Letters to Russell, Keynes, and Moore*. Edited by G. H. von Wright, with B. F. McGuinness. Oxford: Basil Blackwell.

Zahar, Elie. 1973. "Why Did Einstein's Programme Supersede Lorentz's?" *British Journal for the Philosophy of Science* 24:95–123, 223–62.

Zeller, Eduard. [1876] 1881. *A History of Greek Philosophy*. 4th ed. Translated by S. F. Alleyne. London: Longmans, Green.

Ziman, John. 1976. *The Force of Knowledge*. Cambridge: Cambridge University Press.

Zimmerman, M. [1962] 1969. "The 'Is-Ought': An Unnecessary Dualism." In *The Is/Ought Question*, edited by W. D. Hudson, 83–91. London: Macmillan.

Znaniecki, Florian. 1940. *The Social Role of the Man of Knowledge*. New York: Columbia University Press.

Index